To

Patty Mill,

the late Jessie Morrison, and the late Calum Morrison

Brief Contents

Contents

Preface

The first edition of *The Tourism System* was published in 1985. Subsequent editions have seen numerous changes. This sixth edition is no exception. The business of tourism is constantly evolving. This edition incorporates changes in the tourism system relating to destinations, channels of distribution, tourist markets, and modes of transportation.

Each chapter includes new quotes, "Quick Trips" and student activities. The quotes have been carefully selected to illustrate points made in the chapters and serve as the basis for discussion of the principles contained in the chapters. Quick trips have been written to practically illustrate each learning outcome. They are intended to engage the reader and stimulate discussion. The student activities provide a means for students to get out of the classroom and learn through independent discovery. A new "Trends" feature has been added to each chapter. This feature is a listing of trends related to the chapter topic.

Chapter 1 has an expanded section on the crucial elements that make a destination competitive. What constitutes competitiveness at tourism destinations is a function of the market segment being targeted and the product mix at the destination. Research is noted on the role of protected areas as attractions. This research underscores the importance of a destination's designation as a protected area. This distinction gives the site a name or label that becomes a marker that differentiates the destination from other similar places. A new section has been added on authenticity and cultural commodification.

Chapter 2 provides updated information on the use of tourism satellite accounts (TSAs). A new quick trip has been added on the Okavango Delta in Botswana, and all of the other quick trips have been updated. Chapter 3 includes new and updated information on UNWTO, ICAO, WTTC, OECD, OAS, and many other important tourism organizations. Chapter 4 supplies updated information on IATA and on air transportation agreements among different countries.

Chapter 5 includes new quick trip features on tourism planning by Fáilte Ireland, the Maldives, and the Isle of Wight in England. Chapter 6 contains an interesting new feature on the impacts of climate change on tourism development, and how the government of Canada is helping with human resources development and training for tourism.

Chapter 7 puts a greater emphasis on quality assurance programs in tourism marketing, and on societal marketing efforts in certain countries. New and contemporary examples of positioning and branding in tourism are provided. Additional examples of Internet marketing programs by destinations are incorporated. Fresh and up-to-date examples of promotional and advertising efforts from around the world are found in chapter 8. Chapter 9 has added information on inbound tour operators and travel management by corporations.

Chapter 10 includes new material on the characteristics of the ideal vacation trip. Chapter 12 places additional emphasis on the use of social media and social networking sites, an expanded section on the use of the Internet and the role of "influentials" in triggering demand. Chapter 13 expands on the impact of the Internet and contrasts differences between men and women.

Chapter 14 introduces, for the first time in the text, the subject of geodemographics, a system that segments the market into neighborhood clusters based on socio-economic and behavioral data. Geodemographics is based on the idea that people with similar socio-economic backgrounds and behavioral profiles select neighborhoods that suit their chosen lifestyles. Certain segments account for a disproportionately large amount of travel activity compared to their share of U.S. households. The section on "Visit Friends and Relatives" (VFR) is expanded and broken into several sub-segments. Various niche markets are examined in detail. Finally, there is a detailed section on the use of technology to replace business travel in the United States.

Chinese citizens can only travel to countries given Approved Destination Status (ADS) by their country. Chapter 15 has detailed information on the conditions necessary for a destination to obtain that designation. The impact of climate change on tourist destinations is a new topic as is the impact of terrorist attacks on tourist destinations. A final addition to this chapter deals with the world's emerging tourism destinations with increased emphasis on China and India.

Acknowledgments

There are several people who helped the two authors in their early studies on the subject of tourism. In particular, we would like to acknowledge our lecturers and advisors at The Scottish Hotel School who gave us our first taste of tourism as an academic field of study. These included *David Pattison, Joyce Lloyd, Kit Jenkins,* and *Roger Carter.* At Michigan State University, *Robert McIntosh* influenced us with his knowledge and dedication to tourism, and to his students. We both greatly admire Dr. McIntosh's pioneering work in publishing the first edition of *Tourism: Principles, Practices, Philosophies* in 1971.

Several people have reviewed previous editions of *The Tourism System.* We have greatly appreciated their viewpoints and acted upon many of their suggested improvements. These include *Brian King* of Victoria University of Technology, *Don Getz* of the University of Calgary, *Chris Cooper* of the University of Nottingham, and *Jonathan Goodrich* of Florida International University.

The assistance of many fine students has helped both of us steal the time to write various parts of this book. In particular, we would like to acknowledge the help of *Krissy Fergus, Analisa Fisher, Rachel Weinhouse,* and *Margot Duchowny.*

The assistance of *Judy Zhu* and *Patricia Robert* of Belle Tourism International Consulting is acknowledged for the fine work on the background research for the quick trips.

About the Authors

Robert Christie Mill, Ph.D., CHA, CHE

Robert Christie Mill is a professor in the School of Hotel, Restaurant and Tourism Management at the University of Denver. His teaching career began in 1972 at Niagara University. He subsequently served on the faculties of Lansing Community College and Michigan State University. Dr. Mill holds a Ph.D. and M.B.A. from Michigan State University and a B.A. from the University of Strathclyde's Scottish Hotel School. He is also a Certified Hotel Administrator and a Certified Hospitality Educator.

His industry experience includes positions with Trust House Forte in Europe, on board ship as a cook with Canadian Pacific, and as assistant to the vice president of Manpower Development with the Inter-Continental Hotel Corporation in New York City.

A two-time Fulbright lecturer to India and Hungary, Dr. Mill has conducted over 100 workshops in 16 states and 13 countries for the management and employees of various companies, industry groups and government organizations including the World Tourism Organization, the American Hotel and Motel Association, and the National Restaurant Association. In addition, he has worked as a member of tourism development project teams for Kintyre in Scotland, Northern Ireland, Algeria, and Tunisia.

Dr. Mill is the author of five books, co-author of a sixth, and chapter contributor to an additional eight in the areas of tourism and hospitality operations. Titles include *The Tourism System; Tourism: The International Business; Managing for Productivity in the Hospitality Industry; Restaurant Management: Customers, Operations, Employees; Resorts: Management and Operations;* and *Managing the Lodging Operation.* In addition, he is the author of scores of refereed articles in academic journals in addition to being an extensive contributor to the trade press.

Alastair M. Morrison, Ph.D., CDME, CTME

Alastair M. Morrison is the CEO of Belle Tourism International Consulting, Ltd. (BTI) and a Distinguished Professor Emeritus of the Department of Hospitality and Tourism Management at Purdue University, West Lafayette, Indiana, U.S.A. Professor Morrison has had a wide variety of experience in the global tourism industry. Most recently he has provided marketing and development advice in Australia, Bahrain, China, Ghana, Honduras, Hong Kong SAR, India, Italy, Jamaica, Macau SAR, Malaysia, New Zealand, Poland, Russia, Scotland, Singapore, Slovenia, Sri Lanka, Thailand, Trinidad & Tobago, and Vietnam.

Professor Morrison has developed and facilitated training programs on behalf of the UN World Tourism Organization (UNWTO) for eight South Asian countries and the China-Tibet Tourism Bureau; European Union; the U.S. Agency for International Development; and Destination Marketing Association International (DMAI). He is the Co-Founder and Co-Director of the Certified Destination Management Executive (CDME) program.

Professor Morrison is the author of three leading books in the areas of tourism marketing and development, and hospitality and travel marketing. In an analysis by Ryan (2005), Professor Morrison was placed among the five most prolific contributors in the world to the academic journals in tourism management. Professor Morrison is an Editorial Board Member of several major hospitality and tourism academic research.

Professor Morrison has received several teaching awards and honors at Purdue and his name has been entered in Purdue's Book of Great Teachers. In 1998, the International Society of Travel & Tourism Educators (ISTTE) selected Professor Morrison as the recipient of the Lifetime Achievement Award for his contributions to tourism education. In addition, he has been elected as a Fellow of the world's most elite organization of tourism scholars, the International Academy for the Study of Tourism (IAST).

As former Associate Dean for Learning and Director of Purdue University, Professor Morrison was responsible for undergraduate and graduate education. Prior to joining the Purdue faculty, he worked in Canada as a management consultant in hospitality and tourism, most recently as President of The Economic Planning Group of Canada (EPG).

He is a Visiting Professor at the Department of Hospitality and Tourism Management, University of Strathclyde, Scotland and was the Queensland Tourist & Travel Corporation Visiting Lecturer at James Cook University in Queensland, Australia. He teaches regularly on tourism marketing and promotion at Hong Kong University, and at IULM (Milan) and AILUN (Sardinia) in Italy.

Professor Morrison is active in several major industry associations. He has served as Chairman of the Travel & Tourism Research Association (TTRA)– Canada Chapter, Board member of the CenStates TTRA Chapter, Vice President of the International Society of Travel and Tourism Educators (ISTTE), and Chairman of Association of Travel Marketing Executives (ATME). He was awarded the distinction as one of the first recipients of the Certified Travel Marketing Executive (CTME) designation from ATME. He has designed and presented the *Destination Marketing Planning, Travel Information & Research, International Tourism & Convention Marketing,* and *Communications and Technology in Destination Management* courses for the Destination Marketing Association International (DMAI) as part of its Certified Destination Management Executive (CDME) Program and is a Co-Director of that program.

Tourism

AN OVERVIEW OF THE TOURISM SYSTEM

A tourist is someone who travels to see something different,
and then complains when things are not the same.

Holloway, C. (1994)

WHAT IS TOURISM?

In writing this book, we set out to do two things: Describe how tourism works and indicate how people can use this knowledge to make tourism work for them, their destination areas or businesses. Our first challenge was to put a label on the phenomenon about which we wanted to write.

Tourism is a difficult phenomenon to describe. The authors have trouble in thinking of tourism as an industry. Wells (1989) defines an industry as a "number of firms that produce similar goods and services and therefore are in competition with one another." In no sense of the word does this describe a *tourism industry*. While there is intense competition in tourism, especially in the post 9/11 environment, many businesses and other types of tourism organizations offer complementary rather than competing products and services. An airline, hotel, restaurant, travel agency, and attraction do not compete with each other. They complement each other and combine to offer visitors a satisfying vacation or business trip.

However, the idea of a tourism industry gives some unity to the idea of tourism. It enhances the image, credibility, and political acceptance of tourism. Tourism's image is *ambiguous* to many scholars and certainly to the "person on the street." For example, scholarly arguments are common as to whether the label should be "tourism" or "hospitality." Most ordinary people are astonished to find out that it is possible for a person to pursue a career in "tourism." While many attempts have been made to define tourism in the past 35 years, there is no single definition that is universally accepted. There is a link between travel, tourism, recreation, and leisure, yet the link is fuzzy. All tourism involves travel, yet not all travel is tourism. All vacation travel involves recreation, yet not all tourism is recreation. All tourism occurs during leisure time, but not all leisure time is spent on tourism activities. Defining tourism as an industry helps people to get a clearer picture of what tourism is all about. With a clearer image comes a better understanding.

The idea of a tourism industry gives those involved a feeling of *greater credibility and respectability*. It builds a sense of belonging and camaraderie. It allows comparisons with other industries such as agriculture and manufacturing. It establishes tourism's standing in the "pecking order" of economic activities. This is certainly useful and builds a greater public awareness of the broad scope and impacts of tourism.

The idea of a tourism industry is *politically attractive.* One of tourism's strengths is that its benefits are felt by many businesses, organizations and people. Visitor spending finds its way into many pockets and purses. At first glance, this might seem an ideal way to get political support for the planning, development, management, and marketing of tourism. However, this apparent strength has been a huge challenge for those interested in tourism. As tourism touches so many businesses and people in varying degrees, its overall impacts are difficult to measure. There is no single industry code for *tourism* under the North American Industry Classification System (NAICS).

The system of *Tourism Satellite Accounts (TSA)* was introduced to better reflect the impacts of tourism throughout an economy. The Bureau of Economic Analysis (BEA) in the United States describes its system of TSAs as follows (Bureau of Economic Analysis, 2009):

> "The Travel and Tourism Satellite Accounts (TTSAs) present a detailed picture of travel and tourism activity and its role in the U.S. economy. These accounts present estimates of expenditures by tourists, or visitors, on 24 types of goods and services. The accounts also present estimates of the income generated by travel and tourism and estimates of output and employment generated by travel and tourism-related industries. The accounts are updated annually and have been expanded to provide quarterly estimates of the sales of goods and services to travelers and employment attributable to those tourism sales."

Many people whose lives or businesses are touched by tourism are mainly engaged in other activities. The storekeeper sells to visitors and residents. While they may know that tourism affects them, it is often difficult to evaluate how much it does. From a political standpoint, the idea of a tightly defined tourism industry allows organizations to demonstrate the impact and importance of tourism. This results in more effective lobbying with governments which brings greater political support and assistance for tourism.

Yet, tourism is not an industry. Tourism is *an activity.* In this we are supported by the United Nations Department of Economic and Social Affairs Statistics Division (2008) who state that tourism "is a social, cultural and economic phenomenon related to the movement of people to places outside their usual place of residence, pleasure being the usual motivation." It cannot then be just one industry, since these activities are intertwined among several industries. Tourism takes place when, in international terms, people cross borders for leisure and business for less than one year. Tourism also occurs within each country, as people travel certain distances from their home environments for pleasure or business trips. The study of tourism is the study of this activity or phenomenon and its effects. The business of tourism is the business of encouraging this type of activity and taking care of people while they are engaged in tourism.

The World Tourism Organization (UNWTO), Madrid, Spain, is a specialized agency of the United Nations. UNWTO's definition of tourism is the most widely accepted around the world. "It comprises the activities of persons traveling to and staying in places outside their usual environment for not more than one consecutive year for leisure, business and other purposes not related to the exercise of an activity remunerated from within the place visited" (World Tourism Organization, 2009). UNWTO identifies the following branches of tourism:

- **Inbound tourism:** Visits to a country by non-residents of that country
- **Outbound tourism:** Visits by the residents of a country to other countries
- **Internal tourism:** Visits by residents and non-residents within a country (domestic + inbound international)
- **Domestic tourism:** Visits by residents within their own country
- **National tourism:** Visits by the residents of a country to other countries plus visits by residents within their own country (domestic + outbound international)
- **International tourism:** The combination of inbound and outbound tourism for a particular country

A variety of other definitions have been offered for tourism. Although tourism is not an industry, it does incorporate a variety of different types of tourism businesses and organizations. These can be divided into sectors and include (Leiper, 1990; Middleton, 1988; Morrison, 2009):

- **Accommodations, food service, and retailing:** Restaurants and food services of various types, hotels, resorts, guest houses, bed and breakfasts, farmhouses, apartments, villas, flats, condominiums and vacation ownership (timesharing), vacation villages, conference center resorts, marinas, ecolodges and other specialist accommodations, shops of various types including duty free

- **Association sector:** International, regional, national, and state trade and travel associations
- **Attractions and events sector:** Theme parks, museums, national parks, wildlife parks, gardens, heritage sites, festivals and events
- **Convention and exhibition sector:** Convention and exhibition centers, congress centers, auditoriums
- **Destination marketing sector:** National tourist offices, state, provincial and territorial tourist offices, regional travel or tourism organizations, convention and visitor bureaus, local tourist authorities, tourism associations
- **Miscellaneous sector:** Recreational facility operators, providers of travelers' checks and insurance, tourism educators, travel writers, publishers of travel guides and books, and other businesses that serve travelers' needs
- **Regulatory and coordinating sector:** Government agencies and nongovernmental organizations that regulate and coordinate different aspects of tourism, e.g., World Tourism Organization and International Civil Aviation Organization
- **Transportation carrier sector:** Airlines, shipping lines, ferry services, railways, bus and motor coach operators, and car rental companies
- **Travel trade intermediary sector:** Tour operators and wholesalers, retail travel agents, convention/meeting planners, corporate travel departments, incentive travel planners, and consolidators

WHY USE A SYSTEMS APPROACH FOR THE STUDY OF TOURISM?

Many people talk about the subject of this book as "the tourism industry." You have already heard that there are at least three good reasons for talking about tourism as an industry. However, the authors choose to characterize tourism as a *system*, rather than as an industry. This is done for several reasons. The first is to emphasize the *interdependency* in tourism; that it consists of several interrelated parts working together to achieve common purposes, which we call *the tourism system*. The tourism system is like a spider's web—touch one part and reverberations are felt throughout the system.

The tourism system approach is based upon *general systems theory*. The father of general systems theory was a biologist, Ludwig von Bertalanffy. He defined a system

as "a set of elements standing in interrelation among themselves and with the environments." Von Bertalanffy (1973) also suggested that general systems theory was "a way of seeing things that were previously overlooked or bypassed."

The authors are not the first to talk about a *tourism system*. Two of the pioneers of the concept were Clare Gunn, Emeritus Professor of Texas A&M University and Neil Leiper of Southern Cross University in Australia. Gunn (1994) describes the *functioning tourism system*, consisting of the supply side of attractions, services, promotion, information, and transportation, and states that:

> No matter how it is labeled or described, tourism is not only made up of hotels, airlines, or the so-called tourist industry but rather a system of major components linked together in an intimate and interdependent relationship.

Leiper (1990) believes that a *tourism system* consists of five elements: a human element (tourist), three geographical regions (traveler-generating region, transit route, and tourist destination region), and an industrial element (the travel and tourism industry). Although Leiper acknowledges the term "industry" in his system, he firmly supports the need to more holistically view tourism as a system rather than as an industry:

> Unfortunately, many persons closely involved with the business of tourism hold a dogma that tourism is an industry. The dogma has been reiterated in academic literature. The origins of this belief are understandable, but that does not mitigate the flawed thinking.

Clearly, it is very easy to use a "laundry list" approach to describe tourism; describing one by one the businesses that obviously are part of tourism such as airlines, hotels and resorts. However, this approach fails to include local communities, and other businesses and organizations affected by tourism, that may or may not see themselves as part of the so-called "tourism industry." For example, many people working for hotels and restaurants do not feel they are part of tourism. Their business begins with customers walking in the front door: They fail to examine the question "Why are they walking in our front door?" This *myopic* view has meant that many organizations have ended up being reactive to changes that have occurred outside their front doors, rather than being proactive and anticipating future changes in tourism. For a student beginning to study tourism, it is important to get "the bigger picture" right away. The *Tourism System Model* framework of the book provides a more comprehensive view of tourism: it captures "the big picture."

A second reason for using a systems approach is because of the *open system* nature of tourism. The tourism system is not a rigid form: rather, it is dynamic and constantly changing. New concepts and phenomena such as space tourism are always arriving in tourism. Adventure travel, dynamic packaging, destination branding, destination management, ecotourism, strategic alliances, sustainable tourism development, tourism satellite accounting, and voluntourism are just a few of the relatively new concepts introduced to tourism. Tourism is greatly affected by external influences such as politics, demographics, technology, war, terrorism, crime, and disease. For example, changes are constantly sweeping through tourism as a result of many years of terrorism and political uncertainty, and due to technological innovations. The tragedy of 9/11 traumatized tourism in the United States and elsewhere, as did the bombings and terrorist acts aimed at travelers in Bali, Madrid, London, Egypt, and Jordan. The outbreak of SARS in 2003 had a catastrophic effect on tourism in Hong Kong, China, Taiwan, and Canada, while the later emergence of "bird flu" continued to weaken travelers' confidence levels through 2005. The following quote underlines the susceptibility of tourism to outside influences:

> Thailand's battered tourism sector could shed up to 200,000 jobs this year, industry experts warned as violent street battles in Bangkok triggered mass cancellations. Anti-government demonstrators who forced the cancellation of a major Asian summit on the weekend shifted their campaign to the capital, clashing with security forces Monday in defiance of a state of emergency. (AFP, 2009)

As each year passes, tourism is becoming more and more complex to describe. Therefore, a third reason for the system is the *complexity and variety* in all aspects of tourism. For example, there are thousands of specialized tours and packages available for travelers today; you can select from a menu that ranges from archaeology to zoology. There is an enormous variety of approaches to each type of tourism business and organization. For example, travel trade intermediaries seldom play just one role today; with the removal of airline commissions, many travel agents have become tour wholesalers and operators. "Laundry list" approaches to tourism fail to reflect the great complexity present in tourism in the first decade of the twenty-first century. Above all, you will learn that it is difficult to put each part of tourism into its own pigeonhole. It just does not work that way any more.

Competition in today's tourism is both fierce and intense. Huge multinational companies are vying for business on a global scale. International brands such as McDonald's and Starbucks know no boundaries. Destination areas are competing with others with marketing budgets unprecedented in size. The systems approach better displays the great level of *competitiveness* present in tourism today. Grasping the full implications of the tourism system has led many previously competitive organizations and destination areas to acknowledge the similarity of their goals and form *partnerships*. For example, the BestCities Global Alliance is a long-term joint marketing effort by Cape Town, Copenhagen, Dubai, Edinburgh, Melbourne, San Juan, Singapore, and Vancouver with the following goal:

> BestCities Global Alliance is the world's first and only convention bureau alliance with eight partners on five continents. Our vision is to be recognized internationally for being innovative and setting and delivering the world's best convention bureau practices for the meetings industry. (http://www. bestcities.net, 2009)

Tourism involves an interaction of many organizations and people, whose goals and interests are sometimes not compatible. The fifth reason for using the systems approach is to acknowledge a level of *friction and disharmony* in tourism in the early twenty-first century. A monumental struggle is taking place in how tourism services are distributed. Lured by the economics, convenience and speed of new technologies such as the Internet, many suppliers and transportation carriers are *bypassing* the traditional channels of distribution, especially retail travel agencies. Airlines have forsaken the restrictions of government agencies in teaming up with foreign airlines to form *global strategic alliances*. The government stranglehold on tourism marketing in many destinations is being challenged, as private-sector businesses, associations, and nonprofits are demanding a greater say. Local residents are questioning the "development at all costs" paradigm as they see precious local environments and ecosystems being threatened.

The spider moves when its web shakes and another insect is trapped. Likewise a change in one part of the tourism system often causes a change in another part of the system. Therefore, the final reason for using the systems approach is because of the need for *responsiveness* in a specific system part to changes in another system part. Tourism is dynamic and ever changing. The linkages in the system represent the feedback mechanisms between pairs of system parts that allow changes to be assimilated. Expanding the spider's web metaphor just once more might provide a good example of the feedback-response mechanism. An intelligent spider may recognize that the larger the web, the more insects that are caught. Feedback from travelers through research studies has shown that more visitors are tending to favor multi-destination over single-destination trips. Tourism destination areas are responding by joining together in multi-destination partnerships and new *regional destination brands* to better accommodate this change in demand. By grasping "the bigger picture," former marketing foes are becoming friends, with each partner having the potential to get a larger share of the visitor market.

THE PARTS OF THE TOURISM SYSTEM

The *Tourism System Model* described in this book consists of four parts—*Destination*, *Marketing*, *Demand*, and *Travel*. The authors started this book with *Destination* out of choice, but it could easily have begun with *Travel*, *Demand*, or *Marketing*.

PART 1: DESTINATION—PLANNING, DEVELOPING, AND CONTROLLING TOURISM

> **1.**
>
> **DESTINATION: PLANNING, DEVELOPING, AND CONTROLLING TOURISM**
>
> AN IDENTIFICATION OF THE PROCEDURES THAT DESTINATION AREAS FOLLOW TO SET POLICIES, PLAN, CONTROL, DEVELOP, AND CATER TO TOURISM, WITH AN EMPHASIS ON SUSTAINABLE TOURISM DEVELOPMENT

Every destination area that chooses to encourage tourism must be prepared to handle the inflows of visitors, and to deal with the challenge that tourism has the potential of generating both positive and negative impacts. A *destination mix* is assembled consisting of attractions and events, facilities, infrastructure, transportation, and hospitality resources. *Tourism policies* and *tourism plans* are developed. The many different *tourism organizations* involved in these processes are described. A *legislative and regulatory framework* is required to ensure that the tourism policy and plan are implemented properly, and that im-

pacts are controlled. The process of *tourism development* and the analysis of individual tourism project development opportunities are explained.

LINK 1: THE TOURISM PRODUCT. The linkage between Parts 1 and 2 (*Destination* and *Marketing*) is called the *tourism product*. Again, a change in the destination may cause a change in marketing, and vice versa. For example, the staging of a mega-event or the introduction of a new major attraction (*Destination*) may result in a shift in the marketing of the destination area (*Marketing*), as is the case with the Beijing Summer Olympics in China in 2008 and the opening of Hong Kong Disneyland in September 2005. If a travel intermediary begins to send larger groups (*Marketing*), this may require a change in the size of accommodations and other facilities and services (*Destination*).

PART 2: MARKETING—STRATEGY, PLANNING, PROMOTION, AND DISTRIBUTION

Now in the second part of the system, destination areas must reach people in the market and encourage them to travel by using marketing principles and techniques. The *uniqueness* of tourism marketing is explained. The processes of *market segmentation* and *positioning*, and the application of the *product life cycle*, are described. A step-by-step procedure for marketing is introduced. Marketing success depends to a large extent on effective communications through *promotion*, and through the selection of the right *distribution channels* (online and traditional travel trade intermediaries). The different types of *destination marketing organizations* and *travel trade intermediaries* are reviewed. The trend toward greater *electronic distribution* is highlighted.

> **2.**
>
> **MARKETING: STRATEGY, PLANNING, PROMOTION, AND DISTRIBUTION**
>
> AN EXAMINATION OF THE PROCESS BY WHICH DESTINATION AREAS AND TOURISM BUSINESSES MARKET SERVICES AND FACILITIES TO POTENTIAL CUSTOMERS WITH AN EMPHASIS ON THE EFFECTIVE USE OF PROMOTION AND DISTRIBUTION CHANNELS

LINK 2: THE PROMOTION OF TRAVEL. The link between Parts 2 and 3 (*Marketing* and *Demand*) is called the *promotion of travel*. A change in the marketing approach may cause a change in the market. For example, an advertising campaign conducted by the U.S. Department of Commerce (*Marketing*) in the United Kingdom in mid-December 2004 to mid-March 2005 increased by 16 percent the intent of those British residents that were aware of the ads (*Demand*) versus those who were unaware of them (U.S. Department of Commerce, 2005). Often, it is the other way around, there is a shift in demand, and marketing is changed accordingly. When people started to take shorter vacations (*Demand*), tourism destinations and suppliers began to offer short-break and weekend getaway packages (*Marketing*).

The *Tourism System Model* is a simple model. The actual situation in tourism is much more complex. There are subsystems within the overall system. For example, Gunn's (1994) *functioning tourism system* might be considered a subsystem for *Destination* (Part 1). The *hospitality and travel marketing system* developed by Morrison (2009) displays a possible subsystem for *Marketing* (Part 2).

PART 3: DEMAND—THE FACTORS INFLUENCING THE MARKET

Part 3 of the book is devoted to demand or the factors that influence people in making travel decisions. A consumer behavior approach is used to describe the travel decision-making process. People decide to travel if they have learned that travel satisfies their needs, if they perceive that future travel will satisfy needs, and if they are able to travel based upon their external constraints including money, time, and other family and work commitments. Travelers' buying decision processes are described. Insights are shared on how tourism marketers can influence demand.

The staging of a mega-event like the Summer Olympics in Beijing in 2008 may result in a major shift in the marketing of the destination area. http://en.beijing2008.com/.

3.

DEMAND: THE FACTORS INFLUENCING THE MARKET

A CONSUMER BEHAVIOR APPROACH TO MARKET DEMAND EMPHASIZING THE INTERNAL AND EXTERNAL INFLUENCES ON TRAVELERS INCLUDING NEEDS, MOTIVATION, AND PERCEPTION; THE ALTERNATIVES TO TRAVEL; THE MARKETING BY TOURISM ORGANIZATIONS; AND THE PROCESS BY WHICH TRAVELERS MAKE BUYING DECISIONS

LINK 3: THE TRAVEL PURCHASE. The linkage between Parts 3 and 4 (*Demand* and *Travel*) is called the *travel purchase*. An arrow pointing in both directions,

clockwise and counterclockwise, characterizes it. This means that each of the two parts (*Demand* and *Travel*) may influence the other part. For example, new segments in the market may emerge based upon special interests or characteristics of groups of people (*Demand*). These people may decide to take advantage of exploring these special interests or mixing with other people of similar characteristics while traveling (*Travel*). For example, organizations such as Ambassadors for Children in Indianapolis, Indiana arrange trips for people interested in volunteer vacations (voluntourism). A new travel mode may be introduced or become more popular (*Travel*). Space tourism is clearly an example of this, but as of now only the wealthiest of people (*Demand*) have been able to afford it.

PART 4: TRAVEL—THE CHARACTERISTICS OF TRAVEL

When the decision has been made to book a travel trip, a set of decisions are taken on whom to travel with; and where, when, and how to get to the destination. Trends in the business and pleasure/personal travel segments are identified. Flows of travelers among destinations are described. Modes of transportation are discussed along with their trends and future prospects.

LINK 4: THE SHAPE OF TRAVEL. The linkage between Parts 4 and 1 (*Travel* and *Destination*) is called the *shape of travel*. It is the combination of who is traveling (travel market segments), and where, when and how they are traveling. Again, a change in either *Travel* or *Destination* may cause a response in the other part of the system.

THE TOURISM SYSTEM MODEL

The four system *Parts* and four *Links* combine in the *Tourism System Model* shown in figure I.1. The model is displayed in this way to emphasize the interactions and interdependency among the four *Parts* of the system. The four-way arrow in the middle of the model indicates that interactions happen between other pairs of system *Parts* (*Demand* and *Destination*, *Travel* and *Marketing*).

The *Tourism System* goes beyond a mere description of tourism and its basic principles. Principles, concepts, and theories from disciplines such as psychology, economics, planning, and marketing that influence tourism are incorporated in the book. Students will realize that tourism is a *multidisciplinary* field in which many contributions are valued and made. In examining the *Parts* and *Links* within *The Tourism System*, those involved in tourism can see where they fit, who is affected by their actions, and how they are affected by the actions of other system participants.

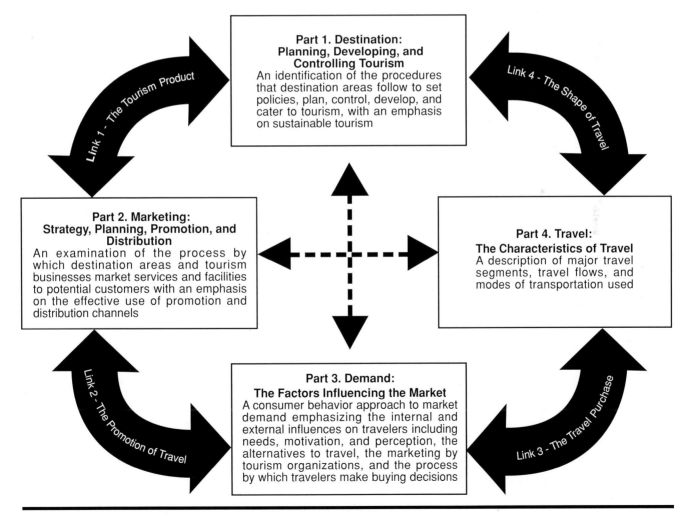

Figure I.1 The Tourism System Model.

TERMINOLOGY

In this book, *travel* refers to the act of moving outside of one's usual environment for business or pleasure, but not for commuting or traveling to or from school. *Tourism* is the term given to the activity that occurs when people travel. This encompasses everything from the planning of the trip, the travel to the destination, the stay itself, the return, and the reminiscences about it afterward. It includes the activities the traveler undertakes as part of the trip, the purchases made, and the interactions that occur between *host* and *guest* in the destination area. In sum, it is all of the activities and impacts that occur when a visitor travels.

The term *recreation* overlaps in many ways with tourism. Recreation is what happens during an individual's leisure time. *Leisure time* is the time people have discretion over. During leisure time people can do what they want. The activities that people engage in during leisure time are known as recreation. Some say that to be recreation, the activity should be constructive and pleasurable. This might involve either aspect to recreation. A game of tennis or golf two miles from home after work would constitute recreation. If one were to drive one hundred miles to a resort for the weekend, the game of tennis would be part of tourism and the golfer would be on a *trip*. A tourism trip does not have to include an overnight stay in the destination area. To avoid the sometimes negative connotations associated with the word "tourist," the term *visitor* has been used throughout this book.

REFERENCES

AFP. 2009. Thai tourism sees 200,000 job losses over crisis, http://www.google.com/hostednews/afp/article/ALeqM5jEe3c3wR19MTHCpCoRnguPzfFUqQ.

Beijing Organizing Committee for the Games of the XXIX Olympiad. 2008. http://en.beijing2008.com/.

Bertalanffy, L. V. 1973. *General Systems Theory: Foundations, Development, Applications.* New York: G. Braziller.

BestCities Global Alliance. 2009. http://www.bestcities.net/.

Bureau of Economic Affairs. 2009. U.S. Travel and Tourism Satellite Accounts, http://www.bea.gov/industry/iedguide.htm#TTSA.

Gunn, C. A. 1994. *Tourism Planning: Basics, Concepts, Cases.* 3rd ed. Washington, DC: Taylor & Francis.

Leiper, N. 1990. *Tourism Systems: An Interdisciplinary Perspective.* Palmerston North, New Zealand, Massey University.

Middleton, V. T. C., A. Fyall, M. Morgan, and A. Ranchhod. 2008. *Marketing in Travel and Tourism.* Oxford, England: Butterworth-Heinemann.

Morrison, A. M. 2009. *Hospitality and Travel Marketing.* 4th ed. Clifton Park, NY: Delmar Cengage Learning.

United Nations Department of Economic and Social Affairs, Statistics Division. 2008. *International Recommendations for Tourism Statistics 2008.* 16–17.

U.S. Department of Commerce. 2005. *First-Ever U.S. Department of Commerce International Tourism Promotion Campaign Successfully Influenced British Travelers to Visit the United States.* Washington, DC: Office of Travel & Tourism Industries, http://www.tinet.ita.doc.gov/tinews/archive/20051011.html.

Wells, A. T., and J. G. Wensveen. 2004. *Air Transportation: A Management Perspective.* 5th ed. Brooks/Cole Cengage Learning.

Tourism

YESTERDAY, TODAY, AND TOMORROW

Travel leads to understanding. It increases the chances for peace, and, therefore, it increases the chances of a better life for all.

Former President Bill Clinton

YESTERDAY: THE HISTORICAL DEVELOPMENT OF TOURISM

For tourism to occur, there must be people who have the ability (both in terms of time and money), the mobility, and the motivation to travel. While the era of mass tourism is a relatively recent one, an individual's propensity and ability to travel has been advanced by numerous developments throughout time.

In pre-industrial times much of the motivation for travel was to develop trade. As empires grew, the conditions necessary for travel began to develop. Ancient Egyptians traveled for both business and pleasure. Travel was necessary between the central government and the territories. To accommodate travelers on official business, hospitality centers were built along major routes and in the cities. The ancient Egyptians also traveled for pleasure. Public festivals were held several times a year. Travel was also for curiosity—people visited the great tombs and temples of the pharaohs.

Assyria comprised the area now known as Iraq. As the empire expanded from the Mediterranean in the West to the Persian Gulf in the East, mobility was made easier to facilitate moving the military. Roads were improved, markers were established to indicate distances, and posts and wells were developed for safety and nourishment. Even today the influence of military construction aids pleasure travel. The U.S. interstate highway system was developed initially to facilitate transportation in the event of a national emergency.

While previous civilizations had set the stage for the development of travel, the Greeks and, later, the Romans brought it all together. In Greek times water was the most important means of moving commercial goods. This combined with the fact that cities grew up along the coast to ensure that travel was primarily by sea. Travel for official business was less important as Greece was divided into independent city-states. Pleasure travel existed in three areas: For religious festivals, for sporting events (most notably the Olympic Games), and to visit cities, especially Athens.

Travel was advanced by two important developments. First, a system of currency exchange was developed. Previously, travelers paid their way by carrying

> Boil it, peel it, cook it, or forget it.
>
> *Standard traveler's adage*

9

various goods and selling them at their destinations. The money of Greek city-states was now accepted as international currency, eliminating the need to travel with a cargo of goods. Second, the Greek language spread throughout the Mediterranean area, making it easier to communicate as one traveled.

Travel flourished in Roman times for five reasons: The control of the large empire stimulated trade and led to the growth of a large middle class with the money to travel; Roman coins were all the traveler had to carry to finance the trip; the means of transportation—roads and waterways—were excellent; communication was relatively easy, as Greek and Latin were the principal languages; and the legal system provided protection from foreign courts, thereby ensuring the safety of the traveler.

The sporting games started by the Greeks were copied in the gladiators' fights to the death. Sightseeing was also popular, particularly to Greece, which had become a part of greater Rome and was the place to see. Touring was also popular to Egypt, site of the Sphinx and the pyramids, and to Asia Minor, scene of the Trojan War. Aristotle visited Asia Minor before establishing his school for students. A final development was that of second homes and vacations associated with them. Villas spread south to Naples, near the sea, the mountains, or mineral spas.

As the Roman Empire collapsed in the fifth century, roads fell into disuse and barbarians made it unsafe to travel. Whereas a Roman courier could travel up to one hundred miles a day, the average daily rate of journey during the Middle Ages was twenty miles. It was not until the twelfth century that the roads became secure again. This was due to the large numbers of travelers going on pilgrimages. Pilgrims traveled to pay homage to a particular site or as an atonement for sin. In other cases, pilgrims journeyed to fulfill a promise made when they were sick.

The next important factor in the history of travel was the Renaissance. As society moved from a rural to an urban base, wealth grew, and more people had the money to travel. Pilgrimages were still important, though journeys to Jerusalem declined due to the growth of Protestantism in Europe. The impetus to travel to learn was aided by the arrival of Renaissance works from Italy. Stable monarchies helped ensure travelers' safety.

The beginning of the sixteenth century saw a new age of curiosity and exploration, which culminated in the popularity of the *Grand Tour*. The Grand Tour was initially a sixteenth-century Elizabethan concept, brought about by the need to develop a class of professional statesmen and ambassadors. Young men traveled with ambassadors over Europe to complete their education. The practice continued to develop in the seventeenth and eighteenth centuries until it became fashionable. No gentleman's education was complete until he had spent from one to three years traveling around Europe with a tutor.

The Grand Tour began in France, where the young man studied French, dancing, fencing, riding, and drawing. Before Paris could corrupt the morals or ruin the finances, the student headed for Italy to study sculpture, music appreciation, and art. The return was by way of Germany, Switzerland, and the Low Countries (Holland, Belgium, and Luxembourg). The Grand Tour reached its peak of popularity in the 1750s and 1760s but was brought to a sudden end by the French Revolution and the Napoleonic Wars.

In the late eighteenth century and early nineteenth century, two major factors affected the development of tourism. Increased industrialization accounted for both of them. First, the industrial revolution accelerated the movement from rural to urban areas. This produced a large number of people in a relatively small area. The desire or motivation to escape, even for a brief period, was there. Associated with this was the development of steam engines in the form of trains and steamships. This allowed the means of mobility to escape. Because of the proximity of the coast to the major urban areas, it was only natural that train lines extended in these directions. However, the vast majority of visitors to the seaside were day-trippers. It was well into the second half of the eighteenth century before the working classes in Britain had regular holidays and sufficient income to use their leisure time to travel.

The development of spas was largely due to the members of the medical professions. During the seventeenth century, they began to recommend the medicinal properties of mineral waters. The idea originated, however, with the Greeks. Spas on the continent of Europe were developed two to three hundred years before their growth in England. Development occurred because of three factors: The approval of the medical profession, court patronage, and local entrepreneurship to take advantage of the first two.

Patronage by court helped establish spas as the place to be. Today we talk about *"mass follows class"*— the idea that the masses are influenced in their choices of vacation spots by people they consider influential. Today film stars seem to have taken over the role of influencer.

The number of people who could afford to "take the waters" was rather small. By the end of the seventeenth century the influence of the medical profession had declined, and spas were more for entertainment instead of health. Their popularity continued, however, into the nineteenth century. It is possible today to drink from the mineral waters at Bath in England. Hot Springs in Arkansas and Glenwood Springs in Colorado still attract many visitors. Additionally, many Eastern European towns proclaim the beneficial effects of mud packs and hydrotherapy.

The medical profession, the British court, and Napoleon all helped popularize the seaside resort. The original motive for sea bathing was for reasons of health. Dr. Richard Russell argued that sea water was effective against such things as cirrhosis, dropsy, gout, gonorrhea, and scurvy and insisted that people drink a pint of it. It is worthy to note that the good Dr. Russell was a physician in Brighton, a resort close to London and on the water. Brighton's fame was assured after the patronage of the Prince Regent, who later became George IV. Similarly, Southend and Cowes are associated with Princess Charlotte and Queen Victoria respectively.

The growth of the seaside resort was stimulated by the French Revolution and the Napoleonic Wars. As stated earlier both put an end to the Grand Tour; those who would have taken the Grand Tour could not travel to the Continent. The now fashionable seaside resorts were the alternative. Toward the end of the nineteenth century, the seaside resorts in Europe became the palaces for the working classes due to the introduction of paid holidays and better wages.

The term *holiday* comes from holy days—days for religious observances. Ancient Rome featured public holidays for great feasting. As Europe became Christian, certain saints' days and religious festivals became holy days when people fasted and prayed and refrained from work. After the Industrial Revolution, the religious holidays gradually became secularized, and the week's holiday emerged. The vacation was negotiated between employer and workers and was again due to the economic and social changes brought about by the Industrial Revolution. It made sense to take the holidays during the warmer summer months. For the employer, it was advantageous to close the entire factory down for one week rather than face the problems of operating with small groups of people absent over a longer period of time. Still today certain weeks are associated with the general holidays of specific cities or towns.

Prior to World War I, the principal mode of domestic transportation was the railway. This meant that development was concentrated at particular points. Regional development occurred with particular resorts growing to serve specific urban areas. Mass production of the automobile, as will be seen later, allowed the dispersion of destination developments.

Tourism in the United States developed for the same reasons as in Europe. At first, travel was limited by the need for transportation. The first development of note was that of resorts. With the encouragement of physicians, resorts like Saratoga in New York became fashionable by the early 1800s. The ocean also became attractive for health reasons initially, although amusements soon sprang up as well.

The development of the railway opened up the country to travelers. By the 1870s, the completion of the Erie Railroad spurred the development of Niagara Falls as a honeymoon paradise. The vast river network of the country's interior allowed the development of steamboat excursions, particularly gambling and amusement trips, between New Orleans and St. Louis.

The Industrial Revolution produced a class of wealthy people who had the time to travel. Touring became popular. Many took the Grand Tour while, for most in the South, an American-style grand tour to the North took a comparable amount of time and money. Three attractions were paramount: Northern cities, historical sites (of the American Revolution and the Civil War), and resorts.

By the late 1800s, the West was attracting not only Easterners but also Europeans who came to see the natural beauty and hunt buffalo. Foreign travelers were also fascinated by travel for religious reasons; many wanted to visit the places where the various religious sects had sprung up.

In the United States, the late nineteenth and early twentieth centuries were characterized as days of high society. The population was rural and centered in the Northeast and Midwest. Many of the 50 million people lived in large families with a strong puritanical work ethic and a belief in self-denial. A sixty-four-hour workweek with Sundays off was the norm. Much of the working class's leisure time was centered around the church. For the wealthy, travel was by railroad and ship to luxury hotel resorts and large second homes. Only the wealthy few were able to travel overseas. By the end of the 1800s, the twelve-hour workday had been reduced to ten hours. *Vacations* were beginning to be recognized. While travel had been for the few, now it began to come within the reach of more people.

Between the world wars, today's consumer society and an era of mass recreation emerged. The 130 million people in the United States spread increasingly to the West Coast and a rural-urban population emerged. Families were smaller, a fifty-hour workweek was common, and more workers were given paid vacations. The development of the automobile allowed the freedom to travel and led to the emergence of the motel. Attractions and facilities became more dispersed as people were not restricted in their movements by the use of public transportation. More middle-class people purchased second homes and saw leisure time as something that was a privilege to enjoy. In Europe, legislation was passed giving paid vacations.

Mass tourism as we know it today is a post-World War II phenomenon. Women who had to work during the war felt more independent; men and women who traveled overseas to fight wanted to return as visitors; travel overseas was encouraged as part of the U.S. attempt to aid war-torn European economies. The introduction of the passenger jet reduced travel time from the United States to Europe from five sailing days or twenty-four flying hours to eight hours; and surplus propeller airplanes were made available to charter operators to transport travelers, not troops, as airlines rushed to purchase new jet aircraft.

The 1960s marked the *democratization of travel*. In the United States, the growth of the population—the baby boomers—together with the forty-hour workweek that increased numbers of three-day weekends and higher levels of disposable income, enabled large numbers of people with the time and money to indulge themselves. Travel was a right. A *hedonistic attitude* (pleasure for the sake of pleasure) increasingly overtook the self-denial of the work ethic.

Temporarily stunned by the *energy crises* of the 1970s and the Gulf War in the early 1990s, tourism continued to grow. The late 1970s and 1980s saw the development of higher divorce rates and single-parent families, together with an increased accent on individual awareness and self-improvement. For many, the indulgence was replaced by a concern for physical fitness.

TOURISM TODAY: AT A CROSSROADS

Tourism at present is greater in size and scope than it ever has been. The World Travel and Tourism Council (WTTC) estimates that tourism will have a global value of $10.8 trillion by 2018, while the World Tourism Organization (WTO) forecasts that there will be 1.6 billion tourists by 2020 (www.futureoftourism.com/travel-trends.htm). Despite natural disasters such as the Indian Ocean tsunami and man-made problems including bomb attacks in London, Turkey, Egypt, Bali and India, tourism has proven to be very resilient. The impact of these events has been temporary shifts in travel flows. People are still traveling.

In 2009, tourism continued to face very challenging external forces. According to the UNWTO (2009):

> "2008 will clearly go into the history books as a year of turbulence and contrasts . . . the growth in international tourist arrivals has slowed drastically worldwide, under the influence of an extremely volatile and unfavorable global economy—due to factors such as the credit crunch, the widening financial crisis, commodity and oil price rises, and massive exchange rate fluctuations."

The sustainable development movement has gained a strong foothold in tourism. The Internet and the Web are in the intermediate stages of revolutionizing how travel information is distributed and how trips are booked.

TOURISM TOMORROW: AN OPTIMISTIC VIEW

The World Travel & Tourism Council (WTTC) in March 2009 acknowledged the challenges and uncertainties that tourism was facing. However, WTTC also noted several positives about tourism and things to look forward to (WTTC, 2009):

- Tourism is a major contributor to job creation and poverty alleviation.
- Fuel prices will be lower.
- The increasing popularity of short break trips will continue.
- There will be more outbound travel from China, India, and Brazil.
- The world tourism economy will continue to grow from 2009 to 2019.

Optimistic projections of international travel must be weighed against concern about the factors that have fueled tourism's growth. According to Professor Harold Goodwin, Director of the International Center for Responsible Tourism at Leeds Metropolitan University, the growth of tourism has been the result of increased prosperity, longer vacations, and inexpensive fuel. He notes that all three are under attack with increased numbers of people in jobs without holiday rights, more and more people not taking their full vacation entitlement because of the pressures of work, and fluctuating oil prices.

It may be that future growth is contingent upon alternative sources of power and improved technology. If high oil prices increase the cost of air travel, we may see more people staying closer to home. Those who do fly to distant destinations may stay longer in order to "justify" in their own minds the higher price of the ticket.

Some suggest that the Internet and virtual reality will act as a substitute for actual travel. It is difficult, however, to substitute the sounds, sights and feel of being in another place. Justin Francis suggests that "Where do you want to go?" should be replaced with "What do you need from a holiday?" (www. futureoftourism.com/travel-trends.htm). Shifting the focus from destination to need satisfaction represents a true customer orientation, an approach that will be suggested throughout this book.

Does tourism sow the seeds of its own destruction? Unplanned development can cause a destination to lose its attractiveness to visitors. However, there is increased evidence of destinations taking their own destinies into hand through codes of environmental ethics to protect their futures for generations of visitors to come. Because less developed countries are especially vulnerable to development pressure, the answer for them may well be to concentrate on quality rather than quantity.

Many of these themes are picked up again in *The Tourism System* as you progress through the book. Above all, you will see that the future of tourism is very exciting. Tourism's future holds great challenges for many professionals and superb career prospects for the tourism students of today. It is hard to grasp that the Grand Tour of Europe can be taken on your personal computer through the Web. The great train journeys of yesteryear are being reinvented in luxurious rail tours. How long will it be before space tourism is common? While the routes may be similar, the journeys of the future will be different from those of the past. Bon voyage!

PART ONE

Destination

PLANNING, DEVELOPING, AND CONTROLLING TOURISM

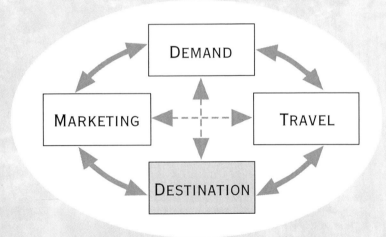

The characteristics of travel to a destination area contribute to shaping how the destination functions and what it provides for visitors. Part One of *The Tourism System* examines an area's destination mix which, in part, reflects the market segments it serves, the geographic origins of visitors, and visitors' modes of transportation. The destination must develop a tourism policy and plan, and the legislation and regulations to control tourism. It must carefully develop tourism to minimize any adverse impacts.

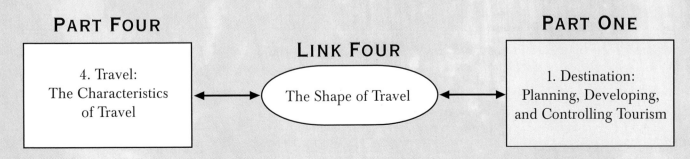

PART FOUR

4. Travel:
The Characteristics
of Travel

LINK FOUR

The Shape of Travel

PART ONE

1. Destination:
Planning, Developing,
and Controlling Tourism

chapter 1

The Destination Mix

ATTRACTIONS AND SERVICES
FOR THE TRAVELER

I love to travel,

But hate to arrive.

Hernando Cortez

PURPOSE

Students will be able to identify the strengths and deficiencies of a tourism destination.

LEARNING OBJECTIVES

- ✓ Explain the interdependencies between the five destination mix elements.
- ✓ Identify the important elements of attractions, facilities, infrastructure, transportation, and hospitality required for a tourism destination.
- ✓ Identify the crucial elements that make a destination competitive.

OVERVIEW

At a destination there is a mix of interdependent elements. The elements are interdependent because in order to produce a satisfying vacation experience, all elements must be present. The destination is composed of:

- Attractions
- Facilities
- Infrastructure
- Transportation
- Hospitality

Attractions draw visitors to an area. Facilities serve the needs of the visitors while away from home. Infrastructure and transportation are necessary to help ensure accessibility of the destination to the visitor. Hospitality is concerned with the way in which services are delivered to the visitor.

ATTRACTIONS

The central aspects of tourism are attractions. Attractions, by definition, have the ability to draw people to them. Although attractions for the visitor concern the satisfactions perceived from various experiences, the task for the developer and designer is to create an environment made up in part of "attractions" that will provide an opportunity for the visitor to enjoy a visit. In discussing destination attractiveness, two ideas emerge. First, there are two universal attributes—climate and natural scenery—that

> Worth seeing? Yes; but not worth going to see.
>
> Samuel Johnson

serve as the primary definition of the attractiveness of a destination. Second, additional factors unique to the destination, are recognized by tourists. The addition at a site of factors other than attractions (services, transportation, hospitality) will help ensure that enjoyment.

Attractions have many characteristics. As mentioned above, they tend to draw visitors to them—they aim to serve the recreational needs of visitors. They can to a large extent be developed anywhere and act as a growth inducer, tending to be developed first in a tourist region.

SCOPE

The way in which attractions are characterized has implications for development and marketing. Attractions can be characterized in terms of their scope, ownership, permanency, and drawing power. A typology is suggested in figure 1.1. Destinations may be primary or secondary (sometimes called stopover or touring destinations). A *primary destination* is one that is attractive enough to be the primary motivation for tourism visits and one that is aimed at satisfying visitors for several days or longer. A *secondary* or *stopover destination* is either an interesting or necessary place to visit on the way to a primary destination, and it aims at satisfying visitors for one to two days. It may be interesting enough to attract tourists on their way somewhere else, or it may, in fact, be a required stop on the way to a final destination. Certain areas can be primary destinations for one segment of the market or stopover destinations for other segments.

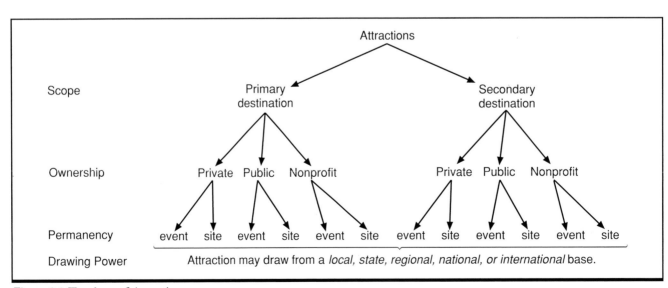

Figure 1.1 Typology of Attractions.

Attractions at a primary destination have to have sufficient breadth of appeal to entice visitors to stay for many days. There has to be sufficient things to do and see to keep all members of the party occupied. At a stopover destination, the length of stay will be shorter and the need for a diversity of attractions is less. From a marketing viewpoint, the primary destination or attraction seeks fewer visitors staying longer periods of time, compared to the secondary destination that relies on attracting larger numbers for shorter periods of time. In terms of location, primary destinations tend to be oriented toward the location of the market (Disney World) or to the site of the resource (Aspen). Secondary destinations, although located between visitors and resources, are more reliant on their accessibility to transportation networks.

OWNERSHIP

The form of ownership of the attraction has great implications for tourism. Approximately 85 percent of all U.S. outdoor recreation lands are owned by the federal government. The agencies that manage this land often do not have tourism as a primary use of the land. Their outlooks will determine the degree to which tourism and recreation are encouraged.

The nonprofit sector is usually oriented to some aspect of the social good. Yet when nonprofit organizations get involved in work for the social good, such as historical preservation, their efforts can have great implications for tourism. Limited tourism may be a vehicle for getting sufficient revenue to continue the historical work. Care must be taken to ensure that the means does not become the end. The nonprofit organization involved may back out of the project and the resource may become overcommercialized and lose its original appeal.

The private sector's motivation is that of profit making. The wise manager will realize that short-run profit maximization may be detrimental to the long-run success of the attraction and the destination.

PERMANENCY

Site attractions concern attractions of a physical nature. They are largely permanent, with their locations being fixed. *Event attractions* are rather short in duration, and their location can be changed. Site attractions are more dependent upon the resource base. Event attractions can be developed at places more convenient to the market. Because site attractions cost more to develop in terms of both time and money than do event attractions, new tourist regions can conceivably develop event attractions as a way of publicizing the area and bringing in cash to help finance more permanent site attractions.

DRAWING POWER

Attractions may also be defined in terms of the distance from which they are able to draw people. Attractions may be locally, statewide, regionally, nationally, or internationally significant. The rating is inclusive in that a national attraction will draw from the state and local levels, also. If proposed and existing attractions can be objectively viewed in terms of their drawing power, appropriate strategies for the marketing of existing attractions and a mix of future attractions can be developed. Attractions do not become attractions for the purpose of tourism until a certain amount of development has occurred to make the natural resource accessible to and attractive for visitors.

Although tourists are motivated to visit a destination to satisfy various needs and wants, they are also motivated to visit a destination because of certain characteristics. The characteristics that attract tourists are:

- Natural resources
- Climate
- Culture
- History
- Ethnicity
- Accessibility

NATURAL RESOURCES. The natural resources of a destination provide an excellent asset to sell to tourists. When studying the landscape or scenery of an area, it is important to note not only the natural resources but also the human imprints on the area; for this is also part of the scenery. In this respect, it is important to point out that any change in one aspect of the scenery changes the whole landscape.

Research into the role of protected areas as attractions indicates the importance of a destination's designation as a protected area in giving the sight a name or label that becomes a marker that differentiates the destination from other similar places. The national park label, for example, is better known than the world heritage label. However, the world heritage designation—once it becomes better known—might appeal to tourists who live far away. Such people are likely to concentrate on must-see attractions, and the world heritage name implies a certain degree of importance and exclusivity.

For many markets, an outstanding natural resource has been, and still is, sandy beaches. © 2009 deb22. Used under license from Shutterstock, Inc.

High expectations are set in the mind of the tourist (Reinius and Fredman, 2007).

For many markets, an outstanding natural resource has been, and still is, sandy beaches. In urban areas, where children do not have the opportunity to run free in safety or the chance to see the sea, an exodus occurs on weekends and holidays to spots offering such attractions. So it is that Jones Beach becomes a weekend mecca for Manhattan residents, while Manitoba advertises 100,000 lakes, together with soft warm sands and sparkling blue waters.

Two important points should be stressed when considering scenery. First, from the visitor's viewpoint, there is no cost for it. A beautiful sunset, Niagara Falls, the Grand Canyon—these cost the visitor nothing. The second point is concerned with the variety of scenery. Variety in an area can be an important selling point. In this way, Britain with a variety of views and types of countryside every few hundred yards can compete—successfully so—with such dwarfing structures as the Canadian Rockies and the Swiss Alps.

CLIMATE. Climate is perhaps the most common marketing theme used as the basis for selling a tourism area once it has suitable visitor attractions. Although a region in some cases can be sold largely on the basis of climate, for maximum effect the area must be readily accessible to large concentrations of population. One reason for the popularity of California's coastline resorts is their proximity via automobile to millions of people. Florida, meanwhile, to attract vacationers from the northeastern and the north central states, must advertise that its sun is only an hour or so away by plane.

In addition to ready accessibility, the destination area should promise something that visitors cannot get at home. In a populous center, where most people live with enough disposable income to travel, one market segment may be attracted by warm sunshine at a time when it is cold and gloomy at home, while another segment may seek accentuated winter conditions of a ski resort. Conversely, when the population centers are sweltering with summer heat, one market segment may head for the seashore—Maine, Oregon, Florida, or even the Caribbean—for cooling breezes, while another segment wants a mountain area, whether it's New Hampshire, the Canadian Rockies, Scotland, or Switzerland.

When considering summer weather, the most comfortable living is in the populous temperate zones of the Mediterranean, which have warm, sunny, and dry climates. Tropical conditions are too hot and too wet to sell solely on this basis, so that selling of tropical climates must be amplified with a number of other attractions, which is the case of the Caribbean.

An interesting corollary of climate advertising is that those who have left home want to be kept informed about the bad conditions they have fled. In Florida and Puerto Rico, hotels post weather conditions in northern cities during the winter. In summer, it may also be cooler in Florida and Puerto Rico than it is back home because of ocean breezes.

Recreational activities are undertaken considering the combination of natural resources and climate on hand. Over the past several years we have seen a remarkable growth in recreational pursuits in general and participative recreational pursuits in particular. This has resulted in a decline in the business of many sedentary holiday areas and the upsurge of resorts offering sporting facilities. The type of recreation facilities offered is usually determined by the nature of the surrounding countryside: skiing requires mountains, water sports need water, and so on. However, we are seeing the introduction of artificial ski slopes, "dry" ski slopes, artificial lakes for boating and fishing, and artificially stocked waters and bird and hunting grounds. Dubai even features an indoor ski area constructed in an extremely arid region.

The important point to remember in selling an area on its recreational facilities is to sell a variety of pursuits, not just one. This way one does not rely solely on one sport, one market, or one season for one's business.

CULTURE. Each country has its own unique culture—a state of manners, taste, and intellectual development. Some countries are found to be more interesting culturally and better developed than others. Culture is, for practical tourism purposes, interwoven with history. Today's way of life is tomorrow's culture.

Thus, although one can "sell" the way of life of the people of a foreign land, that way of life must be radically different from the visitor's own to induce excitement and the desire to view it.

America and the Americans have always exhibited, perhaps because of their relatively young existence, an almost insatiable appetite for historical culture. With a fusing in this country of so many races from so many different lands, these groups have jealously clung to preserving their own ethnic culture. Today, however, these cultures are not guarded quite so tightly, but are sold to the rest of the country. Williamsburg, the Pennsylvania Dutch, and western ranch country demonstrate this feature remarkably well.

Each country has its own unique culture that is interwoven with history. © 2009 David Hughes. Used under license from Shutterstock, Inc.

HISTORICAL RESOURCES. Historical resources may be defined by function into the following subdivisions:

1. War
2. Religion
3. Habitation
4. Government

Past wars hold a fascination for many people. Depending on the chronological distance from the event, the emotions aroused range from morbid curiosity and excitement to sorrow and remembrance. Thus, people throng to the Tower of London and Edinburgh Castle to see the chamber of horrors and the bottleneck dungeons, excited by the thought of such distant gory deeds. The most popular World War II sites in Europe are Margraten in the Netherlands, Omaha Beach Ceremony in France on the site of the D-Day

landings in Normandy in 1944, and the Luxembourg City Cemetery, where General George S. Patton Jr. lies buried. In America, the popularity of Arlington Cemetery in Washington, DC, attests to the national feeling of remembrance for those who died for their country, while the site of the World Trade Center bombings in New York City continues to draw those wishing to pay their respects. After many years, Vietnam is now becoming a popular tourist destination.

Since the times of the earliest pilgrimages and the travelers in Chaucer's Canterbury Tales, pilgrims have made journeys to shrines, monuments, and cathedrals in the name of their Lord. Although religion can be a tremendous selling force, it can act negatively for the country. The obvious present example is in Northern Ireland, where past demonstrations against parades commemorating William of Orange's defeat of the militant Catholics have erupted into long, and sometimes bloody, battles that have served to disrupt trade, industry, and tourism from progressing into the area.

Religion forms the basis for the Outdoor Biblical Museum in Nymegen, Holland, which is a beautiful and moving attempt to bring all faiths to a point where they can worship together. Visitors walk along narrow paths cut through a forest to arrive at a scene from the Bible. A minimum of figures and a natural landscape leave the visitor awestruck by the simplicity of it all.

From the simple house tour to the elaborate view of Buckingham Palace, humans' natural curiosity to see the trappings of others' homes is a marketable item. Thousands flock to the homes of Anne Hathaway and William Shakespeare, or to the houses of George Washington and Abraham Lincoln, in an attempt to achieve some sense of rapport with the memory of these famous people. However, one need not be numbered among the dead to enjoy this admiration and visitation. The White House and Buckingham Palace are favorite tourist stops while, in Britain, many stately homes are being opened to the public, and the promise of dining with a duke and thereafter spending the night in one of the state rooms is an appealing attraction to many. After the success of the movie *Lord of the Rings*, the New Zealand Tourist Board began promoting the various sites where the movie was filmed.

Visitors can be encouraged to visit places where fictitious people lived. There is a *Sound of Music* trip to Salzburg while Romania's tourism authority offers a tour to Dracula's Transylvania (now a part of Romania).

A nation's capital will always hold a fascination for those who desire to see where the decisions are made.

The Houses of Parliament are as well known as the House of Representatives and the Kremlin. The chance to see the country's leaders in session is an experience few visitors would miss. Even on the state and local levels, council sessions can become the focal point of an educational tour, while the City Hall "you can't fight" may also be visited.

ETHNICITY. The United States is a cosmopolitan mixture of first-, second-, and third-generation Scots, Irish, Dutch, Germans, Russians, and so on. As such, it is easy to appeal to people's basic sentimentality to coax them "back to the homeland." The ethnic groups may be classified as first and later generations. For the first generation, no development is needed at all, because these people wish to see the area they left just as they left it.

However, first-generation travelers will generally stay with friends, and one finds that it is the later generations that will spend more money in a particular spot. This latter group of travelers, experiencing a different environment, will require some of the creature comforts afforded them at home. It should not be thought, however, that the only viable market for this kind of promotion consists of present-day U.S. citizens, though many examples of such marketing exist. One of the definite movement channels that can be readily traced is that from Ireland to New York and Boston.

In North America itself, Michigan's Tulip Festival, the Highland Games at Alma, the Beer Festival at Frankenmuth, and the weekly summer ethnic concerts in downtown Detroit show the success of a campaign on this asset.

It is possible also to spotlight movements within a country. In the United States, it is estimated that one out of every five Americans moves each year. Nor are these movements random. States like Florida, Nevada, Arizona, and California have attracted decennial population increases in the order of 50 to 80 percent, and states like Arkansas and West Virginia have suffered population decreases in the order of 6 to 10 percent. There may well be a significant market to be reached through the sentimental pull of old friends and places.

ACCESSIBILITY. The last item to consider in this section is accessibility. Though germane to every asset listed above, certain areas owe their popularity—and some their very being—to the fact that they are readily accessible to large urban areas. The development of Brighton, England, as a weekend and holiday resort despite its completely stony beach is due to its proxim-ity to London with a potential market of over 8 million people.

The accessibility of an area to a particular market should be measured in terms of time, cost, frequency, and comfort. Although attention should be paid to each factor, an area can sell on its comparative advantage in providing exceptional services in one or a combination of several of the above factors at the expense of another.

Traveling to Europe by plane, for instance, may be less comfortable than sea travel, but Europe is more accessible in terms of time and frequency of service. An advertisement for a sea ferry declares, "All that divides Scotland and Ireland is two-and-a-half hours." The motorist immediately knows how long it will take him to get to Ireland, and a seemingly large and time-consuming obstacle—the Irish Sea—becomes a mere two-and-a-half hour expressway.

Part of Mexico's appeal to the U.S. market is its accessibility in terms of cost—not necessarily in terms of cost to reach the country, but in terms of what can be bought there. A two-week vacation in Mexico may be more accessible in terms of cost than fourteen days in the United States.

Other areas have become attractions because of the difficulty in reaching them. In those few cases in which lack of accessibility increases the attractiveness, the end result (the destination) should be somewhat spectacu-lar—a magnificent view, great food, or a wonderful culture.

Overall, two patterns of attractions have emerged (Hu and Ritchie, 1993). First, some aspects have universal importance in influencing the evaluations tourists have of how attractive a destination is. Scenery, climate, and price are most critical. Second, there are certain aspects of a destination whose importance depends on the type of destination and vacation experience being provided. Culture, as an attraction, is more important to certain types of tourists than to others. Thus, a destination should emphasize its culture to those visitor segments to whom this is important rather than to all segments of the market.

DEVELOPMENT AND DESIGN

Gunn (1972) has suggested several design principles to guide the development of attractions. It is important to remember that the dependencies of the attraction vary. Certain types of attractions, such as ski areas and battlefields, are extremely dependent upon the resource base, but others, such as theme parks, are much less so. All attractions are, to some extent, dependent upon their relationship to the visitor's origin, upon their accessibility, and upon the number of facilities and services available. In terms of the visitor origin, the time relationship may be more important than the distance relationship. Zones of visitor origin will differ, depending upon the mode of transportation considered. A two-hour zone, for example, may include visitors one hundred miles away by car and five hundred miles away by plane.

As noted earlier, accessibility, although important, is more crucial to the touring destination because the time available is a major constraint.

Services and facilities tend to grow up to support the developed attraction. However, if a service center is already developed, its location may affect the development of a new attraction.

Attractions tend to be clustered for several reasons. First, there is an increased desire on the part of visitors to do more in one place. Second, clustering allows a destination a better opportunity to satisfy more people. To explore a major theme fully, a variety of different attractions may be required. A group of museums, each exploring part of an overall theme, is more effective than one. A cluster of different but related historic buildings may be necessary to explore and explain a particular time in history fully. Different rides, clustered into a theme park, are necessary to appeal to all of the senses.

The extent of clustering depends upon the type of destination involved. For the primary destination, clustering is obviously more important. This is particularly true if accessibility is dependent upon modes of transportation oriented toward mass tourism. Destinations that rely on visitors arriving by plane, boat, or train will be apt to develop more clusters of attractions than those appealing to the motorist.

> Every year it takes less time to fly across the Atlantic and more time to drive to the office.
>
> Anonymous

EVENTS

Events can be developed for several reasons. Events may be staged to make money; celebrate particular holidays, seasons, or historical events; provide cultural or educational experiences; or unite and give a feeling of pride to a particular community. An event may seek to combine these reasons. It is important that objectives be developed, agreed upon, and ranked, in order that subsequent conflicts over strategy can be solved by referring to the action that will help to achieve the most important objective.

A Do-It-Yourself Kit has been developed on behalf of Arts Victoria in Australia to allow festival organizers to determine the economic impact of festivals or events. This is done through a determination of the value added to the gross regional product by visitors to the region, locals who stay in the region rather than going outside and festival organizers obtaining funds from both within and outside of the region that would not have been obtained had the event not taken place.

A survey of seven festivals ranging from one to ten days in duration found an economic impact from $26,000 to just over $3.3 million (Jackson et al., 2005).

FACILITIES

While attractions draw visitors from their homes, facilities are necessary to serve these visitors away from home. Facilities tend to be oriented to attractions in their locations because of the need to locate close to where the market will be. They tend to support rather than induce growth and, hence, they tend to be developed at the same time as or after the attractions are developed. The relationship between attractions and other elements of a tourism destination is suggested in figure 1.2. A certain level of services is necessary for a destination to be considered by a visitor. If the level of services is lacking, that destination will not be considered. However, the mere presence of these facilities and other services, by themselves, will not bring visitors. Attractions must be present for this to occur. If people feel a destination is not safe they will not visit. However, the fact that a destination is regarded as safe will not, in and of itself, induce travel. Attractions are necessary.

It is possible for an attraction to be a facility. A case in point would be a well-

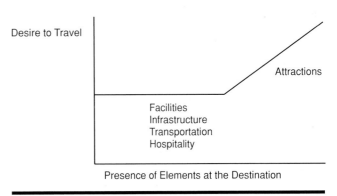

Figure 1.2 The Importance of Destination Elements.

known resort hotel that not only serves to draw people to an area but satisfies their needs as well.

LODGING

While away from home, the visitor needs to eat and sleep. Sleeping accommodations can range from hotels of an international standard and condominiums, to campgrounds and the homes of friends and relatives. Lodging accounts for between one-fifth and one-fourth of total visitor expenditures, despite the fact that almost half of U.S. visitors stay in the homes of friends and relatives when taking a trip. It is vital to the success of a tourist region that a sufficient quantity of accommodations of the right quality be provided for visitor needs.

The type of accommodation provided will be determined primarily by the characteristics of the market segment being sought. Some prefer the full-amenity type of property. In destination areas these properties will tend to have greater demands placed on them in terms of room size and services offered because guests will be staying a long time. Visitors whose prime motivation is to see friends and relatives will likely stay with them.

The type of accommodation provided is also partly determined by what the competitors are providing. A key concept to remember in marketing is that the facilities provided should be at least equal to those provided by the competition for the same market. The type of lodging is also determined by the transportation used by visitors to the destination. In Roman times, resting places were determined when the horse, not the rider, was tired. In the United States in the early seventeenth century, taverns were located about fifteen miles or one day's carriage ride apart. The development of rail travel led to accommodation clusters near the stations. An increase in auto travel encouraged the roadside motel, but the growth of air travel has led to clusters of hotels and motels around airports.

FOOD AND BEVERAGE

More of the tourist dollar is spent on food and beverage than on any other service. It is probably no coincidence that those states highest in per capita eating place sales are also top tourist states. The type of food service provided will be related to visitor needs. Many areas have successfully developed menus indigenous to the area to promote local economy foods, while they also use the local items as a unique selling point.

QUICK TRIP 1.1

A Grave Attraction

The Holocaust is considered a dark spot on the history of the world. Some people are convinced that such a tragedy never occurred; most wish it never happened, but some want to remember and experience the horrors. Auschwitz was the largest Nazi concentration and extermination camp. This camp was the backdrop for some of the world's greatest tragedies, the place where over one million people were murdered. In two consecutive months, almost half a million Jews were exterminated there. The other parts of Auschwitz were dedicated to labor and experiments. More than 50 percent of those not sent to the extermination part of Auschwitz died from starvation, inhuman living conditions, disease, punishment, medical experiments, and labor that exceeded physical boundaries. On July 2, 1947, the Polish Parliament turned Auschwitz into a museum, and it has been preserved for decades. Millions of tourists visit this site each year, each sharing different backgrounds and religious beliefs. The tour guides take visitors by the gas chambers, the abandoned suitcases, prosthetic limbs, human hair, shoes, and glasses, reminders of the innocent lives that were extinguished here.

THINK ABOUT THIS:

1. What makes this an attraction?
2. Should this be considered an attraction?
3. Is this attraction somehow dishonoring those who died there? Is it honoring them?
4. Is it important to keep reminders of the past to prevent a repeat in the future?

Source: Auschwitz: A Grim Reminder of the Holocaust. *Tourism Review*, 2008: 7–8. Retrieved 7 May 2008, http://www.tourism-review.com.

SUPPORT INDUSTRIES

Support industries refer to the facilities provided for visitors in addition to lodging, food, and beverage. These may include souvenir or duty-free shops (for goods), laundries and guides (for services), and festival areas and recreational facilities (for activities).

Support industries can either be subsistence-related by providing staple needs or requirements or pleasure-related by providing impulse or entertainment purchase opportunities.

Tourism support industries include small businesses such as souvenir shops. © 2009 Whaldener Endo. Used under license from Shutterstock, Inc.

For tourism, support industries tend to be small businesses. This fact can be both positive and negative for the destination area. It can be positive in that the encouragement of small businesses will allow for the wide distribution and sharing of the financial benefits of tourism with those in the community. On the other hand, small businesses may lack the capital and expertise required to provide a quality part of the vacation experience. Several considerations can assist in maximizing the potential of support industries. It is important that the support industries be located in places accessible to visitors. It will be necessary to observe or predict visitor movement patterns to locate facilities to serve them optimally. The number and types of facilities offered will also have to be determined relative to visitor needs. Facilities should be provided that match the quality and price level of lodging, food, and beverage operations that should themselves be provided in light of visitor expenditure levels.

If a sufficient number and mix of services are provided, the supply may actually stimulate demand or increase the length of stay of visitors by offering such a number of attractive alternatives that they will have enough things to buy and do to encourage them to stay longer. At the same time, too many facilities at one place may mean that there is insufficient sales volume to ensure a reasonable rate of return for the businesses involved.

The two primary techniques for helping ensure the effective development of support industries are:

1. Zoning and operating regulations enforced by law
2. Ownership or control exercised through leasing of facilities to individual entrepreneurs

QUICK TRIP 1.2

Green Hotels–Is Green Here to Stay?

A recent trend in helping the environment has made its way into the hospitality arena. In Colorado, several hotels are evaluating the pros and cons of going green. Some say that it helps the environment and saves money, while others say it is not possible to see the benefits of going green yet. Increasing research has shown that the amount of money to be saved from going green is extraordinary. The Oxford Hotel in Denver, part of Sage Hospitality Resources LLC, has taken several strides to become green. From installing low-energy lighting to energy-efficient thermostats, hotel officials estimate the annual savings will be approximately $26,000 per year. More and more guests are asking about the hotel's green practices before they stay there. Many companies will only book at hotels that are environmentally friendly. Many experts are saying that people will pay more for a green hotel, while others are saying that if people are paying that much money, they want their sheets changed every night and they want their miniature shampoo bottles.

THINK ABOUT THIS:

1. Is going green simply the latest trend?
2. Will the green incentive last? If not, what do you think will be the next trend?
3. Would you choose to stay at one hotel over another because it is green?

Source: Leavitt, N. Colorado Hotels Ponder Economics of Going Green. *Denver Business Journal*, 2008. Retrieved 7 May 2008, http://denver.bizjournal.com/denver/stories/2008/02/04/story7.html.

The methods can, in fact, be combined with good results. People at destination areas may designate certain areas as being appropriate for tourist-support industries, and within those areas they may lay down restrictions as to theme, design, building height, and density; and they may place restrictions on signs in order to ensure the development of a destination that has attractions and facilities that meet expectations of the visitor market sought. The problem can also be effectively managed if a developer or public agency owns a large tract and establishes control through requirements in the lease agreement.

INFRASTRUCTURE

Attractions and facilities are not accessible to visitors' use until basic infrastructure needs of the destination have been met. Infrastructure consists of all the underground and surface developmental construction of a region and comprises:

- Water systems
- Communication networks
- Health care facilities
- Power sources
- Sewage/drainage areas
- Streets, highways
- Security systems

There has been some criticism of tourism's overreliance on a fully developed infrastructure. In certain parts of the world, newly discovered tourist destinations may be able to satisfy visitor needs without developing a full infrastructure system. The lack of modern highways may, in fact, be an added attraction for some kinds of visitors. As a destination attracts more visitors, the increase in numbers may actually stimulate the development of the infrastructure. In most cases, the reverse is true. Infrastructure development is necessary to stimulate the development of tourism.

The infrastructure of an area is shared by both visitors and residents. An upgrading of the elements of the infrastructure primarily for the purpose of attracting visitors will benefit the host population. The development of infrastructure is almost always a public-sector responsibility. It is one way that the public sector has created a climate suitable for tourism development.

The development of a proper infrastructure requires engineering input, but it is wise to consider the reports of engineers in light of the effects on tourism. The best placement of a coast road from an engineering perspective may not be the best route for visitor viewing.

The important parts of a tourist infrastructure are the following:

- **Water**—Sufficient quantities of pure water are essential. A typical resort requires 350 to 400 gallons of water per room per day. An eighteen-hole golf

QUICK TRIP 1.3

Accessible Travel

Infrastructure is what is necessary for tourists to visit attractions. One group of tourists that need special forms of infrastructure is people who are handicapped. Have you ever thought about how a person in a wheelchair travels on an airplane? How about a paraplegic person? Rex Airline, out of Australia, has passed guidelines that would require a disabled person to travel with a caretaker. The airline argues that it is not fair for the flight attendant to have so much time taken up with a disabled person and that often flight attendants hurt their backs lifting disabled persons. The infrastructure for a handicap destination must be different from that of a normal person. This includes curb cuts, audible crosswalk signals, ramps, and elevators. In the United States, 12.9 percent of persons ages twenty-one to sixty-four have a disability. That is a big portion of people who are not thought about when the infrastructure of destinations is planned.

THINK ABOUT THIS:

1. Is it worth expanding the infrastructure of destinations to include disabled persons?
2. Are there certain areas that should not be changed for handicap accessibility?
3. What aspects of infrastructure need to be altered to accommodate handicapped and disabled tourists?

Sources:

Accessible World of Travel. *Tourism Review,* 2008. Retrieved 7 May 2008, http://www.tourism-review.com.

Summary: Prevalence by State: Ages 21 to 64. *2006 Disability Status Report: United States.* 3–5. *Rehabilitation Research and Training Center on Disability Demographics and Statistics.* 2007. Cornell U. Retrieved 7 May 2008, http://www.DisabilityStatistics.org.

course will require 600,000 to 1 million gallons of water per day, depending on the region in which it is located.

- **Power**–The important considerations are that adequate supplies of power be available to meet peak-load requirements, that continuity of service be ensured, and that, if possible, the type of power supplied be compatible with that used by the target markets of the destination.

- **Communication**–Despite the fact that many visitors may wish to get away from it all, it is necessary for most that telephone and/or internet access be available. The lack of telephones in hotel rooms will deter visitors from staying at a particular property because of the security aspect.

- **Sewage/drainage**–Sewer demand is often placed at 90 percent of domestic water demand. Although water-storage reservoirs and sewage treatment plants can be designed on the basis of maximum average demand, transmission lines must be designed on a basis of maximum peak demand.

- **Health care**–The type of health care facilities provided will depend on the number of visitors expected, their ages, the type of activities in which they will engage, and local geographic factors. Ski areas will tend to specialize in broken bones, for example.

- **Security**–While on vacation visitors are in an unfamiliar environment. Because of this, the need for assurances regarding their safety is important. Especially when traveling long distances and to foreign countries, the image gained of the destination may be distorted. Europeans, for example, are fed television programs that sensationalize the U.S. crime scene. This creates an image of the United States as a place filled with violence. In addition, the costs of medical care are so expensive that concerns about health in foreign countries may generate additional fears. Insecurities about food, water, or police protection may dissuade visitors from visiting. It is necessary that the basic needs for security be considered and ensured to make the potential visitor feel secure prior to and during the vacation.

TRANSPORTATION

The transportation infrastructure at a destination has been shown to positively contribute to tourist numbers (Khadaroo and Seetanah, 2007). A complete transport system consists of four elements (Prideaux, 2000):

QUICK TRIP 1.4

The Mini World Has a Huge Problem

Dubai, the capital of the United Arab Emirates, for years has been sustained by profits from oil reserves. Each year these wells produce $1.5 billion worth of revenue for the tiny country; however, by the year 2016, the oil is expected to run out. Once a small fishing village, Dubai has managed to get itself on the map not only from its natural resources but also from its inventive nature to make Dubai a world-class tourism destination. As there is not much oceanfront property in Dubai, the country has built three palm-shaped, man-made islands that span out from the coast, creating miles of new oceanfront property. While the palms were massive projects in and of themselves, in 2003, Dubai announced that it would be reproducing the world, but in islands, two miles off the coast. The world islands will be in an area of about twenty-four square miles, or the size of Manhattan. The project is projected to cost $14 billion and require 350 cubic meters of sand and 320 million tons of rock, enough to build five pyramids. The three hundred islands that make up the world were originally forecast to house about three thousand people as a very exclusive neighborhood. However, the price tag of $38 million for an island has scared off most individuals, so resorts have invested a fortune in building on these islands. The projected population of this area is now 250,000. As the world has no direct connection to the mainland, all transportation to the islands must be done by boat. The experts are now developing a system that will safely transport these individuals, with the possible use of water taxis, water ferries, and global positioning systems. The transportation of this project is a logistical nightmare. The world islands will become the largest berth and will need over twenty-four thousand parking spots for boats.

THINK ABOUT THIS:

1. Currently, there are no ways of regulating boat traffic; how would you manage that amount of boats in such a small area?

2. What types of technology would you utilize to make this project more accessible?

Source: Incredible Islands: Dubai. Man-made. *National Georgraphic*. Spring 2008.

Modes–Road, sea, air, and rail. The distance between the origin and the destination will influence the mode used. Tourists are concerned about cost, time and distance covered in deciding which mode to use. It is important to consider travel to and from the destination as well as travel **at** the destination. One study indicates that car-borne visitors to a national park spend more than public transport users (Downard and Lumsdon, 2004). The authors suggest that, once the visitors reach the park, slowing them down generates more income for the local economy. They suggest moving away from a focus on volume through the park as a measure of economic success. A tour through the park with one stop generates less income than a series of stops throughout the transportation corridor. A "hop on–hop off" type of bus service is likely to generate more income.

The way–Roadways, seaways, airways, and railways. The availability of first-class roads adds greatly to the accessibility of a region. Some areas have, in fact, refused to upgrade their road systems in order to slow down tourism development. The effect of a highway system was noted by the U.S. Department of Transportation when it estimated that the development of the U.S. interstate system meant that the distance that could be safely driven in one day increased from 350 to 500 miles.

There are certain ways to make use of the highway more interesting to tourists.

1. Provide close-range view of local scenes.
2. Change the elevation.
3. Develop viewpoints and overlooks.

A scenic highway can bring visitors to an area. © 2009 Thomas Barrat. Used under license from Shutterstock, Inc.

> It is said that about 20 percent of the population fear flying, even though statistically it is the safest form of transport.
>
> Travel/Tourism, The War Cry, 1 May 2004

4. Independently align dual-lane highways to fit into the land contour.
5. Selectively thin trees to reveal views.

It is crucial to consider to what extent resident (or local) traffic is to be integrated with tourist (or regional) traffic. It may be desirable to design a dual system of higher-speed lanes flanked by roads for low-speed local traffic. Roads should be engineered for safety, taking appropriate measures designed to safeguard the highway user.

Terminals–There should be a degree of coordination between the three modes of air, rail, and bus to facilitate passenger transfer between modes. Directional and informational signs should be easy to see and of a uniform design throughout the mode. O'Hare Airport in Chicago used to have a desk above which was a sign that read "Multilingual assistance available." Any tourist able to read the sign had no need of the services being provided. A security system should be in place to prevent theft of luggage and/or misclaiming of checked bags at terminals. Personnel should be available to assist passengers, particularly the aged, the handicapped, and non-English-speaking passengers. Complete information should be provided on the location, fares, schedules, and routes of local transportation services.

Technology–Changes in technology determine competition between the modes, price, speed, comfort and safety. Intelligent Transportation Systems (ITS) uses a variety of technologies to better manage ground transportation. Included are such things as information systems and automated traffic management techniques. In the Acadia National Park in Maine, a variety of technologies are being used to improve operation of the Island Explorer bus system (Daigle and Zimmerman, 2004).

Two-way voice communication allows drivers to be in touch with dispatchers who can pinpoint the location of buses through automatic vehicle locators. Electronic bus departure signs allow passengers to know how long it will be before a bus arrives. Parking lots are monitored and the amount of traffic is recorded at park entrances to improve bus allocation. Visitors find the system easy to use and indicate that the information helps reduce the stress and uncertainty of travel.

The influence of transportation elements on a destination are as follows (Prideaux, 2000):

- The distance from origin to destination influences the transportation mode chosen in that the greater the distance between the origin and the destination, the more likely it is that air transportation will be used.
- The major factors influencing transportation access costs are fare costs, travel time, and distance traveled.
- As distance between origin and destination increases, travel costs increase and are more important in the vacation decision.
- There are hidden costs involved in traveling (e.g., meal and lodging expenses). Identifying these costs may lead tourists to substitute one mode for another.
- The development of international markets requires access to international airports. This is especially true when there are sea gaps or long surface travel is necessary.

HOSPITALITY RESOURCES

Hospitality resources refer to the general feeling of welcome that visitors receive while at a destination area. It is the way that visitor services are delivered by service providers, as well as the general feeling of warmth from the general resident population. It is a combination of a certain amount of knowledge and a positive attitude that results in specific hospitable behaviors. The way in which services are delivered is particularly important because tourism is consumed on the spot. Sales and service occur at the same time. Although excellent service cannot totally make up for a hard bed, tough steak,

QUICK TRIP 1.5

Hospitality in Africa

Globally, tourism accounts for 231 million jobs; and by 2020, the tourism industry is forecast to become worth $2 trillion. Lately a trend has developed that brings tourists to Africa in search of new experiences. Tourism is one of the only exports that do not exploit the region; it gives investors a chance to develop this area, giving the local people more jobs, resulting in a better quality of life. There is a low entry barrier in the tourism industry in Africa compared to entering into business with Natural Resources in Africa. If Africa wants a slice of this booming export, it must increase hotel rooms and hospitality. Another obstacle that Africa has to overcome is the lack of hospitality education throughout the continent. There are very limited educational resources to facilitate the development of Africa into a tourism-driven continent. According to the Small Business Administration, poor customer service is among the top reasons customers desert businesses. Chris Bryant, a former training director and spokesman for Nordstrom Department Store and The Ritz-Carlton Company, says that it is essential for a company to develop a core set of values. As with all international business ventures, culture clash can be a problem; but with such limited infrastructure in Africa, will the difference in culture prove to be too much?

THINK ABOUT THIS:

1. If Africa really wants to grow its tourism industry and, specifically, hospitality, do you think that for most African countries there will be enough people willing to get into the industry?
2. Will training and educating local people on hospitality be too difficult?
3. Would it be easier to simply bring in more international help?
4. Would that decrease the authenticity of the attraction?
5. Do you think that the communities would welcome these visitors or be resistant to the change?

Sources:

Alleyne, S. Destination Africa: A look at how tourism could change the face and economics of Africa. *Black Enterprise,* 2008. *Student Resource Center Gold.* Gale. Cherry Creek High School Lib., Greenwood Village, CO. Retrieved 7 May 2008, http://infotrac.galegroup. com/itweb/?db=SRC-1.

Dixon, A. With a smile: Customer service affects every aspect of your business. *Black Enterprise,* 2008. *Student Resource Center Gold.* Gale. Cherry Creek High School Lib., Greenwood Village, CO. Retrieved 7 May 2008, http://infotrac.galegroup.com/itweb/?db=SRC-1.

bumpy bus ride, or rainy weather, poor service can certainly spoil an otherwise excellent vacation experience. In the broader sense, visitors will have a much more rewarding vacation if they feel welcomed by the host population and will certainly feel awkward and unhappy if they feel resented. The best and least expensive way to reach any type of tourist market is to do such a good job of ensuring that tourists have such a great experience that they tell their friends about it when they return home.

Hospitality resources can be improved by, in effect, training tourism personnel to be hospitable and encouraging positive feelings toward tourism and visitors on the part of the general public. These two aspects will be dealt with separately.

HOSPITALITY TRAINING

A program of hospitality training is generally aimed at motivating service providers to be hospitable in their dealings with visitors. The assumption is that providing more hospitable service will result in a more satisfied visitor who will be inclined to return and/or spread positive reactions through word-of-mouth advertising to other potential visitors. To achieve hospitable service on the part of service providers, it may be necessary to change their present behavior. Many believe that a change in behavior is brought about by a change in attitude and an increase in the level of knowledge. The three aspects of attitude are toward self, toward others, and toward the subject matter.

> The average tourist wants to go to places where there are no tourists.
> Sam Ewing

ATTITUDE TOWARD SELF. If an individual's self-esteem, or attitude toward self, is low, that individual will tend to behave in such a way that the feedback from others will confirm this low opinion of himself or herself. Traditionally, tourism businesses have lacked prestige. Those who work in tourism have, by association, lacked prestige. Behavior is thus precipitated that will reinforce this feeling. The key then is to change the individual's perception of self in order to improve behaviors. If service providers can be made to believe that their work and they themselves are important, the hope is that their work and specifically their actions toward visitors will reflect this new feeling. This aspect can be put into practice by highlighting the vital part that service providers play in ensuring a positive vacation experience. If service providers can be viewed as hosts and host-

Florida

Florida is no longer the hot spot that it once was. Gary Sain, president and CEO of Orlando/Orange County Convention & Visitor Bureau, says that Florida is "competing with much more choice, easier choice." European visitors can go to Greece or Spain for less money than traveling across the ocean to Florida. The weak dollar is helping Florida's attraction to international visitors, but it might not be enough. A focus on Florida's smaller towns that are being marketed as the "Real Florida" has been started as well, but Florida makes itself competitive by focusing on niche markets. Florida has started targeting niche markets such as African Americans and Hispanics. It is also looking to the gay, lesbian, bisexual, and transgender (GLBT) market to increase its competitiveness. Research by Witeck-Combs Communications in Washington, DC, has shown that the GLBT tourists spend on average $260 more than their heterosexual counterparts. Fort Lauderdale has become one of the top GLBT destinations, and Orlando has developed what is now known as "Gay Days." Florida has a gay-market sales manager who has been working with Visit Florida for over three years.

THINK ABOUT THIS:

1. A key aspect of defining a destination as competitive is that the destination must increase tourism expenditure in a profitable way while enhancing the well-being of the residents of the destination. Is Florida's plan of targeting these niche markets enhancing the quality of life for the residents?

2. Is this plan preserving the natural capital?

Source: Miracle, B. Global Competition: Florida officials hope to gain an edge by focusing on niche markets. *Florida Trend*, 2008. *Student Resource Center Gold.* Gale. Cherry Creek High School Lib., Greenwood Village, CO. Retrieved 7 May 2008, http://infotrac.galegroup.com/itweb/?db=SRC-1.

esses rather than just employees, their self-image may be raised. Stress should be placed on the fact that dealing with and serving people is, indeed, a most difficult task. Visitors often bring demands with them that are difficult to satisfy. Although it is relatively easy to deal with a satisfied guest, it is very challenging to deal with visitors who are dissatisfied or extra demanding. The ability to create a satisfied guest is a very demanding task. Those people who can do this have skills that should be highly regarded by themselves as well as by others.

ATTITUDE TOWARD OTHERS. The second aspect of attitude relates to attitude toward others. An individual's feelings toward people that she or he comes into contact with will affect, positively or negatively, behavior toward them. The task is to assist the service provider in developing positive feelings toward fellow employees and visitors that will result in positive behavior toward the visitors. This can be achieved by training the individual in the importance of teamwork and interdependence in getting the job done. Oftentimes employees are not aware of all the people and actions that are necessary to ensure a satisfied guest. It is important that employees see where they fit into the big picture of a satisfied visitor, not only to see how important their role is, but also to be aware of the interfacing roles of others.

It is obviously important to consider the employee's attitude toward visitors. The key to the development of positive attitudes toward visitors is being able to develop the ability to put oneself in the visitor's place. Role-playing can be successfully used for this purpose. If a service provider can empathize with the visitor, accept visitors as they are, understand that for them this vacation is something that they have saved for all year, and appreciate how tired they may be after a long trip, then the attitude is likely to be more positive.

ATTITUDE TOWARD SUBJECT MATTER. The third aspect of attitude concerns attitude toward subject matter. The individual who does not believe in the work being done will display a negative attitude that will be reflected in poor service toward the guest. A positive attitude on the part of service providers toward visitors can come about only when employees are made aware of how important tourism is to their state, country, city, and property. By being aware of the amount of revenue, jobs, and taxes generated and the dispersion of the visitor dollar throughout the community, employees may become convinced of the economic and social significance of the industry of which they are a part.

The hope is that more hospitable behavior will come, in part, from a better self-image, more empathy with others, and a positive attitude about tourism's role in the community. To precipitate a change in attitude, it is necessary to raise the knowledge level of the individual. This may be done in group sessions or through a variety of audiovisual means.

A hospitable service provider will result in a more satisfied visitor.
© 2009 Phil Date. Used under license from Shutterstock, Inc.

TEACHING SPECIFIC BEHAVIORS

A second theory of behavior change is that a change in behavior affects attitudes. If people can be trained in specific desired behaviors and act them out, the positive feedback they receive will result in a positive attitude. The task is to develop specific behaviors that will be termed hospitable and instruct employees in these behaviors. If the employees act out these hospitable behaviors, the positive reactions (tips, recognition, advancement, and so on) will result in positive attitudes toward hospitality. To this end, employees can familiarize themselves with the surrounding attractions and services (to be able to give advice or directions). Some attractions will have an open house for those involved in tourism to acquaint them by means of a mini-familiarization tour. Sessions can cover both verbal and nonverbal behavior. Employees are often unaware of the negative messages their facial expressions or posture give.

By means of this joint approach—attempting to change attitudes about self, others, and tourism through increasing the level of knowledge and teaching specific hospitable behaviors—an attempt is made to raise the hospitality level of service providers.

COMMUNITY AWARENESS PROGRAMS

Although the visitor is most directly affected by the degree of hospitality shown by service providers, the overall feeling of welcome within a community will also enhance or detract from the vacation experience. Residents of a destination area cannot be trained to act in a hospitable way toward visitors, but a community awareness program can help develop a more positive attitude toward the visitor. The objectives of such a program are twofold: to build acceptance of tourism and to build an understanding of the visitor.

An acceptance of tourism cannot be built unless the benefits of tourism are made relevant to members of the community. The benefits of tourism are many, yet many people do not realize that they are positively affected by it. To some it may mean a summer job, while to others tourism may ensure that a playhouse can survive year-round for the cultural benefit of the community. It is necessary to communicate to each part of the community messages that are important and relevant to them. An understanding of who the visitor is can assist in a greater acceptance of the visitor. Knowing why people visit the area might result in a renewed civic pride.

There are different ways to communicate with the local community. Public meetings can be held to discuss particular problems. Some areas have successfully organized a speaker's bureau consisting of tourism community leaders who talk to community groups. Information sheets and newsletters, though infrequently used, can be distributed to the general public. Some communities have shown the effect of tourism by giving two-dollar bills in change to visitors to distribute throughout the area. In the off-season in Niagara Falls, Ontario community groups can tour many of the tourist attractions free of charge. Whatever methods are used, the objective remains to create a feeling of welcome for the visitor within the community.

AUTHENTICITY AND CULTURAL COMMODIFICATION

Closely related to the idea of hospitality are the concepts of authenticity and cultural commodification. It is argued by some that authenticity is a Western concept associated with the past and that contrasts with modernity. Tourists travel to experience a culture that is different from their own. Tourists from developed countries who travel to lesser developed destinations search for the "real" or authentic country and people. At the destination, there may be pressure to keep the original way of life to appeal to tourists. In Eastern Indonesia, the local government has enacted legislation to "protect" local culture. Villagers are denied the rights to have windows or electricity in their homes to keep the village "authentic."

When local culture is turned into an attraction for tourists, it becomes a commodity. When culture commodification is thus sold, it can lead to a loss of authen-

ticity. There may be pressure—subtle or otherwise—to keep the "old ways" in order to attract tourists. This can lead to a lack of economic development for the community.

The flip side is that tourism can make people proud of their culture. Local people can use that identity and pride to become empowered in their own communities (Cole, 2007).

COMPETITIVE DESTINATIONS

A tourist destination is made up of all the elements just described. However, these elements are there for a purpose—to attract, satisfy and have return numbers of tourists. This does not occur in a vacuum as destinations compete with each other in both a domestic and international arena. The objective, in seeking to be competitive, is to deliver "goods and services that perform better than other destinations on those aspects of the tourism experience considered important by tourists" (Dwyer and Kim, 2002). It has also been argued that destinations need to shift from an emphasis on high-quality offerings to providing staged opportunities for involvement that create memorable experiences.

There is no widely accepted concept of destination competitiveness. Rather, what constitutes competitiveness at tourism destinations is a function of the market segment being targeted and the product mix at the destination (Enright and Newton, 2005).

Ritchie and Crouch, who have written extensively on the subject, define competitiveness thus: "[W]hat makes a tourism destination truly competitive is its ability to increase tourism expenditure, to increasingly attract visitors while providing them with satisfying, memorable experiences, and to do so in a profitable way, while enhancing the well-being of destination residents and preserving the natural capital of the destination for future generations" (Ritchie and Crouch, 2003, p. 2).

There are various ways to measure the competitiveness of tourist destinations. One way is to survey tourist perceptions of different destinations. This approach can get to the factors that tourists consider important. One such method was conducted by FutureBrand, a division of Interpublic Group. They collected information from over twenty-six hundred respondents and over fifty experts. Information was collected in eight areas. These areas and the top countries in each are:

■ Attractions: Diversity and quality things to see and do—Australia, Canada, Italy, Spain, United States

- Authenticity: Unique character of the destination—Australia, Canada, New Zealand
- Culture: Arts, crafts, cultural environment—France, Italy, Greece, Japan, Spain, United Kingdom
- Ethos: Customs, beliefs, mores, and history—France, Italy, Greece, Japan, United Kingdom
- Geography: Natural resources and typography—Australia, Canada, France, Italy, New Zealand, United States
- Infrastructure: Technology, communications, transportation, and health care—Canada, France, Italy, United Kingdom, United States
- Governance: Political freedom, safety, and security—Australia, Canada, France, New Zealand, United Kingdom, United States
- Economy: Standard of living—Australia, Canada, France, Italy, Japan, United States

Useful as this list is, it only covers a limited number of countries. Other studies use published data to develop an index of competitiveness. These studies also tend to consider only a small number of destinations.

One model of destination competitiveness (Dwyer et al., 2004) suggests the following indicators against which destinations can be compared:

- Destination management
- Nature-based resources
- Heritage resources
- Quality service
- Efficient public services
- Tourism shopping
- Government commitment
- Location and access
- E-business
- Night life
- Visa requirements
- Amusement/theme parks

Pine and Gilmore (1999) lay out the tourist experience at the destination as having four components: active participation, passive participation, absorption, and immersion. Absorption brings the experience into the mind of the tourist while immersion involves being part of the experience itself. The experience desired will have implications for what is offered at the destination to make it competitive in the mind of the tourist. The passive participant looking for absorption wants to be entertained while the active participant seeking absorption wants to learn something new. Passive participants looking for immersion want an esthetic experience that

allows them to be in the environment without altering the way it is presented to them. The active participant seeking immersion, on the other hand, wants an escapist experience that has an effect on what they see. The point is that destination competitiveness needs to consider the experience the tourist is seeking.

The overall attractiveness of a destination is a combination of supply (the elements at the destination) and, as noted here, demand—how important these elements are to potential tourists. The importance of considering both supply and demand is noted in research on the attractiveness of the State of Virginia. The Shenandoah Valley ranked first on measures of demand attractiveness and fifth on supply measures. That is, tourists thought the services and facilities in the region were average, while measures of supply were below average. The region may promise more than it can deliver. Improvements in supply need to be made. Where supply measures are greater than demand measures—such as at Chesapeake Bay—a suggestion is offered to increase the number of tourists by making them aware of the potential of the area (Formica and Uysal, 2006).

The cultural background of the tourist is part of this equation also. Asian tourists prize the quality of interpersonal relationships in evaluating service encounters while Western tourists place more value on goal completion, efficiency, and time savings. What is "good service" to one group may not be regarded as good to another. Employees at the destination should be given cultural training to make them conscious of the need to deliver service in a way that will be appreciated by people from a variety of cultures (Tsang and Ap, 2007).

For a destination to become competitive, tourism officials start with the attractions, facilities, infrastructure, transportation and hospitality. Taking into account the forces in the larger environment that define or influence the potential of the destination to be competitive (existing tourist demand, the global or macro environment and the competitive micro environment), tourism officials manage the destination—develop policy, plan, develop and market the destination—in an attempt to become more competitive than other destinations seeking the same segments of tourists.

The Formica and Uysal (2006) study discussed earlier sought to identify the factors that differentiated Virginia as a tourist destination. The authors found that four factors account for two-thirds of the variance: tourism services and facilities, cultural/historical factors, rural lodging, and outdoor recreation.

A comprehensive effort was undertaken in Ontario to put the elements of a premier-ranked destination into a systems framework (Genest and Legg, 2002). The three dimensions of the framework are identified as Product, Performance and Futurity. The Product piece identifies the high quality tourist experience as consisting of:

- Distinctive core attractions
- Quality and critical mass
- Satisfaction and value
- Accessibility
- Accommodation base

The performance dimension identifies how the destination's success is measured by:

- Visitation
- Occupancy and yield
- Critical acclaim

Finally, the futurity dimension indicates that success of the destination is sustained by:

- Destination marketing
- Product renewal
- Managing within carrying capacities

The most comprehensive index using published data for over two hundred countries is the Competitiveness Monitor (CM) developed by the World Travel and Tourism Council (WTTC) and the Travel Research Institute at the University of Nottingham. The model uses eight indicators:

- Price: Hotel prices and purchasing power parity
- Infrastructure: Road development and access to sanitation facilities and drinking water
- Environment: Population density, carbon dioxide emission, and ratification of environmental treaties
- Technology: Use of Internet, telephone mainlines, and mobile phones; and export of technology
- Human resources: Quality of the labor force
- Openness: Openness to international trade
- Social development: Quality of life at the destination
- Human tourism: Impact of tourism on the economy and the sum of tourist arrivals and departures as a ratio of the population of the destination country

Not all indicators are given the same weight. Social development technology, and price are given the highest weights while human tourism indicators and environment are given the lowest in order to arrive at an aggre-

gate index. As might be expected, developing countries do better than developed countries in terms of price. North American and Scandinavian countries are more competitive in terms of infrastructure, technology, and social development indicators while African and former Soviet Union countries are the least competitive. Openness tends to favor smaller countries. On the basis of this research, the most tourism competitiveness destinations are (Gooroochurn and Sugiyarto, 2005):

- United States
- Sweden
- Norway
- Finland
- Australia

It is proposed that the competitiveness of a tourism destination can be explained as follows (Ritchie and Crouch, 1993):

TOURISM COMPETITIVENESS = f (Destination Appeal, Destination Management, Destination Organization, Destination Information, Destination Efficiency)

The appeal of a destination itself is a combination of two factors: the characteristics of a region that make it attractive to visit compared to the deterrents or barriers to travel. The determinants of *destination attractiveness* are outlined in table 1.1 while the deterrents to visitation of a destination are presented in table 1.2. The more the attractiveness outweighs the barriers, the greater will be the appeal.

Destination management is a measure of how effective the marketing and management efforts are to maximize the positive attributes of the destination while minimizing the negatives or barriers. From a marketing perspective, managers at the destination attempt to select appropriate segments of the market and persuade people in those segments to visit the destination, in part through the development of a strong image and a believable promotional effort in selling the destination. Packages need to be developed and alliances made with tour wholesalers and retailers.

At the same time, management efforts should be aimed at making it as easy as possible for visitors to travel to and enjoy the benefits of the destinations. This includes efforts to reduce requirements for entry and measures to help ensure visitor safety.

Destination organization is a function of various internal organizational actions and the creation of *strategic alliances* aimed at improving the destination's attractive-

Table 1.1
Determinants of Destination Attractiveness

Natural Features
e.g. General topography
      Scenery

Climate
e.g. Temperature
      Amount of sunshine, rain

Culture and Social Characteristics
e.g. Traditions
      Style of architecture
      Local foods

General Infrastructure
e.g. Roads
      Sewerage, water, electricity

Basic Services Infrastructure
e.g. Shopping
      Car maintenance

Tourism Superstructure
e.g. Lodging
      Information

Access and Transportation Facilities
e.g. Distance and time to get there
      Frequency, ease and quality of transportation

Attitudes about Tourists
e.g. Warmth of welcome
      Ease of communication

Cost/Price Levels
e.g. Value for money
      Exchange rates

Economic and Social Ties
e.g. International trade
      Common culture, language, religion

Uniqueness
e.g. One-of-a-kind attractions or events

Source: Ritchie, J. R. B., and G. I. Crouch. 1993. Competitiveness in international tourism: A framework for understanding and analysis. *The Tourist Review*, 35: 53–56.

Table 1.2
Deterrents to Visitation of a Destination

Security and Safety
e.g. Political instability
      High crime rate

Health and Medical Concerns
e.g. Poor sanitation
      Lack of reliable medical services

Laws and Regulations
e.g. Visa requirements
      Currency controls

Cultural Distance
e.g. Inability to communicate
      Restrictions on behavior

Source: Ritchie, J. R. B., and G. I. Crouch. 1993. Competitiveness in international tourism: A framework for understanding and analysis. *The Tourist Review*, 35: 57.

by the European Travel Commission. In recent years, the United States and Canada have formed similar unions for the purpose of sharing research findings.

In today's increasingly sophisticated business environment, decisions need to be made based on the best information available. This information includes internal information, aimed at assisting the destination better manage the tourism product, and external marketing information that allows the destination to adapt to changing market conditions. The principal components of an internal *destination management information system* are (Ritchie and Crouch, 1993):

■ Visitor statistics detailing patterns of tourist behavior
■ Performance measures that identify problems
■ Economic, social, and environmental impacts
■ Information to monitor and track the attitudes of local people toward tourism

At the same time, market research is necessary to focus on such things as market segmentation, the forecasting of tourist demand, visitor satisfaction ratings, the effectiveness of advertising, and the development of new products and services.

Finally, there is a series of activities that can contribute to how well tourism services are delivered to the visitor. The quality or value of the services provided should be equal to or greater than the price charged. This might involve setting standards for specific types of businesses and monitoring the extent to which these standards are reached. It might mean supporting education and training programs aimed at increasing the service abilities of employees. It might also involve educa-

ness to tourists. Because tourism impacts many sectors of a destination, its economic advantages are spread widely. However, as a result of this structure, the various businesses that comprise tourism tend to be small, fragmented, and unfocused. Thus, it is argued, there is a need for some kind of umbrella organization—such as a National Tourism Organization or, at a more local level, a Convention & Visitors Bureau—to act as a coordinating body for both public and private tourism interests. At the same time, given the increasingly global environment, tourism concerns, even at the national level, can no longer be resolved alone. There are economies of scale to be gained by pooling resources and working together. In Europe, for example, individual countries contribute to a joint market research effort conducted

tional campaigns aimed at residents, indicating the benefits to them of tourism development. At the same time, it is important for tourism businesses to be productive and profitable. Cost-benefit analyses have to be done before different services can be introduced to ensure that they can be delivered in a way that is not only satisfying to the guest but profitable to the business.

BENCHMARKING

Benchmarking is a useful tool that destinations can use to gain a competitive advantage in the marketplace.

QUICK TRIP 1.7

St. Moritz–The Cradle of Winter Tourism

Today, St. Moritz is one of the most prestigious holiday destinations, but it was not always so. In the early sixteenth century, St. Moritz was hailed by a famous doctor for the powerful mineral spring water, claiming to cure all. From there, bath houses were built, and slowly people started to return to the beautiful area. In 1855, Johannes Badrutt pioneered hotels in the area and St. Moritz became the hot spot for royalty. Royalty usually only came during the summer holidays, leaving the town mostly deserted during the winter. The story goes that Badrutt made a bet with four of his English guests that if they came back during the winter and did not enjoy themselves he would pay for all of their accommodations and travel. The English came back, but with more people, and stayed until Easter. This marked the birth of year-round tourism in St. Moritz. Ice-skating, curling, bobsledding, and skiing began to fill the travelers' time. By 1913, a railway was built over the Alps to increase accessibility to the town. By 1968, a car-parking house was constructed with a capacity for five hundred cars. The year 1979 marked the first ever golf tournament on a frozen lake. Royalty and celebrities continue to flock to St. Moritz as the ultimate hot spot for all vacations. This sets the bar for the best winter resort.

THINK ABOUT THIS:

1. Using all six elements of a destination, explain why St. Moritz is successful.

Source: History. *St. Moritz: Top of the World.* Retrieved 7 May 2008, http://www.stmoritz.ch.

They can do so by continuously measuring the elements, services and practices at a specific tourist destination with those destinations recognized as being the leaders in tourism.

The end objective is not to compare but, acting on the comparison, to take action in order to improve what is available and how it can be utilized for the benefit of visitors. As such, there are three steps involved (Kozak, 2004):

1. Measures of performance are identified and appropriate data are collected.
2. The destination is benchmarked against recognized destinations recognized as industry leaders.
3. New ideas that come from the comparison are put into practice.

PERFORMANCE MEASUREMENT. The measure of performance might be such things as the number of complaints received, the level of satisfaction, the number of refunds requested and the number of repeat visits (Kozak, 2004).

There is a four-part process involved.

1. A performance measure is established on items important to the destination visitors;
2. performance is measured;
3. a desired standard is set to benchmark against; and
4. the overall performance of the destination based on the total of the performance measures used is evaluated.

DESTINATION BENCHMARKING. Benchmarking can be internal (comparison to the destination's prior performance), external (comparison to a similar destination recognized as performing at a superior level) or generic (comparison to generally-accepted international standards).

NEW IDEAS. The key at this point is for those at the destination to improve elements of and service and practices at the destination that will improve visitor satisfaction and that will result in a competitive advantage.

An example can be found in examining deep-sea sports fishing in Gran Canaria, one of the Canary islands off the north-west coast of Africa (Meian-Gonzalez and Garcia-Falcon, 2003).

Experienced and committed enthusiasts of the sport as well as tourism professionals were surveyed to determine which types of services are important to deep-sea sports fishers and how Gran Canaria stacked up against the competition. The top resources are:

- Abundant fishing resources
- Suitable for this class of sports fishing
- Well-equipped charter boats
- Suitable accommodation
- Knowledge of and compliance with the rules of the International Game Fish Association (IGFA)
- Well trained charter boat crews
- Non-polluted environment
- Proximity of the fishing grounds to the marina
- Easily accessible airport
- Sporting atmosphere
- Marinas in good condition
- Peace and quiet
- Hospitality and good restaurants

The major competitors are identified as Madiera, Cape Verde and the Azores. Cape Verde is considered to have more fishing resources because of the warmer waters, while Madiera has slightly better accommodation and restaurants. The quality of the charter boats and crews and compliance with (IGFA) rules are consid-

ered equal. Gran Conaria is advised to make improvements in accommodation, restaurants, boats and crews and rule compliance. Although it outpaces Cape Verde in all these areas, that destination has to be considered a serious competitor because of the warmer waters, something that Gran Conaria cannot duplicate.

The subject of how a destination can effectively use its resources will be covered in great depth in the next several chapters.

SUMMARY

To be a successful tourist destination there must be a blend of certain elements. Attractions are the first and most important of these. While attractions are needed to bring people in, they must have adequate facilities, infrastructure, and transportation alternatives to make their stay comfortable. Finally, hospitality on the part of local people will help ensure a satisfied customer who will want to return.

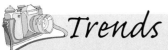 *Trends*

Top Ten Luxury Travel and Lifestyle Trends

Karen Weiner

1. Traditional demographics won't define luxury consumers who will display luxury status outwardly via symbols.
2. Relationships with family take center stage on vacation.
3. Creativity checks in—companies will need to innovate.
4. Concierges are king—a lack of time and information overload combine to create a market for specialists who help arrange our lifestyles.
5. Altruism and responsibility are back—the need to link oneself to a higher cause.
6. Health, well-being, and looking good move up in financial priorities.
7. Saving time is the next great luxury.
8. Cultural events are big news.
9. The affluent are tired of product and want unique experiences.
10. People want more space when they travel—in airline seats and hotel rooms.

ACTIVITIES

1. If you had a friend from another country coming to your home country, where would you tell them to go and why? According to the five characteristics that make a destination, identify two different tourism destinations, one that you would describe to a friend as the best destination in your country, and another destination that you would not recommend to anyone.

2. Make a brochure for a fellow student on how to create a successful tourism destination.

3. Focus on one characteristic of the destination in Activity 2 and identify five ways to advance or improve this characteristic for tourism today.

INTERNET ACTIVITIES

4. Go to http://www.youtube.com and access a video clip from the television show *The Jetsons*. Watch the video and then predict advances in the tourism market from transportation to infrastructure that will change within the next twenty and one hundred years.

5. Using Google Earth (http://earth.google.com), find a location on the globe that you have never heard of. Then research the tourism in the area. If a tourism market is already established, explain why it is established. If there is not a market, explain what the location needs to do to become a destination.

REFERENCES

Cai, L., and R. Woods. 1993. China's tourism—service failure. *Cornell Hotel and Restaurant Administration Quarterly*, 34 (4): 30–39.

Cole, S. 2007. Beyond authenticity and commodifaction. *Annals of Tourism Research*, 34 (4): 943–960.

Daigle, J. J., and C. A. Zimmerman. 2004. The convergence of transportation, information technology, and visitor experience at Acadia National Park. *Journal of Travel Research*. 43: 151–160.

Downard, P., and L. Lumsdon. 2004. Tourism transport and visitor spending: a study in the Norta York Moors National Park. *U.K. Journal of Travel Research*, 42: 415–420.

Dwyer, L., and C. Kim. 2002. Destination competitiveness: A model and determinants. *Capitalizing on Travel Research for Marketing Success*. 33rd Annual Conference Proceedings of the Travel and Tourism Research Association.

Dwyer, L., R. Mellor, Z. Livaic, D. Edwards, and C. Kim. 2004. Attributes of destination competitiveness: a factor analysis. *Tourism Analysis*, 9: 91–101.

Enright, M., and J. Newton. 2005. Determinants of tourism destination competitiveness in Asia Pacific: comprehensiveness and universality. *Journal of Travel Research*, 43: 339–350.

Formica, S., and M. Uysal. 2006. Destination attractiveness based on supply and demand evaluations: an analytical framework. *Journal of Travel Research*, 44: 418–430.

FutureBrand, country brand index. Presentation at the World Travel Market, London, November 12, 2007.

Genest, J., and D. Legg. 2002. Premier-ranked tourist destinations: development of a framework for analysis and its self-guided workbook, *Capitalizing on Travel Research for Marketing Success*. 33rd Annual Conference Proceedings of the Travel and Tourism Research Association.

Gooroochurn, N., and G. Sugiyarto. 2005. Measuring competitiveness in the travel and tourism industry. *Tourism Economics*, ii (1): 25–43.

Gunn, C. A. 1972. *Vacationscape: Designing Tourist Regions*. Austin, TX: The University of Texas.

Gunn, C. A. 1979. *Tourism Planning*. New York: Crane, Rusak and Company, Inc.

Jackson, J., M. Houghton, R. Russell, and P. Triandos. 2005. Innovation in measuring economic impacts of regional festivals—a do-it-yourself kit. *Journal of Travel Research*, 43: 360–367.

Khadaroo, J., and B. Seetanah. 2007. Transport infrastructure and tourism development. *Annals of Tourism Research*, 34 (4): 1021–1032.

Kozak, M. 2004. Introducing destination benchmarking: a conceptual approach. *Journal of Hospitality & Tourism Research*, 28 (3): 286–287.

Mathews, W. 1993. How to treat international visitors as guests. *Travel & Tourism Executive Report*, 14: 5–7.

Mazanec, J. A., K. Wöber, and A. H. Zins. 2007. Tourism destination competitiveness: From definition to explanation? *Journal of Travel Research*, 46: 86–95.

Meian-Gonzalez, A., and J. Garcia-Falcon. 2003. Competitive potential of tourism in destination. *Annals of Tourism Research*, 30 (3): 720–740.

Oh, H., A. M. Fiore, and M. Jeong. 2007. Measuring experience economy concepts: Tourism applications. *Journal of Travel Research*, 46: 119–132.

Pine, B. J. II, and H. J. Gilmore. 1999. *The Experience Economy: Work Is Theater & Every Business a Stage*. Boston, MA: Harvard Business School Press.

Prideaux, B. 2001. The role of the transport system in destination development. *Tourism Management*, 21: 61.

Reinius, S., and P. Fredman. 2007. Protected areas as attractions. *Annals of Tourism Research*, 34 (4): 839–854.

Ritchie, J. R. B., and G. I. Crouch. 1993. Competitiveness in international tourism: A framework for understanding and analysis. *The Tourist Review*, 35: 60.

Ritchie, J. R. B., and G. I. Crouch. 2000. Are destination stars born or made: Must a competitive destination have star genes? 31st Annual Conference Proceedings of the Travel and Tourism Research Association. 306–315.

Tsang, N. K.-F., and J. Ap. 2007. Tourists' perceptions of relational quality service attributes: A cross-cultural study. *Journal of Travel Research*, 45: 355–363.

ADDITIONAL READINGS

Attractions: The Heart of the Travel Product, Center for Survey and Marketing Research, University of Wisconsin–Parkside, Box 2000, Kenosha, WI 53141, February 1992.

Heritage, Tourism and Society, D. T. Herbert, ed., Mansell Publishing Ltd., 125 Strand, London Wc2R 0BB, U.K., 1995.

Nature-Based Tourism: An Annotated Bibliography, W. Whitlock and R. H. Becker, Regional Resources Development Institute, Clemson University, 265-B Lehotsky Hall, Clemson, SC 29634-1005, 1991.

Tourism Historic Places, P. Baker, National Trust for Historic Preservation, 1785 Massachusetts Avenue, NW, Washington, DC 20036, 1995.

SURFING SOLUTIONS

http://www.all-hotels.com/ (Hotels)
http://www.cdc.gov/travel/ (Center for Disease Control)
http://www.cuisinenet.com/ (Restaurants)
http://www.festivals.com/ (Festivals)
http://www.timeout.co.uk/ (City guides)
http://www.ypb.com/travelmonitor/NLTM.html/ (National Leisure Travel Monitor, YP&B/Yankelovich Partners)

ACRONYMS

AAA (American Automobile Association)
FEEE (Foundation for the Environmental Education of Europe)

chapter 2

Tourism Impacts on the Economy, Society, Culture, and Environment

THE NEED FOR SUSTAINABLE TOURISM DEVELOPMENT

Today the business volume of tourism equals or even surpasses that of oil exports, food products or automobiles. Tourism has become one of the major players in international commerce, and represents at the same time one of the main income sources for many developing countries. This growth goes hand in hand with an increasing diversification and competition among destinations.

UN World Tourism Organization (2009), http://www.unwto.org/aboutwto/why/en/why.php?op=1,
accessed January 4, 2009

PURPOSE

Having learned about the economic, social, cultural, and environmental impacts of tourism on destination areas, students will be able to suggest ways that the benefits of tourism can be maximized.

LEARNING OBJECTIVES

- ✓ Explain the three major economic impacts of tourism on destination areas and how these impacts are measured.
- ✓ Describe the strategies to maximize the economic impact of tourism and how tourism's role in economic development can be analyzed.
- ✓ Discuss the potentially negative social and cultural impacts of tourism on destination areas.
- ✓ Identify the positive social and cultural impacts that may result from tourism.
- ✓ Describe the potentially negative environmental impacts of tourism on destination areas.
- ✓ Identify the positive environmental impacts that tourism development can foster.
- ✓ Explain the principles of sustainable tourism development.

Overview

Tourism has had significant impacts upon destination areas throughout the world. This chapter explores the potential economic, social and cultural, and environmental effects of tourism upon destinations and suggests strategies to maximize tourism's positive impacts. Tourism may be one of several alternative economic development options available to a destination area. The characteristics of tourism compared to other development possibilities are examined. Three major types of economic impacts of tourism are described. Suggestions are given to help destinations develop policies for maximizing tourism's positive effects, while minimizing the negative impacts.

Although tourism brings significant economic advantages to destination areas, it can cause adverse social and cultural changes, and damage natural environments. In other ways, tourism can benefit the local environment, society, and culture. The concept of sustainable tourism development is recommended as a broad guiding strategy for all destinations.

The Role of Tourism in Economic Development

The increasing fascination with tourism worldwide in the past fifty years has been motivated largely by its potential economic benefits for communities of all sizes. Many of the early books and articles about tourism emphasized the economic impact of tourism, especially in its economic development role for developing countries. In the four decades since the first English-language textbooks on tourism were published, a more balanced view of tourism's impacts has emerged. Today, it is widely recognized that tourism can have negative impacts on communities by adversely affecting the environment, society, and culture. While this chapter begins with a review of the role of tourism in economic development, this does not suggest that these economic impacts are any more important or significant than the other positive or negative impacts of tourism.

The potential economic benefits of tourism are a major attraction for many countries, states, provinces, territories, regions, counties, cities, and other communities. In particular, tourism development is seen as an attractive policy alternative to promote economic growth and diversification. This especially has been the case for developing countries where three pro-tourism arguments are identified. First, the demand for international travel continues to grow within the developed nations of Europe, North America, and the Asia-Pacific region. Second, as household incomes in the developed countries increase, the *income elasticity of demand* for tourism means that the demand for international travel will increase at a faster rate. Third, developing countries need *foreign exchange earnings* to spur their own economic development and to satisfy the rising expectations of their growing populations.

Traditionally, the developing (or so-called *Third World*) countries have tended to rely upon agriculture and other natural resource–based industries for economic growth. For example, the CIA *World Factbook* (2008) estimated that agriculture employed between 56 percent and 76 percent of all the people in the five Asian nations of Bangladesh, India, Myanmar, Nepal, and Vietnam from 2001 to 2005. In contrast, the service sector in 2006 employed 76 percent of the people in Canada and 75 percent in Australia in 2004. Full agricultural growth is a key to industrialization and further economic and employment growth. Recognizing that almost all developing countries have followed *import-substitution* (the substitution of locally produced products for those presently imported), the World Bank stresses the need to reward exports with incentives. A basic problem, however, with a reliance on agricultural development is that the developing country can easily be overly dependent on a few specific types of crops or animal products. The prices of these crops or products are unpredictable and affected by weather, disease, and outside manipulation by large buyers from the developed countries.

Another economic policy option is to promote the development of manufacturing facilities. However, the development of the manufacturing sector is not always a viable option. The potential problems with manufacturing may include:

- The processing of raw materials is directly related to the base amount available in the area, and possible projects are likely to be few for all but the most richly endowed nations.
- For industries aimed at import substitution, the relatively small size of domestic markets restricts growth.

> **South Africa's New Gold**
> *Tourism has become one of the most important sectors in South Africa following the end of apartheid, creating almost a million jobs and overtaking gold exports as an earner of foreign currency.*
>
> Liz Smailes, PATA Compass, November/December 2008, page 50

- Developing countries are characterized by chronic shortages of skilled labor.
- For export-oriented industries, products have to face full international competition, in terms of price and quality, as well as in marketing sophistication.

One example of the problems of industrialization in a lesser-developed country is in the small West African nation of The Gambia. Some 75 percent of its labor force is employed in agriculture, forestry, and fishing. The country has one major cash crop, groundnuts, which occupy 60 percent of its crop land. Industrialization through the development of manufacturing businesses and tourism represent the two major economic development options available to this "one-crop economy." However, according to Thompson, O'Hare, and Evans (1995), "Industrialization in The Gambia is negligible given the lack of indigenous skills, low levels of literacy, low purchasing power of the domestic market, poorly developed fuel and power resources and inadequate transport facilities." Tourism was first introduced to The Gambia in the 1960s and now contributes substantially to its economy. The Gambia is quite close to Europe and now is one of the most popular West African tourism destinations for Europeans.

Tourism faces similar problems to manufacturing in developing countries. However, many countries have the basic "raw materials" for tourism, such as scenery and rich histories and cultures. In addition, there are usually fewer restrictions on international travel than on international trade. The distance of the destination from the market is becoming less of a problem and indeed may be an attraction to certain groups of travelers who are seeking the exotic and unexplored. When compared with primary industries such as agriculture, mining, and forestry, tourism prices are more under the control of the seller than of the buyer. The Organization for Economic Cooperation and Development (OECD) has concluded that tourism provides a major opportunity for growth in countries that are at the intermediate stage of economic development, experiencing rather fast economic growth and requiring more foreign-exchange earnings. China would be a good example here; as its economy has boomed, so has its tourism development. However, OECD cautions, "In developing economies, the relative advantages of backwardness like the low labour costs open the world market for tourism products. However, these advantages are somewhat diminished by the market power of the travel industry. The more peripheral a country is the higher it depends on the big firms of the travel industry such as airlines, tour operators and hotel industry" (OECD, 2001).

Tourism has particularly attracted attention in its role as an *invisible export*. As an invisible export, tourism differs from international trade in physical products in several ways:

- The "consumer" collects the product from the exporting country (destination), thereby eliminating any freight costs for the exporter, except in cases in which the airline used belongs to the destination country.
- The demand for the pleasure (vacation travel) segment of tourism is highly dependent on non-economic factors, such as natural disasters, terrorism, political troubles, and changes in the popularity of countries and resort areas created mostly by media coverage. At the same time, international tourism is usually both *price-elastic* and *income-elastic*. Therefore, shifts in prices or household incomes normally result in more-than-proportional changes in pleasure travel.
- By using specific fiscal measures, the exporting (destination) country can manipulate exchange rates so that those for visitors are higher or lower (normally the latter in order to attract a greater number of visitors) than those at other foreign trade markets. Also, visitors are permitted to buy in domestic markets at the prices prevailing for the local residents (the exceptions being the duty-free shops for visitors operated in many countries).
- Tourism is multifaceted and directly affects several sectors of the economy (such as hotels and other forms of accommodations, shops, restaurants, local transportation firms, entertainment establishments, and handicraft producers) and indirectly affects many others (such as equipment manufacturers, utilities, and agricultural producers).
- Tourism brings many more nonmonetary benefits and costs (i.e., social, cultural, and environmental) than other export industries.

It is argued that tourism, when compared to manufacturing, is not a "smokestack" business. In other words, tourism development does not require the development of the types of factories that often pollute local environments. This position must be carefully weighed against the realization that tourism also has contributed to the environmental degradation of many parts of the world.

The Contributions and Negative Effects of Tourism

The Production and Consumption Branch of the United Nations Environment Programme (UNEP) has published some very useful information on the potential advantages and disadvantages of tourism development from an economic viewpoint. The following are identified as contributions that tourism can make to economic conservation:

- **Foreign exchange earnings:** Tourism expenditures and the export and import of related goods and services generate income to the host economy and may stimulate the investment required to finance growth in other economic sectors.
- **Contribution to government revenues:** Direct and indirect taxes earned on tourism.
- **Employment generation:** The rapid expansion of international tourism has created many new jobs.
- **Stimulation of infrastructure development:** Tourism can encourage local governments to invest in providing better water and sewage systems, roads, electricity, telephone, and public transportation systems; all of which may help improve the lives of local residents.
- **Contribution to local economies:** Tourism may create significant local tax revenues, as well as other direct and indirect spending and employment.

Tourism in the Bahamas creates a significant share of total employment and generates significant tax revenues for the government.
© 2009 Ovidiu Lordachi. Used under license from Shutterstock, Inc.

UNEP also points out that there are "many hidden costs to tourism, which can have unfavorable economic effects on the host community. Often rich countries are better able to profit for tourism than poor ones." The agency identifies the following as the potential negative economic impacts of tourism:

- **Leakage:** The direct income is the amount of tourist spending left after taxes, profits, and wages are paid outside the area and after imports are bought. The subtracted amounts are referred to as leakage.
- **Enclave tourism:** Enclave tourism is "when tourists remain for their entire stay at the same cruise ship or resort, which provides everything they need and where they will make all their expenditures, not much opportunity is left for local people to profit from tourism."
- **Infrastructure costs:** Local governments and taxpayers may have to make a significant investment in the infrastructure to serve tourism.
- **Increase in prices:** The demand for goods and services from tourists can increase the prices that have to be paid by local residents, whose incomes remain constant.
- **Economic dependence of the local community on tourism:** Too much emphasis on tourism can put unnecessary stress on a local economy and local people, who must perform well to sustain the industry.
- **Seasonal character of jobs:** Tourism jobs are often seasonal, and this can lead to job insecurity.
- **Other industry impacts affecting tourism:** Economic crises in generating countries can adversely affect the economies of the host countries.

THINK ABOUT THIS:

1. How can a small or developing country maximize the potential economic benefits of tourism, while also limiting the potential negative effects?
2. What can a country do to discourage enclave tourism or at least to minimize its negative effects?
3. What can a country do to help alleviate the problems caused by the seasonality of employment in tourism?

Source: United Nations Development Programme. 2002. Economic Impacts of Tourism, http://www.uneptie.org/pc/tourism/sust-tourism/economic.htm.

ECONOMIC IMPACTS OF TOURISM

Tourism has several potential economic impacts on destination areas. Generally, these impacts fall into three categories:

1. Increasing foreign exchange earnings
2. Increasing income
3. Increasing employment

Government Revenue in Canada Attributable to Tourism, 2007

Government revenue from tourism activities in Canada reached $19.7 billion in 2007, up 4.3% from one year earlier. The increase was driven by higher revenues from domestic tourism spending, as the revenue directly related to tourism exports fell for the third straight year. Tourism spending by residents accounted for three-fourths ($14.5 billion) of the total while the balance ($5.1 billion) stemmed from spending by non-resident visitors to Canada.

Statistics Canada (2008), page 9

INCREASING FOREIGN EXCHANGE EARNINGS

Many countries have embraced tourism as a way to increase foreign exchange earnings to produce the investment necessary to finance growth in other economic sectors, particularly in manufacturing. Some countries have required visitors to bring in a certain amount of foreign currency for each day of their stay and do not allow them to take it out of the country at the end of their vacation. However, there is a danger of overstating the foreign exchange earnings generated by tourism unless the import factor is known. The value of goods and services that must be imported to service the needs of tourism is referred to as *leakage*. The money spent leaks from the destination's economy and must be subtracted from foreign exchange earnings to determine the true impact. In Australia, there has been considerable debate about the true economic impact of the growing number of Japanese travelers, especially to places such as Sydney, the Gold Coast, and Far North Queensland. Some have argued that, although the Japanese spend the most per capita of all international groups within Australia, many of the services they purchase are owned by Japanese companies including package tours, hotels and resorts, duty-free shops, and attractions such as cruise operations. Stated another way, it is perceived that there is a large leakage factor to the Japanese economy for Japanese visitor expenditures in Australia.

Leakage occurs from at least six factors. The extent to which a destination can minimize leakage will determine the size of the foreign exchange earnings. Leakage occurs first from the cost of goods and services that must be purchased to satisfy the needs of visitors. If a Japanese visitor wants to eat sushi or sashimi, and if the fish and seafood have to be imported, the costs of the fish and seafood are import costs that must be deducted from earnings. Local manufacturing or handicraft industries may also import part of their raw materials to produce goods for visitors. This is a cost that needs to be subtracted from the foreign exchange earnings from souvenir sales and the sales of other locally produced products.

A second leakage occurs when importing goods and materials for infrastructure and buildings required for tourism development. The use of materials indigenous to the host destination not only reduces import costs but also adds a distinctive look to the local architecture and building interiors.

Payments to foreign *factors of production* represent a third leakage. Commissions have to be paid to overseas tour operators and travel agents. If foreign capital is invested in the country's tourism, interest payments, rent, and profits may have to be paid to those outside the country. The amount of local ownership and control is crucial in this regard. Foreign-owned chain hotels will often be staffed, stocked, and furnished by people, food, furnishings, fixtures, and equipment from the home country.

A fourth leakage is the expenditure for promotion, public relations/publicity, and similar services abroad. The cost of maintaining a national tourist office (NTO) in an origin country can be substantial and needs to be set against the foreign exchange earnings from that country.

Fifth, there are several ways that *transfer pricing* can reduce foreign exchange earnings. If visitors make purchases in the country of origin for services to be delivered at the destination, the transfer payments need not be made for the services provided. If a tourism company is multinational, payments may be recorded in the country of visitor origin rather than in the destination country, thereby reducing profits and taxes in the destination country. As mentioned earlier, this has been the case with Japanese travelers to Australia who often purchase their packages from Japanese tour operators who buy services from Japanese-owned hotels, resorts, and attractions located in Australia. Purchases by a foreign-owned hotel within the host country may be made from a foreign-owned subsidiary at inflated rates to reduce the taxable income in the destination country. The use of credit cards and traveler's checks can mean that local banks are not able to participate in the exchange.

Sixth, foreign exchange earnings can be reduced when host governments exempt duties or taxes for foreign-owned companies or offer financial inducements to attract investment.

Unfortunately, for many developing countries that desperately need foreign exchange earnings, the import content of tourism is often very high, especially for small countries and island nations. Some small-island nations may have an import content in tourism of over 50 percent.

A critical issue for destination areas is to determine the net foreign exchange earnings from different types of visitors and types of tourism purchases within the destination. Visitors with high household incomes may be few and spend large amounts of money, but they may require a substantial infrastructure and facilities with high import costs. Is this better for the destination than mass-market visitors who arrive in greater numbers and spend less per capita, but who require fewer imported goods and services? The import proportion can vary significantly by type of tourism purchase.

Initially, the foreign exchange cost is high as a destination begins to develop its tourism potential. Materials have to be imported and incentives given to attract investment. After this heavy initial cost period, foreign exchange costs gradually diminish for a period and then tend to increase again. This is mainly due to the *demonstration effect*. The demonstration effect occurs when local residents, exposed to goods imported for visitor use, begin to demand those goods for themselves. This automatically increases the demand for imports and is shown in figure 2.1. To what extent the cost of the demonstration effect should be "charged" to tourism is

debatable. As incomes rise and as communications through media, such as cable television and the Internet, now instantly relay messages across the globe, people increasingly are exposed to many new products and services.

INCREASING INCOME

The most popular method for estimating the income generated from tourism is by determining the income multiplier for the destination. *Income multipliers* measure the amount of local income generated per unit of visitor expenditure (Wanhill, 1994). There are two main techniques used for measuring the multiplier effect: the *ad hoc* or *simple multiplier* and *input-output analysis*.

THE *AD HOC* OR SIMPLE MULTIPLIER. Tourism generates revenues or income within the destination. The amount of income generated is difficult to determine because tourism is comprised of many different sectors of the economy. Additionally, many small businesses are involved, which leads to great problems in gathering precise data.

Visitors make an initial round of expenditures in the destination area. These expenditures may be for lodging, food, beverages, entertainment, clothing, gifts and souvenirs, personal care, medicines, cosmetics, photography, recreation, tours, sightseeing, guides, local transportation, and miscellaneous other items. These expenditures are received as income by local tour operators, handicraft sellers, hotel operators, restaurants, and other tourism businesses. In the second round of expenditures, the tourism businesses use some of the money

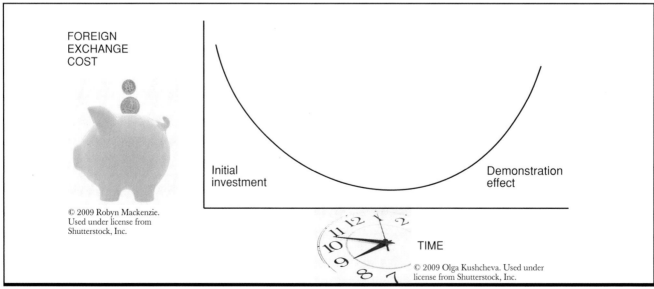

© 2009 Robyn Mackenzie.
Used under license from
Shutterstock, Inc.

© 2009 Olga Kushcheva. Used under
license from Shutterstock, Inc.

Figure 2.1 Foreign Exchange Cost over Time.

to purchase goods, pay wages and salaries, and other expenses. The income in the next (third) round may be spent or saved. For example, employees who have received wages or salaries may spend some of that on rent or food, and may put some into their savings. The money paid for goods in the third round may be spent on the producer's raw materials such as seed, fertilizer, and imported raw materials. Any money spent on imports leaks out of the destination's economy. This process continues until the additional income generated by a new round of transactions becomes zero.

The major message that one gets from studying the multiplier effect is that it is wrong to just measure what visitors spend in the destination area. There are three levels of income that must be analyzed:

1. **Direct:** The first round of spending by visitors in the destination area
2. **Indirect:** The second round of expenditures by businesses who receive the first round of visitor spending

Standard Multiplier Analysis

The standard multiplier approach is the simplest and least expensive way to calculate multipliers (Leitch and Leistritz, 1985). The formula for calculating the standard income multiplier is:

$$Income\ Multiplier = \frac{1}{1 - (MPC \times PSY)}$$

The marginal propensity to consume *MPC* locally represents the proportion of local income spent within the locality. One can make a crude estimate of the *MPC* by asking "what proportion of people's incomes is likely to be spent locally?" Empirical estimates vary from 0.20 to 0.80.

PSY is the proportion of a tourist expenditure dollar that becomes income to local households, which typically ranges from 0.25 to 0.75. This variable measures how much local labor, interest, and profit is involved in the final price of the product. For example, one would expect to see a higher *PSY* in locally operated tourism businesses that hire mostly local people than in international chains that employ more nonlocal residents (Blakely, 1994).

The standard multiplier approach has been used in tourism studies since the 1960s. The early works by Zinder (1969) estimated a high tourism sector multiplier relative to other industrial sectors. Further empirical work showed that the tourism industry did not provide the vigorous growth effect suggested by these early studies. While these studies were being scrutinized, the opinion that the tourism industry has a greater than average multiplier was still held.

The standard multiplier approach has been criticized for its oversimplification. However, no other model can approach the export base techniques (standard multiplier approach) in terms of inexpensiveness and simplicity (Pfister, 1976).

The multiplier effect of tourism shows the total economic impacts on the local economy. © 2009 Andresr. Used under license from Shutterstock, Inc.

THINK ABOUT THIS:

1. What can a country do in order to increase the size of its tourism multipliers?
2. Does everyone in a country or community recognize the multiplier effect of tourism? Why or why not?

Sources:

Blakely, E. J. 1994. *Planning Local Economic Development: Theory and Practice,* 2nd ed. Thousand Oaks, CA: SAGE Publications, Inc.

Leitch, J. A., and F. L. Leistritz. 1985. Techniques for assessing the secondary impact of recreation and tourism. In D.B. Propst, *Compiler, Assessing the Economic Impacts of Recreation and Tourism.* Southeastern Forest Experiment Station, North Carolina.

Lin, T., and F. D. De Guzman. 2007. *Tourism for Pro-Poor and Sustainable Growth: Economic Analysis of Tourism Projects.* Manila, Philippines, 15–16.

Pfister, R. L. 1976. On improving export base studies. *Regional Science Perspectives,* 6: 104–113.

Zinder, H. 1969. *The Future of Tourism in the Eastern Caribbean.* Washington, DC: Zinder and Associates.

3. **Induced:** The third and subsequent rounds of expenditures after the second round

The total income impact of tourism equals the sum of the direct, indirect, and induced impacts. If the multiplier is found to be 2.0 then the indirect plus the induced are equal to 1.0. If the multiplier is calculated at 1.73, then the indirect plus the induced are 73 percent of the direct.

The size of the multiplier depends upon the extent to which the various economic sectors are linked to one another. This is a function of the diversity of activities within the destination. When tourism operators buy goods and services mainly from other local economic sectors, there is a smaller propensity to import and the multiplier ratio is higher than if the reverse was true.

The size of the destination has a great influence on the size of the income multiplier. For example, most smaller island economies have income multipliers of less than 1.0. Larger countries with developed economies, such as Turkey and the United Kingdom, have higher multipliers in the range of 1.5 to 2.0.

The simple multiplier has been criticized by some experts. It is best used in small countries with relatively small economies. The simple multiplier model does not take into account the fact that the destination country may increase export sales to other countries from which it presently imports. Although it may be necessary to import certain items to cater to visitors, once visitors return to their home countries they may want food, beverages, or other items from the destination country (e.g., wine from South Africa, cheese from the Netherlands). Second, the model fails to account for the new investment in the destination country resulting from the additional income generated.

A visitor's purchase of local handicrafts indirectly affects other sectors of the economy. © 2009 Jean Schweitzer. Used under license from Shutterstock, Inc.

INPUT-OUTPUT ANALYSIS. A more serious criticism of the simple multiplier model is the assumption that each type of income has the same effect. To remedy this it is necessary to break the increase in expenditures into component elements to analyze the effect of each element separately. This is done through a technique called *input-output analysis*. Input-output analysis is a method of looking at these interactions among different economic sectors and determining the effects of any possible changes. It is a means of analyzing inter-industry relationships in the production process in a destination area's economy (Frechtling, 1994). An input-output table shows how transactions flow through an economy in a given time period. A matrix is developed, the rows of which show the total value of all the sales made by each sector of the economy (or industry) to all the other sectors. The columns of the matrix show the purchases made by each sector from each of the other sectors.

There are also problems associated with input-output analysis. It is extremely difficult and expensive to get sufficient data for a detailed model, largely because visitor spending affects so many sectors of the economy. Analysis is suitable for only the short- and medium-term. Last, it is argued, input-output analysis makes too many unrealistic assumptions. It assumes that supply is elastic. Any increases in demand will require more output than can be met by purchases from the economic sectors that supplied the previous supply. It is unlikely that this will happen in the short-run because of production hindrances. Input-output analysis assumes that production functions are linear in form and that trade patterns are stable. It assumes that when production increases, purchases of imports will be made in the same proportions and from the same sources as before, negating any thought of *economies of scale.*

Additionally, input-output analysis assumes that increases in income will be spent on the same items and in the same proportions as previously. In reality, none of these assumptions are likely. Certainly, input-output analysis can show the economic impacts of different kinds of visitors, which assists in target market selection. It can also show short-term economic effects compared with the effects of other sectors of the economy. Other tools are needed to demonstrate the best long-term policy option for investment in the various available economic sectors.

ECONOMIC IMPACT MODELS. In addition to the multiplier methods, some destination areas have developed *economic impact models* that reflect their specific needs. For example, the U.S. Travel Data Center has developed the Travel Economic Impact Model (TEIM). In Canada, the Conference Board's Canadian Tourism Research Institute (CTRI) has developed the Tourism Economic Assessment Model (TEAM). This model estimates the direct, indirect and induced economic impact for around sixty measures, including employment, wages and salaries, and gross domestic product (GDP); and by categorical industry output. The TEAM model is used by several Canadian convention and visitors bureaus (CVBs) and provincial tourism agencies. These models gather data on visitor expenditures and tourism employment, and then simulate the economic impacts that follow from these direct effects.

INCREASING EMPLOYMENT

A major argument for encouraging tourism development is that it produces many jobs. Tourism creates primary or *direct employment* in such areas as lodging, restaurants, attractions, transportation, and sightseeing operations. *Indirect employment* is also created in construction, agriculture, and manufacturing. The amount of indirect or secondary employment depends upon the extent to which tourism is integrated with the rest of the local economy. The more integration and diversification that occurs, the more indirect employment generated.

Tourism is considered to be more *labor-intensive* than other industries. For this reason, it is often argued that tourism deserves special developmental support. The degree of labor intensity can be measured in terms of the cost per job created or the employment/output ratio. The employment/output ratio is the number of workers employed divided by the contribution of tourism to the national income. Although research conclusions are not unanimous, the cost per job created in tourism has been found to be no less than in other economic sectors. A major reason is because tourism is also *capital-intensive*. The heavy costs of providing necessary infrastructure and building structures drastically increase the cost of creating jobs.

In the early stages of tourism development, the cost per job created is likely to be high due to the capital costs required. Similarly, the capital/output ratio is high because of the low volume of visitors in the initial stages of tourism development. As the destination country develops and as more visitors are attracted, the capital/output ratio declines. The cost per job created is reduced due to the experience and organization of those in the destination. In addition, as tourism increases, physical development takes place in facilities that require less investment than the construction of international-level hotels and resorts. Jobs are created at a lower average cost. In the third stage of tourism development, the average cost per job created may increase due to higher land prices and increased engineer-

ing costs because of the necessity of using sites that are more difficult to develop. In addition, as tourism increases in importance, more infrastructure (roads, electrical and sewerage services, etc.) may be necessary as the tourism plant becomes more spread out geographically. The increased demand for infrastructure may be caused by the larger numbers of visitors in the destination area.

The cost per job created depends upon the type of facility constructed. The cost is greater for a luxury hotel than for a smaller, more modest property. However, a luxury hotel offers more job opportunities per room and higher employment/output ratios than smaller properties. The larger properties are more inclined to use imported labor especially for managerial positions. The key to maximizing the economic and job returns is to use materials and personnel indigenous to the destination area while maintaining standards of quality acceptable to visitors.

Several additional criticisms of tourism as an employer have been made. Tourism is a highly seasonal business in many destination areas. To ensure a balance between market demand and staff requirements, tourism businesses tend to adopt one of two strategies. Employees are either laid off during the low season, or additional employees are imported from other regions during the high season. With the first approach, tourism cannot provide a meaningful job to a resident. With the second approach, there is an increased need for housing for employees who spend most of their wages outside of the destination area. Thus jobs and income are lost to the local area.

Because tourism relies so heavily upon people for delivering a service, productivity gains are difficult to come by. The national output may be difficult to improve if tourism becomes a dominant part of the economy, particularly if the host destination lacks a strong industrial sector, where productivity gains are easier to obtain.

ECONOMIC DEVELOPMENT CONSIDERATIONS AND ANALYSIS

Apart from the three major types of economic impacts, destination areas need to consider the long-term economic development consequences of tourism. Issues that need to be analyzed are the attractiveness of tourism development versus other forms of economic development and the contributions of tourism to regional economic development.

COST/BENEFIT ANALYSIS

Cost/benefit analysis is a technique used to determine which economic sector produces the most benefit in terms of foreign exchange, employment, taxes, or income generated relative to the costs of development. The factors of production are valued at their *opportunity cost*; the marginal value of their next best use. It is then possible to compare several investment options. The social cost/benefit analysis of a project determines the average annual rate at which benefits accrue to society. Critics of cost/benefit analysis argue that the results are too dependent upon the appropriateness of its assumptions. It is not possible to check actual performance against prediction.

STRUCTURAL ANALYSIS

As growth occurs, long-term economic changes can be tracked through structural analysis. Three different processes must be studied:

1. Accumulation processes (investment, government revenue, education)
2. Resource allocation processes (structure of domestic demand, production and trade)
3. Demographic and distribution processes (labor allocation, urbanization, demographic transition, income distribution)

Recently, countries have tended to become primary or industrial specialists, have balanced production and trade, or have moved through the process of import substitution. Insufficient work has been done to determine the development pattern of a country's economy as it builds its tourism sector. Early work suggests that there is a danger of developing tourism at the expense of other exports such as agriculture. For maximum eco-

nomic impact, care must be taken to achieve as much integration of tourism with the national economy as possible.

SATELLITE NATIONAL ACCOUNTING

One of the traditional problems in analyzing the true economic impacts of tourism is that it is not considered to be an industrial sector of its own in national accounting systems. The Standard Industrial Classification (SIC) systems in many countries split tourism up into other industry sectors, e.g., airlines to transportation and restaurant sales to retailing. In 1993, the United Nations Statistics Division produced a publication called the *UN System of National Accounts* that recommended the creation of a *satellite accounting system* for complex service sectors such as tourism. The World Tourism Organization and the World Travel & Tourism Council (WTTC) support the concept of analyzing tourism through a satellite account for tourism. In essence, this means adding up the impacts of tourism that have traditionally been allocated to other economic sectors.

TOURISM AND REGIONAL DEVELOPMENT

Can tourism help regional development by producing income and jobs in areas previously lacking in economic development opportunities? Many people feel that this is a key role of tourism. However, tourism normally requires a heavy investment in infrastructure. This means that the cost of developing tourism in a rural or outlying area that needs economic development may be as great as for agriculture or manufacturing.

MODIFYING THE HOST DESTINATION'S SOCIOECONOMIC STRUCTURE

Tourism development can change the economic structure of a destination area. Although such changes can easily be integrated into the economy of a developed nation, the effects in a lesser-developed country are more profound. Stresses can occur when the old and the new exist side by side. Traditional methods of farming and primitive industries contrast with modern hotels and polished entertainment for visitors. This may cause a movement away from traditional forms of employment. The fisherman turned tour-boat entrepreneur and farm girl turned waitress undergo not only a change in income but a change in status. The fisherman's catch is lost to the local people, but his own income may increase. The waitress may view her task of serving as a

The U.S. Travel and Tourism Satellite Accounts

The Bureau of Economic Analysis (BEA) in the United States maintains the satellite accounts for travel and tourism in the country. The BEA defines Satellite Industry Accounts as "statistical frameworks that are designed to expand the analytical capacity of the national income and product accounts and the input-output accounts and to supplement these accounts by focusing on a particular aspect of economic activity."

The travel and tourism industry—as measured by the real output of goods and services sold directly to visitors—grew for the sixth consecutive year in 2007, according to the most recent statistics from the travel and tourism satellite accounts of the BEA. These revised estimates show increases in real direct output of 1.9 percent in 2007, 3.1 percent in 2006, and 2.9 percent in 2005. The slowdown in 2007 is larger than previously reported and reflects an upward revision of 0.6 percent point to the growth in 2006. Employment in the tourism industry accelerated, increasing 1.7 percent in 2007 after increasing 0.6 percent in 2006 and 1.0 percent in 2005.

Other highlights from the travel and tourism satellite accounts include the following:

- Inbound tourism grew 15.8 percent in 2007, and outbound tourism grew 4.8 percent. As a result, net exports of travel and tourism nearly tripled to $18.4 billion in 2007 from $6.7 billion in 2006.
- Current-dollar total tourism-related output increased 5.8 percent to $1.32 trillion in 2007 from $1.25 trillion in 2006.
- Prices for tourism goods and services increased for the fifth consecutive year in 2007, increasing 3.6 percent after increasing 4.2 percent in 2006.
- Real output slowed or turned down in fourteen of twenty-four commodities in 2007, including traveler accommodations, international passenger air transportation, and gambling.

Tourism has an expansive positive impact on the U.S. economy. © 2009 T-design. Used under license from Shutterstock, Inc.

THINK ABOUT THIS:

1. Although travel and tourism are significant economic activities in the United States, the total contribution to national GDP is small, percentage wise. What challenges does this pose for U.S. tourism in making tourism a greater economic priority?
2. What is the ratio of indirect to direct outputs for travel and tourism in the United States? What does this imply about the interdependence of travel and tourism with other sectors of the U.S. economy?
3. How interdependent are the individual components of travel and tourism in the United States?

Source: Bureau of Economic Analysis. 2008. U.S. Travel and Tourism Satellite Accounts for 2004–2007.

throwback to earlier colonial times or may look at the newfound job as a cleaner and less arduous way to earn a living. The satisfaction for locals may depend upon the range and type of jobs available and the opportunity for advancement. The problem of seasonal employment is a major concern.

As with any other economic development, tourism encourages workforce migration, with the corresponding possibility of breaking down the traditional family unit. It does appear that, even though migration occurs, family ties and responsibilities are maintained.

> **Using Satellite Accounting to Measure the Economic Impacts of Tourism**
>
> *The purpose of a tourism satellite account is to analyze in detail all the aspects of demand for goods and services associated with the activity of visitors; to observe the operational interface with the supply of such goods and services within the economy; and to describe how this supply interacts with other economic activities.*
>
> 2008 Tourism Satellite Account: Recommended Methodological Framework, *Commission of the European Communities, Eurostat (2008), page iii*

Tourism development can cause profound changes within a society in terms of economic power. Tourism businesses attract women and young people who gain a higher level of economic independence. Great tension can occur, particularly in traditional societies, because of this shift in the economic resources within the host destination. It is not known whether such changes result in negative effects on families.

Finally, tourism can change the value and land ownership patterns. As tourism develops, the value of potential sites increases and land speculation happens. Some destination regions take steps to prevent unhealthy land speculation. Land sold to outsiders results in a short-term profit to the local landowner. However, the land may be lost forever to agricultural production or local recreational use, and control of the land goes out of the community. Tourism may force local indigenous people off of their traditional lands. Such has been the fate of the Masai tribes of Kenya and Tanzania. According to Krotz, "Tourism is the push that is chasing the Loita Masai, just as it is pushing indigenous local peoples in many places of the world" (Krotz, 1996).

Many impacts of tourism are direct, such as the raising of land values, while others are indirect (the demonstration effect when imports increase through local resident exposure to goods imported for visitor consumption). Many of these changes would occur no matter what type of economic development took place. Whether these changes are good or bad is often a value judgment. The important point is to realize that these impacts are likely to occur, decide whether or not they are desirable for the destination area, and plan accordingly.

MAXIMIZING TOURISM'S POSITIVE ECONOMIC IMPACTS

If a policy is adopted to maximize the positive economic impacts of tourism, the key is to maximize the foreign exchange earnings, income, and employment within the destination area. This means tourism development and marketing to bring in more money from visitors, and organizing tourism to minimize the leakage of both money and jobs. Tourism development is discussed in chapter 6 and tourism marketing is the focus of chapters 7–9.

The development of tourism may force people off of their traditional lands. © 2009 James Steidl. Used under license from Shutterstock, Inc.

> **Tourism's Contribution to the Australian Economy 1997–98 to 2006–07**
>
> *Tourism has an important place in the Australian economy. In 2006–07 tourism directly contributed A\$38.9 billion to Gross Domestic Product (GDP) including A\$32.3 billion in Gross Value Added (GVA). Tourism is a labour intensive industry and generates many jobs for Australians; 483,000 people were directly employed in the Australian tourism industry in 2006–07.*
>
> *Tourism Research Australia (2008), page 1*

ENCOURAGING IMPORT SUBSTITUTION

One of the strategies for minimizing leakage from the destination's economy is import substitution. A major economic problem, especially for lesser-developed countries, is the lack of linkages from tourism to other sectors of the economy. Foreign exchange earnings can be increased if ties can be developed between tourism and primary, manufacturing, and other service businesses. The economic feasibility of local development can be investigated in industries ranging from handicrafts to furniture. The industries showing most promise can be supported through specific subsidies, grants, or loans. Also, quotas or tariffs can be placed on the importation of goods that can be developed locally. However, this strategy may invite retaliation from other countries or regions.

IMPLEMENTING INCENTIVE PROGRAMS

The use of local architecture, design, and materials can be encouraged through incentive programs. Financial and fiscal incentives may cause an inflow of capital, both local and foreign, necessary to develop the tourism destination mix. The types of incentives for tourism development are discussed in chapter 6. Unfortunately, incentives are often given on the basis of what the competition is offering rather than on what is best for the destination area. As a result, capital-intensive activities may be encouraged when, for many destinations, the problem is a surplus of labor. Several other difficulties can arise. The easy importation of materials may make it more difficult for local industries to develop. Destination areas have found that it is difficult to phase out tax concessions. Managers may lose interest in the project or let the quality standards run down as the tax holiday comes to a close. Care must be taken to ensure that the burden of risk is borne not only by the local government, but also by local or outside investors as well. Before implementing an incentive strategy a destination should:

1. Examine the performance of other countries' incentive programs in light of their resources and development objectives.
2. Research the actual needs of investors.
3. Design codes of investment concessions related to specific development objectives, with precise requirements of the investors (such as in terms of job creation).
4. Establish targets of achievement and periodically monitor and assess the level of realization of such targets.

DEALING WITH MULTINATIONAL TOURISM COMPANIES

As tourism has developed, the opportunity has arisen for the global expansion of large tourism companies, particularly hotels, airlines, restaurants, travel agencies, and tour operators. These multinational companies (multinationals) have been criticized for operating to benefit their own profitability at the expense of destination areas.

Most multinational tourism companies have head offices located in the developed countries. A large proportion of the world's hotels are owned or affiliated with companies headquartered in the United States, France, and the United Kingdom. There is a trend toward more hotel ownership by Japanese and Hong Kong SAR companies, especially in the Asia-Pacific region. Problems arise for the destination countries when the multinational corporations have no financial investment in the hotels. Many overseas chain hotel and resort properties are operated without any foreign equity involvement. The chains' control is exercised through management contracts or franchise agreements.

It is possible that a foreign-owned hotel can engage in policies that run counter to the national tourism plan. The chances of this happening are lessened with a direct financial involvement of the overseas company. Likewise, the criticism that a specific type of international property is out of context with the host country must be viewed in the context of the target market. If a country has correctly identified the type of visitors it is seeking, it may seek a larger "international" facility. In general,

however, multinational corporation hotels usually generate lower foreign exchange receipts than do local hotels; especially the smaller locally owned and managed properties. The criticism that foreign-owned properties import too much seems to be ill-founded.

However, there has been no clear evidence that the import content would have been less if the hotel had been developed by a local developer. Hotels seem to be willing to purchase food locally if prices are competitive and supplies are assured.

Another concern among host countries has been that a foreign-owned hotel allows limited opportunity for local employees to reach positions of responsibility. International hotel chains usually employ a core of expatriate managers. Some management contracts will stipulate that within, say, three to five years the management team must be made up of locals. It appears that foreign ownership of hotels is of greatest benefit to a country in the early stages of tourism development. At this point, the destination can really benefit from the foreign know-how. Maximization of benefits comes from direct financial involvement of the multinational business in the development of local managerial and supervisory talent.

Most countries in the world still have a national airline owned by the government. Visitors generally prefer to travel by an airline of their country of origin rather than by the airline of the destination country. Because of the perceptions of quality and safety, this is particularly true for travel to a lesser-developed country. Almost every charter airline is owned and operated by companies in developed countries. Although some countries do not allow charter aircraft to use their airports, the development of mass tourism often requires the development of charter traffic.

Tour operators can wield a great deal of influence over destinations. Operators have the ability to direct large numbers of visitors to particular destinations. If a country has made a decision to develop mass tourism—and has built the infrastructure and facilities to service these visitors—it must attract sufficient numbers of visitors to use and pay for the facilities. In this situation, a country can become dependent on large tour operators who have the ability to influence where people vacation. In Europe and North America, a large percentage of the charter tour market is becoming controlled by a smaller number of tour companies. The larger foreign operator dealing with the mass market is more likely to bypass local inbound tour operators and deal directly with the local hotels and attractions. If hotel supply is greater than demand, accommodation operators may be forced

The Economic Impact of Tourism in China and Hong Kong

By 2020, the People's Republic of China is predicted to become the world's tourism superpower, leading all destinations in international tourism arrivals and in outbound tourists as well. In 2006, the World Travel & Tourism Council (WTTC) released a very comprehensive report, The Impact of Travel & Tourism on Jobs and the Economy: China and China Hong Kong SAR. This report includes two simulated Tourism Satellite Accounts (TSAs) and economic forecasts for China and Hong Kong.

The Canadian Tourism Commission defines a TSA as "a statistical tool that measures the total economic and employment impact of tourism, allowing researchers to directly compare the impacts of tourism with those of other industries and from country to country." The WTTC adds that travel and tourism "is an industrial activity defined by the diverse collection of products (durables and nondurables) and services (transportation, accommodations, food and beverage, entertainment, government services, etc.) that are delivered to visitors." The WTTC TSA economic impact models include the following elements:

Travel and Tourism Consumption:

1. Personal travel and tourism (resident spending on travel and tourism)
2. Business travel (spending by industry and government on travel and tourism)
3. Government expenditures—individual (spending by government agencies to provide visitor services, e.g., immigration/customs)
4. Visitor exports (spending by international visitors on goods and services in the subject country)

Travel and Tourism Demand:
Includes Travel and Tourism Consumption plus:

1. Government expenditures, collective—spending by government agencies on tourism promotion, aviation administration, security services, resort area sanitation services, etc.

The Terra Cotta Warriors in Xi'an: One of China's major tourism attractions. Photo by Alastair Morrison.

(continued)

2. Capital investment—capital spending by the private and public sectors to provide facilities, equipment, and infrastructure to visitors
3. Exports, nonvisitor—consumer goods sent abroad for ultimate sale to visitors or capital goods sent abroad for use by industry service providers (e.g., cruise ships, aircraft)

Employment:

1. Travel and tourism industry employment (jobs with face-to-face contact with visitors)
2. Travel and tourism economy employment (travel and tourism industry employment plus jobs with industry suppliers (e.g., food suppliers), government agencies, manufacturing and construction, and supplied commodities)

The following two tables show the TSA figures for China and Hong Kong for 2006, along with the forecast for 2016. According to research conducted for the purpose of this report, China has the potential to become one of the world's great tourism economies—in terms of inbound, domestic, and outbound travel. This follows the opening of its markets to the outside world and its entry into mainstream economic and political circles such as the World Trade Organization. Having prepared these forecasts, the WTTC stated that "although the version for China's ascension is extraordinary and bold, and historical experience has clearly demonstrated the Chinese Government's ability to deliver on its promises, the scope and depth of effort necessary for China to build a world-class tourism economy are staggering."

China	2006	2016
Personal Travel & Tourism	776.7*	2,839.9
Business Travel	274.8	1,022.2
Government Expenditures	72.4	166.9
Capital Investment	1,058.2	3,329.4
Visitor Exports	288.7	693.6
Other Exports	299.5	1,044.1
Travel & Tourism Demand	2,770.3	9,096.0
T&T Industry GDP	496.8	1,629.7
T&T Economy GDP	2,358.9	7,537.0
T&T Industry Employment	17,383.2	20,444.9
T&T Economy Employment	77,600.5	89,990.3

*All figures are in billions of Renminbi, except employment in forecast number of jobs.

Hong Kong	2006	2016
Personal Travel & Tourism	112.6*	281.2
Business Travel	29.5	64.4
Government Expenditures	9.4	14.3
Capital Investment	51.8	145.8
Visitor Exports	115.0	276.4
Other Exports	131.8	349.1
Travel & Tourism Demand	450.1	1,131.2
T&T Industry GDP	50.5	114.8
T&T Economy GDP	257.2	642.1
T&T Industry Employment	167.7	208.9
T&T Economy Employment	549.4	769.5

*All figures are in billions of Hong Kong $, except employment in forecast number of jobs.

THINK ABOUT THIS:

1. What are the major challenges that the Chinese government will face in tourism destination management in the next ten to fifteen years?
2. How can Hong Kong capitalize on the huge growth of tourism that will occur in Mainland China?
3. How should China and Hong Kong minimize the negative impacts of tourism that may accompany such rapid growth?

Source: World Travel & Tourism Council. 2006. The impact of travel & tourism on jobs and the economy in China and China Hong Kong SAR.

to promise rooms at uneconomic rates or else face a total loss of business. If destination areas become totally dependent on foreign tour operators, they risk losing control of tourism development. Also, foreign exchange revenues may suffer. Destination areas benefit more from short-haul tourism than from long-haul. In addition, by dealing with operators who focus on smaller but more specialized markets, there is more chance that local inbound operators will be used.

To maximize foreign exchange earnings, many countries have placed restrictions on spending. Countries have limited the amount of their own currency that visitors can bring into and take out to ensure that foreign currency is used to pay bills within the destination. Visitors may be required to pay hotel bills in foreign currency. Before being allowed into the country, visitors may have to show that they have enough money for their stay, or they may even be required to enter with a specified amount of foreign currency for each day of their visit. Foreign tour operators will often barter with operators of local facilities to avoid an exchange of cash. Destination countries may require that tour operators pay in foreign currencies for services in the host country. In other cases, tour operators may issue vouchers in the country of origin for services to be provided at the destination. Some destination countries require that these vouchers be cashed by the service provider inside the host country.

SOCIETAL AND CULTURAL IMPACTS

Tourism involves the movement of, and contact between, people in different geographical locations. In sociological terms this means (Shankland Cox Partnership, 1974):

■ Social relations between people who would not normally meet
■ The confrontation of different cultures, ethnic and religious groups, values and lifestyles, languages, and levels of prosperity
■ The behavior of people released from many of the social and economic constraints of everyday life
■ The behavior of the host population, which has to reconcile economic gain and benefits with the costs of living with strangers

The degree to which conflict occurs between hosts and guests depends upon the similarity in their standards of living, the number of visitors, and the extent to which visitors adapt to local norms.

Negative Impacts of Tourism in Myanmar (Burma)

Attending cultural shows and displays that are put on for solely tourists' benefit as this can have the impact of devaluing the importance of the cultural activity. In some cases, especially for the ethnic communities, the people themselves may not choose to be tourist attractions and may not receive any of the benefits. This is particularly true for the Padaung 'long neck' villagers where many women and girls who would not otherwise wear the rings, are forced to do so in the name of potential tourist revenue.

http://www.voicesforburma.org/ responsible-tourism/negative-impacts-of-tourism, accessed January 4, 2009

The social and cultural impacts of tourism are both negative and positive. Figure 2.2 identifies some of the potential negative social and cultural impacts of tourism on a destination area.

One of the most recognized groups of social problems is that caused by sex tourism. There has been a history of this type of tourism especially in certain countries of Southeast Asia. This trade in the human flesh has led to other problems including the spread of AIDS and child prostitution (Chon and Singh, 1994) in countries like Thailand. So great is the problem of child prostitution that the World Tourism Organization issued a policy statement in 1995, *The Statement on the Prevention of Organized Sex Tourism*, and a global organization known as ECPAT (End Child Prostitution and Trafficking) has been established.

Tourism also produces positive social and cultural impacts on a destination. If destination areas recognize that indigenous cultures attract visitors and serve as a unique factor in distinguishing them from other destinations, attempts may be made to keep culture and traditions alive. In some cases, traditional ways and goods may be restored because willing buyers (visitors) can be found. The Aaraya women of Cuna, Panama, had to be taught to sew the traditional dress of their culture. The skill had been lost. In London, England, many theaters can survive only because

HUMAN	SOCIAL	CULTURAL AND HERITAGE
Damage to family structures and subsistence food production	Encouragement of urbanization and emigration	Commercialization of traditional welcome and hospitality customs
Displacement of local people to make way for airports, resorts, nature reserves, historical and other attraction sites, and other tourism development projects	Friction between locals and visitors because of overcrowding and lack of access for residents to recreational areas	Loss of cultural authenticity (e.g., vulgarization of traditional crafts, importation of foreign cultural influences)
Encouragement of behaviors such as begging, touting, and other harassment of visitors	Increase in health risks through diseases such as AIDS and influenza	Overcrowding and damage to archaeological and historical sites and monuments
	Increase in drug abuse and prostitution	
	Open antagonism and crimes against visitors	

Figure 2.2 Potentially Negative Social and Cultural Impacts of Tourism on a Destination Area.

A cultural performance like this in Shaoxing, China, not only entertains visitors but also helps preserve the community's traditions. Photo by Alastair Morrison.

of the influx of visitors. In other areas, festivals are staged for visitors by the community—these festivals help to keep its culture alive. Thus, entertaining the visitor may be the impetus for the performing of cultural activities or the production of goods, but the effect on the local community is that of preserving part of the traditional culture.

However, again there are some potentially negative sides to this. First, a process of *cultural involution* can take place. The modernization of an area and a people can be halted because of visitor demand for the old ways. Tourism in essence can encourage local people to remain artisans at the expense of industrial modernization. Second, the authenticity of culture packaged for the visitor may be questionable. Many people feel that when a cultural event is prepared for visitor consumption, its original, often spiritual, meaning is lost. In the United States, the moving of certain historic celebrations (Columbus Day, Washington's Birthday, and so on) to Mondays to give more three-day weekends throughout the year delighted many people in tourism. The purpose of the celebrations, however, was lost. In a smaller destination, such changes in festivals, foods, and traditional ways of life have a greater impact.

Tourism's effect on architecture has largely been to the detriment of local styles. Part of this pressure comes from visitor demands, part from the multinational companies who seek economies of scale in construction, and part from the host countries themselves who see the building of international-level hotels and resorts as a step toward modernity. A decision to build in the local style using materials indigenous to the area gives the region a different selling point while reducing economic leakage.

Tourism appears to act as a medium for social change (because of the contact between host and guest) rather than as the cause itself. The host/guest interaction offers the opportunity for each to learn more of the other, and as such, it can contribute to a greater understanding between peoples. Each destination area must weigh the social and cultural gains (e.g., revived local arts and crafts, theater, exposure to new ideas, etc.) against the potential losses (e.g., overcrowding, a cheapening of the culture, increases in crime, etc.).

ENVIRONMENTAL IMPACTS

While tourism's economic impacts have been accepted for decades, it is only more recently that the potential adverse environmental effects of tourism have been widely recognized. This came at a time when much greater attention worldwide was being given to environmental conservation and climate change. There are many cases around the world where tourism has been a direct contributor to environmental degradation. Often these negative impacts occur when the level of visitor use is greater than the environment's capacity to cope with this (known as the carrying capacity). The types of negative environmental impacts that may be found are shown in figure 2.3.

Social and Cultural Impacts of Tourism in the Okavango Delta, Botswana

In Botswana (located in southern Africa), tourism was almost non-existent at her independence in 1966. However, by 2000, it had grown to be the second largest economic sector, contributing 4.5 percent to Botswana's Gross Domestic Product. Most of Botswana's tourists (that is, photographic tourists and safari hunters) visit the Okavango Delta (an inland wetland) and rich wild life habitat located in northwestern Botswana. On average, about fifty-thousand tourists visit the Okavango Delta annually. A study of tourism showed that the development of tourism in the Okavango Delta had both positive and negative sociocultural impacts on local communities. Its positive sociocultural impacts include:

- The improvement of various local services such as entertainment, health, telecommunications, and banking
- Local government administration, infrastructure development such as tarred roads, airports and airstrips, hotels and lodges
- The participation of local communities in community-based tourism and natural resource management

Tourism development in the Okavango Delta also has negative sociocultural impacts that threaten the quality of life among local people. These impacts include:

- Enclave tourism, racism, relocation of traditional communities, breakup of the traditional family structure and relationships
- Increase in crime, prostitution, and the adoption of the Western safari style of dress
- A traditionally unacceptable "vulgar" language by young people

The Okavango Delta is one of Botswana's major tourist attractions and is the world's largest inland delta. © 2009 Johan 1966. Used under license from Shutterstock, Inc.

THINK ABOUT THIS:

1. What can the Okavango Delta do to try to eliminate these negative social and cultural impacts of tourism?
2. How can foreign tourists alter their own behaviors to reduce the negative impacts of local people in Okavango Delta?
3. Is it inevitable in the future that tourism will be a major contributor to the homogenization of societies around the world? Why or why not?

Source: Mbaiwa, J. E. 2004. The socio-cultural impacts of tourism development in the Okavango Delta. *Journal of Tourism and Cultural Change*, 2 (3): 163–184.

Researchers in the city of Sochi on Russia's Black Sea coast found that tourism was contributing to air and noise pollution in this resort area (Lukashina et al., 1996). Sewage pollution is a major problem for many older Mediterranean resort areas (Romeril, 1989). The increasing popularity of trekking in Nepal's Annapurna region is leading to pollution along the trekking trails and contributing to deforestation. The development of tourism is threatening the nesting sites of loggerhead

turtles in Turkey and Greece (Doggart and Doggart, 1996).

While tourism is increasingly being criticized for its adverse environmental effects, it can have positive impacts on the local ecology. For example, greater protection of specific ecosystems may result to support tourism. This may mean that other harmful economic activities, such as commercial fishing around reef systems, logging operations in forests, excessive clearing

Changes of Land Use
Changes in traditional land uses, loss of open space, displacement of local residents, deterioration in community character

Congestion and Air Pollution
Congestion of pedestrians and vehicles with vehicle transmissions (lead and CO^2) causing air pollution

Contribution to Worldwide Environmental Problems
Contribution to problems such as global warming through aircraft and other transportation emissions

Deterioration and Disturbance of the Natural Ecology
Damage to land and marine flora and fauna, degradation of habitats on land and in the water, disturbance of biotic communities

Deterioration of Archaeological, Historical, Architectural, and Natural Sites
Adverse impacts on sites through littering, vandalism, desecration, and souvenir taking

Impacts of Foot Traffic
Loss of vegetation and habitats through excessive trampling, permanent changes to man-made monuments and natural features (e.g., sand dunes, rocks, coral reefs)

Pollution of Beaches, Lakes, Rivers, and Underground Water
Pollution resulting from improper sewage and solid waste disposal

Visual Clutter
Unsightly developments consisting of poorly designed, intrusive buildings and signs

Insufficient Utility Services Capacity
Lack of infrastructure capacity during peak periods for water supply, power, telecommunications, and sewage disposal

Figure 2.3 Types of Negative Environmental Impacts.

© 2009 riekephotos. Used under license from Shutterstock, Inc.

and runoffs from agriculture, may be limited or eliminated. Some of the visitor expenditures to enjoy natural environments may be reinvested in research and better conservation programs. A greater emphasis on the natural environment to support tourism may result in a greater understanding among local people of environmental issues.

SUSTAINABLE TOURISM DEVELOPMENT

The key to achieving an acceptable balance between the positive and negative impacts of tourism seems to be in adopting the principles of sustainable tourism develop-

ment. According to the World Commission on Environment and Development (1987), sustainable development "meets the needs of the present without compromising the ability of future generations to meet their own needs." Chapter 6 reviews this concept in detail. The three main principles of sustainable tourism development are (McIntyre, 1993):

1. **Ecological sustainability** ensures that tourism development is compatible with the maintenance of essential ecological processes, biological diversity, and biological resources.
2. **Social and cultural sustainability** ensures that tourism development increases people's control over their lives, is compatible with the culture and values of people affected by it, and maintains and strengthens community identity.

New Zealand Drafts a Tourism Strategy Until 2015
In managing our destinations, there is a need to recognise the value to the tourism industry of New Zealand's iconic vistas, scenic views and the natural state of much of our environment. As development pressures build for a range of reasons (from wind farms to housing) efforts must be made to protect the environment and those features that form a crucial part of the New Zealand experience. Tourism is dependent on the preservation and quality of New Zealand's natural environment. Where possible, values important to tourism such as vistas, water quality and coastal access should be identified, and mechanisms established to protect them.

New Zealand Ministry of Tourism (2007), page 48

The Global Code of Ethics for Tourism

In December 2001, the United Nations adopted the resolution for a *Global Code of Ethics for Tourism.* According to Francesco Frangialli, Secretary-General of the World Tourism Organization, "With international tourism forecast to nearly triple in volume over the next twenty years, members of the World Tourism Organization believe that the Global Code of Ethics for Tourism is needed to help minimize the negative impacts of tourism on the environment and on cultural heritage while maximizing the benefits for residents of tourism destinations."

The following ten articles outline the principles embedded in the Code of Ethics:

- Article 1: Tourism's contribution to mutual understanding and respect between people and societies
- Article 2: Tourism as a vehicle for individual and collective fulfillment
- Article 3: Tourism, a factor of sustainable development
- Article 4: Tourism, a user of the cultural heritage of mankind and a contributor to its enhancement
- Article 5: Tourism, a beneficial activity for host countries and communities
- Article 6: Obligations of stakeholders in tourism development
- Article 7: Right to tourism
- Article 8: Liberty of tourism movements
- Article 9: Rights of the workers and entrepreneurs in the tourism industry
- Article 10: Implementation of the Global Code of Ethics for Tourism

The Global Code of Ethics developed by the World Tourism Organization (UNWTO) set important guidelines for all countries to follow.

Article 3 specified the following five principles for sustainable tourism development:

1. All the stakeholders in tourism development should safeguard the natural environment with a view to achieving sound, continuous, and sustainable economic growth geared to satisfying equitably the needs and aspirations of present and future generations.
2. All forms of tourism development that are conducive to saving rare and precious resources, in particular water and energy, as well as avoiding so far as possible waste production, should be given priority and encouraged by national, regional, and local public authorities.
3. The staggering in time and space of tourist and visitor flows, particularly those resulting from paid leave and school holidays, and a more even distribution of holidays should be sought so as to reduce the pressure of tourism activity on the environment and enhance its beneficial impact on the tourism industry and the local economy.
4. Tourism infrastructure should be designed and tourism activities programmed in such a way as to protect the natural heritage composed of ecosystems and biodiversity and to preserve endangered species of wildlife; the stakeholders in tourism development, and especially professionals, should agree to the imposition of limitations or constraints on their activities when these are exercised in particularly sensitive areas: desert, polar, or high-mountain regions, coastal areas, tropical forests or wetlands, propitious to the creation of nature reserves or protected areas.
5. Nature tourism and ecotourism are recognized as being particularly conducive to enriching and enhancing the standing of tourism, provided they respect the natural heritage, and local populations and are in keeping with the carrying capacity of the sites.

(continued)

An emphasis on the natural environment to support tourism may result in better conservation measures among local people. © 2009 vita khorzhevska. Used under license from Shutterstock, Inc.

3. **Economic sustainability** ensures that tourism development is economically efficient and that resources are managed so that they support future generations.

The objectives of sustainable tourism are to improve the quality of life of the host community, provide a high quality experience for the visitor, and maintain the quality of the environment on which both the host community and the visitor depend (McIntyre, 1993).

SUMMARY

Tourism can have significant and beneficial economic impacts on destination areas. The three major categories of economic impacts are increasing foreign exchange earnings, increasing income, and increasing employment. A variety of techniques can be used to measure tourism impacts including multipliers, input-output analysis, and cost-benefit analysis. Tourism development has modified the socioeconomic structures of many destination areas and affected societal and cultural values. These impacts have in many cases been negative, and tourism has been widely criticized for permanently altering the societies and cultures of some destinations. Tourism has been a major contributor to environmental degradation in many parts of the world.

This highlights the inherent conflict in the tourism system between economic development and societal, cultural, and environmental values. It is vitally important for those involved in tourism policy-setting and planning to recognize and give equal consideration to both the potential positive and negative effects of tourism. The principles of sustainable development must be followed. Above all, local people must play a key role in determining the future of tourism in their communities.

The Impacts of Tourism on Climate Change

It underscored the need for the tourism sector to rapidly respond to climate change if it is to develop in a sustainable manner, which will require actions to: mitigate greenhouse gas emissions from the tourism sector, derived especially from transport and accommodation activities; adapt tourism businesses and destinations to changing climate conditions; apply existing and new technologies to improve energy efficiency; and secure financial resources to assist regions and countries in need.

Climate Change and Tourism: Responding to Global Challenges, *UN World Tourism Organization (2008), page vii*

Trends

How to Limit Adverse Impact on Climate Change When Traveling

1. *Fly wisely*: Minimize air travel and stay in your destination longer.
2. *Travel light*: Keep luggage to a minimum, taking only what you really will need. Do not take things to the destination that will become waste.
3. *Book responsibly*: Select tourism companies that have good sustainability practices.
4. *Before you leave*: Turn off the lights and unplug appliances at your home.
5. *While you are there*: Turn off the lights and air conditioner in your room; unplug appliances when you leave the room.
6. *Greener way to get around*: Use public transportation and alternative modes of transport (e.g., walk or bicycle, take a horse or camel).
7. *Eat local*: Dine at local restaurants or buy locally produced foods at grocery stores.
8. *Save water*: Reuse towels in bathroom; save water when showering, shaving, cleaning teeth, etc.
9. *Save money and charge your trip sustainably*: Use rechargeable batteries whenever possible on your trip.
10. *Offset the avoidable footprint*: Contribute to credible carbon-offsetting programs and other energy-saving initiatives.

Source: The International Ecotourism Society (TIES). 2008. 10 things you can do to conserve energy when you travel, http://www.ecotourism.org.

ACTIVITIES

1. You have been asked to do a presentation on the impacts of tourism in your local area. Describe what steps you would take and whom you would consult to determine the economic impacts of tourism within your local area?
2. Which agencies would you contact to determine the extent and types of environmental and sociocultural impacts of tourism on the area?
3. Conduct a small survey of local area residents to find out their opinions on the most significant tourism impacts. What are your results and conclusions?

INTERNET

ACTIVITIES

4. What are the major sources of online information about the economic impacts of tourism that you would analyze?
5. Which Web sites would provide you with the best sources of information of the environmental impacts of tourism?
6. Which Web sites would provide you with the best sources of information of the sociocultural impacts of tourism?

REFERENCES

Archer, B. H. 1989. Tourism and island economies: Impact analyses. In *Progress in Tourism, Recreation and Hospitality Management*, C. P. Cooper (ed.). London: Bellhaven Press. 125–134.

Archer, B. H. 1995. The impact of international tourism on the economy of Bermuda. *Journal of Travel Research*, 34 (2): 27–30.

Archer, B. H., and J. E. Fletcher. 1990. Tourism: Its economic significance. In *Horwath Book of Tourism*, M. Quest (ed.). London: The MacMillan Press. 10–25.

Ashley, C., H. Goodwin, and D. Roe, 2001. *Pro-Poor Tourism Strategies: Expanding Opportunities for the Poor*. Pro-Poor Tourism Briefing No. 1. London: Overseas Development Institute.

Cater, E. 1993. Ecotourism in the Third World: Problems for sustainable tourism development. *Tourism Management*, 14: 85–90.

Chon, K. S., and A. Singh. 1994. Environmental challenges and influences on tourism: The case of Thailand's tourism industry. In *Progress in Tourism, Recreation and Hospitality Management*, C. P. Cooper and A. Lockwood (eds.). Chichester, England: Wiley. 81–91.

Cooper, C. P., and I. Ozdil. 1992. From mass to "responsible" tourism: The Turkish experience. *Tourism Management*, 13 (6): 377–386.

Crotts, J. C. 1996. Theoretical perspectives on tourist criminal victimisation. *Journal of Tourism Studies*, 7 (1): 2–9.

Department of Environmental Affairs and Tourism. 1996. *White Paper: The Development and Promotion of Tourism in South Africa*. Pretoria: Government of South Africa.

Doggart, C., and N. Doggart. 1996. Environmental impacts of tourism in developing countries. *Travel & Tourism Analyst*, (2): 71–86.

Fielding, K. A., P. L. Pearce, and K. Hughes. 1992. Climbing Ayers Rock: Relating visitor motivation, time perception and enjoyment. *Journal of Tourism Studies*, 3 (2): 49–57.

Fletcher, J. E. 1989. Input-output analysis and tourism impact studies. *Annals of Tourism Research*, 16: 514–529.

Frechtling, D. C. 1994a. Assessing the impacts of travel and tourism: Introduction to travel economic impact estimation. In *Travel, Tourism, and Hospitality Research*, J. R. B. Ritchie and C. R. Goeldner (eds.). New York: John Wiley and Sons, Inc. 359–365.

Frechtling, D. C. 1994b. Assessing the impacts of travel and tourism: Measuring economic benefits. In *Travel, Tourism, and Hospitality Research*, J. R. B. Ritchie and C. R. Goeldner (eds.). New York: John Wiley and Sons, Inc. 384–385.

Glasson, J., K. Godfrey, and B. Goodey. 1995. *Towards Visitor Impact Management*. Aldershot, England: Avebury.

Hughes, H. L. 1994. Tourism multiplier studies: A more judicious approach. *Tourism Management*, 15: 403–406.

Hunter, C., and H. Green. 1995. *Tourism and the Environment: A sustainable relationship?* London: Routledge.

Joppe, M. 1996. Sustainable community tourism development revisited. *Tourism Management*, 17: 475–479.

Kennedy, D. 1993. Tourism and the environment–What follows? *PATA Occasional Papers Series*, (5): 1–9.

Krotz, L. 1996. *Tourists: How Our Fastest Growing Industry Is Changing the World*. Boston: Faber and Faber.

Laws, E. 1995. *Tourist Destination Management: Issues, Analysis and Policies*. London: Routledge.

Lim, E. 1991. New Zealand tourism and the economy. Wellington: New Zealand Tourism Department.

Lukashina, N. S., M. M. Amirkhanov, V. I. Anisimov, and A. Trunev. 1996. Tourism and environmental degradation in Sochi, Russia. *Annals of Tourism Research*, 23: 654–665.

Lundberg, D. E., M. H. Stavenga, and M. Krishnamoorthy. 1995. *Tourism Economics*. New York: John Wiley & Sons, Inc.

McIntyre, G. 1993. *Sustainable Tourism Development: Guide for Local Planners*. Madrid: World Tourism Organization.

Manning, E. W., and T. D. Dougherty. 1995. Sustainable tourism: Preserving the golden goose. *Cornell Hotel and Restaurant Administration Quarterly*, 36 (2): 29–42.

May, V. 1991. Tourism, environment and development: Values, sustainability and stewardship. *Tourism Management*, 12: 112–118.

Organization for Economic Cooperation and Development. 2001. Summary and Recommendations, Seminar, "Tourism Policy and Economic Growth," http://www.oecd.org/.

Pearce, P. L., G. Moscardo, and G. F. Ross. 1996. *Tourism Community Relationships*. Trowbridge, England: Pergamon.

Romeril, M. 1989. Tourism: The environmental dimension. In *Progress in Tourism, Recreation and Hospitality Management*, C. P. Cooper (ed.). London: Bellhaven Press. 103–113.

Shankland Cox Partnership. 1974. *Tourism Supply in the Caribbean: A Study for the World Bank*. Washington, DC: The World Bank.

Stronza, A., and J. Gordillo. 2008. Community views of ecotourism. *Annals of Tourism Research*, 35 (2): 448–468.

Teo, P. 1994. Assessing socio-cultural impacts: The case of Singapore. *Tourism Management*, 15: 126–136.

Thompson, C., G. O'Hare, and K. Evans. 1995. Tourism in The Gambia: Problems and proposals. *Tourism Management*, 16: 571–581.

Vellas, F., and L. Becherel. 1995. *International Tourism*. New York: St. Martin's Press.

Wanhill, S. 1994. The measurement of tourist income multipliers. *Tourism Management*, 15: 281–283.

World Bank. 1979. Development in perspective: World Bank assessment. *Tourism International Air Letter*.

World Commission on Environment and Development. 1987. *Our Common Future*. Oxford: Oxford University Press.

World Tourism Organization. 1996. *Agenda 21 for the Travel and Tourism Industry: Towards Sustainable Development*. Madrid: World Tourism Organization.

WTTC. 2004. *The Caribbean: The Impact of Travel and Tourism on Jobs and the Economy*. London: World Travel and Tourism Council.

Zeng, B. 2006. The role of tourism in eliminating poverty in China: A review of literature. *Tourism Tribune*, 21 (2): 89–94.

SURFING SOLUTIONS

http://www.abs.gov.au/ (Australian Bureau of Statistics)

http://www.bea.gov/ (Bureau of Economic Analysis, United States)

http://www.canadatourism.com/ (Canadian Tourism Commission)

http://www.conferenceboard.ca/ctri/ (Canada Tourism Research Institute, Conference Board of Canada)

http://www.ecpat.net/EI/index.asp (ECPAT International)

http://www.ilo.org/gloabl/lang--en/index.htm (International Labour Organization)

http://www.oecd.org/ (Organization for Economic Cooperation and Development)

http://www.tia.org/ (Travel Industry Association)

http://www.tra.australia.com/ (Tourism Research Australia)

http://www.unwto.org/ (United Nations World Tourism Organization)

http://www.wefa.com/ (Global Insight, Inc.; DRI-WEFA)

http://www.wttc.org/ (World Travel & Tourism Council)

ACRONYMS

CTC (Canadian Tourism Commission)

CTRI (Canadian Tourism Research Institute, Conference Board of Canada)

ECPAT (End Child Prostitution and Trafficking)

ILO (International Labour Organization)

NTO (national tourist office or organization)

OECD (Organization for Economic Cooperation and Development)

TEAM (Tourism Economic Assessment Model)

TEIM (Travel Economic Impact Model)

TSA (Tourism Satellite Account)

UNEP (United Nations Environment Programme)

UNWTO (United Nations World Tourism Organization)

WEFA (formerly Wharton Economic Forecasting Associates, now DRI-WEFA)

WTTC (World Travel & Tourism Council)

chapter 3

Tourism Policy and Organizations
GOVERNMENT INVOLVEMENT IN TOURISM

If Marco Polo (1254–1324) is the father of early tourism policy, we have to wait another 700 years
to reach a place in history where we can identify the beginnings of modern tourism policy.
It has taken place at different stages in different parts of the world.

Tourism Policy and Planning: Yesterday, Today and Tomorrow, *David L. Edgell, Maria Delmastro Allen,
Ginger Smith, Jason R. Swanson, Butterworth-Heinemann (2007), page 42*

PURPOSE

Having learned about government involvement in tourism and tourism policy, students will be able to
explain the roles of tourism organizations operating at different geographic levels throughout the world.

LEARNING OBJECTIVES

✓ Identify the reasons for government involvement and the roles of government in tourism.
✓ Describe the elements of a tourism policy model and how they are used to form a tourism policy for
  a destination.
✓ Explain the roles of global tourism organizations, including the World Tourism Organization
  (UNWTO).
✓ Explain the roles of multicountry regional organizations.
✓ Explain the roles of national tourism organizations.
✓ Explain the roles of state, provincial, and territorial government tourism organizations.
✓ Explain the roles of regional and local tourism organizations.

OVERVIEW

A tourism policy is established to guide the development of tourism in a destination area. Because of the potential importance of tourism to the destination, government involvement is desirable for establishing and implementing tourism policies. This chapter examines the governmental frameworks at different levels within which tourism policy is established and implemented. The roles played by government agencies in tourism are reviewed and a model for establishing tourism policy is given.

Tourism policy is implemented through the efforts of many tourism organizations. The number of tourism organizations involved in tourism around the world has been expanding. The roles of global, multi-country, national, state, provincial, territorial, regional, and local tourism organizations are examined.

REASONS FOR GOVERNMENT INVOLVEMENT IN TOURISM

There are several reasons why government agencies are involved in tourism. First, there are *political reasons*. Tourism involves travel across national boundaries. Governments must get involved with policies and procedures on the entry and exit of foreign travelers and nationals. The encouragement of tourism can be used for political purposes by furthering international relations between two countries or as a way of enhancing the national and international image of a country. For example, Japan, embarrassed by its huge international trade surplus during the 1980s, initiated the *Japan Ten Million Programme* to encourage Japanese people to take trips to foreign countries. This policy is quite different from other countries that are concerned about their international travel deficits (the differences between what their residents spend abroad and what foreigners spend in their countries on travel) and balance of payments.

Second, there are *environmental reasons* for government involvement. Tourism is based on such things as the scenery, history, and cultural heritage of a destination.

One of the dangers of tourism is, in making destinations more acceptable to foreign markets, the true nature of the natural, social, and cultural environments may be permanently damaged, altered, or lost. Therefore, among other things, governments must encourage adoption of the principles of sustainable tourism development.

Third, as discussed in chapter 2, there are *economic reasons* for government involvement in tourism. Tourism generates income, creates jobs, helps in economic diversification, complements certain local industries, is an export, and provides foreign exchange earnings. To enhance these economic advantages to the destination area, government agencies must get involved.

The extent of government involvement in tourism varies from country to country. The greater the importance that the government attaches to tourism, the greater is the involvement. For example, government involvement in tourism is much greater in the Bahamas, where visitor spending represents about 60 percent of the Gross Domestic Product (*CIA World Factbook,* 2008), than in the United States, which has a much more diverse economy. The existing conditions in a country, including the political, economic, and constitutional system, also affect the type and amount of government involvement in tourism. For example, the level of involvement in socialist countries such as China and Vietnam is greater than in countries that are predominantly free-enterprise systems.

The level of economic development is another important factor determining the extent of government involvement. The greater the economic development of a country; the less the need for government involvement. The maturity and financial capabilities of the private sector are important factors. The greater the capability of the private sector, the less is the need for government involvement. In the United States, politicians have argued that tourism businesses are so highly developed, sophisticated, and resourceful that there is little need for the federal government to be involved in tourism development or marketing. This philosophy was clearly demonstrated through the closure of the U.S. Travel and Tourism Administration (USTTA) in 1996.

New Tourism Policy for Europe
The renewed tourism policy, proposed by the Commission in 2006, aims to help the industry meet a number of challenges while promoting overall competitiveness. Those challenges include facing up to Europe's ageing population; growing external competition, consumer demands for more specialised tourism, and the need to develop more sustainable and environmentally friendly practices. The revised policy seeks to produce more and better jobs by nurturing conditions that will help tourism grow strongly in the coming years.

Tourism, *European Commission, Enterprise and Industry (2008), http://ec.europa.eu/enterprise/tourism/index_en.htm, accessed January 4, 2009*

Tourism Coordination
Tourism Policy-Setting and Tourism Planning
Tourism Legislation and Regulation
Tourism Infrastructure Development
Tourism Operations
Tourism Development Stimulation and Control
Tourism Marketing and Research
Tourism Training and Education

Figure 3.1 Eight Potential Roles of Government in Tourism.

GOVERNMENT ROLES IN TOURISM

There are eight key roles that government agencies play in tourism (figure 3.1). The extent of government involvement actually varies by country. In the United States, for example, government tourism organizations are mostly involved in tourism marketing and research. In Canada, they play a wider role and typically lead the process of tourism planning, while making extensive contributions in tourism training and education. In less-developed nations of the world, government tourism agencies play a more "hands-on" role in tourism development and operations.

TOURISM COORDINATION

Government agencies often play a coordinating function. Coordination is necessary among the many governmental bodies concerned with different aspects of tourism. For example, immigration may decide to relax the frontier formalities to expedite the entry of visitors into the country. This helps tourism. The agency responsible for drug enforcement may be against this proposal; for fear that it will increase the flow of drugs, as well as visitors, into the country. Some kind of coordination is necessary. Coordination is also required among government agencies at the national, state, provincial, territorial, and local levels. To be truly effective, tourism within a country must be coordinated so that all regions are working toward the same tourism vision and goals. For the same reason, coordination is necessary among the government, the private sector, and nonprofit organizations. Many educational and cultural organizations, although they do not have tourism as a core focus, provide resources that attract visitors. The private sector is very involved in tourism. To avoid duplication of effort, it is vital that goals and strategies

be coordinated. The overall responsibility for tourism needs to be assigned to a specific agency dedicated to tourism.

TOURISM POLICY-SETTING AND TOURISM PLANNING

Government agencies are involved in developing tourism policies and plans. Among other things, these policies and plans indicate the sectors of tourism to be developed, the appropriate rates of growth, sustainable tourism development procedures, and the sources of capital needed for expansion. The key is to balance the development of supply (attractions, facilities, transportation, infrastructure, and human resources) and the promotion of demand (the number of visitors) while maintaining the principles of sustainable tourism development. Government's tourism planning role is explained in chapter 5.

Bhutan Strictly Limits Tourist Arrivals but Still Benefits from Tourism

Bhutan adopts a policy of controlled tourism, hence its arrival figures are small compared to its South Asian counterparts (21,094 in 2007; 22,380 projected for 2008). Still, tourism is one of the growing foreign exchange earners of the country.

Asian Tourism Guide 2008/2009, Bhutan, TTG Asia (2008), page 7

TOURISM LEGISLATION AND REGULATION

An important role of government is as a legislator and regulator. Government legislation can affect the number of paid vacation days during the year and hence the amount of discretionary paid time available for vacations. Policies on passports and visas also directly affect tourism. Visitors are required to have official visas when traveling to several countries (e.g., China and India). Government influence may also be felt through regulations on operating a tourism business. In some countries, tour operators, travel agents, and guides must be licensed. Businesses have safety and health regulations to abide by; they also have to meet zoning, building, and licensing requirements. The need to protect the environment and other resources that attract visitors may result in restrictions regarding the use of fragile natural resources. Visitors are no longer allowed to enter certain European monuments (e.g., Stonehenge in England), and park systems often have certain areas set aside as wilderness where use is severely limited. This role is fully reviewed in chapter 4.

TOURISM INFRASTRUCTURE DEVELOPMENT

Governments are expected to provide the infrastructure and transportation facilities (roads, airport facilities, sewage disposal, electricity, water, and other essential

Having great transportation facilities and infrastructure is crucial to tourism development. © 2009 Tyler Olson. Used under license from Shutterstock, Inc.

services) for tourism development in destination areas. These services are crucial to tourism development and cannot be provided by private developers without government assistance. Again, there is a special need for this assistance from government in less-developed countries.

TOURISM OPERATIONS

Many governments are involved through the ownership and operation of certain attractions, facilities, and services. Typically, this involvement is limited to national and state park systems, historic and government sites, monuments, and buildings. Many countries still operate state-owned airlines, but there is a definite trend toward the privatization of national carriers. Governments own and operate chains of hotels in India, Greece, Spain, and Portugal. Government ownership and operation of hotels and resorts is not very prevalent in the developed countries. An exception to this rule is found within certain national, state, and provincial parks in the United States and Canada. Governments also may act as inbound tour operators such as in China.

TOURISM DEVELOPMENT STIMULATION AND CONTROL

Governments stimulate tourism development in different ways. Government agencies identify tourism project development opportunities and seek developers for these projects. Financial and fiscal incentives, such as low-interest loans or non-payment of taxes for a specified period of time ("tax holidays"), are offered to induce private-sector investment in tourism. Governments

must also introduce and enforce development controls to ensure that the environment is not harmed and that all other procedures and codes have been followed. This role is discussed in detail in chapter 6.

TOURISM MARKETING AND RESEARCH

Governments sponsor research that benefits all tourism organizations and businesses. For example, research may be conducted on the characteristics of a particular foreign market. The results are made available to tourism businesses that develop plans to attract this market. Governments stimulate tourism by spending money on marketing. The marketing covers the entire country, state, province, or territory. It usually consists of travel promotion aimed at generating visitor demand. In some cases, it may also involve investment promotion aimed at encouraging capital investment for tourism attractions and facilities. The marketing role of government is highlighted in chapters 7 through 9.

TOURISM TRAINING AND EDUCATION

Another important role played by government agencies is the provision of training and education programs for tourism. Some programs focus on training at the skill levels and this includes the many national governments that operate their own hotel and restaurant training schools, including Bahrain and Sri Lanka. Other agencies, including Fáilte Ireland, assist with the development of training programs (courses, seminars, workshops) and materials (books, manuals, guides, audio and videotapes, CD-ROMs, Web sites) for management. Some governments are concerned with the establishment of minimum standards or competencies that tourism employees must meet. This is a very common practice for tour guide qualification in several countries. In addition, several governments operate training programs for foreign retail travel agents including Tourism Australia and Tourism Ireland.

TOURISM POLICY FORMULATION

Whether governments like it or not, they need to become involved in tourism. To guide the government's own programs, along with the actions of private and nonprofit organizations, it is essential that a top priority becomes the establishment of a tourism policy.

A statement of tourism policy provides a set of guidelines for all those directly and indirectly involved in tourism by specifying the broad goals and objectives, priorities, and actions that provide the basis for the future development of tourism. Despite this need to establish a tourism policy as a precursor for future tourism planning and development, many government agencies have yet to develop tourism policy statements (Baum, 1994a).

The model presented in figure 3.2 illustrates the process by which a tourism policy is formulated. The many needs of a destination, such as creating employment, economic diversification, and resource protection and conservation, are identified by using research techniques. Tourism goals reflect these overall needs, but they are constrained by the existing market and resource factors. A series of strategies and programs flows from the overall policy aimed at achieving the tourism goals and satisfying needs.

DESTINATION AREA NEEDS AND TOURISM GOALS

Goals for tourism have to be set before policy statements can be developed. In so doing, it is crucial that

these tourism goals not be set in isolation. For example, there is a very close link between tourism and recreation. It can be argued that tourism is a form of recreation involving overnight travel or travel a certain distance away from home. In addition, both visitors and residents often share the same recreational facilities.

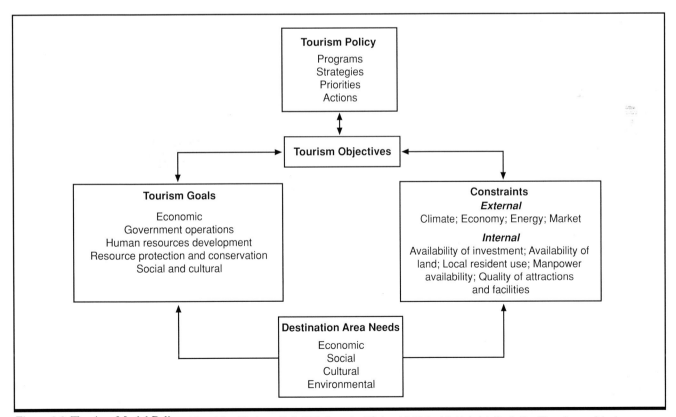

Figure 3.2 Tourism Model Policy. Adapted from Matthews, H. G. 1978. *International Tourism: A Political and Social Analysis.* Cambridge, Massachusetts: Schenkman Publishing Company; Scottish Tourist Board. 1975. *Planning for Tourism in Scotland: Preliminary National Strategy.* Edinburgh: Scottish Tourist Board; U.S. Senate. 1978. *National Tourism Policy Study: Ascertainment Phase.* Washington, DC: Committee on Commerce, Science and Transportation.

Tourism goals must complement broader economic, social, cultural, and environmental needs of the destination area. They must support broad national or regional interests. Against the backdrop of these national interests, tourism goals can be developed in six categories:

1. Economic
2. Government operations
3. Human resources development
4. Market (demand) development
5. Resource protection and conservation
6. Social and cultural

CONSTRAINTS

Before more specific objectives can be developed for the six categories of goals, it is necessary to consider certain constraints to tourism. These constraints are external and internal to the destination area.

External constraints are those outside the direct control of the destination, while internal constraints can be influenced by the tourism policy. Because the volume of demand for travel is closely related to levels of disposable income, policy is constrained by general economic conditions in the visitor-generating countries. A stagnant economic situation suggests that a destination should plan for limited growth and a policy of improved quality rather than quantity of resources.

Policy is also constrained by the world energy situation. The price and supply of oil affect destination regions that rely upon automobile visitors. The overall effect of an increase in the price of gas or uncertainty over gasoline supplies may be a reduction in the number of auto-based visitors, a redistribution of visitors to more accessible areas, and a more center-based vacation than a touring one. The increased cost of jet fuel may also have an upward effect on the price of airline travel, and this can have a negative impact on travel to destinations. This has important policy implications for the development of facilities and the encouragement of public transportation.

The potential of various travel market segments also influences policy. For example, the best potential for increased travel to certain parts of the Caribbean is from Europe because of its increased affluence and shorter-duration air trips. This suggests that Caribbean nations develop policies encouraging more European flights to their countries. Another example is the recent expansion of outbound travel by residents of Mainland China. This has encouraged many countries to seek the Approved Destination Status (ADS) from the government of the People's Republic of China. For example, in 1999 Australia and New Zealand were among the first Western countries to be granted this status by China, allowing them to receive groups of Chinese leisure travelers. This has allowed Australia to receive many more travelers from Mainland China.

Climatic factors constrain the types of tourism that can be developed. For example, the climate of Scotland is regarded unfavorably by many people in Britain. To a certain extent the image is not totally justified and may be remedied by promoting the seasons when the climate is conducive to holiday-making. If poor weather limits vacation activities, the implication for policy-makers is to develop more wet-weather facilities.

Internal constraints influence tourism policy, but can be modified by the tourism policy that is established. The quality of attractions and available facilities limits the type of visitors that can be attracted. For example, visitors from developed countries are accustomed to private bathrooms in hotels. If these are lacking, a policy implication may be to provide financial incentives for modernization by building more rooms with private bathrooms. Facilities that have been built without private bathrooms may not be eligible for such aid.

Tourism policy cannot be separated from recreation and leisure policy. The use of attractions and facilities by local residents has to be considered as a possible constraint to tourism policy. In urban areas it may be that only a small portion of the recreational capacity will be available for visitors, particularly on weekends. However, some cultural and recreational facilities may be available to the local community only because of the support from visitor demand. The extensive theater facilities in London are a prime example. Many of these theaters rely upon visitor traffic to make them commercially viable. If this demand was not present, many theaters would be forced to close and this resource would be lost to the local population.

The availability of land and investment capital is also of concern to destination areas. In smaller countries and regions such as Singapore and the island of Tobago, difficult decisions must be made regarding appropriate land uses. In both Canada and the United States, considerable controversy has arisen over the proposed uses of public land for parks or other wilderness or recreational uses. The scarcity of investment capital raises particular problems for many destination countries, especially the lesser-developed nations. The lack of money for investment can hold back tourism development, but the attraction of foreign capital may result in a loss of local control and leakages from the economy. This problem is felt not only by countries but also by local areas within a country that seek financing from domestic sources of capital. Decisions to expand, contract, build, or close are made by executives outside the community.

The availability of human resources constrains tourism policy. Tourism is a people business. The characteristics of tourism create unique employment problems. Tourism jobs are often seasonal, part-time, or low-

paying. In order to deal with the public from another social class and culture, it may be necessary to learn different behaviors or different ways of serving food than those used in homes in the host country. In some cases, foreign hotel companies, before opening overseas properties, have to support the development of schools for training local employees in methods of serving their nationals.

QUICK TRIP 3.1

A Vision and Tourism Policy for Tourism in Belize

Ask most people who are knowledgeable about tourism to name a few of the top ecotourism destinations in the world and it is very likely that Belize will be among them. The government of Belize, through the Ministry of Tourism and the Belize Tourism Board, has developed a tourism vision and policy for the country to ensure that it remains in this enviable position.

The country's vision for tourism was revised in 2005 and is the foundation for the policy. It is "to develop a vibrant and progressive tourism industry through a responsible approach, which embraces a strong 'eco-ethic' and effective destination management that seeks to improve the quality of life for all Belizeans." The Belize Tourism Policy itself identifies a set of "Critical Success Factors" that must be satisfied:

- Government's commitment through the declaration of and positioning of tourism as a national priority sector in its national development agenda
- Government's commitment to the broad policies, growth strategies, and subsequent tourism master plan
- Effective public/private sector partnership for the development of policies and strategies
- Private sector commitment to establishing export ready products
- Involved, informed private sector participation
- Access to investment capital
- Creating a balance between all sectors of the industry
- Institutional strengthening of public and private entities to develop and deliver the tourism master plan

Additionally, the Belize Tourism Policy includes a set of "Guiding Principles" that explain how tourism should be developed and managed:

1. All tourism activity will be designed to improve the quality of life enjoyed by Belize's citizens.
2. An appropriate balance between the two main segments of the Belize tourism sector, stayover and cruise, will be established to ensure that the destination positioning Belize has established in the global tourism sector is not compromised.
3. Government will foster a positive environment for the tourism sector and meaningful local participation in the sector.
4. Tourism sector planning and management will be based on partnerships and collaboration.
5. Local communities will play a meaningful role in the tourism sector, one that ensures economic, social, and cultural benefits to each participating community.
6. Tourism policy and development programs will be integrated with national economic, social, and cultural policy.
7. Development of the tourism sector will be market-driven.
8. Government will insist on the application of business practices in the management of the destination.

(continued)

In 2007, Belize received 251,655 foreign tourists, almost 61 percent of whom were from the United States and 13.6 percent from Europe. Almost 95 percent of these visitors came to Belize for vacations. Belize also welcomed 623,031 cruise visitors in 2007, almost all on same-day visits. With a 2007 population of 291,800 Belize has three times as many tourists as residents.

The Belize Tourism Board is the country's main agency in charge of tourism marketing and development. Its mission statement is that it "is a statutory Board within the Ministry of Tourism, which represents a strategic partnership between government and the private sector to develop, market, and implement tourism programs that will fulfill the emerging needs of our local industries and the international tourism marketplace for the benefit of Belize and Belizeans."

The Belize Tourism Board has a very well-planned approach to tourism marketing and development.

THINK ABOUT THIS:

1. What are the major challenges facing a small country such as Belize in maintaining the quality and integrity of its natural and cultural attractions?

2. What are some potential goals and objectives that Belize could set for tourism based on this broad Tourism Policy?

3. Given its focus on specific niche markets like ecotourism, how should Belize's marketing activities differ from those of other countries with a broader range of target markets?

Sources:

Belize Tourism Board. 2005. *Belize Tourism Policy, 2005*.

Belize Tourism Board. 2006. *Action Plan 2006–2007*.

Belize Tourism Board. 2008. http://www.belizetourism.org/.

TOURISM OBJECTIVES

After considering the external and internal constraints, more specific tourism objectives are articulated. At this point, it is not unusual to find that conflicts arise between goals or within goals. For example, should casino gaming be encouraged? To do so may be consistent with tourism's economic goals, but may conflict with a country's social or cultural goals, or religious beliefs.

In setting its tourism policy in 1988, the government of Trinidad and Tobago stated that it "will not permit the establishment of gambling casinos and/or any similar activities that are likely to have undesirable consequences for the society" (Trinidad & Tobago Tourism Development Authority, 1988). Although the government recognized the earning potential of casinos, the potential social costs were considered too great. The same is also true in the People's Republic of China, which only allows legalized casino gaming in the Macau SAR and on overnight gambling cruises leaving from Victoria Harbour in Hong Kong.

Conflicts can also arise within goals. For example, encouraging more foreigners to go to existing visitor ports of entry may help to improve the international balance of payments thus helping achieve part of an economic goal. However, this may not be compatible with another economic goal of maximizing regional economic development. Only when local residents weigh what is best for their community and what meets their needs, are such conflicts solved in the best interests of the community.

Although there is great potential for casinos in many destinations, some governments feel the social costs are too great. © 2009 Yuri Arcurs. Used under license from Shutterstock, Inc.

TOURISM POLICY

The tourism objectives, carefully formulated to complement the tourism goals, constitute the main element of the tourism policy for a destination area. Edgell (1990a) has developed a Model National Tourism Policy, which contains the following components:

- Encourage the orderly, fair, and reasonable development of tourism resources.
- Ensure the availability of public tourism training, to increase the skills and productivity of the tourism labor force and to broaden access to employment opportunities in tourism.
- Encourage the modernization and competitiveness of the accommodation sector.
- Maximize the "income effects" of international tourism by encouraging and taking steps to reduce foreign exchange leakage.
- Ensure the availability of reliable, convenient transport services between the host country and the main tourism-generating countries and between the host country and other countries in its region.
- Expand off-season tourism and thereby increase the productivity of the accommodation sector and reduce layoffs within tourism and tourism-related enterprises.
- Facilitate the entry and exit of visitors at all ports of arrival by simplifying and expediting passenger inspection procedures.
- Encourage the development of industries that supply goods and services to hotels.
- Establish tax incentives to attract investment in tourism-related enterprises such as hotels, sightseeing services, marinas, car rental firms, and airlines.

- Identify national goals to which tourism can contribute.
- Identify tourism objectives to which other economic sectors can contribute.
- Ensure that all government departments contribute to tourism development.
- Develop a periodic tourism master plan to guide government agencies in the implementation of the national tourism policy.
- Create a better understanding among the nation's residents and civil servants of the importance of tourism to the nation's economy; and foster a spirit of hospitality and friendliness toward visitors.
- Promote tourism in a manner that fosters visitors' understanding and respect for the religious beliefs, customs, and ethnic traditions of the nation's residents.
- Monitor visitor impact on the basic human rights of the nation's residents and ensure equal access by visitors and residents to public recreational resources.
- Ensure the protection of wildlife and natural resources and the preservation of geological, archaeological, and cultural treasures in tourism areas.
- Encourage, assist, and coordinate, where possible, the tourism activities of local and area promotional organizations.
- Ensure that the national tourism interest is fully considered by public agencies and the national government in their deliberations; and harmonize, to the maximum extent possible, all national activities in support of tourism with the needs of the general public, the political subdivisions of the nation, and tourism businesses.

TOURISM STRATEGIES AND PROGRAMS

Having established the tourism policy, government officials and others involved in tourism can begin the task of developing tourism strategies, plans, programs, and perhaps also the required legislation and regulations, to achieve the policy's stated objectives. Chapter 4 considers the legislation and regulations required to support tourism and other policy areas. Chapter 5 examines how the tourism planning process results in programs and actions to support policy goals and objectives. Examples of such programs include establishing specific government financial incentives for tourism development, setting immigration rules, and developing tourism marketing programs targeting specific market segments.

TOURISM ORGANIZATIONS

There is an enormous and ever-expanding group of tourism organizations around the world that either set tourism policies or try to influence them. One way of classifying these organizations is by their geographical scope. The following are the major geographical groupings of tourism organizations:

- Global organizations
- Multicountry regional organizations
- National tourism organizations
- State, provincial, and territorial tourism organizations
- Regional tourism organizations
- Local tourism organizations

GLOBAL ORGANIZATIONS

The first group is global in scope. Some of these organizations are primarily involved with tourism-related matters including the World Tourism Organization (UNWTO), International Civil Aviation Organization (ICAO), and the World Travel & Tourism Council (WTTC).

WORLD TOURISM ORGANIZATION (UNWTO), MADRID, SPAIN. The only official organization that represents governmental interests on a worldwide basis is the World Tourism Organization (UNWTO). The World Tourism Organization is a specialized agency of the United Nations and the leading international organization in the field of tourism. It serves as a global forum for tourism policy issues and a practical source of tourism know-how. The forerunners to WTO were the International Congress of Official Tourist Traffic Associations (ICOTTA) set up at The Hague (Netherlands) in 1925 and the International Union of Official Travel Organizations (IUOTO), which was established in 1947. The ICOTTA and the IUOTO were created to promote tourism for the economic, social, and cultural advancement of all nations. The WTO, an intergovernmental organization in tourism, was approved by IUOTO members in 1970 and was officially launched in January 1975. Based in Madrid since 1976, the WTO was transformed into a specialized agency of the United Nations in 2003. The UNWTO has 160 member countries and territories and more than 350 Affiliate Members from local governments, tourism associations, and the private sector companies. The UNWTO states that it plays "a central and decisive role in promoting the development of responsible, sustainable, and universally accessible tourism, paying particular attention to the interests of developing countries" (World Tourism Organization Web site, 2008).

The UNWTO's main programs are:

- **Information and Communications:** Within this program area, the components are: (1) media; (2) documentation resources and archives; (3) fairs and communications assistance; and (4) publications and e-library. One of the units involved here, the Documentation Resources Department, promotes and facilitates access to tourism information for UNWTO members and other institutional partners through appropriate mechanisms and effective information support services. There is also a dedicated media section of UNWTO.
- **Education and Knowledge Management:** The UNWTO Education, Training, and Knowledge Management Department implements UNWTO's

---

Netherlands Change Policy to Go after the Outbound Markets from China and India

The Dutch Economy Ministry plans to invest 50 million Euros in the next three years to boost tourism in the country, with a focus on attracting more tourists from rapidly growing economies like China and India, the Ministry said Monday. Presenting the national tourism policy for the next three years in the seaport of Scheveningen Monday, Dutch State Secretary for Economic Affairs Frank Heemskerk said tourism promotion in recent years have focused on an increase in the number of foreign tourists.

New Dutch tourism strategy aimed for Chinese, Indians, China.org.cn (2008), http://www.china.org.cn/international/cultural_sidelines/2008-06/10/content_15709908.htm, accessed January 5, 2009

program of work in education and training. It also coordinates the activities of the UNWTO Education Council as well as the UNWTO Themis Foundation with a goal of achieving tourism competitiveness and sustainability through excellence in tourism education.

- **Development Assistance:** The Department of Development Assistance at UNWTO "dedicates itself to meet the specific needs of the Member States and to support them in their efforts to develop and promote the tourism industry as an engine for socioeconomic growth and poverty alleviation through the creation of employment." The seven strategic objectives of the department are:

1. Build up a stronger, healthier, and more efficient tourism sector.
2. Optimize socioeconomic benefits of tourism.
3. Alleviate poverty at the grassroots level.
4. Promote sustainable livelihoods.
5. Preserve, conserve, and enhance cultural and natural heritage.
6. Involve local communities in the development process.
7. Foster public-private partnership.

China to Create 100 Million Jobs in Tourism by 2015
China plans to increase the number of tourism employees to 100 million by 2015 and boost the development of the industry by offering tax breaks and fortifying infrastructure. The employee boost will almost double the current 60 million people in the industry, according to a joint statement by six government departments including the National Development and Reform Commission and China National Tourism Administration.

Tourism to provide 100 million jobs, Shanghai Daily (August 28, 2008), page B2

The department provides technical assistance to member countries on the following:

- Identification and assessment of potential tourism development areas
- Establishment of coherent frameworks for long-term sustainable tourism development
- Preparation of national and regional Tourism Development Master Plans
- Development of community-based tourism
- Alleviation of poverty through tourism
- Development of rural tourism and ecotourism
- Development of human resources for tourism
- Formulation and implementation of appropriate marketing and promotional strategies

---

Namibia has a Community-Based Tourism Policy
Tourism has become the fourth largest income earner in Namibia, and has created about 10,000 jobs. It is a vital industry but must benefit the local residents of the areas that tourists visit. This will lead to higher living standards and encourage people to conserve the environment. Tourism is dependent on the environment—an environment which is not cared for, with little wildlife and other resources will not attract visitors to the country. It is therefore important to consider the environment when planning new developments. With this in mind, the Ministry of Environment and Tourism has drawn up the Community-based Tourism Policy. The policy explores ways in which communities can benefit from the tourism industry to promote social and economic development and conservation in communal areas.

Community Based Natural Resource Management (CBNRM), Namibia's Community Based Tourism Policy, *Ministry of Environment and Tourism, Namibia (2009), http://www.met. gov.na/programmes/cbnrm/cbtourism_guide.htm,* accessed January 4, 2009

- Strengthening of institutional capacities of national tourism administrations (NTAs)
- Adjustment and improvements in existing tourism regulations in accordance with international standards
- Stimulation and promotion of public-private partnerships
- Establishment of hotel classification systems
- Deployment of information technology in tourism

This department is responsible within the UNWTO Secretariat for the implementation of ST-EP projects that focus on the contribution of tourism to poverty alleviation and improve the capacities of NTAs and local authorities in developing countries to design and implement poverty reduction policies, plans and projects, through the development of sustainable tourism.

- **Sustainable Development:** There are several UNWTO initiatives in this program area: (1) providing guidelines for policy making and planning; (2) coordinating destination-specific activities (coasts and islands; ecotourism and protected areas; cultural and urban sites; and rural and community-based tourism); (3) advising of cultural, social, and ethical aspects of tourism; (4) assisting with poverty reduction efforts through tourism; and (5) implementing global initiatives (e.g., climate change and tourism; Global Code of Ethics for Tourism, etc.).
- **Competitiveness and Trade in Tourism Services:** This program area involves four aspects of tourism:

(1) quality and standards; (2) investment; (3) trade in tourism services; and (4) safety and security.

- **Market Intelligence and Promotion:** The mission of the Market Intelligence and Promotion Department is to provide the members of UNWTO with information on the qualitative and quantitative knowledge of tourism markets, identifying market trends and effective techniques of tourism promotion and its evaluation.
- **Statistics and Tourism Satellite Account:** The mission of the Department of Statistics and Tourism Satellite Account (TSA) is to foster the development of national Systems of Tourism Statistics (STS), the international comparability of tourism statistics, and the macroeconomic analysis of tourism.
- **Risk and Crisis Management:** This unit maintains the Tourism Emergency Response Network.
- **Coordination in Destination Management:** Organizes conferences and other meetings related to destination management.
- **Conferences:** Organizes the General Assembly (every two years), meetings of the Executive Council, and various Technical Conferences.
- **E-Tourism:** The UNWTO has initiated several activities related to the impact and use of the Internet in tourism.

There are several groups within UNWTO that are responsible for its policies and programs. The UNWTO Secretariat consists of the Secretary General of UNWTO and the full-time UNWTO staff (about 110 people) located in Madrid. There is also a Regional Support Office for Asia-Pacific located in Osaka, Japan. The General Assembly, held every two years, brings together all members to consider UNWTO's policies and programs. The UNWTO has six Regional Commissions for Africa, the Americas, East Asia and the Pacific, Europe, the Middle East, and South Asia who oversee the implementation of UNWTO programs in their respective regions. The third UNWTO body is the Executive Council, consisting of around thirty-six members. The Executive Council meets at least twice a year to take whatever measures are necessary to implement the decisions and recommendations of the previous General Assembly. There are also several special committees that advise the UNWTO on specific issues (e.g., the Sustainable Development of Tourism Committee).

Although its members include many developed countries, such as Canada, France, Germany, Italy, and Japan, the UNWTO places a special emphasis on tourism in developing countries. The UNWTO has three membership categories: full, associate, and affili-

ate. In October 2008, the UNWTO had 154 member countries and seven associate members (including Hong Kong, Macau, and Puerto Rico). The UNWTO had more than 350 affiliate members, which include international and regional tourism bodies, such as the Pacific Asia Travel Association (PATA) and the Caribbean Tourism Organization (CTO), and private sector tourism companies, associations, and educational institutions.

There are other United Nations agencies that have roles that affect tourism. These include the International Labour Organization (ILO) based in Geneva, Switzerland; The U.N. Environment Programme (UNEP); and the U.N. Conference on Trade and Development (UNCTAD). The ILO has a Hotel and Tourism unit within its Enterprise & Cooperative Development Department that organizes training and education programs in developing countries. The World Bank (International Bank for Reconstruction and Development), the International Finance Corporation, the International Monetary Fund, and the Multilateral Investment Guarantee Agency are other agencies that provide assistance to tourism development on a worldwide basis.

INTERNATIONAL CIVIL AVIATION ORGANIZATION (ICAO), MONTREAL, CANADA. The International Civil Aviation Organization (ICAO) was established in December 1944 through *The Convention on International Civil Aviation* (also known as the Chicago Convention). The ICAO is made up of representatives from the gov-

---

Helping to Eliminate Poverty through Tourism

Poverty alleviation has become an essential condition for peace, environmental conservation and sustainable development, besides being an ethical obligation in an affluent world, where the divide between poor and rich nations seems to have increased in recent years. The potential for tourism to play a significant role in the alleviation of poverty is increasingly recognised by international bodies and national governments. Its geographical expansion and labour intensive nature support a spread of employment and can be particularly relevant in remote and rural areas where many of the poor live. UNWTO statistics show the growing strength of the tourism industry for developing countries. In 2005, international tourism receipts for developing countries (low income, lower and upper middle income countries) amounted to US$ 203 billion. Tourism is one of the major export sectors of developing countries, and is the primary source of foreign exchange earnings in 46 of the 49 Least Developed Countries.

Sustainable Tourism—Eliminating Poverty, About ST-EP, UN World Tourism Organization (2009), http://www.unwto.org/step/about/en/step.php?op=1, accessed January 6, 2009

ernments of approximately 190 contracting states. The principal task of the ICAO is to promote worldwide civil aviation. The ICAO is a United Nations specialized agency and provides the global forum for civil aviation. The ICAO pursues its vision of safe, secure, and sustainable development of civil aviation through cooperation amongst its member states. To implement this vision, the ICAO has established the following strategic objectives for the period of 2005 to 2010:

- **Safety:** The objective is to enhance global civil aviation safety and is achieved through the following actions:
  1. Identify and monitor existing types of safety risks to civil aviation and develop and implement an effective and relevant global response to emerging risks.
  2. Ensure the timely implementation of ICAO provisions by continuously monitoring the progress toward compliance by states.
  3. Conduct aviation safety oversight audits to identify deficiencies and encourage their resolution by states.
  4. Develop global remedial plans that target the root causes of deficiencies.
  5. Assist states to resolve deficiencies through regional remedial plans and the establishment of safety oversight organizations at the regional or subregional level.
  6. Encourage the exchange of information between states to promote mutual confidence in the level of aviation safety between states and accelerate the improvement of safety oversight.
  7. Promote the timely resolution of safety-critical items identified by regional Planning and Implementation Groups (PIRGs).
  8. Support the implementation of safety management systems across all safety-related disciplines in all states.
  9. Assist states to improve safety through technical cooperation programs and by making critical needs known to donors and financial organizations.
- **Security:** The objective is to enhance global civil aviation security and is achieved through the following:
  1. Identify and monitor existing types of security threats to civil aviation and develop and implement an effective global and relevant response to emerging threats.
  2. Ensure the timely implementation of ICAO provisions by continuously monitoring the progress toward compliance by states.
  3. Conduct aviation security audits to identify deficiencies and encourage their resolution by states.
  4. Develop, adopt, and promote new or amended measures to improve security for air travelers worldwide while promoting efficient border crossing procedures.
  5. Develop and maintain aviation security training packages and e-learning.
  6. Encourage the exchange of information between states to promote mutual confidence in the level of aviation security between states.
  7. Assist states in the training of all categories of personnel involved in implementing aviation security measures and strategies and, where appropriate, the certification of such personnel.
  8. Assist states in addressing security-related deficiencies through the aviation security mechanism and technical cooperation programs.
- **Environmental Protection:** The objective is to minimize the adverse effect of global civil aviation on the environment. Here the measures include minimizing the adverse environmental effects of global civil aviation activity, notably aircraft noise and aircraft engine emissions.
- **Efficiency:** The objective is to enhance the efficiency of aviation operations by addressing issues that limit the efficient development of global civil aviation:
  1. Develop, coordinate, and implement air navigation plans that reduce operational unit costs, facilitate increased traffic (including persons and goods), and optimize the use of existing and emerging technologies.
  2. Study trends, coordinate planning, and develop guidance for states that support the sustainable development of international civil aviation.
  3. Develop guidance and facilitate and assist states in the process of liberalizing the economic regulation of international air transport, with appropriate safeguards.
  4. Assist states to improve efficiency of aviation operations through technical cooperation programs.
- **Continuity:** The objective is to maintain the continuity of aviation operations by identifying and managing threats to air navigation:

1. Assist states to resolve disagreements that create impediments to air navigation.
2. Respond quickly and positively to mitigate the effect of natural or human events that may disrupt air navigation.
3. Cooperate with other international organizations to prevent the spread of disease by air travelers.

- **Rule of Law:** The objective is to strengthen law governing international civil aviation:
  1. Prepare international air law instruments that support the ICAO's Strategic Objectives and provide a forum to states to negotiate such instruments.
  2. Encourage states to ratify international air law instruments.
  3. Provide services for registration of aeronautical agreements and depositary functions for international air law instruments.
  4. Provide mechanisms for the settlement of civil aviation disputes.
  5. Provide model legislation for states.

The ICAO is governed by a council composed of thirty-six contracting states. An assembly of all contracting states is held once every three years, with the last being in 2007. The Secretariat, consisting of ICAO's full-time staff, works in its Montreal headquarters.

Two other important groups in air transportation worldwide are the International Air Transport Association (IATA) with headquarters in Montreal and the Air Transport Action Group (ATAG) based in Geneva, Switzerland. The IATA is a global association of approximately 230 airlines with a mission "to represent, lead, and serve the airline industry" (IATA, 2008).

The ATAG was created in 1990 and is funded by IATA, Airbus Industrie, and Boeing. It has over eighty member organizations from airlines, airports, and many other parts of tourism. The ATAG produces a variety of publications including air traffic forecasts and special reports such as *The Economic and Social Benefits of Air Transport.*

WORLD TRAVEL & TOURISM COUNCIL, LONDON, ENGLAND. The World Travel & Tourism Council (WTTC) was founded in 1990 and is a private-sector membership organization that provides a "forum for business leaders in the Travel & Tourism industry. With Chief Executives of some one hundred of the world's leading Travel & Tourism companies as its Members, WTTC has a unique mandate and overview on all mat-

---

> **US$2.5 Billion Loss for 2009—Worst Revenue Environment in 50 Years for Airline Industry**
>
> *The International Air Transport Association (IATA) announced its forecast for 2009 showing an industry loss of US$2.5 billion. All regions, except the US, are expected to report larger losses in 2009 than in 2008.*
>
> *"The outlook is bleak. The chronic industry crisis will continue into 2009 with US$2.5 billion in losses. We face the worst revenue environment in 50 years," said Giovanni Bisignani, IATA's Director General and CEO.*
>
> *International Air Transport Association (2008), http://www.iata.org/pressroom/pr/2008-12-09-01.htm, accessed January 4, 2009*

---

ters related to Travel & Tourism. WTTC works to raise awareness of Travel & Tourism as one of the world's largest industries" (WTTC Web site, 2008). The WTTC has a president and a small staff in London.

The WTTC's report, *Progress and Priorities 2007/08, World Travel & Tourism Council,* describes its three areas of activity as follows:

1. **Global Activities:** The WTTC addresses challenges and opportunities that affect all sectors of the global tourism industry. The council is empowered to provide an effective voice for the industry and its dialogue with governments around the world. The WTTC's global activities include the *Global Travel & Tourism Summit* and the *Tourism for Tomorrow Awards.* The WTTC policies are drawn up by the executive committee and implemented from the council's headquarters in London, England.
2. **Regional Initiatives:** Regional activities are conducted in countries and regions that have great potential for tourism development, but that lack the framework or resources to achieve growth. The objective is to translate WTTC's mission into action by working with governments, local leaders, and WTTC global members with a regional presence, to identify and eliminate barriers to growth. For example, the WTTC recently put a focus on the Former Yugoslav Republic of Macedonia.
3. **Economic Research:** Tourism is one of the world's most important and fastest growing economic sectors, generating quality jobs and substantial wealth for economies around the globe. The WTTC undertakes extensive annual macro-economic research, which assesses the current and projected impact of tourism on 176 national economies around the world. The latest research shows that the industry currently generates 238 million jobs and contributes nearly 10 percent of global GDP.

The WTTC's vision for world tourism is expressed in its publication, *Blueprint for New Tourism*, and has three elements. The *Blueprint* makes the following calls to action:

1. Governments recognizing travel and tourism as a top priority
2. Business balancing economics with environment, people, and cultures
3. A shared pursuit of long-term growth and prosperity

One of the WTTC's major activities since its establishment has been economic research on tourism. The WTTC uses Tourism Satellite Accounting (TSA) to produce estimates of tourism's economic impact for the world, regions of the world, and for individual countries. Quick Trip 2.4 provides a description of the WTTC's TSA for China and Hong Kong.

In 2007, the WTTC launched a worldwide campaign to draw more attention to climate change and the environment. The council plans to continue the dialogue about the effects of tourism on climate change, and vice versa.

MULTICOUNTRY REGIONAL ORGANIZATIONS

There is an increasing number of organizations that represent groupings of countries interested in tourism. Some of these are primarily governmental organizations and others are composed mainly of private-sector members. As the trend toward *regionalization* continues from 2009 onward, the number of these types of organizations will grow. There are two subgroups of these organizations: organizations in which tourism is just one part of a broader mandate (e.g., the OECD) and organizations that specifically address tourism (e.g., the PATA).

ORGANIZATION FOR ECONOMIC COOPERATION AND DEVELOPMENT, PARIS, FRANCE. The Organization for Economic Cooperation and Development (OECD) was created for reasons of general economic growth and stability. It has thirty-two member countries that are "committed to democratic government and the market economy and provides a forum where governments can compare and exchange policy experiences, identify good practices, and promote decisions and recommendations." In May 2007, the OECD countries invited

The WTTC *Blueprint for New Tourism.*

Chile, Estonia, Israel, Russia, and Slovenia to begin discussions on joining the OECD and offered enhanced engagement, with a view to possible future membership, to Brazil, China, India, Indonesia, and South Africa.

The OECD's mission is to help governments and society realize the full benefits of globalization, while addressing the economic, social, and governance challenges that go with it. The OECD puts a high priority on interpreting emerging issues and identifying policies that can help policy makers.

The OECD is one of the world's largest and most reliable sources of comparable statistical, economic, and social data. Its databases span areas as diverse as national accounts, economic indicators, trade, employment, migration, education, energy, and health. These databases include statistics of tourism for OECD member countries that are published in its biennial volume of *Tourism in OECD Countries: Trends and Policies.* This publication shows that tourism is a significant economic activity in OECD member countries: "Tourism, a key driver of globalization, accounts for between 2 and 12 percent of GDP, between 3 and 11 percent of employment, and about 30 percent of services exports" (OECD, 2008).

There is a Tourism Committee within the OECD under its Centre for Entrepreneurship, SMEs, and Local Development. The Tourism Committee acts as "a forum of exchange for monitoring policies and structural changes affecting the development of international tourism and promotes a sustainable economic growth of tourism." Each year, the senior OECD member tourism policy makers get together and discuss significant industry developments and take action when necessary. They assemble materials on tourism policies and contribute to the work of other OECD units. The Tourism Committee works cooperatively with the World Tourism Organization (UNWTO), the European Union, and the International Labour Organization. The Tourism Committee also maintains communications with nonmember countries. Through consultations and by organizing seminars, the committee provides a discussion forum for industry, academia, and other groups. The Statistical Working Party, which meets annually, was created in 1971 to provide member countries with the needed background materials for the development of tourism policies.

The OECD employs twenty-five hundred people in Paris, including economists, scientists, and lawyers. The OECD was founded in 1961 and took the place of the former Organization for European Economic Cooperation, which was set up to administer U.S. and Canadian aid to Europe under the Marshall Plan after World War II. The original core members were from North America and Europe, but membership has now been significantly widened.

ORGANIZATION OF AMERICAN STATES, WASHINGTON, DC.

The Organization of American States (OAS) brings together the countries of the Western Hemisphere to strengthen cooperation on democratic values, defend common interests, and debate the major issues facing the region and the world. It is "the region's principal multilateral forum for strengthening democracy, promoting human rights, and confronting shared problems such as poverty, terrorism, illegal drugs, and corruption" (OAS Web site, 2008). The OAS plays the leading role in fulfilling the mandates agreed to by the hemisphere's leaders through the Summits of the Americas. The Charter of OAS was signed in 1948 by the United States and twenty Latin American countries. The OAS has thirty-five member states (Cuba's membership is currently suspended) and has granted permanent observer status to the European Union and around fifty other countries.

The OAS plays an active role in tourism in the Caribbean, in Central America, and in South America. Within the Department of Trade and Tourism is the Tourism and Small Enterprise Section, and this section:

- Provides support to member states in the area of tourism services as they relate to trade, competitiveness, and sustainable development
- Provides support to other areas of the General Secretariat engaged in activities related to tourism
- Formulates, evaluates, and executes technical cooperation projects in the area of tourism and sustainable growth and development
- Facilitates the exchange of information and promotes public/private sector cooperation in the area of tourism as it relates to trade
- Conducts research and analysis of the tourism sector and its relationship with trade
- Provides support to the Inter-American Tourism Congress, the main forum for formulating hemispheric tourism policy
- Collaborates with international, regional, and subregional bodies as well as nongovernmental organizations and the private sector in the area of tourism

- Identifies and promotes best practices in the use of information and communication technologies and Internet-based resources to enhance the competitive performance of small and medium enterprises

EUROPEAN UNION AND EUROPEAN COMMISSION, BRUSSELS, BELGIUM.

The European Union consists of twenty-seven countries (Austria, Belgium, Bulgaria, Cyprus, Czech Republic, Denmark, Estonia, Finland, France, Germany, Greece, Hungary, Ireland, Italy, Latvia, Lithuania, Luxembourg, Malta, the Netherlands, Poland, Portugal, Romania, Slovakia, Slovenia, Spain, Sweden, and the United Kingdom), and another three candidate countries (Croatia, Former Yugoslav Republic of Macedonia, and Turkey). The EU Web site (2008) describes it as a unique economic and political partnership between twenty-seven democratic European countries. It is not a state intended to replace existing states, but it is more than any other international organization. The EU is, in fact, unique. Its member states have set up common institutions to which they delegate some of their sovereignty so that decisions on specific matters of joint interest can be made democratically at the European level. This pooling of sovereignty is also called "European integration."

The European Commission is one of the institutions of the European Union. Within the EC, several Directorate-Generals (or DGs) have been created, and the one concerned with tourism is the Enterprise and Industry DG. This DG contains a Tourism Unit that has four major areas of action:

1. Promote the competitiveness and sustainability of European tourism.
2. Improve the regulatory environment for tourism.
3. Enhance the understanding and visibility of tourism.
4. Support the promotion of European destinations.

ASIA-PACIFIC ECONOMIC COOPERATION, SINGAPORE.

The Asia-Pacific Economic Cooperation (APEC) was created in 1989 and has since become a primary vehicle for promoting open trade and economic cooperation among the countries of the Asia-Pacific region. It has twenty-one members that include Australia, Canada, Chile, China, Japan, Mexico, New Zealand, the United States, and several Southeast Asian countries. The original three objectives of the APEC were to:

1. Develop and strengthen the multilateral trading system.

The European Union Communities.

2. Increase the interdependence and prosperity of member economies.
3. Promote sustainable economic growth.

The APEC created a Tourism Working Group at its seventh meeting in Japan in 1995. The Tourism Working Group brings together government tourism officials from APEC member countries to share information, exchange views, and develop areas of cooperation on tourism-related policies. In July 2000 in Seoul, Korea, the APEC Tourism Working Group established the following four policy goals to foster the development of tourism and enhance its contribution in the region:

1. Removal of impediments to tourism business and investment

2. Increased mobility of visitors and demand for tourism goods and services
3. Sustainable management of tourism outcomes and impacts
4. Enhanced recognition and understanding of tourism as a vehicle for economic and social development

MULTICOUNTRY REGIONAL TOURISM ORGANIZATIONS

Several multicountry regional tourism organizations have been established to assist in the development and marketing of tourism in different parts of the world. These include the Caribbean Tourism Organization

(CTO), the Confederación de Organizaciones Turísticas de la América Latina (COTAL), the European Travel Commission (ETC), the Pacific Asia Travel Association (PATA), and the South Pacific Tourism Organization (SPTO). Although these organizations all are aimed at promoting tourism in specific geographic areas, they differ in their membership compositions and structures. For example, the PATA is more of an industry association, while the SPTO is more of a grouping of national government tourism agencies.

The Pacific Asia Travel Association (PATA) was established in 1951 to promote Pacific Asia's tourism destinations, products, and services. The PATA's headquarters are in Bangkok, and it is a not-for-profit membership association. Its mission is to act "as a catalyst for the responsible development of the Asia Pacific travel and tourism industry. In partnership with PATA's private and public sector members, we enhance the sustainable growth, value, and quality of travel and tourism to, from, and within the region" (PATA Web site, 2008). PATA has one hundred government, state, and city tourism agency members, fifty-five airlines and cruise line members, and several hundred other travel industry company members. There is also a worldwide network of more than thirty PATA chapters, and thousands of other travel industry professionals belong to these chapters.

The PATA is engaged in a wide variety of activities. For example, it holds the annual PATA Travel Mart trade show, as well as a Tourism Strategy Forum. The PATA collects and disseminates important tourism statistics and research for the Asia-Pacific through its Strategic Intelligence Center (SIC), including forecasts of travel to the region.

Regional marketing partnerships covering several different countries are on the increase. These initiatives do not necessarily involve creating permanent organizations. They include El Mundo Maya (The Mayan World) in Mexico and Central America, the Silk Road partnership involving twenty-eight different countries,

QUICK TRIP 3.2

The Caribbean Tourism Organization

The Caribbean Tourism Organization (CTO) was created in January 1989 from a merger of the Caribbean Tourism Association (founded in 1951) and the Caribbean Tourism Research and Development Centre (founded in 1974). The CTO is an international development and marketing agency in tourism with its headquarters in Barbados. The CTC also has marketing offices in the United States, Canada, and the United Kingdom.

The CTO's purpose is "to increase significantly the inclusion of the Caribbean region in the set of destinations being considered by travelers. CTO envisions the global recognition of the Caribbean as a growing set of places and experiences that people feel compelled to enjoy in their lifetime." The primary goal of the CTO is to provide to and through its members the services and information necessary for the development of sustainable tourism for the economic and social benefit of the Caribbean people. This is accomplished through the following and other initiatives:

- Providing an instrument for close collaboration in tourism among the various territories, countries, and other interests concerned
- Developing and promoting regional travel and tourism programs to and within the Caribbean
- Providing members with opportunities to market their products more effectively to both the Caribbean and the international tourism marketplaces
- Assisting member countries, particularly the smaller member countries with minimal promotion budgets, to maximize their impact through the collective CTO forum
- Carrying out advertising, promotions, publicity, and information services calculated to focus the attention of the public upon the Caribbean as one of the world's outstanding tourist destinations
- Providing a liaison for tourism matters between member countries
- Providing a sound body of knowledge on tourism through data collection, collation, and research
- Creating processes and systems for disseminating and sharing tourism information
- Providing advice, technical assistance, and consultancy services with respect to tourism
- Providing training and education for Caribbean nationals and for international travel agents

(continued)

The CTO has several distinct program areas, which include: (1) Caribbean Regional Sustainable Tourism Development; (2) CTO HR Development; (3) CTO Information Management and Research; (4) CTO Sustainable Tourism; (5) CTO Marketing; and (6) CTO United Kingdom. The CTO's members include thirty-four destination countries, as well as private tourism businesses (airlines, cruise lines, tourism organizations and associations, tour operators, and media and destination management companies). These include popular destinations such as Aruba, the Bahamas, Barbados, Bermuda, Jamaica, Puerto Rico, Trinidad & Tobago, and the Virgin Islands, plus the South and Central American destinations of Belize, Guyana, Suriname, and Venezuela.

Among its marketing and promotional activities, the CTO has created an Internet site for visitors, http://www.caribbeantravel.com/, and a corporate site for members and others, http://www.onecaribbean.org/. The former includes a very useful interactive trip planner and booking engine for visitors to the Caribbean, while the corporate site gives detailed information on CTO programs and member information.

The steel drum band is a distinctive sound from Caribbean tourism.
© 2009 Lisa F. Young. Used under license from Shutterstock, Inc.

THINK ABOUT THIS:

1. What unique challenges does the CTO have in serving such a diverse range of destinations?

2. What special issues does the CTO face, given the multilingual nature of its member countries?

3. The largest share of world cruising occurs in the Caribbean. What unique policy issues are raised for the Caribbean region and individual countries due to the fast growth in Caribbean cruising?

Sources: Caribbean Tourism Organization. 2008. http://www.onecaribbean.org/ and http://www.caribbeantravel.com/.

the Jewels of the Mekong area in Southeast Asia, and the Heritage Necklace Circuit in Southeast Asia.

DEVELOPMENT AGENCIES AND BANKS. The last group of regional organizations is specialized development agencies and banks that provide funding for tourism development. These include the World Bank (Washington, DC), the African Development Bank (Abidjan, Ivory Coast), the Asian Development Bank (Manila, Philippines), the Caribbean Development Bank (Barbados), the European Bank for Reconstruction and Development (London, England), the European Investment Bank (Luxembourg), the Inter-American Development Bank (Washington, DC), the Islamic Development Bank (Jeddah, Saudi Arabia), the Japan Bank for International Cooperation (Tokyo), the Nordic Development Fund (Helsinki, Finland), and the OPEC Fund for International Development (Vienna, Austria).

Some of these banks are referred to as Multilateral Development Banks (MDBs) since they provide financial support and professional advice for social and economic development activities in developing countries. These include the World Bank, the African Development Bank, the Asian Development Bank, the European Bank for Reconstruction and Development, and

the Inter-American Development Bank. Often the types of projects that receive assistance are large-scale infrastructure and transportation system developments. Some of the agencies have specific policies and programs for tourism.

NATIONAL TOURISM ORGANIZATIONS

The tourism policy of a country is developed and implemented by its national tourism administration (NTA) and/or its national tourist office (NTO) (also sometimes referred to as a national tourism organization). These are the official national bodies responsible for the development and marketing of tourism in specific countries. The national tourism organization is either one body or responsibilities are split between two organizations, the NTA and NTO. The marketing responsibilities are given to the NTO and all other responsibilities including policy-making and planning are given to the NTA (Morrison et al., 1995). This division of tourism responsibilities is found in both Australia and New Zealand. Australia's NTO is Tourism Australia and its NTA is the Department of Resources, Energy, and Tourism. In New Zealand, the NTO is the New Zealand Tourism Board and the NTA is the Ministry of Tourism. The roles of these organizations vary according to the governmental status they are given in specific countries. It may be governmental and part of the civil service system as an *independent ministry*, such as in the Bahamas and Belize. It may also be a named section of a shared ministerial portfolio such as in Australia.

Second, the NTO may be a *governmental agency* or bureau responsible for tourism and set within a larger department. Examples here include the Sernatur (Servicio Nacional de Turismo) in Chile, the Singapore Tourism Board, and the Tourist Authority of Thailand. Generally, a governmental agency has less influence and status than the ministry form. Tourism bodies with a governmental status have the broadest range of functions of national tourism organizations.

Third, the official tourism organization may be a *quasi-public government-funded commission, board, or authority,* such as Tourism Australia, VisitBritain, Canadian Tourism Commission, Hong Kong Tourism Board, Fáilte Ireland, New Zealand Tourism Board, and South African Tourism. These are sometimes referred to as *statutory bodies* or "quangos" (quasi non-governmental organizations). These organizations are governed by independent boards of directors drawn from private-sector tourism businesses and nonprofit organizations. A key advantage of the government-funded commission or board is that is has greater management flexibility in dealing with the commercial aspects of tourism marketing and promotion. A closer liaison with the private sector and other non-governmental organizations is possible with this type of arrangement. Because of the public-private partnership nature of this type of organization, there has been a trend for more countries to adopt this type of structure.

Last, the official tourism organization may be a private association indirectly supported by government funding. This approach is not found very often. A major advantage of having a governmental agency as a national tourism organization is that it has the authority within government to represent tourism and develop and implement tourism policy.

The roles of national tourism organizations (NTOs) affect both the supply and demand for all elements of the tourism destination mix. On the supply side, pro-

Parfois, ne rien faire est utile.

Canada

The Canadian Tourism Commission is considered to be one of the best NTOs in the world.

grams include *conducting inventories and assessments of the destination mix* prior to the development of a national tourism plan. NTOs coordinate the *national tourism planning* process. NTOs develop and operate programs to improve the quality of different elements of the destination mix. This includes protecting the environment through a national park system and other measures to encourage sustainable tourism development. Governments may establish *minimum standards* for hotels, attractions, tour operators, and tour guides. NTOs operate *training and education programs* to increase professionalism in tourism and improve hospitality skills. A very good example of this is the *KiwiHost* program (http://www.kiwihost.co.nz), which was originally introduced by the NTO in New Zealand. The program began in 1991 with the aim of setting a national standard for service in tourism. By 2008, approximately 250,000 people in New Zealand had received the service training. When another agency sets policy that affects tourism, the NTO may have some advisory input into that policy.

Although the government's role in economic activities in free-market economies is generally confined to *legislation and regulation*, the role of the government in socialist countries is quite different, although the differences are now becoming less obvious. In socialist countries, governments have traditionally been involved in owning and operating visitor attractions and facilities, as well as in controlling domestic travel agencies and inbound tour operators. Developing countries lacking private capital and expertise often find it necessary for the government to develop, own, and manage facilities and attractions. To further ensure the proper supply, some governments provide *financial incentives* for the development of facilities and attractions, and for human resources development to educate and train local residents for tourism.

On the demand side, NTOs are involved in *facilitation, marketing research, marketing,* and *representation* in foreign countries. The role of the NTO in facilitation tends to be an advisory one, commenting on the effect of government policies regarding visas, passports, and customs formalities on visitor demand. NTOs are primarily known for their roles in marketing, especially in attracting foreign visitors to their respective countries, and in sponsoring or generating tourism marketing research

Tourism Australia

Tourism Australia is a statutory authority of the Australian government, which promotes Australia as a tourism destination internationally and domestically and delivers research and forecasts for the sector. Tourism Australia reports to the Cabinet Minister with responsibility for tourism, the Hon. Martin Ferguson AM, MP.

Established on 1 July 2004, Tourism Australia brings together the collective skills and knowledge of four separate organizations: the Australian Tourist Commission, See Australia, the Bureau of Tourism Research, and the Tourism Forecasting Council.

The roles of Tourism Australia are to stimulate sustainable international and domestic demand for Australian tourism experiences through industry leadership and coordination; and to influence the actions of the industry's tourism and travel marketing by:

- Championing a clear destination marketing strategy
- Articulating and promoting a compelling tourism destination brand
- Facilitating sales by engaging and supporting the distribution network
- Identifying and supporting the development of unique Australian tourism experiences, especially indigenous
- Promoting Australia as a leading sustainable business events destination
- Gathering and communicating reliable market intelligence and insights for improved decision making
- Working with partners who can extend Tourism Australia's influence

Tourism Australia's main goal is "build Australia's market share of targeted travelers through increasing demand."

The Tourism White Paper is an Australian government tourism initiative, designed to achieve industry growth and provide greater synergy across all areas. It provides the framework for structural change to more effectively support Australia's tourism industry. The Tourism White Paper is designed to:

- Improve international marketing strategies and effectiveness through a greater focus on regional dispersal and a revitalized Brand Australia
- Support domestic tourism marketing and promotion, including regional tourism promotion
- Improve tourism information, research, and forecasts to more effectively serve the needs of the industry.

According to the document:

"This White Paper proposes a suite of measures, underpinned by structural reform, to position Australia as a world leader in the provision of tourism goods and services and as a 'Platinum Plus' destination that will bring in increased tourism revenue by providing a value-for-money experience second to none."

In 2007, Australia welcomed 5.2 million international visitors age fifteen years and over, which was an increase of 2 percent over 2006. These visitors stayed for an average of thirty-one days in Australia. Over 1 million (1,119,000) of these visitors were from New Zealand; 749,000 were from the United Kingdom; 586,000 were from Japan; 465,000 were from the United States; and 353,000 were from Mainland China.

Australia's Ayers Rock (Uluru) is one of its prime outback attractions. © 2009, used under license from Shutterstock, Inc.

(continued)

data. Some agencies, including New Zealand Tourism Board, have no direct supply-side functions and are also not involved in the marketing of tourism to their own residents (domestic tourism). Others such as the Singapore Tourism Board have traditionally had both supply- and demand-side functions. The promotional role of national tourism organizations are reviewed in detail in chapter 8.

STATE, PROVINCIAL, AND TERRITORIAL TOURISM ORGANIZATIONS

Overall, the role of state, provincial, and territorial tourism organizations worldwide seems to be increasing in importance. Tourism organizations are present throughout the world in the states, provinces, or territories within and associated with countries. Different types of organizational structures are found here as well. The most common organizational structures are statutory bodies and independent or semi-independent tourism ministries, departments or divisions. Examples of the first type are Enjoy England, Hawaii Visitors and Convention Bureau, VisitScotland (Scottish Tourist Board), Wales Tourist Board, and Tourism Queensland in Australia. In Hawaii, leadership is provided by the Hawaii Visitors & Convention Bureau, a private, nonprofit corporation that has a contract with the state government to handle all of Hawaii's tourism marketing and research. There is a state government tourism office known as the Hawaii Tourism Authority.

As was the case with the NTOs, there is a definite trend toward creating public-private partnerships and away from government-only state, provincial, and territorial tourism organizations. Visit Florida in the United States is a good example of this trend and it was founded in 1996. It is not a government agency but,

rather, the operating company of the Florida Commission on Tourism. The activities of Visit Florida include:

- Coordinating direct mass media marketing to consumers, both domestically and internationally
- Working with the world's major travel writers and broadcasters and producing print and broadcast promotions
- Interfacing with the professional travel trade and consumers; attending and facilitating the presence of the Florida tourism industry at travel trade shows worldwide
- Maintaining international representation in the United Kingdom, Europe, Canada, Latin America, and Japan
- Compiling the state's official air and auto visitor numbers, tracking tourism trends, and conducting surveys to assess the effectiveness of advertising and marketing efforts

All of Hawaii's tourism marketing and research is handled by the Hawaii Visitors and Convention Bureau, a private, nonprofit corporation. © 2009 Kato Inowe. Used under license from Shutterstock, Inc.

■ Operating the state's five Official Florida Welcome Centers at I-10 in Pensacola, U.S. 231, I-75, I-95, and the Florida Capitol

The roles of these organizations tend to parallel those of their respective NTOs but, in this case, at the state, provincial, and territorial levels. Some of the fifty states in the United States, the ten Canadian provinces, and the two Canadian territories have an agency officially responsible for tourism. The six Australian states, the Northern Territory, and the ACT also have official tourism organizations. In the United Kingdom, Enjoy England, VisitScotland, Wales Tourist Board, and the Northern Ireland Tourist Board support the efforts of VisitBritain by marketing their areas. A state tourism organization system is also found in India and a provincial tourism administration/bureau system is found in China.

The primary role of state, provincial, and territorial tourism organizations is *domestic travel promotion*; promoting their destinations to their own residents and the residents of nearby states, provinces, or territories. However, these organizations are becoming more involved in international travel promotion and are spending more to attract foreign visitors. This is certainly the case with the state and territorial tourism organizations in Australia and the national agencies in the United Kingdom. Additionally, these organizations are playing an increasingly important role as a cooperative partner with their NTOs.

A traditional marketing role of these organizations has been in *generating and fulfilling inquiries* through media advertising. Many of these organizations also provide travel information at *travel information* or *welcome centers* that they operate. Some of them have marketing offices in other parts of the country and overseas. They set up promotional booths at travel trade and consumer travel shows, fairs, or exhibitions. They host travel writers, retail travel agents, and tour wholesalers visiting their state, province, or territory on *familiarization trips*.

These organizations make significant investments in *marketing research,* gathering statistics on ongoing visitor volumes and on other special tourism research studies. The level of research effort has been increasing as these organizations try to more precisely target marketing programs and to measure the effectiveness and impacts of their marketing activities.

Many state, provincial, and territorial tourism organizations play a role in *tourism development* and in the *training and education* of tourism employees. This is especially true in Australia and Canada where significant investments have been made in tourism planning and

stimulating the development of new attractions and facilities, and in the improvement and expansion of existing ones. Canadian and Australian organizations have also had a well-established role in educational and training programs to upgrade management and other employee skills.

Almost all these organizations play some role in encouraging *package tour development and promotion*. In some cases, this has involved financial and or technical assistance with package or tour development. Many of these organizations have cost-sharing programs that provide grants to local groups to promote tourism to their communities.

REGIONAL TOURISM ORGANIZATIONS

The next level of tourism organizations found in several countries is at the regional level. Some states, provinces, and territories cover very large geographic areas (e.g., the state of Queensland in Australia and the Province of Ontario in Canada). The economic and social priorities, and destination mixes are quite different from region to

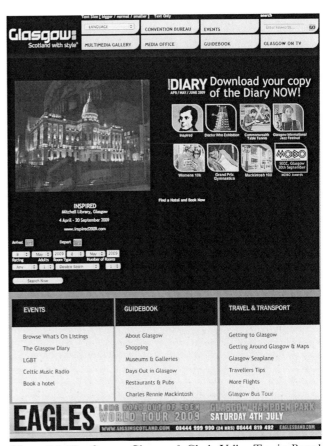

Figure 3.3 The Greater Glasgow & Clyde Valley Tourist Board has established an excellent Web site to support tourism in Scotland's largest city and the surrounding Clyde Valley.
http://www.seeglasgow.com.

region. In these situations, it is very desirable for groups of communities to prepare their own policies and plans for tourism development and marketing. This may lead to the creation of a system of regional tourism organizations (RTOs).

Regional tourism organization systems are found in Canada, Australia, and the United Kingdom, and in some states within the United States. In many cases, these systems have been initiated by state and provincial tourism organizations to increase the effectiveness of regional tourism marketing and development. Often, RTOs are created as nonprofit associations. RTOs are generally partly funded by state or provincial grants and by membership dues from private-sector tourism busi-

nesses and local tourism organizations. RTOs perform roles similar to their state, provincial, or territorial tourism organizations, especially in the area of tourism promotion.

LOCAL TOURISM ORGANIZATIONS

The final group of tourism organizations is found at the individual community level. Around the world, the number of communities forming these organizations is increasing rapidly. There are many different organizational formats for local tourism organizations. The tourism organization may be within the local government structure and be funded completely by local govern-

---

QUICK TRIP 3.4

Canadian Tourism Human Resource Council (CTHRC)

The CTHRC is part of a network of tourism human resource development organizations across Canada. Established in 1993, the CTHRC addresses labor market issues and promotes professionalism in the Canadian tourism sector. Collectively, council members work on behalf of 164,000 businesses that make up the sector. The CTHRC brings together tourism businesses, labor unions, associations, educators, and governments to coordinate human resource development activities in support of a globally competitive and sustainable Canadian tourism sector. Through its *emerit*® tourism training brand, the council provides resources that include:

- More than fifty national occupational standards
- Online and paper-based training tools
- National professional recognition
- Professional certification for twenty-six occupations

In each province and territory, the council's local partner delivers its entire range of *emerit*® tourism training programs and products including national occupational standards, occupation-specific training, business planning and "how to" tools, and the national professional certification and other recognition programs. The CTHRC partners also deliver the Ready-to-Work program and promote their career-planning and awareness initiatives.

Peggy's Cove is one of the most distinctive attractions in Canada's maritime province of Nova Scotia. © 2009 Norman Pogson. Used under license from Shutterstock, Inc.

THINK ABOUT THIS:

1. What do you think are the major benefits of Canada's tourism training network across the country?
2. What are some of the potential challenges for the Canadian Tourism Human Resource Council in cooperation with its provincial partners in order to guarantee uniform service levels across the country?
3. How would you describe the importance of tourism human resources development to a country like Canada?

Source: Canadian Tourism Human Resource Council. 2008. http://www.cthrc.ca/eng/index.aspx.

ment. It may be a public-private partnership with some funding from both the local government and private-sector tourism businesses. The local tourism organization may have little or no direct local government funding, but receive its budget from user taxes, private-sector memberships, or grants from states or provinces.

States and provinces are often instrumental in the creation of local tourism organizations and in helping maintain their operations. States and provinces can assist local efforts by passing legislation enabling communities to collect taxes to support local promotional activities. In the United States, this is usually in the form of a *room* or *innkeeper's tax*, but some cities derive support from a tax on alcoholic beverages, car rentals, entertainment and gaming, or tickets, or from an earmarked sales tax. States or provinces can provide matching (cost-sharing) grant funds, either for general purposes or for activities specified by the state or provincial government. The types of activities receiving such funding are usually such things as promotion and public relations, familiarization tours for tour wholesalers and travel writers, brochure preparation, tourism planning studies, and marketing research projects.

Room taxes are a common method of obtaining funding for local tourism organizations. This requires passage of a county or city ordinance after state or provincial enabling legislation has authorized counties or cities to establish such a tax. Room tax proposals are often resisted by local lodging groups as an unfair tax on only one segment of tourism. However, local residents are inclined to be supportive since these are taxes paid by the visitor, not the resident, i.e., they represent a *user-pay* approach. Counties and cities in some cases also receive an allocation from the general funds of the city, county, or state or province.

Another common method of financing local tourism organizations is through *membership programs*. Dues are often set on a sliding scale based upon the mem-

ber's volume of business or the number of employees. An ongoing task of a membership organization is to convince local businesses that it is worth their time and money to belong. Some communities obtain money through a variety of fund-raisers including special dinners or events such as races and auctions. These events require a great deal of effort as well as the support of many local people and businesses. However, they provide a focal point for increasing community support for tourism.

SUMMARY

Governments around the world have selected to take a leadership role in tourism planning and development because of the potential economic, social, cultural, and environmental impacts of tourism. The amount of involvement depends upon such factors as the political philosophy of the government and the maturity of the destination area. A tourism policy must be established to guide the tourism destiny of the country, region, state, or province. Without a policy and a mechanism for implementing it, tourism will increase or decline at the destination in a haphazard and potentially negative manner.

To bring a tourism policy into effect, there must be an organization responsible for its implementation. There are various levels of tourism policy and, therefore, a variety of policy-implementing agencies spread throughout the world. For example, the World Tourism Organization (UNWTO) has a global responsibility for tourism, while there are several multicountry regional tourism organizations. Within an individual country, there is usually a national tourism organization (NTO), state, provincial, or territorial tourism organizations, regional tourism organizations, and local tourism organizations.

 *Trends*

Trends Affecting Policies of Tourism Destinations within Europe

1. The aging population and increased concern for health and wellness are likely to lead to increasing demand for health tourism products and spas.
2. There will be more demand for independent travel and less demand for traditional packaged holidays.
3. Because of global climate change, the costs of maintaining certain natural areas, such as beaches and ski slopes, will significantly increase.
4. There will be more future demand for shorter holiday trips.
5. The need will grow for more information on product sustainability.
6. More government tourism agencies and tourism operators will emphasize environmental and social responsibility.
7. There will be a more competitive global environment for tourism.
8. The raising of retirement age levels will slow the growth in travel by seniors.
9. The more experienced travelers will demand higher-quality experiences and service at all levels of expenditure.
10. Volunteer tourism will continue to grow in popularity.

Source: European Travel Commission, *Tourism Trends for Europe*.

ACTIVITIES

1. Select a group of tourism organizations in your country, at either the city/county, regional, or state/provincial/territorial level. Choose a group of up to ten of these with a good geographic distribution.
2. What are the tourism policies and goals of each of these organizations?
3. What are the organizations' major programs and activities?

INTERNET

ACTIVITIES

4. Find and analyze these organizations' Web sites. What types of information are provided on the Web sites?
5. Do these Web sites provide information of the organizations' tourism policies and goals? Which Web sites provide the best information on these topics, and why?
6. Overall, which of the Web sites do you feel are the most effective? What are your reasons for this assessment?

REFERENCES

Baum, T. 1994a. The development and implementation of national tourism policies. *Tourism Management*, 15: 185–192.

Baum, T. 1994b. National tourism policies: Implementing the human resource dimension. *Tourism Management*, 15: 259–266.

Bramwell, B., and L. Rawding. 1994. Tourism marketing organizations in industrial cities: Organizations, objectives and urban governance. *Tourism Management*, 15: 425–434.

Bramwell, B. 2005. Actors, networks and tourism policies. In *Tourism Management Dynamics, Trends Management and Tools*, D. Buhalis, and C. Costa (eds.). Oxford: Elsevier. 155–163.

Bramwell, B., and D. Meyer. 2007. Power and tourism policy: Relations in transition. *Annals of Tourism Research*, 34 (3): 766–788.

Braunlich, C. G., A. M. Morrison, and R. Feng. 1995. National tourist offices: Service quality expectations and performance. *Journal of Vacation Marketing*, 1: 323–336.

Choy, D. L. 1993. Alternative roles of national tourism organizations. *Tourism Management*, 14: 357–365.

Department of Environmental Affairs and Tourism. 1996. *White Paper: The Development and Promotion of Tourism in South Africa.* Pretoria: Government of South Africa.

Dredge, D. 2006. Policy networks and the local organization of tourism. *Tourism Management*, 27: 269–280.

Edgell, D. L., Sr. 1990a. *Model National Tourism Policy.* Washington, DC.

Edgell, D. L., Sr. 1990b. *International Tourism Policy.* New York: Van Nostrand Reinhold.

Edgell, D. L., Sr. 1993. *World Tourism at the Millennium: An Agenda for Industry, Government and Education.* Washington, DC: U.S. Department of Commerce.

Edgell, D. L., Sr. 1999. *Tourism Policy: The Next Millennium.* Champagne, IL: Sagamore Publishing.

Fayos-Sola, E. 1996. Tourism policy: A midsummer night's dream? *Tourism Management,* 17: 405–412.

Gee, C. Y., J. C. Makens, and D. J. L. Choy. 1997. *The Travel Industry,* 3rd ed. New York: Van Nostrand Reinhold.

Gil-Pareja, S., R. Llorca-Vivero, and J. A. Martinez-Serrano. 2007. The impact of embassies and consulates on tourism. *Tourism Management,* 28: 355–360.

Greenwood, J. 1993. Business interest groups in tourism governance. *Tourism Management,* 14: 335–348.

Hall, C. M. 1994. *Tourism and Politics: Policy, Power and Place.* Chichester, England: John Wiley & Sons, Inc.

Hall, C. M., and J. M. Jenkins. 1995. *Tourism and Public Policy.* London: Routledge.

Hawes, D. K., D. T. Taylor, and G. D. Hampe. 1991. Destination marketing by states. *Journal of Travel Research,* 30 (1): 11–17.

Hawkins, D. E., and S. Mann. 2007. The World Bank's roles in tourism development. *Annals of Tourism Research,* 34 (2): 348–363.

Johnson, P., and B. Thomas, eds. 1992. *Perspectives on Tourism Policy.* London: Mansell Publishing.

Judd, D. R. 1995. Promoting tourism in U.S. cities. *Tourism Management,* 16: 175–187.

Lavery, P. 1992. The financing and organization of national tourist offices. *EIU Travel & Tourism Analyst,* 4: 84–101.

Long, J. 1994. Local authority tourism strategies—a British perspective. *Journal of Tourism Studies,* 5 (2): 17–23.

Long, P. T., and J. S. Nuckolls. 1994. Organizing resources for rural tourism development: The importance of leadership, planning and technical assistance. *Tourism Recreation Research,* 19 (2): 19–34.

McGibbon, J. 2000. *The Business of Alpine Tourism in a Globalising World.* Rosenheim, Germany: Vetterling Druck.

McIntosh, R. W., C. R. Goeldner, and J. R. B. Ritchie. 1995. *Tourism: Principles, Practices, Philosophies,* 8th ed. New York: John Wiley & Sons, Inc.

Morrison, A. M., C. G. Braunlich, N. Kamaruddin, and L. A. Cai. 1995. National tourist offices in North America: An analysis. *Tourism Management,* 16: 605–618.

Owen, C. 1992. Building a relationship between government and tourism. *Tourism Management,* 13: 358–362.

Pearce, D. 1992. *Tourist Organizations.* Harlow, Essex: Longman Group U.K.

Pforr, C. 2006. Tourism policy in the making: An Australian network study. *Annals of Tourism Research,* 33: 87–108.

Richter, L. K. 1993. Tourism policy-making in South-East Asia. In *Tourism in South-East Asia,* M. Hitchcock, V. T. King, and M. J. G. Parnwell (eds.). London: Routledge. 179–199.

Stevenson, N., D. Airey, and G. Miller. 2008. Tourism policy making: The policymakers' perspectives. *Annals of Tourism Research,* 35 (3): 732–750.

Trinidad & Tobago Tourism Development Authority. 1988. *Tourism Policy.* Port of Spain: Trinidad & Tobago Tourism Development Authority.

World Tourism Organization. 1997. *Budgets of National Tourism Administrations.* Madrid: World Tourism Organization.

SURFING SOLUTIONS

http://www.atag.org/ (Air Transport Action Group)

http://www.apec.org/ (Asia Pacific Economic Cooperation)

http://www.canadatourism.com/ (Canadian Tourism Commission)

http://www.cotal.org.ar/ (Confederation of Latin American Tourism Organizations)

http://www.culture.gov.uk/ (Department for Culture, Media and Sport, United Kingdom)

http://www.enjoyengland.com/ (Enjoy England)

http://europa.eu/ (European Union portal)

http://www.iata.org/ (International Air Transport Association)

http://www.icao.org/ (International Civil Aviation Organization)

http://www.ret.gov.au/Pages/default.aspx (Department of Resources, Energy and Tourism, Australia)

http://www.ilo.org/global/lang--en/index.htm (International Labour Organization)

http://tinet.ita.doc.gov/ (ITA Office of Travel & Tourism Industries, United States)

http://www.nitb.com/ (Northern Ireland Tourism Board)

http://www.oas.org/ (Organization of American States)

http://www.oecd.org/ (Organization for Economic Cooperation and Development)

http://www.onecaribbean.org/ (Caribbean Tourism Organization, Barbados)

http://www.pata.org/ (Pacific Asia Travel Association)

http://www.southafrica.net/ (South African Tourism)

http://www.spto.org/ (South Pacific Tourism Organization)

http://www.tourism.australia.com/ (Tourism Australia)

http://www.tourismnewzealand.com/ (Tourism New Zealand)

http://www.tq.com.au/ (Tourism Queensland)

http://www.un.org/ (United Nations)

http://www.visitbritain.org/ukindustry/ (VisitBritain)

http://www.visiteurope.com/ (European Travel Commission)

http://www.visitflorida.com/ (Visit Florida)

http://www.visitscotland.com/ (VisitScotland)

http://www.unwto.org/ (World Tourism Organization)

http://www.wtbonline.gov.uk/ (Visit Wales/Wales Tourist Board)

http://www.wttc.org/ (World Travel & Tourism Council)

ACRONYMS

APEC (Asian Pacific Economic Cooperation)

ATAG (Air Transport Action Group)

COTAL (Confederación de Organizaciones Turísticas de la América Latina)

CTC (Canadian Tourism Commission)

CTO (Caribbean Tourism Organization)

CVB (convention and visitors bureau)

EC (European Commission)

ETC (European Travel Commission)

EU (European Union)

GATS (General Agreement on Trade in Services)

GATT (General Agreement on Tariffs and Trade)

IATA (International Air Transport Association)

ICAO (International Civil Aviation Organization)

ILO (International Labour Organization)

ICOTTA (International Congress of Official Tourist Traffic Associations)

IUOTO (International Union of Official Travel Organizations)

NAFTA (North American Free Trade Agreement)

NTA (national tourism administration)

NTO (national tourism organization or national tourist office)

OAS (Organization of American States)

OECD (Organization for Economic Cooperation and Development)

NGO (nongovernment organization)

PATA (Pacific Asia Travel Association)

RTO (regional tourism organization)

SAARC (South Asian Association for Regional Cooperation)

SATOUR (South African Tourism)

SME (small- and medium-size enterprises)

SPTO (South Pacific Tourism Organization)

TA (Tourism Australia)

TCSP (Tourism Council of the South Pacific)

UNCTAD (United Nations Conference on Trade and Development)

UNDP (United Nations Development Programme)

UNEP (United Nations Environment Programme)

UNWTO (United Nations World Tourism Organization)

USTTA (U.S. Travel and Tourism Administration)

WTTC (World Travel & Tourism Council)

chapter 4

Tourism Regulation

CONTROLLING TOURISM

Government Regulation Is Mandatory

Government regulation in the tourism sector is nevertheless necessary to ensure that adequate controls are in place to address and protect the interests of the individual citizen.

Fiji Government Online Portal (2007), http://www.fiji.gov.fj/publish/page_9313.shtml, accessed January 5, 2009

PURPOSE

Having learned the reasons for government legislation and regulations, students will be able to describe the types of legislation and regulations that are found in tourism.

LEARNING OBJECTIVES

✓ Explain why the government role in establishing tourism-related legislation and regulations is both essential and controversial.
✓ Identify and explain the multilateral and bilateral agreements affecting tourism.
✓ Explain the common reasons for introducing tourism-related laws and regulations in destination areas.
✓ Identify the categories and types of tourism legislation and regulation found in destination areas.
✓ Describe specific forms of destination area legislation and regulations.
✓ Discuss the purposes and results of airline deregulation.
✓ Explain the steps that private-sector businesses in tourism are taking to promote self-regulation.

OVERVIEW

The role of the government in regulating tourism is regarded by many as essential and by some as controversial. This chapter explores the many ways in which tourism is regulated by government.

At the multicountry level, there are a number of international agreements and treaties that affect tourism. The most significant of these involve air travel among countries. Multilateral and bilateral agreements affecting tourism are discussed in this chapter.

The categories and types of tourism legislation and regulations found in tourism destination areas are identified. Common reasons for introducing these measures are described. The chapter explains in more detail some of the major types of tourism-related legislation and regulations. The trend toward the deregulation of airlines is discussed. Attempts by tourism businesses at self-regulation are reviewed.

GOVERNMENT ROLE IN CONTROLLING TOURISM

One of the government roles in tourism identified in chapter 3 is setting and enforcing various forms of legislation and regulations. This role is both essential and controversial in most free-enterprise-system destination areas. It is essential because governments cannot totally rely upon the private sector to effectively control and regulate tourism; it is often controversial because the private sector feels that governments go too far in enforcing regulations.

Around the world, a multitude of government agencies have programs and regulations that directly or indirectly affect tourism. Countries with socialist or communist governments regulate tourism very comprehensively. The complexity of the tourism regulatory framework in most destination areas is a direct reflection of tourism itself. Visitors cross international borders; are exposed to all of the cultural, historic, man-made, and natural resources of the destination area; and must be catered to in a safe, secure, and hygienic fashion. It is no surprise that a variety of government agencies have tourism-related regulations and not just one.

> **Tourism Industry in Australia Getting More Government Regulation**
>
> *Few sectors have experienced as much turmoil in recent years as the tourism and hospitality industry. With volatile world events causing a global downturn in the airline industry, combined with local impacts such as rising public liability insurance premiums, tourism operators have endured a difficult time. The industry continues to deal with changes brought about by increased government regulation.*
>
> Tourism & Hospitality, Deacons (2008), http://www.deacons.com.au/industries/tourism-hospitality, accessed January 5, 2009

Governments are involved in tourism for political, environmental, and economic reasons. The roles of governments in tourism include coordination, policy-setting and planning, legislation and regulation, infrastructure development, operations, development stimulation and control, marketing and research, and training and education. The emphasis given to each of these eight roles varies from destination to destination, but it is usually related to the importance attached to tourism as an economic activity. The actions of those in government have to be supported by various bodies of law (legislation) and specific regulations to have legitimacy in democratic societies. It is with the actual enforcement of the laws and with the structuring of regulations that the most controversy and conflict occurs between the private sector and government in the tourism system.

In introducing legislation and regulations, governments act in the general interests of their citizens and visitors. They do so to protect and conserve their destination area's natural, historical, and cultural resources, to ensure the health and safety of visitors, and to protect visitors from unscrupulous business practices. In these respects, the value of a government's role cannot be questioned.

However, government agencies are often accused of being too bureaucratic, of developing unnecessary "red tape," and of going too far in their policing efforts. This is especially true when the political pendulum and public sentiment swing more toward the free-enterprise approach, as they have in the airline industry worldwide. Governments have been sharply criticized for hindering the development of tourism destination areas because of their lengthy and complex project approval processes. Certainly, government agencies seldom appear to act or react with the speed with which the private sector requires.

The lack of coordination and cooperation between government agencies in their policies and programs is often quite prevalent in tourism. This is a reflection of the diversity of the tourism system itself and of the unavoidable conflicts between the goals of some agencies, such as natural resource conservation versus tourism promotion and development agencies. Any destination area with a vital interest in tourism should take steps to bring about the highest amount of coordination and cooperation among its government agencies.

MULTILATERAL AND BILATERAL AGREEMENTS

In addition to the layers of national, state, provincial, territorial, regional, county, and municipal legislation and regulations, there are certain agreements that have been reached among foreign countries which have a direct impact upon tourism. These are called *multilateral agreements* meaning that several countries have signed and agreed to abide by the codes of conduct in the agreements. These agreements are increasingly leading to the liberalization of trade and travel among countries; a trend that will be beneficial to tourism in the future.

MULTILATERAL AIR AGREEMENTS

Perhaps the most significant multilateral agreements for tourism are those that relate to air travel. The embryonic period for these air travel agreements was during World War II. The *five freedoms* of international air travel were first discussed at an international civil aviation conference in Chicago in 1944 (the *Chicago Convention*) and were:

1. **Right of transit:** The freedom to fly over another country without stopping
2. **Right of technical stop:** The right to stop at another country's airport for fuel and servicing
3. **Right to discharge passengers:** The right to discharge passengers at another country's airport
4. **Right to pick up passengers:** The right to pick up passengers from another country's airport and return them to their homes
5. **Right to discharge and load passengers:** The right to discharge passengers at another country's airport and to then load passengers for countries farther on

Although these freedoms had considerable support, especially from the United States, they were never agreed to universally. This meant that there was a need to establish bilateral agreements between pairs of countries. The formation of the International Civil Aviation Organization (ICAO) in 1944 and the International Air Transport Association (IATA) in 1945 paved the way for the development of bilateral agreements. ICAO is an organization of national governments and an agency of

> **Mumbai Terror Claims New Target, Tourism Industry**
>
> *The travel industry though, is not too optimistic. First the financial meltdown and then the Mumbai attacks have hit the industry hard. Immediately after the attacks, most business travellers postponed their trips and most holidaymakers simply cancelled bookings.*
>
> Mumbai Terror Attack, Akanksha Banerji, IBNLive.com India (2008), http://ibnlive.in.com/news/mumbai-terror-claims-new-target-tourism-industry/80715-7.html, accessed January 4, 2009

the United Nations; IATA is a trade association that represents the airlines.

Chapter 3 indicates that approximately 190 countries, including Australia, Canada, South Africa, the United States, and the United Kingdom belong to the ICAO. The ICAO pursues a vision of safe, secure, and sustainable development of civil aviation through cooperation among its member states. For the period up to and including 2010, its strategic objectives concern: (1) safety, (2) security, (3) environmental protection, (4) efficiency, (5) continuity, and (6) rule of law.

In 2008, 230 airline companies belonged to the IATA, several of which were government-owned airlines. Any company offering a scheduled international air service may belong to the IATA. The IATA's mission is to represent, lead, and serve the airline industry (IATA Web site, 2008):

- Represent: The IATA seeks to improve understanding of the industry among decision makers and increase awareness of the benefits that aviation brings to national and global economies. It fights for the interests of airlines across the globe, challenging unreasonable rules and charges, holding regulators and governments to account, and striving for sensible regulation.

- Lead: The IATA's aim is to help airlines help themselves by simplifying processes and increasing passenger convenience while reducing costs and improving efficiency. The groundbreaking *Simplifying*

Agreements among countries allow for smooth and safe passenger transportation around the world. © 2009 Fred Goldstein. Used under license from Shutterstock, Inc.

the Business initiative is crucial in this area. Moreover, safety is the IATA's number one priority, and the IATA's goal is to continually improve safety standards, notably through the IATA's *Operational Safety Audit* (IOSA). Another main concern is to minimize the impact of air transport on the environment.

- Serve: The IATA ensures that people and goods can move around the global airline network as easily as if they were on a single airline in a single country. In addition, it provides essential professional support to all industry stakeholders with a wide range of products and expert services, such as publications, training, and consulting. The IATA's financial systems also help carriers and the travel industry maximize revenues.

The IATA's priorities in 2008 were (IATA Web site, 2008):

Safety
- Implement IATA Safety Audit for Ground Operations (ISAGO), conducting at least sixty station audits and eight headquarters audits.
- Develop plan to address future airline training and qualification requirements.

Environment
- Achieve a reduction of at least 6 million tons of CO_2 from operations and infrastructure.
- Implement a strategy to reach carbon-neutral growth.
- Develop standards and guidelines for an industry carbon offset program and pilot it with at least six airlines in four different regions.

Simplifying the Business
- Achieve 100 percent **e-Ticketing** penetration in IATA *Billing and Settlement Plan* (BSP) on 1 June 2008 and implement a program to eliminate remaining paper documents by developing an *electronic multipurpose document* (EMD).
- Ensure that 130 airports offer *Common Use Self-Service* (CUSS) facilities by the end of 2008 and that two hundred airlines are *Bar Coded Boarding Pass* (BCBP)-enabled.

- Implement e-freight pilots at eight additional locations (fourteen total) by the end of 2008.
- Conduct two pilots in each area of *Fast Travel*.
- Launch the *Baggage-Management Improvement Programme* (BIP) at six airports.

Financial
- Achieve savings/cost avoidance of $1.5 billion in industry taxes, charges, and fuel fees, including at least $800 million in real cost reduction.
- Launch four new initiatives to reduce airline costs and improve service.

> **Government Red Tape after 9/11 Devastates American Tourism Industry**
>
> *While tourism is rising rapidly in much of the world, it is falling in America, thanks to the hassle that our government puts foreign tourists through when they seek to visit our country. In response to the terrorist attacks on 9/11, our government, rather than focusing on terrorists, stepped up its hassling of harmless foreign visitors to the U.S.*
>
> Hans Bader, OpenMarket.Org (2007), http://www.openmarket.org/2007/11/19/government-red-tape-after-911-devastates-american-tourism-industry/, accessed January 5, 2009

In 1979, the IATA was reorganized into a "two-tier" organization. First, the IATA is a trade association that represents airlines. Second, the IATA handles *tariff coordination* for passenger fares, cargo rates, and travel agent commissions for international air travel. More than one hundred of the IATA's members are tariff coordination members including most of the major airlines in North America, Europe, and the Asia-Pacific region. The IATA sets rates on international routes to which all member airlines agree. The IATA operates a *Clearing House* for air-ticket coupons that allow passengers to fly internationally on several airlines while requiring only one flight coupon. When a passenger travels on two or more airlines on a trip, this is called *interlining*. Here is how the IATA Web site described the Clearing House in 2008:

> "The IATA Clearing House provides a competitive, seamless secure service providing an efficient on-time settling of interline accounts between the world's airlines, airline-associated companies, and Travel Partners.
>
> Offsetting of mutual transactions can reduce hundreds of bilateral, multi-currency transactions for passenger, cargo, baggage, catering, ground-handling, and other services to one single payable or receivable amount.
>
> Each week, 350+ members and participants of the IATA Clearing House settle multimillion dollar transactions. An interclearance agreement with the U.S.-based Airlines Clearing House (ACH), allows for 450+ airlines and participants to settle

their accounts through this IATA service. Around 80 percent of the annual multibillion dollar interline transactions are settled through the netting process thus requiring minimal movement of funds, assuring high credit and currency protection to its users."

Unlike the national regulatory agencies, the IATA does not certify airlines, award routes, or act on market exit decisions. These powers remain with the national governments and their regulatory authorities. The IATA acts in an advisory capacity on mutual problems and issues facing the commercial airlines around the world. The IATA specifies its areas of activity as (IATA Web site, 2008): (1) airline and aircraft operations; (2) airport and air navigation services; (3) cargo; (4) economics; (5) environment; (6) finance; (7) passenger and commercial activities; (8) policies, regulations and standards; (9) safety and security; (10) simplifying the business; and (11) travel and tourism.

Within the "economics" activity area, the IATA collects data on worldwide airline passenger and freight volumes and trends. In fact, the IATA is one of the most important sources of statistics on international air travel.

The "travel and tourism" activity area covers all of the IATA's interactions with travel agencies, including IATAN (International Airlines Travel Agents Network), a nonprofit subsidiary of the IATA. The IATAN accredits airline-appointed travel agencies and travel sales intermediary (TSI) travel agencies in the United States. The IATAN's mission is, "to promote professionalism, administer meaningful and impartial business standards, and to provide cost-effective products and services that benefit the travel industry" (IATAN Web site, 2008). It also operates the *IATA/IATAN ID Card Program* for individual travel agent staff members. The IATA also oper-

ates Billing and Settlement Plans (BSPs) for travel agencies. In 2008, the IATA had BSPs in 160 different countries.

Many multilateral agreements have been agreed to by countries on airlines' liabilities for passenger injuries and damage or loss of baggage. Three of the major agreements are the *Warsaw Convention*, the *Hague Protocol*, and the *Montreal Agreement*. The Warsaw Convention dates back to 1929 and constitutes the main body of international rules in this respect. The United States accepted the Warsaw Convention regulations in 1934; Canada and the United Kingdom are other adherents to it. Several Central American and South American countries are not members of the treaty. The Hague Protocol and the Montreal Agreement represent international agreements that have raised the dollar limit on an airline's liability to an individual passenger. In 1999, the Montreal Convention was signed into being and replaced the Warsaw Convention. The Montreal Convention partially removed the previous limits of liability of airlines in aircraft accidents where passengers are injured or killed. A two-tier system of compensation was approved: (1) the airline is found to be at fault in the accident (unlimited liability applies); (2) a payment of around $135,000 per passenger irrespective of the airline's fault.

In more recent times, governments, especially the United States, have been advocating more liberalization of international air travel through the signing of bilateral and multilateral "Open Skies Agreements." A discussion of these follows, but in general they are an attempt to lessen the regulations in international air travel.

BILATERAL AND PLURILATERAL AIR AGREEMENTS

A *bilateral agreement* is an agreement struck between two national governments. The U.K.–U.S. *Bermuda Agreement* of 1946 was the benchmark bilateral air travel agreement. Bilateral air agreements mainly address the questions of which airlines can fly between two countries and to which airports they are allowed to fly. Since 1946, approximately 4,000 bilateral air agreements have been signed and registered with ICAO. Bilateral air services agreements usually contain provisions on:

- Traffic rights: Routes airlines can fly, including cities that can be served within, between, and beyond the bilateral partners
- Capacity: Number of flights that can be operated or passengers that can be carried between the bilateral partners

---

China and Taiwan Open up Direct Access Routes for Tourism by Air and Sea on December 15, 2008

Taiwanese planes and ships set off yesterday on the first direct journeys between China and Taiwan in 60 years, marking a new era in relations between the rivals.

The inaugural Trans Asia Airways airliner took off carrying 148 Taiwan tourists and businesspeople for the 80-minute flight across the 160-km (100-mile) Taiwan Strait to Shanghai. At the same time, a China Eastern Airlines plane left Shanghai for Taipei. That means that travellers will no longer need to switch planes at a third point—usually Hong Kong or Macau—before proceeding to their destination.

Direct flights between China and Taiwan mark new era of improved relations, *Times Newspapers (2008),* http://www.timesonline.co.uk/tol/news/world/asia/ article5346905.ece, accessed January 6, 2009

- Designation, ownership, and control: Number of airlines the bilateral partners can nominate to operate services and the ownership criteria airlines must meet to be designated under the bilateral agreement (This clause sometimes includes foreign ownership restrictions.)
- Tariffs (prices): Some agreements requiring airlines to submit ticket prices to aeronautical authorities for approval
- Other clauses addressing competition policy, safety, and security (Department of Infrastructure, Transport, Regional Development and Local Government, Australian Government, 2008)

These bilateral agreements are sometimes loose and often mask ongoing disputes between two countries over air services. The 1973 bilateral agreement between the United States and Canada was a good example. It was indicative of the inherent problems of a tourism system in which the market or political philosophies of nations are quite different. In 1978, the United States began the process of deregulating its domestic airline industry and has been a strong proponent of an open skies airline policy internationally. For some years, Canada maintained a policy of protecting its airline companies. Canada's refusal to completely open up the international air border between itself and the United States led in 1983 to a serious dispute over a proposed package of heavily discounted fares to be offered by Air Canada (the government-owned airline at the time) to several cities in the southern United States. The U.S. Civil Aeronautics Board's obstinacy in not allowing these fare schedules caused many Canadians pre-booked on these flights to cancel their trips. The destination areas within the southern United States suffered because of the loss of potential income from the Canadian travelers. In 1995, a new bilateral air agreement between Canada and the United States, known as the *Open Skies Agreement*, was signed. This agreement allows full market access for the airlines of both countries between airports in the two countries.

In 2008, the United States had ninety "Open Skies" country partners, with whom the government had signed either bilateral or multilateral agreements for passenger air transportation. Canada has such agreements with approximately seventy-nine countries and Australia had sixty-seven bilateral air services agreements in 2008. According to the U.S. Department of State, Open Skies agreements set liberal ground rules for international aviation markets and minimize government intervention. Provisions apply to passenger, all-cargo, and combination air transportation and encompass both scheduled and charter services. Key provisions often include: (1) free market competition (no restrictions on international route rights; number of designated airlines; capacity; frequencies; or types of aircraft); (2) pricing determined by market forces (a fare can be disallowed only if both governments concur—"double-disapproval pricing"—and only for certain, specified reasons intended to ensure competition); (3) fair and equal opportunity to compete; (4) cooperative marketing arrangements (designated airlines may enter into code-sharing or leasing arrangements with airlines of either country, or with those of third countries, subject to usual regulations. An optional provision authorizes code sharing between airlines and surface transportation companies); (5) provisions for dispute settlement and consultation (model text includes procedures for resolving differences that arise under the agreement); (6) liberal charter arrangements (carriers may choose to operate under the charter regulations of either country; (7) safety and security (each government agrees to observe high standards of aviation safety and security, and to render assistance to the other in certain circumstances); and (8) optional 7th Freedom All-Cargo rights (provides authority for an airline of one country to operate all-cargo services between the other country and a third country, via flights that are not linked to its homeland) (U.S. Department of State Web site, October 2008).

Plurilateral air services agreements are used in situations in which groups of countries get together to negotiate and sign such agreements. For example, in 2007, the United States and the twenty-seven countries of the European Union began to negotiate a plurilateral air services agreement. Canada also began negotiating a similar agreement with the European Union countries in 2007.

Airlines are increasingly forming *strategic alliances* with foreign airlines in an attempt to gain greater access to foreign countries (e.g., Star Alliance; One World Alliance; and Sky Team Alliance). This strategy allows the airlines to avoid the intergovernmental restrictions imposed by bilateral and plurilateral agreements. These alliances have been very popular in the United States, where outbound international passenger volumes have increased. *Code sharing* is one of the facets of these alliances. This arrangement allows one airline to use its own two-character code (e.g., AA for American Airlines) to advertise a flight as its own in travel agent computer reservation systems, when the flight is actually being operated by its partner airline (e.g., China Eastern Airlines).

Historically, one of the reasons for restrictions of airline operations was the protection of government-owned airlines (also known as *national flag carriers*). The need for these restrictions is becoming less as more countries are *privatizing* national carriers. There has also been a trend in airports to allow these to be operated by companies and authorities that are autonomous of government. This trend has been led by countries such as the United Kingdom, Australia, and Canada.

WORLD TRADE ORGANIZATION, GATT AND GATS

The General Agreement on Tariffs and Trade (GATT) is a treaty and represents the world's only multilateral agreement on the rules for international trade. The first agreement was signed in 1947. Generally, the purpose of GATT is to remove barriers to international trade. There have been several rounds of negotiations since

QUICK TRIP 4.1

The Changing Face of Air Travel: Strategic Airline Alliances

The 1990s and early 2000s were periods of rapid change in the international airline business. Some of the major trends included the privatization of national airlines and airports, the creation of "open skies agreements" between nations, and the formation of several major airline strategic alliances. Behind many of these trends has been the gradual relaxing of government regulation and control of how the airline business operates.

According to Lu (2007), strategic alliances involve a wide range of cooperation among airline partners, including cooperative sales and marketing, sharing of airport facilities, technical cooperation, common purchasing, slot exchanges, code-sharing agreements, combined consumer reservation system displays, schedule cooperation, and integration of pricing. These shared activities help airlines to expand their service network, provide more seamless transportation, expand their lounge service, increase frequency and capacity, and increase the value of their frequent flyer programs. However, it is argued by some that these arrangements give the members a "cartel-like" power that may result in anti-competitive practices such as price-fixing.

At the end of 2008, three major international strategic alliances were in operation and these were as follows:

1. One World Alliance: American Airlines, British Airways, Cathay Pacific, Finnair, Iberia, Japan Airlines (JAL), Lan-Chile, Malev, Qantas, and Royal Jordanian–http://www.oneworld.com/
2. Star Alliance: Air Canada, Air China, Air New Zealand, All Nippon Airways (ANA), Asiana Airlines, Austrian Airlines, British Midland (BMI), EgyptAir, LOT Polish Airlines, Lufthansa, Scandinavian Airlines (SAS), Shanghai Airlines, Singapore Airlines, South African Airways, Spanair, Swiss International Air Lines, TAP Portugal, Thai, Turkish Airlines, United, and U.S. Airways–http://www.staralliance.com/en/travellers/

3. Sky Team Alliance: Aeroflot, AeroMexico, Air France, Alitalia, China Southern, Continental Airlines, Czech Airlines, Delta, Korean Air, and Northwest Airlines–http://www.skyteam.com/EN/index.jsp

THINK ABOUT THIS:

1. What are the potential benefits to airline passengers of open skies agreements?
2. What are the major advantages to individual airlines of belonging to a strategic alliance group?

The Star Alliance is the largest global alliance of international passenger airlines. Source: Star Alliance Services GmbH.

3. How will the growth in strategic alliances, further privatization of airlines and airports, and more liberalization of air travel between countries affect international air travel in the future?

Sources: Web sites of the airline strategic alliances; Lu, C.-J. 2007. The Cartel-Like Practices vs. Application of Antitrust/Competition Law. *Aerlines Magazine*.

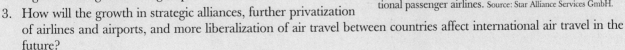

1947, with the latest known as the Uruguay Round in 1986–1994. The final stages of the Uruguay Round resulted in an agreement to create the World Trade Organization. Today, the World Trade Organization (WTO), established in 1995 and headquartered in Geneva, "deals with the rules of trade between nations at a global or near-global level" (World Trade Organization Web site, 2008). In July 2008, the WTO had 153 member countries (including Australia, Canada, China, the United Kingdom, and the United States, but not Russia).

Another outcome of the Uruguay Round was the General Agreement on Trade in Services (GATS). According to the World Trade Organization's publication, *GATS–Fact and Fiction*, it "is among the World Trade Organization's most important agreements. The accord, which came into force in January 1995, is the first and only set of multilateral rules covering international trade in services." GATS will liberate trade in services and could have a major impact on tourism. GATS may result in free market access to suppliers of tourism services in foreign countries and equivalent treatment to domestic businesses. Barriers to market entry such as quotas and licenses may be removed. It should be noted that government services and the air transport sector are not covered in GATS. The WTO highlights the importance of trade in services and GATS in this statement, "Ranging from architecture to voice-mail telecommunications and to space transport, services are the largest and most dynamic component of both developed and developing country economies. Important in their own right, they also serve as crucial inputs into the production of most goods. Their inclusion in the Uruguay Round of trade negotiations led to the General Agreement on Trade in Services (GATS). Since January 2000, they have become the subject of multilateral trade negotiations" (WTO Web site, 2008). In 2008, negotiations among the WTO members were still continuing on how exactly to implement GATS.

HOTEL CLASSIFICATION, RATING AND GRADING

Hotel classification on an international level also represents a tacit attempt by several nations to regulate standards within another important component of the tourism system. The World Tourism Organization (UNWTO) has historically taken the lead role in this regard. It was given this authority in 1963 when the United Nations Conference on International Travel and Tourism asked it to draft these standards. The main

rationale for setting these was that "traveling problems can be eased to a considerable extent if hotels of a particular category in all countries were to present more or less the same characteristics of comfort and service" (World Tourism Organization, 1969).

Although many countries appear to agree in principle with the classification method and criteria that the UNWTO has developed, many have chosen to create their own classification and grading/rating systems because they have found the UNWTO guidelines to be too broad for their purposes. For example, the International Hotel & Restaurant Association (IH&RA) based in Geneva, Switzerland, disagrees with the concept of an international hotel classification system for these reasons (IH&RA Web site, 2008):

- Following an extensive audit and analysis of worldwide grading systems, the IH&RA contends that current national hotel classification and grading systems already give an indication of the level of standard offered by a hotel in that country or region, enabling consumers to make an informed choice.
- The IH&RA believes that setting up an international hotel classification scheme is an unfeasible and ill-founded undertaking. Hard and fast quantitative criteria (e.g., room size, height of ceiling, construction standards, language proficiency) vary from country to country and even more so from one geographic region to another. Qualitative crite-

The hotel classification system in Germany. Source: Deutschen Hotelklassifizierung. 2009. http://www.hotelsterne.de/uk/.

ria remain highly subjective, particularly as regards delivery of services. In addition, the IH&RA notes that consumers already have access to a broad array of guides and, more recently, to Internet-based sources of information. The fact that tour operators and other bodies, including online travel agencies, often establish their own rating systems, providing enhanced, current evaluations, further supports the position of the IH&RA.

As the IH&RA notes, there are a number of private-sector accommodation and restaurant rating schemes in operation around the world, and these have helped travelers to better determine quality standards in unfamiliar destinations. These include the systems operated by Michelin and the motoring organizations in several countries.

Several countries are using national classification and or grading/rating systems for lodging facilities. For example, these include almost all of the national tourism agencies in Europe, and the system operated by the China National Tourism Administration (CNTA) in Mainland China.

WORLD HERITAGE LIST, UNESCO

The United Nations Educational, Scientific and Cultural Organization (UNESCO), is an agency of the United Nations concerned with education, science, and cultural and natural heritage. At its 1972 General Conference, an international agreement was signed titled the *Convention Concerning the Protection of the World Cultural and Natural Heritage*. The primary purpose of this agreement was to define and conserve the world's heritage by drawing up a list of sites whose outstanding values should be preserved for all humanity and to ensure their protection through a closer cooperation among nations (UNESCO World Heritage Centre Web site, 1997). In 2008, there were 878 sites around the world on the UNESCO *World Heritage List* (679 cultural; 174 natural; and 25 mixed). Some of the well-known tourism attractions on the list include the Canadian Rocky Mountain National Parks; Ayers Rock-The Olgas, and the Wet Tropics of Queensland (Australia); the Galapagos Islands (Ecuador); the Cathedral of Notre Dame in Paris; the Taj Mahal; Machu Picchu (Peru); the Kremlin and Red Square (Russia), the Old and New Towns of

The Leshan Giant Buddha is one of the sites on UNESCO's World Heritage List. Photo by Alastair Morrison.

Edinburgh (United Kingdom); and Grand Canyon National Park (United States).

UNESCO describes the importance of WHL sites as follows:

"Heritage is our legacy from the past, what we live with today, and what we pass on to future generations. Our cultural and natural heritage are both irreplaceable sources of life and inspiration. Places as unique and diverse as the wilds of East Africa's Serengeti, the Pyramids of Egypt, the Great Barrier Reef in Australia, and the Baroque cathedrals of Latin America make up our world's heritage."

The World Heritage Committee was established under the Convention as a statutory body. The committee, consisting of twenty-one member countries, selects new sites for the World Heritage List and helps to protect the sites with assistance from the World Heritage Fund. The day-to-day management of the convention has been given to the UNESCO World Heritage Centre located in Paris. Evaluations of new sites are done with the assistance of the International Council on Monuments and Sites (ICOMOS) for cultural sites, and the World Conservation Union (UCN) for natural sites. Both of these organizations are located in Paris.

UNESCO maintains another list called the *List of World Heritage in Danger*. This list includes sites that are placed in danger because of civil disturbances or through environmental threats. For example, in 2007 these sites included 30 of the 878 on the World Heritage List, including the Galapagos Islands (Peru); Samarra Archaelogical City (Iraq); and Niokolo-Koba National Park (Senegal).

FREE TRADE AGREEMENTS

There are many other treaties and agreements governing trade and travel procedures among countries. These also play a key role in the tourism regulatory framework of destination areas. One of the major forces here in recent years has been the creation of *free trade areas* such as the European Economic Community (EEC) and the North American Free Trade Agreement (NAFTA). Australia and New Zealand have signed a Trans-Tasman Mutual Recognition Arrangement (TTMRA).

The World Heritage List Recognizes the World's Cultural and Natural Treasures

The World Heritage List (WHL) includes many of the world's best-known tourist attractions including the Pyramids in Egypt, the Great Wall and Terracotta Warriors in China, the Great Barrier Reef and Kakadu National Park in Australia, the Acropolis in Greece, Vatican City, Canada's Rocky Mountain National Parks, Britain's Stonehenge and the Tower of London, and Yellowstone National Park and the Statue of Liberty in the United States. Many other listed sites may not be household names but fit UNESCO's definition of global, cultural, and natural treasures.

UNESCO has developed an elaborate list of WHL selection criteria. There are separate sets of selection criteria for cultural properties and natural properties. The criteria for selection as a WHL-listed cultural property are that a site must:

I. Represent a masterpiece of human creative genius.
II. Exhibit an important interchange of human values, over a span of time or within a cultural area of the world, on developments in architecture or technology, monumental arts, town planning or landscape design.
III. Bear a unique or at least exceptional testimony to a cultural tradition or to a civilization that is living or that has disappeared.
IV. Be an outstanding example of a type of building, architectural or technological ensemble, or landscape that illustrates (a) significant stage(s) in human history.
V. Be an outstanding example of a traditional human settlement, land use, or sea use that is representative of a culture (or cultures) or human interaction with the environment, especially when it has become vulnerable under the impact of irreversible change.
VI. Be directly or tangibly associated with events or living traditions, with ideas, or with beliefs with artistic and literary works of outstanding universal significance. (The committee considers that this criterion should preferably be used in conjunction with other criteria.)

To make the WHL, natural properties must meet one of the following selection criteria:

VII. Contain superlative natural phenomena or areas of exceptional natural beauty and aesthetic importance.
VIII. Be outstanding examples representing major stages of earth's history, including the record of life, significant ongoing geological processes in the development of landforms, or significant geomorphic or physiographic features.
IX. Be outstanding examples representing significant ongoing ecological and biological processes in the evolution and development of terrestrial, freshwater, coastal, and marine ecosystems and communities of plants and animals.
X. Contain the most important and significant natural habitats for in situ conservation of biological diversity, including those containing threatened species of outstanding universal value from the point of view of science or conservation.

In 2008, the World Heritage List had 878 sites in total, including 679 cultural, 174 natural, and 25 mixed sites in 145 state parties.

THINK ABOUT THIS:

1. What are the potential advantages to a destination if it receives a World Heritage Listing from UNESCO?
2. Are there any dangers that receiving such a listing might pose and, if so, what are these?
3. What steps can a destination take to ensure that these sites are protected from environmental damage from human impacts?

The Pyramids of Egypt are on the World Heritage List.
© 2009 mmmm. Used under license from Shutterstock, Inc.

Source: UNESCO WHL Web site. 2008. http://whc.unesco.org/en/criteria/ and http://whc.unesco.org/en/list.

The North American Free Trade Agreement (NAFTA)

The implementation of the North American Free Trade Agreement (NAFTA) began on January 1, 1994, and involves trade among Canada, Mexico, and the United States. Article 101 of NAFTA established a free trade area covering the three countries. The objectives of this agreement are to:

a. Eliminate barriers to trade in, and facilitate the cross-border movement of, goods and services between the territories of the parties.

b. Promote conditions of fair competition in the free trade area.

c. Increase substantially investment opportunities in the territories of the parties.

d. Provide adequate and effective protection and enforcement of intellectual property rights in each party's territory.

e. Create effective procedures for the implementation and application of this agreement, for its joint administration and for the resolution of disputes.

f. Establish a framework for further trilateral, regional, and multilateral cooperation to expand and enhance the benefits of this agreement.

It is expected that NAFTA will eventually benefit tourism by simplifying border entry procedures among the three countries. For business travel, simplified procedures will be introduced to expedite business travel including granting eligible business people with temporary entry without prior approval.

THINK ABOUT THIS:

1. How will NAFTA benefit tourism among the three North American nations (Canada, Mexico, and the United States)?

2. In what ways has the creation of the European Union affected travel among its member countries?

3. Are there any potentially negative impacts on tourism of opening up these types of trade areas? If so, what are these impacts?

Source: NAFTA Secretariat. 2008. http://www.nafta-sec-alena.org/DefaultSite/index_e.aspx.

Source: NAFTA Secretariat.

REASONS FOR DESTINATION AREA LEGISLATION AND REGULATIONS

Every country has a myriad of laws and regulations that affect tourism. These are established by various levels of governments from national to local. Laws and regulations allow governments to implement tourism policies and plans (chapter 5), to fulfill government roles in tourism (chapter 3), and to control the impacts of tourism (chapter 2).

There are several categories of laws that impact tourism. These vary from country to country. According to Goodwin and Gaston (1992), there are eight different classifications of laws that impact tourism in the United States:

1. Judicial and administrative law
2. Common and statutory law
3. Common and civil law
4. Public and private law
5. Substantive and procedural law
6. Contract and property law
7. Tort and criminal law
8. Law and equity

Many of the laws that directly affect tourism in most countries are in the statutory law category. These are laws created by acts of lawmaking bodies (governments). There are tort and criminal laws that impact tourism; most often when frauds are committed against travelers and people buying land for recreational purposes. Some of the most common reasons for introducing tourism-related laws and regulations are as follows.

CONTROLLING THE ENTRY OF FOREIGN VISITORS AND GOODS. There is a need in every country to

---

OTTI Looks after U.S. Tourism Policy Issues

The Office of Travel and Tourism Industries (OTTI) plays an active role in domestic and international policy issues as they relate to the U.S. travel and tourism industry. From a domestic policy perspective, OTTI serves as the Secretariat for the Tourism Policy Council. The Tourism Policy Council (TPC) is an interagency committee established by law for the purpose of ensuring that the nation's tourism interests are considered in Federal decision-making. Its major function is to coordinate national policies and programs relating to international travel and tourism, recreation, and national heritage resources that involve Federal Agencies.

Tourism Policy, ITA Office of Travel & Tourism Industries (2009), *http://tinet.ita.doc.gov/about/tourism_policy.html*, accessed January 6, 2009

introduce laws and regulations regarding the entry of foreign nationals and goods from other countries. Protecting the national health interest is one of the reasons for immigration regulations and procedures, as is the detection of the flow of illegal drugs and potential terrorist threats against a country.

CONTROLLING THE QUALITY OF THE VISITOR EXPERIENCE.

Laws and regulations may be introduced to ensure that visitors have a high quality experience in the destination area. For example, the use of some wilderness areas (e.g., scenic rivers) may be regulated so that the user's experience of the wild is not spoiled by there being too many other visitors. Laws may be introduced to protect foreign visitors from being harassed or abused by local people who are begging or touting services and products.

ENSURING TRAVEL SAFETY.

Many laws and regulations are in force to ensure the safety of people traveling by air, rail, road, and sea. Regulatory agencies are created within each country to control and enforce safety standards. For example, many countries have a maritime regulatory agency that ensures the safety of all watercraft through programs of licensing and regular inspections. Other nations and states have regulations to ensure safety in adventure travel activities.

ESTABLISHING TOURISM ORGANIZATIONS.

Laws are often passed to establish new tourism organizations. For example, the Tourism Australia Act 2004 established Tourism Australia. The Canadian Tourism came into being as a result of the Canadian Tourism Commission Act 2000.

GAMING CONTROL.

Laws are introduced at various levels of government to control the development of gaming operations including casinos and lotteries. Some countries and states strictly prohibit different forms of gaming due to social or religious reasons. Other governments allow only certain forms of gaming, e.g., casinos on riverboats; casino gaming on cruise ships outside of territorial waters.

MAINTAINING BUILDING STANDARDS.

Building codes are introduced to ensure that building materials and specifications meet required standards.

MAINTAINING OPERATING STANDARDS.

Governments introduce licensing and registration systems to maintain the operating standards in different parts of tourism. These may include regular inspection programs to ensure continued conformance to standards. Accommodation grading or rating systems are an example of this type of system.

PROTECTING THE TRAVELER.

A variety of laws and regulations are introduced to protect visitors. These include fire safety laws for hotels, regulations on the safe handling of food, and laws to protect travelers from fraud and financial failures of travel trade companies. Other laws protect consumers from deceptive advertising practices. Regulations may also be in force to protect the safety of visitors when engaging in certain activities (e.g., adventure travel activities such as whitewater rafting and ballooning) and attending certain types of attractions (e.g., amusement parks with rides). Laws are also introduced to protect people when they are purchasing condominium resort offerings including timesharing.

PROTECTING THE ENVIRONMENT AND CULTURE.

There are many laws and regulations dealing with environmental protection and conservation. These include laws creating national or state park systems, shoreline protection systems, regulations on sewage disposal systems, and other measures to protect physical environments. For example, the Kingdom of Bhutan in the Himalaya Mountains strictly controls the number of foreign visitors into the country in order to control the impacts of tourism.

RAISING FUNDS FOR TOURISM.

Some laws are introduced to institute taxes or other levies to provide for

---

UK Government Report Recommends Space Tourism Rules Should Help Industry

Regulation of suborbital and orbital tourism should be developed in phases to facilitate the new space industry's growth, according to the UK's Science and Technology Facilities Council (STFC). In a draft report for its partner, the British National Space Centre (BNSC), the STFC recommends that the UK government adopt a phased approach to regulation as the industry develops. The report suggests that the regulatory regime should facilitate the industry's development that BNSC should work with industry to assess evaluation methods for spaceflight vehicles, ground infrastructure and crew and tourists and that BNSC should seek an international framework and identify mutual recognition agreement opportunities for launch licensing. It also says that spaceflight participants should fly at their own risk.

Rob Coppinger, FlightGlobal (2009), http://www.flightglobal.com/articles/2008/06/03/224404/uk-government-report-recommends-space-tourism-rules-should-help-industry.html, accessed January 5, 2009

tourism marketing and development. In the United States, uniform innkeepers' laws at the state level provide the mechanism for funding local convention and visitors bureaus.

SUPPORTING PHYSICAL PLANNING GUIDELINES. Laws and regulations are introduced to control land use. The zoning regulations and building permit systems in force in many municipalities are a good example.

TYPES OF DESTINATION AREA LEGISLATION AND REGULATIONS

Before describing specific types of tourism legislation and regulations, it is useful to classify them into different groups. One method of classification is to group the tourism legislation and regulations into *functional areas*, such as those related to the protection of the environment, those related to economic development, and those related to frontier controls. Another means of classification is to group on a *sector basis* by identifying the legislation and regulations that relate to airlines, hotels, travel agents, and other tourism businesses. In this respect, *horizontal legislation or regulations* are those items that affect every sector, whether it be a tourism or non-tourism one, such as income tax and labor

It is important to regulate the use of wilderness areas in Canada to protect the local species and also the visitors. Source: Canadian Tourism Commission.

legislation. *Specific legislation or regulations* are those items that relate directly to a specific sector. An example of this is a grading system for hotels. Figure 4.1 illustrates commonly found legislation and regulations classified on a sector-by-sector basis in tourism.

FORMS OF DESTINATION AREA LEGISLATION AND REGULATIONS

There are certain forms of legislation and regulation that are encountered in most destination areas. These include legislation and regulations governing the following:

- Accommodation standards
- Alcohol sales laws and regulations
- Civil aviation regulations
- Environmental protection and conservation regulations
- Health regulations
- Innkeeper liability laws
- Retail travel agency, tour wholesaler, and operator regulations
- Regulations on safety in activity participation
- Timesharing laws and regulations

ACCOMMODATION AND FOOD SERVICES	TRAVEL AGENTS, TOUR WHOLESALERS, TOUR OPERATORS	AIRLINES, RAILWAYS, BUSES, SHIPS, AND OTHER CARRIERS	ATTRACTION OPERATORS, ADVENTURE TRAVEL OPERATORS
Alcohol sales and regulations	Definition of responsibilities and limitations	Control of fares and tariffs	Regulation of safety procedures
Building and zoning codes	Regulations and licensing of travel agents, tour wholesalers and operators	Control of route entry and exit	Licensing or registration of operators
Classification, grading, and rating of hotels and other establishment types	Regulations of promotions	Labor and taxation legislation	Inspection and licensing of equipment
Fire safety regulations and codes	Labor and taxation legislation	Licensing of carriers	Licensing or certification of guides
Health safety regulations and codes		Limitation of weights and capacities	
Liability laws with respect to guests and their belongings		Negotiation of services	
Labor and taxation legislation		Regulation of safety procedures	
		Subsidization of routes	

Figure 4.1 Types of Legislation and Regulation.

ACCOMMODATION STANDARDS

One of the aspects of tourism that receives much attention from governments around the world is the standards of accommodation facilities. Some countries have introduced mandatory *classification and grading systems* for accommodation, while others operate similar programs on a voluntary basis. For example, the Republic of Ireland operates a compulsory accommodation and grading system. Fáilte Ireland (The National Tourism Development Authority) operates the system, which covers hotels, guest houses, youth hostels, holiday camps, caravan and camping sites, holiday cottages, and holiday apartments.

ALCOHOL SALES LAWS AND REGULATIONS

Regulations are required over the sale and consumption of alcohol. This is accomplished mainly through the licensing of establishments that are allowed to

---

QUICK TRIP 4.4

VisitScotland's Quality Assurance Scheme

VisitScotland has a comprehensive quality assurance scheme that assesses serviced and self-catering accommodation, visitor attractions, caravan and camping, and hostels. The awards of star levels are based on the standard of welcome, hospitality, and service provided. The rating is not based upon the size of the property or the range of facilities available.

A trained inspector visits the properties on a yearly basis and grades them. For the accommodation properties, the star levels represent the following:

- 1 star: Acceptable
- 2 stars: Good
- 3 stars: Very good
- 4 stars: Excellent
- 5 stars: Exceptional

VisitScotland says the following about its quality assurance scheme (VisitScotland Web site, 2008):

One of the beautiful lochs of Scotland. © 2009 Graham Lumsden. Used under license from Shutterstock, Inc.

"Our assessments of accommodation give a clear idea of the standards of hospitality, service, cleanliness, accommodation, comfort and food you can expect. The five-star grading schemes give you all the reassurance you want—quickly and clearly.

Our schemes help you distinguish between the quality of the accommodation and the range of facilities on offer. They also demonstrate the variety of accommodation types—from B&Bs, self-catering and holiday parks through to hotels and restaurants with rooms."

Scotland is not alone in the United Kingdom in offering such a system for rating tourism facilities and attractions. The Wales Tourist Board, Enjoy England, and the Northern Ireland Tourist Board have similar schemes.

THINK ABOUT THIS:

1. What are the advantages of using quality as the basis for rating or grading accommodation properties and attractions?
2. What are the potential challenges or difficulties in implementing a scheme like this based on quality?
3. Why have countries such as the United States not introduced accommodation and attraction rating or grading systems like those found in the United Kingdom?

Source: VisitScotland. 2008. http://www.visitscotland.com/quality-assurance/.

One of the main goals of regulating the sale and consumption of alcohol is to prevent injuries that may result from alcohol abuse. © 2009 Yuri Arcurs. Used under license from Shutterstock, Inc.

sell alcohol and where alcohol consumption is permitted. One of the main goals of licensing is to prevent injuries that can result from the abuse of alcohol through car accidents, fights, and other anti-social behavior. A second reason is to prevent the sale of alcohol to underage customers, to people who are already intoxicated, and to habitual drunkards (Cournoyer, Marshall, and Morris, 1993). Typically, licenses to sell alcohol are granted by state, provincial, or territorial governments.

CIVIL AVIATION REGULATIONS

Almost every country in the world has a government regulatory agency that controls air travel. In the United States, this is the Federal Aviation Administration (FAA). Canada has the Transportation Safety Board, Australia has the Civil Aviation Safety Authority (CASA), and both the United Kingdom and New Zealand have a Civil Aviation Authority (CAA). One of the major roles of these regulatory agencies is to ensure the highest levels of safety when flying and when on the ground at airports.

One of the most talked about trends in civil aviation during the 1980s and 1990s was *airline deregulation*, meaning the relaxation of regulations governing the operation of commercial airlines. The deregulation of the domestic airlines in the United States is a benchmark case study for many other regions of the world. The United States established the Civil Aeronautics Board (CAB) in 1938 through the Civil Aeronautics Act. Its mandate was to protect the safety of the public and to maintain the viability of the U.S. airline industry. The CAB was given the authority to determine which airlines could operate in the United States, which routes they could operate, and what fares they could charge. It

was given powers over airline schedules, airline profit margins, and the types of working relationships permissible. Since its inception, the CAB was probably the most influential regulatory agency in the United States with respect to tourism.

The successful passage of the Airline Deregulation Act in October 1978 was a very significant event for U.S. tourism. This act was historically unique since it was the first time that the U.S. government virtually abolished its role in the economic regulation of an industry. The decision to wind up the powerful CAB came after much public criticism of the agency and of its perceived over-regulation of the airline industry. The general concern was that the CAB had gone too far in trying to maintain the viability of the airline industry and was beginning to engage in activities that were not beneficial to the traveling public. Another major problem with the CAB was its tardiness in responding to proposals presented by individual airline companies. During the long lag time, airlines often changed their minds about their proposals or they lost the benefit of the marketing opportunity they were seeking. The Airline Deregulation Act of 1978 envisaged that the CAB would be completely phased out by January 1985. The CAB "sunset" timetable included the loss of its authority over route entry in 1982 and its jurisdiction over tariffs and pricing in 1983. The CAB ceased to be at the end of 1984.

According to the General Accounting Office Report on Airline Deregulation: Changes in Airfares, Service Quality, and Barriers to Entry, the results of airline deregulation were (GAO, 1999):

- Average airfares declined by 21 percent from 1990 to 1998.
- The overall quality of air service improved for airports serving large and medium-large communities.
- Results were mixed for airports serving small- and medium-size communities.
- Some airports had restrained competition, and airfares at these airports were consistently higher than those at comparable airports without the airport-created constraints.

The U.S. air travel experiment, which was motivated by the desire to let the marketplace operate more freely to the ultimate benefit of travelers, has had its advantages and disadvantages. As the GAO report indicates, several new airlines were created and some of these introduced more discounted air fares for travelers. Several new airlines failed or were absorbed by the larger airline companies. Airline competition definitely increased. There were some consumer concerns with the quality of airline services and the safety of air travel. Airports and airplanes became more crowded, and overbooking was encountered more often.

Maynard (2008), in a *New York Times* article, points out that the architects of airline deregulation in the United States did not predict three resulting strategies that have been applied by almost all major airlines: (1) frequent-flier programs; (2) hub-and-spoke systems; and (3) airline strategic alliances. She argues that these strategies have given major airlines greater competitive power. In addition, the proposed mergers of major air-

QUICK TRIP 4.5

International Civil Aviation Organization

The International Civil Aviation Organization, a U.N. specialized agency, is the global forum for civil aviation. The ICAO works to achieve its vision of safe, secure, and sustainable development of civil aviation through cooperation among its member states.

To implement this vision, the organization has established the following Strategic Objectives for the period 2005–2010:

A. Safety: Enhance global civil aviation safety.
B. Security: Enhance global civil aviation security.
C. Environmental protection: Minimize the adverse effect of global civil aviation on the environment.
D. Efficiency: Enhance the efficiency of aviation operations.
E. Continuity: Maintain the continuity of aviation operations.
F. Rule of law: Strengthen law governing international civil aviation.

These objectives reflect the status, role, and responsibilities of the ICAO as the:

■ Leader in the development and promotion of SARPs and in auditing compliance with them
■ Institution facilitating and assisting its contracting states in the implementation of SARPs, Air Navigation Plans, and ICAO policies
■ Promoter of global air transport policies for an efficient international civil aviation system
■ Ultimate venue for crisis management in international civil aviation
■ Body dealing with the development and diffusion of international air law and with the settlement of international civil aviation disputes
■ Central institution for global governance in civil aviation

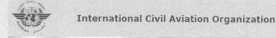

International Civil Aviation Organization

ICAO CARBON EMISSIONS CALCULATOR

ICAO has developed a methodology to calculate the carbon dioxide emissions from air travel for use in offset programmes.

The ICAO Carbon Emissions Calculator allows passengers to estimate the emissions attributed to their air travel. It is simple to use and requires only a limited amount of information from the user.

The methodology applies the best publicly available industry data to account for various factors such as aircraft types, route specific data, passenger load factors and cargo carried.

For additional information, please see the accompanying methodology to the ICAO Carbon Emissions Calculator.

You can find your carbon footprint by entering your city of origin and destination

From: [   ]   To: [   ]

My ticket is: ● Economy Class   ○ Premium Class (Economy Premium, Business, or First)

Number of passengers: 1 ▾

Click here to read the ICAO Methodology

ICAO Carbon Emissions Calculator. Source: International Civil Aviation Organization, http://www2.icao.int/en/carbonoffset/Pages/default.aspx.

THINK ABOUT THIS:

1. What are some of the major issues facing regulatory bodies such as the International Civil Aviation Organization?
2. What are the major challenges facing an organization such as the International Civil Aviation Organization in developing regulations and controls for the emerging space tourism business?
3. One of the major trends in commercial aviation in recent years has been the privatization of airports. What are the major advantages of privatizing airports, and what are the potential disadvantages?

Source: International Civil Aviation Organization. 2008. http://www.icao.int/.

lines, such as Delta and Northwest (approved by shareholders in September 2008), will lead to greater concentration of the domestic airline industry.

ENVIRONMENTAL PROTECTION AND CONSERVATION REGULATIONS

Governments at all levels have introduced laws and regulations aimed at promoting environmental protection and conservation. These measures help support the role of governments in sustainable tourism development. Among the most important laws are those that have ini-

National Parks protect and conserve precious natural areas for future generations. © 2009 Danny Warren. Used under license from Shutterstock, Inc.

tiated systems of national parks. Two of the landmark pieces of such legislation in the world are the Yellowstone National Park Act of 1872 in the United States and the Rocky Mountain Parks Act of 1887 in Canada, which established its first national park surrounding Banff, Alberta. The National Parks Act followed in Canada in 1930 and in 1953 the Historic Sites and Monuments Act was passed. The 1930 Act stated that only such uses would be permitted within national parks that would "leave them unimpaired for the enjoyment of future generations" (Parks Canada, 1979). This clause has been quite controversial since some of Canada's national parks such as Banff, Lake Louise, and Jasper are

QUICK TRIP 4.6

South Africa's Regulation of the Management of Boat-Based Whale Watching and Protection of Turtles

In the Republic of South Africa, Environment Affairs and Tourism (EAT) aims to lead sustainable development of its environment and tourism for a better life for all through:

- Creating conditions for sustainable tourism growth and development for the benefit of all South Africans
- Promoting the conservation and sustainable utilization of our natural resources to enhance economic growth
- Protecting and improving the quality and safety of the environment
- Promoting a global sustainable development agenda

In July 2008, EAT published a Government Gazette called "Regulation of the Management of Boat-Based Whale Watching and Protection of Turtles." The objectives of these regulations are to:

1. Promote the economic growth of the boat-based whale watch industry and the sustainable nonconsumptive use of whales and dolphins, particularly for ecotourism.
2. Improve the regulatory and compliance framework pertaining to this specific industry.
3. Redress past racial and gender discrimination in the boat-based whale watching industry.
4. Provide for control over the boat-based viewing of whales and dolphins so that these activities may take place in a manner that does not threaten the safety of individuals or the well-being of the whales and dolphins.
5. Provide for control over the number of boat-based whale and dolphin watching operations in order to manage any adverse impact on whale and dolphin behavior and to protect whales and dolphins.
6. Provide for control over the viewing of turtles and to protect and minimize any adverse impacts on turtles.

(continued)

Viewing turtles is a major attraction for tourists, but it is even more important to protect the habitats and minimize the impacts on these magnificent animals. © 2009 Alexey Stiop. Used under license from Shutterstock, Inc.

among the nation's major tourist attractions and most favored destinations, particularly for foreign visitors.

In England in 2006, the government created Natural England to conserve and enhance the natural environment, for its intrinsic value, the well-being and enjoyment of people, and the economic prosperity that it brings (Natural England Web site, 2008). Natural England has the responsibility for designating national parks and areas of outstanding natural beauty.

State, regional, county, and municipal governments usually have the authority to regulate land uses and to acquire land within their jurisdictions. Historically, these powers have been passed on to local governments at the city, town, and county levels. Cities, towns, and counties exercise these powers through the development of municipal plans, the enforcement of zoning regulations, and the operation of building permit systems.

HEALTH REGULATIONS

Governments introduce rules to protect visitors and residents from the risk of disease and illness resulting from exposure to food and water. Several countries insist that travelers from infected areas of other countries show proof of vaccination against certain diseases (e.g., yellow fever). The outbreak of Severe Acute Respiratory Syndrome (SARS) in 2003 in China and Hong Kong, which was spread by travelers to Canada and other countries, brought a new level of world awareness to the interaction of tourism, travel, and the spread of disease. This resulted in the screening of air passengers in many Asian airports. For example, an estimated CAD $7.55 million was spent on airport passenger screening in

Canada from March 18 to July 5, 2003. The threat of the spread of avian (bird) flu is another major health concern in tourism. There is an obligation on the part of governments and tourism businesses to warn travelers of the risks of contracting certain diseases and precautions that are advisable to reduce such risks.

It is essential that governments protect people from food-borne illnesses when they eat in restaurants. This role is accomplished through regular inspections by health inspectors and rules regarding the storage, cooking, and handling of food and beverages. Often, this role is performed by local government agencies that have the right to close down establishments that do not meet standards.

AIRPORT AND AIRLINE SECURITY AND SAFETY

Airports and airplanes have been the targets of terrorists for many years, but it took the incidents of September 11, 2001 to truly awaken most people to the need for tighter security at airport terminals and on planes. The Madrid train bombings in March 2004 and the subway and bus bombings in London in July 2005 again sensitized the world that travelers and tourists are prime targets for extremists of all types. Previous research has shown a clear negative correlation between acts of terrorism and volumes of visitors to affected areas or sites. Therefore, government authorities and transportation companies must continue to introduce regulations, systems, and procedures that give further protection to the world's growing flow of tourists.

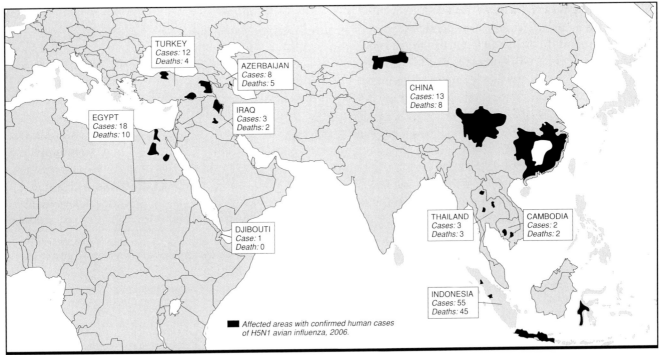

The World Health Organization Tracks Cases of Bird Flu. Source: World Health Organization.

INNKEEPER LIABILITY LAWS

Most destinations have a variety of laws and regulations that indicate the extent of the liability of accommodation establishment operators for the personal injury of guests and the loss of guest possessions. These measures include fire safety laws that impose rules regarding the construction and operation of accommodation establishments. One of the major problems facing accommodation operators is how to protect guests' property when they are on the premises. Thefts from guest rooms and vehicles are quite common in tourism. In some countries, under common law, innkeepers have "absolute liability" for any loss of guest property. Other accommodation operators install elaborate security systems including guest room safes and electronic door card key systems.

RETAIL TRAVEL AGENCY, TOUR WHOLESALER, AND OPERATOR REGULATIONS

Travel trade intermediaries are another part of tourism that is frequently covered by tourism legislation and regulations. These measures are introduced to protect consumers from fraudulent practices and from the financial failure of tour wholesalers, tour operators, retail travel agencies, and other organizations that sell

travel services. There has been a definite trend toward more regulation in this area as the numbers of travel-related frauds are increasing, especially with the growing reliance on the Internet. Often these programs require travel companies to be licensed or register with a government agency before they are allowed to operate. They may also be required to post a bond or pay into a compensation fund.

The Province of Ontario in Canada provides a good example of the regulation of travel trade intermediaries. The Travel Industry Act of 2002 required all travel agencies and wholesalers operating in Ontario to be registered. The Travel Industry Council of Ontario (TICO) was established by the Ontario Government to administer the 2002 Act that covers all of the twenty-eight hundred travel agencies and wholesalers registered in Ontario. The TICO's mission is "to promote a fair and informed marketplace where consumers can be confident in their travel purchases" (TICO Annual Report, 2008). Additionally, TICO administers an industry-financed Travel Compensation Fund. This fund compensates customers of registered companies if they become bankrupt or insolvent, or protects customers from the failure of an airline or cruise line associated with the registered companies.

In the United Kingdom, the Civil Aviation Authority (CAA) grants licenses to companies that provide package vacations that include flights. These are called

Air Travel Organisers' Licenses (ATOLs). Every ATOL holder is examined each year to ensure that it is financially sound. In 2008, the CAA had to deal with the failure of a major tour company, the XL Leisure Group U.K. Australia operates a national system of travel agent licensing and a Travel Compensation Fund to reimburse travelers if a licensed travel agency goes bankrupt or becomes insolvent. The Travel Compensation Fund is Australia's "primary means of providing compensation to eligible travelers who suffer loss as a result of the financial collapse of a participating travel agency business. The TCF helps guard against the failure of participating travel agency businesses through financial monitoring of agency accounts" (Travel Compensation Fund Web site, 2007).

REGULATIONS ON SAFETY IN ACTIVITY PARTICIPATION

There are many situations around the world in which travelers are exposed to danger within destination areas. These include when people are traveling by road, rail, and by water, and when visitors are engaging in certain activities that may result in injuries or death. Scenic boat trips, motor coach tours, scenic rail trips, and guided four-wheel drive trips are examples of tourism offerings where travelers are exposed to a certain level of physical danger. An element of danger is also present when riding on roller coasters and other equipment at theme and amusement parks. The trend toward the increasing popularity of adventure travel places more people each year in situations of personal risk.

The rapidly increasing popularity of adventure travel in many parts of the world has inevitably led to an increase in accidents involving travelers. These have

Adventure travel, with activities such as rafting, is increasing in popularity every year. Safety regulations are needed to protect adventure travel participants. © 2009 Pokrovskaya Elena. Used under license from Shutterstock, Inc.

occurred in activities including ballooning, kayaking, jet-boating, and white water rafting. Some destinations that are quite dependent on adventure travel are concerned about the negative publicity these incidents create for tourism. New Zealand is one of these countries and it is well known for its adventure activities. As a result of a number of fatalities in 1995 involving foreign visitors, the Tourism Policy Group conducted an analysis of the safety of adventure tourism operators. The report stated that "the Ministry of Commerce's primary concern is whether there is a potential for long term damage to occur to tourism if New Zealand is perceived by overseas travelers as unsafe" (Tourism Policy Group, 1996). This shows that the government not only has a responsibility to protect the safety of visitors, but that failure to perform this role may have a negative effect on tourism marketing.

TIME-SHARING LAWS AND REGULATIONS

Another part of tourism that has received considerable attention has been the condominium real estate developments within resort areas, particularly *time-sharing* projects. The early history of these projects in many countries involved several cases of fraud and misleading sales claims. Several governments moved to protect customers from such abuses. For example, in the United States, Nebraska was the first state to introduce a time-sharing act to protect its citizens against any misleading claims of time-sharing resort developers in Nebraska and elsewhere.

Brits Advised to Check Insurance if Participating in Extreme Activities in NZ

We strongly recommend that you obtain comprehensive travel and medical insurance before travelling. New Zealand offers an extensive range of extreme activities and if you intend to participate in activities e.g.: bungee jumping, water boarding or white water rafting, you should ensure that your travel insurance covers these types of activities. You should check any exclusions, and that your policy covers you for all the activities you want to undertake.

Travel advice by country, New Zealand, *Foreign & Commonwealth Office*, UK Government (2007), http://www.fco.gov.uk/en/travelling-and-living-overseas/travel-advice-by-country/asia-oceania/new-zealand, accessed January 6, 2009

SELF-REGULATION IN TOURISM

A government's main control over individual tourism business operators is through mandatory licensing or registration, which may or may not be supported by a system of regular inspections or reviews. Government licensing or registration systems operated by government protect travelers from tourism operators or operations that are unsafe, incompetent, or financially unstable. An alternative to this type of government control is to have tourism businesses regulate themselves. This may be done through private-sector associations or specially created organizations. There has been a definite trend around the world toward more self-regulation in tourism. The types of programs that can be used to maintain professional and other standards in tourism include:

ACCREDITATION. Accreditation is a process by which an association or agency evaluates and recognizes a program of study or an institution as meeting certain predetermined standards or qualifications (American Society of Association Executives). The appointment of travel agents by organizations such as IATA is an example of this approach.

CERTIFICATION. Certification applies to individuals who work for tourism businesses. It is a process by which an individual is tested and evaluated to determine his or her mastery of a specific body of knowledge, or some portion of a body of knowledge (American Society of Association Executives). Certification usually follows after a course of study and after the individual has gained a prescribed number of years of experience. In the United States, for example, the National Restaurant Association offers certification programs on food sanitation standards and alcohol service (the ServSafe Food Safety and ServSafe™ Alcohol programs).

CODES OF ETHICS OR PRACTICE. Trade associations may develop codes of ethics or codes of practice to which they require members to adhere. Chapter 7 indicates that several travel agency associations (including ASTA, AFTA, and ABTA) have developed codes of ethics for their members.

CONSUMER PROTECTION PROGRAMS. A trade association establishes a program to protect travelers in the event of the bankruptcy or insolvency of any of its

European Tour Operators Association

The ETOA was founded in 1989 by a group of tour operators who wanted representation in Europe. After nineteen years, the ETOA still remains the only trade association offering European level representation for the interests of inbound and intra-European tour operators, wholesalers, and their European suppliers.

Today, the ETOA is the voice of European inbound travel, with over four hundred members including leading international tour operators, online travel agents, and wholesalers whose business is to bring passengers into Europe. In 2006, ETOA members brought $3.6 billion of revenue to Europe.

The ETOA's aim is the following:

- To create commercial opportunities between buyers and sellers in the travel industry and act as a forum for cooperation between members
- To influence European tourism legislation so that it ensures that members are provided with a viable environment in which to do business
- To keep members informed of the latest developments in the issues that affect their business

When tour operators belong to associations such as the ETOA, this tends to indicate that they support the highest professional standards in the industry sector. This offers the consumer some level of assurance about the professional competency of a member company.

THINK ABOUT THIS:

1. What are the major benefits to a tour operator in belonging to the European Tour Operators Association?
2. What are the traveler benefits from using an ETOA's member tour operator?
3. What can smaller tour operators do to reassure potential clients of their financial stability?

Europe is the leading tourism destination region in the world. © 2009 My-New-Images. Used under license from Shutterstock, Inc.

Source: European Tour Operators Association. 2008. http://www.etoa.org/.

Quality Is Not Everything, but without Quality, Everything Is Nothing

Quality is increasingly becoming the key competitive tool in the tourism sector. More and more often, guests and customers are opting for those products and services that allow them to be certain of receiving high quality and value for money. Promoting and ensuring quality in tourism is one of the Swiss Tourism Federation's main concerns, both as regards its own services and for the tourism sector as a whole. This is why the STF has been entrusted with managing the joint "Quality Label for Swiss Tourism" programme.

Quality in Swiss Tourism, *Swiss Tourism Federation* (2009), http://www.swisstourfed.ch/index.cfm/fuseaction/show/path/1-2.htm, accessed January 4, 2009

members. All members are required to participate in this program. A self-imposed program may obviate the need for a government agency to introduce one. The consumer protection plan operated by the U.S. Tour Operators Association (USTOA) is a good example of this.

Self-regulation tends to be a more popular form of control among private businesses. For example, there has been a proliferation of professionalism certification programs in North America. These now cover association executives, corporate travel managers, hotel managers and sales executives, meeting planners, retail travel agents, and tour planners (Morrison, Hsieh, and Wang, 1992). The Certified Travel Counselor program offered for retail travel agents by The Travel Institute is one of the oldest of these programs, having started in the mid 1960s. However, programs such as these are most effective if all members of the group participate in the program, and many of these programs in tourism are voluntary. Associations are often reluctant to enforce mandatory conditions of membership for fear that businesses will not join and membership revenues will be lost. In addition, it is essential that visitors understand the program objectives and the value of using businesses participating in the program.

SUMMARY

Experience has shown that tourism development can have both positive and negative impacts on a destination area. Tourism also affects and is influenced by the national interests of a country including its natural and cultural resources and its immigration laws and policies. For these and other reasons, it is essential that govern-

ments play a role in developing legislation and in regulating specific parts of tourism.

All tourism destinations have many laws and regulations that affect tourism. Many of these are introduced to protect visitors and residents, as well as the environmental and cultural heritage of the destination.

There has been a strong global trend toward freer trade and travel among countries. This will have a positive influence on world tourism in the future. There has also been a definite trend toward deregulating parts of tourism and toward the privatization of previously government-operated organizations. The United States has been a leader in this regard having removed its regulation on airlines. Another trend that shows the increasing maturity and professionalism in tourism is the move toward greater self-regulation through accreditation, certification, and consumer protection programs. The development of programs such as these, along with more deregulation and privatization, may mean that the government influence on tourism will diminish in the future.

REFERENCES

American Society of Association Executives. (n.d.). *Accreditation, Certification, & Standardization: Definitions & Principles.* Washington, DC: ASAE.

Basan, L., and D. Magas. 2007. Tourism Destination Management Company (DMC): A central actor of a destination and a milieu. *Tourism and Hospitality Management,* 13 (3): 615–626.

CERT. 1993. *Tourism and Travel in Ireland.* Dublin: Gill & Macmillan.

Cournoyer, N. G., A. G. Marshall, and K. L. Morris. 1993. *Hotel, Restaurant, and Travel Law: A Preventive Approach,* 4th ed. Albany, NY: Delmar Publishers.

Del Rosso, L. 1995. Travel sellers laws are a reality in more states than ever. *Travel Weekly,* 54 (98): 18–22.

Department of Foreign Affairs and International Trade. 1996. *Canada, the North American Market and NAFTA.* Ottawa: DFAIT.

Dilts, J. C., and G. E. Prough. 1991. Travel agent perceptions and responses in a deregulated travel environment. *Journal of Travel Research,* 29 (3): 37–42.

Edgell, D. L., Sr. 1993. *World Tourism at the Millennium: An Agenda for Industry, Government and Education.* Washington, DC: U.S. Department of Commerce.

Fredericks, A. 1985. The ripple effect. *Travel Weekly,* 44 (48): 6–7.

General Accounting Office. 1996. *GAO Report: Airline Deregulation.* Washington, DC: GAO.

General Accounting Office. 1999. *GAO Report: Airline Deregulation: Changes in Airfare, Service Quality, and Barriers to Entry.* Washington, DC: GAO.

Trends

Trends Affecting Tourism in Protected Areas

1. Park visitation will increase.
2. Park tourism leads to increased public participation and collaboration.
3. Increasing education levels in society lead to demands for increasing sophistication in park management and park services.
4. A population shift in the developed world toward increasing numbers of older citizens results in significant change in activities, settings, and experiences sought by visitors.
5. Increased accessibility of information technology means the potential, current and past visitors will be better informed and knowledgeable about what leisure opportunities exist, the current state of management, and the consequences of management actions.
6. Increasing availability of information technology profoundly influences park visitation.
7. Advances in the technology of travel and reductions in costs result in increased demand for park and protected area opportunities distant from one's residence.
8. The increase in park area, number of parks, and park visitation exceeds the capability of many park management institutions.
9. Park management shifts gradually from government agency structures, with centralized financial control, to parastatal forms, with flexible financial management.
10. Park management funding increasingly shifts from government grants to park tourism fees and charges. This results in higher levels of visitor focus in management.

Source: Eagles, Paul F. 2004. "Trends affecting tourism in protected areas." Working Papers of the Finnish Forest Research Institute 2.

ACTIVITIES

1. Analyze the strategic alliances among airlines in your region of the world. Which airlines are involved in these partnerships? What are the benefits to the partner airlines?
2. In what ways are the airlines cooperating (e.g., code sharing, sharing of equipment and facilities)?
3. What are the potential benefits of these partnerships to airline passengers? Do you think that the number of strategic alliances will grow in the next five years? Why or why not?

INTERNET

ACTIVITIES

4. Find the Web sites of these strategic airline alliances. What passenger services and benefits are offered through these Web sites?
5. What are the benefits to each of the strategic alliance partners in having its airline's information on these Web sites?
6. For those airlines that do not belong to the strategic alliances, what are the major challenges of not being part of these cooperative programs both offline and online?

Goodwin, J. R., and J. R. Gaston. 1992. *Hotel and Hospitality Law: Principles and Cases*, 4th ed. Scottsdale, AZ: Gorsuch Scarisbrick, Publishers.

Hiemstra, S. J., and J. A. Ismail. 1992. Analysis of room taxes levied on the lodging industry. *Journal of Travel Research*, 31 (1): 42–49.

Inskeep, E. 1991. *Tourism Planning: An Integrated and Sustainable Development Approach*. New York: Van Nostrand Reinhold.

International Civil Aviation Organization. 1996. *The World of Civil Aviation 1995–98*. Montreal: ICAO.

Mihalic, B. J. 1992. Tourism impacts related to EC92: A look ahead. *Journal of Travel Research*, 31 (2): 27–33.

Miller, J. R. 1987. *Legal Aspects of Travel Agency Operation*, 2nd ed. Albany, NY: Delmar Publishers.

Morrison, A. M., S. Hsieh, and C. Y. Wang. 1992. Certification in the travel and tourism industry: The North American experience. *Journal of Tourism Studies*, 3 (2): 32–40.

Parks Canada. 1979. *Parks Canada Policy*. Ottawa: Parks Canada.

Rose, A. 2004. Do we really know that the WTO increases trade? *American Economic Review*, 94: 98–114.

Stanton, J., and C. Aislabie. 1992. Local government regulation and the economics of tourist resort development: An Australian case study. *Journal of Tourism Studies*, 3 (2): 20–31.

Tourism Policy Group. 1996. *Safety Management in the Adventure Tourism Industry: Voluntary and Regulatory Approaches*. Wellington, New Zealand: Ministry of Commerce.

Vellas, F., and L. Becherel. 1995. *International Tourism*. New York: St. Martin's Press.

Williams, A., and V. Balaz. 2000. *Tourism in Transition. Economic Change in Central Europe*. London: Tauris.

World Tourism Organization. 1969. *International Hotel Classification*. Madrid: World Tourism Organization.

World Tourism Organization. 1991. *Food Safety in the Tourism Sector*. Madrid: World Tourism Organization.

SURFING SOLUTIONS

http://www.caa.co.uk/ (Civil Aviation Authority, United Kingdom)

http://www.casa.gov.au/ (Civil Aviation Safety Authority, Australia)

http://www.faa.gov/ (Federal Aviation Administration, United States)

http://www.failteireland.ie/ (Fáilte Ireland)

http://www.iata.org/ (International Air Transport Association)

http://www.iatan.org/ (International Airlines Travel Agent Network)

http://www.icao.org/ (International Civil Aviation Organization)

http://www.icomos.org/ (International Council on Monuments and Sites, Paris)

http://www.iucn.org/ (The World Conservation Union)

http://www.kingdomofbhutan.com/ (Kingdom of Bhutan)

http://www.nafta-sec-alena.org/ (NAFTA Secretariat)

http://www.pc.gc.ca/ (Parks Canada Agency)

http://www.tc.gc.ca/ (Transport Canada)

http://www.tico.on.ca/ (Travel Industry Council of Ontario)

http://www.tourism.govt.nz/ (Ministry of Tourism, New Zealand)

http://www.tsb.gc.ca/ (Transportation Safety Board of Canada)

http://www.unesco.org/ (UNESCO)

http://whc.unesco.org/ (UNESCO World Heritage List)

http://www.ustoa.com/ (United States Tour Operators Association)

http://www.visitscotland.com/ (Visit Scotland)

http://www.who.int/ (World Health Organization, Geneva)

http://www.wto.org/ (World Trade Organization, Geneva)

ACRONYMS

ABTA (Association of British Travel Agents)

AFTA (Australian Federation of Travel Agents)

ASTA (American Society of Travel Agents)

ATOL (Air Travel Organizer's License)

BSP (Billing and Settlement Plan)

CAA (Civil Aviation Authority, United Kingdom)

CAB (Civil Aeronautics Board, United States)

CASA (Civil Aviation Safety Authority, Australia)

EEC (European Economic Community)

EU (European Union)

FAA (Federal Aviation Administration, United States)

GAO (General Accounting Office, United States)

GATS (General Agreement on Trade in Services)

GATT (General Agreement on Tariffs and Trade)

IATA (International Air Transport Association)

IATAN (International Airlines Travel Agent Network, IATA)

ICAO (International Civil Aviation Organization)

ICOMOS (International Council on Monuments and Sites)

IUCN (World Conservation Union)

NAFTA (North American Free Trade Agreement)

OAS (Organization of American States)

TC (Transport Canada)

TICO (Travel Industry Council of Ontario)

TSB (Transportation Safety Board of Canada)

TTI (The Travel Institute)

UNESCO (United Nations Educational Scientific and Cultural Organization)

UNWTO (United Nations World Tourism Organization)

USTOA (U.S. Tour Operators Association)

WHO (World Health Organization)

WTO (World Trade Organization)

chapter 5

Tourism Planning

SELECTING AMONG ALTERNATIVES
FOR THE FUTURE OF TOURISM

Failing to plan is planning to fail.

Famous business saying
Source and date unknown

PURPOSE

Having learned about the reasons and purposes for tourism planning, students will be able to describe a process for planning tourism in a destination area.

LEARNING OBJECTIVES

✓ Describe the reasons for tourism planning and the consequences of unplanned development of tourism.
✓ Explain the reasons for tourism planning.
✓ Identify the barriers to tourism planning.
✓ Explain the purposes of tourism planning.
✓ Describe the steps in the tourism planning process.
✓ Explain the major components of a destination area's market potential and the research techniques that can be used to assess market potential.
✓ Describe and differentiate among tourism position statements, vision statements, goals, strategies, and objectives.

OVERVIEW

Because of the wide-ranging effects of tourism on a destination, it is vital that development be undertaken within the context of a plan. This chapter deals with the planning process as a method for selecting among future alternatives for a destination. Reasons are given why tourism planning should take place and the consequences of unplanned development are described. The purposes of planning are explained and barriers to planning are examined in an attempt to understand why planning is sometimes neglected. The steps of a tourism planning process are described.

THE DESTINATION AREA WITH AND WITHOUT TOURISM PLANNING

> **Good Looks Are Not Everything or Enough in British Columbia**
> *But it's not enough to look at our beautiful province and high-profile events and pat ourselves on the back for a job well done. With a thoughtful and comprehensive plan, we can build on timing and opportunity to move the tourism industry to the next level of worldwide recognition.*
>
> *This is why the government of British Columbia has developed the Tourism Action Plan. It is our commitment to helping the tourism industry take full advantage of these golden opportunities, our growing reputation, our spectacular natural resources and our talented and committed workforce, to build for the future.*
>
> Province of British Columbia's Tourism Action Plan, Ministry of Tourism, Sports and the Arts (2007), page vi

REASONS FOR TOURISM PLANNING

There are many good reasons for tourism planning. Gunn (1994), in his authoritative book on tourism planning, suggests five basic reasons:

1. Tourism development has both negative and positive impacts.
2. Tourism is more competitive than ever before and there has been a proliferation in the promotion of tourism destinations.
3. Tourism is a more complicated phenomenon than it was previously thought to be.
4. Tourism has damaged many natural and cultural resources.
5. Tourism affects everyone in a community and all people involved in tourism should participate in the tourism planning process.

The negative and positive impacts of tourism are well demonstrated through the *destination life cycle* concept (Butler and Waldbrook, 1991; Getz, 1992). This concept suggests that the evolution of all destination areas follows several predictable stages. In Butler's view, the destination life cycle has seven distinct stages (see figure 5.1):

1. **Exploration:** Small numbers of adventurous visitors are attracted by the area's natural and cultural attractions. There is little or no infrastructure for tourism.
2. **Involvement:** Local investment in tourism and tourism advertising starts. Visitor numbers begin to increase and government agencies start to develop the infrastructure.
3. **Development:** There is a rapid growth in visitor numbers as the destination becomes heavily advertised. The type of visitors attracted changes to the less adventurous. Fabricated attractions replace natural and cultural ones. External investment replaces local.
4. **Consolidation:** Growth in visitor numbers begins to slow. Tourism becomes "mass market" and advertising is aimed at attracting new markets and correcting seasonality.
5. **Stagnation:** The destination area is no longer fashionable as peak visitor numbers are reached. There is a heavy reliance on repeat visitors. The carrying capacity limits on resources are reached. Occupancy rates are low and there are frequent changes in tourism business ownership.

An area's natural environment can begin the destination life cycle by bringing new visitors to the area. © 2009 Elisei Shafer. Used under license from Shutterstock, Inc.

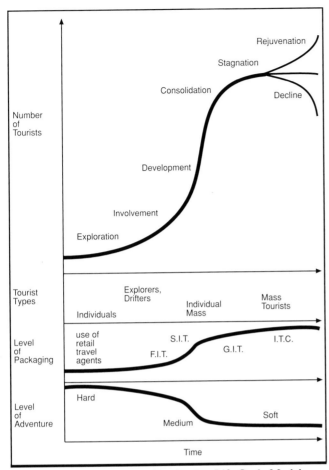

Figure 5.1 Butler's Tourism Destination Life Cycle Model.

6. **Decline:** The tourism infrastructure becomes run down as visitor numbers decrease. External investors begin to pull out.

7. **Rejuvenation:** New attractions are developed or new natural resources are used to reverse the negative trends in visitor arrivals.

Tourism researchers have used destination life cycle models to examine many destinations ranging from the Isle of Man in Britain to Wasaga Beach in Ontario (Getz, 1992). It should be easy to relate to destination areas around the world that fit into each of these categories. Antarctica and Bhutan could be good candidates for the first two stages. Heavily developed destinations such as Acapulco in Mexico, Waikiki Beach in Hawaii, and Australia's Gold Coast perhaps belong in the third and fourth stages. Some of the traditional seaside beach areas of Australia, Britain, and the United States are in the decline stage. The gambling resort destinations of Atlantic City, Macau and Las Vegas could be good examples of rejuvenation, where new attractions have drawn different types of visitors than previously.

Another destination life cycle model that has been popular in tourism is the one developed by Plog (1973). Plog's hypothesis is that destination areas tend to rise and fall in popularity according to the whims of those in the predominant *psychographic groups* to which they appeal at different stages in their development histories. A new and exotic destination tends to appeal first to Plog's *allocentric* group; the innovators in travel markets who seek out uncrowded and unique destinations. As the destination area becomes more widely publicized and better known, it loses its appeal to the allocentrics and they are replaced by the *midcentrics*, who greatly outnumber the allocentrics in the population. Plog relates the midcentric appeal stage in the destination area's history to the maturity phase of the product life cycle where sales volumes are at their peak. Basically, the destination area can be said to have mass market appeal at this point. Eventually as time progresses, this destination area also loses its appeal to the midcentrics, and they are replaced by the *psychocentrics* who, like the allocentrics, represent a much smaller proportion of the population. According to Plog, the psychocentric stage is the final point in the destination area's life cycle; it has lost its appeal to both the market innovators and the mass market. One of the most important messages of the Plog hypothesis is that destination areas can "carry with them the potential seeds of their own destruction" if they allow themselves to become over-commercialized and to forsake the unique appeals that made them popular in the first place.

Although Plog's concept appears to suggest that all destination areas eventually face the same fate, the years of experience that have been gained since it was first publicized have shown that there have been several exceptions to this rule. This experience indicates that destination life cycles can be extended if change is anticipated, and if steps are taken to adapt to the change. One of the core functions of tourism planning is to provide the basic framework to allow the destination area to cope with change.

Facing Adversity Michigan Decided to Develop a Strategic Tourism Plan

The decision to initiate this effort to develop a comprehensive strategic plan for Michigan's tourism industry was made at a time when the industry was facing an extended period of adversity linked to projected long term economic weakness and slow population growth in its prime markets.

Michigan Tourism Strategic Plan 2007–2011, *Michigan Tourism Industry Planning Council (2007), page 5*

The most important lesson from studying destination life cycle models is not which destination fits where, but rather that the future of every tourism destination needs to be carefully charted. Tourism planning helps the destination make better choices for the future. It may help the destination avoid undesirable changes to natural environments and to the community's social and cultural values.

CONSEQUENCES OF UNPLANNED DEVELOPMENT

What can happen if a destination area does not get involved in tourism planning? The examples are numerous and well-documented, especially as they relate to tourism's damaging impacts on many physical environments and local peoples. Some of the symptoms of a lack of tourism planning are shown in figure 5.2. The observers of tourism as an activity have done a good job of describing these negative impacts, particularly as they relate to environmental degradation and adverse cultural and social effects. In some cases, the lack of adequate tourism planning is as much to blame for these problems as tourism itself.

BARRIERS TO TOURISM PLANNING

Not every tourism destination in the world has a tourism plan. With so many good reasons for tourism planning, one might wonder why not. The simplest answer is that there are often many barriers to tourism planning and they include:

- The objections to the principle of tourism planning.
- The costs of conducting tourism planning processes can be high.
- The complexity of tourism and the large number of government agencies involved.
- The diversity of tourism businesses.
- The seasonality of tourism in many destinations.
- The high ownership turnover in tourism businesses.

The first barrier is that some people are against tourism planning in principle, particularly within the developed countries. This is especially true in parts of the Asia-Pacific region, Europe, and North America, where tourism has existed for many years without any formal tourism planning. Many business people view tourism planning as an encroachment into their domain of activ-

Types of Impacts	Symptoms of Lack of Tourism Planning
Physical	■ Damage or permanent alteration of the physical environment ■ Damage or permanent alteration of historical and cultural landmarks and resources ■ Overcrowding and congestion ■ Traffic problems
Human	■ Less accessibility to services and visitor attractions for local residents resulting in local resentment of tourism activity ■ Dislike of visitors on the part of local residents ■ Loss of cultural identities ■ Lack of education of tourism employees in skills and hospitality ■ Lack of community awareness of the benefits of tourism
Marketing	■ Failure to capitalize on new marketing opportunities ■ Erosion of market shares due to the actions of competitive destination areas ■ Lack of sufficient awareness in prime markets ■ Lack of a clear image of destination area in potential markets ■ Lack of cooperative advertising among tourism businesses ■ Inadequate capitalization on packaging opportunities
Organizational	■ Fragmented approach to the marketing and development of tourism, often involving "competitive" splinter groups ■ Lack of cooperation among tourism businesses ■ Inadequate representation of tourism's interests ■ Lack of support from local government authorities ■ Failure to act upon important issues, problems, and opportunities of common interest to tourism
Other	■ Inadequate interpretation and guiding services ■ Inadequate programs of directional signs ■ Lack of sufficient attractions and events ■ High seasonality and short lengths of stay ■ Poor or deteriorating quality of facilities and services ■ Poor or inadequate travel information services

Figure 5.2 Symptoms of a Lack of Tourism Planning.

ity, and they are skeptical of its ultimate value to them. They point out that tourism has already succeeded without a formal tourism plan.

The high cost is a second barrier to tourism planning. Because effective tourism planning must be based upon detailed resource analysis and market research, it often becomes a very expensive process. Governments generally are required to fund tourism planning efforts on behalf of everyone involved. Private-sector businesses often object to this, believing that the money is better spent on more marketing or promotion of the destination.

A third barrier is the complexity of tourism and the large number of government departments whose activities affect tourism. Tourism planning is often made more difficult because the policies of these departments are not coordinated and indeed are sometimes in direct conflict with one another. Additionally, tourism is not a readily identifiable industry; it is an activity that cuts across many other industries. Although the front-line recipients of visitors' expenditures, such as hotels, resorts, airlines, car rental agencies, campgrounds, commercial attractions, and restaurants are obvious, others including retail shops, banks, and municipal governments are not normally seen as being part of tourism. Another complication is that some tourism businesses receive their income both from visitors and from local residents.

A fourth barrier to planning is that tourism is often characterized by having a few very large and a multitude of smaller businesses. There is also a tendency for individual operators to categorize themselves as being in particular business segments (e.g., the "hospitality industry" or the state park system) rather than acknowledging their broader role in tourism. Other problems encountered in planning tourism include the seasonality of business activity and the relatively high ownership turnover.

Despite these barriers to tourism planning, an increasing number of plans are produced each year around the world. Indications are that tourism planning will be given a higher priority in the future and that more destinations will become involved in planning. As they become involved, they will have at their disposal the prior planning experience of many other areas and thus a more refined "technology" of tourism planning.

PURPOSES OF TOURISM PLANNING

Tourism as an activity in a destination is created through the existence of unique attractions and events.

> **Safeguarding a World Treasure at Australia's Kakadu National Park**
>
> *The (tourism) vision states "Kakadu National Park is one of the great World Heritage parks, recognised universally as a place with:*
>
> - *a living Aboriginal culture—home to Bininj/Mungguy*
> - *extraordinary natural landscapes and a rich variety of plants and animals*
> - *enriching and memorable experiences for visitors*
> - *a strong and successful partnership between traditional owners, governments and the tourism industry, providing world's best practice in caring for country and sustainable tourism."*
>
> *Kakadu National Park Draft Tourism Master Plan 2008–2014, Kakadu Board of Management (2008), page 6*

These may include beaches, natural scenery, parks, historical buildings and landmarks, unique cultural characteristics, unique local events and festivals, and outdoor sports and recreation activities. If a destination area wants to maintain tourism as a long-term economic activity, it must use tourism planning to preserve and enhance these special factors that made it different from all other destinations in the first place. It must practice *sustainable tourism development.* Tourism planning has five basic purposes:

1. Identifying alternative approaches
2. Adapting to the unexpected
3. Maintaining uniqueness
4. Creating the desirable
5. Avoiding the undesirable

Figure 5.3 shows the planning considerations and potential outcomes that accompany each of these five planning purposes.

A unique local festival may create tourism as an activity in a destination. © 2009 Peter Hansen. Used under license from Shutterstock, Inc.

<table>
<tr>
<td>

Identifying alternative approaches

Marketing

Development

Organization of tourism

Community awareness of tourism

Support services and activities

</td>
<td>

Adapting to the unexpected

General economic conditions

Energy supply and demand situation

Values and lifestyles

Performance of local industries

Government legislation and
regulations

Technological advancements

</td>
<td>

Maintaining uniqueness

Natural features and resources

Local cultural and social fabric

Local architecture and heritage

Historical monuments and landmarks

Local festivals, events, and activities

Parks and outdoor sports areas

</td>
</tr>
<tr>
<td colspan="1">

Creating the desirable

Sustainable tourism development

High level of community awareness of the benefits
of tourism

Clear and positive image of area as a tourism
destination

Effective organization of tourism

High level of cooperation among tourism
organizations and businesses

Effective marketing, directional sign and travel
information programs

</td>
<td colspan="2">

Avoiding the undesirable

Friction and unnecessary competition

Hostile and unfriendly attitudes of local residents towards visitors

Damage or undesirable permanent alteration of natural features and
historical resources

Loss of cultural identities

Loss of market share

Stoppage of unique local events and festivals

Overcrowding, congestion, and traffic problems

Pollution

High seasonality

</td>
</tr>
</table>

Figure 5.3 Purposes of Tourism Planning.

One of the most important of these purposes of tourism planning is to avoid the negative physical, human, marketing, organizational, and other impacts that can occur when planning is not practiced. Tourism is definitely not the answer to every destination area's economic and social problems, and every community should not pursue tourism. Where the decision is made to develop tourism, it is much more likely to be successful if planning is done.

ROLES AND RESPONSIBILITIES IN TOURISM PLANNING

Historically, tourism planning appears to have originated in Europe. France, Ireland, and the United Kingdom were among the pioneers of tourism planning, with all three nations being involved in some form of tourism planning in the early 1960s. Canada was also in the forefront of tourism planning, its efforts originating in the late 1960s and early 1970s. Following the lead of these developed countries, tourism planning quickly was adopted in several developing nations in Africa and Asia. Many tourism master plans are prepared in the People's Republic of China every year. Other countries such as Australia, New Zealand, and South Africa have invested heavily in tourism planning at the national, state, and regional levels. Interestingly, the United States has seen little organized tourism planning to date and

certainly lags behind Canada and Mexico in this respect.

Tourism is important to governments around the world and is a mainstay of many private-sector businesses. It affects local communities and involves numerous nonprofit organizations. Tourism planning is most effective when it is highly participatory and has the input of the widest range of groups and citizens in a community. Past experience has shown that this process produces the best results and that plans are more likely to

---

Japan Plots a Future Strategy for Its Tourism

- *Increase the number of international visitors to 10 million by 2010, with a long-term goal of equaling the number of Japanese overseas travelers (7.33 million in 2006)*

- *Increase the number of international conferences held in Japan by over 50% by 2011, with the aim of becoming the top host nation of international conference in Asia (168 conferences in 2005)*

- *Increase the duration of Japanese domestic travel by 1 night per person by 2010, to 4 nights annually (2.77 nights in 2006)*

- *Increase the number of Japanese overseas travelers to 20 million by 2010, with the aim of promoting mutual international exchange (17.53 million in 2006)*

- *Increase domestic travel spending to ¥30 trillion by 2010, through the creation of new demand brought about by improved environment for smooth travel and diverse service offerings by increased productivity in the tourism industry (¥24.4 trillion in 2005)*

Tourism Nation Promotion Basic Plan: Basic goals, Japan Tourism Agency (2008), http://www.mlit.go.jp/kankocho/en/vision/plan.html, accessed January 4, 2009

be successfully implemented if communities and the private-sector tourism businesses are actively involved in the planning process. "Top-down" planning exercises by government agencies, or their hired consulting firms, have failed miserably in many parts of the world. These plans were developed in a vacuum, without adequate community and private-sector input. The participants in the tourism planning process and their potential roles are shown in figure 5.4.

Tourism planning needs to happen at many levels. Tourism plans have been developed for areas that include parts of several countries. An example would be the plan developed for the ASEAN nations in Southeast Asia. Planning takes place at the national level within a country and also at the state, provincial, or territorial levels. Tourism planning also occurs at the regional and local levels. Finally, planning can be done for specific resort areas or sites.

The starting point for the tourism planning process in a specific country is with the development of a *national tourism policy*. In chapter 3, a tourism policy model was described, and it was suggested that a

---

The Development of a Tourism Master Plan for Papua and New Guinea Involved Many People
This Report has been developed through an extensive public consultation exercise, which has included 14 stakeholder workshops, attended by over 400 participants across the country, as well as extensive discussions with individual stakeholders. In addition two Issues papers and a Draft Report were released and written submissions received from a variety of stakeholders.

Papua and New Guinea Tourism Sector Review and Master Plan 2007–2017, *PNG Tourism Promotion Authority (2006), page 4*

---

national tourism policy is a combination of the principles upon which a nationwide course of action for tourism is based. The tourism policy represents the basic foundation upon which more specific goals, strategies, objectives, and plans are developed. All tourism planning efforts must be complementary to the national tourism policy. National tourism policies and tourism plans must have definite time spans and be evaluated and modified when these time periods expire. Change is inevitable and continuous, and tourism policy making and planning have to be dynamic processes. Tourism policies tend to be more broad-scale than tourism plans, and they usually are valid for a greater number of years. The life span of a tourism plan is normally not more than three to five years.

Some classification of tourism planning terminology is necessary. First, it should be realized that the terms *tourism plan, master plan for tourism*, and *tourism strategy* are often used to refer to the same thing. In this book, the authors refer to the entire task as being tourism planning, irrespective of whether the eventual result is called a tourism strategy or a tourism plan or a tourism master plan. Under this definition, all tourism planning exercises produce alternative tourism strategies and a tourism plan. The tourism plan itself is a very specific course of action, and the tourism strategies are the alternative approaches available to achieve the tourism planning goals.

STEPS IN THE TOURISM PLANNING PROCESS

Tourism planning takes place at a variety of levels in a destination. However, the approaches used in producing the plans follow a similar step-by-step pattern. There are seven steps in the tourism planning process:

1. Background analysis
2. Detailed research and analysis
3. Synthesis and visioning
4. Goal-setting, strategy selection, and objective-setting
5. Plan development
6. Plan implementation and monitoring
7. Plan evaluation

Government Tourism Officials
Coordinate the tourism planning process; fund tourism planning; provide liaison among all parties involved.

Local Community Residents
Identify community values; indicate satisfaction levels with tourism and acceptable future changes in tourism; provide opinions and suggestions.

Nonprofit Organization Representatives
Ensure consideration of programs of related nonprofit organizations; provide opinions and suggestions.

Other Government Agency Officials
Ensure consideration of policies and programs of related government agencies.

Tourism Organization Representatives
Ensure consideration of programs of tourism organizations; provide opinions and suggestions.

Tourism Business Operators
Provide opinions and suggestions.

Tourism Consultants
Facilitate the tourism planning process; conduct research and analysis; write tourism plan.

Developers and Investors
Develop project conceptual plans; fund feasibility studies; provide investment funds.

Figure 5.4 Tourism Planning Participants and Roles.

STEP 1: BACKGROUND ANALYSIS

Steps	Activities	Participants	Outcomes
■ Review of government policies, goals, objectives and programs ■ Inventory of existing destination mix elements and components ■ Description of existing tourism demand ■ Review of strengths, weaknesses, problems, and issues with tourism	■ Resource inventory ■ Government policy and program review ■ Research of secondary sources of information ■ Pooling of opinions and group workshops	■ Government tourism officials ■ Selected tourism business operators ■ Selected tourism organization representatives ■ Officials from other key government agencies ■ Local residents ■ Representatives from nonprofit groups ■ Tourism consultants	■ Catalog of government policies, goals, objectives, and programs ■ List of destination mix elements and components ■ Description of past visitor profiles ■ Description of major tourism strengths, weaknesses, problems, and issues

Figure 5.5 Tourism Planning Process: Background Analysis.

BACKGROUND ANALYSIS

Each of the seven steps in the tourism planning process involves a variety of steps, activities, participants, and outcomes, and these are illustrated for the Background Analysis step in figure 5.5.

The first step in the tourism planning process could be classified as being a *situation* or *SWOT analysis* that produces the basic direction for the succeeding steps. This is a logical starting point for most tourism plans because most destination areas have some level of existing tourism activity, as well as regulatory and policy frameworks for tourism.

GOVERNMENT POLICIES, GOALS, OBJECTIVES, AND PROGRAMS. In establishing a national tourism plan, the national tourism policy must be considered first. Also if a state, province, or territory has a tourism policy, then it must be carefully reviewed at the outset of the plan. Chapter 3 mentioned that tourism policy goals normally fall into six categories: economic, government operations, human resources development, market development, resource protection and conservation, and social and cultural. For example, in 2003 the Prime Minister of Japan announced a new tourism policy for the country. The new policy was thought necessary because of an imbalance between overseas Japanese travelers (16.83 million in 2002) and inbound foreign tourists to Japan (6.14 million). This resulted in four broad policy initiatives (Japan Tourism Policy Web site, Ministry of Land, Infrastructure and Transport, 2005):

■ Doubling of inbound tourism
■ Encouraging Japanese tourists (to travel in Japan)
■ Enhancing the attractiveness of Japan and local regions
■ Encouraging local efforts to build tourism

Because other government agencies, apart from those directly involved in tourism have policies, goals, and objectives that affect tourism, these must also be considered in the Background Analysis step. Existing tourism-related programs or activities of government and private-sector tourism associations and organizations are also identified.

EXISTING DESTINATION MIX ELEMENTS AND COMPONENTS. The Background Analysis produces an inventory of the area's destination mix elements. Figure 5.6 provides a description of these destination mix elements and their components. Some would say that these destination mix elements and components constitute the existing *tourism product* of the destination area.

EXISTING TOURISM DEMAND. Next, the Background Analysis step involves a description of existing tourism demand in the destination area using published *secondary sources* of information. This information provides a profile of the major characteristics of past visitors (see figure 5.7).

The quantity and quality of this information is determined by the priority that the destination area has given to tourism market research in the past. If gaps are found in the available information, these are usually identified in the Background Analysis step and an attempt is made to fill them in the Detailed Research and Analysis step.

TOURISM STRENGTHS, WEAKNESSES, PROBLEMS, AND ISSUES. The final step in the Background Analysis is a review of the major strengths, weaknesses, problems, and issues of tourism within the destination area. This is an important scene-setting step for the remainder of the tourism planning process, and it is introspective, critical, and objective. It involves a variety of indi-

QUICK TRIP 5.1

Fáilte Ireland West: Regional Tourism Development Plan, 2008–2010

Following the recent reorganization of regional tourism structures, Fáilte Ireland West, as part of the National Development Authority, is charged with delivering increased tourism benefits to the counties of Galway, Mayo, and Roscommon. The purpose of the reorganization was to increase effective local delivery of key tourism objectives, as contained in the National Development Plan and Fáilte Ireland's Product Development Strategy. The total number of visitor bed nights to the region in 2006 was estimated at 11 million, with overseas visitors accounting for 61 percent of these.

In developing the background for the tourism plan, the Fáilte Ireland prepared a SWOT (strengths-weaknesses-opportunities-threats) analysis, which produced the following major conclusions about Fáilte Ireland West tourism:

Strengths	Weaknesses
■ Galway: major accommodation and transport hub ■ Air services via three airports ■ Internal access via road, rail, and ferries ■ Image and awareness ■ Heritage towns (e.g., Westport) ■ Arts, events including performing arts ■ Atlantic Islands ■ Game angling ■ National Parks ■ Adventure Centers ■ Coastline and beaches ■ Lough Key ■ Tourist-oriented shopping	■ Decline in rural visitation ■ Increasing concentration of overseas holiday bed nights in Galway City ■ Lack of rural transport ■ Roscommon tourism product base ■ Signposting ■ Road infrastructure ■ Countryside access ■ Product integration and cross-selling ■ Lack of a major performance venue ■ Limited island accommodation

Opportunities	Threats
■ Walking, cycling, and outdoor opportunities ■ Western corridor (rail and road) ■ Extension of regional air services ■ Gaeltacht and Irish culture ■ Historic houses, parks, and gardens ■ Better telling of the story ■ Linkages of inland waterway systems	■ Continued greater concentration of overnights in Galway City ■ Galway City over-exploitation ■ Rural accommodation base continues to decline ■ Environmental degradation ■ Increasing road traffic volumes ■ Urban sprawl ■ Water-supply quality ■ Loss of direct air services

THINK ABOUT THIS:

1. What partnership approach should Fáilte Ireland West develop to enhance the function in tourism product development and marketing?

2. What can Fáilte Ireland West do to solve the threat of continued greater concentration of overnight stays in Galway City?

3. What measures should Fáilte Ireland West take to deal with environmental degradation?

Source: Fáilte Ireland. 2008. West Tourism Development Plan 2008–2010.

The west coast of Ireland is a place full of scenic beauty with a rich culture and heritage. © 2009 Keith Murphy. Used under license from Shutterstock, Inc.

Attractions and Events
- Accessibility (proximity to markets)
- Climate (contrasts with market areas' climates)
- Culture (beliefs, attitudes, habits, traditions, customs, forms of behavior)
- Historic resources (government, habitation, religious, war)
- Natural resources (landscapes, scenery, beaches, lakes and rivers, flora and fauna, other unique natural features)

Facilities
- Lodging
- Food and beverage
- Support industries (souvenir and handicraft shops, duty-free shops, guides, festival areas, recreational facilities, laundries)

Infrastructure
- Telecommunication networks
- Health care facilities
- Power sources and systems
- Sewage disposal and drainage systems
- Water resources and systems

Transportation
- Transportation terminals
- Roads, streets, highways, and parking systems
- Railway systems, water transportation systems, public transportation systems

Hospitality Resources
- Community attitudes toward tourism
- Hospitality and service quality training programs
- Population and workforce
- Travel information centers

Figure 5.6 Destination Mix Elements and Components.

Activity Participation and Facility Use
Activity participation, usage of facilities (such as accommodation, attractions, events, and recreational facilities)

Demographic and Socioeconomic
Age, gender, income, education, occupation, family life cycle stage

Geographic
Geographic origins, geographic destinations

Information Sources and Media Use
Sources of travel information used, media habits

Travel Planning and Arrangements
Length of trip planning period, types of travel arrangements preferred (e.g., group versus independent travel)

Travel Trip
Expenditures, length of stay, number of previous visits, timing of visit, transportation used, trip purposes, travel party composition, travel party type (e.g., family with children, singles, tour groups, business groups)

Figure 5.7 Past Visitor Profile Factors and Characteristics.

viduals, including government tourism officials, officials from other key government agencies, selected tourism business operators, selected tourism organization representatives, and local citizens. This exercise is likely to be

The carrying capacity of a beach is hard to measure. © 2009 Monkey Business Images. Used under license from Shutterstock, Inc.

most objective and productive if a broad variety of opinions and interests are sought. Private consulting organizations specializing in tourism are often used as facilitators in the planning process. These consultants inject a degree of objectivity and broad tourism experience that may not be readily available in the destination area itself.

Another step that is taken in some tourism plans at this point is staging a series of *public meetings* with citizen groups in the destination area. These sessions are essential in determining community attitudes and awareness levels of tourism, and the types of future directions that citizens want for tourism.

DETAILED RESEARCH AND ANALYSIS

A good tourism plan cannot be developed without research. Tourism plans that are prepared without research tend to reflect the subjective opinions of their authors and to perpetuate existing situations. Research is conducted in four areas: resources, activities, markets, and competition. The basic level of research during the Background Analysis step helps to pinpoint where the more detailed research needs to be focused (figure 5.8).

RESOURCE ANALYSIS. Using the inventory of destination mix elements and components (figure 5.6) as a base, the first step involves the preparation of maps identifying the location of key resources. With the mapping completed, the *carrying capacities* of the resources are then measured. Although the capacities of some of the tourism resource components are easily measured (such as in guest rooms, restaurant seats, camp sites, and golf courses), the capacities of others (such as boating lakes/rivers, beaches, and historical landmarks) are not.

Steps	Activities	Participants	Outcomes
■ Resource analysis ■ Activity analysis ■ Market analysis ■ Competitive analysis	■ Resource mapping ■ Resource capacity measurement ■ Limits of acceptable change process ■ Resource classification ■ Primary market research ■ Activity identification and evaluation ■ Identification and evaluation of competition	■ Government tourism officials ■ Physical planners ■ Market researchers or survey specialists ■ Tourism consultants	■ Maps showing the disposition of tourism resources ■ Capacity measurements for resources ■ LAC standards ■ Description of scope of appeal of resources ■ Research results on potential markets ■ Inventory of tourism and recreation activities ■ Competitive strengths and weaknesses

Figure 5.8 Tourism Planning Process: Detailed Research and Analysis.

Another approach that can be used in resource analysis is the *Limits of Acceptable Change* (LAC). Gartner (1996) suggests a nine-step procedure for using LAC in tourism:

1. **Identify area issues and concerns:** Ask local residents and visitors to indicate the types of activities and acceptable levels of development.

2. **Define and describe tourist activity opportunity classes:** Determine acceptable and unacceptable developments for specific areas or zones.

3. **Select indicators of resource change:** Select indicators of change in biological, social, and other resource areas.

4. **Inventory existing conditions:** Find out the existing conditions using the indicators for each type of resource in specific areas or zones.

5. **Specify standards for resources and social conditions:** Determine tolerable limits of change for each indicator and each resource.

6. **Identify alternative opportunity class allocations reflecting area issues and concerns and existing resource and social conditions:** Review and perhaps revise acceptable or unacceptable developments for specific areas or zones based on information collected for various indicators.

7. **Identify actions needed for each alternative:** Identify alternative actions for each area or zone to keep them within the LAC.

8. **Evaluate and select a preferred alternative:** Assess and pick a preferred set of actions for each area or zone by conferring with local residents and visitors.

9. **Implement the preferred alternative and monitor conditions:** Institute the preferred alternative and monitor to ensure that the LAC standards are not exceeded.

The final stage of the resource analysis is *resource classification*. This represents a ranking or grading of the scope of appeal of the tourism resources of the destination area. Thus, individual resources or zones within the destination are normally defined as being of international, national, regional, or local significance, or as having international, national, regional, or local market appeal.

ACTIVITY ANALYSIS. The second step is the *activity analysis*. Activities include all of the things that the visitor can do in the destination area, ranging from outdoor recreational pursuits, such as alpine skiing, to more passive activities, such as shopping and viewing scenery. Every destination area has a variety of existing activities and potential activities not yet being capitalized upon. As the activities available at the destination are often a prime motivating factor to travel, this exercise can be useful in identifying new demand generation opportunities. The activities are classified by range of appeal (local, regional, state, national, or international). It also is essential to identify the seasons and months of the year in which the activities can be pursued. Because many destination areas suffer from seasonality of demand, this helps to pinpoint those activities that will generate demand outside of peak periods.

MARKET ANALYSIS. A good tourism plan incorporates some *primary research* on the existing and potential mar-

One way to research potential visitor markets is to have potential visitors complete online surveys. © 2009 by Noam Armonn. Used under license from Shutterstock, Inc.

kets for the destination area. The market research carried out in the Background Analysis step was based upon already available information (secondary research). The primary research is done by conducting one or more surveys of existing and potential visitors. Surveys of existing visitors are normally done while the visitors are within the destination area. In addition to gathering visitor profile data as shown in figure 5.7, they are useful in producing the following information:

- Awareness of area attractions and other destination mix elements and components.
- Constraints or barriers to return visits.
- Expenditures within the destination area.
- Images of the destination area.
- Identification of attractions and other items that will increase the likelihood of return visits.
- Likelihood of return visits.
- Motivations for travel to the area.
- Ratings of attractions, facilities, services, and other destination mix elements.

- Satisfaction with trips.
- Sources of information used in planning trips and during trips.

Most often, the personal interview technique is used in these surveys of existing visitors, either at exit or entry points, or at key tourism facilities, attractions, and events.

The Background Analysis and Detailed Research and Analysis steps provide clues as to the sources of potential new market demand for the destination area. The eight main components of a destination area's market potential are shown in figure 5.9. In addition to the potential markets shown in figure 5.9, the destination may concentrate on attracting current pleasure travelers as future pleasure travelers (i.e., encouraging repeat visits). Another potential market may be in attracting current business travelers as future pleasure travelers.

A variety of techniques are available to research potential visitor markets. These include personal interviews, focus groups, telephone interviews, mail and faxed questionnaires, and online surveys. Research can be directed toward the individual pleasure travelers in a specific geographic market (sometimes called *household surveys*) or be aimed at travel trade intermediaries (retail travel agents, tour wholesalers, tour operators, incentive travel planners, corporate travel departments, and convention and meeting planners) and other travel opinion leaders (club, association, and affinity group executives). This research helps to determine:

- Awareness of area attractions and other destination mix elements and components
- Competitive destinations
- Images of the destination area
- Likelihood of future visits to the destination area
- Steps needed to generate business from these potential visitors

PLEASURE TRAVELERS		
Existing Geographic Markets ■ Increase market penetration. ■ Develop new market segments.		New Geographic Markets ■ Attract existing market segments. ■ Attract new market segments.
BUSINESS TRAVELERS		
Existing Geographic Markets ■ Increase market penetration. ■ Develop new market segments.		New Geographic Markets ■ Attract existing market segments. ■ Attract new market segments.

Similar potential may exist for VFR, personal travelers, and other market segments.

Figure 5.9 Components of a Destination Area's Market Potential.

New Zealand's Tourism Planning Toolkit

The Ministry of Tourism in New Zealand has developed a *Tourism Planning Toolkit* for local community authorities to apply. This wonderful resource has been placed on the Web making it really easy to use in developing local tourism plans.

The Toolkit includes:

- **Situation Analysis Toolkit:** Visitor demand; public sector infrastructure; natural assets; visitor satisfaction; tourism industry inventory; economic impact; community tourism
- **Strategic Planning Toolkit:** Local authority planning; working with the tourism industry; infrastructure planning
- **Implementation Toolkit:** Tourism partnerships; project design, appraisal and development; tourism project evaluation; event development funding and evaluation
- **Monitoring Performance Toolkit:** Performance indicators

It contains many very useful checklists for local authorities to fill out, and the following is an example from the Situation Analysis Toolkit element on visitor demand.

Checklist—Key Tourism Information for Local Authorities

Information	Yes	No	Unsure/ Partially
1. The number and type of visitors to the area			
2. The economic benefits provided for your area by visitors			
3. The number and range of accommodation facilities in the area			
4. The number of attractions and activities in the area			
5. The forecast number of visitors to the area for the next five years			
6. The impact on accommodation and attraction requirements from the forecast visitor increases/decreases			
7. The views of visitors on the quality of their experience to the area			
8. The views and opinions of residents in respect to the current levels of tourism in the area			
9. The views and opinions of residents in respect to the forecast levels of tourism in the area			
10. The capacity of current infrastructure and services to cope with existing and future demand from visitors			
11. The impact of visitors on the environment			
12. The level of satisfaction of the tourism industry with maintenance and development of tourism infrastructure and services in the area			

If you have answered "No" or "Unsure/Partially" to any of the above, you will need to access available resources and potentially undertake surveys identified in this section of the Toolkit to obtain the base information required to prepare a strategic plan or address specific issues.

THINK ABOUT THIS:

1. Could destinations outside of New Zealand use this Toolkit? Why or why not?
2. What are the major benefits to a country like New Zealand from having an assistance program such as this?
3. Should the New Zealand Ministry of Tourism be concerned about others having access to these materials on the Web? Why or why not?

Source: Tourism Planning Toolkit. 2005. The Ministry of Tourism, New Zealand, http://www.tourism.govt.nz/tourism-toolkit/tkt-structure.html.

New Zealand is a fantastic destination for adventure travel and outdoor recreation. © 2009 Falk Kienas. Used under license from Shutterstock, Inc.

Research also provides an opportunity to "market test" new ideas for tourism attractions and events, tours or packages, hotel and resort developments, and new activity ideas that have been identified earlier in the planning process.

Another important aspect of the Detailed Market Analysis is an evaluation of the likely impact of *future travel trends* on the destination area. The information on these trends comes from a variety of available *futures* research studies and ongoing *tracking* research programs on travel trends. It is a fairly common practice at this point in the tourism planning process to forecast tourism demand volumes for the period of the tourism plan. For example, the *New Zealand Tourism Strategy 2015* forecasts a 4 percent increase each year in international visitor arrivals for the next seven years (New Zealand Ministry of Tourism, 2007).

When the forecasts are ready, a supply (capacities of resource components) and demand (forecast demand volumes) matching exercise is carried out. This step helps those in the destination area determine where there are likely to be shortfalls in different tourism resources and where there could be problems in preserving tourism resources due to excessive demand levels.

COMPETITIVE ANALYSIS. No destination area is without competition and a tourism plan must consider the *competitive advantages* and future plans of competitors. It is most useful to

define competitive markets in terms of their relative distance from prime geographic markets. Those destination areas closer to a prime market are often referred to as being *intervening opportunities*; the visitor must pass them to reach the subject destination area. For example, Hawaii is an intervening opportunity for tourism in Australia, while Canada's Yukon Territory and British Columbia are for tourism in Alaska. The research described earlier assists in identifying the most competitive destinations, their strengths and weaknesses, and the steps that can be taken to make the subject destination area different from its competitors. In the *Hawaii Tourism Strategic Plan: 2005–2015*, the Hawaii Tourism Authority identified Florida and Las Vegas as major competitors. The Plan noted that both of these competitive destinations were investing heavily in advertising, research, and product development.

Other types of research and analysis may be needed. This may include an evaluation of the tourism organizations, community tourism awareness levels, and the tourism marketing programs of the destination area. The Background Analysis step indicates the degree of emphasis to be given to these factors. For example, in some areas, organizational problems or conflicts may be so acute that they require detailed research and evaluation.

SYNTHESIS AND VISIONING

The third step of the tourism planning process represents the point in which the major conclusions from all of the previous work are formulated (figure 5.10). Some tourism planning experts consider it to be one of the most important and creative steps in the process.

A comprehensive tourism plan produces recommendations on five topics:

1. **Development or product development:** Physical changes in the destination area including new attractions, facilities, infrastructure, travel information and interpretive centers, and transportation systems.
2. **Marketing:** Changes to past marketing programs involving new marketing strategies, positioning approaches, packaging and tours, distribution, and promotional programs.

Steps	Activities	Participants	Outcomes
■ Preparation of prelimi-nary position statements ■ Preparation of vision statements	■ Information assembly ■ Writing of position statements ■ Writing of vision statements ■ Group workshops	■ Government tourism officials ■ Selected tourism business operators ■ Selected tourism orga-nization representatives ■ Officials from other key government agencies ■ Local residents ■ Tourism consultants	■ Position statements on current conditions ■ Vision statements of desired future situations ■ Critical success factors (CSFs)

Figure 5.10 Tourism Planning Process: Synthesis and Visioning.

3. **Tourism organization:** Changes to government and non-government organizations involved in tourism.

4. **Community awareness of tourism:** Programs to increase community resident awareness of the benefits of tourism.

5. **Support services and activities:** Changes in travel information center systems, directional sign pro-grams, scenic tour systems, interpretive services, hospitality and service training programs.

POSITION STATEMENTS. The first step in the synthesis phase is the preparation of *position statements* for each of these five topics. The position statement describes the existing situa-tion (*Where are we now?*) with respect to development, marketing, organiza-tion, community awareness, and other support services and activities. One of the participating groups is given the responsibility for preparing preliminary position statements, usu-ally either the tourism consultants or government tourism officials. These are then reviewed and discussed by all participants, and a consensus is reached on the final wording of the statements. Position statements may be simply ex-pressed in one sentence or be documented in several pages of text. A simple position statement on develop-ment could be "our destination area has historically been developed to appeal to a summer/warm weather market; facilities to attract tourism at other times of the year have not been constructed."

> **China Plans to Be a Tourism Superpower by 2020**
>
> *China intends to become a world power in tourism by 2020. It sees tourism as a means to achieve its major goal of building a prosperous society during the 11th Five-Year Plan from 2006 to 2010. To attain these goals, China sees an urgent need to lift the industry's quality across the board and define the path for a healthy and sustainable growth in the future.*
>
> The 11th Five-Year Plan for the China Travel Industry: Extracts and Sum-mary, English Version, *China National Tourism Administration and Pacific Asia Travel Association. (undated).*

VISION STATEMENTS. The second step is known as *visioning* in which the desired future situation for tourism is determined (*Where would we like to be?*) The desired future states are expressed in terms of *vision statements* that reflect future tourism development, marketing, or-ganization, community awareness, and support services and activities. In our simple example this could be "it is our desire to have year-round tourism facilities in our destination area." Tourism plans provide the "bridge" between the present situation and desired future situa-tions in a destination area. They provide the means to the end. To accompany the vision statements, it is useful to identify *critical success factors* (CSFs) or condi-tions that must be met for the tour-ism vision to be realized.

GOAL-SETTING, STRATEGY SELECTION, AND OBJECTIVE-SETTING

Now that the destination area has defined its future vision for tourism, goals, strategies, and objectives are defined (figure 5.11).

TOURISM GOALS. Tourism goals, strategies, and objectives must be complementary to tourism policy goals and objectives. The major policy goal for tourism may be to stimulate employment, income, and economic development through tourism; an economy-oriented policy approach to tourism. Another destination area suffering from overcrowding or an already too rapid pace of develop-ment may select a more conservation-oriented ap-proach. Remember that a tourism plan has a relatively

Steps	Activities	Participants	Outcomes
■ Definition of tourism goals ■ Identification of alternative strategies and selection of desired strategies ■ Definition of tourism objectives	■ Goal setting ■ Strategy mapping ■ Writing of goals, strategy statements, and objectives ■ Group workshops	■ Government tourism officials ■ Selected tourism business operators ■ Selected tourism organization representatives ■ Officials from other key government agencies ■ Local residents ■ Tourism consultants	■ Statements of tourism goals ■ Maps or other visual presentations of alternative strategies ■ Strategy statements ■ Rationale for selected strategies ■ Statement of tourism objectives

Figure 5.11 Tourism Planning Process: Goal-Setting, Strategy Selection, and Objective-Setting.

QUICK TRIP 5.3

The Maldives Third Tourism Master Plan, 2007–2011

The Maldives, consisting of 1,190 islands formed into twenty-six natural atolls, has become one of the most popular holiday destinations in the world. Each island with its unique shape is rimmed by white sandy beaches sparkling in the sun alongside crystal clear lagoons and dazzling underwater gardens making it a perfect natural combination for an ideal tropical holiday destination.

The Maldives has shown remarkable performances in tourist arrivals in the year 2006 with over 600,000 visitors and an annual growth rate of 52.3 percent. After the impacts of the December 2004 tsunami, throughout the year 2005 tourist arrivals showed a negative trend. However, by December 2005, it had started to recover, and since then there have been impressive improvements in tourist arrivals.

The Maldives Third Tourism Master Plan, 2007–2011, was officially launched in August 2007 at a ceremony held in Hanimaadhoo, Haa Dhaalu Atoll. The thrust of the Maldives Third Tourism Master Plan is on expanding and strengthening Maldives tourism as an instrument of economic and social development in a manner that benefits all Maldivians in all parts of the country. The plan stresses the development of the industry along the lines of sustainability, adopting environmentally and socially

The Maldives is a tropical paradise located in the Indian Ocean. © 2009 sf2301420max. Used under license from Shutterstock, Inc.

responsible tourism practices. Accordingly, the plan emphasizes developing tourism in harmony with nature, facilitating and enhancing private-sector investment, developing human resources, creating greater employment opportunities, and diversifying markets and products.

Contrary to previous plans, the Third Tourism Master Plan is formulated as a "living document" to ensure its responsiveness to rapid changes in the Maldivian economy and global trends in the industry.

THINK ABOUT THIS:

1. What types of tourism goals could be developed based upon these vision and mission statements?

2. How should the Maldives adjust its tourism strategies in the rapidly changing world economic environment like the financial crisis in 2008?

3. How should the Maldives diversify its markets and products to improve its international competitiveness and reach?

Source: Ministry of Tourism and Civil Aviation, Republic of Maldives. 2008. http://www.tourism.gov.mv/.

short life span, usually three to five years, and its goals should be achievable within that time period. A destination area with an economy-oriented policy approach may wish to obtain the maximum economic impact from tourism within the term of the plan. This area will probably adopt a goal that emphasizes the development and marketing of those regions or specific resource components likely to produce the greatest economic return within the planning period; it will concentrate on its major strengths. Yet another destination may have an economy-oriented approach but be more concerned with spreading the economic benefits of tourism more evenly throughout its regions. Its goal might be to concentrate on the development and marketing of those regions with the lowest levels of existing tourism activity.

TOURISM STRATEGIES. Once the planning goals are defined, a variety of strategies can be used to achieve them. Within a specific destination area, it should also be realized that different strategies may be used for the regions within it. Some regions may have economy-oriented strategies and some may have conservation-oriented strategies.

A commonly found tourism development strategy involves dividing the destination into destination zones, touring corridors, and other areas. This can be applied to many geographic areas, including countries, states, provinces or territories, counties, and regions within counties. As well as being visually displayed through maps, a strategy is verbalized in a series of strategy statements. A comprehensive strategy incorporates in these statements the five elements of development, marketing, organization, community awareness of tourism, and support services and activities. Again, a strategy translates the existing conditions in these five elements

into the desired future situations. For example, a destination area highly dependent on one specific geographic market for visitors may wish to adopt a strategy of diversifying its geographic markets, thereby reducing its dependence on one market. Those in a destination area with the planning goal of increasing the economic benefits of tourism to a specific region may select a strategy to increase visitation to that region.

TOURISM OBJECTIVES. The tourism plan objectives flow logically from the selected strategy and support specific tourism goals. The objectives are more short-term than the goals and are more measurable.

PLAN DEVELOPMENT

The next step of the tourism planning process is the development of the plan itself. The plan details the programs and activities needed to achieve the goals, implement the strategy, and attain the objectives (figure 5.12).

New Jersey Launches a New 10-Year Tourism Master Plan in 2009

Gov. Christine Todd Whitman announced a 10-year tourism master plan yesterday that would emphasize the state's cultural and rural attractions, partly through overseas advertisements. Tourists are spending more money and more nights in the state. Tourism spending rose by 6 percent in 2007, to $25.5 billion from $24 billion, while overnight stays increased by 9 percent. To highlight the new master plan, Governor Whitman also announced that the old slogan, "New Jersey and You . . . Perfect Together," would be displayed in a redesigned silhouette of the state that includes the barrier islands.

Tourism Plan Cites Cultural Attractions,
New York Times (January 5, 2009)

STEP 5: PLAN DEVELOPMENT

Steps	Activities	Participants	Outcomes
▪ Description of programs, activities, roles, and funding ▪ Writing of tourism plan reports	▪ Plan detailing ▪ Report writing ▪ Report presentations ▪ Report review and revisions	▪ Government tourism officials ▪ Selected tourism business operators ▪ Selected tourism organization representatives ▪ Officials from other key government agencies ▪ Local residents ▪ Tourism consultants	▪ List of programs and activities ▪ Description of government and private-sector roles and responsibilities ▪ Funding requirements and sources ▪ Description of specific development projects and marketing initiatives ▪ Plan schedule and timetable ▪ Tourism plan reports

Figure 5.12 Tourism Planning Process: Plan Development.

Isle of Wight–The 2020 Vision for Tourism

The impact of tourism on the Isle of Wight is extensive. The island's economic, environmental, and social well-being is fundamentally influenced by the way in which the tourism industry operates.

Tourism is worth over half a billion pounds to the island's economy. It currently generates 360 million pounds of direct tourist expenditure, 25 million pounds from visiting yachts, and an additional 150 million pounds through the multiplier effect on suppliers and income-induced spending. It also supports over 20 percent of the jobs on the island.

The local strategic Partnership's 2020 vision for the island is a progressive island built on economic success, high standards and aspirations and a better quality of life for all. This can be translated into the following long-term key objectives for tourism on the Isle of Wight:

- A better employer–better paid, skilled, and satisfied workforce
- Radically less seasonal–longer, flatter patterns of business
- Increased wealth creation–higher spend from visitors, more profitable businesses
- Higher quality–across the whole spectrum of visitor experience
- Higher levels of repeat business–more satisfied and motivated customers
- More acceptable locally–tourism seen as a credible part of the economy and positive contributor to the quality of life on the island
- Enhancing and protecting the environment–ensuring that key assets are not spoiled by over development or excessive use

THINK ABOUT THIS:

1. In this plan, Isle of Wight has a long-term vision of higher levels of repeat business. What are some of the major challenges that Isle of Wight will face in achieving this vision?

2. The Isle of Wight is a small island located in the south of the United Kingdom. Which unique problems do smaller and more compact destinations like the Isle of Wight encounter in sustaining tourism growth in the long term?

3. What steps can a destination such as the Isle of Wight take to reduce the seasonality of its tourism demand?

4. The tourism industry plays an extremely important role in the island's economy and society. How can Isle of Wight maintain sustainable tourism development?

The Isle of Wight was one of Queen Victoria's favorite holiday spots.

Source: Isle of Wight. 2005. The 2020 Vision for Tourism.

PROGRAMS, ACTIVITIES, ROLES, AND FUNDING. A comprehensive plan deals with the five topics of development, marketing, organization, community awareness, and support services and activities. The tourism plan takes the objectives and specifies the activities, programs, and other steps required to achieve them (see figure 5.13).

TOURISM PLAN REPORTS. Once it has been laid out in this detail, the tourism plan is then written up in formal reports, either by a private tourism consulting firm or by government tourism officials. The tourism plan reports are often presented in two parts. The first is a summary report containing the plan itself, and the second is a more detailed technical report providing all of the research, findings, and conclusions. The reports are usually prepared in draft and are reviewed and revised by government and tourism business representatives prior to being finalized for publication and for public presentations.

Outcomes and Results
The expected results and outcomes of the tourism plan.

Activities and Programs
The programs and activities required to achieve each objective.

Development Projects
The specific development projects needed to achieve certain objectives.

Budget
The money required to carry out specific programs and actions and the sources of these funds.

Marketing Initiatives
The specific marketing initiatives needed to achieve certain objectives.

Monitoring and Evaluation Procedures
The monitoring and evaluation procedures for judging the success of the plan.

Roles and Responsibilities
Roles and responsibilities of government, tourism businesses, tourism organizations, and others.

Schedule and Timetable
The schedule and timetable for carrying out specific programs and activities.

Figure 5.13 Tourism Plan Elements.

PLAN IMPLEMENTATION AND MONITORING

Many tourism plans have been written but never implemented. Why would so much good work and money be wasted? The answer is that plan implementation has been given inadequate attention. Responsibilities for the tourism objectives must be clearly allocated to specific organizations or people. The funds must be available to carry out the activities and programs in the plan (figure 5.14).

PLAN IMPLEMENTATION. The implementation of the plan occurs according to its schedule. The overall responsibility for coordinating its implementation is usually given to a governmental tourism agency. Proposed development projects and other proposals requiring physical changes are reviewed in feasibility studies and environmental impact assessments (EIAs). The process of development is discussed in full detail in chapter 6.

New marketing plans are written and implemented. These plans may involve creating a new positioning approach (image) and branding for the destination, potential market development, the creation of new tours or packages, new distribution strategies, and promotional programs. The tourism plan may also call for changes in existing tourism organizations or for the creation of new tourism organizations. New programs may be designed to increase community awareness of tourism and to improve the destination's hospitality resources.

PLAN MONITORING. While the plan is being implemented the coordinating agency continually checks to ensure that progress is made as was originally planned. Monitoring is done for each tourism goal and for every objective that supports this goal. Modifications to the plan may be required if inadequate progress is made toward achieving certain goals and objectives.

PLAN EVALUATION

Plan evaluation occurs after the term of the tourism plan has expired. The basic purpose of plan evaluation is to determine if the goals and objectives of the tourism plan were achieved. If they were not achieved, an

STEP 6: PLAN IMPLEMENTATION AND MONITORING

Steps	Activities	Participants	Outcomes
■ Plan implementation ■ Plan monitoring	■ Feasibility studies ■ Environmental impact assessments ■ Marketing plan development ■ Implementation of development projects ■ Improvements to infrastructure and transportation ■ Improvements in hospitality resources and community awareness programs ■ Organizational changes	■ Government tourism officials ■ Selected tourism business operators ■ Selected tourism organization representatives ■ Officials from other key government agencies ■ Developers ■ Tourism consultants	■ Feasibility studies ■ Environmental impact assessments ■ Marketing plans ■ New organizational structures in place ■ New developments ■ New hospitality resource and community awareness programs ■ New support services and activities ■ Progress reports on plan implementation

Figure 5.14 Tourism Planning Process: Plan Implementation and Monitoring.

analysis is conducted to determine the reasons for nonperformance (figure 5.15).

PERFORMANCE ON GOALS AND OBJECTIVES. The actual performance related to each individual goal and objective is measured. A variety of indicators may be used that involve evaluation research of different types.

This might include surveys of visitors, local residents, and tourism business operators to determine their attitudes to the changes resulting from the plan's implementation. Specific measurement indicators such as visitor numbers and expenditures may also be used in the evaluation. Meetings are scheduled to discuss the findings of the tourism plan evaluation.

STEP 7: PLAN EVALUATION

Steps	Activities	Participants	Outcomes
■ Measure performance against each goal and objective ■ Analyze reasons for nonperformance	■ Gathering of performance indicators ■ Surveys of local residents ■ Surveys of local tourism business operators ■ LAC measurements ■ Marketing plan evaluation	■ Government tourism officials ■ Selected tourism business operators ■ Selected tourism organization representatives ■ Officials from other key government agencies ■ Local residents ■ Tourism consultants	■ Performance indicators for each goal and objective ■ Local resident attitude surveys ■ Tourism business operator surveys ■ LAC results ■ Marketing plan evaluation results ■ Suggestions for future tourism planning processes

Figure 5.15 Tourism Planning Process: Plan Evaluation.

QUICK TRIP 5.5

Major Goals for Tourism in Hawaii until 2015

Tourism is vitally important to the state of Hawaii. In 2003, it provided one in every five jobs in Hawaii, and by 2007 it was expected to produce 17.3 percent of the Gross State Product and 26.4 percent of all tax revenues. As the leading industry in the state, its future planning is of the highest priority.

The Hawaii Tourism Authority (HTA) is the state agency with overall responsibility for tourism. HTA was established in 1998 and was given the following mandates:

■ Create a vision and develop a long range plan for tourism in Hawaii.

■ Develop, coordinate, and implement state policies and directions for tourism and related activities taking into account the economic, social, and physical impacts of tourism on the state and its natural resources infrastructure; provided that the authority shall support the efforts of other state and county departments or agencies to manage, improve, and protect Hawaii's natural environment and areas frequented by visitors.

■ Develop and implement the state tourism strategic marketing plan, which shall be updated every three years, to promote and market the state as a desirable leisure and business visitor destination.

■ Have a permanent, strong focus on marketing and promotion.

■ Conduct market development-related research as necessary.

■ Coordinate all agencies and advise the private sector in the development of tourism-related activities and resources.

■ Work to eliminate or reduce barriers to travel in order to provide a positive and competitive business environment, including coordinating with the Department of Transportation on issues affecting airlines and air route development.

(continued)

- Market and promote sports-related activities and events.
- Coordinate the development of new product lines with the counties and other public and private sectors including the development of sports, culture, health, education, business and ecotourism.
- Establish a public information and educational program to inform the public of tourism and tourism-related problems.
- Encourage the development of tourism educational, training and career counseling programs.
- Establish a program to monitor, investigate, and respond to complaints about problems resulting directly or indirectly from the tourism industry and taking appropriate action as necessary.

The HTA has developed the *Hawaii Tourism Strategic Plan: 2005–2015*. The following goals were set in the plan:

1. **Access:** Maintain and improve transportation access, infrastructure and services to facilitate travel to, from, and within Hawaii
2. **Communications and Outreach:** Facilitate interaction among all visitor industry stakeholders that improves the lines of communication and enhances greater understanding of roles, values, and concerns
3. **Hawaiian Culture:** Honor and perpetuate the Hawaiian culture and community
4. **Marketing:** Develop marketing programs that contribute to sustainable economic growth
5. **Natural Resources:** Respect, enhance, and perpetuate Hawaii's natural resources to ensure a high level of satisfaction for residents and visitors
6. **Research and Planning:** Perform collaborative research and planning for use in the development of programs, policies, and plans that will positively contribute to the state's economy, benefit the community, and sustain Hawaii's resources
7. **Safety and Security:** Achieve a safe Hawaii visitor experience
8. **Tourism Product Development:** Provide a diverse and quality tourism product unique to Hawaii that enhances the Hawaii visitor experience and enriches residents' quality of life
9. **Workforce Development:** Ensure a sufficient and highly qualified workforce that is provided with meaningful careers and advancement opportunities

In the plan, four measures of plan success are identified:

1. Resident sentiments
2. State and county tax receipts
3. Visitor spending
4. Visitor satisfaction

Many destinations have traditionally set some of their tourism goals and objectives in numbers of visitor arrivals. This has become almost a standard practice in tourism. Despite its popularity, this may not be the optimum approach to market selection and emphasis since different markets have varying levels of contribution to the economy. It will be noticed that the HTA's emphasis is on visitor spending and not on arrivals.

THINK ABOUT THIS:

1. What are the major advantages of focusing on visitor expenditures rather than visitor arrivals in setting goals and objectives in tourism plans?
2. What are the potential dangers or limitations of just using the expenditure-based approach to setting tourism goals and objectives?
3. How important is it for a destination like Hawaii to measure residents' sentiments about tourism and how might the results influence future tourism plans?

The goals for Hawaii's tourism recognize the importance of preserving Hawaii's rich cultural traditions. © 2009 Chiyacat. Used under license from Shutterstock, Inc.

Source: Hawaii Tourism Authority. 2005. Hawaii Tourism Strategic Plan: 2005–2015, http://www.hawaii.gov/tourism/tsp.html.

The final outcome of evaluation becomes a major input into the next round of tourism planning. Specific recommendations are made based upon the lessons of this tourism planning process. The most important questions that need to be answered are: What goals were achieved? What goals were not achieved? Why were these goals not achieved? What should be done differently the next time tourism planning is done? The tourism planning process has come full cycle.

SUMMARY

Every destination area interested in tourism must use the tourism planning process. Although tourism planning can be hard work, time consuming, costly, and difficult to sell, it is an essential activity in today's rapidly changing business environments. The absence of tourism planning in a destination can lead to irreversible economic, social and cultural, and environmental damage and to loss of market share. There are many barriers to tourism planning in every destination area, but the rewards resulting from an effective tourism planning process far outweigh the efforts needed to surmount these. Empirical evidence throughout the world clearly shows that the "model" destinations for successful tourism are those that have embraced the tourism planning concept.

REASONS FOR NONPERFORMANCE. It is highly likely that not all of the tourism goals and objectives will be achieved. The important thing here is to determine the reasons for nonperformance on specific goals and objectives. Nonperformance may result for many reasons such as unexpected changes in world events, the inability to attract private development funding, or unanticipated competitive strategies and programs.

RECOMMENDATIONS FOR FUTURE TOURISM PLANNING. It is useful at this point to rewrite the position statements that were prepared earlier in the Synthesis and Visioning step. This allows the participants to evaluate if the vision statements were realized.

 *Trends*

Trends in Sustainable Tourism Planning: The Seven Es

1. *Environment:* Managing natural and physical environments as well as the human-nature interactions
2. *Economics:* Promoting financial profitability without destroying or depleting the natural capital and eroding the cultural values of the host community
3. *Enforcement:* Implementing, managing, and monitoring of plans, legislative and other regulatory measures, and voluntary codes of conduct
4. *Experience:* Enhancing tourist satisfaction, experience, and knowledge provided by the attractions
5. *Engagement:* Involving the stakeholders including the host community in planning, decision making, and implementation
6. *Enquiry:* Conducting research through scientific enquiry on the technical and social implications of tourism on the conservation of natural and cultural heritage including environmental protection
7. *Education:* Improving understanding about the natural and cultural environments as well as visitor use and impacts

Source: Catibog-Sinha, C., and J. Wen. 2008. Sustainable tourism planning and management model for protected natural areas: Xishuangbanna Biosphere Reserve, South China. *Asia Pacific Journal of Tourism Research*, 13 (2): 145–162.

ACTIVITIES

1. Arrange an interview with an official of a local tourism organization to discuss the topic of tourism planning. Begin the discussion by asking this person about the perceived value of tourism planning for the local area. Has a tourism plan ever been completed for the area? If not, why has a plan never been prepared? Ask the person to describe how he or she thinks a tourism plan could be developed.

2. If a plan has been completed, what process was used for its development? Who coordinated the tourism planning process and what other parties were involved?

3. Has the implementation of the plan been successful? Why or why not?

INTERNET
ACTIVITIES

4. Do an Internet search and collect information on an assortment of tourism plans for a variety of different geographic areas.

5. What are the most effective plans and what is the reason for your evaluation?

6. What can your local area learn and apply on the basis of your review of these plans?

REFERENCES

Alipour, H. 1996. Tourism development within planning paradigms: The case of Turkey. *Tourism Management*, 17 (5): 367–377.

Butler, R. W. 1980. The concept of a tourist area cycle of evolution: Implications for management of resources. *Canadian Geographer*, 24 (1): 5–12.

Butler, R. W., and L. A. Waldbrook. 1991. A new planning tool: The tourism opportunity spectrum. *Journal of Tourism Studies*, 2 (1): 2–14.

Ding, P., and J. Pigram. 1995. Environmental audits: An emerging concept in sustainable tourism development. *Journal of Tourism Studies*, 6 (2): 2–10.

Frechtling, D. C. 2001. *Forecasting Tourism Demand*. Oxford: Butterworth and Heinemann.

Gartner, W. C. 1996. *Tourism Development: Principles, Processes, and Policies*. New York: Van Nostrand Reinhold.

Getz, D. 1986. Models in tourism planning. *Tourism Management*, 7: 21–32.

Getz, D. 1992. Tourism planning and the destination life cycle. *Annals of Tourism Research*, 19: 752–770.

Gunn, C. A. 1994. *Tourism Planning: Basics, Concepts, Cases*, 3rd ed. Washington, DC: Taylor & Francis.

Hall, D., M. Smith, and B. Marciszewska. 2006. Introduction. In *Tourism in the New Europe: The Challenges and Opportunities*, D. Hall, M. Smith, and B. Marciszweska (eds.). 3–19.

Ivanovic, S., and E. Mrnjavac. 2007. Logistics and logistics processes in a tourism destination. *Tourism and Hospitality Management*, 13 (3): 531–546.

Keane, M. 1997. Quality and pricing in tourism destinations. *Annals of Tourism Research*, 24: 117–130.

Kelly, M. 1998. *Tourism Planning: What to Consider in Tourism Plan Making*. Proceedings of the 1998 National Planning Conference.

Krotz, L. 1996. *Tourists: How Our Fastest Growing Industry is Changing the World*. Boston: Faber and Faber.

Laws, E. 1995. *Tourist Destination Management: Issues, Analysis and Policies*. London: Routledge.

Long, P. T., and J. S. Nuckolls. 1994. Organizing resources for rural tourism development: The importance of leadership, planning and technical assistance. *Tourism Recreation Research*, 19 (2): 19–34.

Manning, E. W., and T. D. Dougherty. 1995. Sustainable tourism: Preserving the golden goose. *Cornell Hotel and Restaurant Administration Quarterly*, 36 (2): 29–42.

Murphy, P. E. 1988. Community driven tourism planning. *Tourism Management*, 9: 96–104.

Pearce, D. 1992. *Tourist organizations*. Harlow, Essex: Longman Group U.K.

Pike, S. 2002. Destination image analysis: A review of 142 papers from 1973 to 2000. *Tourism Management*, 23: 541–549.

Plog, S. G. 1973. Why destination areas rise and fall in popularity. *Cornell Hotel and Restaurant Administration Quarterly*, 14 (3): 13–16.

Ritchie, J. R. B. 1993. Crafting a destination image: Putting the concept of resident-responsive tourism into practice. *Tourism Management*, 14: 379–389.

Stynes, D. J., and C. O'Halloran. 1987. *Tourism Planning*. East Lansing, MI: Tourism Information Series No. 2, Cooperative Extension Service, Michigan State University.

Tosun, C., and C. L. Jenkins. 1996. Regional planning approaches to tourism development: The case in Turkey. *Tourism Management*, 17: 519–531.

SURFING SOLUTIONS

http://app.stb.gov.sg/asp/abo/abo.asp (Singapore Tourism Board)

http://english.visitkorea.or.kr/enu/SI/SI_EN_3_2_1. jsp?cid=590898 (Korean Tourism Organization)

http://www.hawaiitourismauthority.org/ (Strategic Tourism Plan for Hawaii: 2005–2015, Hawaii Tourism Authority)

http://www.mlit.go.jp/sogoseisaku/kanko/english/overview. html (Japan Tourism Policy Web site)

http://www.tourismtrade.org.uk/MarketIntelligenceResearch/
?url=/research (VisitBritain Research, Statistics on Tourism
Research for the United Kingdom)

http://www.tourism.govt.nz/ (New Zealand Ministry of
Tourism)

http://www.tourismtrade.org.uk/ (VisitBritain corporate site)

ACRONYMS

CSF (critical success factor)
EIA (environmental impact assessment)
LAC (limits of acceptable change)
STD (sustainable tourism development)

chapter **6**

Tourism Development

BUILDING A SUSTAINABLE FUTURE
FOR TOURISM

Costa Rica Gets It Right in Tourism Development

Costa Rica has developed an environmentally sound and lucrative ecotourism industry that has allowed it to protect its vast natural treasures while bringing economic opportunities to typically disadvantaged rural areas. While the industry has faced difficulties in reconciling its environmental ideals with the growing demand for ecotourism and the temptation for profit-seeking, the environmental and economic benefits of ecotourism have far outweighed these drawbacks.

The Pros and Cons of Ecotourism in Costa Rica, *Julie Dasenbrock (2001),*
http://www.american.edu/TED/costa-rica-tourism.htm#general, accessed January 6, 2009

PURPOSE

Having learned about the concept and principles of sustainable tourism development, students will be able to describe a process for evaluating individual tourism project development opportunities.

LEARNING OBJECTIVES

✓ Explain the concept and principles of sustainable tourism development.
✓ Describe the main forms of tourism development.
✓ Discuss government and private-sector roles in tourism development.
✓ Describe the role and types of government incentives for tourism development and the criteria for government financial assistance.
✓ Describe the objectives and steps in completing a pre-feasibility study and an economic feasibility study.
✓ Identify the two main groups concerned with the results of economic feasibility studies and discuss the questions they typically want answered.
✓ Explain the purposes of preparing an environmental impact assessment.

OVERVIEW

This chapter begins by describing the concept and principles of sustainable tourism development. The link between tourism development and tourism planning is emphasized. The tourism development roles of the private sector and government are outlined. Sources of financial assistance from government and the private sector are examined. A process for analyzing individual tourism development projects is described. Particular attention is paid to the analysis of the project from the economic feasibility and environmental impact viewpoints.

BUILDING A SUSTAINABLE FUTURE FOR TOURISM

SUSTAINABLE TOURISM DEVELOPMENT

Chapter 2 emphasizes the need to control the impacts of tourism through the application of the principles of sustainable development. According to Manning and Dougherty (1995), sustainable development "means the use of natural resources to support economic activity without compromising the environment's carrying capacity, which is its ability to continue producing those economic goods and services." The origination of the sustainable development concept is attributed to the 1980 World Conservation Strategy and the 1987 World Commission on Environment and Development (The Brundtland Commission).

The concept of sustainable tourism development (STD) is the application of the basic principles of sustainable development to tourism, which is highly dependent on the natural resources of destination areas. STD first started to be talked about in the early 1990s. Butler (1993) provides a good definition of STD as:

> Tourism which is developed and maintained in an area (community, environment) in such a manner and at such a scale that it remains viable over an indefinite period and does not degrade or alter the environment (human and physical) in which it exists to such a degree that it prohibits the successful development and well-being of other activities and processes.

> **Tourism Operators Not Just in It for Themselves**
> *The principles of responsible tourism encourage tourism operators to grow their businesses whilst providing social and economic benefits to local communities and respecting the environment.*
>
> A Practical Guide to Tourism Destination Management, *UN World Tourism Organization (2007), page 14*

It should be noticed that STD is not just concerned with natural and physical environments, but recognizes the need to maintain the cultures and lifestyles of local peoples. The World Tourism Organization (UNWTO) has prepared recommended STD guidelines in *Sustainable tourism development: Guide for local planners* (McIntyre, 1993). This UNWTO report recommends that tourism needs to be developed to satisfy three broad principles (Ding and Pigram, 1995):

1. To improve the quality of life of the host community
2. To provide a high-quality experience for visitors
3. To maintain the quality of the environment on which both the host community and the visitors depend

It is generally accepted that all tourism developments should respect the concept and principles of sustainable tourism development. However, there remains a practical problem of defining exactly what sustainability means. Gartner (1996) states the STD concept is hard to operationalize and that "there is yet no consensus on what it really means, let alone how to implement a sustainable tourism policy." It could be argued that the massive Walt Disney World development in Orlando, Florida, is not sustainable, yet it has already thrived for almost forty years. Some have suggested that ecotourism or alternative tourism are the only types of developments to ensure sustainability. This has been hotly debated by others who state that some forms of ecotourism also harm the physical environment and local cultures (Ioannides, 1995). While this debate will continue for many years to come, the STD concept does, if nothing else, heighten the need for careful development planning that assesses all of the potential impacts of a tourism project development opportunity.

FORMS AND IMPACTS OF TOURISM DEVELOPMENTS

There are many different forms of development that have occurred in tourism destinations around the world. According to Gartner (1996), all physical developments in tourism inevitably transform local environments. Some tourism experts refer to the scale of transformation as being from low-impact to high-impact developments. Low-impact or "soft" tourism developments are

Climate Change and Tourism–Responding to Global Challenges

The Report on "Climate Change and Tourism–Responding to Global Challenges," which was commissioned to an international team of experts by the World Tourism Organization (UNWTO), the United Nations Environment Programme (UNEP), and the World Meteorological Organization (WMO), provides a synthesis of the state of knowledge about current and likely future impacts of climate change on tourism destinations around the world, possible implications for tourist demand, and current levels and trends in greenhouse gas (GHG) emissions from the tourism sector. It gives an overview of policy and management responses of adaptation to climate change and mitigation of tourism's emissions. The report also summarizes the main results of a series of events focused on climate change and tourism that took place in the second half of 2007.

The following measures are recommended in the destination tourism development:

Coastal and Island Destinations
- "Soft" coastal protection to prevent erosion (e.g., reforestation of mangroves, reef protection)
- Enhanced design, site selection standards, and planning guidelines for tourism establishments
- Integration of climate change factors into regulatory frameworks for tourism development, such as Environmental Impact Assessment for tourism infrastructure and establishments
- Implementation of tourism development plans within the framework of Integrated Coastal Zone Management (ICZM) processes and spatial planning such as zoning
- Shade provision and crop diversification
- Reduction of tourism pressures on coral reefs
- Water conservation techniques, such as rainwater storage, the use of water-saving devices, or wastewater recycling
- Diversification of the tourism product to less-climate-dependent and seasonal activities, such as ecotourism
- Education/awareness-raising among tourism businesses and their staff, as well as tourists
- Awareness and preparedness to face extreme climatic events and disasters at the national and local levels through improved coordination between disaster management offices, tourism administrations, businesses, and host communities
- Improved provision of climatic information to the tourism sector through cooperation with national meteorological services
- Insurance coverage (or alternative schemes) for the recovery of infrastructural and other damage
- Drainage and watershed management to reduce flood and erosion risks
- Support of protected area management, and other means of the conservation of coastal ecosystems in order to enhance their resilience

Mountain and Winter Tourism Destinations
- Stimulate product and seasonal diversification, e.g., creating spas, all-year tourism
- Implement snow-making, and make it more efficient
- Groom ski slopes to reduce snow depth requirements
- Preserve glacier areas
- Move ski areas to higher altitudes or to colder north slopes
- Improve insurance cover in the face of extreme events and natural disasters (e.g., avalanches)
- Promote industry partnerships (integration within resorts, cooperation between resorts) to reduce economic vulnerability and share the cost of snow-making
- Educate and raise awareness among tourists about the impacts of global environmental change on the Alpine landscape
- Combine mitigation and adaptation measures into integrated and coherent strategies
- Improve water use and protect Alpine watersheds
- Improve emergency preparedness, implement and improve warning and evacuation systems, and put avalanche prevention infrastructure into place

(continued)

Nature-Based Destinations

- Develop response plans, i.e., water supply planning (in drought-susceptible destinations); develop risk assessment and preparedness strategies; and implement early warning systems (e.g., for flooding)
- Improve adaptive capacity of authorities and managers of protected areas through capacity building initiatives, especially in biodiversity hotspots of LDCs and developing countries
- Establish scientific monitoring survey programs to assess ecosystem changes and take necessary protection measures (monitoring activities could especially focus on species and habitats most vulnerable to climate change impacts and most important for tourism activities)
- Promote product diversification, for example, opening up new "micro destinations" and attractions within and adjacent to an already popular national park or heritage site; diversification is especially important where key elements of the nature-based product are threatened (e.g., polar bear watching in Northern Canada)
- Carry out re-design or redefinition of protected areas, for example, revision of zoning of certain areas, extending protected area to a larger surface, creation of migratory corridors to allow threatened species to more easily find new geographic ranges
- Reduce or remove external stresses such as pollution and, in the case of marine resources, agricultural runoff
- Promote the application of integrated tourism carrying capacity assessment techniques (considering physical, economic, environmental, sociocultural and managerial aspects) in protected areas as tools for tourism planning
- Improve visitor and congestion management to prevent overuse of sites and physical impacts of visitation
- Promote mitigation options among environmentally conscious ecotourists, e.g., through offsetting their trips to nature-based tourism destinations
- Ensure active participation of local communities living within or near protected areas, in policy making and management processes
- Take into consideration local and traditional knowledge to develop coping and adaptation strategies
- Develop replicable methodologies and share knowledge across nature-based destinations

THINK ABOUT THIS:

1. What influence will climate change make on tourism destination development, especially those that are nature-based?
2. Do you think that climate change will have an influence on cultural-based tourism destinations?
3. How important are the education and training of tourism employees in encouraging the sustainable tourism development concept?

Source: World Tourism Organization. 2008. http://www.unwto.org/.

Global warming is a major challenge facing the world and tourism as well. © 2009 digitalife. Used under license from Shutterstock, Inc.

usually smaller-scale and are designed to meet ecologically-sustainable tourism development (ESTD) principles (Moscardo, Morrison, and Pearce, 1996). The goals and characteristics of ecologically sustainable tourism are shown in figure 6.1.

Some refer to low-impact or "soft" tourism developments as alternative tourism and compare this to the more high-impact mass tourism and resort tourism (Doggart and Doggart, 1996). Mass tourism is where thousands of visitors concentrate in particular areas and this requires large-scale investment in accommodation, infrastructure, and services. Examples include parts of Florida (e.g., Orlando and Miami); Bali in Indonesia; Pattaya and Phuket in Thailand; the beach areas of France, Italy, and Spain; and the Surfers Paradise area of Australia's Gold Coast. Resort tourism includes self-contained or integrated projects like the typical Club Med village. The high-impact tourism development projects have the potential of causing major transformations in local environments and peoples. Mathieson and Wall (1982) identify four undesirable situations that may result from high-impact developments which are poorly planned and developed:

1. **Architectural pollution:** The development of new architectural forms that are not compatible with local environments and cultural heritage. While spectacular, the mega-resort developments in Las

Goals
- To improve material and nonmaterial well-being of communities
- To improve intergenerational and intragenerational equity
- To protect biological diversity and maintain ecological systems
- To ensure the cultural integrity and social cohesion of communities

Characteristics
- *Tourism* that is concerned with the quality of experiences
- *Tourism* that has social equity and community involvement
- *Tourism* that operates within the limits of the resource (This includes minimization of impacts and the use of effective waste management and recycling techniques.)
- *Tourism* that maintains the full range of recreational, educational, and cultural opportunities within and across generations
- *Tourism* that is based on activities that reflect the character of the region
- *Tourism* that allows the guest to gain an understanding of the region visited and that encourages guests to be concerned about and protective of the host community and environment
- *Tourism* that does not compromise the capacity of other industries or activities to be sustainable
- *Tourism* that is integrated into local, regional, and national plans

Source: Ecologically Sustainable Development Working Group. (1991). *Final report: Tourism.* Canberra: Australian Government Publishing Service.

Figure 6.1 Goals and Characteristics of Ecologically Sustainable Tourism.

Vegas are hardly compatible with the heritage of Nevada.

2. **Ribbon development and sprawl:** Strip development that follows along coastlines or on either sides of roads leading to important attractions. Sprawl is when development expands continuously from the site of the original attraction.

3. **Infrastructure overload:** The visitor use of infrastructure systems, including power and sewage disposal, is greater than the capacity of these systems.

4. **Traffic congestion:** Traffic volumes exceed the capacity of the local road and highway systems.

The problems caused by unplanned mass tourism are very real and have been witnessed around the world. Many alternatives to mass tourism have been

> **Power up, but Step Lightly**
> *Travel is a powerful engine of change. It broadens perspectives, erases boundaries, and encourages diversity. It opens you up to values and ways of living that are at once unfamiliar and illuminating. Travel is a powerful force for good, and yet through our sheer numbers alone, we travelers often unwittingly put delicate human and natural ecosystems at risk.*
>
> Editor's Note 11.07, *Nancy Novogrod, Travel + Leisure (2007), http://www.travelandleisure.com/articles/editors-letter-november-2007, accessed January 4, 2009*

suggested, especially for less-developed countries (LDCs). One of the most talked about alternative in the past twenty years has been ecotourism. There are many definitions of ecotourism, with most emphasizing natural environments and a concern for local peoples. The Canadian Environmental Advisory Council definition of ecotourism is (Wight, 1993a):

> Ecotourism is an enlightening nature travel experience that contributes to the conservation of the ecosystem while respecting the integrity of host communities.

Another interpretation of ecotourism (Kersten, 1997) based on an analysis conducted in Germany is that it aims to:

- Deter or minimize negative environmental and sociocultural impacts.
- Take place within "relatively untouched" natural areas.
- Contribute to the conservation of areas.
- Improve the local economy of adjacent communities.
- Primarily address visitors who maintain a certain "nonconsumerism," nature-loving, and ethical conscience toward tourism.

The increasing popularity of ecotourism has led to the development of a specialized form of accommodation known as ecolodges and to the creation of tour operators and tours that concentrate on nature and local cultures.

THE LINK BETWEEN TOURISM PLANNING AND TOURISM DEVELOPMENT

The tourism planning process in chapter 5 produces goals, strategies, and objectives for tourism development, marketing, organization, community awareness of tourism, and other support services and activities. The tourism development portion of the plan provides overall guidelines for development and outlines broad development concepts. These overall tourism development guidelines ensure that when development occurs it supports the area's economic, social and cultural, and environmental policies and goals. Specific guidelines describing the basic characteristics of the scale, quality, and types of development are written.

The tourism planning process also identifies individual project development opportunities worthy of in-depth research through feasibility studies and environmental impact analyses. The term "tourism product" is used for all categories of project development opportunities, both commercial and noncommercial. The economic feasibility and environmental impact of commercial (profit-making) project development opportunities is established with the techniques described in this chapter. The noncommercial development opportunities may include support facilities like travel information centers, infrastructure, transportation, and nonprofit attractions such as museums and other historic landmarks. The advisability of proceeding with these projects cannot be measured through an economic feasibility study since they may produce little or no revenue. These projects may be analyzed using a technique known as cost/benefit analysis, or are assessed for their contributions to the achievement of the tourism plan's goals and objectives.

GOVERNMENT AND PRIVATE-SECTOR PARTICIPATION IN TOURISM DEVELOPMENT

GOVERNMENT AND PRIVATE-SECTOR ROLES

Both the government and the private sector have important roles to play in tourism development. The private sector's main role is to develop and operate tourism facilities and services for visitors while maximizing financial returns. In today's more enlightened times,

companies accept that they have social and environmental responsibilities that they must uphold in achieving profit goals.

Not all tourism project development opportunities are identified in the tourism planning process. Many project ideas emerge from the private sector itself through sponsored research studies and assessments of supply and demand relationships. Idea generation is, therefore, a key role of the private sector.

The entrepreneurial role is the heart of the private sector's involvement in tourism development. This role embraces idea generation, development project implementation, financial risk-taking and investment, and the management of operations. The private sector also provides the specialized technical skills required in the development process through tourism consultants, market research firms, economists, environmental and social impact experts, architects, engineers, designers, lawyers, project managers, and builders. The private sector, through its financial institutions, other corporate lenders, and individual citizens, provides a large proportion of the financing for the investment in tourism development projects.

Nonprofit organizations (or the volunteer sector) play an important role in tourism development in most destinations. These organizations include convention and visitors bureaus, chambers of commerce, travel associations, foundations, historical and cultural societies, recreation and sports associations, service clubs, community associations, and religious groups. While their roles vary, non-profits typically are involved in operating attractions (such as pioneer villages, historic buildings, museums, and art galleries); creating and running events and special meals; providing travel information services; and financing the development of community-

Many private campground operators feel that government should not be in the campground business. © 2009 Burcu Arat Sup. Used under license from Shutterstock, Inc.

oriented facilities (such as recreation and community halls, historical and cultural centers, and trail systems).

The most widely-accepted function of government in tourism development is as a stimulator or catalyst for development. Governments complement the efforts of the private sector and nonprofit organizations. The World Tourism Organization (UN-WTO) recommends as a general principle that governments should not try to do what the private sector is able and willing to do. Although this is a generally accepted principle in many countries, there are still many cases of overlapping activities and conflict between the government and the private sector. In some countries, the federal, state or provincial, and local governments are involved in the operation of parks, most of which include camping facilities. Many private campground operators feel that the government-operated facilities offer unfair competition and that the government should not be in the campground business. Another area of contention often found is in the provision of boat-docking facilities where both the private sector and government agencies operate competitive facilities. A further area of direct competition is that of government-owned airlines versus private air carriers.

There are several valid reasons behind the reversal in the government and private-sector roles in tourism development. The most important is that it is not always reasonable to expect tourism to develop in the manner and at the speed contemplated in the tourism plan if left entirely to the private sector. Government agencies often find themselves with a more direct role in tourism development for the reasons shown in figure 6.2.

Delivering a Country Brand

For the traveler, every in-country experience adds to or detracts from the overall impression of the destination. From the airport conditions, the simplicity of customs procedures and the cost of a cab to the ease of conducting business, the friendliness of the locals and the quality of the hotel service, a perception is being created about what the country is (or isn't) about.

COUNTRY BRAND INDEX 2008: Insights, Findings & Country Rankings, FutureBrand (2008), page 32

Due to profitability concerns, several provinces within Canada and states in the United States are directly involved in the resort business. These include the states of Indiana and Kentucky, where inns have been developed within certain state parks. In these parks, the inns are owned by the state government and are either operated by the state government or by the private sector through a management contract or lease arrangement.

The social tourism function of governments is a widely accepted phenomenon in several countries in Europe and elsewhere. For example, France has established a network of "village de vacances" (family-oriented resorts) and "gites familiaux" (family homes in resort settings) for its disadvantaged citizens.

Another major role of governments is as a regulator of tourism developments. Governments must ensure that developers follow all the laws, procedures, and codes in planning and constructing projects. This may mean that developers are required to conduct environmental impact analyses and to involve local residents in a process of consultation.

ROLE OF GOVERNMENT FINANCIAL INCENTIVES IN TOURISM DEVELOPMENT

One of the major hurdles that all tourism projects face is securing the financing needed for their development.

Ireland Has an Excellent Approach to Tourism Development

Fáilte Ireland, the National Tourism Development Authority was established under the National Tourism Development Authority Act, 2003 to guide and promote tourism as a leading indigenous component of the Irish economy. The organisation provides strategic and practical support to develop and sustain Ireland as a high-quality and competitive tourist destination. In this context, our mission is broadly: "To increase the contribution of tourism to the economy by facilitating the development of a competitive and profitable tourism industry."

Fáilte Ireland (2007), http://www.failteireland.ie/, accessed January 6, 2009

Bankruptcy
Existing tourism facility becomes bankrupt and cannot be sold on the market; the government is obliged to acquire the facility.

Pilots or Demonstration Projects
Government wants to encourage private-sector development by pioneering new types of development through "demonstration" or "pilot" projects.

Profitability Concerns
Private sector is unwilling to finance a project because of limited profit potential; the government has given this project a high priority due to its regional economic contributions or its pivotal role in stimulating tourism.

Social Tourism
Government wants to provide low-cost vacation opportunities for disadvantaged groups within the population, such as the poor, the sick, and the aged.

Figure 6.2 Reasons for Government Involvement in Tourism Operations.

Many tourism projects have been economically feasible but have not been developed because the developers were not able to attract the right amount or types of financing. The number of government agencies providing specific financial incentives for tourism projects has greatly increased on a worldwide basis. This is part of governments' role as stimulators of tourism development.

Government financial incentives for tourism projects can be classified into two broad categories. Fiscal incentives are special allowances for income tax or other tax purposes. Direct and indirect incentives constitute the second main category, and include a wide variety of programs aimed at easing the financing requirements

of projects. The basic objective of most of these incentive programs is to help businesses implement tourism development projects that, without assistance, may be abandoned or seriously delayed. On a global basis, all levels of government are involved in providing these types of incentive programs. Figure 6.3 provides a description of the types of financial incentive programs provided by government agencies to tourism development projects.

Because most government departments providing these financial incentives receive more applications for assistance than their budgets can handle, it is inevitable that not all projects that request monetary help receive it. In certain cases, this results in these projects not proceeding any further. A government agency involved in providing financial incentives, technical, or other assistance to individual tourism projects establishes a set of project selection criteria. These criteria assist the agency in identifying those projects that merit assistance and screening out other projects that are not as desirable. Typically, criteria fall into the categories shown in figure 6.4.

PRIVATE SECTOR FINANCING FOR TOURISM DEVELOPMENT

Although governments are playing a greater role in providing financing to tourism projects, it is the private sec-

Categories of Incentives	Types of Incentives
Fiscal Incentives	■ **Tax holidays or deferrals.** Government agency defers the payment of income taxes or other taxes for a predetermined time period. ■ **Remission of tariffs.** Government agency relaxes or removes import duties on goods and services required by the project. ■ **Tax reductions.** Government agency lowers the normal tax rates that would be paid by the project.
Direct and Indirect Incentives	■ **Nonrefundable grants.** Reduces a project's capital budget. ■ **Low-interest loans.** Reduces the amount of interest that the project must pay during its operating life. ■ **Interest rebates.** Government agency rebates a portion of the project's interest costs during its operating life. ■ **Forgivable loans.** Government agency loans funds to the project and then "forgives" all or part of these over an agreed-upon time period; this acts like a phased nonrefundable grant. ■ **Loan guarantees.** Government agency guarantees a loan given to a project by a private financial institution. ■ **Working capital loans.** Government agency loans funds to meet the working capital needs of a project. ■ **Equity participation.** Government agency purchases some of the available shares in the project, and becomes an equity investor. ■ **Training grants.** Government agency provides a nonrefundable grant to the project for staff training purposes. ■ **Infrastructure assistance.** Government agency assumes the costs of some or all of the infrastructure required for the project. ■ **Leasebacks.** Government agency purchases land, buildings, or equipment and then leases them to the project. ■ **Land donations.** Government agency donates land free of charge to the project.

Figure 6.3 Categories and Types of Government Incentives.

Tourism Development Incentives in Kentucky

The Commonwealth of Kentucky recognizes the tourism industry as a vital component to its economic well-being. To encourage the private development of tourism activities, the State of Kentucky provides financial incentives for approved projects. There are currently two incentive programs available for major tourism projects, the Kentucky Tourism Development Act and Tax Increment Financing.

Kentucky Tourism Development Act
This legislation is the first of its kind in the nation and provides the opportunity for developers of approved projects to recover up to 25 percent of their development costs over a ten-year period. While other states have attempted to duplicate this legislation, none have experienced the success of Kentucky. Projects utilizing the program include a $32 million aquarium, a $100 million speedway, and a $4 million glass artisan's facility, among others. This program has encouraged the development of privately owned tourism attractions having investments totaling in excess of $372 million.

The Act defines eligible projects (tourism attractions) as:

- Cultural or historical sites
- Recreation or entertainment facilities
- Areas of scenic beauty or distinctive natural phenomena
- Entertainment destination centers
- Kentucky crafts and products centers
- Theme restaurant destination attractions
- Lodging, when any of the following are applicable:
  - Built in conjunction with a tourism attraction and the tourism attraction costs more than the lodging facility
  - Built on state or federal parks and recreational lands
  - Involves restoration or rehabilitation of a historic structure
  - Involves the restoration, rehabilitation, or upgrading of lodging facilities having no less than five hundred rooms with project costs exceeding $10 million

Projects that do not qualify are strictly retail businesses and recreational facilities that are used primarily by local residents and are not a likely destination for out-of-state travelers.

Tax Increment Financing
For projects of a larger scale, Kentucky continues to show its support through Tax Increment Financing. This program provides the developer of an approved project the ability to recoup up to 25 percent of their project costs over a twenty-year period. Two projects totaling $200 million have received approval under this legislation.

Boating is a major tourism and recreational activity on Kentucky's lakes. © 2009 Anne Kitzman. Used under license from Shutterstock, Inc.

Projects applying for benefit under the Tax Increment Financing legislation must meet the following requirements:

- Be a tourism attraction or recreational or commercial facility.
- Represent new economic activity in the Commonwealth.
- Have a minimum capital investment of $10 million.
- Create no less than twenty-five new full-time jobs for Kentucky residents.
- Have a net positive economic impact for the State of Kentucky.
- Generate no less than 25 percent of its annual revenues through out-of-state visitors.
- Result in a unique contribution to or preservation of the economic vitality and quality of life of a region of the Commonwealth.
- Be not primarily devoted to the retail sale of goods.

(continued)

Competitive Impact
Project complements, rather than competes with, existing tourism businesses and does not seriously jeopardize the financial viability of any individual business.

Compliance with Policies and Plans
Project complies with the destination's tourism policies and plans.

Developer and Operator Capabilities
Project developers and operators are capable of successfully developing and operating the business.

Economic Contributions
Project creates significant levels of income and employment benefits.

Environmental Impacts
Project is developed in compliance with existing legislation and regulations governing the conservation and protection of the environment (sustainability guidelines).

Equity Contributions
Where the project is profit making, the investors have sufficient equity to inject into the venture.

Feasibility
Where the project is profit making, it is economically feasible.

Sociocultural Impact
Project does not jeopardize the social well-being of local residents.

Tourism Impact
Project adds to the destination's tourism potential by creating an attraction, by improving the area's capacity to receive and cater to visitors, or by being beneficial to tourism in some other way.

Figure 6.4 Criteria for Government Financial Assistance.

Ghana's Tourism Developments Have a Clear Purpose
Tourism development in Ghana is comprehensively aimed at a broad and desirable range of domestic, sub-regional African and international tourists. The Government is pursuing quality tourism development that is internationally competitive and compatible with Ghana's social values and environmental setting. It aims to attract tourists, who show respect for the country's history and environment. Emphasis is placed on tourism to help in the conservation of the country's historical and environmental heritage. Apart from the economic benefits, tourism is used to present Ghana's unique cultural, historical and environmental heritage to the international community and to educate Ghanaians about their own heritage. The government intends to use tourism as an alternative development strategy to help address broad national issues.

Business & Investment, *Ghana Tourism (2009),*
http://www.touringghana.com/investments/index.asp,
accessed January 6, 2009

tor that supplies the majority of the financing. These private sources range from individual citizens to major institutional lenders such as banks, trust companies, credit unions, insurance companies, and other commercial finance companies. Typically, a private financing source requires that the following five criteria be met before lending money to tourism developers:

1. Previous management experience in tourism and an established credit record within the management development team

2. Proof of economic feasibility via an independent economic feasibility study
3. Adequate collateral or security for the funds to be borrowed
4. Adequate equity invested by the owners of the project
5. Proof of stability in the tourism destination in which the project will operate

Tourism development projects require equity from owners and investors as well as borrowed capital (debt). These individuals are the true "risk takers" in the development, and they are rewarded with profits for a return on their investments. Not all projects are able to secure the types and amounts of private financing that they require, although they may have successfully survived all of the earlier screening mechanisms.

ANALYSIS OF INDIVIDUAL PROJECT DEVELOPMENT OPPORTUNITIES

Individual project development opportunities in tourism are either generated through the tourism planning process or by the private sector independent of this process. In destinations without tourism plans, governments may also be involved in identifying development opportunities for private-sector investment. Although these development opportunities can have the potential of satisfying tourism planning goals and considerable initial appeal to those in the private sector, they may be undesirable due to financial, environmental, social, cultural, or other reasons. All individual tourism project development opportunities must be carefully analyzed before proceeding with construction.

There are many types of tourism project development opportunities. Projects differ in their ability to generate financial profits. Projects such as hotels and commercial attractions are inherent profit-generators. Profit-generating projects are analyzed in economic feasibility studies. Other projects, such as travel informa-

tion centers and infrastructure, generate no direct financial returns. However, these projects are essential to an area's destination mix. Other projects are the subject of cost/benefit analyses or other types of contribution analysis studies. Some tourism projects involve building construction (superstructure) or the development of transportation and essential public services (infrastructure); others require only human resources and equipment (such as guided canoe or ecotourism trips).

Despite differences in the tourism project ingredients, individual project opportunities can be analyzed by using similar techniques. Figure 6.5 shows a tourism project evaluation system. There are several decision points in project analysis in which further consideration of a tourism development project may be terminated. These include:

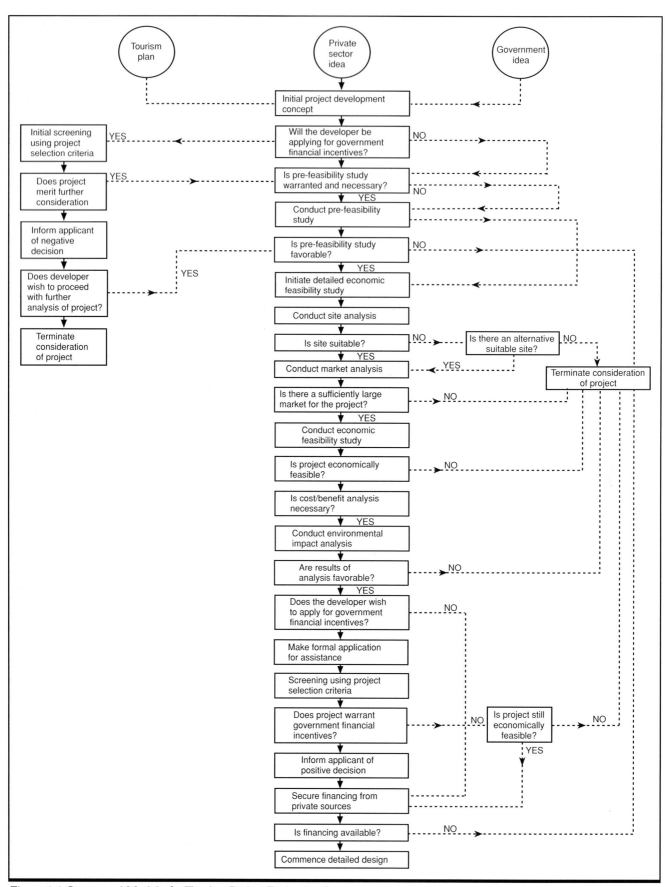

Figure 6.5 Conceptual Model of a Tourism Project Evaluation System.

- A pre-feasibility study produces negative results.
- The site for the project is unsuitable and no alternative site is available.
- The market analysis indicates that the market is not large enough to support the project.
- The project is not economically feasible.
- The environmental, social or cultural impacts are unacceptable.
- The results of a cost/benefit analysis are negative.
- The government decides the project does not qualify for financial assistance and it is not feasible without these government incentives.
- Sufficient financing from the private sector cannot be secured.

PRE-FEASIBILITY STUDY

A pre-feasibility study determines whether a detailed economic feasibility study is justified and which topics this detailed study should address. Because detailed economic feasibility studies are costly and time-consuming, pre-feasibility studies can be extremely valuable to developers. The objectives of a pre-feasibility study are to determine whether:

- The information available is adequate to show the project will not be viable or will not be attractive to investors or lenders.
- The information available indicates that the project is so promising that an investment decision can be made on the basis of the pre-feasibility study itself; that is, a detailed study is not needed.
- A preliminary assessment of potential environmental, social or cultural impacts shows that these potential impacts are significant and unacceptable to the local community.
- Aspects of the project are so critical to its viability that they must be analyzed as part of the detailed economic feasibility study.
- The availability of factors critical to the viability of the project (such as the availability of a specific site) must be confirmed prior to doing a detailed economic feasibility study.

Pre-feasibility studies can be completed by private developers, by government agencies considering financing projects, or by private consulting organizations on behalf of the developers or government agencies. In some cases, the tourism development component of the tourism planning process produces pre-feasibility analyses of key tourism project development opportunities.

DETAILED ECONOMIC FEASIBILITY STUDY

If a project survives the pre-feasibility screening, it should then be analyzed through a detailed economic feasibility study. The majority of tourism development project economic feasibility studies are carried out by private consulting organizations on behalf of private developers, investors, or government agencies, or a combination of these parties.

Although many successful tourism development projects have been developed without detailed economic feasibility studies, as have many that have not proven successful, these analyses are vital to many people involved in the development process including the developers, investors, potential lenders, and government agencies. Other players involved in the process may include management companies interested in operating the projects on behalf of the developers and investors under management contracts or leases. The potential lenders may fall into two groups: those providing the construction (interim) financing, and those providing the long-term (permanent) financing.

An economic feasibility study is a study to determine the economic feasibility of a tourism development project opportunity. A project is economically feasible if it provides a rate of return acceptable to the investors in the project. A market study is one component of an economic feasibility study which analyzes the project's market potential. Because of the need to acquire an unbiased opinion on a project's viability, economic feasibility studies are prepared by an independent third party and not by the developers, investors, or the potential lenders. Many lenders, including both private financial institutions and government agencies providing financial assistance programs, require that these independent studies be completed before they will seriously consider projects.

An economic feasibility study is designed to answer the questions, shown in figure 6.6, that are of concern to the participants in the development process. The economic feasibility study has another important use for developers. It produces recommendations on the scale, sizes, facility types, and quality levels of operation. These recommendations are based upon the size and expectations of the market from the market study. At a later date in the development process, these findings will be used as the basis for the architect's preliminary drawings.

SITE ANALYSIS. Although not all tourism development project opportunities require physical site loca-

Developers and Investors

- Which of several alternative site locations is the most appropriate?
- Is a specific site appropriate for the development?
- If not, is there another site available that would be suitable?
- Is market demand large enough to support the project?
- What are the optimum scale and components of the project?
- What style of operation and quality levels should be provided?
- What revenues and expenses will the project experience?
- What will the capital costs be?
- Will the project produce a satisfactory return on investment?
- Should the developers and investors proceed with further analysis?

Lenders

- All of the above questions should be of concern to the lenders, and:
  - How much money will be loaned to the developers and investors?
  - Do the developers and investors have sufficient equity to invest in the project, given the financing required?
  - Will the project produce sufficient operating profits and cash flow to cover the interest and principal payments when they become due?

Figure 6.6 Questions Addressed in a Feasibility Study.

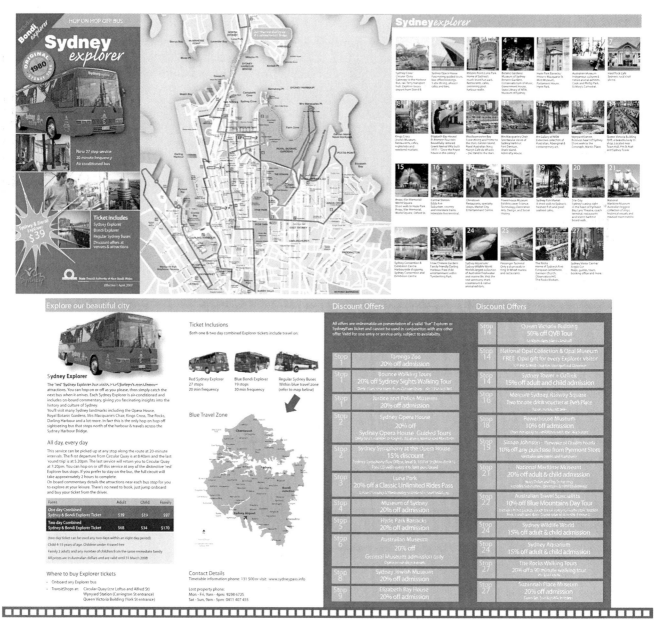

The Sydney Explorer bus service is an important tourism development.

What Questions Should a Feasibility Study Answer?

According to Gary R. Warnell at Michigan State University, a feasibility study is a tool that addresses the question, "Will the expected returns from a proposed venture be sufficient to justify the initial investment?" However, the Office of the Governor Economic Development & Tourism in Texas puts the questions answered in a feasibility study into a wider business planning context in its *Tourism Tip Sheet: Developing a Tourism Related Business*. This document identifies ten "mileposts" or sequential steps for the tourism project developer:

1. Establishing a vision
2. Concept planning
3. Site requirements and site selection
4. Feasibility study
5. The business plan
6. Operations plan
7. Marketing plan
8. Partnership plan
9. Finance plan
10. Implementation

The feasibility study should determine the expected return on investment in a tourism development project. © 2009 Arne Trautmann. Used under license from Shutterstock, Inc.

It defines a feasibility study as a tool that answers the question if a project "is capable of achieving financial success based upon a financial, market, and site analysis."

The government in Bulgaria requires the developers to answer the following five broader questions in a study of project feasibility:

1. What is the tourism potential of the area (location, attraction)?
2. What is the current level of tourism development in the location and surrounding area?
3. How important is tourism for the social and economic development of the location and the surrounding area?
4. What are the potential markets for the area, how will the location/area be promoted, and what trends are foreseen?
5. What impacts will the project have on further development of the area and how will its sustainability be ensured?

THINK ABOUT THIS:

1. How do these questions and steps differ from those outlined in this chapter?
2. How do the five broader questions suggested by the government in Bulgaria help with tourism planning in destinations?
3. How should the developers create a vision for their project?

Sources:

Ministry of Regional Development and Public Works, Republic of Bulgaria. 2005. http://www.mrrb.government.bg/pdocs/doc_1192.doc.

Office of the Governor Economic Development & Tourism, Texas. 2004. *Tourism Tip Sheet: Developing a Tourism Related Business*.

Warnell, G. R. 2002. *Feasibility analysis in tourism*. Michigan State University Extension Service.

tions, a very large proportion do. An economic feasibility study can either specify a site (site specific), if a specific site location has been chosen for the project, or determine if an appropriate site exists within a given geographic area.

A tourism project site usually requires specific characteristics to be successful. This is not true of all sectors of an economy, as there are many "footloose" enterprises that are not location-dependent. In tourism, location has an extremely important bearing upon financial viability.

A hotel in the city should be close to tourist or business attractions, such as shopping or convention centers. © 2009 Zsolt Nyulaszi. Used under license from Shutterstock, Inc.

The characteristics or criteria for site selection and evaluation vary with the type of tourism project under consideration. For example, a proposed new alpine ski area is dependent on the snow conditions and slope characteristics in a given location, while an urban hotel requires proximity to a concentration of industry and commerce. Similarly, a motor hotel requires ease of access and proximity to highways, while the placement of tennis courts is dictated by the wind and sun conditions at the site. The first step in the site analysis is to identify the criteria that are crucial to the project. Tourism development project site criteria or characteristics can be divided into three categories:

- Market-related criteria
- Physical characteristics
- Other criteria

Figure 6.7 provides a master list of individual criteria within each of these categories. The identification of the most important site characteristics for a project is crucial. This requires a familiarity and experience

Criteria	Site Characteristics	Site Characteristics
Market-Related Criteria	**Proximity and Accessibility to:** ■ Attractions and events ■ Competitors ■ Facilities (accommodations, restaurants, shopping) ■ Potential visitor markets ■ Transportation facilities	**Visibility:** ■ If required, is site visible to potential visitors? ■ If required, is site sufficiently private?
Physical Characteristics	**Aesthetics:** ■ Adjoining lands and land uses ■ Focal points ■ Noise ■ Scale ■ Variety (features, forms, colors) ■ Views **Geology and Geomorphology:** ■ Bedrock type ■ Geologic history ■ Water-table level and quality ■ Infrastructure availability: —Energy sources —Sewage disposal system —Transportation facilities and systems —Water supply (drainage and flooding problems, lakes and seas, natural springs, rivers and streams, waterfalls and cascades) **Natural Conditions:** ■ Ability to support specific types of recreational activities ■ Climate and micro-climate (humidity, precipitation, purity of air, seasons, sunshine and clouds, temperatures, winds)	**Soils and Topography:** ■ Depths ■ Slopes ■ Soil types ■ Vegetation: —Clearing problems —Ground cover type —Tree types —Visual and physical condition **Wildlife and Fish:** ■ Effects of development on these ■ Species and types **Other Site Characteristics:** ■ Dimensions and shape ■ Geographical orientation ■ Height above sea level ■ Length of shoreline ■ Rights of way and easements
Other Criteria	■ Availability of a suitable quality of land for project ■ Availability of staff accommodation ■ Cost of land ■ Labor laws and labor relations history ■ Manpower availability	■ Social and economic characteristics of host area ■ Sources and types of financial assistance in host area ■ Zoning laws and other government regulations

Figure 6.7 Master List of Site Selection Criteria.

with the particular project type, and a broad knowledge of construction and site engineering. Ideally, a multidisciplinary team consisting of a specialized tourism consultant, engineer, environmental and social impact experts, landscape architect, and architect should be used.

When a specific site has not been selected, a "long list" of potentially suitable sites is identified and these sites are ranked on their compatibility with the project. This ranking can be done by attaching a weighting factor to each site selection characteristic and giving each site a numerical score for that characteristic. The weighting factor reflects the relative importance of each site characteristic, and the numerical score (say on a 0 to 10 basis) indicates the quality or quantity of that characteristic for the site. The multiplication of the weighting factor and the numerical score provides a final score for each characteristic at each alternative site. The final scores for all characteristics are added to give a total score for each alternative site. The most appropriate site for the project is the one earning the highest total score.

The evaluation of sites for certain tourism projects requires a high degree of specific technical expertise. Generally, these projects are highly dependent on the characteristics of the natural resource base and have high construction costs, such as alpine skiing areas and large full-service marina projects. Private organizations specializing in site evaluations for projects are normally contracted to perform these analyses.

An economic feasibility study may be terminated after the site analysis if an essential site characteristic is missing or if some insurmountable legal or zoning restriction or other barrier to development is found. The study moves on to the market analysis if this is not the case.

Market Analysis. The market analysis portion of an economic feasibility study is often the most costly and time-consuming element. The costs and time required are dependent on the mix of primary and secondary research conducted. Secondary research is the analysis of available, published sources of information and is far less expensive than primary research. Market surveys aimed at producing new information and conclusions for the project are classified as primary research. Although pre-feasibility studies are often based only on secondary research, detailed economic feasibility studies must contain a mixture of both secondary and primary research.

The market analysis starts with the collection and review of secondary sources of information since this

provides a clearer focus on the type and scope of primary market research needed. With the growing attention being given to tourism on a worldwide basis, the amount of available tourism research is enormous. An analysis of secondary sources in tourism can be time-consuming and exhausting, unless the researcher knows about the major tourism journals, reference centers, libraries, and online sources of information.

When the review of secondary sources of information is complete, a primary research plan is drawn up and implemented. This may involve conducting a variety of surveys. It requires that the researchers have a thorough understanding of marketing research techniques. The survey methods include:

- Questionnaires (personal interview, telephone, mail, fax, online, or self-administered)
- Focus group
- Delphi method

Questionnaires are the most frequently used instruments in tourism project feasibility studies. Researchers direct their questions to potential visitors or to the managers of competitive or similar operations. In the latter case, the questions are aimed at gathering information on the facilities and services offered, and on the existing market volumes and characteristics through such competitive performance statistics as room occupancy rates or attendance figures. The common factor in all questionnaires is that they require responses (written or oral) to questions (written or oral). The three major advantages of questionnaires are versatility, speed, and cost. Questionnaires are versatile because almost every research problem can be addressed, including the respondent's knowledge, opinions, motivations, and intentions. The use of questionnaires is usually faster and cheaper than the observational method of research. The observational method is a process of observing and studying the behavior of people, objects, and occurrences rather than of questioning people to get the same information.

Telephone surveys have higher response rates than mail surveys.
© 2009 Andresr. Used under license from Shutterstock, Inc.

The questionnaire method has recognized limitations. Respondents may be unwilling to provide the information. They may not agree to be interviewed or refuse to answer specific questions. Mail surveys typically have low response rates with sometimes as many as 90 percent of the questionnaires not being returned. Skilled and experienced researchers can bring the response rates up to 40 percent or more. Personal and telephone surveys have higher response rates. A second disadvantage of questionnaires is that the respondent may be willing to cooperate but is unable to provide accurate answers to some questions. For example, the respondents may not have thought through their motivations for particular purchases or activities. A third limitation of questionnaires is that the respondent may intentionally supply incorrect or inaccurate information. Some respondents may give the types of answers that they think the researchers want, or they may deliberately give misleading information. Others may answer in a particular way so as not to be embarrassed or to have their egos damaged. Respondents may also wrongly interpret the meanings of particular questions and may give less than satisfactory answers.

Broad-scale questionnaire surveys, although relatively inexpensive when compared to other market research techniques, can be very expensive if they are conducted at the individual household level. This is particularly true if the potential users reside in countries distant from the destination area. Unlike consumer product research, market research using broad-scale questionnaires may encounter difficulties in determining the exact geographical origins of potential users of a

> The relationship between politics and tourism is not primarily concerned with political parties and elections and their influence on tourism policy, although this is, of course, an aspect of the politics of tourism. The study of politics is inexorably the study of power.
>
> Hall, C. M. (1994),
> Tourism and Politics, 2

tourism project and their relative proportions. Because there are these problems in defining the statistical universe, it is also extremely difficult to accurately state what the size and structure of a sample should be.

Due to the unique challenges in conducting surveys of potential users of proposed tourism projects, it is common to survey people in the channels of distribution (retail travel agents, tour wholesalers, and tour operators) and other travel decision-makers (such as convention-meeting planners, corporate travel managers, and association executives) or to utilize the focus group or Delphi methods as a supplement to questionnaire surveys.

The focus-group method involves bringing together a small group of people (ideally eight to twelve) in one place and asking them to focus upon the research topic. The research team supplies an experienced focus group moderator. The objectives of these sessions are to get the group to reach consensus on questions posed by the moderator. The focus group can be drawn from householders in general, or each participant may have common characteristics, such as being convention-meeting planners, retail travel agents, tour operators, tour wholesalers, or club executives. Because focus-group participants tend to interact with one another and because there is a greater opportunity to explore individual preferences and attitudes, this method overcomes some of the drawbacks of questionnaires. Focus-group participants are often prescreened before being invited to the meetings.

The Delphi method is often used for forecasting and futures exercises in tourism, but it can also be applied to a tourism development project. It can also be called the "knowledgeable panel" method since it involves recruiting a team of experts on a particular topic. The team acts as a sounding board on alternative approaches, ideas, or concepts. The Delphi group participants do not have to meet in person, but each one is required to give responses to a variety of written propositions prepared by the researchers, such as "What probability do you attach to this resort succeeding at this location?" (Provide a probability percentage between 0 percent and 100 percent.)

Another type of research that has been used for some tourism projects is analogy research. This does not involve any surveying of potential visitors; it means doing detailed research on the performance of comparable (or analogous) operations. By studying the success of comparable projects, conclusions are drawn on the likely success of the proposed project. Because many factors contribute to a tourism business' success, analogy research must be applied with great caution.

In economic feasibility studies, it is often necessary to forecast demand for either the project itself or for the destination area in general, or for both. There are many forecasting techniques available to the researcher. Forecasts are divided into time spans that are considered to be accurate. There is general agreement that there are four basic forecasting horizons: short-term (one day to two years), medium-term (between two and five years), long-term (between five and fifteen years), and futurism (over fifteen years). For example, the extrapolation method is thought only to be useful for short-term forecasts, while correlation techniques are considered to be good for short-, medium-, and long-term forecasting.

The forecasting of potential market demand for a project usually covers the medium-term to long-term forecasts, that is, the initial five to fifteen years of operation. This seems appropriate since the critical financial years of a purely commercial project are its first one to ten years. Most commercial tourism projects are expected to reach their full financial and operating potential within their first five years of operation and to pay back their investor's equity within ten years. Also the present value concept dictates that the earlier the financial returns are received from a project the greater is their contribution to economic feasibility.

The actual forecasting of potential demand levels for a tourism development project can be approached through several different methods (figure 6.8). It is advisable to use two or more of the methods shown in figure 6.8 and then to cross-check their results. Once a technically acceptable potential market demand forecast has been developed, an initial judgment can be made as to whether the market is of sufficient size with the appropriate characteristics to support the project. This requires considerable experience with the business type being considered. It has to be very clear that the potential demand levels are large enough to make the project viable. For example, if a hotel requires an annual occupancy percentage of 70 percent to be viable, and the potential demand generates an occupancy rate of only 30 percent in the project's fifth year, the proposed hotel will not be viable. In most cases, this judgment is not so obvious, and more analysis needs to be done to determine if the demand levels justify the investment.

ECONOMIC FEASIBILITY ANALYSIS. The economic feasibility analysis determines if a tourism development project can produce a satisfactory financial return for investors. It is composed of the following seven steps:

Alternative Scenario
Uses either the calculation, market share/penetration, or survey/potential demand quantification methods and produces optimistic, realistic, and pessimistic scenarios of potential demand levels.

Analogy
Assumes that the project will achieve certain demand levels based upon the known performances and penetration levels of similar projects elsewhere.

Calculation
Projects potential demand by using "rules-of-thumb" or consumer expenditures and behavior patterns.

Market Share or Market Penetration
Calculates total market demand and the project's share of total demand by using information from competitive facilities, historic demand growth rates, and anticipated future occurrences, or other forecasting techniques.

Survey and Potential Demand
Quanitifies total potential demand by using the results from questionnaire or other survey methods, by "grossing up" from the sample size taken.

Figure 6.8 Forecasting Methods and Approaches.

1. Project description: The components, scale and sizes, and quality levels required to capture the potential market demand
2. Pricing: The unit prices and rates to be charged
3. Revenues: The market demand levels multiplied by unit prices and rates
4. Expenses and profits: The operating expenses and profits
5. Capital costs: The capital budget (or total required investment) for the project
6. Cash flow: The capital expenses, net income, and cash flow
7. ROI: The rate of return on investment

The forecasts of potential market demand and the desires and expectations of people interviewed provide the key inputs for detailing the project concept. The project concept describes the components, scale, sizes, and quality levels of facilities and services needed to satisfy the potential demand. Unit prices and rates are then prepared.

The next two steps are referred to as the production of forecast or *pro forma* income statements indicating the estimated revenues, operating expenses, and operating profits for the project. When estimating revenues, the total potential demand is broken down into segments, and the applicable unit prices and rates are multiplied by the resulting volumes in each segment. The operating expenses include the costs of operating the project, such as the cost of food and other merchandise for resale, labor, marketing, energy, and repairs and maintenance. Publications containing average business performance statistics can be helpful in estimating these operating costs. Greater individual accuracy occurs when the forecaster is familiar with the type of business under consideration, and when detailed staffing schedules and other operating standards are developed for the project.

There are other ongoing expenses that the project will encounter, and these all relate to the capital investment in the development. To estimate these expenses requires that a capital budget be prepared first. A capital budget is a detailed, itemized forecast of the capital investment required by the project. For a tourism development project, these costs include building construction, professional fees, infrastructure, recreational facilities, furniture, fixtures and equipment, interim financing, contingencies, and miscellaneous other items. The most realistic capital budgets are produced by a multi-disciplinary team consisting of specialized tourism consultants, civil engineers, quantity surveyors, interior designers, architects, and landscape architects. The capital budget is prepared by identifying all of the capital costs that will be encountered, and then pricing each item. A contingency factor, normally between 10 and 20 percent, is added to cover unforeseen cost overruns or overlooked items. Once the capital budget is complete, the capital-related expenses for the project are calculated. These expenses include financing charges on long-term debt, depreciation, municipal/local government taxes, and insurance premiums on fixed assets. The capital-related expenses are deducted from the operating profits to give net income figures (after tax

profit) and cash flow forecasts. The net income and cash flow projections cover the useful life of the project.

One or more financial analysis techniques are used to measure the rate of return produced by these forecast net income and cash flow levels. Most experts in the field favor present value yardsticks that use the discounted cash flow (DCF) method, especially the net present value (NPV) and internal rate of return (IRR) techniques. The present value concept implies that money has a time value. Thus, a dollar, euro, or pound received today is worth more than a dollar, euro, or pound received a year from now, since the cash received today can be reinvested to produce a higher overall return. With present value methods, the cash received in profits in the earlier years are more valuable than those earned in later years. Both the NPV and IRR techniques use cash flow figures as a basis for projections and discount the value of future cash flows at certain assumed rates of return. Based upon the rates of return predicted, a decision is made as to whether the tourism development project is economically feasible. If the rate is less than what the investors require, the project is not economically feasible.

The positive impact of government financial incentives upon a project's economic feasibility has not been discussed. Many tourism projects, which are not economically feasible with only private-sector financing, are developed because of the injection of government financial assistance. These incentives increase the rates of return for investors by reducing the interest burden on projects or reducing financing costs in some other way. In many cases, the increases are great enough to change a project into a feasible venture. However, if a project is not feasible and there is no possibility of receiving government financial assistance, it will probably be terminated at this point.

COST/BENEFIT ANALYSIS

Profit-making projects that are found to be economically feasible may or may not have to be further analyzed using cost/benefit analysis. Cost/benefit analyses are useful for evaluating noncommercial tourism projects that generate no direct revenues or that have, at best, operating revenues equaling operating expenses. Cost/benefit analyses are done by or on behalf of government agencies. They help these agencies measure and weigh all of the costs and benefits of alternative projects. The agencies are then able to determine which project will produce the largest net economic benefits for society as a whole.

A proposed casino may have great potential for financial return, but a government may decide the social costs are too high. © 2009 Monkey Business Images. Used under license from Shutterstock, Inc.

Economic feasibility analyses are just one aspect of cost/benefit analysis. There are several financial analyses or capital budgeting techniques available that permit comparisons between alternative projects. In purely financial terms, the project that creates the highest rate of return for its investors is the best alternative. However, from a government viewpoint, the size of the return on private investors' capital cannot be the only criterion for support. A government agency has broad-scale economic, environmental, social, and cultural responsibilities that have to be considered before giving financial assistance or other support to a project. For example, a proposed casino may generate spectacular returns for investors, but a government agency may feel that such a project will undermine the social well-being of the destination area.

A cost/benefit analysis attempts to weigh the quantifiable and nonquantifiable costs and benefits of a tourism project against each other. Some subjectivity and judgment has to enter into this because there can be no single measurement or set of measurements of a project's overall worth to a destination area. Assuming that the cost/benefit analysis results are positive, the project can progress to the next level of evaluation. Some project developers may wish to apply for government financial assistance, while others may go ahead without such assistance.

ENVIRONMENTAL IMPACT ANALYSIS

The purpose of an environmental impact assessment (EIA) is to identify in advance factors that may affect the ability to build a proposed tourism development and the environmental attributes that will be affected by the development (Manning and Dougherty, 1995). Three objectives of an EIA are (Ecologically Sustainable Development Working Group, 1991):

1. Identify risks, minimize adverse impacts, and determine environmental acceptability
2. Achieve environmentally-sound proposals through research, management, and monitoring
3. Manage conflict through the provision of a means for effective public participation

Many countries require that EIAs be conducted before final government approval is given. These analyses are usually paid for by the developers and conducted by expert consultants. The consultants attempt to predict and evaluate the impact of the tourism development project on various environmental attributes (e.g., beaches and coastlines, wetlands, flora, and fauna). They also recommend environmental safeguards that must be taken to ensure that the development does not cause the adverse impacts that have been predicted. Governments often require that the developer and their consultants establish a process of public input into the EIA.

There is growing public concern for the impact of developments on the environment. Around the world, several proposed tourism projects have been vigorously opposed by conservation and other interest groups. So great has been the protests that the developers have given up on the projects. There can be no doubt that these types of public opposition on environmental grounds will continue in the future as society becomes more environmentally sensitive. This will place an even greater premium on careful planning by developers and the adoption of "best environmental practices."

Tennessee Cares about Sustainable Tourism Development

The State of Tennessee is committed to a Sustainable Tourism effort to preserve and protect our state's unsurpassed natural beauty while encouraging the growth of the tourism industry in Tennessee.

Tennessee Department of Tourist Development (2009), http://www.tnvacation.com/sustainable/, accessed January 6, 2009

DETAILED DESIGN AND CONSTRUCTION

In the final stages of realizing a tourism development project, various levels of architectural designs and drawings are prepared. Normally, this procedure includes:

- Preparation of preliminary architectural concepts
- Preparation of a preliminary architectural design
- Preparation of a final architectural design
- Construction

At each of the first three stages, the drawings become increasingly more detailed and exact. When the final drawings have been approved, the project moves into construction.

SUMMARY

The tourism plan for a destination area provides overall guidelines for development, and identifies project development opportunities worthy of more in-depth analysis through economic feasibility studies, cost/benefit analyses, and environmental impact assessments. Governments play a key role in ensuring that developers abide by the overall guidelines and the broad development concepts are realized. Government agencies are also playing an ever-increasing role in stimulating the development of tourism project opportunities through many types of financial incentive programs.

Only a small proportion of tourism project development opportunities actually reach the construction stage, as most are unable to meet certain criteria or to secure the necessary financing. Many are screened out because they are not economically feasible or due to environmental impacts that are expected to be adverse and unacceptable.

Trends

Development Trends in Sectors of Tourism

1. Cruise lines are continuously adding new amenities and facilities in their new ships (e.g., Internet service, climbing walls, skating rinks).
2. Passenger railway systems are adding more high-speed train services.
3. Aircraft are getting bigger and faster (e.g., Airbus A380).
4. Lodging companies are increasingly using brand extensions supported by online retail merchandising (e.g., Westin's Heavenly Bed®).
5. Canal systems around the world are being transformed for more tourism and leisure use.
6. Ferry companies are adding larger and more modern vessels.
7. More indoor waterpark resorts are being developed.
8. Restaurants are increasingly being co-branded and placed in different types of locations.
9. Airports are placing greater attention on retail shopping areas and other passenger services.
10. Buses and motor coaches have increasing comfort and sophistication.

Source: Morrison, A. M. 2009. *Hospitality and Travel Marketing*, 4th ed. Clifton Park, NY: Delmar.

ACTIVITIES

1. You are asked to prepare an economic feasibility study on a new tourism development project in your area. What are the major steps that you would include in this economic feasibility study?
2. What printed secondary sources of information would be the most useful in doing this study?
3. What primary research would you consult in preparing the study (e.g., surveys, focus groups)?

INTERNET
ACTIVITIES

4. How would you use the Internet to gather information on the potential markets for the new tourism development project?
5. Identify up to five comparable projects that you could analyze online that would provide good benchmark information for your project. Analyze these comparable projects and prepare your results.
6. How would you use the Internet to get information on the likely capital costs of this project?

REFERENCES

Bramwell, B. 1991. Sustainability and rural tourism policy in Britain. *Tourism Recreation Research*, 16 (2): 49–51.

Butler, R. W. 1993. *Pre- and Post-Impact Assessment of Tourism Development*. Tourism research: Critiques and challenges. New York: Routledge. 135–155.

Cater, E. 1993. Ecotourism in the Third World: Problems for sustainable tourism development. *Tourism Management*, 14: 85–90.

Ding, P., and J. Pigram. 1995. Environmental audits: An emerging concept in sustainable tourism development. *Journal of Tourism Studies*, 6 (2): 2–10.

Doggart, C., and N. Doggart. 1996. Environmental impacts of tourism in developing countries. *Travel & Tourism Analyst*, (2): 71–86.

Ecologically Sustainable Development Working Group. 1991. *Final Report: Tourism*. Canberra: Australian Government Publishing Service.

Gartner, W. C. 1996. *Tourism Development: Principles, Processes, and Policies*. New York: Van Nostrand Reinhold.

Glasson, J., K. Godfrey, and N. Goodey. 1995. *Towards Visitor Impact Management*. Aldershot, England: Avebury.

Gunn, C. A. 1994. *Tourism Planning: Basics, Concepts, Cases*, 3rd ed. Washington, DC: Taylor & Francis.

Hall, C. M. 1994. *Tourism and Politics: Policy, Power and Place*. Chichester, England: John Wiley & Sons, Inc.

Harrison, D. (ed.). 1992. *Tourism & the Less Developed Countries*. London: Bellhaven Press.

Inskeep, E., and M. Kallenberger. 1992. *An Integrated Approach to Resort Development: Six Case Studies*. Madrid: World Tourism Organization.

Ioannides, D. 1995. The flawed implementation of sustainable tourism: The experience of Akamas, Cyprus. *Tourism Management*, 8: 583–592.

Jurdana, D. S., and Z. Susilovic. 2006. Planning city tourism deveopment: principles and issues. *Tourism and Hospitality Management*, 12 (2): 135–144.

Kersten, A. 1997. *Community Based Ecotourism and Community Building: The Case of the Lacandones (Chiapas)*. http://txinfinet.com/mader/planeta/0597/0597lacandon.html.

Khadaroo, J., and B. Seetanah. 2008. The role of transport infrastructure in international tourism development: A gravity model approach. *Tourism Management*, 29: 831–840.

Lane, H. E., and D. Dupré. 1997. *Hospitality World: An Introduction*. New York: Van Nostrand Reinhold.

Laws, E. 1995. *Tourist Destination Management: Issues, Analysis and Policies*. London: Routledge.

Lindberg, K., and D. E. Hawkins (v. 2). 1998. *Ecotourism: A Guide for Planners & Managers*. North Bennington, VT: The Ecotourism Society.

Lundberg, D. E., M. H. Stavenga, and M. Krishnamoorthy. 1995. *Tourism Economics*. New York: John Wiley & Sons, Inc.

Mann, S. 2005. *Development through Tourism: The World Bank's Role*. Washington, DC: World Bank.

Manning, E. W., and T. D. Dougherty. 1995. Sustainable tourism: Preserving the golden goose. *Cornell Hotel and Restaurant Administration Quarterly*, 36 (2): 29–42.

Mathieson, A., and G. Wall. 1982. *Tourism: Economic, Physical, and Social Impacts*. New York: Longman Scientific & Technical.

McIntyre, G. 1993. *Sustainable Tourism Development: Guide for Local Planners*. Madrid: World Tourism Organization.

Moscardo, G. M., A. M. Morrison, and P. L. Pearce. 1996. Specialist accommodation and ecologically sustainable tourism. *Journal of Sustainable Tourism*, 4 (1): 29–52.

Pearce, D. 1992. *Tourist Organizations*. Essex, England: Longman Group U.K.

Peet, R., and E. Hartwick. 1999. *Theories of Development*. New York: Guilford Press.

Prideaux, B. 2000. The role of the transport system in destination development. *Tourism Management*, 21: 53–63.

Sharpley, R., and D. Telfer. 2002. *Tourism and Development: Concepts and Issues*. London: Channel View.

Smith, V. L., and W. R. Eadington (eds.). 1992. *Tourism Alternatives: Potentials and Problems in the Development of Tourism*. Philadelphia: University of Pennsylvania Press.

Swarbrooke, J. 2002. *The Development & Management of Visitor Attractions*, 2nd ed. Oxford: Butterworth-Heinemann.

Vellas, F., and L. Becherel. 1995. *International Tourism*. New York: St. Martin's Press.

Weaver, D. B. 2000. A broad context model of destination development scenarios. *Tourism Management*, 21 (3): 217–224.

Weiler, B., and C. M. Hall (eds.). 1992. *Special Interest Tourism*. London: Bellhaven Press.

Whelan, T. (ed.). 1991. *Nature Tourism: Managing the Environment*. Washington, DC: Island Press.

Wight, P. A. 1993a. Sustainable ecotourism: Balancing economic, environmental and social goals within an ethical framework. *Journal of Tourism Studies*, 4 (2): 54–65.

Wight, P. A. 1993b. Ecotourism: Ethics or eco-sell? *Journal of Travel Research*, 31 (3): 3–9.

World Tourism Organization. 2004. *Indicators of Sustainable Development for Tourism Destinations*. Madrid: WTO.

SURFING SOLUTIONS

http://www.kentuckytourism.com/industry/Incentives.htm (Kentucky Department of Travel)

http://www.bigvolcano.com.au/ercentre/ercpage.htm (Big Volcano Ecotourism Resource Centre, Australia)

http://www.ecotourism.org/ (The International Ecotourism Society, United States)

http://www.gov.ie/tourism-sport/ (Department of Arts, Sport and Tourism, Ireland)

http://ec3global.com (EC3 Global/Green Globe)

http://www.tourismconcern.org.uk/ (Tourism Concern, United Kingdom)

http://www.un.org/esa/sustdev/sdissues/tourism/tourism.htm (United Nations sustainable development position on tourism)

http://www.wtbonline.gov.uk/ (Wales Tourist Board)

Acronyms

CHT (cultural heritage tourism)
EIA (environmental impact assessment)
EU (European Union)
ESTD (ecologically sustainable tourism development)

IRR (internal rate of return)
LDC (less-developed country)
NPV (net present value)
ROI (return on investment)
STD (sustainable tourism development)
UNWTO (United Nations World Tourism Organization)

PART TWO

Marketing

STRATEGY, PLANNING, PROMOTION, AND DISTRIBUTION

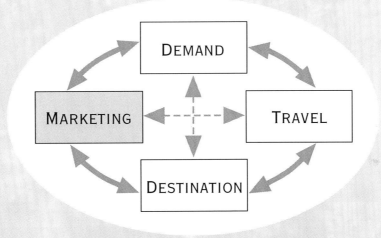

The destination mix of an area becomes its tourism product, shaped by market demand as well as its tourism policy, plan, legislation and regulations, and tourism development. Part Two of *The Tourism System* examines the strategies, procedures, and techniques that a destination area can use to market its tourism product in such a way as to have an effective influence on demand.

chapter 7

Tourism Marketing

BRINGING ALL OF THE PARTS
OF TOURISM TOGETHER

Destination Branding Needs to Be Brought into Reality

To lift a destination brand from the pages of a strategic plan, put meaning behind words
of a promise and bring it into existence requires a unique plan of action.

Destination BrandScience, Duane Knapp and Gary Sherwin,
Destination Marketing Association International (2005), page 53

PURPOSE

Having learned about the basic principles and concepts of marketing as applied to tourism, students will be
able to describe the procedures that should be used in marketing tourism destinations and organizations.

LEARNING OBJECTIVES

✓ Describe the differences between the marketing of tourism services and traditional product
marketing.
✓ Compare and contrast the different approaches to marketing associated with production, selling,
marketing, and societal marketing orientations.
✓ Explain the concept of market segmentation and how target markets are selected.
✓ Define positioning and explain how it is used in tourism.
✓ Explain the product life cycle concept and how it applies to tourism.
✓ Describe each of the steps of the marketing planning process in tourism.
✓ List and describe the elements of the marketing mix.

OVERVIEW

The marketing of tourism services is unique. This chapter begins by reviewing the factors that make tourism marketing different from the marketing of other products and services. Several definitions of tourism marketing are provided that emphasize the need for a marketing orientation and market segmentation. A five-step procedural model for marketing planning is described. Through the process of market segmentation, target markets are selected, and an appropriate marketing mix for each target market is selected. The elements of the marketing mix are described.

TOURISM MARKETING IS UNIQUE

The challenges in tourism marketing are unique and different from those of traditional product marketing. These differences are the result of the characteristics of tourism supply and demand (see figure 7.1 on page 170). Tourism is a combination of personal services and certain physical facilities and products. An *intangible experience* is offered, not a physical good that can be inspected before it is bought. Because tourism is a service business, production and consumption take place at the same time. In manufacturing, goods are produced, stored, and sold. The inventory process for products serves as a way of linking these stages of production and consumption. Tourism supply cannot be stored. Unlike a can of food which, if it is not sold one day can be sold the next, airline seats, hotel rooms, cruise ship berths, places on an escorted tour, and restaurant seats not sold today are lost forever. Tourism is a highly *perishable* commodity. While the "tourism inventory" cannot be stored and adjusted to changes in demand, the capacity to produce tourism services must be developed ahead of time. This puts great pressure on tourism developers to effectively plan the proper amounts of facilities and to keep them as fully used as possible. This creates another kind of challenge: Tourism supply is relatively fixed. The resources and infrastructure of a destination cannot change as quickly as can visitor demand.

A second factor that makes tourism unique is that the service provided is a *mixture of several services and some facilities and products.* For example, most travel trips have information, transportation, lodging, food and beverage, attraction, and activity components (the destination mix concept discussed in chapter 1). These components are offered by different organizations and may be marketed directly to the visitor by each organization or combined into a package where the services are supplied by a group of organizations. This lack of one single organization's control over the entire travel trip experience means that a great deal of *interdependence* exists among tourism organizations. For the visitor to leave having had a satisfactory experience, every tourism organization must have performed to the same standard. One bad service experience can spoil an otherwise perfect vacation or business trip. Therefore, the marketing success of each organization in the tourism service chain is dependent on the efforts of the other organizations providing all the other trip components.

A third unique feature of tourism is that the organizations that market tourism destinations usually have *little control over the quality and quantity of services provided.* Destination marketing organizations (DMOs) such as convention and visitors bureaus and state and national tourism organizations are seldom directly involved with the operation of tourism businesses providing visitor services. While these organizations are held accountable for the successful marketing of all the destination's tourism offerings, they must rely on the other tourism organizations to provide satisfactory experiences for visitors.

Fourth, the guest's satisfaction is a *function of the staff providing the service.* Tourism is a people business; people providing personal services to other people. Because of the great amount of variation in human personalities, it is very difficult to always provide a consistent quality of service. It is impossible to fully standardize tourism services. As one person has said, although we may want to, "You can't paint a smile on a human being's face." The tourism organizations that invest most heavily in hospitality skills and other types of service training are the ones most likely to enjoy the greatest success.

A fifth factor that makes tourism different from other industries is the role of *travel trade intermediaries.* Because visitor services are located at a distance from potential customers, specialized intermediaries—organizations that operate between the producer and the visitor—are required to bridge the gap. Additionally, since

> **75% of the Canadian Tourism Commission's Budget Goes Into International Marketing**
> *Approximately three-quarters of the CTC's (Canadian Tourism Commission) overall budget (C$76.5 million in 2008) is dedicated to marketing Canada internationally. The CTC also invests a portion of its resources to inspire Canadians to explore their own country, as opposed to travelling abroad.*
>
> Factsheet, The CTC's Mandate, Canadian Tourism Commission (2008), http://mediacentre.canada.travel/, accessed January 4, 2009

New Zealand Has Quality Management

New Zealand has constantly shown concern for the development of its tourism industry. Most recently, November 2007, an updated *Tourism Strategy* was presented, emphasizing the importance of the industry and its excellence.

Accepted by most tourism professionals and this book is the idea that tourism does not have a comprehensive system for quality control. The elevated number of services and products used by and offered to the tourist, along with the constant creation of unique experiences, increases the difficulty of quality management. New Zealand, with its Qualmark®, tries to amplify the degree to which it can guarantee quality.

Qualmark®

For the best holiday experiences—look for the Qualmark®—New Zealand tourism's official mark of quality.

Whether you're looking for places to stay, things to do or ways of getting around, the Qualmark® provides the quality assurance you need. Qualmark® assured businesses can be found across New Zealand.

When you see the Qualmark® it means that those businesses have been independently assessed against a set of national quality standards. It identifies professional and trustworthy businesses so you can book and buy with confidence.

The Tourism New Zealand Board has involved itself directly with the operation of tourism-dependent businesses and services, through keeping a close eye on these company's operations. Items like cleanliness, safety, security, and comfort are thoroughly accessed and rated. The ratings granted by the Qualmark® are divided as follows:

Stars	Description
★ ★+	**Acceptable.** Meets customers' minimum requirements. Basic, clean, and comfortable accommodation
★★ ★★+	**Good.** Exceeds customers' minimum requirements with some additional facilities and services
★★★ ★★★+	**Very good.** Provides a range of facilities and services and achieves good to very good quality standards
★★★★ ★★★★+	**Excellent.** Consistently achieves high quality levels with a wide range of facilities and services
★★★★★	**Exceptional.** Among the best available in New Zealand

These star ratings are meant to give the tourist an idea of what to expect from the business while the company gains higher credibility, visibility, and, potentially, higher profitability. The label is directly linked to the achievement of the *2015 Tourism Strategy Outcomes*. The number one desired outcome is:

NEW ZEALAND DELIVERS A WORLD-CLASS VISITOR EXPERIENCE–by improving quality, offering better booking systems and information, raising recognition of i-SITEs by visitors, raising awareness of Qualmark® as a mark of quality, making improvements to monitoring of visitor satisfaction and perceptions of quality, ensuring infrastructure meets demand, coordinating domestic tourism planning, and supporting and encouraging Maori tourism.

In today's tourism system, this initiative demonstrates the commitment to provide the best possible experiences, products, and services for all the involved stakeholders.

New Zealand offers a high-quality environment for visitors. © 2009 urosr. Used under license from Shutterstock, Inc.

THINK ABOUT THIS:

1. Will initiatives like the Qualmark® redress the assumption that quality management in the tourism industry is impossible? Why or why not?

(continued)

2. In an industry that is constantly growing, there are many companies directing their products to the tourist segment. How can quality labels affect buying processes? Are they truly worthwhile?

3. This quality label is a result of New Zealand's identification of a need expressed by the market. Which are the other labels and destinations that have shown this kind of project?

4. Are there any underlying advantages for marketing a destination with a quality label?

Sources: Tourism New Zealand Board and Qualmark® Official Web sites, 2008: http://www.newzealand.com/travel/qualmark/qualmark_home.cfm, http://www.nztourismstrategy.com/ and http://www.qualmark.co.nz/.

many tourism organizations are small, they cannot afford to set up their own retail outlets in every visitor's hometown. In most industries, the producer exerts great control over every stage in the development and delivery of the product. There is *no physical distribution process* in tourism. In the place of physical distribution is a network of professional travel trade intermediaries and the Internet. These skilled, knowledgeable travel trade intermediaries can influence, if not determine, which services are offered, to whom, when, and at what price.

The sixth factor that makes tourism different from other industries relates to demand. Tourism demand is *highly elastic, seasonal* in nature, and is influenced by *subjective factors* such as taste and fashion as well as more objective factors such as price and the physical attractions at the destination. In many cases, the services and experiences sought can be provided by any number of destinations or organizations. For example, many destinations around the world offer unique natural

> **The DMO and CVB Executives' Dilemma**
> *Imagine a job where you are hired and evaluated by one group of people and funded by another. The group evaluating you sees your work responsibilities as properly focused on short-run, industry-specific results because members of the group are themselves evaluated on these results. But the group funding you sees your work responsibilities as focused on long-term, community-wide results, as members of this group are evaluated that way. To make this job more challenging, imagine that neither group understands the perspective of the other.*
>
> Marketing Destination Marketing Organizations, *(2008), page 1,*
> *Robert C. Ford and William C. Peeper*

environments together with interesting flora and fauna. However, during the late 1980s to 2010, the Central American countries of Costa Rica and Belize became very popular and somewhat "fashionable" nature-based tourism destinations.

Finally, the *intangible* nature of tourism services means that the visitor's travel experiences exist only in memory after the trip is over. Many products can be reused several times after they are bought. Many products have guarantees or warranties; tourism services do not. While vacation photographs, videos, and souvenirs help visitors remember their trips, a re-purchase is necessary to enjoy a similar trip experience again. This places a greater onus on tourism organizations to deliver satisfactory experiences to their customers.

TOURISM MARKETING DEFINED

There are many definitions of marketing but few specifically address the unique characteristics of marketing tourism services. One of the definitions designed to fit tourism is that "marketing is a management philosophy which, in light of tourist demand, makes it possible through research, forecasting and selection to place tourism products on the market most in line with the orga-

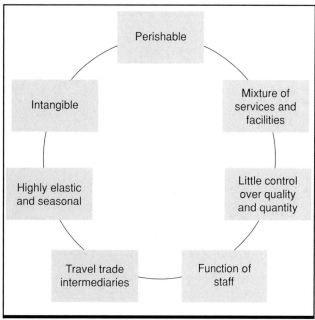

Figure 7.1 The Unique Features of Tourism Marketing.

nization's purpose for the greatest benefit" (World Tourism Organization, 1975). This definition suggests several things. First, it indicates that marketing is a way of thinking about a situation that balances the needs of the visitor with the needs of the organization and the destination. A marketing orientation is needed to meet this requirement. Second, the definition stresses tourism research and forecasting that culminate in the selection of target markets (market segmentation). Third, the concepts of positioning and the product life cycle ensure the proper placement of tourism services on the market and suggest the appropriate marketing strategies and plans.

Other definitions of marketing emphasize the need for a *systems approach* and recommend a step-by-step process for marketing tourism services. "Marketing is a continuous, sequential process through which management in tourism plans, researches, implements, controls, and evaluates activities designed to satisfy both customers' needs and wants and their own organization's objectives. To be effective, marketing requires the efforts of everyone in an organization and can be made more or less effective by the actions of complementary organizations" (Morrison, 2009). This second definition indicates that marketing should be an ongoing concern in a tourism organization, not just a one-time effort each year. It also suggests that marketing should involve everyone in the organization, not just the marketing department. Five key functions of marketing are identified as:

1. Planning
2. Research
3. Implementation
4. Control
5. Evaluation

The interdependency of tourism organizations in providing satisfying visitor experiences is also highlighted in this definition.

Another important characteristic of marketing is identified in a third definition: "Communicating to and giving the target market customers what they want, when they want it, where they want it, at a price they are willing to pay. Any business that does this will fulfill its twofold purpose of creating and keeping customers and, in turn, will produce revenue" (Lewis and Chambers, 2000). This definition emphasizes that it is not enough to attract first-time visitors. Bringing people back for repeat visits is at least equally important to a tourism organization.

MARKETING ORIENTATION

As an essential first step in marketing, an overall marketing orientation must be developed to guide marketing efforts. This philosophy sets the tone for every subsequent decision. Although several different orientations are possible, experience has shown that they are not all equally effective.

Some organizations' marketing efforts are guided by a *production orientation*. With a production orientation, the greatest emphasis is placed on the services or products provided to the visitor. For example, a destination area may have many physical, historical, and cultural resources. The extent to which the destination's resources are better than those of its competitors determines, in part, how many people visit the destination. This orientation was used at one time by the local authorities in a town on the south coast of England. They decided in the late 1960s to print brochures only in English. It was pointed out that a major potential market was the French residents across the English Channel. The reply was given that if the French wanted to visit, then they should be interested enough to learn to read English in order to understand what was available. Although it cannot be denied that resources are important, a total emphasis on tourism supply fails to recognize the visitor's needs and expectations. A production orientation is only successful if there is a surplus of demand over supply (which rarely happens in the modern, highly competitive tourism environment). In this case, the destination or company that offers the best product will get the visitor. An old adage says "Build a better mousetrap,

What's Going on at the Head Office of the Hong Kong Tourism Board?

At a management level, the HKTB maintains a close watch on global tourism trends, keeps track of competitors' activities, conducts extensive market research and analysis, and develops the Board's overall marketing, business development and product development strategies. Meanwhile, various Head Office departments also provide worldwide support in key areas, such as corporate communications and public relations, marketing communications, strategic planning and research, industry training and human resources, financial management, systems management and administration. Other Head Office departments provide services that benefit Hong Kong's tourism-related industries at a local level. These include organising or coordinating events aimed at visitors; developing tour itineraries; providing visitor information and services; and promoting quality services and good hospitality.

About HKTB: Structure and Management, *Hong Kong Tourism Board (2008),* http://www.discoverhongkong.com/eng/about-hktb/structure-management.html, *accessed January 4, 2009*

and the world will beat a path to your door." Often referred to as the "better-mousetrap fallacy," this form of competitive advantage is normally short-lived in today's business climate.

When supply exceeds demand, the problem becomes "How can I sell all these mousetraps?" The number of destinations actively seeking tourism has increased as has the number of travel destinations throughout the world with easy accessibility. The emergence of more professional destination marketing organizations, tour operators, and travel agencies has increased the intensity of competition for the visitor dollar, euro, and pound. It has meant that destination areas can no longer sit back and wait for visitors to come to them. Visitors must be convinced of the benefits of traveling to a particular destination. This has caused a shift in orientation from emphasizing the product to intensified selling. The emphasis in this orientation is on promoting what is available for sale. Yet, this *sales orientation* still focuses on the needs of the seller— How can we sell more product?—rather than on the visitor's needs and wants—What will satisfy the visitor? The first priority here is to convince potential visitors that what is available for sale will please them.

A newer development is an orientation in which the needs and wants of the visitors are the first priority for the marketer. This is called a *marketing orientation*. A tourism organization begins with the needs and wants of the visitor and attempts to provide the services to satisfy them. It involves being open when the visitor wants it to be open; serving breakfast when the visitor wants it rather than when it is convenient for management; providing the kind of experiences that visitors want rather than what we feel they should have. It is realizing that, using the earlier metaphor, an individual does not want to buy a mousetrap; rather she wants to kill mice. Some say this is an exercise in "putting yourself in the visitor's shoes"; always trying to see things from the visitor's viewpoint. If and when a better way is developed of satisfying a need, people are likely to try it. This marketing orientation will be reinforced later when an emphasis will be placed on the satisfaction of needs and wants.

Many tourism organizations have come to realize that they have a responsibility to society and local communities as well as to their visitors. Strictly concentrating on their visitors' needs and wants may cause long-term damage to the environment, society, and local communities. For example, fast-food companies are beginning to shoulder some *social responsibility* by improving (or at least providing more information on) the nutritional content of menu items and using recyclable mate-

The tourism organization responsible for marketing this beach can use a marketing orientation, which places the needs and wants of visitors as the first priorities; but it must also protect the beach from overuse and pollution. © 2009 Varina and Jay Patel. Used under license from Shutterstock, Inc.

rials in their packaging. Beer companies and distilleries have joined the movement against drunk driving by developing advertisements that emphasize the consequences of drinking and driving.

Having a sense of social and community responsibility is especially important in tourism. A marketing orientation that concentrates solely on visitors' needs is not the ideal philosophy, even for the visitors themselves. A tourism destination relies on the resources of its community, which both visitors and residents share. To become totally marketing oriented, all aspects of the community would have to be oriented toward satisfying visitors' needs and wants. The risk for the community is that by orienting totally for visitors' needs, the needs, integrity, and long-term interests of the community and local residents may be harmed. Consider the situations explored in earlier chapters of destination areas that have adapted to the needs of the visitor and, in the process, have lost their uniqueness, heritage, and natural resources while receiving a relatively poor economic return on investment. Destination areas that adapt their resources to satisfy visitors' needs may lose the very thing that makes them attractive and unique in the first place. The visitor is the ultimate loser, as more and more destinations take on an increasingly similar and familiar appearance.

The erosion of natural, historic, and cultural resources is not the only potential pitfall of tourism development. In the late 1980s, the Caribbean, long a favorite destination of North American and European visitors, began to realize that tourism contributed to social problems such as increased prostitution, drug trafficking, and the spread of AIDS. The Barbados Board

Honduras and Societal Marketing

Through marketing orientation, tourism can become a solution for many destinations. Theoretically speaking, a well-planned destination can guarantee a sustainable income through the activity, guaranteeing well-being. Many regions' revenues, however, are based on the exploration of their natural resources. This module of development does not offer long-term sustainability due to the utilization of finite income sources.

The region of La Moskitia (Mosquito Coast–Honduras), has rich indigenous cultures and is covered by tropical rainforests. Nonetheless, the main source of income was the depredation of terrestrial and marine resources. The intense and continuous exploration caused a noticeable decline of resources, attracting international attention. The region's habitants realized that their income and future could be at risk.

The natives of the *Río Plátano* Biosphere Reserve (a 2-million-acre UNESCO World Heritage Site) within La Moskitia, joined forces to preserve their home. La Ruta Moskitia Ecotourism Alliance (LARUMO Alliance) was created. This program unites the efforts of six indigenous groups and an international conservation organization (RARE) in an attempt to decrease predatory activities and help the local people to develop sustainable activities, such as ecotourism.

The region's tourism-oriented organization has resulted in *ecotourism enterprise groups* (tours, lodging, dining, and transportation services). Every enterprise employs ten to twenty native people. Capacity building, training, and self-empowerment are the bases of each group. The employees receive monthly salaries and share annual profits. All the funds received through tourism are kept by the local population. These funds are used, in part, to reinvest in the activity, amplifying and enhancing available infrastructure.

Product development is a constant concern and an important component of the project's competitiveness.

This community-based project has resulted in poverty alleviation, biodiversity conservation, and sustainable tourism. The La Ruta Moskitia Ecotourism Alliance has created at least 150 rural community jobs and supports more than 750 immediate family members.

For this reason, La Ruta Moskitia has become an attractive destination for adventure and ecotravelers and a model to be used by other regions struggling for their survival and the preservation of their resources.

This initiative has won the Investor in People Award of the 2008 Tourism for Tomorrow Awards (WTTC). The award is given to an ecotourism enterprise that supports sustainable economic alternatives for local communities and helps protect the ecosystem and cultural integrity.

THINK ABOUT THIS:

1. La Moskitia has shown a future-oriented development strategy. What could have happened if a sustainable source of income was not developed? What could happen if their tourism-oriented strategies are not comprehensive to local necessities?

2. By winning the People Award of the 2008 Tourism for Tomorrow, La Ruta Moskitia has attracted positive media. What can other communities learn from the experience of La Ruta Moskitia?

3. With current tourism trends, is this type of project a new trend within the industry? What regions are more likely prone to this type of development?

4. What are the benefits for the visitor of the La Ruta Moskitia? Are there any disadvantages?

Sources: 2008. http://www.wttc.org; 2008. http://www.tourismfortomorrow.com; 2008. http://rareconservation.org; 2008. http://www.larutamoskitia.com.

Honduras offers a great mix of different types of attractions for visitors, including Copan. © 2009 Sam Chadwick. Used under license from Shutterstock, Inc.

of Tourism acted on this problem by airing television commercials that warned against harassing visitors on beach fronts to buy drugs (Hart, 1989).

The best solution to these potential problems with tourism is to develop a marketing approach that focuses on the satisfaction of visitor needs and wants while respecting the long-term interests of the community. This approach is referred to as a *societal marketing orientation*. This orientation provides for planning, development, and marketing activities that focus on the needs of the visitor, but that also consider the effects of these activities on the long-term interests of the community before any action is taken. It is also known as encouraging *sustainable tourism development* (as discussed in chapter 2).

All marketing activities are influenced by the orientations of those people directly responsible for marketing. It is essential that these individuals' decisions reflect a predetermined philosophy or corporate culture that provides an overall guide for the development and marketing efforts of the destination or organization.

MARKET SEGMENTATION

Another important marketing decision is the selection of groups of potential visitors with whom we wish to do business. *Market segmentation* is a recognized and universally accepted way of analyzing tourism markets and selecting from among them. Market segmentation is a process through which people with similar needs, wants, and characteristics are grouped together so that a tourism organization can use greater precision in serving and communicating with these people. Market segmentation is a two-step process: (1) deciding how to group all potential visitors (the *market segments*), and (2) selecting specific groups from among these (the *target markets*) to pursue.

Market segmentation is based on four assumptions. First, the market for a service is made up of several segments whose members have distinctive needs and preferences. In other words, not all visitors are alike. Second, potential visitors can be grouped into segments whose members have similar and identifiable characteristics. Third, a single travel trip offering, such as a Caribbean cruise, appeals to some segments of the market more than others. Fourth, destinations and organizations can make their marketing more effective by developing specific travel trip offerings for specific segments of the market. A cruise package may suit one group of potential visitors, while a white water rafting trip may appeal more strongly to another group.

The process of segmenting the tourism market should be the basis for *strategic* (long-term) marketing decisions. Market segmentation is more than a process for analyzing demand. It is a management tool that leads to specific marketing decisions. The development of a marketing strategy begins with the identification of market segments and their characteristics. A tourism organization or destination may decide to develop unique offerings for every potential visitor market segment. However, limitations of time and money usually prevent this. Time and money can be saved by offering one basic option to everyone, such as Club Med used to do in the 1950s, 1960s, and 1970s. Although this one option undoubtedly appeals to some potential visitors, it will not to others. The compromise is to separate visitors into segments with similar characteristics and produce offerings geared to the needs of certain selected segments.

SELECT MARKET SEGMENTATION METHOD

Two overall types of methods used to segment tourism markets are:

1. *Forward segmentation* (a priori methods).
2. *Backward segmentation* (a posteriori methods) (Smith, 1989; Pearce, 1989).

Forward segmentation methods have traditionally been the most frequently employed in tourism primarily because they are the easier of the two to use. Here, the marketer predetermines the segmentation base or bases to be used for market segmentation, for example purpose-of-trip and/or geographic origin. Usually the marketer acts on information such as previous research studies by others that suggest an *a priori* segmentation base is a key factor in determining visitor behavior. For example, it is a common practice in international tourism to treat the residents of each tourism-generating country as unique target markets. In addition, most practitioners make the a priori decision to address business and pleasure travelers as two separate and distinct target markets.

Backward segmentation methods, including using factor-cluster analysis, result in segments derived from the application of specific statistical analysis techniques to sets of visitor data. The marketer does not predetermine the segments; the statistical analysis suggests them. In an analysis of Hong Kong residents, five distinct travel segments were identified on the basis of preferred sets of vacation activities:

1. Visiting friends and relatives
2. Outdoor sports activity
3. Sightseeing
4. Entertainment
5. Full-house activity

The study used the cluster analysis technique to maximize the heterogeneity between the clusters and maximize the homogeneity within each individual cluster (Hsieh, O'Leary, and Morrison, 1992).

IDENTIFY MARKET SEGMENTATION BASES AND SEGMENTS

A viable visitor market segment must meet the following criteria by being:

- **Measurable.** Can the number of potential visitors within the segment be estimated with a reasonable degree of accuracy?
- **Accessible.** Can these visitors be reached with specific promotional techniques or media? Can they be reached and influenced by existing or potential travel trade distribution channels, or by the Internet?
- **Substantial.** Are there sufficient numbers of visitors in this visitor market segment to justify a tailor-made marketing effort?
- **Defensible.** Are the visitor market segment's characteristics different enough to justify separate marketing activities and expenditures just for them, or can they be grouped with one or more other target markets? If competitors decide to use more of a mass marketing approach, will this have an adverse effect on us?

A vacation destination would be marketed differently to families with children than to groups of young single people. © 2009 Monkey Business Images. Used under license from Shutterstock, Inc.

- **Durable.** As the market develops, will this visitor market segment maintain its uniqueness, or will these differences disappear with time?
- **Competitive.** Do we have a relative advantage over the competition in serving this visitor market segment?
- **Homogeneous.** Are the people within the visitor market segment similar enough?
- **Compatible.** Is the visitor market segment compatible with the other visitor market segments that the organization or destination attracts?

Many bases or characteristics are used to segment the tourism market. Seven general categories are:

1. Demographic and socioeconomic
2. Geographic
3. Purpose of trip
4. Behavioral
5. Psychographic
6. Product related
7. Channel of distribution (see figure 7.2).

DEMOGRAPHIC AND SOCIOECONOMIC SEGMENTATION. Many early segmentation studies in tourism used demographic and socioeconomic statistics as the basis for forming market segments. These remain the most commonly used today due to the relative ease of acquiring the statistical data, the comparability of the information through census as well as media-generated data, and the fact that the data are easy to understand and apply. For example, age and income have been very successful predictors of recreation participation. However, the use of only demographic data to segment markets

| **Demographic and Socioeconomic** |
Age, education, gender, income, family size and composition, family life cycle stage, social class, type of residence/home ownership status, second home ownership, race or ethnic group, occupation

Geographic
Country, region, market area, urban/suburban/rural, city size, population density, ZIP Code or postal code, neighborhood

Purpose of Trip
Regular business travel; business travel related to meetings, conventions, exhibitions, and congresses; incentive travel; visiting friends and relatives; close-to-home leisure trips; touring vacation; city trip; outdoors vacation; resort vacation; cruise trip; visit to theme park; festival or event visit

Behavioral
Volume of use, frequency of use, usage status, use occasions, brand loyalty, benefits sought, lengths of stay, transportation modes used, expenditure levels, experience preferences, activity participation patterns

Psychographic
Lifestyle, attitudes/interests/opinions, values

Product Related
Recreation activity, equipment type, price level, type of hotel/resort property

Channel of Distribution
Principal function, area of specialization, size and structure, geographic location

Figure 7.2 Tourism Market Segmentation Bases and Characteristics.

has come under attack. The rapidly changing nature of society makes it impossible to rely solely on these data as a means of developing a marketing strategy. Just because a segment of people are within a particular age or income group does not necessarily mean they have similar travel preferences. Also, socioeconomic information does not give the marketer sufficient information about

Family life cycle is a composite of marital status, age, and the numbers and ages of children at home. © 2009 Monkey Business Images. Used under license from Shutterstock, Inc.

likes and dislikes to properly position the tourism destination or organization in the marketplace.

Greater success has been found in using demographic criteria that are *multivariate* (using two or more demographic variables). Status, for example, includes dimensions of income, education, and occupation. Family life cycle is a composite of marital status, age, and the numbers and ages of children at home. Life cycle segmentation has proven to be an effective way of segmenting in a number of tourism and recreation cases.

It is unlikely that segmentation on the basis of demographics will ever be abandoned. Although other segmentation bases provide information useful for strategic decisions on what to offer in the way of tourism services, it is still necessary to communicate with an individual market segment. For all its shortcomings, demographic segmentation offers one of the best ways to access a specific segment of the market.

Geographic Segmentation. Geographic considerations are very important to tourism. Much of the attractiveness of a visitor destination is based on contrasting cultures, climates, or scenery. This implies there being a certain distance between origin and destination. This book has already discussed the crucial role in tourism the accessibility of a destination plays. To date, destinations have used geographically-based studies solely to identify primary, secondary, and in some cases, tertiary markets. National and state tourist organizations tend to use geographic segmentation for the purposes of guiding promotional efforts. National tourism statistics have traditionally been collected by country of origin and marketing priorities are set according to the contributions of each country to total arrivals.

Another important aspect of geographical segmentation along with demographics is that both provide the means of access to target markets. In marketing, it is essential to know where potential customers live or work in order to communicate with them (see figure 7.3, page 183).

Purpose-of-Trip Segmentation. The established tradition in tourism is to divide the market into two broad purpose-of-trip segments: (1) business and (2) pleasure/personal travel markets. A modified version of this approach was used in a segmentation study of a hotel located in Singapore. Two broad segments were first defined: (1) the group segment and (2) the individual segment. The group segment was then further subdivided into group tours, conventions, corporate meetings, and airline crews. The individual segment consisted of corporate, full-rate and miscellaneous, frequent travelers, and group inclusive tours (GITs). The research for this study showed that purpose of trip was a better way of differentiating segments than nationality or income (Mehta and Vera, 1990).

BEHAVIORAL SEGMENTATION.
Behavioral segmentation divides customers by their usage rates, benefits sought, use occasions, usage status and potential, and brand loyalty (Kotler et al., 1999). Usage rate was increasingly used by the tourism industry in the 1980s and 1990s, especially as greater attention became focused on frequent travelers.

The Japanese and Korean honeymooner markets have drawn special attention among destinations in the Asia Pacific region. © 2009 WizData, Inc. Used under license from Shutterstock, Inc.

Heavy-half segmentation is an example of usage-rate or use frequency segmentation. Some attempts have been made in recreation and tourism to use this segmentation base. Heavy-half segmentation refers to the idea of segmenting a market on the basis of quantity purchased or consumed. As with other types of products, however, heavy-half segmentation has been found lacking. A major problem is that the characteristics of the heavy half (the major purchasers) have been found to be similar to those of the light half. Similar difficulties have been found with segmentation on the basis of brand loyalty.

Benefit or attribute segmentation is becoming a very popular segmentation base in tourism. It involves segmenting a market according to the relative importance assigned to benefits that visitors expect to realize after purchasing the product. The relative importance of specific product benefits to prospective visitors is determined. Clusters of people are formed who attach similar degrees of importance to the same product benefits. The results can have important ramifications for developing new products and advertising messages. However, it is necessary to develop demographic profiles of the benefit clusters to reach them.

Use-occasion segmentation is enjoying greater popularity in tourism. Perhaps the best example of this is

> **Malaysia Wants More Medical Tourism**
> *Since January (2008), Malaysia has extended stays from 30 days to six months and introduced multiple-entry visas to allow travelers arriving for surgery access to rehabilitation and follow-up care.*
>
> Highlights 2008, Malaysia,
> S. Puvaneswary, TTG Asia (2008), page 6

the growing number of resorts and destinations pursuing the honeymooner market. Here, the use-occasion is a honeymoon. The Japanese honeymooner market has drawn special attention among destinations in the Asia Pacific region. Destinations such as Australia, Hawaii, Hong Kong, and Singapore have been particularly successful in appealing to Japanese honeymooners.

PSYCHOGRAPHIC SEGMENTATION.
Although expensive to use and difficult to carry out, this newer technique of market segmentation can be very helpful in describing visitors. It is especially useful in highly specialized and extensively developed markets where psychographic profiles supplement the information gained from simpler analyses. Demographic data may be likened to the bones of a skeleton; psychographic data represents the flesh. The bones form the basis of the structure, but it is only by covering the form with flesh that the features become recognizable. Information about an individual's attitudes, interests, and opinions gives a much clearer picture of the people in a market segment.

The VALS™ (Values and Life Styles) program is one most widely recognized application of psychographic segmentation in the United States. There are other psychographic or lifestyle segmentation methods available including the Prizm NE and Acorn system.

PRODUCT-RELATED SEGMENTATION.
A major advantage of segmenting by means of product-related variables is that the information gained is directly related to the particular tourism service under consideration. Indeed, a major flaw in some studies is that information is sought from the potential visitor that deals with general benefits sought or, in the case of psychographic segmentation, general attitudes about types of products and services, rather than about specific products and services.

CHANNEL-OF-DISTRIBUTION SEGMENTATION.
This chapter has already indicated that tourism's distribution

channels are unique and play a more powerful role than the intermediaries in other industries. Chapter 9 provides a detailed description of these distribution channels. It is important to recognize that these intermediaries should be segmented by the other tourism organizations that depend upon them for business. Intermediaries vary according to their principal function (e.g., retailing versus wholesaling travel services), area of specialization by travel service, market segment, or destination (e.g., cruise-only travel agents, corporate and ethnic travel agencies), size and structure (e.g., large franchised travel agency chains versus the small independent retailer), online versus offline, and, of course, geographic location.

While segmentation schemes for distribution channels have received little attention from tourism researchers, the traditional and newer online intermediaries are of great importance to tourism. Most organizations that target travel intermediaries in their marketing use a two-step process:

1. Identify the target market of travelers
2. Then select the intermediaries who serve these target markets.

SELECT TARGET MARKETS

Once market segments have been identified and profiled, the tourism destination or organization must select the target market or markets that it wants to attract and serve. This decision is based upon an analysis to determine which segments will produce the greatest benefits and which the destination or organization can serve best. The analysis involves four concerns:

1. **Income potential and yield:** What is the current and future potential for income from this segment? Income is a combination of the number of current and potential visitors and their current and potential per-person spending.
2. **Competition:** To what extent does competition exist for the segment in question? How strong is our advantage compared to competitors?
3. **Cost:** How much investment is required to develop services to attract this segment and to communicate with its members?
4. **Ability to serve:** Are the financial and managerial capabilities in place to design, promote, and distribute the appropriate services and satisfactorily serve this market segment?

The segments chosen become the destination's or organization's target markets. Developing marketing programs to meet the needs of these target markets should begin with a technique known as *positioning*.

POSITIONING

Positioning is a relatively new concept in marketing. Most experts agree that its origins date back to around 1972 and a series of articles written by advertising executives Al Reis and Jack Trout. These articles were later expanded into a book titled, *Positioning: The Battle for Your Mind*. In these authors' own words, "Positioning is what you do to the mind of the prospect" (Ries and Trout, 1981). Other authors have elaborated on this original definition including Lewis and Chambers (2000) who say that positioning is "the consumer's mental perception of a product, which may or may not differ from the actual characteristics of a product or brand." Most experts agree that the purpose of positioning is to create a perception or *image*–to establish a position–in the targeted visitor's mind. Since the objective is to influence the individual visitor's perception of the destination or organization, there is a clear link to the psychological dimensions of perception discussed in chapter 12. Effective positioning is expected to grow in importance as the tourism destinations and organizations competing for visitors continue to increase.

In using positioning, the logical place to start is with the questions "Do we have a position in our potential visitors' minds?" and, if so, "What is that position?" Answering these questions must involve some marketing research. Focus group research done in Los Angeles for the Tahiti Visitor Board showed that a variety of misperceptions were hindering further tourism growth from the Southern California market. These were that Tahiti was fourteen to sixteen hours from Los Angeles (rather than just eight); it was an isolated, single-island nation (it actually has 130 islands); it has limited accom-

---

Down Under, but at the Top In Destination Marketing
Tourism Australia, and its predecessor the Australian Tourist Commission, has been vigorously marketing Australia internationally as a tourist destination for more than 40 years. During this time Australia has established a reputation as an innovator in tourism marketing and has built one of the world's most successful and desirable destination brands.

A Uniquely Australian Invitation, Tourism Australia (2008), http://www.tourism.australia.com/Marketing.asp?sub=0413, accessed January 5, 2009

Is the Visiting Friends and Relatives Market Really Worth the Effort?

When selecting target markets, many tourism destination marketers choose to overlook the visiting friends and relatives (VFR) market. Why? There is a fairly common assumption that VFRs are the "penny-pinchers" of tourism, staying at the homes of family and friends and spending very little elsewhere in the communities they are visiting. Some recent figures suggest that these assumptions are quite far off the mark.

The Hong Kong Tourism Board (HKTB) collects statistics on expenditures by origin country of visitors. The highest spending overnight visitors are from the Americas at HK$5,744 per visitor in 2007. Surprisingly, overnight visitors from Mainland China ranked in fourth place in spending, ahead of visitors from North Asia, South Asia, and Southeast Asia. Each overnight visitor from Mainland China spent HK$5,193 in 2007. This statistic is surprising because a much higher proportion of the Mainland visitors stay in the homes of family and friends, while foreign visitors mainly stay in commercial accommodations. Twenty-nine percent of the Mainlanders in 2007 listed VFR as their principal purpose of trip to Hong Kong, compared to the all overnight visitor average of 19 percent and the Americas' 12 percent.

Although tourists from Mainland China spend less on accommodation, they spend more on other product and service categories. This idea is based on the preceding facts and the results of the Overnight Visitor Spending by Spending Category analysis conducted by the HKTB. The results show that tourists from the Americas spend, on average, 48 percent of their total expenditure on hotel receipts (accommodations), while tourists from Mainland China spent only 10.6 percent. Nevertheless, Mainlanders spend more on shopping, 72.6 percent, far more than any other market area.

The situation in Hong Kong adds further credence to what several tourism researchers discovered during the 1990s. For example, Morrison, Verginis, and O'Leary (2000) found that long-haul VFR travelers from Germany and the United Kingdom spent significant amounts at their destinations; 6,329 DM for the German travelers and £2,114 for the British travelers (these figures were for 1995 and included the cost of travel to the destinations). What is particularly noteworthy from this study is that the German and British VFRs outspent all others in terms of retail shopping, a similar finding to that of the HKTB for the Mainland Chinese.

While conventional destination marketing wisdom suggests writing off VFRs as a low-yield target market, these research statistics challenge this position. The lesson is clear—assumptions about target markets are not a good substitute for good research information.

THINK ABOUT THIS:

1. What are some of the common assumptions that marketers tend to make about the VFR market?

2. Why can it be misleading and dangerous to follow these assumptions when making decisions on selecting target markets?

3. What types of research should a destination conduct to make sure that it has accurate information on the contributions of each potential target market?

A significant portion of visitors from Mainland China to Hong Kong is for VFR. Photo by Alastair Morrison of Star Ferry to Central Pier.

Sources:

Hong Kong Tourism Board. 2008. Tourism Expenditure Associated to Inbound Tourism: Jan–Dec 2007; Visitor Profile Report: Jan–Dec 2007. http://partnernet.hktourismboard.com.

Morrison, A. M., C. Verginis, and J. T. O'Leary. 2000. Reaching the unwanted and unreachable: An analysis of the outbound, long haul German and British visiting friends and relatives market. *Tourism and Hospitality Research: The Surrey Quarterly Review*, 2 (3): 214–231.

modations; and it is difficult to get there (Covey, 1988). Another study about India as a travel destination highlighted two significant misperceptions: not many people in India speak English and there are few first-class hotels there (Kale and Weir, 1986). The message from these two examples should be clear; the flow of information to visitors is imperfect and it is a major error to assume that they have an accurate image or perception of the destination or organization.

The next step in positioning is to determine whether the visitor's perception or image needs to be established, changed, or reinforced. Here, two forms of positioning can be used: objective positioning and subjective positioning. With *objective positioning*, the destination or organization attempts to tailor-make its services and products to match the needs and wants of a selected target market or markets. Some refer to this as "product-market matching." The emphasis is placed on adding or modifying one or more objective characteristics of the services or facilities being offered. For example, a destination that decides to pursue the scuba diving market will need to add dive shops, dive boats, dive maps, diving guides/instructors, and other services required by this specialized target market. Once the objective attributes have been altered to suit the target market, these changes must be communicated to potential visitors through various types of consumer and travel intermediary promotions. The following are some examples of objective positioning statements in tourism:

The Arizona Office of Tourism positions the state on its well-known landmark, the Grand Canyon. http://www.arizonaguide.com.

- Arizona: "Grand Canyon State"
- Hawaii: "The Islands of Aloha"
- Lapland: "Vitality from nature"
- Nepal: "Naturally Nepal. Once is not enough."
- Qantas: "The Spirit of Australia"
- SuperClubs: "The World's Only Super-Inclusive Resorts"

Subjective positioning is an attempt to form, reinforce, or change the potential visitor's image without altering the physical characteristics of the services and products offered. Subjective positioning normally follows objective positioning. It is often used when research shows that there are misperceptions about a destination or organization, or when a negative image has developed through adverse publicity or for other reasons. This is usually called "*repositioning.*" When Tahiti discovered its distance misperception, an advertising campaign was launched stating that it was just "*Two and a half hours beyond Hawaii and fifty years behind it.*" Another major application of subjective positioning is to communicate emotional appeals and messages, rather than rational (objective). The following are some examples of subjective positioning statements in tourism:

A destination that wants to promote scuba diving needs to provide all of the services and equipment required by this specialized market.
© 2009 Yuri Arcurs. Used under license from Shutterstock, Inc.

- Brazil: "Sensational!"
- India: "Incredible India"
- Jamaica: "Once you go, you know"
- Jiangsu Province: "To taste Jiangsu is to know China"
- Queenstown, New Zealand: "Pure inspiration"
- Singapore: "Uniquely Singapore"
- Victoria, Australia: "You'll love every piece of Victoria"
- Windstar Cruise Line: "180° from Ordinary"

Once the decision is made to use either or both objective and subjective positioning, the next step is to determine how this will be communicated to potential travelers and travel trade intermediaries. There are at least six broad positioning approaches:

1. Positioning on specific product features
2. Positioning on benefits, problem solution, or needs
3. Positioning for specific usage occasions
4. Positioning for user category
5. Positioning against another product
6. Positioning by product class dissociation (Kotler, 1984)

The following are examples of each of these positioning approaches:

- **Positioning on specific product features:** "No artificial ingredients" (Costa Rica Tourist Board)
- **Positioning on benefits, problem solution, or needs:** "Now everyone can fly" (AirAsia)
- **Positioning for specific usage occasions:** "Romance me" (Fiji Visitors Bureau)
- **Positioning for user category:** "Where business and aloha meet" (Hawaii Visitors and Convention Bureau)
- **Positioning against another product:** "Avis: We try harder" (Avis Rent-A-Car System)
- **Positioning by product class dissociation:** "The spice of the Caribbean" (Grenada Board of Tourism)

PRODUCT LIFE CYCLE

The concept of the product life cycle (PLC) is useful in choosing, attracting, and serving target markets. The PLC concept suggests that a destination, service, or product moves through four distinct stages: *Introduction, growth, maturity,* and *decline.* In chapter 5, the various stages were described from a planning perspective. It is important that the destination or organization examines the PLC concept at two different levels. First, at what stage in the PLC is our part of tourism? Second, at what stage in the PLC is our own destination, service, or product? Since the spectacular growth of international tourism in the 1970s and before, year-to-year increases have been much more modest, suggesting a maturing of the industry. In the developed countries, some parts of the industry such as domestic airlines and hotels are also in the maturity stage.

It is important to identify the PLC stage situation because the effectiveness of different marketing strategies varies by stage. For example, in

The Fiji Visitors Bureau has done an outstanding job of positioning the nation of islands as a wedding and honeymoon destination. http://www.bulafiji.com/romanceme/.

Costa Rica has been very successful in positioning its natural features with the statement "No Artificial Ingredients." http://microsites.visitcostarica.com/.

stages of the industry and its own offerings, position these effectively within the minds of the targeted potential visitors. Having made these decisions, specific marketing programs using pricing, services and products, promotions, and distribution channels (marketing mixes) are designed. The process used to develop marketing mixes should be systematic; it should follow a step-by-step procedure known as the *marketing planning process*.

Marketing planning implies a future orientation. It involves identifying suitable marketing goals and objectives as well as determining the most appropriate marketing strategies to achieve these goals and objectives. Marketing planning takes place at two levels: *strategic marketing planning* for three to five years or more in the future, and *tactical marketing planning* for the next year. Both levels of planning must be closely integrated with the other.

A model of the marketing planning process containing five basic questions has been suggested by Morrison (2009) (see figures 7.3 and 7.4). The five questions are:

1. Where are we now?
2. Where would we like to be?
3. How do we get there?
4. How do we make sure we get there?
5. How do we know if we got there?

WHERE ARE WE NOW?

The planning of marketing must begin by addressing the question "Where are we now?" This involves a thorough analysis of the existing situation. Marketing goals, strategies, and objectives should not be defined until this analysis has been completed. Many marketing experts refer to this step as a *situation analysis* or *SWOT* (strengths, weaknesses, opportunities, threats) analysis. The factors that should be analyzed include the marketing environment, development goals and strategies, services, products and destination mix, market profile, and competition.

SCAN THE MARKETING ENVIRONMENT. Planning must be accomplished within the framework of the

---

No Pain, No Gain, In Spain

After 50 years of uninterrupted growth, Spain's overbuilt and relatively expensive resorts seem ill-placed to cope with a downturn, at a time of increasing competition from cheaper, less crowded destinations like Croatia and Turkey.

Economy causes tourism to feel the pain in Spain, Ben Harding, *Shanghai Daily* (September 6, 2008), page B5

---

the maturity stage, more emphasis must be placed on drawing business away from competitors, or on finding new target markets or uses.

Butler and Waldbrook (1991) describe a cycle of development apparent in tourist destinations that is based on the traditional product life cycle. The seven stages of development are: exploration, involvement, development, consolidation and stagnation, followed by either decline or rejuvenation (see figure 5.1). There is a link between the type of visitors attracted to a destination and its development as it changes to attract greater numbers of tourists (Butler and Waldbrook, 1991).

MARKETING PLANNING PROCESS

A tourism destination or organization must segment the market using the most appropriate methods and bases, select target markets and, taking into account the PLC

Marketing Planning Process Steps	Techniques and Concepts	Outcomes and Results
1. Where are we now?	Environmental scan Situation analysis	Strengths and weaknesses Challenges, opportunities, threats Visitor market profile Competitive analysis
2. Where would we like to be?	Visioning Market segmentation Positioning	Vision, goals, and objectives Marketing strategy Target markets Positioning approach
3. How do we get there?	Marketing mix	Marketing plan (eight Ps)
4. How do we make sure we get there?	Control	Progress reports Marketing plan modifications
5. How do we know if we got there?	Evaluation	Marketing effectiveness or accountability

Figure 7.3 Tourism Marketing Planning Process Model.

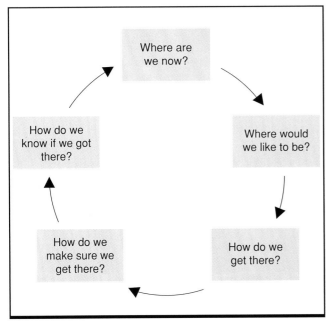

Figure 7.4 A Systems Approach to Tourism Marketing.
Adapted from Morrison. 2009.

external environment that is constantly changing, but over which the marketing manager has little or no control. The technique of identifying and analyzing the impact of external environmental forces is known as *environmental scanning*. The basic reason for doing an environmental scan is that it is better to anticipate change before it happens than to react to change after it has happened. This can be accomplished by answering these key questions: What are the major trends? Will they affect us and how will they affect us? How much will they affect us? How will they affect our closest competitors? What should we do differently in the future to adapt to these trends and their likely impacts?

The environmental forces to be scanned should include legislation and regulation; political situations; social and cultural characteristics; economic conditions; technology; transportation; and competition at a macro level. For a tourism organization or destination that attracts visitors from several countries, an environmental scan is needed for each individual visitor-generating country.

The first of the forces to be considered is the *legal and regulatory environment*. Certain countries, including South Korea and China, have in the past placed legal restrictions on their residents that have hampered the flow of outbound tourism. Residents may be restricted from traveling, or they may be unable to take more than a certain sum of money out of the country. Political factors must also be considered. Tensions or hostilities between the country of origin and the country of destination will affect marketing success. A good example of this is the uneasy relationship between Cuba and the United States. It is important to consider the social and cultural characteristics of the host destination's residents including educational backgrounds, traditions, religions, and the overall way of life. Most international travel is generated from countries with higher educational standards, from societies regarded as more cultured, and from countries having a higher degree of industrialization.

The pace of *technological change* within tourism and society in general is accelerating. Profound changes are resulting from the direct and indirect impacts of new technologies, including the use of the Internet and particularly the Web. Tourism is rapidly transforming from dependence on paper-based information to dependence on electronic information (e.g., e-tickets). Other technologies that are having a significant impact are global distribution systems (GDS), computerized reservation systems (CRS), and video- and tele-conferencing using satellite and other technologies.

Another important factor is *transportation* and other aspects of *accessibility* such as documentation requirements. The destination must be accessible to visitors from generating countries or regions. The current and projected *economic conditions* in generating countries are a factor of great importance in tourism. It is essential that there are enough people in the country who can afford to travel. China's increasing affluence, for example, has attracted much greater attention from destinations in the Asia Pacific region and elsewhere. The *exchange rate* between the host country and generating countries is another key economic concern. Past history has shown that major exchange rate shifts have a direct impact on travel volumes between specific pairs of countries.

Although commonly overlooked, the destination or organization's *macro-competition* should be analyzed. These are not head-to-head competitors, but represent the other products and services competing for the same disposable income. For example, the purchase of an expensive home entertainment system may take the place of a foreign vacation trip. A new car purchase may result in less frequent and shorter vacations being taken. There are potential substitutes for travel and they should be taken into consideration in marketing planning.

CONSIDER THE DEVELOPMENT GOALS AND STRATEGIES.
The marketing plan should be just one part of the overall *strategic plan* for the destination or organization, and just one element in the comprehensive tourism plan for a destination area. Tourism is one, and only one, strategy for development. As noted in chapter 2, tourism can be used as a political, social, and economic force. Yet, other alternatives are available. A comprehensive plan for tourism must be consistent with the overall planning and development goals and strategies for the destination area.

EVALUATE SERVICES, PRODUCTS, AND THE DESTINATION MIX.
One of the principal outcomes of a situation analysis is the determination of the destination's or organization's strengths and weaknesses, especially when compared to its closest competition. Competition is defined as anyone who serves the same target market or markets. The situation analysis reviews the destination's or organization's services and products, target markets, and competition. A tourism destination should compare the five components of its *destination mix* against those of its closest competitors:

- Attractions (natural resources, climate, cultural and historical resources, ethnic attractions, accessibility, manmade attractions)
- Facilities (lodging, food and beverage, support industries)
- Infrastructure (freshwater supply, sewage disposal systems, communications systems, road systems, health care facilities, energy systems, security systems)
- Transportation (airports, railway systems, cruise ship terminals, bus transportation)
- Hospitality (hospitality training programs, friendliness of local residents, overall service levels)

PREPARE A VISITOR MARKET PROFILE.
The crucial task is to develop a profile of the visitor and then to project that profile into the future by considering trends in the country or region of origin. The profiling task should address the questions and provide the visitor characteristics shown in figure 7.5.

When the existing target markets have been profiled, consideration is then given to new visitor target markets. Jones (1996) suggests that four categories of potential new visitors should be analyzed:

1. **Existing market segments:** Other people from existing target markets that have not yet visited the destination or used the service. For example, if most people in the existing market come from within a five-hundred-mile radius, potential markets may be discovered from areas within five hundred miles from which visitors do not yet come (e.g., specific cities or communities).

2. **Proximate potential market segments:** Past visitors to nearby destinations who have similar characteristics to existing target markets. These people have used a region and have demonstrated an interest in what it has to offer.

Malaysian Borneo (Sabah) Gets Serious About Nature Tourism Marketing

We are fully committed to continually improve our processes and activities towards achieving our vision, mission and targets in Sabah.

VISION
To achieve a minimum 1% of the total global tourism receipts by the year 2020.

MISSION
To market position Sabah, Malaysian Borneo as the premier nature adventure destination in the world.

Customer Charter, Sabah Tourism Board (2009), http://www. sabahtourism.com/corporate/about-us/1-7-customer-charter/, accessed January 6, 2009

Topics	Questions	Characteristics
WHO?	Who are they? Who makes the travel decision? Who helps them with travel decisions?	Behavioral characteristics Demographic/socioeconomic Influence of travel trade intermediaries Psychographic
WHERE?	Where do they live? Where do they travel within the destination? What other destinations do they visit?	Geographic characteristics Travel routes and patterns
WHAT?	What do they buy?	Services, products, facilities Usage of packages or tours
WHY?	Why do they travel? What do they like to do?	Activity preferences Motivations
WHEN?	When do they travel? When is the travel decision made? How long do they stay?	Length of stay Planning or "lead" time Seasonality of demand
HOW MANY?	How many of them are there? What are the sizes and composition of travel parties?	Market size Trip party size
HOW?	How do they make travel plans?	Booking preferences Use of travel trade

Figure 7.5 Components of a Visitor Market Profile.

3. **Expanded potential market segments**: Travelers who want similar products and services to that offered by the destination, but who have not yet visited the region. These might include special-interest markets such as adventure travel, golf, and scuba diving.

4. **Potential market segments for additional/enhanced products**: New visitors that would be attracted if new attractions or facilities were added. Examples might include a casino operation, convention center, golf courses, or guided nature tours.

ANALYZE COMPETITION. It is very important to analyze the marketing programs, positioning, and overall management of competing destinations or organizations, and to compare this with those of the subject destination or organization. What image do competitors have in the minds of potential customers? How successful were their past marketing programs? What have been their most successful marketing efforts? Do they have a cohesive, experienced, and marketing-oriented management team?

DETERMINE STRENGTHS AND WEAKNESSES. The culmination of this analysis is the identification of competitive strengths and weaknesses (What is there that is better than competitors?). The typical broad approach in marketing is to build upon and enhance competitive strengths and to take steps to address and improve upon weaknesses.

WHERE WOULD WE LIKE TO BE?

The second step in marketing planning is to define what the tourism destination or organization wants to achieve in the future. This is accomplished by considering alternative approaches to marketing for the next three to five years. The process involves defining a vision, establishing marketing goals, selecting target markets, creating a positioning approach, and setting marketing objectives.

DEFINE A VISION AND VISION STATEMENT. When the situation analysis is completed, the tourism organization or destination now must describe where it wants to be in the future. The first step in sketching the desired future situation should be the determination of a *vision* and *vision statement* for the destination or organization. According to Ritchie (1993), the visioning process consists of three distinct stages:

1. Envisioning of an image of a desired future organizational state, which
2. When effectively communicated to followers
3. Serves to empower those followers so they can enact the vision

In some ways, a vision is like a *super long-term goal* that becomes the foundation for defining the whole program of marketing action.

While there are few specific guidelines as to what a vision statement should include, it should at a minimum be measurable. The following are examples of vision statements for tourism destinations:

- **London, England:** "By 2016, London will be recognized as the leading global city for tourism and as a constantly evolving destination. London will deliver a high-quality visitor experience, continually surprising and exciting our visitors with a vibrant, contemporary, diverse offer in a historically rich environment. Tourism in London will contribute to the economic success of the city and the quality of life for Londoners" (Visit London Limited, 2008).
- **Canada:** The CTC is Canada's national tourism marketing organization. Our vision is compelling the world to explore Canada (Canadian Tourism Commission, 2008).
- **South Africa:** For South Africa to be the preferred tourist destination in the world, in order to maximize the economic potential of tourism for the country and its people (South Africa Tourism, 2008).
- **Singapore Tourism Board:** To be a leading economic development agency in tourism, always pushing new frontiers, setting new benchmarks and pioneering best practices (Singapore Tourism Board, 2008).

ESTABLISH TOURISM MARKETING GOALS. A set of *marketing goals* are now required to translate the vision into a program of marketing action for the next three to five years. Marketing goals describe the overall purposes and desired outcomes of future marketing programs. Marketing goals may be statements about the types of target markets to be attracted, images and perceptions to be communicated, marketing partnerships to be created, and forms of tourism development desired. They may set targets for visitor arrivals, expenditures, and foreign exchange earnings. Marketing goals provide the framework for the selection of target markets and the identification of more specific marketing objectives.

SELECT TARGET MARKETS. For marketing goals to be realized there must be a clear strategy about which segments of the tourism market will be targeted in the next three to five years. This involves the use of the *market segmentation analysis.* First, market segments are defined using one or more of the seven segmentation bases discussed earlier: demographic and socioeconomic, product-related, psychographic, geographic, purpose of trip, behavioral, or channel of distribution. The seg-

ments selected as target markets must meet the criteria of being measurable, accessible, substantial, defensible, durable, homogeneous, and compatible. The size (substantiality) of the market can be measured in terms of the number of visitors, the number of visitor nights, or the amount of visitor expenditures. Market segments that are large offer less risk than ones that are relatively small. Other factors that should be considered are the income potential, competition, cost, and the ability to serve potential target markets. The destination or organization should also have some advantage over one or more competitors in serving the target market.

The Fiji Visitors Bureau (FVB) and the Hawaii Visitors and Convention Bureau (HVCB) provide good examples of targeting a specific market segment. FVB has developed special and very attractive pages on its Web site dedicated to the theme of weddings and honeymoons. The HVCB, again using its Web site, takes aim at meeting, incentive, convention and exhibition planners in trying to position Hawaii as an attractive MICE destination. An excellent example of a highly targeted marketing strategy is that used by Contiki Holidays. This tour operator provided escorted tours to various parts of the world for people between ages eighteen and thirty-five.

CREATE A POSITIONING APPROACH. Next, the positioning of the destination or organization for each selected target market must be developed. Positioning should involve answering the following questions: Is there an existing image or perception in potential visitors' minds? What is this image or perception? Is there a need to create, change, or reinforce this image or perception? How should objective or subjective positioning be used to create the desired future positioning? and Which positioning approach should be used?

Tourism New Zealand is considered to be one of the best national tourist offices in the world. With its *100% Pure New Zealand* program it set new standards for positioning and branding a country tourism destination. This positioning emphasizes the unique and spectacular natural scenery in the country's North and South Islands.

SET MARKETING OBJECTIVES. *Objectives* are established for the next year and should meet four tests. First, they must be capable of being measured. Second, they must address a specific target market. Third, they must be stated in terms of a desired result or outcome that relate directly to either the environmental scan,

Why New Zealand Targets the Interactive Traveler

New Zealand's National Tourism Organisation's (NTO) job is to promote New Zealand internationally as a tourism destination. Their target market is what the organization calls the "interactive traveler." These are people who:

- Are regular international travelers
- Consume a wide range of tourism products and services
- Seek out new experiences that involve interacting with nature, social, and cultural environments
- Respect the environment, culture, and values of others
- Are considered leaders by their peers
- Don't mind planning and booking holidays directly
- Prefer authentic products and experiences
- Are health conscious and like to "connect" with others
- Enjoy outdoor activity
- Are sociable and like to learn
- Have high levels of disposable income

They are more likely to be 25 to 34 or 50 to 64, and not have any children at their homes. Additionally, they make great use of technology, including computers and the Internet. Interactive travelers research tourism destinations very thoroughly. They do much of the gathering of travel information on the Web.

Why has New Zealand decided to focus on this particular target market? Tourism New Zealand provides four reasons:

1. **Financial constraints:** New Zealand has a limited budget for promotion to would-be visitors. The bigger the target, the further we have to spread our budget and the less impact we will make. Tourism New Zealand's marketing will be more effective if we make a bigger impact with a smaller target.

2. **Finite resources:** New Zealand can't increase the amount of natural tourism assets it has. Rather than trying to simply increase the volume of visitors, we need to focus our messages on the people who most appreciate what we have, and can help us to maintain a high-quality visitor experience.

3. **Proposition match:** As a place to have a holiday, New Zealand is more attractive or relevant to certain people than others. It's logical to attract the visitors who have the greatest chance of being highly satisfied. They'll go home and tell their friends.

4. **Strategy 2010:** New Zealand has clearly defined long-term goals for tourism that will be achieved more readily if we focus on a particular group of travelers.

New Zealand is regarded as an outstanding adventure travel destination. © 2009 Ben Heys. Used under license from Shutterstock, Inc.

THINK ABOUT THIS:

1. What types of activities within New Zealand are likely to be the most appealing to these interactive travelers?

2. Which of the segmentation bases do you think Tourism New Zealand is using and what are your reasons for this?

3. Make a visit to Tourism New Zealand's consumer travel Web site, http://www. purenz.com. How well does this site appeal to the characteristics of the interactive travelers as described here?

Source: Tourism New Zealand. 2008. Why Does New Zealand Target the Interactive Traveller? Why a Target Market? http://www. newzealand.com/.

This Web site by the Hawaii Visitors and Convention Bureau is targeted toward the meetings, incentives, conventions, and exhibitions (MICE) segment. http://www.meethawaii.com/.

HOW DO WE GET THERE?

The third step is to prepare an action or implementation plan to achieve the marketing goals and objectives. Using the marketing objectives for each selected target market as a basis, marketing mixes are designed and detailed in a written *marketing plan*. Traditional approaches to marketing suggest that a *marketing mix* is comprised of four components: product, price, promotion, and place (distribution). These are called *the four Ps of marketing* (Perreault and McCarthy, 2000). Some authors have suggested that there are additional components to the tourism marketing

situation analysis, or development goals and strategies. Finally, a specific deadline for achievement must be stated. The accountability for marketing should be measured against the degree to which objectives are achieved (see page 195, "How do we know if we got there?").

mix. Because of the uniqueness of tourism marketing, it is recommended that packaging, programming, people, and partnership be considered as four additional marketing mix components (Morrison, 2002). The traditional four Ps then expands to eight Ps (product, price, promotion, place, packaging, programming, people, and

---

QUICK TRIP 7.5

Tourism Marketing Strategies and Priorities for Ontario

The Ministry of Tourism and Recreation in Ontario "supports delivery of high-quality tourism and recreation experiences to Ontarians and visitors to Ontario. Promoting a sustainable, customer-focused tourism industry and an active population helps improve our quality of life, increase pride in our communities, and increase economic growth." It seeks "to increase investment in Ontario's tourism industry by developing appropriate tools to foster an attractive climate in which to invest. Through our agency, the Ontario Tourism Marketing Partnership Corporation, the program markets Ontario as a year-round world-class travel destination. We work in partnership with our agencies, attractions, boards and commissions and the private sector. These partnerships maximize the economic, cultural, and social contributions of our agencies and attractions and stimulate economic growth, job creation, and stronger communities."

The Ministry has developed the *Ontario Tourism Strategy*, a plan for the sustainability and growth of Ontario's tourism industry that charts the course for tourism in the province until 2010. The five strategic directions outlined in this strategy are:

- Embracing a visitor-first philosophy
- Developing destinations and experiences
- Building the image and influence of tourism
- Strengthening strategic marketing
- Developing an "all of government" approach to tourism

(continued)

The following priorities were established for strengthening strategic marketing for 2005–06:

- Complete the Ontario Branding Exercise.
- Conduct marketing partnerships with destination partners (for example, with Toronto, Niagara Falls, Ottawa, Muskoka, Southern and Northern Ontario).
- Improve online experience for consumers.
- Align travel information centers to OTMPC's marketing efforts.
- Agencies and attractions will participate in strategic marketing in their regions.

The overall responsibility for marketing Ontario's tourism rests with the Ontario Tourism Marketing Partnership Corporation (OTMPC), the tourism marketing agency of the government of Ontario. Its vision is "to make Ontario the premier four-season destination by offering our guests satisfying experiences in our diverse nature, communities, and culture."

In 2003, Ontario and particularly Toronto suffered from the effects of the SARS outbreak. The following table shows the drop in overseas visitors to Ontario.

Person Visits in Ontario by Overseas Residents, 1980–2006 by Origin *(in thousands)*

	Overseas Total	United Kingdom	Japan	France	Germany	Other Countries
2000	2,384	488	258	206	190	1,242
2001	2,146	456	195	171	164	1,160
2002	2,014	406	197	135	145	1,131
2003	1,558	343	86	107	112	910
2004	2,049	429	207	118	141	1,154
2005	2,172	454	195	123	143	1,257
2006	2,198	422	182	130	131	1,333

The Ministry, in an attempt to recover from the 2003 drop, introduced the *Ontario Tourism Revitalization Program*, which included an Event Marketing and Development Fund (EMDF) and a Destination Marketing Partnership Fund (DMPF). The program guidelines include the following conditions: "The applicant must demonstrate that in 2003, there was a negative impact of various factors on their event and festival, or on the regional tourism economy. Proposals to the EMDF and DMPF must include information outlining why tourism revitalization assistance is required. For example, information such as comparative analysis for projected attendance, tickets sold, packages sold, the value of sponsorships lost, and projected economic loss for the community as it relates to the event or festival will be required to justify the funding request under the Tourism Revitalization Program."

THINK ABOUT THIS:

1. What are the challenges that face a provincial tourism office in implementing a service quality program within businesses and at other customer-contact points?

2. Why should a tourism office like the one in Ontario be interested in fostering an "all of government" approach to tourism?

3. What can destinations such as Ontario and Hong Kong do to recover from the effects of outbreaks of diseases like SARS?

Ontario places a high priority on tourism development and marketing. © 2009 Gary Blakeley. Used under license from Shutterstock, Inc.

Sources:

Ontario Ministry of Tourism and Recreation. 2005 and 2008. http://www.tourism.gov.on.ca/english/about/index.html.

http://www.tourism.gov.on.ca/english/about/revitalization.htm and http://www.tourism.gov.on.ca/english/about/2004-OTRP-Guidelines-form-e.pdf.

Ontario Tourism Strategy. 2008. http://www.tourism.gov.on.ca/english/tourism_strategy/ont_tourism_strategy-e.pdf.

Number of Person Visits in Ontario, 1980–2006. http://www.tourism.gov.on.ca/english/research/trends/index.html.

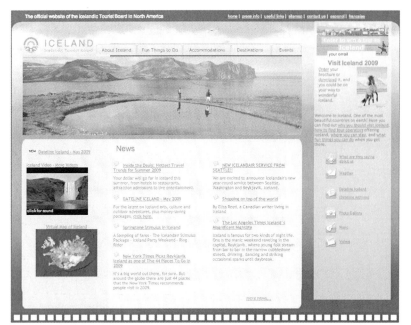

The Iceland Tourist Board positions the country as a pure and unspoiled destination for visitors. http://www.goiceland.org/news.php.

partnership). It is essential that each address the needs and characteristics of people in the selected target markets.

PRODUCT. Travel experiences consist of several different services and products ranging from transportation and lodging to sightseeing and souvenirs. These services and products are usually offered by a variety of tourism organizations. Each organization is dependent on the others to offer an attractive and satisfying overall travel experience. A marketing orientation suggests that services and products be designed to match the needs and wants of the targeted visitors. In addition, the market segmentation concept is based on the assumption that no single tourism destination or organization can provide services and products that will satisfy everyone. An organization must select a target market, and provide a variety of services and products to satisfy the targeted customers' needs. Striking the right balance between providing customized services to appeal to a particular target market, while having enough variety to be attractive to more than one target market, is a difficult decision for tourism marketing managers. The relatively fixed supply of tourism facilities and services, coupled with seasonal fluctuations in demand levels and customer types, make this task more complex.

There should be strong demand for the service or product from at least one core market segment, with the possibility of additional business from other market segments. It may be that the product can expect to break even on the basis of business from the major market segment and produce profit from business from the rest of the market. There may, of course, be a period of time before sales for a new attraction or service reach the break-even point.

New products and services should match the positioning or image of the tourism destination area or organization. They should also complement existing offerings. This does not mean that a destination area must appeal only to one segment of the market and that all its services and products must meet the needs of that market segment. A great deal obviously depends upon the size of the destination area. One part of a destination area may appeal to the younger singles and couples, while another part may be more attractive to seniors. It is important, however, that each individual part of the destination area develop the services, products, and positioning to fit one or more selected target markets.

New services and products must be adequately supported by the available supply of human resources, capital, management expertise, and natural resources. Although new services and products should be based on an identified competitive advantage, they may not be feasible due to a lack of the right quality or quantity of human or financial resources. For example, a destination area may have magnificent mountain terrain suit-

Although the resort's pool may not bring in revenue directly, its availability may increase room business. © 2009 Maksym Gorpenyuk. Used under license from Shutterstock, Inc.

able for skiing but may lack management knowledge in ski-area operations. Experienced management may have to be hired on a permanent or temporary basis before a ski area can be proposed. It is also possible in tourism that certain new services or products may be undesirable for social, cultural, or environmental reasons.

New services and products should contribute to the profit and/or growth of the entire tourism destination or organization. In some cases the new offering may bring in no profit itself, but its provision may contribute to growth. The hotel pool, for example, may cost the operation money while bringing in no direct revenue. However, its availability may bring in additional room business. If the pool is eliminated, this may cause guests to use another hotel or resort. Similarly, a destination may introduce its own airline, not as a revenue-producing venture but as part of a strategy to attract more visitors.

PRICE. In pure economic terms, price is a result of supply and demand. When supply exceeds demand, price will tend to decrease. The reverse is also true. Of greater importance is the extent to which demand changes (as measured by the amount purchased) as price changes–the elasticity of demand. A 5 percent reduction in price may result in a corresponding 10 percent increase in the number of buyers and a subsequent increase in total sales revenue. Demand in this case is elastic. Generally, products aimed at the luxury end of the customer scale are less susceptible to changes in price and tend to be price inelastic. For businesses that are open only part of the year, supply is limited and prices have to be higher (everything else begins equal) than businesses open year round. Because demand is not often uniform throughout the year, it is common to charge higher prices during the peak season and lower prices when demand slackens.

The expected length of the product life cycle and the destination's or organization's position on it also affect pricing decisions. A fad item with an expected short life cycle will have to charge high prices to recoup the investment in a relatively short period of time. A product that expects a longer life can be priced lower.

The price charged is influenced by competition. If a destination's facilities and services are very similar to competitors, its prices must be similar to theirs. The extent to which the destination area or other tourism service is unique influences whether it can charge more than the competition. Related to the influence of competition is the management policy regarding market share. If the decision is made to increase market share, prices will probably be lower than if we decide to "skim" a small number of visitors from several market segments.

Pricing policy is also influenced by the needs of the selected target market. If a tourism destination or organization serves the needs and wants of the market and if those needs and wants are perceived as being important to the members of the market segment, those people will be willing to pay a higher price. The price charged must also be perceived by the market as less than or at least equal to the value received. In some situations the influence of the market seems to go against economic principles. With certain luxury items, demand may increase as price increases. This phenomenon reflects a degree of snobbishness on the part of the market. The feeling may be that the higher the price the greater the perceived value and the greater the demand. But the actual value in the minds of the buyers must still equal or exceed the price paid.

PROMOTION. The topic of promotion is covered in detail in chapter 8. Promotion is the most visible part of

South Africa Tourism joins with other partners in promoting the biggest event for the world's favorite game–2010 FIFA World Cup. http://www. southafrica.info/2010/.

the marketing mix, apart from the services or products themselves. Many people fall into the trap of confusing marketing and promotion, thinking of them as being exactly the same. However, there is much more to marketing than just promotion. The *promotional mix* consists of several elements including advertising, sales promotion, merchandising, personal selling and sales, public relations and publicity, along with Internet marketing. All promotions involve some form of communications with potential customers.

PLACE (DISTRIBUTION). Tourism distribution is unique. In the absence of a physical distribution system, tourism has developed a unique set of *distribution channels* and travel trade intermediaries. These intermediaries influence visitor's choices of tourism destinations and businesses, and require separate attention by the tourism marketer. The choice of specific channels of distribution and intermediaries is influenced by several factors including the target market, type of tourism service or destination, and the location of the services relative to the customers' residences. Chapter 9 provides detailed information on tourism distribution and individual categories of travel trade intermediaries.

NTOs Spend Heavily on Marketing and Advertising
Nearly two thirds of the available NTO budgets is spent on actual costs for marketing. The remaining share is used for operating costs. Between 2004 and 2005 the share of operating costs has lightly decreased, which indicates that available budgets are increasingly spent on direct out of pocket expenses for marketing purposes.

More than 40 per cent of the NTOs marketing budgets is spent in advertising, followed by marketing activities such as "information" and "attending trade fairs", both with a share of just above ten per cent. Around 2.5 per cent of the marketing budget is spent on research.

Structures and Budgets of National Tourism Organizations 2004–2005, *UN World Tourism*

PACKAGING. Packages in tourism are unique. They are especially important because they can be used to help cope with the problems of the immediate perishability of services, and the difficulties of matching demand volumes with supply capacities. Packaging also provides a way to match tourism services and products with visitors' needs. For example, tourism businesses now offer many packages for special-interest groups ranging from anthropologists to zoologists.

Group	Reasons
Visitors	1. Greater convenience (saves time)
	2. Greater economy (saves money)
	3. Ability to budget for trips (makes planning easier)
	4. Implicit assurance of consistent quality (less risk)
	5. Satisfaction of specialized interests
	6. Added dimension to traveling
Participating Businesses	1. Increased business in off-peak periods
	2. Enhanced appeal to specific target markets
	3. Attraction of new target markets
	4. Easier business forecasting and improved efficiency
	5. Use of complementary facilities, attractions, and events
	6. Flexibility to capitalize on new market trends
	7. Stimulation of repeat and more frequent usage
	8. Increased per capita spending and lengths of stay
	9. Public relations and publicity value of unique packages
	10. Increased customer satisfaction

Figure 7.6 Reasons for the Popularity of Vacation/Holiday Packages. Adapted from Morrison. 2009.

Packaging is significant because it brings together many of the elements of the destination mix. Packages combine the services and products of several tourism organizations. The package is more convenient for visitors since it includes several services and products at an all-inclusive price. Other advantages of packages are listed in figure 7.6.

PROGRAMMING. Programming involves special activities, events, or other types of programs to increase customer spending or to give added appeal to a package or other tourism service. Many vacation packages include some form of programming such as escorted ground tours, sports instruction, and entertainment events. A popular approach among travel destinations is to designate particular years for special celebrations and to focus attention on programs that support specific themes. For example, Thailand introduced "Visit Amazing Thailand Year" in 2009.

For example, the Brazil Ministry of Tourism (http://www.braziltour.com) has dedicated a page on its Web site to promote the Carnival that takes place in February and March every year. The Edinburgh and Lothians Tourist Board (http://www.edinburgh.org) promotes the Edinburgh Military Tattoo and the International Festival held in Scotland's capital in August annually.

The Brazil Ministry of Tourism uses programming in promoting Carnival. http://www.braziltour.com/site/en/tour_produtos/internas_submenu.php?id=339&fatherId=6.

PEOPLE (HUMAN RESOURCES). Tourism is a people business. No amount or quality of facilities can make up for poor service. A tourism marketer must ensure that employees are adequately trained in their specific function, and that tourism employees and local residents have hospitable attitudes toward visitors.

PARTNERSHIP. Partnership means *cooperative marketing* programs involving two or more tourism destinations or individual organizations. In an increasingly competitive tourism industry, the pooling of resources with other organizations may provide the added edge necessary for success. Packaging, when it involves two or more organizations, represents one important application of the partnership concept. Cooperative advertising is a second application. For example, the Central American countries of Belize, El Salvador, Guatemala, and Honduras have linked up with Mexico in promoting the Mayan World region (*El Mundo Maya*). This joint marketing program is based on the remaining archaeological sites of the Mayan civilization, which are found in these five countries. Another example of a regional partnership is the joint promotion by the countries of Europe sharing the Alps (Austria, France, Germany, Italy, and Switzerland).

Strategic alliances are another form of cooperation in tourism. These are long-term agreements between companies or countries to invest in joint marketing programs. Strategic alliances have been especially popular among airline companies. Alliances are also being formed among hotels, airlines, and car rental companies to gain competitive advantages through reciprocal frequent traveler award programs, and to provide travelers with greater speed and flexibility (Dev et al., 1996). Good examples of these are the three major airline strategic alliances (Star Alliance, OneWorld Alliance, and SkyTeam Alliance), and the cooperation between the Scandinavian countries in tourism promotion (Denmark, Finland, Iceland, Norway, and Sweden are represented by the Scandinavian Tourist Boards).

The Scandinavian countries' marketing of tourism is a long-term, team effort. http://www.goscandinavia.com/.

There are eight criteria for successful inter-organizational partnerships (Kanter, 1994):

1. **Individual excellence:** All the partners are strong organizations and want something positive from the partnership.

2. **Importance:** The partnership fits with each partner's long-term strategy.

3. **Interdependence:** The partners need each other because they have complementary skills and assets.

4. **Investment:** The partners invest in each other.

5. **Information:** Communication is open among the partners.

QUICK TRIP 7.6

Hawaii Knows the Importance of Partnership Creation

The Hawaii Tourism Authority, established in 1998, is the official advocate for the state's tourism industry. Its mission is:

> To strategically manage Hawaii tourism in a sustainable manner consistent with our economic goals, cultural values, preservation of natural resources, community desires, and visitor industry needs.

One of the core values of the HTA is "collaboration and partnerships." This means leading and supporting partners in the public and private sectors that need to work together on each initiative to achieve the overall vision. Through partnerships, the HTA has found a way to address shoulder periods, increase total number of arrivals, length of stay, and per person daily spending.

The alignment of the HTA's efforts with those of their chosen partners brings greater efficiency to marketing efforts, potentially increasing Hawaii's market share.

During the HTA Tourism Conference, 2008, the results of 2007 tourism were addressed. One of the main concerns presented was the need for *stronger* strategic partnerships. The allies sought include Tour Operators, large Retail Agency Chains, Product Promotions Agencies, and Airlines. It was made clear that each partner must be chosen based on the attractiveness each represents to HTA's target markets and the benefits it can bring to tourism statistics. All selected associates must follow the guidelines and objectives created by the HTA, meaning that their goals and customers must be inline with the needs of Hawaii's Tourism Authority.

THINK ABOUT THIS:

1. Besides what is mentioned in the Quick Trip, how else can the collaboration with industry partners be beneficial to tourism? Are partnerships limited to those acting within the same industry?

2. The HTA specifically mentioned that partnerships with flight carriers are important. Why are these companies singled out? Geographic location and accessibility are important when considering alliances. Are there other destinations that support partnerships for similar reasons?

3. Using common knowledge about Hawaii (features, characteristics, location, etc.), what other company alliances may be interesting?

4. Are there any dangers in creating long-term partnerships?

Source: Hawaii Tourism Authority 2007 Annual Report, HTA 2007 Tourism Conference Presentation–March 2008, http://www. hawaiitourismauthority.org.

The Hawaii Tourism Authority puts a strong emphasis on the importance of partnerships in destination marketing. http://www.hawaiitourismauthority.org/.

6. **Integration:** Partners develop links and shared methods of operation.

7. **Institutionalization:** The partnership is given a formal status.

8. **Integrity:** The partners behave honorably toward each other.

How Do We Make Sure We Get There?

Marketing does not stop after the marketing plan has been written. Steps must be taken to ensure that the plan is successful in achieving its objectives. Progress toward the achievement of objectives must be made as the plan is being implemented. This is done by checking progress at predetermined times to see if things are going as planned. If significant deviations from the expected results are found, it may be necessary to modify the marketing plan. This process is often referred to as *marketing control*.

How Do We Know If We Got There?

The last step in the marketing planning process is to determine *marketing effectiveness*. Results and outcomes are evaluated to determine if the marketing goals and objectives have been attained. It has become popular to refer to this as a procedure to ensure the *accountability* of those responsible for tourism marketing. Marketing effectiveness is measured by accountability or evaluation research.

Summary

The marketing of services is different from the marketing of products. Since tourism is a service business and since it is a unique form of service, tourism requires different types of marketing programs and activities. Tourism marketing has evolved through a series of stages or eras. The current societal marketing era is most appropriate for destination tourism marketing since it goes beyond pure economic considerations and is consistent with the sustainable tourism development concept.

Tourism marketing must follow a systematic marketing planning process. It is important to consider the external marketing environment as well as those factors that the organization or destination can control. Careful attention must be given to market segmentation and the selection of target markets. Every tourism organization needs to choose a unique blend or marketing mix of these factors to meet the needs of its target markets. In tourism, the marketing mix consists of eight elements: products and services, price, place (distribution), promotion, packaging, programming, people, and partnership. Marketing plans must be controlled and evaluated to ensure that they are effective.

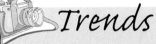 ***Trends***

Marketing Trends in Tourism

1. Increasing use of the Internet and mobile technologies for marketing
2. Greater emphasis on customizing packages including dynamic packaging
3. Growing emphasis on providing "hands-on" and participative activities for visitors to attractions
4. More attention being given to revenue or yield management
5. Growing diversity of special-interest activities and destinations
6. Increasing importance and use of customer databases
7. Partnering with other organizations being given a much higher priority
8. Growing importance of online travel companies
9. Globalizing of communications through the use of multilingual and multicultural approaches
10. Increasing range of short-break and mini-vacation packages being offered

Source: Morrison, A. M. 2009. *Hospitality and Travel Marketing*, 4th ed. Delmar.

ACTIVITIES

1. Pick a segment of the tourism market in which you have an interest. This could be a special-interest market (scuba diving, cuisine, health/spa, etc.) or another type of segment (e.g., families, MICE). Visit a local library or bookstore and try to find as much information as you can in printed format on destinations and travel activities for your chosen market segment.

2. Visit a selection of local travel agencies and ask for information on travel for your chosen market segment. How comprehensive and appealing was the information that the agencies provided?

3. Interview a variety of tourism companies and organizations that are actively marketing to this segment. What types of marketing strategies are they applying in appealing this segment?

INTERNET
ACTIVITIES

4. Identify a set of up to ten tourism Web sites that specifically address your selected market segment.

5. What specific activities and experiences do these Web sites feature for the market segment?

6. In your opinion, which Web sites are the best in appealing to and providing information for the market segment? Why?

REFERENCES

Bigne, E., I. Sanchez, and J. Sanchez. 2001. Tourism image, evaluation variables and after purchase behaviour: Inter-relationship. *Tourism Management,* 22: 607–616.

Butler, R. W., and L. A. Waldbrook. 1991. A new planning tool: The tourism opportunity spectrum. *The Journal of Tourism Studies,* 2 (1): 2–14.

Butler, R. 2006. *The Tourism Area Life Cycle(1).* Ontario: Channel View.

Covey, C. 1988. Tahiti sets out to dispel myths that deter tourists. *Travel Agent Magazine,* March 31: 8–9.

Crissy, W. J. E., R. J. Boewadt, and D. M. Laudadio. 1975. *Marketing of Hospitality Services: Food, Lodging, Travel.* East Lansing, MI: Educational Institute of the American Hotel and Motel Association.

Dev, C. S., S. Klein, and R. A. Fisher. 1996. A market-based approach to partner selection in marketing alliances. *Journal of Travel Research,* 35 (1): 11–17.

Deng, J., B. Xiang, and L. Zhong. 2008. Tourism development and the tourism area life-cycle model: A case study of Zhanjiajie National Forest Park, China. *Tourism Management,* 29: 841–856.

Gallarza, M., S. Gil, and G. Calderon. 2002. Destination image: Towards a conceptual framework. *Annals of Tourism Research,* 29: 56–78.

Gartner, W. C. 1996. *Tourism Development: Principles, Processes, Policies.* New York: Van Nostrand Reinhold.

Gomezelj, D., and T. Mihalic. 2008. Destination competitiveness: Applying different models, the case of Slovenia. *Tourism Management,* 29: 294–307.

Govers, R., F. M. Go, and K. Kumar. 2007. Virtual destination image: A new measurement approach. *Annals of Tourism Research,* 34 (4): 977–997.

Hart, C. 1989. The Caribbean—Caught in a tourist trap. *World Development.* 7–9.

Hsieh, S., J. T. O'Leary, and A. M. Morrison. 1992. Segmentation of the Hong Kong travel market by activity participation. *Tourism Management,* 13: 209–223.

Hyde, K. F. 2008. Information processing and tour planning theory. *Annals of Tourism Research,* 35 (3): 712–731.

Jones, C. B. 1995. *Destination Databases as Keys to Effective Marketing.* San Francisco: Economics Research Associates. http://www.econres.com/.

Kale, S. H., and K. M. Weir. 1986. Marketing third world countries to the Western traveler: The case of India. *Journal of Travel Research,* 25 (2): 2–7.

Kanter, R. M. 1994. Collaborative advantage. *Harvard Business Review,* 72 (4): 96–108.

Kotler, P. 1984. *Marketing Management: Analysis, Planning, Implementation, and Control,* 5th ed. Englewood Cliffs, NJ: Prentice-Hall, Inc.

Kotler, P., J. Bowen, and J. Makens. 1999. *Marketing for Hospitality & Tourism.* Upper Saddle River, NJ: Prentice-Hall, Inc.

Krotz, L. 1996. *Tourists: How Our Fastest Growing Industry Is Changing the World.* Boston: Faber and Faber.

Lewis, R. C., and R. E. Chambers. 2000. *Marketing Leadership in Hospitality,* 3rd ed. New York: Van Nostrand Reinhold.

Mackay, K., and D. Fesenmaier. 2000. An exploration of cross-cultural destination image assessment. *Journal of Travel Research,* 38: 417–423.

Mehta, S. C., and A. Vera. 1990. Segmentation in Singapore. *The Cornell HRA Quarterly,* 31 (1): 80–87.

Morgan, N., A. Pritchard, and R. Pride. 2002. Marketing to the Welsh diaspora: The appeal to hiraeth and home-coming. *Journal of Vacation Marketing,* 9 (1): 69–80.

Morrison, A. M. 2009. *Hospitality and Travel Marketing,* 4th ed. Clifton Park, NY: Delmar Publishers.

Pearce, D. 1989. *Tourist Development,* 2nd ed. Essex, England: Longman Scientific & Technical.

Perreault, W. D., Jr., and E. J. McCarthy. 2000. *Essentials of Marketing: A Global-Managerial Approach,* 12th ed. Homewood, IL: Irwin.

Ries, A., and J. Trout. 1981. *Positioning: The Battle for Your Mind.* New York: Warner Books, Inc.

Ritchie, J. R. B. 1993. Crafting a destination vision: Putting the concept of resident-responsive tourism into practice. *Tourism Management*, 14: 379–389.

Ritchie, J. R. B., and G. Crouch. 2003. *The Competitive Destination: A Sustainable Tourism Perspective*. Cambridge: Cabi Publishing.

Smith, S. L. J. 1989. *Tourism Analysis: A Handbook*. Essex, England: Longman Scientific & Technical.

Travel Weekly. 1997. Australia showing personality in latest ad campaign. *Travel Weekly*, 56 (14): 26.

Trout, J. 1996. *The New Positioning: The Latest on the World's #1 Business Strategy*. New York: McGraw-Hill, Inc.

Wind, Y., V. Mahajan, and R. E. Gunther. 2002. *Convergence Marketing: Strategies for Reaching the New Hybrid Consumer*. Upper Saddle River, NJ: Prentice-Hall.

Woodside, A., and C. Dubelaar. 2002. A general theory of tourism consumption systems: A conceptual framework and an empirical explanation. *Journal of Travel Research*, 41: 120–132.

World Tourism Organization. 1975. *Testing the Effectiveness of Promotional Campaigns in International Travel Marketing*. Ottawa: WTO Seminar.

SURFING SOLUTIONS

http://www.adage.com/ (*Advertising Age* magazine)

http://www.marketingpower.com/ (American Marketing Association)

http://www.stb-asia.com/corporate/index.html (Scandinavian Tourist Board in Asia)

http://www.oattravel.com/gcc/general/ (Overseas Adventure Travel)

http://app.stb.com.sg/asp/index.asp/ (Singapore Tourism Board)

ACRONYMS

CRS (computerized reservation system)
DMO (destination marketing organization)
GDS (global distribution system)
PLC (product life cycle)
SWOT (strengths, weaknesses, opportunities, threats)
TA (Tourism Australia)
VFR (visiting friends and relatives)

chapter 8

Tourism Promotion

COMMUNICATING WITH TARGET MARKETS

Italy's Tourism Image in Need of a Makeover

Bella Italia's image has darkened in recent months under media coverage of reeking mountains of garbage in Naples, adulterated wine, and dioxin-tainted mozzarella. Figures published by the Touring Club Italiano (TCI), a national tourism promotion organisation, show that the country's fall from grace is nothing new, however. The world's tourism champion in 1970 in terms of the number of visitors, Italy has gradually slipped to fifth place.

Tourist paradise Italy looks to burnish tarnished image, Hanns-Jochen Ka, TopTravelNews.com, http://www.topnews.in/travel/tourist-paradise-italy-looks-burnish-tarnished-image-236, accessed January 6, 2009

PURPOSE

Having learned about the general principles of communications and promotion, students will be able to describe a program for implementing a promotion in a tourism destination or organization. They will also be able to explain the roles of destination marketing organizations at all levels.

LEARNING OBJECTIVES

✓ Identify and describe which promotional methods are most effective during the various stages of the visitor's buying process.
✓ Distinguish between informative promotion, persuasive promotion, and reminder messages, and identify when the use of these techniques is most appropriate.
✓ List and describe the main elements in the communication process.
✓ List and describe the elements of the promotional mix.
✓ Identify and explain the procedures involved in implementing a promotional program.
✓ Describe the roles and activities of national tourist offices (NTOs) related to promotion.
✓ Describe the promotional programs operated by agencies at the state, provincial, territorial, regional, and local levels.

OVERVIEW

The process of promotion is a process of communication; communication between seller and buyer. This chapter discusses the promotional mix concept. A link is established between the goals of promotion and the customer's buying process stages described in chapter 11. Appropriate types of promotion are suggested for each of the traveler's buying process stage.

The process of communication is explained. An eight-step program for implementing promotions is described. A target market and promotional objectives need to be established. Once a promotional budget has been set, the message idea and format for the promotion can be designed. A promotional mix and the appropriate media are selected. At each step of the program, controls are used to ensure that promotional campaigns progress as planned and achieve the objectives. It is important to evaluate promotions after they have been implemented to measure their effectiveness and to ensure accountability.

The promotional roles and programs of destination marketing organizations (DMOs) at the national, state, regional, and local levels are described.

PROMOTION = COMMUNICATION

Developing the promotional mix is an exercise in communication. Destination marketing organizations, suppliers of tourism services, and travel trade intermediaries have to communicate messages to potential visitors. Through explicit communications, language and images are used in advertisements and other promotions to create a common understanding between the organization (sender) and the visitor (receiver). Messages can also be transmitted through implicit communications in nonver-

bal means such as gestures and facial expressions, and by non-explicitly communicated items such as prices and the physical characteristics of the facilities provided.

GOALS AND TYPES OF PROMOTIONS

Tourism promotions may have several goals. The ultimate goal of promotion is behavior modification. The first behavioral goal may be to create a booking or sale by convincing the visitor to purchase for the first time. Second, the goal may be to modify the repeat visitor's purchase behavior by having them switch to another destination, package, or service. Third, the goal may be to reinforce existing behavior by having the repeat visitor continue to purchase the same destination, package, or other service. Promotion accomplishes this by informing, persuading, or reminding the visitor about the promoter's services.

The effectiveness of different types of promotions varies with product life cycle (PLC) stage. For example, informative promotions are more important during the first stage of the PLC (introduction) when a new destination or business is entering a market. Potential visitors must be given enough information and knowledge before they will buy. Persuasive promotions try to get a visitor to buy and become the objective during the growth stage of the PLC. In the maturity stage, reminder promotions become important. Visitors have already used the tourism services or been to the destination before. Reminder promotions jog visitors' memories and help keep the tourism destination or organization in the public eye.

PROMOTION AND THE VISITOR'S BUYING PROCESS

The goals of behavior modification are more effectively achieved by matching the three types of promotion with the stages of the visitor's buying process (as discussed in chapter 11). For example, informative promotions are most effective at the earlier buying process stages of attention and comprehension (figure 8.1). Promotional messages must grab the visitor's attention, while providing enough information and convincing arguments to assist with comprehension. The Canadian Tourism Commission does a great job of this in its "*Canada: Keep Exploring*" promotional campaign. Instead of showing just the spectacular Canadian scenery, these promotions show people actively enjoying certain types of experiences in these beautiful destinations.

Singapore Is a Unique Tourism Destination

Uniquely Singapore—Unique is the word that best captures Singapore, a dynamic city rich in contrast and colour where you'll find a harmonious blend of culture, cuisine, arts and architecture. A bridge between the East and the West for centuries, Singapore, located in the heart of fascinating Southeast Asia, continues to embrace tradition and modernity today. Brimming with unbridled energy and bursting with exciting events, the city offers countless unique, memorable experiences waiting to be discovered.

Brand Overview, Destination Singapore, *Singapore Tourism Board* (2005), http://app.stb.gov.sg/asp/des/des05.asp, accessed January 5, 2009

Scotland's Marketing Campaigns, Promotional Mix Elements

Scotland has developed the VisitScotland.com Web site in order to better communicate with its clients. All the efforts being undertaken in name of the industry's continuous expansion are exposed here. One of the driving forces of this initiative is to have all tourism businesses aligned with their national tourism organization, to unify marketing efforts through the dissemination of information. The Web site explains the goals and targets of each marketing campaign, and how it will be conducted.

To begin, the campaign efforts are divided into two large geographic markets, the United Kingdom and Ireland and international.

International markets are important to Scottish tourism. Because foreign visitors tend to stay longer than domestic visitors, their total expenditure during their visit is higher—so while 17 percent of the total number of trips made to Scotland in 2006 were by foreign visitors, they provided around 35 percent of total expenditures by all visitors. Our aim is to continue to increase the number of foreign visitors to Scotland, but especially to increase the value of their tourism expenditure.

Focusing on the international marketing campaign, Scotland has developed a wide range of communications including advertising, advertorial promotions, Web sites, direct marketing, PR, and exhibitions. The goal is to increase brand awareness through the consistent use of key themes, tone of voice, and visual cues. The promotional campaigns (and their respective tools) for 2008/2009 are:

- *Pan European Touring Campaign:* Features direct mail, press inserts and advertorials, online advertising (banners, video streaming, key word advertising on key travel and lifestyle portals and e-newsletters), acquisition leads buys, and press and PR activity (info-screens, press visits, releases, features, and ongoing media relations)
- *Pan European City Breaks Campaign:* Based on regular e-communications, monthly e-blasts (intended to drive traffic to city gateway sites) and above the line activity (e-commerce and PR, online and advertorial festival theme runs, direct mail, and banner ads)
- *U.S. Spring Touring Campaign 2008:* Publicized through advertising on the Web (interactive banners, video streamed banners and key word advertising), advertorials to promote *Win a Scottish Island* sweepstakes (bringing merchandising), and press and PR (year-round program of press visits, releases, features, and ongoing media relations)
- *Date a Hot Scot:* Driven by press and PR, and has its own Web site
- *Swedish Golf Campaign 2007:* Targets the lucrative Swedish golfing market through active participation at golfing events, online advertisements, e-newsletters, incentive drivers, and corporate and consumer PR teams, a more hands-on approach

Hiking on Scotland's highlands and islands is a popular activity among visitors. © 2009 Nikki Bidgood. Used under license from Shutterstock, Inc.

THINK ABOUT THIS:

1. The purpose of having the preceding information accessible to all is an attempt to unify promotional objectives. How could an institution like VisitScotland effectively unite tourism suppliers?

2. Clients are receptive to all promotion campaigns. Agree or disagree? Why? Do limits exist?

Sources: http://www.visitscotland.com/, http://www.scotland.org/, http://www.visitscotland.org/. Scottish Tourism: The Next Decade—A Tourism Framework for Change.

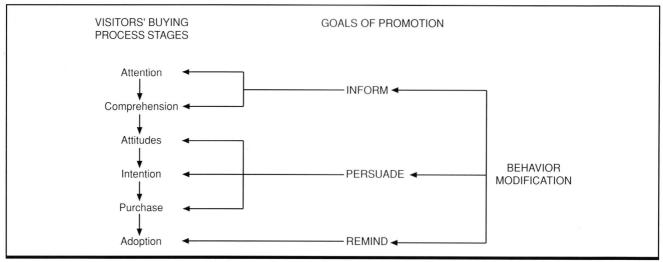

Figure 8.1 Goals of Promotion and the Visitor's Buying Process.

Persuasive promotions work better at intermediate buying process stages (attitudes, intention, and purchase). They can be used to change attitudes, develop intentions to buy, and to initiate purchases. The New Zealand Tourism Board (Tourism New Zealand) provides a good example of this on its Web site. Videos of past visitors' trips and great experiences in New Zealand can be downloaded and watched on the Web site. These are a powerful testimonial for other people considering similar trips to an exciting long-haul destination such as New Zealand.

Reminder promotions are more effective after the first visit to the destination or first use of the organization's services. Reminder promotions help stimulate repeat visits or purchases. A process known as *database marketing* is increasingly being used in tourism to encourage repeat usage. Computer technology that allows the manipulation of relational databases on past and potential visitors is facilitating this process. Cruise line companies and casino operators have been especially successful in building databases and using reminder promotions. There are four major objectives of database marketing (Jones, 1998):

1. To know more about what existing and potential visitors want
2. To reach these visitors and tell them what the destination/organization has to offer
3. To satisfy customers so that they come back and spread the good word (word of mouth)
4. To operate profitably

French Government Tries to Rejuvenate Tourism
The French Government, as part of its strategy to rejuvenate its tourism industry, has created a new France brand that includes a new logo and tagline. The objective was to establish a strong, united visual identity that can be used throughout the industry and to standardize the image of France worldwide. Advisors to the plan wanted a logo that is striking, witty and generous to express three traits that make France unique:

Liberty: independence, creativity, imagination, boldness, spontaneity, a multitude of possibilities
Authenticity: history, heritage, culture, nature
Sensuality: pleasure, Epicureanism, romance, intensity, passion, femininity

The tagline "Rendez-vous en France" is an integral part of the logo. It is a universal term often associated with a romantic rendez-vous that is an attractive concept for all cultures.

The new face of French tourism: New France brand with logo and tagline, FranceGuide.com (2008), http://us.franceguide. com/press/The-new-face-of-French-Tourism.html?nodeID= 422&EditoID=199508, accessed January 6, 2009

Cruise line companies have been successful in building databases and using reminder promotions. Photo by Alastair Morrison.

Return on Investment through Databasing Clients

The return on marketing investment lies hand in hand with the effectiveness of marketing strategies. Communicating with target markets is a critical part of all businesses. In the long run, final results depend on how many potential clients were changed into real customers. The best way to do this uses up-to-date information about the targets.

Hotels, casinos, airports, cruise lines, and others use information systems to support their competitive strategy, personalize and manage customer relations, reward and attract customers, and build more efficient marketing schemes. Information technology (IT) has many uses in this field.

Bill Gates once said, "How you can gather, manage and use information will determine whether you win or lose."

Property management systems (PMSs) are designed to give a competitive edge and increase customer loyalty to hotels. The decision-making process in the hospitality industry is based on informed decisions, decisions that can be supported by appropriate PMSs. One of the leading property management systems offers:

Complete demographic records for guests, business accounts, contacts, groups, agents, and sources. Profiles include addresses, phone numbers, membership enrollments, stay and revenue details, guest preferences, and additional data that make reservations handling and many other activities faster and more accurate.

Software provider Micros Fidelio U.K. offers a "multiproperty, fully integrated hotel system that includes property management, sales and catering, central reservations, revenue management, material management, and back office applications. Our client base includes InterContinental Hotels Group, Hilton International, Marriott International, Four Seasons, Wyndham Hotels, Le Meridien Hotels, and Best Western to name a few."

Developing, storing, and maintaining databases are essential to effective tourism marketing today. © 2009 Silvia Bukovac. Used under license from Shutterstock, Inc.

THINK ABOUT THIS:

1. Information technology and systems are not new to the tourism world. How else can the use of technology be lucrative to marketing and communication?

2. Ethics and privacy are issues discussed frequently. Where do IT-dependent businesses in tourism stand on this topic?

3. In the cruise industry, for example, databasing is used not only for communication but also to enhance the vacationers' experience. How else can IT make tourism more pleasant?

Sources: 2008. http://www.micros-fidelio.co.uk/industry/hotels-resorts/; 2008. http://www.propertysolutions.com; Information Systems for Managers: Texts and Cases by Gabriele Piccoli. 2007.

THE COMMUNICATIONS PROCESS

The communications process is shown in figure 8.2. The sender (tourism destination or organization) sets marketing objectives for the target market (receivers). A budget is established for communications. The message strategy (message idea and format) for the promotion are developed. Based upon the chosen message idea and format, an appropriate promotional mix and medium are selected. Steps are taken to generate responses from the receivers (potential visitors). The responses are compared to the marketing objectives to determine the overall effectiveness of the promotional campaign.

Many destination marketing organizations use *direct-response advertising*, either online or through traditional media. This advertising generates requests for printed collateral materials including visitor guides, calendars of festivals and events, and maps. The process of sending collateral materials to people who request them is known as *fulfillment*. Destination marketing organizations measure the effectiveness of direct-response advertisements by keeping records of the telephone, mail, fax, and electronic (e-mail and Web) inquiries after the advertising has been run. Some agencies go further and determine, through techniques like *conversion studies*, how many inquirers actually visit the destination or use

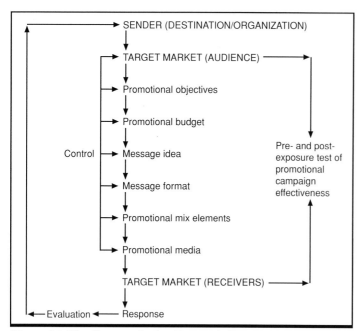

Figure 8.2 The Communication Process in Tourism.

the service after being sent the requested collateral materials.

This analysis only goes part of the way in determining promotional effectiveness. If the response rates do not match objectives, time and money have been wasted. The analysis does not indicate where the problems were; it shows the effects rather than the causes of the problems. Were the objectives set too high? Were the message idea and format appropriate but communicated to the wrong target market? Were the right media used to communicate the message? Was the wrong in-

---

Ireland Launches Aggressive New Overseas Marketing Strategy

Dublin, 26 November 2008: Tourism Ireland today launched details of its €47 million marketing strategy and plans to promote the island of Ireland overseas in 2009, at an event attended by Minister for Arts Sport & Tourism, Martin Cullen TD, and tourism industry leaders. Details of a new three-year global advertising campaign 'Go Where Ireland Takes You' were also previewed at the event. This new campaign, which will launch early next year overseas, will include TV, press and online advertising and will have an estimated annual audience of 200 million potential visitors worldwide. The new press ads have been created through a technique using computer-generated imagery, to create novel infinity maps, which is a first for a tourism agency worldwide. These maps show multiple images or "icons" from around the island of Ireland offering the potential visitor many compelling reasons to visit.

€47m Global Tourism Marketing Plans Launched, Tourism Ireland (2008), http://www.tourismireland.com/Home/about-us/press-releases/€47m-Global-Tourism-Marketing-Plans-Launched.aspx, accessed January 6, 2008

---

formation or images communicated? To avoid these kinds of problems, the communications process must be controlled during every step in the promotional program (see figure 8.2).

IMPLEMENTING A PROMOTIONAL PROGRAM

SELECT THE TARGET MARKET

The process of target market selection was explained in chapter 7. This should include an analysis of published (secondary research) market data and primary research results from such techniques as surveys or focus groups. A target market must be accessible through one or more promotional mix elements, or through a specific type of media. Certain basic information must be available on a target market's demographics and geographic origins (place of residence or business). A target market may be more finely pinpointed by overlaying demographic and geographic characteristics with one or more of five other segmentation bases (psychographics or lifestyles, purpose of trip, product related, behavioral, or channel of distribution). The target market must include people with similar characteristics who are the best prospects for future business. This first element of the tourism communication process can only be effective if a complete market segmentation analysis has been done.

DEVELOP PROMOTIONAL OBJECTIVES

The next step is to establish the objectives for the promotional campaign. To be effective, objectives must be target-market specific, stated as a desired result or outcome, measurable, realistically attainable, and have a deadline for achievement.

When setting promotional objectives, it is important to consider the targeted visitors' buying process stage, as well as the destination or organization's product life-cycle stage. The current level of awareness of the tourism destination or service must be established. If people in the target market are at the intention stage of the buying process, then informative messages are a poor use of time and money. Similarly, the promotion of a new package will not be effective if the intention to buy already exists. By conducting an awareness study, either through a survey or focus groups, the buying process stage of the targeted visitors can be determined. At the attention or awareness stages, the objective may be to expose the message to a specified number of target market members within a specific time period. At the intention stage, the objective may be oriented toward increasing purchases. Controlling this second element in the tourism communication process involves two steps:

1. Ensuring through research that the buying process stage of the target market has been correctly identified.
2. Ensuring that promotional objectives are target-market specific, results-oriented, measurable, reasonably attainable, and time-specific.

ESTABLISH THE PROMOTIONAL BUDGET

The promotional objectives must provide the basic foundation for establishing the promotional budget. This is called the *objective-and-task budgeting method*, which uses a "bottom-up" or zero-based budgeting approach. Only by planning what is required (the tasks or activities) to achieve objectives, can an accurate estimate be made of how much to spend on promotions. Often objectives are based upon how much money the destination or organization has to spend; the "top-down" bud-

> **Technology Is Putting a New Face on Tourism Marketing**
> *The Internet and other new technologies have changed the tourism industry in an unprecedented way, and to a degree that has not been seen in any other sector. The speed of change and development is fast, and keeping pace is becoming more and more of a challenge. Online information is now one of the primary influences on consumer decisions in nearly all major markets.*
>
> Handbook on E-marketing for Tourism Destinations, *UN World Tourism Organization (2008), page xv*

geting or *affordable budgeting method*. Tourism destinations and organizations do not have unlimited funds for marketing and many operate with very small promotional budgets. Despite this, setting marketing objectives after, rather than before, the budget is established can produce objectives that will never be achieved. When a tentative budget amount has been estimated based upon the objectives and tasks (promotional activities), other factors need to be considered. These include the promotional budgets of competitors and the funds available to the tourism destination or organization. All marketing plans and budgets must be flexible enough to allow for changing market conditions and competitive activities; therefore, a contingency amount needs to be attached to the promotional budget.

When preparing the budget, consideration is given to cooperative promotions (*partnerships*) with other organizations. Many destination marketing organizations have extensive cooperative marketing programs, especially with efforts to attract international visitors. The pooling of promotional dollars creates great synergy for all parties involved; in effect, it increases everyone's promotional budget.

QUICK TRIP 8.3

The Canadian Tourism Commission

In contrast with its neighbor to the south, Canada's national tourism office has traditionally enjoyed much greater federal government financial support and an enhanced structure within the political system. The Canadian Tourism Commission (CTC) replaced the federal government's Tourism Canada in 1985. The CTC is a Crown corporation of the federal government, which works in partnership with "the tourism industry and all levels of government" to "compel the world to explore Canada."

In its Strategic Plan 2008–2012 Overview, the CTC states that its goal is "to grow tourism export revenues for Canada." The objectives allied to this goal are:

1. Convert high-yield customers.
2. Focus on markets of highest return on investment.
3. Maintain brand consistency.
4. Research new market opportunities.

To reach these objectives, the CTC should create the following perspectives:

■ Stakeholder perspective: Focused on growing tourism export revenues for Canada together with the rest of the tourism industry

(continued)

- Budget/financial perspective: Indicates whether the strategy, implementation, and execution are resulting in the desired financial returns
- Customer perspective: Identifies the CTC's targeted customers and market segments
- Internal business processes perspective: Focused on day-to-day operations critical to delivering on the organization's value proposition and achieving the desired financial results (These key business processes are research, executing the brand, and focusing marketing efforts on markets of highest return.)
- Learning and growth perspective: Identifies infrastructure and human resources needed

The priorities established follow with explanations:

- *Priority 1: Consumer relevancy*
  The CTC seeks to develop and maintain relevant communication with targeted potential travelers and ensure that the marketing messaging they receive is relevant and addresses their interests and expectations as consumers. In order to accomplish this objective, the CTC needs to reach the right people, at the right time, with the right experience, presented in the right way.

- *Priority 2: Align market allocations to achieve highest return on investment*
  In 2008, the CTC will focus its investments in the United States (including Leisure and MC&IT markets), Mexico, France, Germany, the United Kingdom, Japan, China, South Korea, and Australia. Compared to 2007, some budget reallocation will be implemented to take advantage of growth markets. Specifically, the allocations for U.S. Leisure, the United Kingdom, France, and Germany will increase in 2008.

- *Priority 3: Differentiate Canada*
  Many destinations are competing for the tourist's dollar. Canada needs to stand out from its competitors. The CTC has had enormous success in launching Canada's tourism brand–Canada. Keep Exploring–on the world stage. In collaboration with Canada's tourism sector, the CTC has created a platform capable of differentiating the Canadian travel experience.

- *Priority 4: Leverage media exposure of the Vancouver 2010 Olympic and Paralympic Winter Games*
  The Vancouver 2010 Olympic and Paralympic Winter Games provide unprecedented opportunities to showcase Canada to the world. By leveraging the media exposure afforded by the 2010 Games, the CTC will work with its partners to differentiate Canada's tourism brand and compel the world to explore Canada.

- *Priority 5: Organizational excellence*
  The CTC's two main assets are its people and Canada's tourism brand. Over the next five years, the CTC will continue to strive for organizational excellence through the promotion of these two assets.

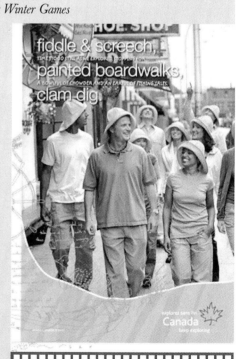

The Canadian Tourism Commission urges visitors to *"Keep Exploring."* Source: Canadian Tourism Commission. 2008.

THINK ABOUT THIS:

1. Why has Canada traditionally had such a well-supported tourism emphasis at the national level while the United States has not?

2. What are some of the major challenges in marketing such a large and geographically diverse country as Canada?

3. Many Canadian tourism officials feel the nation's image is of the three Ms–mountains, moose, and Mounties. In May 2005, the CTC launched Brand Canada with its tag line *Canada. Keep Exploring*. What special difficulties does Canada face in its destination branding and image making given these historical associations that many potential visitors have?

Source: 2008. http://www.corporate.canada.travel/en/ca/index.html?sa_campaign=domains/un/www.canadatourism.com/home.

DETERMINE THE MESSAGE IDEA

Primary research techniques such as focus groups, one-to-one interviews, and surveys can be used to pinpoint the target market's perceptions (images), needs, wants, motives, and expectations. The findings may be used to determine what to communicate in the message (the message idea). Alternative message ideas can be developed and discussed with a sample of people from the target market, perhaps in a small-group setting like a focus group. Based on people's ratings of the alternative approaches, the most effective message idea is chosen. Message ideas must support the positioning approach (image to be communicated) selected by the tourism destination or organization. Control is achieved through this process of pre-testing alternative message ideas; by choosing a message idea that communicates best to representatives of the targeted visitors.

SELECT THE MESSAGE FORMAT

Message ideas can be communicated in many different ways. How a message is communicated to the target market is called the message format or creative format. The objective is to choose a format that effectively communicates the message idea in a way that is understandable, distinctive, and believable for the target market. Advertising agencies are often used to assist with this creative task. The alternative formats that can be used are (Morrison, 2002):

- **Analogy, Association, Symbolism:** The format here is to link the tourism destination or service with an object or concept that supports the message idea. Thai Airways International has used the slogan *Smooth as silk* to emphasize the quality (smoothness) of its in-flight service. The State of Victoria in Australia makes an analogy with a jigsaw puzzle in its *you'll love every piece of Victoria* promotional campaigns.
- **Comparisons:** The tourism destination or service is compared with a specific competitor or against all competition to communicate an important difference. For example, The Palace of the Lost City at Sun City, South Africa, claims to be *The Most Extraordinary Hotel in the World*. Avis' *We try harder* campaign has for many

years compared the car rental company with industry leader Hertz.
- **Fear:** The approach here is to warn potential visitors about doing or not doing something. One classic example of this format is in the credit card business with American Express' *Don't leave home without it* campaigns.
- **Honest-Twist:** This format starts with a statement of fact and then "twists" this fact to the benefit of the advertiser. A classic example is the approach used by Avis. They launched a campaign saying that they were the number two car rental company (behind Hertz); the "honest." Then they said that, because of this, "they try harder" (the "twist").
- **Slice of Life:** These promotions show typical or realistic scenes from everyday life. A popular approach in tourism is to show people in their highly stressed jobs or suffering through very bad weather in their home locations, and then to show them in a very relaxing, warm-weather situation.
- **Testimonials:** Testimonials are endorsements of the tourism destination or service by celebrities, noted experts, past visitors, or travel trade intermediaries. The Cayman Islands used the visit of Michel Cousteau, son of Jacques Cousteau, to promote its scuba diving opportunities. The Hong Kong Tourism Board has used actor, Jackie Chan, in its promotions.
- **Trick Photography or Exaggerated Situations:** Here photographic tricks, graphics, and special

Thai Airways International uses the analogy of *"Smooth as silk"* to describe its service.
http://www.thaiair.com/.

effects are used to emphasize the message idea. A 1991 Qantas advertisement demonstrates this approach. With the heading "We'll move heaven and earth," a map is shown where Australia is much closer to the United States. The message idea seems to be that if you fly transpacific with Qantas, they will make the trip seem much shorter.

Once the message format has been chosen, several alternative approaches to using it may be developed and pre-tested by showing them to groups of people from the target market. Based upon their reactions, the alternative approaches are compared and one of them is selected. To test the promotional effectiveness of the selected approach, surveys of the target market may be conducted after people have been exposed to the message. These surveys can be used to determine what images were conveyed or what was remembered from the message. They may also find out if visitor attitudes toward the tourism destination or organization have changed as a result of being exposed to the promotion.

Select Promotional Mix Elements

Many promotional tools exist to communicate messages to people in the target market. There are five major elements of the promotional mix that can be used separately or together (Morrison, 2002):

1. **Advertising:** Any paid form of nonpersonal presentation and ideas, goods, or services by an identified sponsor.
2. **Personal Selling:** Oral conversations, either by telephone or face to face, between salespeople and prospective customers.
3. **Sales Promotion:** Approaches other than personal selling, advertising, and public relations and publicity where customers are given a short-term inducement to make an immediate purchase or booking, or to communicate with potential visitors or travel trade intermediaries.
4. **Merchandising:** Materials used in-house to stimulate sales including brochures in display racks, signs, posters, photographs, displays, tent cards, and other point-of-sale promotional items.
5. **Public Relations and Publicity:** All the activities that maintain or improve relationships with other organizations and individuals. Publicity is one public relations technique that involves nonpaid communication of information about a destination's or organization's services.

The selection of promotional mix elements varies with the characteristics of the target market, the type of destination or tourism service, and the promotional funds available. The more expensive and complex the service or destination being promoted, the greater is the need for some form of personal selling. While an advertisement may induce a couple to spend a weekend at a resort, a meeting planner choosing a site location for a convention of more than a thousand delegates will require more detailed information and some personal selling. Likewise, a couple planning to take a cruise or an extensive foreign tour will need the advice of an experienced travel agent.

Tourism destinations and organizations usually have four different groups at which they need to direct promotional messages:

1. Visitors
2. Travel trade intermediaries
3. The media
4. The local community (see figure 8.3)

Two of these branches of promotion are called consumer promotions (visitors) and trade promotions (travel trade intermediaries). Consumer promotions can be further categorized into potential visitors, past visitors, and present visitors. Messages also need to be directed at the media (newspapers, magazines, television, and radio stations) and the local community (residents, elected officials, government agencies).

The effectiveness of specific promotional tools varies according to which of the four groups are being targeted (figure 8.3). For example, sales promotions and educational workshops or seminars can be very effective when promoting to travel agents. Advertising on television or in a consumer travel magazine may be more effective in communicating with potential visitors. The emergence of the Web in the mid 1990s provided a vehicle for reaching all four groups.

Most promotional budgets in tourism include amounts for each of the five promotional mix elements. However, the relative proportions of each mix element will vary according to the absolute size of the budget. For example, maintaining a large sales force and placing national-level advertising require a large minimum investment. Many forms of advertising are relatively expensive and advertising typically represents a large share of all promotion spending. For example, a four-color advertisement in a national consumer travel magazine may cost several thousand dollars.

Visitors	Travel Trade/Media/Local Community
Potential Visitors Consumer travel, sports, recreation shows Direct mail and direct fax advertising Help desks Inquiry handling and fulfillment Media advertising Telemarketing Travel videos and films Web site	**Travel Trade Intermediaries** Collateral materials (visitor guides, calendars of events, maps, etc.) Contests and games Direct mail and direct fax advertising Display materials (maps, posters, brochures) Destination "expert" programs Familiarization trips Inquiry handling and fulfillment Newsletters Preferred supplier programs Press releases Recognition and award programs Trade journal advertising Travel trade fairs, shows, exhibitions Workshops and seminars Web site
Past Visitors Direct mail and direct fax advertising Frequent traveler clubs Newsletters Telemarketing Web site	**The Media** Editorials/feature stories Familiarization trips for travel writers Newsletters Photo galleries Press conferences and releases Web site
Present Visitors Hospitality and service training programs Reception and welcoming services Travel maps and literature Travel information centers	**Local Community** Community tourism awareness programs Newsletters Hospitality/service quality award programs Web site

Figure 8.3 Promotional Activities and Communications Channels.

SELECT PROMOTIONAL MEDIA

The appropriate media to communicate the message idea are then selected. The media used in tourism include newspapers, magazines, television (network and cable), radio, the Web, outdoor/transit, and direct mail. Each medium has distinctive advantages and disadvantages. The crucial part of media selection is choosing those that will be seen, read, or heard by the intended target market. Most media companies provided market research statistics on the profiles of their readers, viewers, or listeners. In addition, there are general criteria against which media can be compared to determine which is the most appropriate:

- **Cost Per Contact:** The cost of reaching one person in the target market
- **Cost Per Inquiry (CPI):** The cost of an advertisement divided by the total number of inquiries it generates
- **Cost Per Thousand (CPM):** The cost of reaching 1,000 people in the target market
- **Geographic Selectivity:** The ability to target specific geographic areas

- **Life Span:** The length of time that the target market will be exposed to the message
- **Market Selectivity:** The ability to communicate with specific target markets
- **Noise Level:** The amount of competitive advertising in the medium
- **Pass-Along Rate:** The rate at which people pass along materials (e.g., magazines) to other people
- **Reach:** The total number of people that are exposed to the message
- **Source Credibility:** The credibility or reputation of the medium for accuracy and lack of bias
- **Timing Flexibility:** The amount of lead time required to place the message (shorter lead times give greater flexibility)
- **Total Cost:** The total cost of developing and communicating the message
- **Visual Quality:** The level of quality of the visual presentation, especially when in color

Although the cost per contact is low for television advertising, the total cost is very high. Television allows the tourism advertiser to be geographically selective and select the target market by the specific type of shows or

Although market selectivity is low with newspapers, the total cost, cost per contact, and geographic selectivity are good. © 2009 Stephen Coburn. Used under license from Shutterstock, Inc.

programs. The visual quality of television advertisements can be extremely high. Television suffers from a rather low level of credibility and trust among viewers, however. Because of the tendency to watch television with other people, the noise level tends to be higher than average. Since advertising schedules often have to be decided far in advance, the timing flexibility for television is below average.

Radio offers a medium that is low in total cost and cost per contact. Like television, radio is selective for broad market groups and has high geographic selectivity. The credibility and noise level are similar to those for television. However, the timing flexibility is far greater; radio advertisements can be placed on very short notice.

Newspapers also offer a low total cost and cost per contact. Market selectivity is low, but geographic selectivity is good since it is possible to target specific cities and towns. Certain nationally distributed newspapers allow tourism marketers to pinpoint business travelers, such as *The Wall Street Journal, Globe & Mail, The Australian, London Times*, and the *Daily Telegraph*. The trust factor for newspapers seems to be low, and the visual quality is less than average. To compensate for a high noise level, short life span, and low pass-along rate, newspapers offer a great deal of flexibility in the timing of advertisements.

Magazines have a much higher cost per contact and total cost than newspapers. However, the specialized nature of magazines, the market selectivity, can be very high. The regional editions available for certain magazines offer some geographic selectivity. The visual quality of magazines is much higher than for newspapers, and the noise level is usually much lower. Both the life span and pass-along rate are above-average. The tim-

ing flexibility is low with magazines as they have relatively long lead times for placing advertisements.

Although the total cost of a direct-mail campaign tends to be rather high, the cost per contact varies widely depending upon the quality of the materials to be sent. Market selectivity and geographic selectivity are the highest of all media; direct mailings can be highly personalized. The source credibility is below average due to the ever-increasing volume of junk mail that most people receive. The life span of a direct mail piece tends to be short, especially if the mailing is not highly personalized. The visual quality can be very high and the noise level is low, but increasing. A direct-mail piece can have a strong impact on a purchase decision, again if the message is highly personalized. Timing flexibility can be good with direct mail but is dependent on the type of items to be included in the mailing and their production times.

All of these media, except direct mail, suffer from a lack of personalization; they are mass media. With the emergence of the concept of relationship marketing (building and enhancing long-term relationships with individual visitors and other organizations), a greater emphasis is now being placed on one-to-one communications (Jones, 1998; Peppers and Rogers, 1993) (see figure 8.4). Media that provide for individualized messages are fast growing in popularity in tourism. These include all forms of direct marketing including direct mail and telemarketing (telephone selling). Additionally, the interactive potential of using the Web and other types of Internet marketing has attracted great attention from tourism marketers in recent years. The major advantages of Internet marketing:

- The global reach of the Internet and the twenty-four-hour availability of travel information
- The increased speed of transactions
- The capacity to instantly update information
- The greater ability to make tangible intangible products and experiences
- The ability to gather research information and build customer databases

Turning Away From: Mass Marketing	And Turning Toward: Direct Customer Communications
Socioeconomic	Customer databases
Media placement	Telemarketing/targeted messages
One-way communication	Building customer relationships

Figure 8.4 Changing Approaches to Tourism Marketing and Communications. Source: Jones. 1998.

Ryanair's Polemic Promotions

Ryanair, famous for its low-cost strategies, has become one of Europe's leading airlines. The revenues come from various sources, one of which is promoting partner companies and sponsors. Unconventional spaces of their operation have been transformed into lucrative tools, for instance:

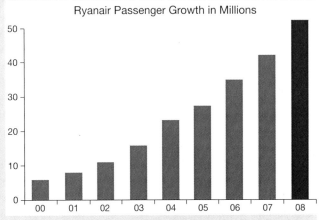

Ryanair Passenger Growth in Millions

Ryanair has enjoyed continuous growth in passenger volumes from 2000 to 2008. Source: Ryanair Ltd. http://www.ryanair.com/site/EN/about.php?page=About&culture=GB&pos=HEAD.

- *Overhead lockers:* The Aeropanel, a new and exciting medium, which gives access to 52 million passengers annually. The interior of the aircraft provides 160 square feet of impactful, interior media space; a unique opportunity to showcase products and services to a captive, receptive, demographically attractive audience. Major brands such as Meteor, ING, and Red Bull have enjoyed highly successful campaigns through this medium.
- *Traybacks:* In-flight tray tables have been given an inset with a patented panel for printed advertisements. Brands can choose to either have a single creative execution or use multiple copies to create an engaging and unique story. Advertisers have benefited from the effectiveness that unparalleled dwell time of forty minutes minimum delivers.
- *Ryanair in-flight magazine:* The monthly magazine carries features directly related to the interests and purchasing habits of Ryanair's unique audience. Elements include engaging destination guides, travel itinerary ideas, property and real estate guides, handpicked hotel reviews, seasonal recreation guides (sun, ski, golf, etc.), consumer product related features, health and beauty tips, technology updates, and personality profiles.

The largest part of Ryanair's revenues are linked to sales. Their strategy base has been to focus on online sales, through their Web site, passing conventional commissioned channels.

To commercialize the company, printed advertisements are used. According to *ABC News* (January 2008), Ryanair has been nicknamed the "bad boy of European airlines" due to its bold advertisements. The Advertising Standards Authority (ASA–U.K.), whose role is to police the rules laid down in the advertising codes, and to apply the advertising codes and uphold standards in all media by being a customer-focused, best-practice regulator, has adjudicated the following ad (January 2008):

Ad

Press ads in the *Herald, Daily Mail,* and *Scottish Daily Mail* were headed "HOTTEST BACK TO SCHOOL FARES." Underneath the heading was a picture of a teenage girl or woman standing in a classroom and wearing a version of a school uniform consisting of a short tartan skirt, a cropped short-sleeved shirt and tie, and long white socks. Body copy stated that one-way fares to Derry, Belfast, Budapest, Grenoble, and Stockholm (Skavsta) were £10 including taxes and charges. A footnote stated "Book until midnight 23.08.07. Subject to availability, terms & conditions. Flights direct from Glasgow (Prestwick)."

Action

Ryanair was asked to withdraw the ad and to ensure that future ads complied with the CAP Code.

This type of ad is not a solitary action but a part of a chain of advertisements generating media attention and publicity.

More recently, Ryanair launched the "Girls of Ryanair" 2008 Calendar. This project has been an integral part of its promotion strategy. The sales made seventy thousand euros and the sum was donated to a charitable cause. The calendar was such a success that the 2008 calendar was sold out in weeks (ten thousand copies), and pre-order options for 2009 calendars are up.

(continued)

- The ease of forming virtual partnerships with related organizations
- The greater ability to build and maintain relationships through improved communications and personalization
- The availability of instant feedback for customers
- The relatively low cost of Internet marketing

The print media (newspapers and magazines) are popular with travel, hotel and resort organizations. Although newspapers are expected to continue to be the most used advertising medium for tourism, their effectiveness is eroding. The travel sections of newspapers tend to be read only after the decision to travel has been made. People who read the travel sections are highly motivated to travel. In order to expand the travel market, other media such as television, radio, direct mail, and the Web will get greater use in the future.

Restaurant companies (especially fast-food chains), hotel chains, and airlines tend to spend the largest amounts on media advertising. Restaurant companies spend the largest proportion of their media advertising budgets on the electronic media, especially on television. Hotels and airlines tend to favor the print media (newspapers and magazines). Destination marketing organizations appear to make the greatest use of magazines and television for their advertising.

MEASURE AND EVALUATE PROMOTIONAL EFFECTIVENESS

The response to a promotion can be measured in terms of changes in the awareness levels of the tourism destination or organization, the way the message is perceived by visitors (see chapter 11), the number of responses, and, if appropriate, the conversion rates. Potential problems are minimized if campaigns are controlled and

effectiveness tested at each step in the promotional program. However, the measurement of promotional effectiveness appears to be something that needs to be improved among tourism organizations. There is a belief among industry experts that many tourism organizations are not doing enough to measure the effectiveness of their promotional campaigns and to be accountable for the funds they are using (Davidson and Wiethaupt, 1989).

There are several specific techniques that can be used to measure promotional efficiency and effectiveness. These include (Davidson, 1994; Koth, 1988; Perdue and Pitegoff, 1994; Pizam, 1994; Siegel and Ziff-Levine, 1994; Woodside and Ronkainen, 1994):

- **Advertising Tracking Studies:** These studies track the awareness levels and images of the tourism destination or organization before and after the placement of the advertising.
- **Cost-Comparison Method:** This method calculates ratios such as cost per inquiry, cost per visitor, and return on investment. These ratios may be produced in a conversion study.
- **Concept Testing:** Small-scale, qualitative studies of rough drawings of message ideas or campaigns.
- **Conversion Studies:** These studies determine how many inquirers from tourism advertising convert to visitors and what are the converted visitors' demographic and travel-behavior characteristics, including length of stay, travel-party size, destination activities, and expenditures.
- **Inquiry and Lead Tracking:** These are measures of promotional efficiency in which records are kept of direct-response advertising inquiries or sales leads (from sales calls or travel and trade shows).
- **Pre-Testing:** Studies that expose samples of the target market to preliminary or finished versions of the proposed promotions.

South African Tourism (SATOUR)

South African Tourism (SATOUR) acts as the tourism-marketing arm of the South African government. SATOUR is a statutory body created by the Tourism Act and performs the role of the national tourism organization (NTO) for the international marketing of South Africa as a preferred tourist destination. SATOUR's key objectives are:

- Increasing tourist volume
- Increasing tourism spending
- Increasing length of stay
- Improving geographic spread
- Improving seasonality patterns
- Improving transformation in tourism

To achieve these key objectives, SATOUR pursues nine core activities:

1. To always understand the market
2. To choose attractive segments
3. To market South Africa to attractive segments
4. To facilitate the removal of obstacles
5. To facilitate the product platform
6. To monitor and learn from tourist experience
7. To build a tourism nation
8. To facilitate strategic alignment of all role players
9. To set standards for the tourism product

In May 2002, SATOUR launched its *Tourism Growth Strategy*; it is currently in its third edition (2008–2010) and has expanded to two other areas (domestic and business tourism growth strategies). SATOUR attributes its recent success to following the strategic directions in its marketing and promotions.

SATOUR reached 9,090,900 arrivals in 2007, up 8.3 percent from 2006. Europe accounted for approximately 65 percent of the overseas visitors; North America for 13 percent; Asia for about 10 percent. The United States continues to be the largest market to South Africa; however, it is interesting to note that India and China were two of the countries with the greatest growth rates in visits to South Africa in 2007 (16.9 percent and 12.9 percent respectively). As of the 2002 growth strategy launch, the number of arrivals has grown 38.8 percent.

THINK ABOUT THIS:

1. What are some of the key challenges that SATOUR faces in marketing a country with South Africa's geographic location?
2. How important is it for South Africa to cooperate with neighboring countries in promoting the concept of visiting South Africa?
3. Is it especially important for a country like South Africa to make effective use of the Web in its tourism promotion? Why or why not?

Sources:

South African Tourism. 2008. http://www.satour.com/; http://www.southafrica.net/satourism/; http://www.southafrica.net/.

South Africa Annual Report 2007 and Tourism Growth Strategy 2008–2010.

Europe accounts for the majority of overseas visitors to South Africa. © 2009 Vatikaki. Used under license from Shutterstock, Inc.

- **Post-Testing:** Studies done after the promotional campaign has ended to determine changes in images, awareness, attitudes, and recall.
- **Travel or Trade Show Audits:** Studies on the past attendance and characteristics of the people who attend consumer travel and travel trade shows.

Broader analyses of marketing effectiveness may measure market share changes, public relations yield ratio, and the ratio of industry and cooperative promotion funding to total funding (Lavery, 1992).

USES OF PROMOTION BY NATIONAL TOURIST OFFICES

A national tourist office (NTO) is the organization officially responsible for the marketing and development of tourism for a country. When there are two national-level tourism organizations, the agency responsible for marketing is usually designated the NTO. The development function is given to a national tourism administration (NTA). According to the World Tourism Organization (2004), 60 percent of the NTOs and NTAs had marketing budgets over $10 million in 2003; employed more than 150 people; and had total operational budgets in excess of $15 million. Some agencies have budgets far greater than this; for example, Tourism Australia received Australian $136.3 million for 2007–08 from its federal government. VisitBritain was allocated £55.1 million in 2007 by the British government. The government decided to trim VisitBritain's allocation, despite the substantial returns on this investment (VisitBritain Web site, 2008):

> VisitBritain is funded by the Department for Culture, Media and Sport (DCMS) through a three-year Funding Agreement. This agreement states the level of funding (grant-in-aid) that the government will provide VisitBritain and sets targets for VisitBritain's performance each year. 2008–09 is the first year of a new Funding Agreement with DCMS. VisitBritain will receive grant-in-aid of £47.9 million. VisitBritain also aims to raise over £20 million nongovernment funding through partnerships and other activities through 2008–09.

VisitBritain consistently achieves a high return on investment. The last available results show that VisitBritain has achieved a return on investment of over 50:1 on its international marketing activity, with many campaigns achieving an even higher return.

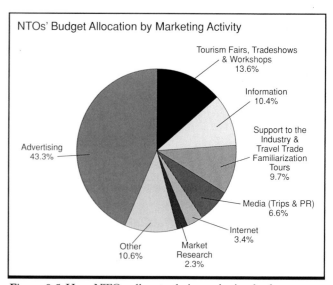

Figure 8.5 How NTOs allocate their marketing budgets.
Source: World Tourism Organization. 2006. *Structures and Budgets of National Tourism Organizations 2004–2005.*

The four most popular promotional activities among these agencies tend to be the production and distribution of brochures and print; operation of a Web site; participating in travel exhibitions, fairs, and trade shows; and international advertising (figure 8.5).

Most NTOs maintain head offices in their own countries and operate a network of offices in other countries. The major proportions of most NTO budgets are spent abroad for the operation of these offices and in promotional programs. NTOs locate in countries that generate most of their international visitor arrivals. The number of offices in a country depends upon the importance of the market and the size of the country. For example, most of the major NTOs have more than one office in the United States, and several have two or more offices in Japan.

There are now several hundred NTOs abroad. A relatively small country, New Zealand operates eleven overseas offices. It is certainly possible to operate overseas marketing campaigns from a head office. Smaller countries with low NTO budgets are forced to do this. Some NTOs contract with sales representative firms or public relations consultants to handle their promotional efforts. Others work through the offices of their national airlines. Some use their embassies or consulates to represent the NTO, but this tends not to be an effective solution. One explanation is that embassies located in the country's capital, are often not in the best places for promoting to potential visitors and travel trade intermediaries (e.g., Canberra in Australia, Ottawa in Canada, and Washington in the United States). It is much more effective to locate NTOs in the country's largest cities (e.g., Sydney, Melbourne, Toronto, Montreal, Vancouver, New York, and Los Angeles).

The first NTO was established in 1901 by the New Zealand Department of Tourism. In their nearly one hundred years of operation, and particularly since the 1960s, the roles of NTOs have evolved and changed (Morrison, Braunlich, Kamaruddin, and Cai, 1995). In their earlier days, the principal function of an NTO was to distribute printed literature to potential visitors. They played a rather passive role as an "order taker" rather than an "order maker." Increased competition from other foreign destinations and travel options (cruises, gambling, and theme parks) forced NTOs to become more aggressive marketers of their countries. The growth in the popularity of tours and packaged vacations also shifted more of the emphasis away from the individual visitor toward travel trade intermediaries. The new electronic media distribution systems, including the Web, also may have a profound effect on the roles of NTOs, as the emphasis on print materials lessens and more people are able to access instant travel information in an electronic form.

National tourist offices staff their foreign offices mainly with their own citizens. A study of NTOs in the United States found that 70 percent of staff was the destination country's citizens and the remainder was locals of the origin country (Morrison et al., 1995).

National tourist offices abroad play the following seven major roles:

1. **Image creation and enhancement role:** To promote a favorable image of the country as a tourism destination, and to maintain or enhance this image.

2. **Literature distribution and fulfillment role:** To increase and make more effective the supply of information on the tourism services and products of the destination.

3. **Marketing research and database development role:** To collect information and create databases that help to increase the effectiveness of marketing decisions.

4. **Package and tour development role:** To increase the availability of the tourist products of the destination by increasing the number of new tour programs and packaged vacations and the capacity of existing ones, or to maintain at targeted levels the number and capacity of such programs.

5. **Partnership development role:** To play a leadership role in the development of marketing and promotional partnerships between transportation carriers, suppliers, travel trade intermediaries, and other businesses in the host country and the originating countries.

6. **Consumer marketing and promotional role:** To secure maximum promotional exposure for the destination mix of the country.

7. **Travel trade marketing and promotional role:** To familiarize travel trade distribution channels with the destination's services and products and stimulate them to increase sales.

IMAGE CREATION AND ENHANCEMENT

Through its promotional programs, an NTO must communicate a distinctive and favorable image (positioning) of the country as a destination. It must seek to maintain and enhance this image, even in the face of adverse publicity.

LITERATURE DISTRIBUTION AND FULFILLMENT

Literature distribution has been a traditional role of all NTOs, and they print large quantities of printed collateral materials to support promotional programs. In recent years, the concept of literature has expanded to information distribution through print, DVDs/CD-ROMs, and the Web. In an analysis of NTO informational materials distributed in the United States, the following five categories of informational materials were identified (Braunlich et al., 1995):

1. Maps
2. Travel planners (also known as travel or visitor guides)
3. Accommodation guides
4. Special event calendars
5. Guides to tour packages

MARKETING RESEARCH AND DATABASE DEVELOPMENT

National tourist offices abroad are increasingly being used to gather marketing research information and to

---

QUICK TRIP 8.6

Most Important Activities of a National Tourist Office Abroad

A study of foreign NTOs located in the United States was conducted by researchers at Purdue University (Morrison et al., 1995). The respondents in this study gave the following rankings to specific NTO activities (scores are out of ten, with ten being most important):

1. Distributing promotional literature to travel trade intermediaries (9.03)
2. Distributing promotional literature to consumers (8.78)
3. Organizing educational/training seminars/workshops for the travel trade (8.69)
4. Developing new packages with the travel trade (8.55)
5. Arranging familiarization trips for travel writers (8.03)
6. Advertising in consumer travel magazines/newspapers (7.94)
7. Arranging familiarization trips for travel trade intermediaries (7.54)
8. Making sales calls on travel trade intermediaries (7.51)
9. Maintaining a computerized database of inquiries (7.45)
10. Exhibiting at travel trade shows (7.40)
11. Advertising in travel trade magazines/newspapers (7.17)
12. Exhibiting at consumer travel shows (5.48)
13. Making sales calls on consumers (e.g., groups) (5.24)

THINK ABOUT THIS:

1. What other potential roles could NTOs play in foreign countries?
2. How should a country measure the effectiveness of these offices?
3. How will the greater use of the Internet affect these offices?

Source: Morrison, A. M., C. G. Braunlich, N. Kamaruddin, and L. A. Cai. 1995. National tourist offices in North America: An analysis. *Tourism Management*, 16 (6): 605–617.

The CNTO represents and markets China in the United States.

---

build databases of travel trade intermediaries, groups, and other types of visitors. The generation of inquiries as a result of direct-response advertising is one good source of databases. Databases may also be bought from mailing list brokers when special-interest markets are to be targeted.

PACKAGE AND TOUR DEVELOPMENT

One way to increase the flow of visitors to a country is to increase the number of tour programs and packaged vacations to that destination.

PARTNERSHIP DEVELOPMENT

Many NTOs try to create marketing and promotional partnerships with tourism and nontourism organizations. The Canadian Tourism Commission (CTC) has an extensive cooperative marketing partnership program that involves other destination marketing organizations and the private sector.

CONSUMER MARKETING AND PROMOTION

A full range of promotional activities was shown in figure 8.3. Recent surveys suggest that NTOs place more emphasis on travel trade than on consumer promotions. Advertising to potential visitors is very important in creating awareness of the country and generating enough interest so that visitors want more information. However, consumer advertising tends to be relatively expensive. The NTOs with larger budgets are able to mount substantial consumer campaigns in certain markets using mainly magazine and television advertising. Smaller-budget NTOs are forced to concentrate on travel trade marketing and use public relations and publicity to promote to the consumer.

TRAVEL TRADE MARKETING AND PROMOTION

An important NTO role is to inform travel trade intermediaries about the country and to familiarize them with its tourism attractions, events, and other resources. One effective way of doing this is through familiarization tours (also called "fams" for short). NTOs organize these educational tours for selected tour wholesalers and retail travel agents. Having experienced the country firsthand, the intermediaries are in a much better position to sell it as a tourism destination. During familiarization tours, the foreign travel trade intermediaries inspect facilities, visit tourism attractions, and make contacts with the local travel trade, who may act as their partners in channeling visitors to the country. Such tours may be conducted in small groups or on an indi-

An effective way to inform travel trade intermediaries about a country's tourism attractions, including its scenic spots, is through familiarization tours. © 2009 Maksym Gorpenyuk. Used under license from Shutterstock, Inc.

vidual basis. Familiarization tours are also often organized for travel writers.

Another major activity of NTOs is exhibiting at travel trade exhibitions or shows. Two of the largest shows in the world are ITB Berlin (held in March each year in Germany) and the World Travel Market (held in November each year in London, England).

Educational workshops and seminars are organized and staged in overseas countries. They bring together all the main components of tourism, such as hotels, travel agents, airlines, and providers of tourist services, from both the generating and the destination country. The main objective of these workshops and seminars is to promote the destination mix of the country to the travel trade and other principals of the generating country. They motivate travel trade intermediaries to increase sales of group tours and FIT (foreign independent tour) travel. They familiarize travel trade intermediaries with the country's facilities and services and the latest developments in tourism. They provide an opportunity for the travel principals of the destination and generating countries to establish working relationships.

Several NTOs have gone further with their trade education efforts to set up training programs that lead to travel agent accreditations. These include the Shamrock Club operated by Tourism Ireland, the Aussie Specialist program operated by Tourism Australia, and the Kiwi Specialist program operated by Tourism New Zealand.

Sales calls are made by NTO staff to retail travel agents and tour wholesalers. The aim of these calls is to assist the travel trade in selling

the country by providing them with information, advice, and promotional collateral materials. To keep the travel trade well-stocked with promotional materials on the country, NTOs have regular direct mailings of brochures and other collateral materials. With this information, the travel trade is in a better position to effectively service client inquiries and promote the country.

Many NTOs establish a permanent channel of communications with the travel trade through the regular distribution of newsletters. The newsletters inform the travel trade about upcoming events, developments in the destination's facilities and services, and other interesting facets of its tourism. As well as maintaining an ongoing relationship, these newsletters also attempt to promote sales by the travel trade to the country.

Some NTOs provide incentives or bonuses in the form of free vacations or gifts. These incentives are often linked with promotional contests or games. These sales promotions are often done in partnership with the main tourism principals of the country (hotel and airline companies).

Promotional evenings may be organized exclusively for members of the travel trade and are basically public relations' exercises. They are often staged in hotels or

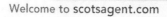

VisitScotland operates the SCOTS Destination Specialist Program, which involves special educational seminars for travel agents and others. http://apps.travelweekly.com/seminars/VisitScotland/main/.

resorts. Food, beverages, and entertainment, often imported from the NTO's country, are provided.

More recently, the operation of sites on the Web has provided instant access to the NTO's information and services. Every major NTO has an official Web site.

STATE, PROVINCIAL, AND TERRITORIAL TOURIST OFFICES

Around the world, wherever there are systems of state, provincial, or territorial governments, tourist offices (STOs) have been created with roughly similar roles to NTOs. These include the provinces and territories of Canada; the states and territory of Australia; the states and territories of the United States; and the provinces of China. The major difference between the promotional activities of these agencies and those of NTOs is that they tend to focus more on domestic travelers than on international. Their primary promotional role is to draw visitors from other states, provinces, or territories within the country. Having said this, it must be realized that several individual states have significant numbers of international visitors and mount extensive international promotion programs. Some states and provinces even operate full-time offices abroad, including the Australian states of Queensland and Victoria. The greater focus on domestic markets means that STOs tend to place less emphasis on travel trade marketing than on consumer marketing. Otherwise, the roles of STOs are similar to those outlined earlier for NTOs.

While these organizations usually have budgets less than their respective NTOs, many still have significant levels of funding. For example, the STO in Hawaii had revenues of $74.4 million in its fiscal year 2007 (Hawaii Tourism Authority, 2007). Tourism Queensland had total revenues of AU$ 70 million in 2006–07, some AU$ 51.5 million of this being contributed by the state government (Tourism Queensland Annual Report 2006–07). Some of the Australian STOs are unique in their operation of travel information centers (which generate retail sales) in other states.

REGIONAL AND LOCAL TOURISM ORGANIZATIONS

Another level of tourism promotion agencies is at the regional level (within states, provinces, or territories) and at the local community level. The format of these agencies varies by country, mainly due to the

organizational structure of government and the physical size of the country, state, province, or territory. In smaller countries such as England and Ireland there tends to be a structure of regional tourism agencies under the NTO. For example, in England there are nine regional tourist boards (East Midlands; East of England; England's Northwest; Heart of England; London; North East England; South East England; South West England; and Yorkshire). The Province of Ontario has twelve regional tourism organizations in the OTAP program (Essex; Southwest Ontario; Niagara Region; South Central Ontario; Toronto and Region; Central Ontario; St. Lawrence Corridor; Ottawa Region;

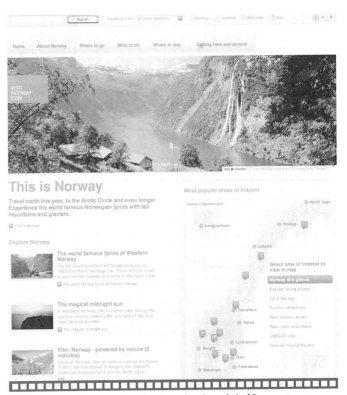

There is a good system of regional tourism boards in Norway. http://www. visitnorway.com/en/Stories/Where-to-go/Where-to-go/.

Eastern Ontario; North-Central; North-East; and North-West).

Another interpretation of the term "region" in tourism is that this represents an area encompassing several different countries and NTOs. For example, the NTOs in the Scandinavian region in Northern Europe operate their international travel promotions in a regional partnership, the Scandinavian Tourist Boards. Other regional partnerships in tourism include El Mundo Maya (the Mayan World) involving the countries of Belize, El Salvador, Guatemala, Honduras, and Mexico in Central America and the Greater Mekong region (Cambodia, China, Laos, Myanmar, Thailand, and Vietnam). The Caribbean Tourism Organization, European Travel Commission, and the Pacific Asia Travel Association are examples of permanent organizations that have been created to encourage the development and promotion of tourism in their multi-country regions.

Some countries, including the United States, have strong local tourism organizations and do not have a formal system of regional tourism organizations. In the United States, the introduction of room taxes by city and county governments has helped to finance an extensive network of local convention and visitors' bureaus (CVBs). The first CVB was opened more than one hundred years ago in Detroit, Michigan. Most of the larger CVBs in the world are members of the Destination Marketing Association International (DMAI) located in Washington, DC. A traditional role of CVBs, as their name suggests, has been to attract business from the MICE markets (meetings, incentives, conventions, and exhibitions). Recently, CVBs have been placing more emphasis on attracting group and individual pleasure travelers.

SUMMARY

Promotion provides the means with which the tourism destination or organization communicates with past and potential travelers. In so doing, the five promotional mix elements of advertising, personal selling, sales promotion, merchandising, and public relations and publicity are used to achieve predetermined objectives. These objectives range from very broad image campaigns to promotions geared to immediately increase revenues. Each of the five promotional mix elements and the available communications media has distinct advantages and disadvantages, and it is important to carefully weigh these against a set of evaluation criteria.

National tourist offices (NTOs) play a pivotal role in promoting their county's tourism attractions, facilities, and services in foreign countries. The role and amount of financial support given to NTOs by their respective governments varies greatly.

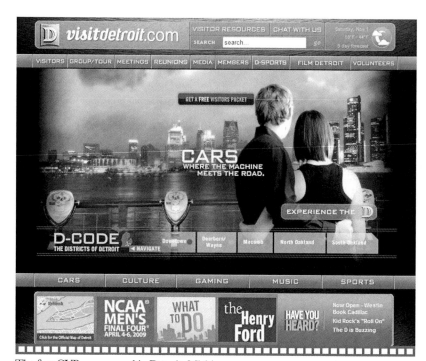

The first CVB was opened in Detroit, Michigan. http://www.visitdetroit.com/.

 *Trends*

Travel Trends Among Australians

1. *Escape:* 75 percent of Australians have been to a foreign country. They have visited an average of eight countries each.
2. *A roof over your head:* Australians rank location as the most important criterion in selecting where to stay.
3. *Show me the money:* Over 600,000 Australians put their entire holiday spending on their credit cards.
4. *Fly by the seat of your computer:* 82 percent and 75 percent of Australians use the Internet to research their domestic and international trips respectively.
5. *Low carb travel:* 76 percent of Australians consider climate change to be a serious issue.
6. *Frisk:* Most Australian travelers support tighter security measures in travel.
7. *Aussie Faves—Favorite overseas countries:* (1) New Zealand, (2) the United Kingdom, (3) the United States
8. *Aussie Faves—Favorite overseas cities:* (1) London, (2) Paris, (3) New York
9. *Aussie Faves—Countries most want to visit:* (1) the United States, (2) the United Kingdom, (3) Canada
10. *Aussie Faves—Favorite Australian destinations:* (1) Gold Coast, (2) Queensland, (3) Tasmania

Source: Australian travel and lifestyle trends, http://www.lastminute.com.au. (Research conducted in August 2007).

ACTIVITIES

1. Select a set of countries or cities that you would most like to visit, and analyze their offline and online promotions. Telephone a selection of travel agencies and ask them for information on the countries or cities you selected. How comprehensive and appealing was the information that the agencies provided?
2. Telephone the DMOs of the countries or cities, and ask them to send you more travel information on their destinations. Which of the DMOs were the most responsive and helpful? How comprehensive and appealing was the information that the DMOs provided?
3. Search for advertisements and other promotions done by the countries or cities in magazines, newspapers, on television, and elsewhere.

INTERNET

4. Find the official tourism Web sites of the countries or cities and rank them according to their attractiveness from your point of view.
5. Which Web sites are the most user-friendly and easy to navigate? Why?

ACTIVITIES
6. Which Web sites provide the most comprehensive and useful information?

REFERENCES

Ahmed, Z. U., and F. B. Krohn. 1990. Reversing the United States' declining competitiveness in the marketing of international tourism: A perspective on future policy. *Journal of Travel Research*, 29 (2): 23–29.

Braunlich, C. G., A. M. Morrison, and F. Feng. 1995. National tourist offices: Service quality expectations and performance. *Journal of Vacation Marketing*, 1: 323–336.

Davidson, T. L. 1994. Assessing the effectiveness of persuasive communications in tourism. In *Travel, Tourism, and Hospitality Research: A Handbook for Managers and Researchers,* 2nd ed., J. R. B. Ritchie and C. R. Goeldner (eds.). New York: John Wiley & Sons, Inc. 537–543.

Davidson, T. L., and W. B. Wiethaupt. 1989. Accountability marketing research: An increasingly vital tool for travel marketers. *Journal of Travel Research*, 26 (4): 42–45.

Dommermuth, W. P. 1989. *Promotion: Analysis, Creativity, and Strategy,* 2nd ed. Boston: PWS-Kent Publishing Company.

Economist Intelligence Unit. 1996. The role and functions of a national tourist office abroad. *International Tourism Quarterly*, 3: 39–58.

Hawes, D. K., D. T. Taylor, and G. D. Hampe. 1991. Destination marketing by states. *Journal of Travel Research*, 30 (1): 11–17.

Jones, C. 1998. *Applications of Marketing in the Tourism Industry.* San Francisco: Economics Research Associates. http://www.econres.com/.

Koth, B. A. 1988. *Evaluating Tourism Advertising with Cost-Comparison Methods.* St. Paul, MN: Minnesota Extension Service, University of Minnesota.

Lavery, P. 1992. The financing and organisation of national tourist offices. *EIU Travel & Tourism Analyst,* 4: 84–101.

Lennon, M. 1995. *Tourism Promotion Using the World Wide Web.* http://info.isoc.org/HMP/PAPER/html/paper.html.

Morrison, A. M. 1987. Selling the USA: Part 1: International promotion. *Travel & Tourism Analyst,* 2: 3–12.

Morrison, A. M., C. G. Braunlich, N. Kamaruddin, and L. A. Cai. 1995. National tourist offices in North America: An analysis. *Tourism Management,* 16: 605–618.

Morrison, A. M. 2009. *Hospitality and Travel Marketing,* 4th ed. Clifton Park, NY: Delmar Publishers, Inc.

Palmer, A., and D. Bejou. 1995. Tourism destination marketing alliances. *Annals of Tourism Research,* 22: 616–629.

Peppers, D., and M. Rogers. 1993. *The One to One Future: Building Relationships One Customer At a Time.* New York: Currency Doubleday.

Perdue, R. R., and B. E. Pitegoff. 1994. Methods of accountability research for destination marketing. In *Travel, Tourism, and Hospitality Research: A Handbook for Managers and Researchers,* 2nd ed., J. R. B. Ritchie and C. R. Goeldner (eds.). New York: John Wiley & Sons, Inc. 565–571.

Petrison, L. A., R. C. Blattberg, and P. Wang. 1993. Database marketing: Past, present, and future. *Journal of Direct Marketing,* 7 (3): 27–43.

Pizam, A. 1994. Methods of accountability research for destination marketing. In *Travel, Tourism, and Hospitality Research: A Handbook for Managers and Researchers,* 2nd ed., J. R. B. Ritchie and C. R. Goeldner (eds.). New York: John Wiley & Sons, Inc. 573–581.

Ronkainen, I. A., and R. J. Farano. 1987. United States' travel and tourism policy. *Journal of Travel Research,* 25 (4): 2–8.

Siegel, W., and W. Ziff-Levine. 1994. Methods of accountability research for destination marketing. In *Travel, Tourism, and Hospitality Research: A Handbook for Managers and Researchers,* 2nd ed., J. R. B. Ritchie and C. R. Goeldner (eds.). New York: John Wiley & Sons, Inc. 559–564.

Travel Industry Association of America. 2005. *Survey of State Travel Offices: 2002–03.* Washington, DC: Travel Industry Association of America.

Woodside, A. G., and I. A. Ronkainen. 1994. Methods of accountability research for destination marketing. In *Travel, Tourism, and Hospitality Research: A Handbook for Managers and Researchers,* 2nd ed., J. R. B. Ritchie and C. R. Goeldner (eds.). New York: John Wiley & Sons, Inc. 545–557.

SURFING SOLUTIONS

http://www.canadatourism.com/ (Canadian Tourism Commission)

http://www.econres.com/resources/issue_papers.aspx (Economics Research Associates Issue Papers)

http://www.failteireland.ie/ (Fáilte Ireland)

http://www1.messe-berlin.de/vip8_1/website/MesseBerlin/htdocs/www.fair.itb-berlin.de/index_e.html (ITB Berlin)

http://www.satour.com/ (South African Tourism)

http://www.tourismaustralia.com/ (Tourism Australia)

http://www.tourisminfo.govt.nz/ (New Zealand Tourism Board)

http://www.visitbritain.com/corporate/ (VisitBritain)

http://www.world-tourism.org/ (World Tourism Organization)

http://www.wtmlondon.com/ (World Travel Market, London, England)

ACRONYMS

CTC (Canadian Tourism Commission)
CVB (convention and visitors bureau)
DMO (destination marketing organization)
ITB (International Tourism Exchange, Berlin)
MICE (meetings, incentives, conventions, and exhibitions)
NTO (national tourist office or organization)
PLC (product life cycle)
SATOUR (South African Tourism)
STO (state tourist office)
TA (Tourism Australia)
TDAP (Tourism Development Action Programs)
TNZ (Tourism New Zealand)
TQ (Tourism Queensland)
UNWTO (World Tourism Organization)
WTM (World Travel Market, London)

chapter 9

The Distribution Mix in Tourism

GETTING MESSAGES AND SERVICES TO THE MARKET

It wasn't that long ago when it was impossible to block out the din of the travel agent death knell. The specter of the Internet was vast, looming large and seemingly sucking away travel agent value. Turns out the rumors of the travel agent's demise have been greatly exaggerated.

Travel Agents Strike Back, Once thought to be going way of the dodo, they are more important than ever, *Glenn Haussman, HotelInteractive.com (2007), http://www.hotelinteractive.com/article. aspx?articleID=8680, accessed January 5, 2009*

PURPOSE

Having learned about the tourism distribution system, students will be able to explain direct and indirect distribution, and describe the functions of the main travel trade intermediaries.

LEARNING OBJECTIVES

✓ Describe the tourism distribution system using a diagram to illustrate the relationship of the various tourism organizations involved.
✓ Define direct and indirect distribution, and explain the difference between these two concepts.
✓ Identify and describe the major types of travel intermediaries.
✓ Explain the functions of tour wholesalers and operators, and the economics of the tour business.
✓ Explain the functions of retail travel agencies.
✓ Describe the reasons for creating corporate travel departments and the functions of these departments.
✓ Explain the functions of incentive travel and convention-meeting planners.

OVERVIEW

The next link in the tourism system involves getting messages and services to the market. This is accomplished through the tourism distribution system. The purpose of the tourism distribution channel is twofold: To get sufficient information to the right people at the right time and in the right place to allow a purchase decision to be made, and to provide a mechanism whereby travelers can make and pay for their purchases. The distribution mix is an important component of the overall marketing mix in tourism.

The concept of vertical integration within tourism distribution channels is discussed. The histories and functions of tour wholesalers and operators, retail travel agencies, corporate travel departments, incentive travel and convention-meeting planners are explained. The implications of changes in electronic distribution systems are reviewed.

TOURISM DISTRIBUTION IS UNIQUE

Airline Tickets Not a Disappearing Act
The airline ticket has not gone away, nor has the GDS. Overall, they are mainstays of the business. But air ticketing continues to decline in the typical agency's business mix, and a new generation of information and booking technologies is giving large and small retailers new alternatives to the old promise of one-stop shopping through the GDS.

2008 Travel Industry Survey, Introduction, *Travel Weekly* special supplement (2008), page 7

The purpose of distribution is to establish a link between supply and demand; between tourism destinations and organizations, and visitors. The distribution system makes tourism services and products available to visitors. Tourism distribution is different than the distribution in other industries. There is no physical distribution since tourism services are *intangible*. Tourism services cannot be physically packaged and shipped to visitors and they cannot be stored in inventory.

While the complexities of transportation and warehousing are eliminated, there are other unique challenges in tourism distribution. Tourism services are *perishable*. The hotel room, airline seat, or cruise berth must be sold each and every day, flight, or sailing.

A tourism sale lost today is lost forever. *Travel trade intermediaries* (organizations that operate between the providers of tourism services and visitors) have a strong influence on visitors' purchase decisions. A major role of travel trade intermediaries is the *packaging* of comple-

mentary tourism services and products to provide a more satisfying travel experience for the visitor. Retail travel agents book airline seats, hotel rooms, cruises, tours and packages, and rental cars and provide individualized packaged vacations in the form of foreign independent tours (FITs). Tour operators assemble these components into packaged vacations or tours and offer these for sale through retail travel agents. The tourism distribution system is different because it includes these and other unique intermediaries that each performs specialized roles. This system communicates promotional messages to potential visitors, along with the necessary factual information, and makes booking easier for the visitor.

DISTRIBUTION'S ROLE IN THE MARKETING MIX

The tourism distribution system or *distribution mix* is a component of the marketing mix; it is referred to as "place" in the traditional 4 Ps of marketing. Distribution mix decisions must be consistent with the overall marketing mix. The goal of the marketing mix is to reach target markets and achieve the objectives for these markets. The distribution mix affects other marketing mix components and is itself affected by these other components. For example, cruise lines rely almost completely on retail travel agents for their bookings. Therefore, the cruise lines' pricing structures must be such as to allow for attractive commission rates for agents.

Promotional approaches need to be adapted to suit the choice of travel trade intermediaries. Because retail travel agents have no inventory, there is no incentive for them to promote specific destinations. The promotional burden rests with destination marketing organizations, transportation companies, and the suppliers of tourism services. In contrast, tour operators carry an inventory of airline seats, hotel rooms, and other tourism services. They have a prior investment (in terms of *blocked space*) with airlines and suppliers in the tour destination areas and are often willing to share the costs of promoting the destination to sell their tours. For the airlines and suppliers of services, the promotional burden is shared through partnerships with tour operators. These partnerships may include joint advertising, joint sponsorship of agent familiarization tours, and other sales promotion activities.

The pricing approaches of tourism suppliers and carriers are influenced by the decision either to distribute directly to the traveler or indirectly through a travel intermediary. When tour operators buy in bulk—such as blocking one hundred rooms per night for three months–they expect and receive lower room rates.

THE TOURISM DISTRIBUTION SYSTEM

DIRECT AND INDIRECT DISTRIBUTION CHANNELS

Tourism distribution is either direct or indirect. *Direct distribution* occurs when a carrier, supplier, or destination marketing organization sells directly to the traveler; *indirect distribution* is when the sale is made through one or more travel trade intermediaries. This produces a rather complex distribution system (see figure 9.1). *Carriers* (airlines, railroad companies, and other transportation providers), *suppliers* (attractions, lodging, cruise line, food service, rental car companies, and gaming facilities), and *destination marketing organizations* face a two-step decision process when selecting their distribution mixes. First, they must make a choice of *distribution channel*. Second, if indirect channels are chosen, they must select specific travel trade intermediaries. McIntosh, Goeldner, and Ritchie (1995) define a tourism channel of distribution as "an operating structure, system or linkages of various combinations of travel organizations through which a producer of travel products describes, sells, and confirms travel arrangements to the buyer." A tourism distribution channel has a twofold purpose: (1) ensuring that travelers obtain the information they need to make trip arrangements and, (2) accepting the bookings and processing the necessary reservations for travelers.

TRAVEL TRADE INTERMEDIARIES

TOUR WHOLESALERS AND OPERATORS. According to the U.S. Tour Operators Association (USTOA) (2002), a *tour operator* is a company whose main business is the planning, packaging, selling, marketing, and promotion of multiple vacation elements, including air or surface transportation arrangements combined with land accommodations. The terms *tour wholesaler* and *tour operator* are often used interchangeably. The *wholesaling* function means assembling or "planning and packaging" the tour. It involves tour planning, preparation, marketing, and reservations. By definition, a wholesaler does not sell directly to the public but receives reservations through other travel intermediaries such as retail travel agencies or airline sales offices. The *operating* part of the tour means managing the tour by providing tour escorts, sightseeing services, or transportation. Many tour operators perform both the wholesaling and operating functions.

A distinction needs to be made between *outbound tour operators* and *inbound tour operators*. *Outbound tour operators* are companies that plan tours and packages for people leaving their own countries. *Inbound tour operators* are tour operators who function in the visitors' tour destinations. They are also called *reception* or *receptive tour operators* or *receptive services operators* (De Souto, 1993), or *destination management companies* or *specialists*. Inbound tour operators (ITOs) normally provide ground transportation, guiding, and welcoming services at the tour destinations. The Inbound Tour Operators Council of New Zealand provides this further explanation of what ITOs do:

> Inbound tour operators provide a vital link between the suppliers of New Zealand tourism product and the overseas travel companies that buy it. As specialists in inbound tourism, ITOC Full Members promote and sell New Zealand travel packages to offshore buyers such as wholesalers, travel agents, meeting planners, and event managers. They also play an important role as tourism "brokers" for overseas travel companies, providing a wide range of services including advice on product, price and availability, coordination of travel arrangements and payments, and supervision of product delivery (ITOC Web site, 2008).

RETAIL TRAVEL AGENCIES. Travel agents handle the sale and reservations of tours, vacation packages, airline tickets, hotel rooms, car rentals,

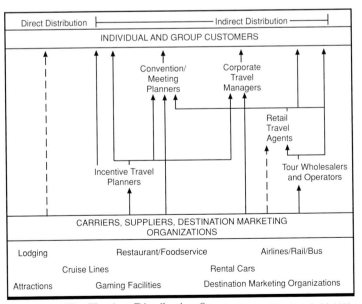

Figure 9.1 The Tourism Distribution System. Source: Morrison, A. M. 2009. *Hospitality and Travel Marketing*, 4th ed.

The ASTA Code of Ethics

The American Society of Travel Agents (ASTA) is one of the oldest and largest travel agency associations in the world. Although ASTA's headquarters are in Alexandria, Virginia, the 20,000 members are located in 140 countries.

ASTA has developed a Code of Ethics that specifies the "responsibilities of all travel agency, travel professional, international travel agency, and international travel professional members." These are:

- **Accuracy.** ASTA members will be factual and accurate when providing information about their services and the services of any firm they represent. They will not use deceptive practices.
- **Disclosure.** ASTA members will provide in writing, upon written request, complete details about the cost, restrictions, and other terms and conditions of any travel service sold, including cancellation and service fee policies. Full details of the time, place, duration, and nature of any sales or promotional presentation the consumer will be required to attend in connection with his/her travel arrangements shall be disclosed in writing before any payment is accepted.
- **Responsiveness.** ASTA members will promptly respond to their clients' complaints.
- **Refunds.** ASTA members will remit any undisputed funds under their control within the specified time limit. Reasons for delay in providing funds will be given to the claimant promptly.
- **Cooperation.** ASTA members will cooperate with any inquiry conducted by ASTA to resolve any dispute involving consumers or another member.
- **Confidentiality.** ASTA members will treat every client transaction confidentially and not disclose any information without permission of the client, unless required by law.
- **Affiliation.** ASTA members will not falsely represent a person's affiliation with their firm.
- **Conflict of Interest.** ASTA members will not allow any preferred relationship with a supplier to interfere with the interests of their clients.
- **Compliance.** ASTA members shall abide by all federal, state, and local laws and regulations.
- **Notice.** ASTA members operating tours will promptly advise the agent or client who reserved the space of any change in itinerary, services, features, or price.
- **Delivery.** ASTA members operating tours will provide all components as stated in their brochure or written confirmation, or provide alternate services of equal or greater value, or provide appropriate compensation.
- **Credentials.** An ASTA member shall not, in exchange for money or otherwise, provide travel agent credentials to any person as to whom there is no reasonable expectation that the person will engage in a bona fide effort to sell or manage the sale of travel services to the general public on behalf of the member through the period of validity of such credentials. This principle applies to the ASTA member and all affiliated or commonly controlled enterprises.

THINK ABOUT THIS:

1. What are the benefits for individual agencies in adhering to the ASTA Code of Ethics?
2. What benefits does this Code of Ethics provide for consumers in using ASTA member travel agencies?
3. What types of practices does this Code of Ethics promote and which unethical behaviors does it try to eliminate?

Source: American Society of Travel Agents. 2008. http://www.astanet.com/about/codeofethics. asp.

The ASTA Code of Ethics describes the responsibilities of travel agency professionals. © 2009 Leah-Anne Thompson. Used under license from Shutterstock, Inc.

cruises, travel insurance, and other related services. The *retail travel agent* is compensated through *commissions* from suppliers, carriers, and other intermediaries such as tour operators; the traveler usually pays nothing for the travel agent's services. Most U.S. travel agencies charge fees to the traveler. The principal value of retail travel agents to travelers is the agents' independence and impartiality, coupled with their knowledge of tourism services and access to the inventory of other tourism organizations. Travelers expect that agents can recommend the best services to fit their travel needs. For suppliers, carriers, destination marketing organizations, and other intermediaries, retail travel agencies represent additional sales outlets for their services and products. For most of them, it would be prohibitively expensive, if not impossible, to establish their own in-house system of nationwide distribution.

Pacific Delight World Tours, a USTOA active member, offers an extensive tour program to China and other destinations. http://www. pacificdelighttours.com/.

A *travel* or *air consolidator* is a special form of travel agency company. According to the U.S. Air Consolidators Association (2008), a consolidator is a travel agency that has negotiated airline rates awarded to them by an airline or airlines. They also work with other retail travel agencies (and sometimes also directly with consumers) to help agencies receive discounted tickets for individual or group travelers. Airlines provide two types of fares to consolidators: (1) net or bulk fares, and (2) commissionable fares (USACA Online Training Course, 2008).

CORPORATE TRAVEL DEPARTMENTS. While traditionally considered as just one aspect of the retail travel agent's business, the growth in business travel has led to the emergence of a new breed of specialized travel agency servicing the corporate traveler; the *corporate travel agency*. At the same time, an increasing number of companies have established in-house *corporate travel departments* to develop company-wide travel policies and to negotiate the best prices on travel. These corporate travel departments are administered by *corporate travel managers*. The National Business Travel Association (NBTA) explains the concept of *travel management* within organizations in the following way (NBTA Web site, 2008):

> Travel management is a specialized business function that balances employee needs with corporate goals, financial and otherwise. Travel management ensures cost tracking and control, facilitates adherence to corporate travel policies, realizes savings through negotiated discounts, and serves as a valuable information center for employees and managers in times when travel is not as smooth and carefree as it used to be.

INCENTIVE TRAVEL PLANNERS. Another recent newcomer to the tourism industry has been the *incentive travel planning company*, a specialized tour wholesaler who primarily serves corporate clients. The trips they arrange are given to certain of their client's employees or dealers as a reward for outstanding sales or work performance. Incentive travel is increasing in popularity as a work-related motivational and marketing tool. Corporations pay for the incentive travel planner's services either through a mark-up on the incentive package or on a fixed-fee basis.

CONVENTION-MEETING PLANNERS. These are employees of corporations, associations, government agencies, and other nonprofit groups who plan and coordinate meetings, conventions, conferences, exhi-

Maritz Inc. is one of the world's oldest and largest incentive travel planning companies. http://www.maritz.com.

bitions, or trade shows. *Convention-meeting planning consultants* are specialized firms that assist planners with on-site negotiations and arrangements.

OTHER INTERMEDIARIES AND ELECTRONIC DISTRIBUTION. Two other intermediaries are travel clubs and sales representatives. *Travel clubs* are groups of individual travelers who use their collective buying power to bargain for discounted prices on tourism services. These include the increasingly popular "last-minute" travel clubs. *Sales representatives* (sometimes called general sales agents or GSAs) are marketing or public relations specialists who represent hotels, resorts, destination areas, and other tourism organizations in foreign countries. These representative firms provide a more economical alternative to having a fully staffed office in each country.

The numbers of ways of distributing travel services have increased in recent years and will

QUICK TRIP 9.2

Sabre–The First GDS

Nowadays, booking a long-haul trip without the use of the Internet is very difficult. Global distribution systems have brought tourism offers directly to the personal computer, telephone, and other electronic devices. GDSs have become essential tools for the travel trade. The major GDSs are dependent on technology to get their offer to their client as quickly and fully as possible. However, you must remember that the Internet has not been around as long as intercontinental voyages.

Sabre Travel Network® is one of the leading providers of innovative travel distribution solutions for travel agencies and suppliers, selling more than $80 billion worth of travel products and services (2005).

The company began its operation in 1960, a partnership between IBM and American Airlines.

For more than 40 years, Sabre Travel Network has been developing innovations and transforming the business of travel. From the original Sabre® system in the 1960s, to Sabre® Inform℠ mobile services, an advanced real-time messaging system for travelers, our technology has traveled through time, around the world, and touched all points of the travel industry.

Before 1960, however, airlines reservations were being made and seats were being sold. The reservation system counted on direct telephone contact, handwritten reservations, and a manual tracking of flight schedules, availability, and prices.

The history of the Sabre system began with a chance meeting . . .

American Airlines President C. R. Smith and R. Blair Smith, a senior sales representative for IBM, met on an American Airlines flight from Los Angeles to New York in 1953. Their conversation about the travel industry sparked the idea of a data-processing system that would create a complete airline seat reservation—and make all the data instantly available electronically to any agent, at any place.

Six years later, the airborne exchange of ideas became a reality. American Airlines and IBM jointly announced their plans to develop a Semi-Automated Business Research Environment—better known as Sabre. The revolutionary system was the first real-time business application of computer technology. It enabled American Airlines to leapfrog from handwritten passenger reservation information in the 1950s to an automated system.

(continued)

1960s

In 1960, the first Sabre reservations system was installed in Briarcliff Manor, New York. The mainframe system was state-of-the-art technology and processed 84,000 telephone calls per day.

When the network was completed in 1964, it became the largest, private real-time data-processing system—second only to the U.S. government's system.

1970s

In 1972, the Sabre system was moved to a new consolidated computer center in Tulsa, Oklahoma, that was designed to house all of American Airlines' data-processing facilities.

The Sabre system was installed in a travel agency for the first time in 1976, triggering the wave of travel automation. By the end of that year, 130 locations had received the system. By 1978, the Sabre system could store 1 million fares.

1980s

In 1983, the Sabre system became available to Canadian travel agents.

In 1985, the introduction of easySabre® allows consumers using personal computers to tap into the Sabre system via computer online services to access airline, hotel, and car rental reservations.

The Sabre system was extended to the United Kingdom in 1986, paving the way for widespread international expansion of the system in the next decade.

In 1988, the Sabre system expanded to store 36 million fares, which could be combined to create more than 1 billion fare options.

1990s

In 1999, we introduced Best Fare Finder pricing, which allows travel agents to search for flights based on fare, rather than schedule.

2000s

In 2000, we introduced Sabre® eVoya℠ Webtop as the next generation of travel agency technology tools, making it simple for Sabre Connected℠ agencies to become Internet ready.

The Sabre GDS is a primary component for travel and transportation information for over 50,000 travel agencies, major travel suppliers, Fortune 500 companies, and travel Web sites around the globe. It serves as a distribution source for travel content from more than 400 airlines, approximately 77,000 hotel properties, 32 car rental companies, 11 cruise lines, 35 railroads, and 220 tour operators. The Sabre system provides users with schedules, availability, pricing, policies, and rules, as well as reservation and ticketing capability for travel suppliers.

THINK ABOUT THIS:

1. There are many global distribution systems around the world; however, only a small number are considered leaders. Do these leaders owe their success to strategic partnerships?

2. Products offered by GDSs are varied. What other services do they offer? Are these services an obligation to new coming distribution systems?

3. What can be said about the future of GDSs and travel distribution?

4. GDSs are paid to distribute airline seats around the world. However, the commissionless sales are becoming more and more frequent for travel agents. Can it be said that travel agents have become extensions of airline sales force?

Source: 2008. http://www.sabretravelnetwork.com/about/history.htm.

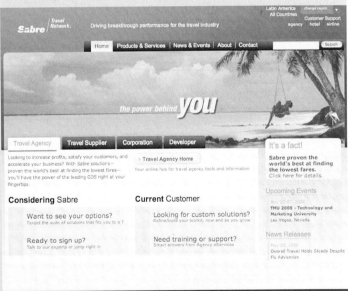

The Sabre Travel Network® has more than fifty thousand travel agency clients. http://www.sabretravelnetwork.com/.

continue to in the future. Some of these distribution methods will involve new organizations entering the tourism industry (e.g., banks and insurance companies) or the creation of new types of service businesses, while others will rely primarily on *electronic distribution* using advances in computer and telecommunications technology.

During the past 30 years, technological advances have had the greatest impact on tourism distribution and the future promises even greater potential for the electronic distribution of tourism information and services. Most retail travel agencies are hooked into airline *computerized reservation systems* (CRS) or *global distribution systems* (GDS), giving them instant access to the inventory of the airlines and other tourism suppliers. Computer software programs and Web sites linked to online database/reservations services are now available to allow travelers to make travel reservations in their own homes or offices via personal computers and telephone lines. For example, there are now several large *online travel agencies* who make travel reservations for people using the Web, including Travelocity and Expedia.

INTEGRATION AND CLASSIFICATION OF CHANNELS

VERTICAL INTEGRATION

Every transportation carrier, supplier, destination marketing organization, and travel intermediary within the tourism distribution system wants potential travelers to have the maximum amounts of exposure and access to their information to encourage inquiries, bookings, res-

---

Expedia Is Climbing to the Top of the Charts in Travel
Travel is one of the largest industries in the world, bringing together people, cultures and destinations across the globe. With more than $17 billion in annual gross travel bookings, Expedia, Inc. plays a leading role in facilitating travel, whether for business or for pleasure, and is committed to providing travelers with the very best resources to serve their travel needs.

Our portfolio of brands includes: Expedia.com®, hotels.com®, Hotwire®, Egencia®, TripAdvisor® and Classic Vacations®. Expedia, Inc.'s companies also operate internationally with sites in Canada, the United Kingdom, Germany, France, Italy, Spain, the Netherlands, Norway, Sweden, Denmark, Australia, Japan and China, through our investment in eLong™.

Expedia, Inc.'s mission is to get the world going by building the world's largest and most intelligent travel marketplace. *Expedia, Inc. (2009), http://overview.expediainc.com/phoenix. zhtml?c=190013&p=overview, accessed January 5, 2009*

---

ervations, and payments. The more direct control an organization has over the distribution of its services (through vertical integration), the greater is the assurance that information will be available and that reservations and payments can be made easily and conveniently. *Vertical integration* refers to the ownership by one organization of all or part of a tourism distribution channel.

HORIZONTAL INTEGRATION

Tourism companies may also expand their power in a distribution channel through horizontal integration. *Horizontal integration* refers to the ownership of similar businesses by one organization in the tourism distribution channel. This happens often in tourism and usually involves a larger company taking over a smaller organization in the same business. Examples of this in the retail travel agency field include American Express' acquisition of Thomas Cook's operations in the United States, and Carlson's acquisition of A.T. Mays in the United Kingdom and Travel Agents International.

CLASSIFICATION OF CHANNELS

Distribution channels can be classified in terms of degree of control into three types: (1) consensus channels; (2) vertically integrated channels commanded by suppliers, carriers, tour operators, retail travel agents, or other intermediaries; and (3) vertically coordinated channels led by suppliers, carriers, tour operators, retail travel agents, or other intermediaries.

CONSENSUS CHANNELS. In a consensus channel, no single type of tourism organization exercises control over the entire distribution system. The many participants work together because they see it in their mutual interest to do so. Distribution channels in North America, the United Kingdom, and Australia tend to be of the consensus type.

VERTICALLY INTEGRATED CHANNELS. Vertically integrated channels are those in which the supplier and retail distribution functions are owned or controlled by a single organization. Because tour operators have historically emerged from the retail travel agency field, vertically integrated channels controlled by retail travel agents are commonly found in the United Kingdom (Thomson Holidays, a division of TUI UK, Ltd.; and the Thomas Cook Group PLC), Germany (REWE Group; TUI AG), and North America (American Express Travel and Carlson Wagonlit Travel).

Integration by the Carlson Companies and the Thomson Travel Group

The Carlson Companies, Inc., based in Minneapolis, Minnesota, provides a good example of vertical and horizontal integration in tourism. Carlson's four major business units are the Carlson Marketing Group, Carlson Wagonlit Travel, CW Government Travel, and Carlson Leisure Group. The company's operations encompass the roles of a tourism supplier (hotels and resorts, restaurants, and cruise ships) and travel trade intermediary (retail travel agencies and incentive travel planning). The specific operations included under the Carlson umbrella include:

- Hotels and resorts: Regent International Hotels, Radisson Hotels & Resorts, Park Plaza Hotels & Resorts, Country Inns & Suites by Carlson, Park Inn Hotels
- Cruises: Regent Seven Seas Cruises
- Restaurants: T.G.I. Friday's and Pick Up Stix restaurants
- Travel agencies: Carlson Wagonlit Travel, Cruise Holidays, America's Vacation Store, Cruise Specialists, Inc., Fly4Less.com, CruiseDeals.com, Results Travel, Carlson Destination Marketing Services, Carlson Leisure Travel Services, SeaMaster Cruises, SinglesCruise.com, CW Government Travel
- Incentive travel and CRM: Carlson Marketing Group, Peppers & Rogers Group, and Gold Points Reward Network

Carlson began its operations in the incentives business in 1938. When it began operating Radisson Hotels, it was practicing vertical integration (moving into the supply side of the tourism distribution channel). The decision to enter the cruise business with the SSC Radisson Diamond was another example of the company becoming more vertically integrated. However, when Carlson acquired the Scottish-headquartered travel agency chain, A.T. Mays, and the Travel Agents International franchise travel agency group, this was horizontal integration (Carlson was already in the travel agency business).

Thomson Holidays is the largest air-inclusive tour operator in the United Kingdom, and is a division of TUI UK Ltd. TUI UK is part of the World of TUI, which is claimed to be the largest tourism and services group in the world. In the 1960s, Thomson purchased the independent British tour operator, Skytours. Later, Thomson acquired the British travel agency group, Lunn Poly, and the charter airline, Britannia Airways. The acquisitions of Lunn Poly and Britannia Airways were examples of vertical integration.

THINK ABOUT THIS:

1. What are the major advantages of vertical integration to companies such as Carlson and Thomson Holidays/TUI UK?
2. What are the potential benefits and disadvantages to the traveler in dealing with vertically integrated travel companies?
3. Will the trend toward greater vertical and horizontal integration in travel continue in the future? Why or why not?

Sources:

Carlson Companies. 2005. http://www.carlson.com/.

Thomson Holidays. 2005. http://www.thomson.co.uk/po/index.jsp.

The Web site of TUI UK. http://www.thomson.co.uk/.

Kayak.com has become one of the leading online travel reservation services.

DISTRIBUTION MIX STRATEGIES

INTENSIVE, EXCLUSIVE, AND SELECTIVE DISTRIBUTION

Each tourism organization must decide on its *distribution mix strategy* or how it will make its services available to potential travelers. The costs of distribution and the need to have the maximum exposure to potential travelers (*market coverage*) suggest using the largest possible number of travel trade intermediaries. However, the image of the services or destination and the motivations of individual travel trade intermediaries favor vertically integrated or vertically coordinated strategies or direct distribution. These strategies provide suppliers, carriers, destination marketing organizations, and travel trade intermediaries with the maximum control over sales and reservations.

The three broad strategy options available are intensive, exclusive, or selective distribution. An *intensive distribution* strategy means maximizing the exposure of travel services by distributing through all available travel trade intermediaries (high market coverage). *Exclusive distribution* occurs when a carrier, supplier, tour wholesaler or operator, or destination marketing organization restricts the number of retail outlets for its services and attempts to have travel agents sell only its services, not those of competitors. This may be accomplished through franchising or ownership of retail outlets (i.e., through a vertically integrated or vertically coordinated approach). *Selective distribution* is a strategy somewhere between intensive and exclusive distribution. More than one but less than all available outlets are used.

FACTORS AFFECTING DISTRIBUTION MIX STRATEGY DECISIONS

For the tourism marketer, the task is to select and design a distribution mix strategy that not only is the most effective in communicating with potential travelers and in accepting reservations, but that is also affordable. The following factors are evaluated in making distribution mix strategy decisions.

MARKET COVERAGE. If a tour operator, supplier, carrier, or destination marketing organization decides not to use the retail travel agency network, an alternative

A tour operator may exert control over the entire channel activity through retail travel agency ownership and the organization of the channel. This system is found in Germany where tour operators control not only their own chain of retail travel agency outlets, which deal exclusively with the products of one operator, but also their own system of general retail and direct mail distribution. TUI AG (Touristik Union International), one of the largest German tour operators, controls a network of travel agencies and a large number of resorts and hotels (around 240 hotels in the TUI Hotels & Resorts group composed of several brands).

VERTICALLY COORDINATED CHANNELS. A vertically coordinated channel led by tour operators is one in which the tour operator's power of control over the channel comes from contractual or financial commitments with retail travel agents. *Franchising* is an obvious example of such a system. In Germany, franchising is a large part of travel distribution. Retail travel agency franchising is also rapidly increasing in popularity in Australia, the United Kingdom, the United States, and Canada. The franchisor of a particular company agrees to retail only through certain retail outlets (its franchisees) and to promote no other methods of distribution. The retail franchisee benefits from the much larger pool of marketing resources of the franchiser and the "name recognition" it shares with the many other franchised agencies under the same umbrella. Carlson Wagonlit Travel is a good example of this in North America, while TravelWorld is a major franchised travel agency in Australia.

distribution network has to be developed. In travel trade terms, this is called *bypassing* the retail travel agency network. This may be a lucrative strategy because the costs of travel agency commissions are eliminated. The use of electronic distribution through the Web and e-mail is facilitating this strategy of dealing directly with travelers. However, in most countries, retail travel agencies offer widespread market coverage that is difficult for one single organization to duplicate.

COSTS. The costs of establishing retail or other direct distribution channels (e.g., a reservations service) are mainly fixed or overhead expenses. Salaries must be paid and offices maintained irrespective of the sales volume generated. Although a part of the compensation of sales representatives may be in the form of commissions, not many people are willing to work on a commission-only basis. In contrast, when working through travel trade intermediaries, only variable costs are incurred. In fact, many travel agency commission payments are made after sales have been made. Fixed costs are reduced to a minimum.

POSITIONING AND IMAGE. The choice of distribution channel must be consistent with the positioning and image of the supplier, carrier, destination marketing organization, or tour wholesaler or operator. An expensive, high-quality tour, destination, or service should be marketed to an upscale demographic market segment through quality intermediaries who cater to upscale travelers.

MOTIVATION OF TRAVEL TRADE INTERMEDIARIES. Each organization within the tourism distribution system has a unique set of objectives and needs. These ob-

The expertise of a travel agent is required to secure bookings on most cruises. © 2009 Rob Marmion. Used under license from Shutterstock, Inc.

jectives and needs are not always compatible and create conflicts and stresses in the tourism distribution system. Travelers want a variety of services and products from which they can select the most satisfying travel experiences. Retail travel agents want to offer travelers a large inventory of destinations and travel services, but need to sell a mix of travel services that produce the maximum commissions. Tour wholesalers and operators want high volume and high profit margins but are concerned about developing tours that motivate retail travel agents to sell them, while representing a minimum level of risk. Suppliers, carriers, and destination marketing organizations want to minimize distribution costs while getting the maximum exposure for their services. They want to generate high traffic volumes and encourage repeat business. The more integration within the channel, the more customer-contact employees are motivated to sell particular services or destinations at the expense of others.

When direct ownership is not feasible or legally permitted, suppliers, carriers, tour wholesalers and operators, and destination marketing organizations use a variety of motivation tactics with retail travel agencies. They offer higher commission rates (*overrides*) for higher volumes of booking. These higher rates of commission may be provided through *preferred supplier* or *vendor* relationships between the two parties. Familiarization tours or training seminars are arranged to increase product knowledge. A variety of sales support services may be provided to travel agents including toll-free telephone "help desks," Web sites, and in-store merchandising displays.

CHARACTERISTICS OF THE TOURISM DESTINATION OR SERVICE. Not all tourism destinations and services are the same. Some tourism services, including domestic airline tickets, are purchased frequently and are often subject to discounting. They may be distributed through large numbers of retail outlets and in a variety of different ways. Other tourism services and destinations, such as long-haul tours and cruises, can be highly priced, are purchased infrequently, and are usually not subject to any discounting. Travelers perceive these services to be distinctive, complex, and expensive. The expertise of the travel agent and personal selling by the agent is required to secure bookings. In this case, the tourism destination or organization should be more selective in its choice of retail travel agency outlets.

ECONOMIC CONCENTRATION. The amount of channel power depends upon the degree of economic concentration among a particular category of tourism organizations. The fewer tour wholesalers or operators serving a particular destination, the greater is the power of these companies in dealing with the destination's suppliers and carriers. This is especially true of smaller, long-haul tourism destinations that do not provide the volumes of visitors to be attractive to many tour companies. Examples of these destinations include Sri Lanka and Bhutan; two countries that are highly dependent on relatively few tour operators.

Germany is a country in which travel is exclusively distributed through vertically integrated channels; there is high economic concentration in the travel trade. According to an FVW survey in 2006, twenty-two German travel companies accounted for 97 percent of the total travel agency sales. These companies exert considerable power over destinations that are highly dependent on German visitors. Japan and South Korea are two other countries in which there is a concentration of power among relatively few travel companies.

There has been a trend away from distributing through as many retail travel agencies as possible (intensive distribution) to being more selective in choosing retailers (selective distribution). Carriers, suppliers, and destination marketing organizations want the maximum sales volumes. For tour wholesalers and operators, volume is even more critical to profitability. This suggests a strategy of using a maximum number of retail travel agencies. However, many tourism destinations and organizations have found that, while it is more risky to deal with a smaller number of travel agencies, the costs of servicing all agencies are prohibitive. Additionally, a small percentage of travel agencies often produce the majority of the business. A strategy of concentrating on agencies that produce most sales results in a more efficient distribution system.

TOUR WHOLESALERS AND OPERATORS

HISTORY

Although tour wholesaling began in the mid-nineteenth century, it was not until the 1960s and 1970s that the packaging of tours increased dramatically. The increase resulted from the development of larger aircraft capable of flying greater distances (the first Boeing 747 flew in 1970). Increased capacity led to lower airfares that stimulated demand for low-cost vacations. Although it is true that demand stimulates supply, supply can also create demand. To meet this demand, tour companies were established to assemble low-cost vacation packages.

CATEGORIES OF TOURS AND PACKAGES

Four main categories of tours and packages are offered by tour wholesalers, tour operators, travel agencies, airlines, and some suppliers:

1. **Escorted tours:** A type of organized tour that includes the services of a tour director who accompanies an individual or group throughout the tour.
2. **Hosted tours:** A type of organized tour that includes the services of a tour host who meets an individual or group at each destination to make local arrangements, but does not accompany the group through the entire tour.
3. **Package tours:** A type of organized, individual or group tour, that includes airfare and some ground transportation arrangements, but does not necessarily include the services of anyone meeting the individual or group at the destination.
4. **Independent tours:** An individualized tour assembled by a travel agent, airline, or tour wholesaler to a specific destination in which the tour patron travels independently with selected family members or friends, but not with groups of strangers.

The term *all-inclusive package* is also used a great deal in tourism. This refers to the complete range of tourism services included in the price of the package. The packages offered by all-inclusive resort chains such as Club Med and Sandals fit into this category, as do the vacations provided by cruise lines.

ECONOMICS OF TOUR WHOLESALING AND OPERATIONS

As mentioned earlier, the independent tour wholesaling and operations business is very concentrated in several countries, with a small number of companies accounting for a large percentage of the total revenue generated. The tour business is also characterized by relative ease of entry, high velocity of cash flow, low return on sales, and the potential for a high return on equity investment.

Taking Advantage of Tours and Packages

Tours and vacation packages offer many important benefits. Key among these is savings. By contracting in bulk for hotels, accommodations, ground transportation, sightseeing tours, meals and other services, tour operators achieve substantial economies. The resulting savings from this volume purchasing are passed on to the traveler.

United States Tour Operators Association (2009), http://www.ustoa.com/advantagesoftours.cfm, accessed January 5, 2009

Vertical Integration of Tour Operators–Pros and Cons

The Pro-Poor Tourism Partnership, "a collaborative research initiative between the International Centre for Responsible Tourism (ICRT), the International Institute for Environment and Development (IIED), and the Overseas Development Institute (ODI)" released a study on the effects of the U.K. outbound tourism market on tourism in poorer countries. The research paper shows the trends of integration, be they horizontal, vertical, or even diagonal, and the impacts on the destination.

Transport, accommodation, catering, and entertainment together compose the founding block of a destinations appeal. The travel trade has made high revenues from the exploration of these. Tour operators especially have found the winning formula. Adopting principles of business administration, economies of scale, and vertical integration have been created making the industry even more lucrative.

Through these strategies, tour operators can achieve enormous buying power and considerable control over the supply and distribution of their products. First, the opportunity for economies of scale (from horizontal integration); second, the ability to control and develop inputs and markets more closely (from vertical integration); and third, the chance to use existing differential advantages to operate profitably in related fields (diagonal integration).

As previously seen, to be vertically integrated means to have one single organization in control of suppliers, distributors, and other components of the channel. All major tour operators have vertical integration as the backbone of their operations and package tours. It is an efficient way to be in command of supplies in terms of quality, availability, access, and price and to reach consumers.

Through vertical integration, a tour operator can incorporate airline and/or accommodation facilities into its company and can thus better manage its costs. Lower prices mean greater market share; being a top company means loyalty from suppliers, even at reduced input prices. Furthermore, suppliers are more inclined to work with larger tour operators, since they are perceived as being less likely to face bankruptcy; but most importantly, they require high volume input.

There are two noteworthy effects of this structure.

1. Leakage. Dividends from tourism activity, in most part, do not stay in the destination.
   Large outbound tour operators have a very low cost structure, paying minimum prices for services provided by local businesses. "Large amounts of the money paid for a holiday remain in, or return to, the generating country."

   In general, small operators do not have as much negotiation power at the destination, meaning that the prices they must pay for the services are considerably higher. This scenario is better for the region's economy; however, it is likely to be unfavorable to the tourist.

   "The extent to which leakages occur varies strongly with the kind of tourism attracted and the degree of reliance on vertically integrated tour operators."

2. No room for small operators. Large operators have dominated the market, leaving little room for small competitors. "Vertically integrated operators capture a large proportion of mainstream package holidays." Many operators have seen themselves forced to specialize their products, avoiding head-on competition with the giants.

THINK ABOUT THIS:

1. Vertical integration presents advantages to the provider. Aside from financial gains, how else is the provider compensated?
2. Are there any examples of both the destination and the TO prospering with the partnership?
3. What is the future of packaged tours?

Source: http://www.propoortourism.org.uk/17_industry.pdf. The UK Outbound Tour Operating Industry and Implications for Pro-Poor Tourism 2003.

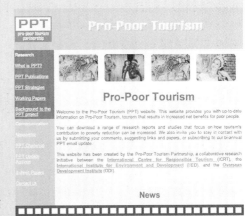

Pro-Poor Tourism

The Pro-Poor Tourism Partnership involves the International Center for Responsible Tourism (ICRT), the International Institute for Environment and Development (IIED), and the Overseas Development Institute (ODI).

EASE OF ENTRY. Some countries, states, or provinces force tour companies to be licensed by a government agency. This is due to a history of tour operator business failures and also to unscrupulous practices of some past operators (e.g., taking deposits from travelers and then disappearing). Several countries require tour operators to have a proven track record of several years of operation and to post bonds to protect their tour patrons in the event of a bankruptcy.

Other countries, including the United States, do not require tour operator licensing by government agencies. Instead, governments constrain tour companies by various regulations or tour operators themselves are self-policing. For example, in the United States, the U.S. Tour Operators Association (USTOA) requires its active members to post a bond of $1 million in trust to protect customers' deposits and payments in the event of the company's closure or bankruptcy. Often members of travel trade associations adopt a *code of ethics* or *conduct* that shows their commitment to ethical business practices that protect travelers. Despite the existence of these measures, in many countries it is relatively easy to become a tour wholesaler or operator. This is a result of the low initial investment required to get started in tour wholesaling.

CASH FLOW. The flow of cash is crucial to a tour wholesaler. The wholesaler signs contracts for bulk quantities of transportation and *ground services* (airport transfers, lodging, meals, entertainment, sightseeing, ground transportation by coach or other means). By contracting in bulk for ground services, the wholesaler receives discounts on regular rates and prices. For example, a wholesaler may contract for two hundred rooms in a hotel every night for three months. The

With an escorted nature tour, the guide, like this one, accompanies the group throughout the tour. © 2009 Creatista. Used under license from Shutterstock, Inc.

ground or *land tour* portion is then marked up by about 10 to 15 percent by the tour wholesaler to provide their profit (Poynter, 1993). The tour wholesaler must also allow for a *travel agent commission*, which may be in the range of 10 to 15 percent of the ground services costs. If air fares are to be included in the tour price, they are then added to the marked-up ground services portion of the tour to arrive at a final tour selling price. The air fares usually cannot be marked up because the commissions go directly to the retail travel agents who are the only ones accredited by the appropriate regulating bodies to sell airline tickets.

The tour wholesaler must make *advance deposits* for ground services to secure them. To offset these advance payments to suppliers (or *vendors*), cash flow or *float* is generated when customers' deposits and final payments are received prior to the tour departure date. Tour wholesalers usually do not pay the outstanding balances for ground service (less the advance deposits) until after the tour. The cash flow (excess of customer deposits and final payments over advance deposits to suppliers) is used to pay the tour wholesalers' operating expenses. Problems arise when the cash flow from one tour has to be used to finance the preparation of another. If demand slows, tour wholesalers with few liquid assets to protect them against cash deficits may become insolvent or bankrupt.

RETURN ON SALES. The average return on sales for an independent tour wholesaler is low and sales volume is the key to profitability. Where airfares are included in the tour price, a significant proportion of tour sales comes from the transportation component, of which 85 percent or more goes to airlines. The tour wholesaler does not receive any of the air ticket revenue. The remaining share of the tour sales price covers the ground services, travel agent commission, and tour wholesaler's profit. Assuming that these represent about 50 to 60 percent of the tour sales price and that travel agents get a 10 to 15 percent commission on the ground services portion, then the tour wholesaler makes a 10 to 15 percent profit on about 40 to 55 percent of the tour sales price. This means that the tour wholesaler's return on sales is low, at about 4 to 8 percent.

In costing a tour, the tour wholesaler must allow for *variable costs* and *fixed costs*. Variable costs fluctuate directly with the number of people on the tour. They include the amounts paid to airlines, ground suppliers, and retail travel agents (in agent commissions). Travel agents receive commissions from the airline (transportation component) and the tour wholesaler (ground services or land tour component). Fixed costs do not vary at all with the number of people on the tour.

They include the tour wholesaler's employee wages and benefits for such items as tour preparation, reservations, record keeping, and accounting. The fixed costs also include promotion expenses, which may encompass brochure printing and distribution costs. Finally, some of the land tour costs are fixed including the cost of the tour director or manager (if the tour is escorted) and the cost of any chartered vehicles (e.g., motor coaches).

RETURN ON EQUITY. Because the capital required to become a tour wholesaler is low, a large return on equity can be made. This potentially high return on equity (tour profits divided by the wholesaler's equity investment) results from the low equity investment and not from the net profit on tour sales (which is relatively low).

FUNCTIONS OF TOUR WHOLESALERS AND OPERATORS

The main function of a tour wholesaler is to combine both transportation and ground services into tours to be sold through retail travel agencies to individual or group travelers. This role is performed by independent tour wholesaling companies. The term wholesaling implies that these companies do not sell directly to the public.

Many tour wholesalers tailor their tour offerings by target market, destination, mode of transportation, or type of activity or special interest. Some wholesalers cater to specific segments of the market (such as national or ethnic groups), while others "mass market" by promoting popular "sun and sand" destinations. Still other wholesalers specialize in developing tours to specific destinations or regions of the world (e.g., AAT Kings Tours, African Travel, Australian Pacific Touring, China Travel Service, Latour Latin America, and Pacific Delight Tours). Some wholesalers specialize in one type of transportation. The majority of tours marketed by independent tour wholesalers involve air travel.

Tour and package development is also done by other types of organizations. Retail travel agents prepare individual (*foreign independent tours* or *FITs*) and group tours (*group inclusive tours* or *GITs*) that they sell to travelers. Airlines and railway companies have wholesaling divisions that put together tours. Companies specializing in incentive travel, cruise lines, travel clubs, educational institutions, and nonprofit organizations (unions, religious groups, associations, and government and quasi-government agencies) also assemble tours and packages.

Some tour wholesalers mass market by promoting "sun and sand" destinations. © 2009 Christian Wheatley. Used under license from Shutterstock, Inc.

A single tour program consists of four parts:

1. Tour planning and preparation
2. Tour marketing
3. Tour administration
4. Tour evaluation

TOUR PLANNING AND PREPARATION. The planning of a tour must begin with some market research. The purpose of this research should be to indicate to the wholesaler which tours will sell and which tour ingredients are essential to attract tour patrons. Both secondary (previously published information) and primary (information collected for the first time) research should be used. The secondary research sources might include the reports of tour operator associations and research organizations, published statistics on arrivals to tourist destinations, directories of tour programs, competitors' brochures, and the wholesaler's own past operating results that show which tours have sold well and been profitable. The primary research steps might include surveying retail travel agents and past and potential tour patrons.

When planning and developing tours for new destinations, tour wholesalers may participate in *familiarization tours* (or FAMs), sponsored by destination marketing organizations, carriers, or suppliers. These trips help the tour wholesaler to determine tour potential, evaluate ground services, and solicit potential government and private-sector partnerships for promoting the tour program. At this point, detailed tour specifications are prepared such as departure dates, tour length, and modes of transportation and ground services to be used. These activities often take place a year to 18 months before the first tour departure date.

The actual *tour program* is usually confirmed from 12 to 15 months prior to the first tour departure. Ground services are negotiated and supplier agreements signed. Transportation commitments are made. When these steps are completed, the tour program can be finalized. The tour price is calculated by taking the negotiated costs for ground services and adding a markup that, when the expected number of tour patrons is considered, is sufficient to cover fixed costs and the tour wholesaler's profit. A checklist for pricing a tour is illustrated in figure 9.2.

Tour _____   Tour Dates _____

Compiled _____   Cancellation Date _____

Revised _____   Gateway _____

A. Variable Costs (per person)

1. Airfare Basis.................... _____   7. State/VAT taxes.............. _____   13. Package........................
2. Surcharges........................ _____   8. Service Charges.............. _____   based on (   )
3. Airport Taxes .... _____   9. Meals............................ _____   14. Insurance..................... _____
4. Transfers........................... _____   10. Meal Taxes & Tips........... _____   15. Publications/
5. Baggage Tips .... _____   11. Sightseeing...................... _____   Postage .... _____
6. Hotel Rooms .... _____   12. Admissions .... _____   16. Miscellaneous................. _____

Single Room Supplement........ _____   Total.................................... _____

B. Fixed Costs (Tour Director)   Include only costs not complemented

1. Transportation.................. _____   7. Sightseeing/...................... _____   12. Passports/Visas.............. _____
   (home/gateway/home)   Admissions   13. Vaccinations .... _____
2. Transportation................... _____   8. Baggage Tips .... _____   14. Currency Conversion....... _____
   (on tour)   9. Insurance......................... _____   15. Miscellaneous................. _____
3. Airport Taxes .... _____   10. Meals/Hotels .... _____   16. Salary .... _____
4. Hotel Rooms .... _____   (Day before/   (days@   )
5. Meals, Taxes, Tips .... _____   Day after tour)
6. Transfers........................... _____   11. Travelers Checks.............. _____   Total.................................... _____

C. Fixed Costs (Group)

1. Chartered Vehicles .... _____   7. Programs......................... _____   13. Administrative .... _____
2. Tolls/Ferries...................... _____   8. Speaker Fee.................... _____   14. Miscellaneous................. _____
3. Sightseeing .... _____   9. Driver Tips .... _____   15. Orientation
4. Admissions....................... _____   10. Brochures...................... _____   16. Fund Raising .... _____
5. Local Guides .... _____   11. Promotion ....
6. Transfers........................... _____   12. Communications .... _____   Total.................................... _____

Grand Total of all Fixed Costs

D. Computations Group Size .... _____   _____   _____

Land Costs

A. Total Variable Costs............................. _____   _____   _____

B. Grand Total of Fixed Costs
   (Divided by Size of Group)................. _____   _____   _____

C. Sum of A and B .... _____   _____   _____

D. Dollar Markup (%)............................. _____   _____   _____

E. Airfare .... _____   _____   _____

F. Sum of C, D, and E .... _____   _____   _____

Selling Price .... _____   _____   _____

E. Minimum number of paying passengers.   _____   Mark-up on Land (D) _____
   _____   Air Commission _____
   Maximum number of paying passengers.   _____   Gross Net _____
   _____   (Per Person)

Source: Howe, R. M. 1980. Analyzing the trip: Checklist of steps. The 1980 Travel Agency Guide to Business and Group Travel. *Travel Weekly*. 110.

Figure 9.2 Tour Price Structure Sheet.

The three columns in part D of figure 9.2 show the cost computations for three different group sizes. The first is the minimum size of group necessary. This would be based upon a specified minimum number of people that the airline or ground service suppliers require to guarantee prices to the tour wholesaler. In some cases, the type of airfare used may necessitate that the wholesaler guarantee a certain minimum number of passengers. The third column shows costs based upon the maximum number of travelers possible on the tour. The costs in the middle column are based on the tour wholesaler's best estimate of the most likely number of tour patrons.

The tour wholesaler's markup is expressed as either a percentage of ground service costs or as a dollar figure. The markup has to be realistic yet also reflect the time and effort involved in organizing the tour. Airfare is added to total ground services costs and markup to arrive at the selling price for the retail travel agent. The final selling price is calculated by adding a retail travel agent commission.

The mechanics of handling reservations and payment are made and brochure production begun. Brochure production is very expensive and part of the production costs may be paid by the airline involved in the tour or one or more of the ground service suppliers. Appropriate commission rates and volume incentives are also negotiated with retail travel agents. At this point, there are typically ten months left before the first tour departs.

TOUR MARKETING. The marketing of a tour is the aspect most crucial to its success. The characteristics of the tour marketing program depend upon the size of the wholesaler and the market segments being targeted. All marketing programs involve brochure distribution, advertising, personal selling, and other sales promotions (e.g., promotional evenings).

Brochures are often large and expensive to produce in high-quality color. While the brochures may be distributed to all travel agencies, it is more efficient to use a selective distribution process. Emphasis should be given to agencies who have provided tour patrons to the wholesaler in the past and especially those that have generated the greatest volumes of past tour patrons. Brochures may also be provided to agencies whose customers fit the profile of the target market for the tour program. Online distribution of brochures in PDF is now commonplace, and this is helping to reduce printing and distribution costs, while also extending the reach of brochures.

Travel trade advertising may be used to promote a specific tour program or to promote the tour wholesaler's overall services. Advertisements placed in travel trade journals, such as *Travel Weekly* are normally factual, describing the tours and giving travel agents booking information. Toll-free telephone numbers, electronic mail numbers, and Web site addresses are included to encourage travel agents to request tour brochures and other sales materials. In addition, tour wholesalers and operators employ sales representatives who concentrate on selling tours to travel agents regarded as the best prospects.

Consumer advertising tends to be less factual and more emotional. Very colorful and eye-catching images are used to attract attention and create interest in the tours. Ads may be placed in consumer travel magazines and usually recommend travelers to book through travel agents. Advertising is also done through direct mail using the tour wholesaler's list of past tour patrons and mailing lists of potential patrons. Again, consumer advertisements tend to be of the direct-response variety, urging potential travelers to request a brochure by a toll-free telephone number, fax number, or through e-mail and Web sites.

Marketing begins nine to twelve months prior to departure and continues until a few days beforehand. Reservations, deposits, and payments are requested from one to two months in advance of the departure. If insufficient advance bookings are made, tours may be consolidated or promotion increased.

TOUR ADMINISTRATION. The administration of a tour begins six months prior to departure. Detailed schedules or worksheets are prepared describing the tour program and a reservation system sufficient to detail the documentation and payment status of each tour patron is set up. Liaison procedures are established between the reservation system and the ground service suppliers at each destination.

Reservations are usually received by telephone, fax, or via computer from retail travel agencies. They are confirmed, recorded, and filed. Deposits and payments are processed and documentation sent to the travel agency for distribution to travelers. Upon completion of the tour, the suppliers are paid. The tour operation part of the tour may be handled by the tour wholesaler or by ground service operators (e.g., inbound tour operators or motor coach companies) or other destination management companies based in the destinations.

TOUR EVALUATION. When the tour is over, the tour wholesaler may evaluate its success through a variety of means. First, it is most important to get each tour patron's opinions on the success of the tour and their satisfaction levels. The tour wholesaler might do this by having each tour patron complete a questionnaire or comment card at the end of the tour or soon after its completion. Second, the wholesaler might contact all the suppliers involved in the tour to get their reactions. Finally, the tour wholesaler needs to complete an internal evaluation to determine the return on investment for each tour.

OPERATING CYCLE

The tour wholesaling and operations business tends to be seasonal. At any one time the wholesaler's staff may be preparing the following year's program while marketing and operating the existing year's offering. To reduce seasonality, tour wholesalers may operate tour programs to several destinations that each has a different seasonal pattern of demand (e.g., winter sports destinations in winter and sun-and-sand destinations in summer).

RETAIL TRAVEL AGENCIES

HISTORY

Thomas Cook is credited with developing the concept of a travel agent in 1841 when he chartered a train to carry people from Leicester to Loughborough, a distance of twenty-two miles, to attend a temperance convention. Today, Thomas Cook is a travel industry giant with five divisions in the United Kingdom, Continental Europe, Northern Europe, North America, and its German airlines.

In the early 1900s, rail travel was the primary mode of transportation for business travelers. Little pleasure travel existed. The travel agent of the day was the hotel porter, who would make reservations for business travelers staying at the hotel. The porter received a commission from the railroad and would add a delivery charge for going to the railroad station to purchase the ticket. The airlines, which first purchased planes with seats for passengers in the late 1920s, saw the railroads as their major competitor for the business market. (The pleasure market would not become significant for another ten years.) The airlines approached the hotel porters, equipped them with ticket stock, and offered a 5 percent commission for making the sale. Little expertise was required as most carriers had only one route and the tickets already contained information about fare ori-

> **Travel Agencies Now Place More Emphasis on Cruise and Pleasure/Leisure Travel Sales**
>
> *CLIA finished 2007 with nearly 16,000 Travel Agency affiliates. The recent reduction in affiliate membership is a reflection of the general consolidation and attrition in the travel agency business. The trend has particularly affected corporate travel and has been accelerated as a result of the airlines reducing/eliminating travel agency base commissions. This is resulting in more travel agencies shifting their focus to cruise and leisure sales.*
>
> *2008 CLIA Cruise Market Overview: Statistical Cruise Industry Data Through 2007,* Cruise Lines International Association (2008), page 9

gin and destination of the flight. The feeling of the carriers was that the porters were providing a ticketing service for business that was already there rather than creating new business. Thus, from the beginning hotel porters and then travel agents were seen as distributors of tickets and entitled to a small commission.

Airlines then began to open their own offices in hotels and this provided large enough traffic volumes to justify the expense. The porters were forced out of business. Airlines restricted the new breed of travel agent from opening offices since they would compete with the airlines' sales offices. After World War II, two trends assisted the growth of retail travel agencies: the expansion of vacation or holiday travel and increasing popularity of international travel. The airlines continued to exert considerable influence over the opening of travel agencies. For example, in the United States prior to 1959, when the so-called need clause was abolished by the Civil Aeronautics Board, a U.S. travel agency could be opened only if it was sponsored by an airline and its opening approved by two-thirds of the airlines represented. The sponsoring airline was responsible for checking that the agency had financial stability, an acceptable location, and staff with sufficient experience. Today, it is necessary for agencies to be appointed by their national and international airline agencies to sell tickets and receive commissions. For example, to book tickets on international airlines, retail travel agents must be approved by IATA (International Air Transport Association).

FUNCTIONS OF RETAIL TRAVEL AGENTS

In essence, retail travel agencies are the department stores of tourism. Around the world, they provide thousands of "travel shops" for suppliers, carriers, destination marketing organizations, and the other travel trade intermediaries. A customer can buy all types of travel

What's New in the U.S. Travel Agency Business?

The Airlines Reporting Commission (ARC) has been providing statistics on the U.S. travel agency business for approximately 25 years. There were over 33,000 retail travel agency locations in the United States in 1997. The ARC statistics show that this number has dropped sharply to under 20,000 in September 2008, including satellite ticket printer (STP) delivery locations.

ARC Statistics

Year Ending in September 2008	
Agent retail locations	17,914
STP locations	1,238
Total sales	$64,413,117,705
Domestic air fare sales	$29,150,803,411
International air fare sales	$26,082,515,435

The ARC is trying to help the travel agency business become more efficient as it transitions in the era of no air ticket commissions and Internet distribution. It is ARC's goal "to help the industry transition from inefficient and costly paper processes, obtain lower costs and greater operating efficiencies through electronic processes." In September 2008, 98.82 percent of all the tickets issued were e-tickets; so it seems that ARC is achieving its goal. It's interesting to note from the *ASTA Agency Profile* for 2008 that their member travel agencies' share of airline sales to total sales has dropped from 56.1 percent in 2000 to 23.8 percent in 2008.

It appears that many people in North America have switched to using the Internet to get travel information and bookings, in preference to using travel agents. The following is what the American Society of Travel Agents (ASTA) says about the benefits of using a travel agent rather than the Internet:

"The Internet can be a powerful tool. It can increase the scope and reach of a consumer's efforts and allow a person to check hundreds of options or research destinations in depth. But to make the Internet work effectively, a person has to understand where to look and what questions to ask, otherwise hours can be wasted surfing the Web and ultimately produce unsatisfactory results. This is where a travel agent can make a world of difference.

A professional travel agent is trained to guide a client through the entire process of planning a trip, whether for business or for leisure. Travel agents take classes, participate in seminars, become destination specialists, and join professional associations, such as ASTA, in order to ensure they make each client's travel experience as personalized, convenient, and memorable as possible. When planning a business trip or family vacation, the Internet can be a valuable resource, but it cannot replace the expertise and guidance of a travel agent. Also, during travel crises, the Internet can't replace a human being who will persist to help a client. Travel agents, meanwhile, can offer a myriad of intermediate options."

THINK ABOUT THIS:

1. What steps have travel agencies taken to make up for lost commissions on booking airline tickets?

2. What have been the effects, both positive and negative, of the Internet on retail travel agencies?

3. What are likely to be the major future challenges to the viability of the travel agencies in the major developed countries?

Sources:

Airlines Reporting Corporation. 2008. http://www.arccorp.com/.

American Society of Travel Agents. 2008. http://www.asta.org/.

The Airlines Reporting Corporation tracks the U.S. travel agency business.
http://www.arccorp.com/index.jsp.

services at an agency including tickets for planes and railways, hotels and resorts, packages and tours, car rentals, and travel insurance. The main functions of retail travel agencies are as follows:

DISTRIBUTION AND SALES NETWORK. Travel agents bring together the sellers and buyers of travel; in this role they can be called "travel brokers." They act as the official "agents" of travel *principals*; the organizations that actually provide the travel services. Travel agents provide an enormous distribution network for suppliers, carriers, destination marketing organizations, and other travel intermediaries.

The United States has the largest concentration of travel agencies. According to the Airlines Reporting Corporation (ARC), there were 17,914 full-service travel agencies and 1,238 satellite ticket printer locations in the United States in September 2008. The greatest growth in the number of travel agencies appears to be in the Asia-Pacific region.

In return for their services, suppliers, carriers, and other travel trade intermediaries pay travel agents *commissions*, which are normally based on a certain percentage of the total value of the reservation. In most countries, travel agency commission rates are in the 5 to 10 percent range. Special arrangements between individual carriers and suppliers, known as *preferred supplier* or *vendor relationships*, allow the travel agents to earn extra points of commission (*overrides*). During the 1990s and into the 2000s, most agencies have been charging their customers *service fees* in an effort to improve profitability in the face of disappearing airline commissions.

RESERVATIONS AND TICKETING. The placement of reservations and the distribution of tickets (mainly for airlines) are traditional roles of retail travel agencies. Reservations and ticketing used to be very time-consuming and labor-intensive but advances in computer and telecommunications technology have speeded up these processes. *Computerized reservation systems* or CRSs, which were first introduced in the early 1970s, have provided travel agents with instant access to an ever-expanding inventory of the services of the airlines, suppliers, and other travel trade intermediaries. Almost all travel agencies today are equipped with CRS systems. While CRS systems began to develop within indi-

vidual countries, they soon became global in their coverage. During the 1990s, four major *global distribution systems* or GDSs emerged (Amadeus, Galileo, Sabre, and Worldspan).

The electronic distribution of airline and other tickets began in the late 1980s. During the 1990s, the concept of *ticketless travel* by air arrived. Also known as *electronic or e-ticketing*, this allows travelers to show up at airline check-ins without a paper ticket. Although many of these reservations are being made by travel agents, travelers are increasingly being able to use electronic ticket through their own personal computers.

In 2008, IATA expected to have 100 percent e-ticketing on its member airlines, so paper tickets are now definitely a thing of the past.

INFORMATION PROVISION AND TRAVEL COUNSELING. The most traditional role of the retail travel agent is that of serving as a "travel expert." Travel agents are a major source of travel information for individual and group travelers. Travel agents are knowledgeable professionals whose advice and counseling is crucial to many travelers. Travelers expect agents to possess a wide knowledge of travel services and companies, along with an in-depth command of world geography.

Throughout the world, travel agency associations are working hard to increase the professionalism of travel agents. The Association of British Travel Agents (ABTA) has introduced the *Accredited Travel Professional* (ATP) program that recognizes individual agents' professional qualifications and experience. The Travel Institute (formerly ICTA) in the United States has offered the *Certified Travel Counselor* (CTC) program since the early 1970s. It now also offers the CTA (*Certified Travel Associate*) and CTIE (*Certified Travel Industry Executive*) professional designations. The Canadian Institute of Travel Counsellors (CITC) is the Travel Institute's equivalent in Canada and offers the *Certified Travel Counsellor* and *Certified Travel Manager* (CTM) programs. The Australian Federation of Travel Agents (AFTA) has established the *Australian Travel Professionals Program*, which offers six categories of certification for travel agents and tour professionals including the CTC.

DESIGN OF INDIVIDUALIZED TOUR ITINERARIES. Another traditional role of the retail travel agent has

---

Corporate Travel Managers Now Take Center Stage

The economic downturn has allowed travel managers to take a front and center role within their companies and has made travel management, as a profession, an important part of every top executive's strategic planning. In many cases, travel managers have been asked to lead company-wide efforts to cut travel costs, track those savings and report them back to senior management.

The Value of Travel Management, *National Business Travel Association (2009), http://www.nbta.org/About/TheValueofManagedTravel/, accessed January 5, 2009*

been the design of individualized tour itineraries for their customers. The preparation of *foreign independent tours* used to be a mainstay source of business for many travel agencies before the issuing of airline tickets and the booking of pre-packaged group tours became more predominant. In this role, the travel agent arranges all the air travel and land arrangements for an individual customer in the traveler's destination of choice.

TRAVEL MANAGEMENT AND CORPORATE TRAVEL DEPARTMENTS

HISTORY

Corporate travel departments are a relatively new phenomenon in tourism. Historically, business travel arrangements within a company were made on a decentralized basis. Each department, division, or unit made its own reservations. In most cases, this meant that many carriers, suppliers, and travel agencies were used by one company. The most important factor in making travel arrangements was the individual traveler's own preferences.

Since about the 1970s, many corporations, government agencies, and non-profits have created their own in-house corporate travel departments. These departments are often administered by full-time *corporate travel managers* who are professionals in the arrangement, negotiation, and control of business travel. The traditional ways of organizing travel were increasingly found to be inefficient as cost control became more critical in worsening general economic conditions. Corporate travel departments were created for three main reasons:

1. To reduce business travel expenses
2. To provide better service to travelers
3. To increase corporate purchasing power in travel (Morrison, Ladig, and Hsieh, 1994)

FUNCTIONS OF CORPORATE TRAVEL DEPARTMENTS

The major function of a corporate travel department is to coordinate and control all of the travel by employees and associates of the organization. The typical roles of the corporate travel department include the following:

NEGOTIATION WITH CARRIERS AND SUPPLIERS.
A primary role of the corporate travel department is to negotiate for the most competitive prices with airlines, hotels, and car rental companies. The central coordination of travel has given many corporations greater purchasing and negotiating power when dealing with the carriers and suppliers. From a fiscal standpoint, it is in the corporation's best interest that the corporate travel department negotiates the lowest possible travel prices.

DEVELOPMENT OF CORPORATE TRAVEL POLICY.
Another important role is the creation of a corporate travel policy outlining the conditions, practices, and processes that must be followed when employees are traveling out of town.

Travel policies should be written and communicated to all employees. The written guidelines cover reservation and ticketing procedures, preferred airlines and travel suppliers, per diems (maximum expenses reimbursed per day), allowable travel expenses, and expense reporting procedures.

The major function of a corporate travel department is to coordinate all of the employee's travel. © 2009 Dmitriy Shironosov. Used under license from Shutterstock, Inc.

MONITORING OF TRAVEL EXPENSES AND TRAVEL POLICY COMPLIANCE.
The corporate travel department is often responsible for setting an annual budget for travel for the company. The control of this budget during the year is exercised by monitoring employee expense reporting and, in particular, ensuring *compliance* with the written corporate travel policies. Since the early 1980s, these departments have helped their organizations gain more control over the use of the growing number of frequent travel reward programs provided by airline, hotel, and car rental firms.

RESERVATIONS AND TICKETING.
Some corporate travel departments act as in-house travel agents and take care of the reservations and ticketing for employees. It

is more common, however, for the reservations and ticketing function to be *outsourced* to retail travel agencies. In many countries, the importance of corporate travel accounts to retail travel agents has greatly increased in the past thirty-five years. The streamlining of corporate travel has brought the independent agent more business and has also provided the basis for the establishment of large *corporate travel agencies* exclusively serving corporations (often called *outplants*). There are also *inplants*— travel agent offices located within the physical premises of corporate clients. Another route followed by some corporations is to themselves become travel agents, operating their own in-house, fully accredited agencies.

MEETING AND INCENTIVE PLANNING. Some corporate travel departments are involved in the organization of corporate meetings and incentive travel trips. In most cases, these tasks are outsourced to other companies that specialize in the organization of meetings and incentive travel. It is also possible that the corporation may employ a full- or part-time meeting planner who may work in a unit outside of the corporate travel department.

MONITORING TRAVEL AGENCY PERFORMANCE. Most corporations work with one or more retail travel agencies. The corporate travel department monitors the performance of these travel agencies both in financial

---

Bringing Amway from China to South Korea

KTO attracts 13,000 of Amway China employees to Korea, expected tourism profits to generate 10 billion Won. On the 3rd December, the Korea Tourism Organization (CEO Oh Jee-chul) reported that an Amway China travel incentive group of 13,000 will be visiting Korea. Amway China has been giving overseas travel incentives to selected outstanding sales employees each year. From March to May of 2009, Amway China will be carrying out their largest scale travel incentive yet, sending more than 13,000 of their best employees to Korea at nine different periods.

Amway China brings their largest successive incentive group to Korea, *KTO News, Korean Tourism Organization* (2008), http://kto.visitkorea.or.kr/enu/ek/content/cms_view_662175.jsp?gotoPage=1&item=all&keyword=, accessed January 6, 2008

---

terms and in employee satisfaction with agency service levels.

As with travel agents, efforts are growing to increase the professionalism and professional recognition of corporate travel managers. Associations of corporate travel executives have been created. In North America, the two major associations representing corporate travel managers are the National Business Travel Association (NBTA) and the Association of Corporate Travel Executives (ACTE). The NBTA has more than one thousand professional travel manager members and several thousand supplier, carrier, and DMO members. The NBTA describes itself as a "global membership organization providing education, information, and advocacy for business travel management professionals." It also operates the Certified Corporate Travel Executive (CCTE) program. The ACTE has a total of six thousand members spread all around the world. The ACTE says that it "is a not-for-profit association established to provide executive-level global education and peer-to-peer networking opportunities. Membership spans all of business travel, from corporate buyers to agencies to suppliers, and accords all sectors equal membership."

INCENTIVE TRAVEL PLANNERS

HISTORY

The first incentive travel trip was offered by the National Cash Register Company of Dayton, Ohio, in 1906. The winners of this award at NCR received a trip to com-

The National Business Travel Association certifies business travel management professionals through its CCTE program. http://www.nbta.org/Education/CertificationCCTE/.

pany headquarters (Ricci and Holland, 1992). Since then incentive travel has enjoyed significant growth—especially since the 1970s. It is used by large- and medium-size corporations to reward company employees, distributors, and sometimes potential customers, typically for outstanding work-related performance. Free travel as a motivational tool is becoming increasingly potent in the developed countries.

Historically, incentive travel trips have been used to recognize outstanding sales performance by company employees as well as dealers and distributors. The number of motivational applications of incentive travel has grown and it is now being used for increasing plant production, encouraging better customer service, improving plant safety, introducing new products, selling new accounts, and enhancing morale and goodwill. The variety of incentive travel offerings has also expanded and now includes more modest weekend vacations as well as the more traditional, once-in-a-lifetime trips to exotic destinations.

FUNCTIONS OF INCENTIVE TRAVEL PLANNERS

The lucrative nature of incentive travel has attracted great interest among all types of tourism organizations including travel trade intermediaries, suppliers, carriers, and destination marketing organizations. The growth of incentive travel has been beneficial for retail travel agents, airlines, hotels, resorts, and other suppliers. It also represents an area of new market potential for national, state, regional, and city tourism marketing agencies. Many airlines, hotel companies, NTOs, and convention and visitors bureaus have established special divisions or departments to serve the growing incentive travel market.

Irish Incentive Travel Planning Wins Big Recognition
Ovation Ireland received the award for an event for the Board of Directors of a South East Asian Financial Institution in collaboration with the Veritas Group, Sydney, Australia. The five day program held in Dublin in October 2007 involved three Michelin Star chef-catered events, escorted walking tours with a local author and historian, company-sponsored day at the races, signature seated dinner in the Gravity Bar of the Guinness Storehouse and an exclusive performance of Handel's Messiah with full baroque orchestra during Dinner at Dublin Castle.

Ovation Ireland wins SITE Crystal Award for "The Most Outstanding Incentive Event 2008", *Ovation Global DMC (2008), http://www.ovationdmc.com/, accessed January 5, 2009*

The outcome of the rapidly growing popularity of incentive travel has been the emergence of a rather complex distribution system. The key players are a small number of full-service *incentive houses* and a growing number of smaller, more specialized *incentive travel planning companies*. The full-service incentive houses provide the full range of incentives, including both merchandise and travel. They include two incentive industry giants based in the United States, Carlson Marketing Worldwide, Minneapolis; and Maritz, Inc., St. Louis, Missouri. The functions of incentive travel planners vary by the type of company but they include the following:

DESIGN AND IMPLEMENTATION OF MOTIVATIONAL PROGRAM. When a company decides to use incentive travel, this is usually done to motivate people to achieve higher levels of work performance. Incentive travel planning companies are engaged to design and implement the incentive travel programs. The first function of the incentive travel planner is usually to design the motivational program. Maritz, Inc., does careful research before program design: "Maritz uses a unique proprietary survey tool that allows us to better understand what motivates the individuals in your program. With this insight, we can help you make choices in destination, format, and activities."

The objective of the motivational program is to excite potential trip winners about the prospect of winning so that they will increase their performance levels. The motivational program may include color brochures, slide shows, videos, or special meetings with presentations on the trip.

DESIGN OF TOUR PROGRAM. Incentive travel planners function as a specialized tour wholesaler. They design incentive tour programs according to their clients' specifications and budgets. Negotiations are made with carriers and suppliers for the trip components. Both domestic and international trips are developed.

TOUR OPERATION. The incentive travel planning company may also operate the incentive travel program including providing tour escorts to accompany the group. More often, however, *destination management companies* (DMCs) or *inbound tour operators* (ITOs) are subcontracted to provide the on-site services to the incentive trip recipients. Often these on-site arrangements include the staging of special activities and events, tours, and elaborately themed meals.

Ovation Global DMC describes DMCs as "specialist service organizations offering unique local knowledge, expertise, creativity, and, above all, contacts in countries all over the world. They are specialists in the depth of their destination management knowledge but also in their strategic understanding of the meetings, incentives, conferences, and events industry."

RESERVATIONS AND TICKETING. The incentive travel company may itself do the reservations and ticketing, if it is accredited by the appropriate airline and supplier agencies. In other cases, these tasks may be given to retail travel agencies. Some retail travel agencies have themselves become involved in planning incentive trips; others simply play the travel fulfillment role by making air and hotel reservations for the incentive travel planning companies.

PROGRAM EVALUATION. Because incentive travel is being used as a marketing tool, it is especially crucial to evaluate the effectiveness of each incentive travel program. The incentive travel planner may assist with program evaluation by comparing program costs to benefits, especially increased sales. For the company sponsoring the trips, it is important to calculate the return on investment. The incentive travel winners may also be surveyed to determine their satisfaction with trips.

Many incentive travel planners, carriers, and suppliers belong to the Society of Incentive and Travel Executives (SITE). SITE describes itself as "the only international, not-for-profit, professional association devoted to the pursuit of excellence in incentives, a multibillion-dollar global industry. SITE provides educational seminars and information services to those who design, develop, promote, sell, administer, and operate motivational programs as an incentive to increase productivity in business" (SITE Web site, 2008). It has over twenty-one thousand members located in eighty-seven countries. Among its educational activities for members, it operates the Certified Incentive Travel Executive (CITE) program.

CONVENTION-MEETING PLANNERS

HISTORY

Another part of tourism that has enjoyed great growth since the 1970s has been the staging of conventions, corporate meetings, congresses, exhibitions and trade shows, and other similar events. This component of business travel is often referred to as the MICE business, an acronym for meetings, incentives, conventions,

> **Internet Travel Search and Shopping Sites Increasing in Importance**
>
> *Search and shopping sites are having a major impact on the travel category, and their power is expected to grow as the slowing economy prompts travelers to spend even more time searching for travel deals," said Cathy Schetzina, technology analyst for PhoCusWright. "This trend underlines the need for travel suppliers and intermediaries to target search marketing and online advertising efforts based on a clear understanding of online travel shopping patterns."*
>
> Travel Media and Referral Sites Attract Nearly Half of the Visits to Travel Web Sites, PhoCusWright inc. (2008), http://www. phocuswright.com/library/pressrelease/523, accessed January 6, 2009

and exhibitions. The increased popularity of these events has benefited all parts of tourism and many destinations throughout the world. As with incentive travel, it has provided the foundation for new types of specialists, called convention-meeting planners, and has created new linkages in the tourism distribution system.

FUNCTIONS OF CONVENTION-MEETING PLANNERS

The major functions of convention-meeting planners are to develop, coordinate, implement, and evaluate conventions and meetings of various sizes and types. There are three distinct stages to this function.

CONVENTION-MEETING PLANNING. Convention-meeting planners prepare and administer budgets for each event. They coordinate the selection of sites, hotels, meeting and exhibit space, and other suppliers. This development of bid packages or *request for proposals* (RFPs) and conduct *site inspections*. They negotiate with hotels, airlines, audiovisual suppliers, meeting facility managers, and other suppliers to get the best deals for their groups. Planners may set up committees to help with the design of speaker, sponsorship, entertainment, and guest programs. Convention-meeting planners design promotions and communicate this information to company employees or association members. For conventions, exhibitions, conferences, and SMERF (social, military, educational, religious, fraternal) markets, this role involves promotions to build attendance to acceptable levels.

ON-SITE COORDINATION. The convention-meeting planner plays a crucial role during the staging of each event as the liaison between the sponsoring association or company and the service providers at the destination.

This person is the key to ensuring that the event runs as it was planned and that unexpected problems are corrected.

CONVENTION-MEETING EVALUATION.

As with incentive travel, the convention-meeting planner must carefully evaluate the success of each event after its completion. A cost-benefit analysis is prepared that may include a comparison of costs with the revenues created through registration and other participant services.

There are several associations of professional convention-meeting planners around the world. In North America, the largest and most important organizations include the Convention Industry Council (CIC), Meeting Professionals International (MPI), and the Professional Convention Management Association (PCMA). CIC operates the Certified Meeting Professional (CMP) program, while MPI offers the CMM (Certification in Meeting Management) designation. The major

---

Hong Kong Introduces New MICE Bureau

Determined to maintain its lead over regional MICE destinations, Hong Kong has launched a dedicated Meetings and Exhibitions Hong Kong (MEHK) bureau and a new global campaign to push its new MICE brand, Hong Kong—Converging Possibilities.

A new approach, additional funding to keep city ahead of MICE game, *TTG Asia, Year-End 2008, December 19–25, 2008, page 10*

---

organization based in Europe is the International Congress and Convention Association (ICCA), located in Amsterdam.

ELECTRONIC DISTRIBUTION SYSTEMS AND THE FUTURE

Technological advances will completely reshape the tourism distribution system of the future, as they have in the past thirty-five years. The electronic distribution of travel services is now a major trend around the globe. One aspect of this has already been mentioned in the form of increased use of computerized reservation systems (CRSs) and global distribution systems (GDSs) by travel trade intermediaries, carriers, and suppliers.

In the early 1990s, the concept of the "information superhighway" began to exert a great influence on travel information dissemination and distribution. This was the decade of the *Internet*, which with the click of a mouse button brought the whole world of travel into the homes and offices of millions of people. The hypertext-based *World Wide Web* gave travelers instant access to information on the services of thousands of travel destinations and organizations around the world. The Web also presented carriers, suppliers, travel trade intermediaries, and destination marketing organizations with the ability to communicate their messages directly to individual customers who were now able to make their own travel reservations and payments through homes or office personal computers. Internet communications through *electronic mail* also became commonplace.

Some retail travel agents fear that advances in electronic distribution and communications systems will cause suppliers, carriers, destination marketing organizations, other travel trade intermediaries, and travelers to bypass them altogether. As the twentieth century closed, all of the major tourism organizations and destinations in the world had established a presence on the Internet and the Web. More people than ever before chose to flip through "electronic brochures"

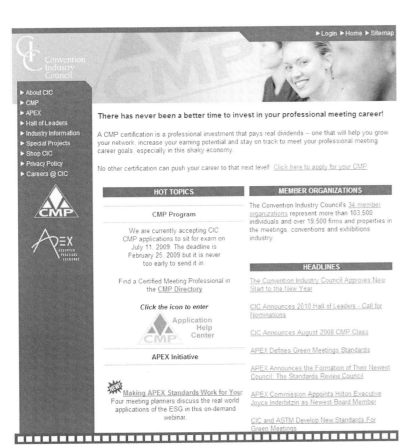

The Convention Industry Council is an umbrella organization representing the meetings, conventions, and exhibitions sector in the United States. http://www.conventionindustry.org/.

on their PCs than to visit their local travel agencies to get the traditional printed copies. New types of *online travel agencies* were established hundreds of miles away from their clients, but linked to them by the Internet.

While some believe that the Internet will cause the eventual demise of the travel agency system, others feel that it is unlikely that systems such as the Web will ever completely displace retail travel agencies. The expertise and personal touch of the knowledgeable travel agent may even become of greater value to travelers overwhelmed by the volume of information on the Internet. Additionally, in some countries, people distrust the secu-

QUICK TRIP 9.6

One Hundred Percent E-Ticketing as of June 1, 2008

Electronic ticketing (e-ticketing), according to ARC, is a method of "selling travel without the issuance of paper flight coupons to the passenger." The fundamental principle is that the ticket is created at the time of sale and is maintained in the database of the ticket issuer, the flight carrier.

The travel trade has issued paper tickets since circa 1930. Electronic tickets began to appear in 1994, and as of June 1, 2008, 100 percent of IATA-issued tickets have become electronic (travel agents in the United States are not part of the IATA mandate and may continue to issue paper tickets after 1 June). According to IATA, to effectively introduce this form of ticketing, airlines had to create "databases, integrated with the airline's passenger service systems, that interfaced with all partners for the real-time processing of passengers by ground handlers and interline partners."

The benefits foreseen pertain to four areas (IATA):

Customers:
- Easier handling of itinerary changes especially for last-minute travel decisions
- More effective use of Internet capabilities for booking travel and check-in
- No more "lost tickets"

Airlines:
- One hundred percent e-ticketing will save the industry at least US$3 billion per year
- Retention of interline revenue as the whole industry implements e-ticketing together
- Continued access to IATA distribution systems

Travel Agents:
- Eliminates costs of ticket printers, maintenance, and ticket distribution
- Removes cost and liability of ticket stock control

Cost Savings:
- US$3 billion annual savings
- An e-ticket costs US$1 to process versus US$10 per paper ticket

THINK ABOUT THIS:
1. U.S. airlines are not under the control of IATA. What are the disadvantages to the industry?
2. What problems will the United States and clients face with this implementation?
3. Why is the e-ticket considered an important step for the air industry?

Ticketless travel was the rule in 2008. © 2009 Franck Boston. Used under license from Shutterstock, Inc.

Sources:

Airlines Reporting Corporation. 2008. http://www.arccorp.com/webhelp/iar/electronic_ticketing_e-ticket.htm.

Air Transport Association. 2008. http://www.iata.org/pressroom/facts_figures/fact_sheets/paper-tickets.htm.

rity of the Internet and prefer to deal personally with local travel agents. It is difficult to say exactly who will eventually be right, but what seems certain is that technology will change the roles of everyone in the tourism distribution system.

Summary

Tourism has a complex worldwide distribution system that gets messages and services out to and back from the market. There are two basic distribution channels in tourism—direct and indirect. Direct channels are when a tourism organization promotes directly to the end user, and accepts the booking or reservation directly. Indirect channels are situations in which an intermediary is used, such as a travel agent or tour operator.

The modern tourism distribution system is both online (via the Web and other parts of the Internet) and offline through traditional channels such as travel agencies and tour operators. Many distribution specialists have emerged to fit particular needs as travel and tourism expanded around the globe. For example, global distribution systems (GDSs) like Sabre and Travelport, and online travel companies such as Expedia and Travelocity, now play an important role. In the offline world, travel management specialists in corporations, incentive travel planners, and destination management companies (DMCs) have also increased in importance.

The tourism distribution system is not just a way of getting tourism out to the market, but also represents an important target market for suppliers, carriers, and

destination marketing organizations (DMOs). Travel trade intermediaries, especially travel agencies, influence consumer choices; so many organizations target them to build business.

The tourism distribution systems in each country are different. In many developed countries, tourism distribution is becoming more integrated, with greater concentration of power among fewer companies. This is likely to continue into the future, especially as further technological innovations improve communications and the speed of transactions.

Trends

Trends in the Distribution and E-Marketing of Tourism Destinations

1. There is rapid growth in the use of the Internet; with broadband use growing at a particularly fast rate.
2. Web searches are now more important than personal recommendation. The Internet is a major and trusted source of travel information.
3. Social networking and user-generated content (e.g., travel blogs) are having an increasing influence on travel sales.
4. Europe and Asia/Pacific have now surpassed the United States in numbers of Internet users.
5. In the future, the growth rate on travel e-commerce (online travel sales) will be greater in Asia/Pacific and Europe than in the United States.
6. There will be more convergence of digital technologies as consumer devices are increasingly capable of integrating several technologies.
7. Consumers will be able to access the Internet for travel information and bookings from an increasing range of devices.
8. DMOs will be able to draw upon the information and features of a growing number of "third-party" sources to enhance the usefulness and functionality of their Web sites (e.g., Google Earth, currency converters, weather forecasts).

Source: U.N. World Tourism Organization. Handbook on E-Marketing of Tourism Destinations, 2008.

ACTIVITIES

1. Select a major tour operator or wholesaler company in your country. Collect the brochures and other printed materials of the company. From these materials, what are the company's specialties in terms of destinations and market segments?

2. What types of tour arrangements does the company offer (e.g., escorted tours, FIT)?

3. Would you or your family be likely to travel with this tour operator? Why or why not?

INTERNET
ACTIVITIES

4. What tours and packages does the company promote on its Web site?

5. Can the tours and packages be bought online? If not, how can they be booked?

6. What customer guarantees or promises does the company offer online?

REFERENCES

Callarisa, L., A. M. Moliner, R. M. Rodrigues, and J. Sanchez. 2007. Travel agency relationship quality. *Annals of Tourism Research,* 24 (2): 537–540.

Cockerell, N. 1991. The European incentive travel market. *EIU Travel & Tourism Analyst,* (4): 76–89.

De Souto, M. S. 1993. *Group Travel,* 2nd ed. Albany, NY: Delmar Publishers Inc.

Friedheim, E. 1992. *Travel Agents: From Caravans and Clippers to the Concorde.* New York: Universal Media.

Fyall, A., C. Callod, and B. Edwards. 2003. Relationship marketing: The challenge for destinations. *Annals of Tourism Research,* 30: 644–659.

Gee, C. Y., J. C. Makens, and D. J. L. Choy. 1997. *The Travel Industry,* 3rd ed. New York: Van Nostrand Reinhold.

Goeldner, C. R., J. R. B. Ritchie, and R. W. McIntosh. 1999. *Tourism: Principles, Practices, Philosophies,* 8th ed. New York: John Wiley & Sons, Inc.

Goldsmith, R. E., S. W. Litvan, and B. Pan. 2008. Electronic word-of-mouth in hospitality and tourism management. *Tourism Management,* 29: 458–468.

Jenkins, D. 1993. *Managing Business Travel.* Homewood, IL: Business One Irwin.

Lang, J. 1994. *The American Express Guide to Corporate Travel Management.* New York: American Management Association.

Mrnjavac, E., and S. Ivanovic. 2007. Logistics and logistic processes in a tourism destination. *Tourism and Hospitality Management,* 13 (3): 531–546.

Mehta, S. C., J. C. M. Loh, and S. S. Mehta. 1991. Incentive-travel marketing: The Singapore approach. *The Cornell H.R.A. Quarterly,* 32 (3): 67–74.

Morrison, A. M., K. A. Ladig, and S. Hsieh. 1994. Corporate travel in the USA: Characteristics of managers and departments. *Tourism Management,* 15: 177–184.

Morrison, A. M. 2009. *Hospitality and Travel Marketing,* 4th ed. Clifton Park, NY: Delmar Publishers.

Poynter, J. M. 1993. *Tour Design, Marketing, & Management.* Englewood Cliffs, NJ: Regents/Prentice-Hall, Inc.

Poynter, J. M. 1998. *Corporate Travel Management.* Englewood Cliffs, NJ: Prentice-Hall, Inc.

Reiff, A. 1995. *Introduction to Corporate Travel.* Cincinnati, OH: South-Western Publishing Co.

Ricci, P. R., and S. M. Holland. 1992. Incentive travel: Recreation as a motivational medium. *Tourism Management,* 13: 288–296.

Shinew, K. J., and S. J. Backman. 1995. Incentive travel: An attractive option. *Tourism Management,* 16: 285–293.

SITE. 2005. *Incentive Travel Factbook.* New York: Society of Incentive and Travel Executives.

Starr, N. 2002. *Viewpoint: An Introduction to Travel, Tourism, and Hospitality,* 4th ed. Upper Saddle River, NJ: Prentice-Hall, Inc.

Vellas, F., and L. Becherel. 1995. *International Tourism.* New York: St. Martin's Press.

Witt, S. F., S. Gammon, and J. White. 1992. Incentive travel: Overview and case study of Canada as a destination for the UK market. *Tourism Management,* 13: 275–287.

SURFING SOLUTIONS

http://www.abacus.com.sg/ (Abacus global distribution system in the Asia Pacific region)

http://www.abta.com/ (Association of British Travel Agents)

http://www.acta.ca/ (Association of Canadian Travel Agencies)

http://www.afta.com.au/ (Australian Federation of Travel Agents)

http://www.amadeus.com/amadeus/amadeus.html (Amadeus global distribution system)

http://www.arccorp.com/ (Airlines Reporting Corporation, United States)

http://www.artaonline.com/ (Association of Retail Travel Agents, United States)

http://www.astanet.com/ (American Society of Retail Travel Agents)

http://www.carlson.com/ (Carlson Companies, Inc.)

http://www.der.com/ (Destination Europe Resources)

http://www.expedia.com/ (Expedia online travel service)

http://www.galileo.com/ (Galileo global distribution system)

http://www.iacvb.org/ (Destination Marketing Association International)

http://www.iata.org/ (International Air Transport Organization) http://www.iatan.org/ (International Airlines Travel Agent Network)

http://www.kuoni.com/corporate-site/ (Kuoni Travel Group)

http://www.maritz.com/ (Maritz, Inc.)

http://www.nbta.org/ (National Business Travel Association, United States)

http://www2.neckermann-reisen.de/nec/index.jsp (Neckermann, Germany)

http://www.sabretravelnetwork.com/ (Sabre global distribution system)

http://www.thomascook.com/ (Thomas Cook Retail Ltd.)

http://www.thomson-holidays.com/po/index.jsp (Thomson/ TUI UK Ltd.)

http://www.tq.com.au/ (Tourism Queensland)

http://www.travelworld.com.au/ (TravelWorld, Australia)

http://www.travelocity.com/ (Travelocity online travel service)

http://www.ustoa.com/ (United States Tour Operators Association)

http://www.world-of-tui.com/en/ (World of TUI)

http://www.worldspan.com/ (Worldspan global distribution system)

ACRONYMS

ABTA (Association of British Travel Agents)

ACTA (Association of Canadian Travel Agencies)

ACTE (Association of Corporate Travel Executives, United States)

AFTA (Australian Federation of Travel Agents)

ARC (Airlines Reporting Corporation, United States)

ARTA (Association of Retail Travel Agents)

ASTA (American Society of Travel Agents)

CCTE (Certified Corporate Travel Executive, NBTA)

CIC (Convention Industry Council, United States)

CITC (Canadian Institute of Travel Counsellors)

CLIA (Cruise Lines International Association)

CRS (computerized reservation system)

CMP (Certified Meeting Professional)

CTC (Certified Travel Counselor)

DMAI (Destination Marketing Association International)

DMC (destination management company)

FAM (familiarization tour)

FIT (foreign independent tour)

GDS (global distribution systems)

GIT (group inclusive tour)

IATA (International Air Transport Association)

ICCA (International Congress and Convention Association)

ITO (inbound tour operator)

MICE (meetings, incentives, conventions, exhibitions)

MPI (Meeting Professionals International)

NBTA (National Business Travel Association, United States)

NTA (National Tour Association, United States)

PCMA (Professional Convention Management Association, United States)

PCO (professional congress organizer)

RFP (request for proposals)

SITE (Society of Incentive and Travel Executives)

STP (satellite ticket printer)

SMERF (social, military, educational, religious, fraternal)

TTI (The Travel Institute)

UFTAA (Universal Federation of Travel Agents' Associations)

USTOA (U.S. Tour Operators Association)

WATA (World Association of Travel Agencies)

chapter 10

Forces Shaping Tourism

CULTURE, TIME, SOCIOECONOMICS, LIFE CYCLE STAGES, PERSONALITY

The World is a book, and those who do not travel read only a page.

Saint Augustine

PURPOSE

Having examined the external environment of specific types of tourists, students will be able to suggest appropriate types of vacations for them.

LEARNING OBJECTIVES

✓ Explain the effects of cultural background on travel decisions.
✓ Explain the effects of time on travel decisions.
✓ Explain the effects of socio-economic background on travel decisions.
✓ Explain the effects of psychographic background on travel decisions.

Overview

Models of behavior have suggested that behavior choices are determined by the types of psychological factors—motivation, perception, learning and attitudes—examined in chapters 11 through 13. However, these factors are, in turn, determined by such things as personality, society and culture, and other such forces external to the individual (see figure 10.1).

This chapter examines these forces. The culture of which we are a part serves as a barometer of general trends within a country, and it exerts social pressure to conform to the broad cultural values presented by the majority of individuals making up that culture. The culture that individuals are part of influences travel motivation, purchase criteria, and purchase alternatives. The amount and type of time available also helps determine if, when, and where we can vacation. Marketers have long segmented the travel market along the socioeconomic criteria of age, income, sex, and education. It is therefore appropriate to determine whether tourism demand differs on these criteria. The characteristic patterns of demand at various stages in the family life cycle are examined, with particular reference to the

> Culture is roughly anything we do and the monkeys don't.
>
> Lord Raglan quotes

effect of children on the family's demand, the demand pattern of the empty nester, and the various barriers to leisure enjoyment at different life-cycle stages. Finally, the role of psychographics in shaping demand is explored. From a marketing viewpoint the segmentation of a target market by lifestyle provides a better picture of the characteristics, likes, and dislikes of the potential visitor.

Whether or not to take a vacation, and the type of holiday chosen, is influenced by a number of factors external to the individual. In this chapter the effect of these variables is examined. Although these factors are explored separately, it should be noted that their effect is often a compound one.

THE EFFECTS OF CULTURE ON TRAVEL

Individuals choose a vacation to satisfy their individual needs and wants (see chapter 11). The way in which these wants are satisfied, however, is heavily influenced by forces external to the individual. As individuals, we

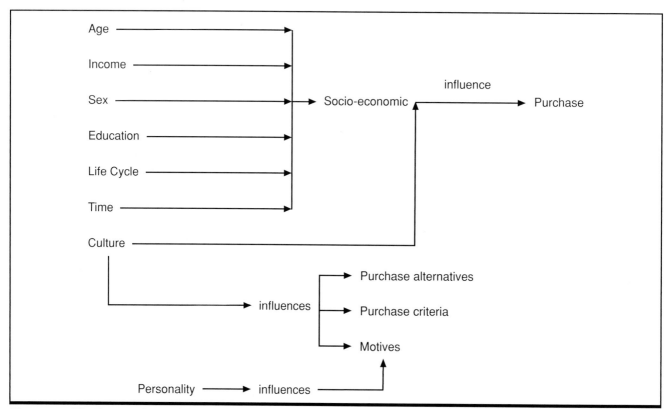

Figure 10.1 The Impact of External Factors on Vacation Purchases.

From a marketing viewpoint, the segmentation of a target market by lifestyle provides a good picture of the characteristics, likes, and dislikes of the potential visitor. © 2009 Maxim Bolotnikov. Used under license from Shutterstock, Inc.

are part of larger social groups by which we are influenced. These groups themselves are part of and influenced by the surrounding culture. *Culture* can be defined as a "set of beliefs, values, attitudes, habits, and forms of behavior that are shared by a society and are transmitted from generation to generation" (Bennett and Kassasjin, 1982). A knowledge of the culture of a country or subculture within that country is important to an understanding of how individuals within that country or subculture will behave. A study of visitors to Korea found, for example, that the motivation to visit Korea, the length of time spent in planning the trip, the sources of information used as well as the length of stay were all significantly influenced by national culture (Kim and Prideaux, 2005).

Although not the only, or even the most important, determinant of how destinations are viewed, different nationalities place different values on specific destination attributes. For example, Japanese business travelers are more interested in the security at a destination than either North American or European business travelers. It may be that the excitement of visiting a destination for the first time gives way to greater concern over services that will make the trip more safe, productive and routine (Suh and Gartner, 2004).

CULTURE AND SOCIETY

Culture has an impact on travel and tourism in five ways (Reisinger and Turner, 1997):

- **Cultural values give individuals rules for behavior.** A culture's overall values determine which goals and behaviors gain social approval or disap-

proval. To the extent that people are concerned about how others think of them, they will be influenced to behave in ways acceptable to society. For these people, society's values determine, in part, what kinds of vacations and what types of behavior on those vacations are acceptable.

- **Cultural values develop certain attitudes and perceptions.** For example, Thailand has long been the recipient of sex tourism. Packages promoted to the Japanese and European markets have included "hostesses" as part of the package. Changing attitudes toward women and sex, together with the fear of AIDS, have resulted in protests against both tourism operators and the visitors themselves. The World Tourism Organization has, in fact, taken a very strong position against such tourism.
- **Cultural values influence how people evaluate the world.** In the United States, many people have developed positive attitudes toward the environment. This change in attitude has been examined in light of its potential for influencing vacation choice. There are those, for example, who have shown that attitudes toward the environment may be a better predictor of what a person does on vacation than demographic information.

The many social institutions of a society are also reflective of its culture. In the United States, for example, the ideas of individual initiative and equal opportunity for all influence the way in which the educational system is organized. The result is a system of mass education with a somewhat liberal child-rearing philosophy. Education is seen as an investment in personal development and success. If vacations are seen as something that will advance a child's progress in society, they will be more attractive to the parents.

- **Cultural differences can impact the level of satisfaction that tourists have with a destination.** The potential for tourist satisfaction is increased when "hosts" at the destination reflect the values of the visiting tourist.
- **Cultural differences can cause difficulties in social interactions.**

Culture affects the social backdrop in the established conventions and practices of society. Society adopts various practices relative to such things as which foods can be eaten, how to entertain, and which gifts are or are not appropriate. It is acceptable, for example, for horse meat to be eaten in France but not in the United States. On the other hand, in most countries of the world, corn is shucked and is considered a food suitable only for animals. While the established dinner hour in the United States is between 6 and 8 p.m., in Spain it is 10 p.m. or later. When attracting or servicing visitors from a culture different from our own, it is necessary to know the established practices to avoid inadvertent behavior.

> Education is when you read the fine print. Experience is what you get if you don't.
>
> Pete Seeger

Last, culture's effect on society is felt in the language people use with one another. It is important to consider not only words, but also gestures, expressions, and other body movements. In Western culture, a smile is a warm signal to further a relationship, but in Asian culture it may be used to cover embarrassment and shame.

QUICK TRIP 10.1

The Year of the Mouse

Disney and China are not often used in the same sentence, but marketers in Hong Kong have been working overtime to make "Mickey" a household name. The classic American theme park being turned Chinese is a feat in and of itself. European and American families have had Disney experiences in the past, but in Hong Kong the parents and the children are discovering Disney together for the first time. While Mickey and Minnie are still in the park, they are dressed in a traditional Chinese new year outfits, and there are several Chinese gods wandering around the park as well. It took a while for the Disney executives to completely understand the Chinese market. During the first two years, attendance was not what was forecasted, and it actually declined. The upcoming year for the Chinese is the year of the rat; Disney is marketing the park with the theme "Year of the Mouse." A mistake that the marketing team made early on was advertising with a family of four, two parents and two children. China only allows each family to have one child, so they quickly changed the marketing campaign to include two grandparents, two parents, and one child. The food sold in Disney's Hong Kong location is deep fried dumplings and turnip cakes instead of the American hot dogs and chicken fingers. The fashions for retail are also changed for the Hong Kong location. Disney is hoping that the year of the mouse and a new redesigned marketing campaign will entice more families to come to a place that has been traditionally an American activity.

THINK ABOUT THIS:

1. How do you think that the Chinese perceived Disney World before they accommodated for their culture? And after they accommodated for the Chinese culture?

Source: Canaves, S. 2008. Main Street, H.K. *The Wall Street Journal*, B1+.

CULTURE AND SOCIAL GROUPS

Social groups have roles or standards of behavior peculiar to each group. These group norms differ from one culture to another. Groups can be classified either as *primary* (family or friends) or *secondary* (unions, fraternities, church, and so on). An individual will belong to more than one group, and consequently, he or she will adopt a role for each social group. These roles may overlap. The surrounding culture will help define for each group the appropriate objects people use to show their membership in the group as well as the relevant status symbols.

Is there a distinct vacation role? One of the attractive features of taking a vacation is that it allows the freedom to be someone other than who we are in everyday life. Traveling to places where we are not known, meeting people who do not know us, allows us to choose how we will behave.

The social role that an individual takes is learned through socialization–the process of social learning by which cultural role expectations are handed down from one generation to another. The link between participation in recreational activities as a child and subsequent participation as an adult has been repeatedly demonstrated. If we also accept that travel is a learned experience, the importance of encouraging travel participation at an early age can be demonstrated. The norms of behavior for a group change by virtue of both internal and external sources. Within a group there are those people (innovators) who are more willing than others to try new things. Usually these group members are better educated, have high incomes, and are more achievement-oriented than others. The innovators also tend to be *opinion leaders* and, as such, highly sought after by marketers. A common saying in explaining destination development is "mass follows class." This phrase suggests that a destination first attracts a relatively small number of high-status individuals whose actions are eventually copied by a larger number of less-innovative others.

Cultural patterns also change by virtue of external forces. As a result of contact with other environments, previous attitudes and behaviors may change. A visit to a foreign country may result in a change in attitude toward the people of that country as well as stimulation of a desire for a cuisine from the destination visited. A vacation in Japan might improve the chance of purchasing Asian dishes upon one's return home.

It can readily be seen that in order to understand a consumer fully, it is necessary to understand the surrounding culture of that consumer. A knowledge of how the culture affects the individual, the social groups to which that individual belongs, and society as a whole will better enable the marketer to sell a travel product. Insight will be gained as to what to say, to whom to say it, and how the message should be phrased. As hosts, we will be better able to understand why visitors act the way they do and be in a better position to anticipate and satisfy their needs and wants.

Innovators are people who are more willing to try new things such as kayak surfing. © 2009 Joe Gough. Used under license from Shutterstock, Inc.

ANALYZING A CULTURE

The cultures of different countries can vary greatly. In order to successfully attract people from a particular country, it is necessary to be aware of these cultural differences.

For example, the literature shows significant cultural differences between Asian and western cultures in the areas of values, rules of social behavior, perceptions, and service (Reisinger and Turner, 1997). In one study comparing Anglo-Americans and Japanese tourists, Anglo-Americans showed a greater preference for separation from in-groups and emotional detachment than did Japanese visitors while Japanese tourists showed a greater attitude toward interdependence and family integrity than did the other group (Lee and Kim, 1999). A marketing effort aimed at people from these cultures

would have to take these differences into account in order to be successful. For example, education is important to people from both cultures. However, East Asians look at education as an investment to help the family; in the United States, it is viewed as an investment in oneself. Thus, while the educational advantages of travel can be marketed to both groups, the approach taken would differ. Messages in East Asia would stress the educational impact on the family and the prestige involved for the family, while the individual benefits would be the focus to U.S. audiences.

In addition, in light of the preceding findings relative to the influence of personal values on activity preferences, we could speculate that, because of their attitudes toward conserving resources, East Asians are less likely to prefer vigorous outdoor activities.

One model for analyzing cultures has been suggested by Hofstede (1985). He has analyzed certain work-related values of over fifty countries. He found that the value patterns dominant in these countries varied along four main dimensions:

1. Individualism versus collectivism
2. Masculinity versus femininity
3. Large or small power distance
4. Strong or weak uncertainty avoidance

On the first scale—individualism versus collectivism—the issue is the closeness of the relationship between one person and other persons. At the individualistic end of the scale, individuals look after their own self-interests and those of their immediate families. At the other end of the scale, the ties between individuals are very tight. People are supposed to look after the interests of their in-group and have no other opinions and beliefs other than those of their in-group. Wealthy countries are on the individualistic side while poorer countries are on the collectivist side. We might speculate that people from countries that score high on individualism would have different motives and behaviors than those from countries with high-collectivist scores. High individualists might be more inclined to travel independently than in groups and to be more motivated by the desire to improve themselves, for example. It has been shown that group oriented recreation activities are relatively more important than individual activities for samples from more collectivist cultures such as Asia and Greece than from more individualistic cultures such as the United States, Australia, and the United Kingdom (Reisinger, 2004).

The second dimension is masculinity versus femininity—the division of roles between the sexes in society.

The point is the extent to which societies try to minimize or maximize the social sex role division. Masculine societies make a sharp division between what men and women should do. In these cases, men always take more assertive and dominant roles, while women take more service-oriented and caring roles. In masculine societies, more importance is given to such things as showing off, achieving something visible, and making money. In feminine societies, more importance is placed on such things as people relationships over money, the quality of life, and preservation of the environment. Masculine countries are Japan, Germany, Austria and Switzerland, some Latin countries, and most Anglo countries. On the feminine side are the Nordic countries. Tourists from more feminine cultures such as Singapore and Thailand attach more importance to socializing and hospitality of hosts than tourists from masculine cultures such as Japan and the United Kingdom (Reisinger, 2004). Placement on this scale would have implications for appropriate marketing appeals. We would expect major decisions, such as for a vacation, to be made by the male in societies that score high on that scale, for example.

> Time is a great teacher, but unfortunately it kills all its pupils.
>
> Louis Hector Berlioz

The third dimension is power distance—how society deals with the fact that people are unequal. Some societies let inequalities grow over time into inequalities in power and wealth, while others try to play down inequalities as much as possible. Asian, African, and Latin American countries have large power index scores (indicating inequalities), while France, Belgium, Spain, and Italy score rather high. The Nordic and Anglo countries score low on this scale. We might expect messages of a more humanitarian and egalitarian type to appeal to cultures low on this scale.

The last dimension is uncertainty avoidance—how societies deal with the fact that time runs only one way. We all have to live with the uncertainty of the future. Some societies teach their people to accept and live with this uncertainty. People will take personal risks rather lightly, will not work so hard, and will be relatively tolerant of behaviors and opinions different from their own. These are weak uncertainty avoidance societies. Others try to control the future through such things as formal and informal rules to protect themselves from the uncertainties of human behavior. In societies like this, the word of experts is relied upon much more heavily than in weak uncertainty avoidance societies. Latin countries score high, while Asian and African countries, with the exception of Japan and Korea, score medium to low. Germany, Austria, and Switzerland

score high, while the Nordic and Anglo countries score low. It might be expected that, in high-scoring countries, the role of opinion leaders (as experts) would be stronger.

It has been shown that Hong Kong consumers are reluctant to make travel purchases online due to the perceived high risk and low convenience factors, together with limited privacy and security (Kolsaker, Lee-Kelley, and Choy, 2004). In another study (Money and Crotts, 2003) consumers with a high risk tolerance tend to use mass media sources. However, even risk-tolerant cultures turn to family and friends for advice. Those in risk-averse cultures prefer packaged tours and vacations. However, against conventional wisdom, they do not plan far in advance. This is likely due to the credibility of the sources, for example, travel agents, they use in planning their vacations.

Safety is more important for those from high uncertainty avoidance cultures such as Singapore and Hong Kong than from low uncertainty avoidance cultures like Greece and Japan (Reisinger, 2004).

Travel risk perception is a function of cultural orientation and psychographic factors. Marketing messages to high-uncertainty cultures such as Greece, Belgium, Portugal and Spain should stress the safety and stability of the destination. Risk-avoidance strategies include such things as traveling in groups as part of a package guided tour, traveling shorter distances to familiar places with risk-free activities (Reisinger and Mavondo, 2005).

Eight specific clusters have been developed and are contained in figure 10.2. While realizing the dangers of stereotyping, the profiles presented here are a useful first step in determining the types of vacation behavior expected from people in these countries. It also suggests that countries in separate segments have cultures sufficiently different to warrant different marketing approaches.

Louden and Britta (1979) have developed a checklist of factors to be considered in analyzing a culture. The analysis would be particularly appropriate before developing a marketing approach to people from different cultures.

✓ Determine relevant motivations in the culture: Which needs do people seek to fulfill? In a comparison of travel motivations for vacations in the United States, for example, Germans were particularly interested in status, while, to the Japanese, people were of prime importance (Shields, 1986).

✓ Determine characteristic behavior patterns: How often are vacations purchased? In Great Britain the annual vacation in the summer is paramount, while those who can afford it take an additional, off-season break. In the United States, on the other hand, there is movement away from the long vacation once a year to several shorter breaks taken more often during the year.

✓ Determine what broad cultural values are relevant to this product: Are vacations, leisure, and recreation thought of in positive terms? In Great Britain, the annual break is seen as very important, something to save for and look forward to all year.

✓ Determine characteristic forms of decision making: Who makes the vacation purchase decision?

When is it made? What information sources and criteria are used in making the decision? As noted above, we would expect the vacation decision to be male dominated in both Japan and Germany. The planning time varies by market segment. Japanese travelers interested in vacationing in Colorado begin planning their trip an average of eleven weeks ahead of time; the British begin twenty-five weeks ahead; and the Germans begin the process thirty-one weeks ahead.

✓ Evaluate promotion methods appropriate to the culture: What kinds of promotional techniques, words, and pictures are acceptable or not acceptable to people of this culture? In Great Britain, for example, the humor is more subtle than in the United States. Advertisements use the double meaning to get the point across in a clever way. Such an approach would probably fail in the United States where the punch line has to be very direct to gain attention.

✓ Determine appropriate institutions for this product in the minds of consumers: Do people tend to purchase vacations directly from suppliers, or are retail travel agents used? What alternatives, acceptable to the consumer, are available for distributing the product? Germans, for example, are more inclined to use retail travel agents than other Europeans when planning vacations to the United States.

1. More Developed Latin
▶ High power-distance
▶ High uncertainty-avoidance
▶ High individualism
▶ Medium masculinity
  ARGENTINA
  BRAZIL

2. Less Developed Latin
▶ High power-distance
▶ High uncertainty-avoidance
▶ Low individualism
▶ Whole range on masculinity
  COLOMBIA
  MEXICO
  VENEZUELA
  CHILE
  PERU

3. More Developed Asian
▶ Medium power-distance
▶ High uncertainty-avoidance
▶ Medium individualism
▶ High masculinity
  JAPAN

4. Less Developed Asian
▶ High power-distance
▶ Low uncertainty-avoidance
▶ Low individualism
▶ Medium masculinity
  PAKISTAN
  TAIWAN
  THAILAND
  HONG KONG
  INDIA
  PHILIPPINES
  SINGAPORE

5. Near Eastern
▶ High power-distance
▶ High uncertainty-avoidance
▶ Low individualism
▶ Medium masculinity
  GREECE
  IRAN
  TURKEY

6. Germanic
▶ Low power-distance
▶ High uncertainty-avoidance
▶ Medium individualism
▶ High masculinity
  AUSTRIA
  GERMANY
  SWITZERLAND

7. Anglo
▶ Low power-distance
▶ Low to medium uncertainty-avoidance
▶ High individualism
▶ High masculinity
  AUSTRALIA
  CANADA
  GREAT BRITAIN
  NEW ZEALAND
  USA

8. Nordic
▶ Low power-distance
▶ Low to medium uncertainty-avoidance
▶ Medium individualism
▶ Low masculinity
  DENMARK
  FINLAND
  NORWAY
  SWEDEN

Figure 10.2 Country Clusters and Their Characteristics. Source: Hofstede, G. 1985.

THE U.S. CULTURE

Many argue that because of the size and diversity of the United States, it is not possible to talk about a national culture. Indeed a number of groups in the United States have managed to maintain elements of their own geographic, religious, and ethnic identities. In addition, any attempt to describe a U.S. culture is fraught with potential charges of promoting stereotypes. Some degree of generalization is possible and desirable, however, if we are to better understand the impact of culture on vacation behavior.

Some of the basic traits of the American culture that have influenced the travel behavior of Americans are (Pizam and Mansfeld, 1999):

QUICK TRIP 10.2

Time Management

The lines of work are blurred every day, and many people aren't sure how to define work. Is it where we go, what we do, or what we have to show for it at the end? Recent studies have shown that the average worker spends one to two hours during each eight-hour workday doing things unrelated to what he or she is being paid for. That equates to approximately fifty extra days of paid vacation each year in addition to the allocated vacation time. The top ways to waste time at work include Web surfing, socializing, and personal business. There are several experts who have made fortunes on helping people and companies become more productive. Merlin Mann, an expert on maximizing productivity, has made a list of helpful strategies called life hacks to help cut through time-consuming problems. These include managing e-mail more productively, qualifying the word "yes," and renegotiating. *Management Today* gives a list of ways to be more productive as well. These tips include when to do which work, how to set agendas, and how to focus.

THINK ABOUT THIS:

1. Would the tourism industries benefit from investing in a program to boost productivity among the workforce?
2. Is there a way that the tourism industries can tap those fifty days that are usually wasted?

Sources:

How to Take Back Your Time and Attention; Merlin Mann, the self-described "head basket case in charge of productivity on the Internet," provides some tips and tricks for taking back control of your life in a breezy and insightful Macworld presentation. 2008. *Information Week. Student Resource Center Gold.* Gale. Cherry Creek High School Lib., Greenwood Village, CO. Retrieved 14 May 2008, http://infotrac.galegroup.com/itweb/?db=SRC-1.

Kirwan-Taylor, H. 2007. The Time We Waited. *Management Today. General Reference Center Gold.* Gale. Cherry Creek High School Lib., Greenwood Village, CO. Retrieved 14 May 2008, http://infotrac.galegroup.com/itweb/.

Vacationing on the Job. 2007. *Money. Student Resource Center Gold.* Gale. Cherry Creek High School Lib., Greenwood Village, CO. Retrieved 14 May 2008, http://infotrac.galegroup.com/itweb/?db=SRC-1.

- Love of originality
- Desire to be near nature
- Individualism
- Social acceptance

It is, in fact, difficult to describe the United States as having only one culture. In *Generations at Work*, Zemke et al. argue that there are four distinct groups in the United States, based on age, who have very different core values.

1. Veterans, born between 1922 and 1943, value dedication and sacrifice, hard work, conformity, law and order, respect for authority, patience, delayed reward, duty before pleasure, adherence to rules and honor (Zemke et al., p. 30).
2. Baby boomers, defined as those born between 1943 and 1960, are optimistic and have a team orientation. They value personal gratification, health and wellness, personal growth, youth, work and involvement (Zemke et al., p. 68).
3. Gen Xers, born between 1960 and 1980, value diversity, thinking globally, balance, technoliteracy, fun, information, self-reliance, and pragmatism (Zemke et al., p. 98).
4. Nexters, those born between 1980 and 2000, are optimistic and confident and value civic duty, achievement, sociability, morality, street smarts, and diversity (Zemke et al., p. 132).

A vacation plan aimed at any of these four groups would have to be adjusted to take the specific cultural values into account.

THE EFFECT OF TIME ON TRAVEL

Time, or rather the availability of time, acts as a major inhibiting factor to travel. The amount of available time and the form in which it is available is, in fact, a major shaper of the destinations that can be visited, the modes of travel that can be used, and the activities that can be engaged in at the destination or en route. The desire to travel and the financial ability to travel are insufficient if one does not have the time to travel. All three factors must be present for travel and tourism to take place.

Our time can be spent in one of three ways (see figure 10.3).

SPENDING TIME

Time is spent in many *maintenance activities*—activities that involve a certain degree of obligation and that are neces-

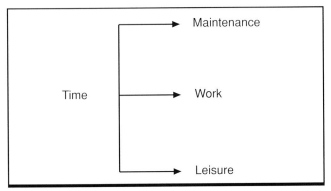

Figure 10.3 Time Divisions.

sary to sustain and maintain life. Included in this definition are such activities as eating, sleeping, maintaining the house, and caring for the lawn. Time can also be spent at work. For many this involves a degree of obligation greater than the time spent in maintenance activities. *Leisure* can be defined, although some people may feel it is a rather simplified definition, as the time remaining after work and maintenance activities have been completed. By its very definition leisure implies that the individual has a level of discretion over how to spend time that is not present in the other two categories. Leisure is often contrasted with the economic activity of work, and is connected with pleasure and a feeling of freedom with a minimum of obligation. Leisure is also seen as inner-directed rather than other-directed. It is the time for one's self. Although leisure time offers opportunities for creativity and personal growth, the accent must be on freedom of choice. Traditionally, researchers have talked about leisure as time spent in productive pursuits. Yet this imposes a value system upon the individual's discretionary time. *Produc-*

Leisure can be defined as the time remaining after work and maintenance activities have been completed. © 2009 Suzanne Tucker. Used under license from Shutterstock, Inc.

tive is a term defined by the researcher. The crucial point is that leisure-time activities are those that are undertaken freely by individuals within their discretionary time.

By seeing time broken down into these three categories, it is easy to demonstrate a relationship between all three. Because time is absolute—there are twenty-four hours in a day, seven days in a week, fifty-two weeks in a year—any change in one of the three parts will automatically affect the others. As the workweek declines, more time is freed for maintenance and/or leisure activities. This is important because in the study of tourism, we are concerned with the use of leisure time, and a recognition that leisure time is bound to the other two concepts helps us to be concerned with changes in those concepts as they might affect leisure time. One important consideration is to contrast production with consumption activities. We can pay someone else to take over a production activity—wash our car. We cannot pay someone to take over a consumption activity—go on vacation for us.

How is time actually spent? In a typical week most time is spent on maintenance activities. This is true for both females and males. The significant difference between the sexes is that females spend more time on housework and necessary home maintenance.

Americans spend on average just over five hours a day on leisure activities. Since 1965, the number of hours the average American works for pay has not changed much (Miller & Associates, 2007, pp. 15, 20). Many companies faced an economic squeeze in the 1980s. Cost-cutting often reduced vacation time. Fearful of losing their jobs, many employees spent less time away from the workplace.

In addition, many companies restructured their labor markets by firing long-term employees and hiring temporary workers. Because vacation time is based on the length of employment, the result was less time off with pay for many people.

Americans themselves seem to agree that they are working harder. A recent survey by online company Expedia indicates that 421 million vacation days were unused by Americans in 2005. Almost one-third of U.S. workers do not use all of their vacation time (*Time*, September 2005, p. A3). Almost half of all Americans work during their days off while almost 40 percent work from home during the holidays. The flip side is that over 40 percent shop online for gifts while at work. The line between work and leisure time is blurring (Miller & Associates, 2007, p. 22). The American Institute of Stress reports that 8 percent of respondents to

Generations

Generations have always been a way to define different markets and characteristic traits. Generational stereotypes have been utilized by the marketing industry for a long time, but this could all be changing. Maddy Dychtwald, senior vice president of AgeWave, a San Francisco-based company that consults with companies on how to market to different generations, says that "[g]enerations no longer define us as they have in the past . . . [p]eople define themselves today by their interests, desires and lifestyles." Instead of targeting a specific generation, AgeWave has moved to analyzing the psychographic aspects of a customer. Another trend touching upon generations is the idea of a multigenerational family trip, one in which grandparents, parents, and children can all have an enriching experience. Even though many indicators show that generational grouping is decreasing, some travel companies continue to market based on age. They believe that the echo boomer generation (those born between 1981 and 2000) are a generational group worth concentrating on. Experts predict that the echo boomer generation is more sophisticated than any other generation and they know what they want and are educated on how to obtain it. It is also predicted that members of the echo boomer generation are not budget travelers, which has piqued the interest of many tourism industries.

THINK ABOUT THIS:

1. Are generational differences really worth focusing on, or are there better ways to target the market?

Source: Del Rosso, L. 2005. Coming of Age: Marketing Travel for the Generations. *Travel Weekly. Student Resource Center Gold.* Gale. Cherry Creek High School Lib., Greenwood Village, CO. Retrieved 14 May 2008, http://infotrac.galegroup.com/itweb?/db=SRC-1.

---

their survey believe that they would be fired or demoted if they took time off work while 17 percent report difficulty in taking a leave of absence due to an emergency.

We might expect that the above distribution would change relative to changes in the family life cycle. This relationship is demonstrated in figure 10.4. In the young and single phase, people are characterized by great physical capacity, disposable time, and few demands on

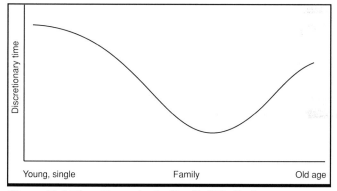

Figure 10.4 Time Phases in the Family Life Cycle.

their income. In the family phase, discretionary income and time decrease, and the physical capacity of the family is limited by that of its weakest member. The third phase is characterized by an excess of discretionary time and a decrease in physical capacity.

We can speculate on the impact this might have on vacation behavior. Young singles would have the time, money, and ability to participate in physically demanding activities. Family activities would be geared to those allowed by the youngest child. Older people would be likely markets during the off-season as well as for last-minute bargains.

In the family phase, activities are geared to those allowed by the youngest child. © 2009 Arne Trautmann. Used under license from Shutterstock, Inc.

HISTORICAL DEVELOPMENT OF LEISURE TIME

The distribution of time between the three categories mentioned has changed over the years. In 1791 Philadelphia carpenters went on strike for the *ten*-hour day. In 1850 the average workweek was close to seventy hours; by 1900 it had declined to about sixty hours; today it is approximately forty. The average number of weekdays enjoyed as paid vacation time varies from country to country. In Austria, Denmark, and Sweden, the workers have thirty paid weekdays of vacation, not counting public holidays. Most European countries give their workers from eighteen to twenty-five paid weekdays off. In contrast, workers in Canada, Japan, and the United States have a measly ten. U.S. manufacturing employees work the equivalent of two months more than those in many European countries.

Since the 1970s, Europeans were willing to accept slower growth in wages in return for fewer work hours and longer vacations. Because of high gains in productivity, economies continued to grow. The situation changed in the 1990s as productivity rates declined. As a result there is increased pressure in various European countries to increase the workweek. In France, where the work week is pegged at twenty-five hours, there is a move to give employees the right to work more hours if they want to increase their paychecks. While many European countries have reduced the average number of hours that people work in an attempt to provide jobs for more people, unemployment rates in many countries remain high (Landler, 2004).

Although, according to many, the workweek has decreased, other factors have prevented more people from seeing an increase in their leisure time. As affluence has increased the incidence of material possessions, much of the reduced work time has manifested itself in increased maintenance time to take care of the new possessions, such as the car and the house. In addition, as cities have grown as a result of the country becoming more urbanized, commuting time to work has increased. A related factor is that, for many, the stress of big-city living means that more time is required before individuals are mentally ready for leisure pursuits. A third factor is that, as the economy moves from primary and manufacturing industries to a service economy, the distinction between work and nonwork becomes increasingly blurred. It is easier for the steel worker to punch out at the end

> If it weren't for caffeine I'd have no personality whatsoever!
>
> Anonymous

> Human beings are the only creatures on earth that allow their children to come back home.
>
> Bill Cosby

of a shift and forget about work problems than it is for the manager of a business.

The time we spend at work is used to gather resources beyond what is needed for survival. This acquisitiveness is the result of cultural training. Anthropologists have found that most hunter-gatherer groups, who live day to day on the resources they can kill or forage and stash very little away for the future, generally work only three to five hours daily. In our "advanced" society, the extra time spent working is to purchase products, and services, including vacations, deemed necessary to our well-being.

Attempts have been made to show a relationship between the type of work and the type of leisure activities engaged in. Leisure has been seen as a compensation for work in that leisure activity is different from work activity. A passive job, for example, may result in active leisure-time activities. A second view is that the development of certain skills and lifestyles learned at work will spill over into a demand for similar kinds of leisure-time activities. The problem, of course, is that any leisure-time behavior can be explained by reference to whichever theory is more appropriate to one's purpose. The link between type of work and leisure activities has not been demonstrated. In fact, several studies have demonstrated that there are no significant differences in leisure activity between workers who are doing what they consider boring jobs and those who are doing more interesting and enjoyable jobs. It does seem clear, however, that the place of leisure in a person's life is becoming more important relative to that of work.

More important than the absolute amount of leisure time available, however, is the way in which it is spent. An individual who finishes dinner at 7 p.m. and plans to go to bed at midnight has five hours of leisure time. The amount of time available limits what activities can be done and where they can be pursued. Leisure time may be thought of as being divided into three categories (see figure 10.5).

Leisure occurs on weekdays, weekends, and on vacations. The importance of this distinction can be illustrated by means of an example. If the workweek were to be reduced by 20 percent, the opportunities for tourism activities would be affected by the way in which the reduction was taken: the workday could be shortened to six-and-a-half hours from eight; the workweek could be shortened from five to four days; one week's paid vacation could be granted in each of three quarters of the

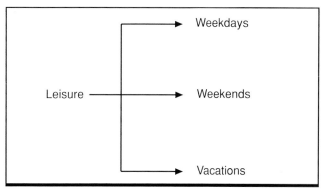

Figure 10.5 Leisure Time Divisions.

year, with one month's vacation in the fourth quarter, and with six months' vacation every five years. All three alternatives represent a cut of 20 percent in the workweek, yet the form in which it is taken affects the opportunities to participate in various activities and to visit various destinations.

It is clear that, although the absolute amount of leisure time may have increased little over the past several decades, the form in which it is being taken is changing. Although most of the gains in leisure in the past century have been taken in the form of a shorter workweek, since 1950 added leisure time has increasingly been taken in blocks of extended periods away from work. Yet the vast majority of full-time U.S. workers still are engaged in a five-day workweek.

> *Life is pleasant. Death is peaceful. It's the transition that's troublesome.*
>
> Isaac Asimov

The concepts of work, leisure, and money are intertwined as far as tourism is concerned. Individuals need both leisure and money to travel. Usually this money is earned by working. Thus, it is necessary to work in order to earn money to engage in leisure-time pursuits. The more one works, the more money is earned (and, therefore, available for leisure activities), but the less time one has to spend and enjoy it. Consumers can thus be thought of as having both a time budget and a money budget, and some make rational decisions in allocating one over the other. The auto worker who takes Friday off to lengthen the weekend for a fishing trip chooses time over money. The college professor who chooses not to teach during the summer, but to travel cross-country also chooses time over money. This idea has been expressed as the principle of *resource value inversion*. As consumers' incomes rise, time becomes increasingly precious to them compared to money. Money, after all, can be saved; time cannot. Combined with this is a perception on the part of many that "time is money."

To what extent are people increasingly unwilling to put off gratification? Are people choosing more time over more money? Several generalizations can be made. First, although Americans desire both more income and free time, it appears that three units of income are preferred for every unit of free time. Second, this preference gap seems to be closing as free time is gradually increasing in importance relative to more income. In times of economic slowdown, this statement does not hold true. Third, the income-free time choice is made within the context of other factors and values associated with an individual's perception of the quality of life. Fourth, the choice between income and free time may be affected by the way in which the free-time options are offered. Some options were demonstrated above with the example of the 20 percent workweek reduction. It appears that most workers prefer free time in the form of extended time away from work.

Much has been made of the effect of a four-day workweek on pleasure travel. However, studies of workers engaged in a four-day, forty-hour workweek have indicated that, because of fatigue from the workweek, most people tended to be more favorably inclined to home-centered relaxation. Another study compared the leisure participation of four-day-a-week and five-day-a-week workers. It found that both sets of workers devoted approximately equal amounts of time to participation in leisure activities. The only difference was that those who worked only four days a week pursued, on average, a greater number of different activities than the five-day-a-week worker. It may be that the extra day offers an opportunity to experiment with new activities, spending less time on each of more activities. This is rather interesting because, if this can be generalized, an extra day of nonwork actually places more time pressure on different leisure activities.

SOCIOECONOMIC VARIABLES AND THEIR EFFECT ON TOURISM DEMAND

AGE

The relationship between tourism and age has two components: the amount of leisure time available relative to age and the type and extent of activities undertaken at various age levels. The amount of leisure time available changes curvilinearly, with the younger and older age groups having proportionately more leisure time.

Yet the amount of available time is, by itself, insufficient to explain age as a factor in tourism behavior. It is safe to conclude that the rates of participation in the overwhelming majority of leisure activities declines with age. There is a greater decline for active recreational activities than for the more passive forms of recreation. Preferred activities among the elderly are the more passive ones such as visiting friends and relatives, sightseeing, fishing, and playing golf. Yet for many retirees, although the number of activities participated in may drop upon retirement, the amount of time spent on each remaining one in terms of participation often increases.

In Japan, people in their twenties have the highest propensity to travel internationally. Membership in birth cohorts is also important. Travel propensities are significantly higher among more recent birth cohorts. Thus, despite the fact that the number of people in their twenties will decline significantly in the near future, the number of Japanese traveling abroad is still expected to rise, albeit at a slower rate of growth than in the past (Sakia et al., 2000).

There appear to be several differences between patterns of travel based on age. Older people tend to represent a smaller share of tourists in proportion to their numbers than do younger people. This may also be influenced by other socioeconomic factors, such as income. Although younger people tend to select more adventurous destinations than do older people, older tourists tend to travel to farther destinations. The older tourists tend to dominate ship travel, spend less than middle-age tourists but more than younger tourists, and, while preferring to travel in the summer (in common with younger travelers), tend to travel more in the spring than do younger tourists. In one study, older people considered restfulness and the historical aspects

of a vacation site more important while younger people emphasized adventure and physical activities. Single people stressed physical activities, meeting new people, and having fun. Married people, on the other hand, put more emphasis on restful and physically refreshing destinations (Kaynak et al., 1995).

GENERATIONAL INFLUENCE

In analyzing the impact of age on travel and tourism, the generational influence must be considered. One

QUICK TRIP 10.4

Bad Time to Be Born

Societies have different standards for what it takes to have children. It actually might not just be societies, but individuals, and different individual preferences. Some adults do not put much thought into having children, but when it happens they make do. Others like to plan and make sure that everything is stable before throwing a child into the mix. In Asia, birthrates have been slowly declining for decades due to different factors such as rapid urbanization and global security. Some experts are calling it the fear factor. Starting in the late 1990s after the Asian financial crisis, external elements have weighed heavier on child-bearing decisions. Because of terrorist bombings and events such as 9/11, young people are starting to be even more uncertain about the future and are less likely to have children. South Korea's fertility rate is the largest two-year decline on record; Hong Kong's fertility rate is among the lowest in the world. People are getting married later and want fewer children. In Taiwan 30 percent of thirty-five-year-olds are unmarried and one out of four of those do not want to have children. Recently, governments have made efforts to boost dating and marriage, but a substantial improvement on the situation has not been reached.

THINK ABOUT THIS:

1. Within the tourism industries, which destinations and activities will suffer if fewer couples marry and/or have children? Which will thrive?

Source: Bad Time to Be Born: Gloom Is Driving down Birthrates among the Asian Tigers. 2004. *Newsweek International. Student Resource Center Gold.* Gale. Cherry Creek High School Lib., Greenwood Village, CO. Retrieved 14 May 2008, http://infotrac.galegroup.com/itweb/?db=SRC-1.

Visiting friends and relatives, sightseeing, fishing and playing golf are preferred activities among the elderly. © 2009 Lisa F. Young. Used under license from Shutterstock, Inc.

large study of U.S. out-of-town vacationers found that the cohort or generational variable is second in importance in explaining commercial lodging usage. Income is rated number one in importance (Peterson and Lambert, 2003).

The generational influence is the common set of shared experiences that all members of a generational cohort went through by those who came of age, approximately between the ages of seventeen and twenty-three, during a particular decade. The three generational cohorts at the turn of the millennium were (Peterson and Lambert, 2003; U.S. Travel Data Center, 1998):

- Matures or Seniors born 1945 and before. They define themselves by the idea of duty having gone through the shared experience of the Great Depression and having survived World War II and the cold war. They are intent on hunting for bargains; they do not like to buy on credit; and they have strong family and community ties.
- Baby boomers, born 1946–1964, are defined by individuality and self-fulfillment as a result of being coddled in their early years and coming of age in the excesses of the 1960s. A very demanding segment, many seek out less traditional vacation destinations.
- Generation Xers born between 1965 and 1978. They are defined as "savvy" because of their exposure to uncertain economic times.
- A fourth cohort—Generation Y (or Nexters)— consists of those born between 1978 and 2004 (sources vary on the exact dates).

An analysis of this information would suggest that the shared attitudes experienced in the formative years continue to have an influence on buying patterns even as the group matures and ages. For example, it might be expected that spending patterns of the Depression babies are forever influenced by the fact that they went through the Depression at an early age. In fact, this group still today uses credit cards less often than do other segments.

There are distinct travel patterns across generations. Overall, domestic household trips are almost twice as likely to be taken for leisure as for business. Generation Y and Matures are the generations most likely to take leisure trips. Trips by Seniors tend to last longer than trips by other generations. They are also most likely to travel out of state and region. Gen-

> America believes in education: the average professor earns more money in a year than a professional athlete earns in a whole week.
>
> Evan Esar

erations X and Y are more active travelers than other generations. Across all generations, dining and shopping are the most popular activities, with Generation X and Y travelers slightly more likely to shop than others. These two groups are also more likely to look for entertainment, sightsee, and take part in nightlife activities. Seniors, on the other hand, are more likely to gamble and take group tours. Boomers and Seniors spend more on travel than do other generations while, as might be expected, travel with children is most common among younger generations.

In terms of the purpose of the trip, baby boomers are the most likely to travel for business while, compared to boomers, visits to friends and relatives are more common among Generations X and Y and Seniors.

In summary, leisure time decreases with age until children leave the nest; then the amount of leisure time increases. This increase continues with retirement. Though participation in physical activities declines with age (together with a corresponding rise in participation in the gentler forms of recreation), interest levels in activities previously participated in remain high. Opportunities may exist for tapping these interests by developing nonparticipatory means of expressing that interest. A skier, for example, may be unable to ski for reasons of age, but may be interested in other related activities such as watching skiers or sharing experiences.

INCOME

Income is obviously an important inhibiting factor in shaping the demand for travel. Indeed, it can be argued that the importance of other demographics is secondary to that of income in that life stage, education, and sex are all determinants of income (Mohsin and Ryan, 2004). A large study of U.S. vacationers found that income, followed by level of education, is the leading influence on out-of-town vacations (Peterson and Lambert, 2003).

It has been demonstrated that income differences account for most of the variance in vacation participation in Europe (Mergoupis and Steur, 2002/2). In fact income, together with other demographic characteristics, explain all of the differences in vacation participation. Not only does travel itself entail a certain cost, but the traveler must pay for services rendered at the destination as well as have money to engage in various activities during the trip. In addition, expenditures may be required in the form of specialized equipment to engage in various recreational activities while at the destination or en route. It is difficult, however, to determine the relative importance of income per se, because this variable is interrelated with other socioeconomic variables. Generally speaking, higher income is associated with higher education, with certain jobs, and with certain age groups. Total family income has risen steadily as more wives have entered the labor force. The fact that family income has risen will have an effect upon tourism demand. Yet the fact that more families have two spouses in the labor force will also affect the shape of tourism demand. Different types of vacations and recreational activities may be demanded because of the time pressures involved in having two working spouses. The difficulty arises in determining the effect of these two interrelated variables on the demand for new tourism and recreation products.

It is important to see that the income spent on travel is spent at the expense of something else (see figure 10.6). Travel expenditures are in competition with other expenditures, some of which are discretionary.

An individual's *personal disposable income* is the amount of income left after paying taxes. After various necessary personal outlays to maintain basic living needs have been spent, an individual has discretion to do with the remainder whatever is desired. A mink coat may be purchased, money may be saved, or a trip taken to Hawaii. It is important to look at income in this way to realize that the trip to Hawaii is in competition not only with a trip to the Bahamas, but also with various other recreational activities and other uses of that discretionary income. As the level of personal income increases, so does the amount of *discretionary income*.

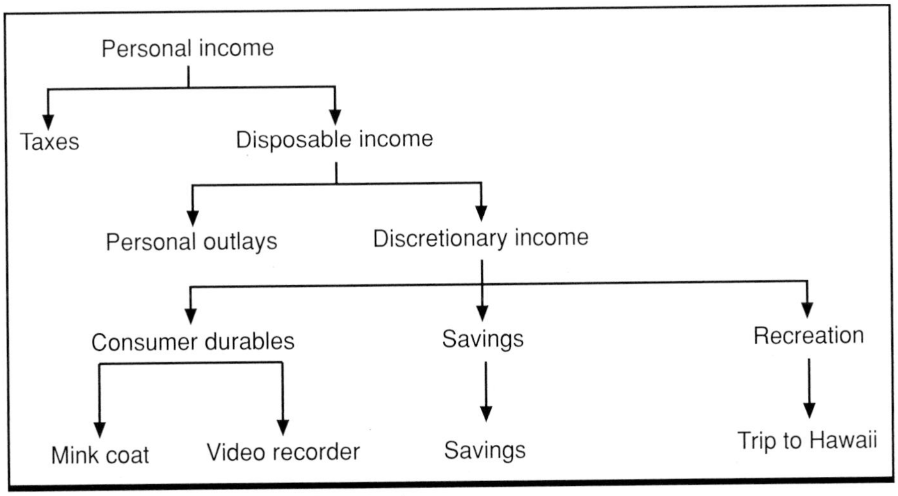

Many studies have attempted to determine the percentage of income spent on recreation as a whole. It appears that at the lower levels of income and education approximately 2 percent of income is spent on recreation. As income increases the proportion spent on recreation increases to between 5 and 6 percent for all education levels. The highest recreation expenditures, 7 percent, are reported by respondents who are heads of households, under forty years of age, and without children. Other studies have indicated a positive correlation between income and recreation expenditures. In fact, it appears that increases in income result in a proportionately greater increase in recreation expenditures. A one percentage point increase in income increases the probability of taking a vacation between 0.20 and 0.30 percentage points. The range in European countries varies from 0.2 percent in Germany to 0.31 percent in Spain, Greece, and Portugal (Mergoupis and Steur, 1999, 2000/2). There is some evidence that higher income has a positive effect on the length of a vacation but the exact impact has not yet been reliably determined (Mergoupis and Steur, 2000/1). As might be expected, higher-income tourists stay longer and spend more per day than do those with lower incomes. The type of recreational activities participated in differs based upon income. Higher-income people tend to participate in activities such as reading, bridge, fencing, squash, and chess; and middle-income people tend to engage in bowling, golf, and dancing. Lower-income families are identified with television viewing, dominoes, and bingo. The implication of these activities is clear to companies who wish to put together travel packages with specific activities involved aimed at particular market segments. A package, for example, aimed at a high-income segment of the market might be built around a recreational activity in which that segment tends to participate.

In addition to the relationship between income and recreation expenditure, some work has been done on the amount of participation in recreation and income. It has been shown that participation in most recreational activities increases as income increases up to a certain point, but declines slightly at incomes higher than this.

The only significant demographic difference between U.S.

Figure 10.6 Personal Income Distribution.

Birth Order and Personality

Have you ever made an assumption about someone based on his or her birth order? Do you assume that only children are spoiled brats? Well, Dr. Kevin Leman has published his findings that link behavior and personality to birth order. Here is what he found:

- Firstborns—Natural leaders and high achievers, this often results in the inability to delegate. This leads to higher stress levels because they want to be in control all of the time. They also at times feel entitled or superior.
- Middle Children—They are usually people pleasers and hate confrontation. They are usually great negotiators, calm and down to earth.
- The Babies—They are often called the cheerleaders as they love to entertain and have excellent people skills. They usually make friends easily and are more likely to take risks. They also have a fairly short attention span.
- Only Children—They are usually task-oriented, organized, and dependable. They can also be demanding and unforgiving, as they don't like to admit when they are wrong.

THINK ABOUT THIS:

1. How would you treat each of these personalities within the tourism industries in regard to advertising or dealing with problems?

Source: Tesh, J. So Does Birth Order Really Affect Your Personality? Rev. of *The Birth Order Connection*, by Dr. Kevin Leman. *The John Tesh Radio Show*. The Tesh Media Group. Retrieved 14 May 2008, http://www.tesh.com.

might be expected, nonworking women have slightly higher participation rates than do employed women, except for such things as going out to dinner and either taking part in active sports or watching sports. There is a clear difference between the sexes in terms of preferred activities. Women are more involved in cultural activities, and men lead in outdoor recreation and playing and watching sports.

One study (Williams and Lattey, 1994) indicates that the traditional responsibilities of females relating to domestic work and child care have led to them viewing leisure activities in a way that are task-oriented rather than time-oriented; social rather than physical; relational as opposed to self-interested. The study specifically dealt with skiing and found that women placed more emphasis on the emotional and social benefits of skiing than on the physical benefits. Women, it was found, are more likely than men to ski if friends and/or family members are involved. The activity is viewed as recreational rather than competitive.

Another study finds that women travel for one of three reasons:

1. Rest/relax
2. Friends
3. Social

The only significant demographic difference identified was employment status. Because the sample was very homogeneous, the authors speculate that generational effect was missing, and it may be that younger women are more likely to desire adventure travel and some degree of physical activity when on vacation. (Pennington-Gray and Kerstetter, 2001).

Significant differences between men and women in souvenir purchases—including merchandise choice and selection factors—have been demonstrated (Combrink and Swanson, 2000). For example, women are more likely to select crafts, postcards, and artistic and authentic clothing than are men. Equally, they are more likely to select merchandise on the basis of appealing colors and design than are men.

domestic and foreign travelers is that of income. A greater percentage of foreign travelers had higher incomes.

GENDER

There are more similarities than differences between the sexes in terms of leisure participation rates. Overall, participation rates in leisure activities do not differ between men and women, although many women engage in slightly fewer activities than do men. As

> My problem lies in reconciling my gross habits with my net income.
>
> Errol Flynn (1909–1959)

EDUCATION

The strong correlation between education as it relates to income has been well-established. Independent of income, however, the level of education that an individual has tends to influence the type of leisure and travel pursuits chosen. The amount of education ob-

Participation in outdoor recreation tends to increase as the amount of one's education increases. © 2009 Varina and Jay Patel. Used under license from Shutterstock, Inc.

tained will most likely determine the nature of both work and leisure-time activities. By widening one's horizons of interest and enjoyment, education influences the type of activities undertaken. Education itself can serve as the primary reason for travel.

Researchers have found that participation in outdoor recreation tends to increase as the amount of education increases. There is also some evidence to suggest that the more educated prefer those activities that require the development of interpretive and expressive skills. Such activities include attending plays, concerts, and art museums, playing tennis and golf, skiing, reading books, attending adult education classes, and undergoing a wilderness experience.

In summary, it appears that the more education people have, the broader their horizons and the more options they can consider. The more-educated travelers also tend to be more sophisticated in their tastes. They may not, however, be bigger spenders. A study of visitors to Hawaii found that visitors with less education spent more per day while on vacation in Hawaii. The authors suggested that the less-educated visitor may equate having fun with spending money.

LIFE CYCLE STAGES

Families evolve through a certain life cycle. The characteristics of the family at the various stages of its life cycle offer certain opportunities or exert various pressures that affect purchase behavior.

Although it has been suggested that this traditional life cycle has become outdated because of changing demographics such as the growing number of "dinks" (double income, no kids) and an increase in single parent families, the Travel Industry Association of America (TIA) has consumer research that shows that travel behavior varies depending on life stages (TIA, 2002). TIA indicates that the three core life stage groups—Singles, Couples and Parents—are defined by combining the demographic variables of children, household composition and marital status. There is additional segmentation based on age and employment to give a total of eleven segments.

The divisions of the family life cycle are shown in table 10.1, together with the respective share of U.S. household trips. Some of the major findings are:

- Although Middle Parent households generate the largest share of trips, they take the same amount suggested by their population size.
- Young Couple, Older Working Couple, and Middle Couple households take more trips than suggested by their respective population size.
- Older, Retired Single households take fewer trips than indicated by their population size.
- Older Retired Single and Older Retired Couple households are more likely to travel for pleasure than are other segments.
- Middle age groups (headed by thirty-five to fifty-four-year-olds) for Singles, Couples and Parents are more likely to take business trips than are other segments.
- Middle Singles are more likely to use air transportation than are other segments.

Table 10.1
A Traditional Family Life Cycle

Stage in Life Cycle	Share of U.S. Household Trips
Young Singles	8%
Middle Singles	8%
Older Working Singles	5%
Older Retired Singles	6%
Young Couples	5%
Middle Couples	13%
Older Working Couples	14%
Older Retired Couples	7%
Young Parents	9%
Middle Parents	23%
Older Parents	2%

Source: *Travel Through the Life Stages.* Washington, DC, Travel Industry Association of America, 2002 Edition, Executive Summary. 3.

- Older Retired Couples and Young Parents are more likely to use auto/truck travel than are other segments.
- Middle Couples and Middle Parents are more likely to stay at a hotel, motel, or bed & breakfast than are other segments.

Other studies have examined the impact of marriage on vacation behavior. They indicate that single people take part in a much wider variety of activities outside the home than do married people. Married life brings about certain changes in leisure habits. Activities that were previously done alone or with friends are participated in less for reasons intrinsic to the activity itself and more for reasons related to the role of being a spouse.

PRESENCE OF CHILDREN

The narrowing of the types of activities participated in is intensified by the presence of children. When a married couple has children, there is a shift from activities engaged in primarily for intrinsic satisfaction to activities that are role-related, such as family activities. Before children came on the scene, the spouse was the chief leisure companion. This companionship is diluted by the presence of children. The presence of children seems to be crucial. Travel is curtailed; more leisure is spent at home; and few new leisure interests are acquired. In at least one case, that of camping, the onset of parenthood has varied effects. Although the addition of young children in a camping family may produce a curtailment of camping activities, the shift to the empty-nest stage produces either an increase or a decrease in the activity. For those couples who enjoy camping, the situation of children leaving the nest may actually increase their participation. For others who saw camping primarily as a family activity, the departure of children from the home may result in less camping.

Most research indicates that family vacation decisions are joint between husband and wife. However, at least one study suggests that, when there are children in the home, the wife exerts more influence over the decision-making process and is more likely to seek information on the possible destination choices than when the couple is childless (Fodness, 1992).

Basic attitudes and behavior patterns of family life established in the early years of the family life cycle affect the future activities of both husbands and wives throughout the marriage (Nickerson, Salcone, and Aaker, 1995). Activities undertaken in the early stages of the life span tend to be repeated throughout life. In addition, the types of vacations taken with parents as a child and during early adulthood serve as a model for future vacations.

For the young child, leisure pursuits are restricted by the dictates of parents and the limitations of money. As children enter school, leisure activities outside the home increase. As children grow older, their leisure habits and attitudes are more heavily influenced by their peers. Because of the high rate of social interaction among young people, leisure fads are easily spread. There is also at this stage an attempt to duplicate the behavior and attitudes of older age groups. Particularly important in this respect are college students, who tend to be leaders, often being the first to try new products and services.

EMPTY NESTERS

As children leave the home, more time and money tend to be available for leisure. Some studies indicate that, in the United States, travel patterns change significantly after age sixty. Up until that time, auto travel is the favored mode of transportation. After that point, travel by bus, plane, or boat is preferred. This can be explained by an increase in available time and money and, perhaps, a reduction in physical abilities.

The empty nesters left behind have been the subject of a focus group study conducted by Plog Research (undated). A focus group consists of a small group of people, usually ten to twelve, getting together for a two-hour discussion. The groups are made up of individuals who have already been screened through questionnaires and interviews to arrive at a group that has members similar to one another in background. The discussion is led by a psychologist who attempts to develop a picture of the needs, interests, and personal psychologies of the group. The findings of the study are revealing. The typical empty nester doesn't think of extended

> The most unfair thing about life is the way it ends. I mean, life is tough. It takes up a lot of your time. What do you get at the end of it? A Death! What's that, a bonus? I think the life cycle is all backwards. You should die first, get it out of the way. Then you live in an old age home. You get kicked out when you're too young, you get a gold watch, you go to work. You work forty years until you're young enough to enjoy your retirement. You do drugs, alcohol, you party, you get ready for high school. You go to grade school, you become a kid, you play, you have no responsibilities, you become a little baby, you go back into the womb, you spend your last nine months floating.
>
> *George Carlin*

Empty nesters usually want to spend more time in fewer places. © 2009 Wolfgang Amri. Used under license from Shutterstock, Inc.

trips by air, especially to foreign destinations. Their thinking is geared to the kinds of trips taken with their children; trips which have typically involved travel by car and visits to friends and relatives. There appears to be a strong desire for travel experiences as a means of self-actualization. Several barriers present themselves. The surface barriers of lack of time and money are true up to a point. For couples who work, scheduling may be a problem, and there is a reluctance toward using all of one's vacation time at once. Financially, although more discretionary income may be available, many empty nesters feel uncomfortable in spending their money on an intangible, such as travel. In addition, they tend to believe that the cost of a trip is more expensive than it really is, estimating the cost at twice the actual one. More than anything, however, they express fear as a barrier to traveling. They are afraid of not knowing how to act in a new environment, of being taken advantage of. In a more subtle way, they feel that travel may be a way for them to learn how to be a couple again. Combined with this, however, is the fear that they may discover that they really do not like each other.

It is necessary to understand the particular inhibiting factors felt by each of these market segments at each stage of the family life cycle in order to be able to offer a product or service that will overcome the barriers and induce purchase behavior. For the empty nesters, for example, a tour would be very appropriate. A package tour relieves the participants of making decisions they may feel inadequate to make. The regular tour may have a negative connotation for them, however. Empty nesters usually want to spend more time in fewer places than many tours offer. Popular kinds of destinations are those that help the empty nesters find their roots. This

appeals to the need to give some meaning to their lives. The tour also helps alleviate some of the fears of being a couple again with no children around. The fact that there are other people around means that the empty nesters do not have to rely totally upon each other for companionship and support during the trip.

A recent study (Cook et al., 2007) identified the characteristics of the ideal vacation trip. Seven lifestage groups were identified based on age, income, and family compositions. The impact of children is seen in the following profiles.

- Young Free, eighteen to thirty-four with no children, would ideally travel to another country.
- Young Families, eighteen to thirty-four with children, are in need of a break from relatives and want romantic time with their spouse. Family obligations come in the way of this ideal.
- Middle Frees, thirty-five to fifty-four with no children, desire "authentic" experiences such as history and heritage destinations where they can enjoy the local culture.
- Middle Families with lower incomes, thirty-five to fifty-four with children and incomes of less than $50,000, see their ideal trip far off in the future. They want time with family, escape, and freedom, and have a great interest in ocean/beach destinations and theme parks.
- Middle Families with higher incomes, thirty-five to fifty-four with children and incomes of $50,000 plus, also have a family orientation. They are interested in spending quality time with their spouse/ partner as well as resting and relaxing. They have unmet needs in the areas of sightseeing, culinary experiences, outdoor activities, and cruising.
- Older Frees with lower incomes, fifty-five and older with no children and incomes less than $50,000, are most concerned about safety, language barriers, and health. Socializing is very important to this segment.
- Older Frees with higher incomes, fifty-five and older with no children and incomes of $50,000 plus. They say that travel is how they define themselves. This segment is the most satisfied with their vacation trips.

BARRIERS TO LEISURE ENJOYMENT

The barriers to leisure enjoyment have been the subject of study by Witt and Goodale (1981). They identified the relationship between various barriers to the enjoyment of leisure and stages in the family life cycle. Understanding these barriers is a crucial step toward knowing what to say, do, and offer to lower those barriers. It was found that the different patterns of change developed over the family life cycle relative to the barriers under discussion. Figure 10.7 illustrates the fact that various barriers (see table 10.2) showed an approximately U-shaped pattern, with the barriers having the least effect when the youngest child was between six and eighteen years of age.

These barriers refer to difficulties in knowing which activities to get involved with and with whom to share participation. This suggests that as children reach school age, parents have more knowledge of what is available and how to utilize those opportunities. It may also be, as mentioned earlier, that their leisure activities are more closely defined for them by the expectation of their role as parents of school-age children. The time when the youngest child leaves home appears to be a critical passage relative to these barriers, a point made in the earlier discussion of the empty nesters.

A second group of barriers exhibit an inverted U-shaped pattern when expressed over the life cycle of the family (see figure 10.8). During the child-rearing period, family obligations increase significantly for women and, to a similar but lesser degree, for men. This fact and the fact that neither parent feels there is

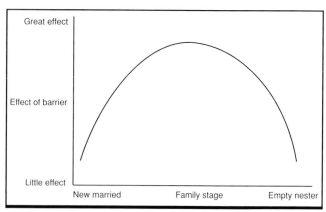

Figure 10.8 Barriers to Leisure Enjoyment at Different Family Stages (Inverted U-Shaped Pattern).

enough free time represent the barriers felt; they increase until children leave the home, and then their effect drops off sharply.

The effect of various barriers has been found to increase as the family goes through various life cycle stages (see figure 10.9). The expectations of family and friends increase for women, but for men they are more constant and less of a limitation over the family life cycle. The feelings of daily stress increase for both sexes as time goes on, while often the feeling of not doing anything stays somewhat constant during the child-rearing stage and increases dramatically when children leave the home. Two other barriers have been analyzed for males only. It has been found that there is an increased effect by males who don't feel fit enough or don't have the physical skills for certain activities. This is reflected in the effect of a falling off in physical skills and fitness levels with age.

Certain points are worthy of note. First, it appears that stages in the family life cycle can help explain and help predict leisure-time behavior. Care must be taken,

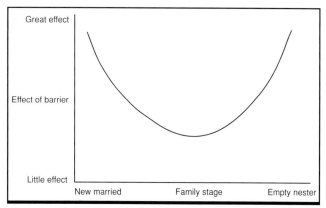

Figure 10.7 Barriers to Leisure Enjoyment at Different Family Stages (U-Shaped Pattern).

Table 10.2
Barriers Exhibiting a U-Shaped Pattern

Not being sure what activities to be involved in
Not knowing what's going on or what's available
Not being sure how to use available resources
Difficulty in planning and making decisions
Not having anyone to do things with
Not being at ease in social situations
Difficulty in carrying out plans

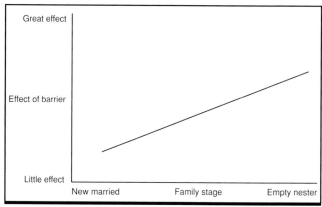

Figure 10.9 Barriers to Leisure Enjoyment at Different Family Stages (U-Shaped Pattern).

however, in the use of correlation or regression techniques for projecting or forecasting leisure activities because of the nonlinear pattern of many of these barriers. Second, it is noted that the family life cycle stage can only explain leisure behavior very partially. Third, it is determined that noting which barriers are predominant at various life cycle stages will enable products, packages, and messages to be targeted to reflect an understanding of these barriers and potential objections of the many market segments.

PERSONALITY

It has been suggested that most people view their vacation as an extension of their personality. Howard and Sheth (1969) have postulated that the effect of personality is felt on two areas—nonspecific motives and the alternatives considered for purchase. They have proposed that the more authoritarian a person is, for example, the fewer alternatives will have to be considered in arriving at a purchase decision. The relationship between personality and nonspecific motives has been explored by various researchers in an attempt to understand existing behavior better and predict future behavior with greater accuracy.

The personality of an individual can be described as "the summation of the characteristics that make the person what he or she is and (that) distinguish each individual from every other individual" (Walters, 1978). It is logical that there is a link between the type of person one is and the type of purchases one makes: A conservative person will tend to make conservative purchases.

PERSONALITY TRAITS

Personality can be thought of as consisting of a variety of traits. Individuals who participate in recreational and tourist activities can be typed in terms of their personality traits in an attempt to determine whether such participants exhibit markedly different personality traits than do non-participants. The purpose of such analysis is to determine whether or not personality can be used as a variable for segmenting the market. If it is found that certain personality traits are dominant in winter vacations, marketers will know better the kind of tourist to appeal to and will gain valuable information as to what to say to appeal to this potential vacationer. To date, the research evidence is inconclusive as to whether or not personality is a significant variable in explaining purchase behavior. Although several studies indicate a strong relationship between personality and consumer

behavior, and a few indicate no relationship, the great majority indicate that any existing correlation is weak.

The relationship between personality and participation in recreational activities is also of interest. As we have seen, recreational activities can serve as a major reason or motivation for vacation travel. If a relationship between certain activities and certain personality traits can be established, an appropriate marketing strategy can be developed.

PERSONALITY TYPES

Often a person is described as having a certain type of personality. Personality types consist of characteristics that, when taken together, form a certain kind of person. One way of typing people is to the extent that they are perceived as being *introverted* or *extroverted*. Introverts look into themselves and tend to be shy and reserved. Extroverts are other-oriented, looking outside the self, and tending to be objective rather than subjective in outlook. Participants in vigorous physical activity in general tend to be extroverts. In fact, outdoor recreational activities in general are not participated in by introverted personality types.

PSYCHOGRAPHICS AND LIFESTYLE

The application of studies of personality to the business world has been hampered because the terminology of personality has come from clinical sources. Psychographics has developed as a way of describing consumer behavior in terms of a distinctive way of living in order to determine whether or not people with distinctive lifestyles have distinctive travel behaviors. Psychographics is the development of psychological profiles of consumers and psychologically based measures of distinctive modes of living or lifestyles.

One study finds that the psychographic makeup of the student travel market can be described by five factors:

1. Cultural values
2. Personality
3. Travel motivation
4. Preferences for activities
5. Lifestyle (Reisinger and Mavondo, 2004)

Stanley Plog developed a model in the 1970s that is designed to explain the types of destinations chosen by people based upon their psychographic characteristics. According to the model, travelers can be described based upon their place on an allocentric/psychocentric continuum. This has since been relabeled *venturesomeness*. Allocentrics, renamed *venturers* by Plog, prefer traveling independently to destinations that have few tourists while psychocentrics, renamed *dependables*, prefer to vacation with tour groups and travel to well developed tourist regions. Venturers tend to be slightly wealthier, more adventurous, extroverted and self-confident, travel more, spending more time away from home, and traveled more as a child (Plog, 1991, 2002).

Plog estimates that 2½ to 4 percent of the U.S. population are pure venturers or pure dependables. The remainder of the population exists along the continuum as near-venturer (16 percent), centric-venturer, centric-dependable (62 percent total for both), and near dependable (16 percent). The relative proportions of these segments may vary by culture.

The personality characteristics used to describe these individuals are represented by three dominant personality traits: territory boundedness, generalized anxieties, and a sense of powerlessness (Griffith and Albanese, 1996).

To this, Plog has added an energy dimension that ranges from high energy to low energy or lethargy (figure 10.10). Dependables tend to be described as being territory bound, experiencing general anxieties, a sense of powerlessness and low energy. The opposite extreme would be true for venturers. The theories underlying Plog's model suggest that, while specific destination choices will vary over time, the general types of destinations chosen will remain the relatively stable.

It is asserted by Plog that people from the East prefer dependable types of travel while those from the West prefer more venturesome types of travel. One study comparing travel behaviors of U.S. and Japanese college students failed to confirm this (Cole and Sakakida, 2003). However, because Japan is moving from a traditionally collectivistic society to an individualistic society, it may not be typical of Eastern society.

In updating his body of work, Plog (2002) finds that:

Plog asserts that people from the West prefer more venturesome types of travel.
© 2009 Jonathan Noden-Wilkinson. Used under license from Shutterstock, Inc.

- Venturers travel more than dependables.
- Different psychographic types engage in different types of leisure activities when on vacation, the participation level rising or falling in a straight line across the psychographic spectrum.

Household income correlates with the amount of leisure travel and is an excellent predictor of spending on a trip. Venturesomeness is a better predictor of the number of trips to be taken as well as the activities to be undertaken on the trips. High risk takers tend to prefer high-energy, outdoor-type activities (Pizam et al., 2004).

It has been shown that demographics are inadequate predictors of nature based vacation behaviors (Murdy, Yiannakis, and Gibson, 2003) and many argue that psychographics is a more useful tool in predicting vacation behavior. Plog concedes that psychographic dimensions are unlikely to displace demographic variables, especially income, in segmenting markets. However, their use can help do the following (Plog, 2002).

- Reposition existing travel products. Repositioning a destination to target near-venturers makes sense since they are a relatively large segment and their behavior influences the 60 plus percent centrics.

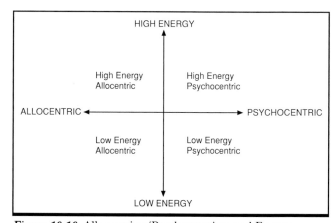

Figure 10.10 Allocentrism/Psychocentrism and Energy Dimensions. Source: Nickerson, N. P., and G. D. Ellis. 1991. Traveler types and activation theory: A comparison of two models. *Journal of Travel Research*, 29 (3): 26.

Renovating Liverpool

Rebuilding a reputation and renovation are difficult tasks, especially for an eight-hundred-year-old port city. Besides being known as the birthplace of the Beatles, Liverpool has a reputation for crime and soccer—not your typical hip destination. A recent poll by Travelodge reports that more than 60 percent of tourists in South England think that Liverpool is "cold, bleak and unsophisticated." However, time and money are being spent trying to change this outlook. Forty million U.S. Dollars (USD) were spent in 2008 on cultural events. In January of 2008, Liverpool received its first large concert venue, seating ten thousand on the waterfront. A 38 million USD cruise terminal was built, along with a 2 billion USD shopping complex. Liverpool has often been known for its art, and many artists are resisting the renovation of Liverpool. Bryan Gray, chairman of the Northwest Regional Development Agency, says that "[m]anaging culture is difficult."

THINK ABOUT THIS:

1. After reading about Liverpool's renovation, what types of people do you think it is trying to attract? Which cultures? People with what time constraints?

2. What socioeconomic categories does its target market fall into?

Source: Jackson, C. 2008. The Next Barcelona. *The Wall Street Journal.* W1. Retrieved 14 May 2008, http://www.wsj.com.

- Develop new travel products to capture the "venturesome" segment.
- Create better marketing messages to appeal to travel segments based on their level of venturesomeness. Travel agents might use this concept to suggest better alternative destinations for their clients. Instead of immediately asking for destination preferences they could ask about previous vacation behavior and examine issues relating to the client's likely place on the venturer–dependable scale. As a result they would be in a position to suggest better alternatives to their clients.

It has been shown that lifestyles vary according to different socioeconomic variables. Although it is beneficial to segment a market on the basis of lifestyle dimensions for marketing purposes, it is necessary to identify the socioeconomic characteristics of these segments in order to reach the target markets effectively.

For example, a study of Spanish tourists identifies that both demographic and psychographic factors have an effect on the decision to take a vacation. Those studied are more likely to take a vacation if their income is high, household size is low, they are age forty-five or less, have an active occupational situation (implies greater budget), are students (more leisure time), live in a large city (need to escape), and have a positive opinion of taking a vacation (psychographic) (Nicolau and Mas, 2005).

SUMMARY

The vacation choices that people make are influenced by, and often constrained by, various factors external to them. The culture of which they are a part and the significant events that helped shape their values all act to determine, in part, when, where, and how they will vacation. The time available also determines if and where people will travel. Developments in paid vacations, as well as advances in technology, have enabled people to take a vacation and have influenced how far they can go with the amount of free time they have.

Demographic and psychographic factors also shape the vacation decision. Early attempts to explain vacation behavior using demographics alone have been found to be incomplete. A full understanding of travel purchases comes from a consideration of both.

Trends

Social Trends Impacting Tourism

1. Personalization: The key will be to provide personalized services to tourists. ChaCha (http://www.chacha.com) is a Web site in beta testing that provides personalized answers to questions including those related to travel itineraries. [Author's note: Holiday Inn offers a choice of four pillow types at many properties: Firm Synthetic, Medium Down, Firm Down, U-Shaped Neck Pillow.]

2. Targeted Segmentation: The baby boomers—those born between 1946 and 1964—are, in fact, two segments: early boomers (born between 1946 and 1953) and late boomers (born between 1954 and 1964). They need to be marketed to separately. The late boomers, also known as Generation Jones, account for 40 percent of all business travelers. They have a Web site specifically targeting them called Boomj.com (http://www.bomj.com).

3. Democratization of Information: Control is moving from suppliers to consumers. The Consumerist (http://consumerist.com) is a blog devoted to consumer complaints and experiences with companies. One hotel company is giving cameras to guests and awarding a prize for the best submitted photo of a hotel stay.

4. Social Networking 2.5: Social connections are being brought into real life. This involves bringing customers together who have shared cultural activities. Hitchsters.com (http://www.hitchsters.com) is a site that brings together people of like interests who want to share a taxi ride to a New York City airport.

5. Life-Story Labeling: People want to know the life story of the products they are using—the footprint of the company. In response, companies are increasingly telling customers and guests what they are doing for the environment.

6. The Experiential Economy: Experiences are replacing goods. In the State of Maine, for example, it is possible to rent a lobster trap for the season. Customers can watch their trap fill up and are sent the lobsters. This extends the vacation experience to the tourists after returning home.

Source: Levine, D. 2007. "Five Cultural Trends Affecting Travel" presentation given at the World Travel Market, London, England. http://www.wtmlondon.com.

ACTIVITIES

1. Explain why Las Vegas' tag line of "What happens in Vegas stays in Vegas" is so appealing to many travelers.

2. Develop a marketing campaign for a tourism attraction targeted toward a specific group with a commercial, slogan, and pamphlet that appeal to someone in another country. Then contrast this marketing campaign for a U.S. citizen in the same demographic target area as you did for another culture.

INTERNET
ACTIVITIES

3. Have you ever gone to a Web site that requires you to choose your country before entering? Go to a Web site such as http://www.Gucci.com, http://www.coca-cola.com, http://www.Nike.com and compare and contrast the differences between the different sites. Explain why these sites have chosen to alter each aspect for the different countries or languages.

4. A culture that is not often considered is cyber culture. There is a digital online world known as second life in which more than one million users have an avatar (online personality). In the form of their avatar, they go through life and interact with other avatars. Is there anything that the tourism industry can do to tap into this cyber culture?

Source: Jurgensen, J. 2008. "Online: My So-Called Second Life." *The Wall Street Journal.* W2. Retrieved 15 May 2008, http://www.wsj.com.

REFERENCES

Bennett, P. D., and H. J. Kassasjian. 1982. *Consumer Behavior.* Englewood Cliffs, NJ: Prentice-Hall, Inc. 123.

Cole, S. T., and Y. Sakakida. 2003. Understanding travel preferences: The case of American and Japanese college students, *Targeted Research: The Gateway to Accountability.* 34th Annual Proceedings of the Travel and Tourism Research Association. CD-ROM, unpaged.

Combrink, T., and K. Swanson. 2000. Souvenir choice and gender: an evaluation of domestic souvenir choice attributes of tourists in the four-corners region of the southwest. 31st Annual Conference Proceedings of the Travel and Tourism Research Association. 378–385.

(September 8, 1996). *Denver Post,* 8G.

Cook, S. D., T. T. Burnett, S. Hopkins, and P. Loeb. 2007. *The Ideal American Vacation Trip.* New York: Travel Industry Association.

Dunn, W. 1993. *1994 Outlook for Generation X/Baby Busters.* Proceedings of the 1994 Outlook for Travel and Tourism. Washington, DC: Travel Industry Association of America. 83–86.

Ferraro, G. P. 1990. *The Cultural Dimension of International Business.* Englewood Cliffs, NJ: Prentice-Hall, Inc. 94.

Fodness, D. 1992. The impact of family life cycle on the vacation decision-making process. *Journal of Travel Research,* 31 (2): 8–13.

Griffith, D. A., and P. J. Albanese. 1996. An examination of Plog's psychographic travel model within a student population. *Journal of Travel Research,* 34 (4): 47–51.

Hofstede, G. 1985. *The Cultural Perspective.* People and Organizations Interacting, A. Brakel (ed.). New York: John Wiley & Sons, Inc.

Undated. *Increasing Your Sales to New and Existing Markets.* Plog Research, Inc.

Jurowski, C., and G. Walker. 1995. *Personal Values and Environmental Attitudes Effect on Pleasure Trip Preferences.* Proceedings of the 26th Annual Conference of the Travel and Tourism Research Association. 193–199.

Kaynak, E., A. Kara, O. Kucukemiroglu, and T. Dalgic. 1995. *Salient Attributes Lead to Travel Preferences: Irish Travelers.* 26th Annual Conference Proceedings of the Travel and Tourism Research Association. 246–253.

Kim, S. S., and B. Prideaux. 2005. Marketing implications arising from a comparative study of international pleasure tourism motivations and other travel-related characteristics of visitors to Korea. *Tourism Management,* 26: 347–357.

Kolsaker, A., L. Lee-Kelley, and P. C. Choy. 2004. The Reluctant Hong Kong consumer: Purchasing travel on-line. *International Journal of Consumer Studies,* 28 (3): 295–304.

Landler, M. 2004. Europe reluctantly deciding it has less time for time off. *New York Times,* CLIII (52,903): C1, C2.

Lee, S. and C. Kim. 1999. Understanding tourist motivations across the globe: Perspective on independent and interdependent self-paradigms. 30th Annual Conference Proceedings of the Travel and Tourism Research Association. 51–55.

Leitel, L., and K. Fergus. 2008. "Vacation compression and comprehensive packaging: What are leisure travelers looking for today?" Term paper for Resort Management course, University of Denver's School of Hotel, Restaurant and Tourism Management.

Louden, D. L., and A. J. D. Britta. 1979. *Consumer Behavior: Concepts and Applications.* New York: McGraw-Hill Book Co. 135–139.

Mergoupis, T., and M. Steuer. 1999. "Holiday Taking and Income," Travel and Tourism Programme Discussion Paper, TTP 1/99, CPNSS, LSE.

Mergoupis, T., and M. Steuer. 2000/1. The Economics of holiday consumption: a survey of the empirical literature. 31st Annual Conference Proceedings of the Travel and Tourism Research Association. 79–88.

Mergoupis, T., and M. Steuer. 2000/2. Holiday taking and income. 31st Annual Conference Proceedings of the Travel and Tourism Research Association. 156–163.

Mohsin, A., and C. Ryan. 2004. Determinants of destination choice: The role of socio-demographic variables. *Tourism Recreation Research,* 29 (3): 27–33.

Money, R. B., and J. C. Crotts. 2003. The effect of uncertainty avoidance on information search, planning, and purchases of international travel vacations. *Tourism Management,* 24: 191–202.

Murdy, J., A. Yiannakis, and H. Gibson. 2003. The confounding effects of demographic variables on predicting nature-based tourist roles across the adult life course. *Targeted Research: The Gateway to Accountability.* 34th Annual Proceedings of the Travel and Tourism Research Association. CD-ROM, unpaged.

Nickerson, N. P., M. L. Salcone, and S. R. Aaker. 1995. Life-span travel patterns. 26th Annual Conference Proceedings of the Travel and Tourism Research Association. 406–411.

Nicolau, J. L., and F. J. Mas. 2005. Stochastic Modeling: A three-stage tourist choice process. *Annals of Tourism Research,* 32 (1): 49–69.

(July–August 1990). Nine Forces Reshaping America. *The Futurist.* 9–16.

Pennington-Gray, L. A., and D. L. Kerstetter. 2001. What do university-educated women want from their pleasure travel experience? *Journal of Travel Research,* 40: 49–56.

Peterson, M., and S. L. Lambert. 2003. A demographic perspective on U.S. consumers' out-of-town vacationing and commercial lodging usage while on vacation. *Journal of Travel Research,* 42: 116–124.

Pizam, A., and Y. Mansfeld, (eds.). 1999. *Consumer Behavior in Travel and Tourism.* New York: The Haworth Hospitality Press. 398.

Pizam, A., G.-H. Jeong, A. Reichel, et al. 2004. The relationship between risk-taking, sensation-seeking, and the tourism behavior of young adults: A cross-cultural study. *Journal of Travel Research,* 42: 251–260.

Plog, S. C. 1991. *Leisure Travel Market: Making it a Growth Market . . . Again!* New York: John Wiley & Sons, Inc.

Plog, S. 2002. The power of psychographics and the concept of venturesomeness. *Journal of Travel Research,* 40: 244–251.

Reisinger, Y. 2004. The Influence of Tourist National Culture on the Importance of Destination Attributes. *Measuring the Tourism Experience.* 35th Annual Conference Proceedings of the Travel and Tourism Research Association. CD-ROM, unpaged.

Reisinger, Y., and L. Turner. 1997. Asian and western cultural differences: the new challenges for tourism marketplaces. 28th Annual Conference Proceedings of the Travel and Tourism Research Association. 110–125.

Reisinger, Y., and F. Mavondo. 2004. Modeling psychographic profiles: A study of the U.S. and Australian student travel market. *Journal of Hospitality & Tourism Research*, 28 (1): 60.

Reisinger, Y., and F. Mavondo. 2005. Travel anxiety and intentions to travel internationally: Implications of travel risk perception. *Journal of Travel Research*, 43: 222.

Richard K. Miller and Associates. *The 2007 Leisure Market Research Handbook*, Loganville, GA.

Sakia, M., J. Brown, and J. Mak. 2000. Population aging and Japanese international travel in the 21st century. *Journal of Travel Research*, 38 (3): 212–220.

Schor, J. B. 1991. *The Overworked American: The Unexpected Decline of Leisure*. New York: Basic Books.

Shields, H. 1986. *Cross-Cultural Differences Among International Travelers: A Market Segment Probe*. Paper presented at the 17th Annual Conference of the Travel and Tourism Research Association.

Suh, Y. K., and W. C. Gartner. 2004. Perceptions in international urban tourism: An analysis of travelers to Seoul, Korea. *Journal of Travel Research*, 43: 39–45.

Travel Industry Association of America. 2006. Travel across the Generations, Executive Summary. Washington, DC.

Travel Industry Association of America. 2002. Travel through the Life Stages, Executive Summary. Washington, DC.

U.S. Travel Data Center. 1988. *Highlights of Discover America 2000*. Washington, DC: Travel Industry Association of America. 5–6.

(October 3, 1990). *Wall Street Journal*.

Walters, C. G. 1978. *Consumer Behavior: Theory and Practice*. Homewood, IL: Richard D. Irwin, Inc. 296.

Williams, P. W., and C. Lattey. 1994. Skiing constraints for women. *Journal of Travel Research*, 33 (2): 21–25.

Witt, P. A., and T. L. Goodale. 1981. The relationship between barriers to leisure enjoyment and family stages. *Leisure Sciences*, 4 (1): 29–49.

Zemke, R., C. Raines, and B. Filipczak. 2000. *Generations at Work*. New York: AMACOM.

SURFING SOLUTIONS

http://www.demographics.com/ (*American Demographics*)
http://www.wfs.org/ (World Future Society)
http://www.plogresearch.com/ (Stanley Plog)
http://www.twcrossroads.com/ (*Travel Weekly*)
http://www.tia.org/ (Travel Industry Association of America)

ADDITIONAL READING

"The Cultural Process," G. Hofstede, in *People and Organizations Interacting*, A. Brakel (ed.). John Wiley & Sons, Inc., New York, NY, 1985.

Leisure Policies in Europe, P. Bramham, I. P. Henry, H. Mommass, and H. van der Poel (eds.). University of Arizona Press, 1230 North Park Avenue, Tucson, AZ 85719, 1993.

Managing Cultural Differences, P. R. Harris, and R. T. Moran, Gulf Publishing Company, 1985.

Sociology of Leisure, J. Dumzedier, Elsevier Scientific Publishing Company, 1974.

World Class Service, G. W. Shames, and W. G. Glover, Intercultural Press, Inc., Yarmouth, Maine, 1989.

PART THREE

Demand

THE FACTORS INFLUENCING THE MARKET

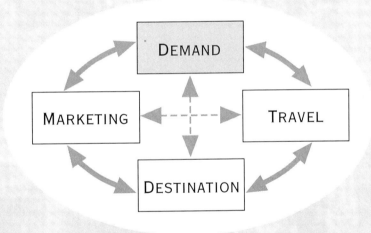

The marketing done by a destination area attempts to influence demand. However, travelers are influenced by many other internal and external factors. Part Three of *The Tourism System* examines these internal and external factors including needs, wants, and motives, perceptions and images, information sources, socioeconomic and family characteristics. It also looks at how people make travel decisions and how they select travel destinations.

chapter 11

Why Do People Take Vacations?

NEEDS, WANTS, AND MOTIVATION

Once the travel bug bites there is no known antidote,
and I know that I shall be happily infected until the end of my life.

Michael Palin

PURPOSE

Based upon an understanding of what motivates people to travel, students will be able to suggest vacation products and communications that will appeal to tourist needs and wants.

LEARNING OBJECTIVES

- ✓ Realize that the key to understanding why people travel is to view travel as a satisfier of needs and wants.
- ✓ Explain, and give appropriate examples of, the role of travel marketers in motivating people to take vacations.
- ✓ Suggest strategies to combat people's given reasons for not taking vacations.
- ✓ Describe how past vacation experiences influence future vacation decisions.

OVERVIEW

The reasons people give for taking vacations are insufficient to explain their travel motivations. In order to market to potential visitors and to serve them at their destinations, it is essential to understand the underlying needs that visitors wish to satisfy when considering a vacation. Vacation behavior is, in fact, determined by such things as motivation, perception, learning, and attitudes—factors that are themselves influenced by personality, culture, and society.

This chapter explores tourism as a satisfier of needs and wants. The relationship between lists in travel literature showing reasons for pleasure travel and Maslow's hierarchy of needs is developed.

Some people hypothesize that people travel if they have learned that travel for a particular reason will help satisfy various needs and wants considered important to them, and if they perceive that, then their needs and wants will be satisfied within the constraints of such things as time, money, and social pressure.

IMPORTANCE OF MOTIVATION

Why do people take vacations? A variety of studies report that tourists travel, for example, to view scenery, to learn about other cultures, or to visit friends and relatives. One study identifies five classes of tourist motives (Bansal and Eiselt, 2004):

1. Climate/atmosphere/environment
2. Relaxation/having a good time
3. Adventure/something new/novelty/curiosity/a desire to experience something firsthand
4. Personal reason, including VFR and prestige
5. Educational, including seeing other cultures, how others live, particular sights

Another study of the "Ideal American Vacation Trip" identifies eight motivational groups:

- Experientials—Enthusiastic travelers interested in a variety of activities that let them immerse themselves in other cultures
- Family focused—Desire to travel more with family members
- Casual travelers—Seeking rest and relaxation
- Trail blazers—Outdoor enthusiasts seeking to connect with nature
- Reconnectors—Interested in rest and relaxation and time with spouse or significant other
- Affluentials—Seeking relaxation, adventure, and luxury
- Back to basics—Frugal travelers looking for rest and relaxation
- Quintessential travelers—Highly motivated by experiences, socializing, and adventure

It is suggested that tourists seek destinations which provide an optimal balance of familiarity-strangeness, stimulation-tranquility, and structure-independence. Familiarity-Strangeness is defined as the degree of similarity/dissimilarity with home culture; Stimulation-Tranquility as the physical or spiritual stimulation versus getting away from it all; and Structure-Independence as the amount of planning involved in order to travel. Along these lines, it has been shown that independent travelers are willing to take risks in selecting vacation alternatives; want to experience the unplanned; and are comfortable with a travel itinerary that seems to just "evolve" compared to being rigidly planned out (Hyde and Lawson, 2003).

This approach to understanding motivation is insufficient for three reasons. First, the visitors themselves may be unaware of the true reasons behind their travel behavior. Individuals are often unaware of the real reasons for doing certain things. A person leaving for a tennis vacation may see the trip as simply a reason to play tennis. When questioned, however, the traveler may reveal that a concern for his or her health prompted the trip. Secondly, a person may not wish to divulge the real reason or motivation behind the trip. For instance, much of the literature mentions "status" as a motivator, yet many travelers will not feel comfortable admitting that a major reason for taking a vacation is that they will be able to impress their friends upon their return home. A third reason that such lists are insufficient for explaining consumer motivations is that they concentrate on selling the product, the stated reason for the trip, rather than on satisfying the needs of the market. But the development of such lists is a necessary first step toward establishing a clas-

> Often I go to some distant region of the world to be reminded of who I really am. There is no mystery about why this should be so. Stripped of your ordinary surroundings, your friends, your daily routines . . . you are forced into direct experience. Such direct experience inevitably makes you aware of who it is that is having the experience. That is not always comfortable, but it is always invigorating.
>
> Michael Crichton, 1988

sification system that will enable us to understand and ultimately predict the visitor's decision-making process.

Dann (1977) noted two stages in a travel decision: *push factors* and *pull factors*. Push factors are internal to the individual, install a *desire* for travel, and are aimed at satisfying various psychological needs. Pull factors are external to the individual, stress benefits of particular destinations, and determine where, when, and how that person vacations. Thus push factors must be present before pull factors can be effective.

It appears that push factors determine *whether* to go, while pull factors determine *where* to go (Lee et al., 2002). A study of Arizona visitors examines the pull factors or destination drivers for that state (Andereck and Knopf, 2004). Cluster analysis indicates the luxury cluster (33 percent) are heavily motivated by climate and such things as resorts/spas, golf, and/or shopping; the nature cluster (29 percent) are primarily motivated by the Grand Canyon and other natural features; the historic/cultural cluster (21 percent); and the indeterminate cluster (18 percent) included respondents who are not primarily motivated by any of the predetermined destination drivers.

Tourists travel to a destination if the benefits offered by the destination (pull factors) are perceived to satisfy the needs of the tourist (Goossens, 2000). To the extent that the destination satisfies these needs the tourist demonstrates loyalty to that destination by coming back to visit and recommending the destination to others (Yoon and Uysal, 2005).

Crompton (1979) identified seven push motives and two pull factors. The push factors were only identified after an in-depth interview. (This gives further support to the argument that visitors may be unaware of what motivates them.) They are escape from a mundane environment; exploration and evaluation of self; relaxation; prestige; regression; enhancement of kinship relationships; and facilitation of social interaction. The pull factors are novelty and education.

It has been shown that a pull factor can satisfy various motivation or push factors (Klenosky, 2002). The study in question showed how a pull factor—a beach—could provide opportunities for (in this case, students on spring break) meeting people and socializing; getting some sun in order to look good and, thereby feel good about oneself; or to enjoy escape and return feeling recharged. A destination seeking to appeal to this segment of the market can plan promotional messages using the beach as the attraction and varying the message to conform to the different motivations of the target.

QUICK TRIP 11.1

What's It Worth?

An eighteen hour and forty-five minute flight from New York to Singapore releases eighty-six hundred pounds of carbon emissions per person. Hannah Karp of *The Wall Street Journal* reports that the average annual carbon emissions for Americans are twenty-six tons. This leads Americans to wonder why they are traveling to see the world if they are compromising its existence in the process. Traveler Nina Williams missed her sister's wedding in September 2008 because she believed so deeply in the environmental issues that traveling entails. Another traveler, Ms. Astyk, has stopped buying her father plane tickets to see his grandchildren. Many Americans have decided to cut down or give up leisure travel entirely because of its impact on global warming. Taking time off of work to relax at home only releases sixty-eight pounds of carbon emissions per day. Environmentally conscience Americans cannot justify leisure travel if it results in the destruction of the earth.

However, taking time off to see family members and being present at important family functions are still very important to most people. The environmental impacts are often set aside because family takes precedence over issues concerning carbon emissions and global warming. How might a person who is concerned about these problems deal with the desire to travel to see family members? If people care about the environment just as deeply as the reason behind their travel, how are they supposed to decide if they should stay or go?

THINK ABOUT THIS:

1. The guest may be able to compromise and still consider the environment without making the decision not to travel to see friends and family. What programs would you implement in your hotel in order to reduce the negative environmental impacts?

2. How could this help travelers feel that they can still claim to be "green" even though they travel?

Sources:

Karp, H. 2008. "The Stay-at-Home Vacation." *The Wall Street Journal.* W3.

Travel Tolls: The Carbon Impact of Various Trips, with the Starting Point New York.

Virgin Atlantic, Environmental Protection Agency. 2008. 1. http://online.wjs.com/media/NoTrav_WSJ121708.gif.

There is some indication that the relative importance of push and pull factors varies by culture. In one study (Yuan and McDonald, 1990) a comparison was made of tourists from four countries: the United Kingdom, Japan, France, and Germany. It was found that both the motivation to travel (push factors) and the specific destination chosen (pull factors) were a product of the culture tourists were from. While the rankings between the motivation factors are similar—novelty and escape are ranked one and two for all four segments—the level of importance attached to the factors varies somewhat. Tourists from France and the United Kingdom give it more importance than do those from Japan and Germany. This suggests that the stress placed on this factor should vary depending upon the country being marketed to. In terms of the pull factors, the rankings for tourists from the United Kingdom and Japan are the same. However, several differences are evident in looking at responses of people from the other countries. For example, those from West Germany place less importance on culture and history while respondents from France find ease of travel to be of less importance.

The relationship between push and pull factors has also been demonstrated in Islamic and Arabic cultures where, in one study, the most important push and pull factors for Saudi tourists are cultural value and religious (Bogari, Crowther, and Marr, 2004).

Another study comparing U.K. and Japanese long-haul travelers found that there is significant variation by culture on both "push" and "pull" factors (You et al., 2000). The three most important 'pull' factors for U.K. travelers are personal safety, see people from a number of ethnic backgrounds or nationalities, and standards of hygiene and cleanliness. The top three for Japanese travelers are outstanding scenery, historical or archaeological buildings and places, and nice weather.

U.K. travelers viewed the following "push" factors, among others, as being more important than did Japanese travelers:

- Knowledge enhancement about places, people, and things
- Getting away from the demands of home
- Being together as a family
- Escaping from the ordinary
- Finding thrills and excitement

> *Seventy-two hours seems to be the maximum time people can stay together without friction developing.*
>
> Dr. Joyce Brothers, quoted in The New York Times

TRAVEL AS A NEED/WANT SATISFIER

The key to understanding tourist motivation is to see vacation travel as a satisfier of needs and wants. Tourists do not take vacations just to relax and have fun, experience another culture, or educate themselves and their children. They take vacations in the hope and belief that these vacations will satisfy, either wholly or partially, various needs and wants. This view of tourist motivations is critical. It is the difference between seeing a destination as a collection of palm trees and hotel rooms for the tourist and seeing it as a means for satisfying what is important to tourists. It is the difference between those travel agents who see themselves as sellers of airline seats and those who view themselves as dealers in dreams.

A MODEL OF BUYER BEHAVIOR

Several researchers have suggested that tourism managers do not make sufficient use of buyer behavior models to assist them in understanding how and why people make vacation purchase decisions. The advantage of such a model is that it helps managers approach the task of influencing vacation behavior in a systematic, focused manner. One useful model is that outlined in figure 11.1. The model suggests that stimuli internal to the individual relating to needs and wants is the beginning of the process. Based on external stimuli the potential traveler is aware (or not) of possible destinations. Destination possibilities are then evaluated as to their viability. Travel to that destination is likely if the traveler

Tourists take vacations with the hope and belief the vacation will satisfy, either wholly or in part, various needs and wants. © 2009 Paul Clarke. Used under license from Shutterstock, Inc.

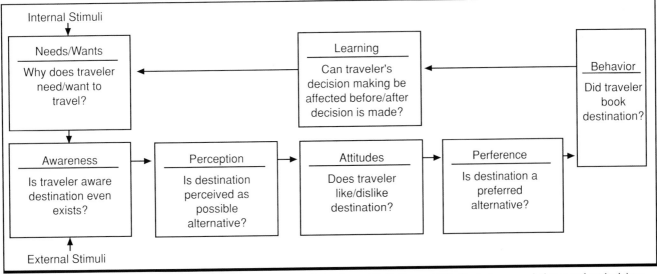

Figure 11.1 Buyer Behavior Model. Source: Baker, K. G., G. C. Hozier, Jr., and R. D. Rogers. 1994. Marketing research theory and methodology and the tourism industry: A nontechnical discussion. *Journal of Travel Research*, 32 (3): 5.

likes the destination and develops a preference for it. As a result of the trip the traveler learns whether or not that experience did, indeed, satisfy the needs and wants previously identified.

> *We used to fly airplanes;*
> *Now we fly people.*
> Jan Lapidoth, SAS

NEEDS, WANTS, AND MOTIVES

A description of the process begins with a consideration of the needs of an individual. When an individual takes a trip, buys a cruise, or rents a cabin, the action is done in hopes of satisfying some *need* of which he or she may only be partially aware. We could provide a better service if we could identify which need or needs the individual is attempting to satisfy. McClelland has suggested that individuals are motivated by the need for achievement, affiliation, or power. Strong relationships have been demonstrated between the need for achievement and adventure tourism and the need for affiliation and cultural tourism (Tran and Ralston, 2006).

A business is not interested so much in a person's needs as in how that person seeks to satisfy those needs. The difference between a need and a *want* is one of awareness. It is the task of the people in marketing to transform needs into wants by making the individual aware of his or her need deficiencies.

A person needs affection, but wants to visit friends and relatives; needs esteem from others, but wants a Mediterranean cruise. In these and other situations people can be made aware through advertisements, for example, that the purchase of an airline ticket to visit parents will result in feelings of love and affection for them, thereby helping satisfy that need.

Although a person may want satisfaction for a need or needs, no action will be taken until that person is motivated.

Motivation occurs when an individual wants to satisfy a need. A motive implies action; an individual is moved to do something. Motivation theories indicate that an individual constantly strives to achieve a state of stability—a *homeostasis*. An individual's homeostasis is disrupted when she or he is made aware of a need deficiency. This awareness creates wants. For the individual to be motivated to satisfy a need, an *objective* must be present. The individual must be aware of a product or service and must perceive the purchase of that product or service as having a positive effect on satisfying the need of which she or he is now aware. Then, and only then, will the individual be motivated to buy. Again, it is the goal of marketing to suggest objectives—cruises, flights, or vacations—to satisfy needs, an awareness of which has already been created. (This process is outlined in figure 11.2.) For example, several years ago an advertisement ran in the Scottish papers showing two little girls with one saying. "Guess

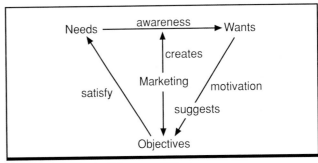

Figure 11.2 Needs, Wants, and Motives.

Discovering Home

I now feel that my once very diffuse cultural identity has been replaced by a much stronger appreciation for my Italian roots.

Alex Catanese

Alex Catanese discovered his Italian roots during a ten-week excursion to Italy. In an article written through Student-Traveler.com, Catanese discusses the importance of finding another home while abroad. He states, "During my stay, I came to feel more like an insider rather than a tourist because I was establishing relationships instead of just passing through." Home may be a place someone has never been. It could be the action of grazing your fingertips along the surface of the Tyrrhenian Sea as the tide is brought forth that invokes the feelings of belonging. It may be the opening of a door and the aroma of homemade bread that greets you as you enter timidly, finding comfort in a place that you only now are seeing for the first time, but has been there all along. As a travel marketer, it is imperative to motivate travelers to take vacations that do not end once they reach their homes and reflect back on the time spent away. They must encourage travel because the experience to be gained is invaluable. It cannot be measured by any currency or length of time. Alex Catanese does not comment on the amount of money he spent, the frustration of a language barrier, or the discomfort of coach travel during the long plane ride to his destination. Instead, he focuses on his deepened understanding of his cultural identity.

THINK ABOUT THIS:

1. It may be possible to write letters to family members abroad and read a text book about the area of your cultural roots. How, as a travel marketer, would you promote the importance of finding one's cultural roots through the act of traveling?

Source: Catanese, A. 2008. Finding Your Roots Abroad: Discovering "Tipicamente Siciliano." *Student Traveler.* 1–2. Retrieved February 2008, http://www.studenttraveler.com/mod-Pagesetter-viewpub-tid-10002-pid-351.html.

what? Next month Grandma and Grandpa are visiting us—from Scotland." The advertisement was promoting flights from Scotland to Canada. It managed to say (between the lines), "We know you love your grandchildren (a need). By showing you this picture we have made you aware of that (a want). By visiting them (an objective) you will satisfy that need for love." In such a way grandparents are motivated to fly to Canada.

Behavior is influenced by a number of things, with motives being only one. We cannot even specify that an individual is motivated at any one time by only one motive. It is important, as we discuss needs and motives individually, to bear in mind that behavior results from the interaction of various motives, one of which may be dominant at any one time as well as interacting with various other socioeconomic and psychographic factors.

Motives may be *specific* or *general*. A general motive would be the end objective, and a specific motive would be a means to reach that end objective. For example, a person may be motivated to take a spa vacation. This,

however, may be no more than an indicator or a more general motive, that of good health. Viewed in this way, it can be seen that good health can be achieved by means other than taking a vacation. We are in competition not only with the next destination, but also with other activities for the consumers' time and money. Although a vacation represents a break from routine for many, that same feeling can also be obtained from decorating the house or laying out a garden. The marketing task is to convince an individual that the purchase of whatever we are selling is the best, if not the only, way of satisfying that need. To the extent that we are successful in accomplishing this, an individual will be motivated to buy.

MASLOW'S NEED THEORY AND TRAVEL MOTIVATIONS. A study of the travel literature indicates that travel motivations can fit into Maslow's hierarchy of needs model. Maslow proposed the following listing of needs arranged in a hierarchy:

1. Survival–hunger, thirst, rest, activity
2. Safety–security, freedom from fear and anxiety
3. Belonging and love–affection, giving and receiving love
4. Esteem–self-esteem and esteem from others
5. Self-actualization–personal self-fulfillment

This hierarchy suggests that lower-level needs demand more immediate attention and satisfaction before a person turns to the satisfaction of higher-level needs. It might be better to think of the hierarchy as a series of nested triangles (see figure 11.3). This representation emphasizes the fact that higher-level needs encompass all lower-level needs. It also illustrates the relative value size of each need better.

There is some indication that the motivation to travel changes with the amount of travel experience that tourists have–the so-called "career ladder" approach (Pearce and Lee, 2005). It may be that less-experienced travelers are motivated by such things as the need for stimulation, personal development and relationships while more experienced tourists are motivated by the desire to experience different cultures and being close to nature. This model will be explored in more detail later in this chapter.

It should be noted that Maslow's model has been criticized on the grounds that the original work was part of a clinical experiment rather than as the foundation for a theory of motivation. Maslow himself expressed some concerns about his own findings. Be that as it may, the fact is that it does seem to explain *why* people vacation. For example, Fakeye and Crompton (1992) identified the following motives for visitors to the Rio Grande Valley of Texas:

Factor 1 Escape from personal, physical, and social problems

Factor 2 Social contacts

Factor 3 Physical self, and intellectual enrichment

Factor 4 Family togetherness and curiosity

Factor 5 Temperature, exploration, and security

These factors seem to mirror Maslow's original list.

In one study comparing Anglo-Americans and Japanese tourists, the two groups differ in the importance of prestige/status, family togetherness, and novelty

QUICK TRIP 11.3

Safety First

When choosing a vacation destination, safety is a primary concern. High crime rates in Mexico may discourage travelers from booking a flight and securing a room. Peter Tarlow, president of Tourism and More Consulting, advises clients against traveling to Mexico, especially Mexico City, because of high kidnapping rates. However, the director of the strategic unit of the Mexico Tourist Board in Washington, Eduardo Chaillo, says that programs have been implemented to reduce the fear of crime in Mexico. A tourism patrol of five hundred to eight hundred green vehicles known as "Green Angels" is available to help tourists on the road. Furthermore, a consumer-protected agency called Profeco is meant to protect visitors on site. He believes that crime in Mexico is no reason not to travel there. From his viewpoint, Mexico City is just like any other big city. It is important for visitors to be aware of possible crime while agencies at all levels of security do everything they can to prevent it.

Unfortunately, crime in most destination areas is not controllable by hotel managers. They cannot assure travelers that between the time they leave the airport and enter the hotel grounds they will not be victims of crime. However, they can control what happens within their facilities.

THINK ABOUT IT:

1. How can property managers design programs to help visitors feel safe when traveling around the local area surrounding the hotel?

2. How can security be assured within and around the hotel?

Source: Godwin, N. 2008. Safety Concerns for Mexico Tourists. *Travel Weekly*. 1–3. Retrieved February 2008, http://www.travelweekly.com/article.

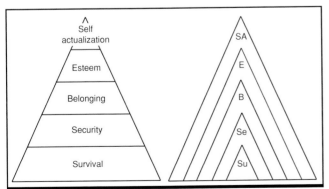

Figure 11.3 Maslow's Hierarchy of Needs. Source: Mitchell, A. 1979. Social Change: Implications of Trends in Values and Lifestyles. VALS Report No. 3.

while there are insignificant differences in knowledge and escape. Japanese tourists show more interdependent characteristics in their travel motivations while Anglo-Americans show more independent characteristics (Lee and Kim, 1999).

Although Maslow's first need listed is *physical*, the other four are *psychological*. To this original list two intellectual words were added:

To know and understand–acquiring knowledge

Aesthetics–appreciation of beauty

The relationship between the physical, psychological, and *intellectual* needs is unclear. It is thought that the intellectual needs exist independently of the others.

Beach and Ragheb (Beach and Ragheb, 1983) used the work of Maslow to divide motivators into the following four types:

1. **Intellectual component:** Extent to which individuals are motivated by such mental activities as learning, exploring, discovery, thought, or imagery
2. **Social component:** Extent to which individuals are motivated by such things as the need for friendship and inter-personal relationships, or the need for the esteem of others
3. **Competence-mastery component:** Extent to which individuals are motivated by such things as the need to achieve, master, challenge, and compete
4. **Stimulus-avoidance component:** Extent to which individuals are motivated by such things as avoiding social contact, seeking solitude, resting and unwinding

The relationship between needs, motives, and references from the tourism literature is shown in table 11.1. Those who say they travel to escape or to relieve tension can be seen as seeking to satisfy the basic survival or physiological need. Such motivation may be for physical or mental relaxation. Vacationers often return from a trip physically exhausted but mentally refreshed. Although there seems to be a difference between those people who take an active vacation and those who opt for a passive vacation, both are motivated by a need for tension reduction.

Passive vacationers are seen as achieving tension relief by giving in or submitting to the surrounding environment. From this submission comes the very relief of tension that will result in their returning refreshed and renewed. The overworked factory worker may relax by lying on a beach for two weeks. The active vacationer achieves tension reduction through physical activity.

The activity can also be seen as being related to achievement and mastery of the environment and, as such, being related to the need for self-esteem. Some people who have jobs that are not physically demanding compensate by engaging in physical activity when on vacation. This illustrates the point made earlier that, at any one time, one may be motivated to satisfy more than one need.

Traveling for reasons of health can be interpreted as a way of attempting to satisfy one's safety needs. By taking care of the body and/or mind, we are protecting ourselves and helping ensure our own longevity. Visits to spas can be seen in this light. Several references specifically link recreation and health, implying a relationship between the two. Some researchers have suggested that travel marketers have a particular responsibility when it comes to selling health as a motivation to travel. They cite Kotler's definition of societal marketing which "holds that the organization's task is to determine the needs, wants and interests of target markets and to deliver the desired satisfactions more effectively and efficiently than competitors in a way that preserves or enhances the consumer's and society's well-being" (1984). Given increased awareness of the relationship between sunbathing and skin cancer; of the impact of tourism development on the environment; and of the spread of AIDS, can and should tourism managers continue to promote the traditional tenets of Sun, Sand, Sea, and Sex?

Hobson and Dietrich (1994) suggest that the challenge is to "create a new image representing health, wealth, and leisure along with different activities which do not promote excessive sun exposure and its inherent dangers to the health of the individual . . . to bring attention to tourists an awareness of the health issues that are faced when traveling . . . showing destination areas

The active vacationer reduces tension through physical activity.

Table 11.1
Maslow's Needs and Motivations Listed in Travel Literature

Need	Motive	Tourism Literature Reference
Physiological	Relaxation	Escape Relaxation Relief of tension Sunlust Physical Mental relaxation of tension
Safety	Security	Health Recreation Keeping oneself active and healthy for the future
Belonging	Love	Family togetherness Enhancement of kinship relationships Companionship Facilitation of social interaction Maintenance of personal ties Interpersonal relations Roots Ethnic Show one's affection for family members Maintain social contacts
Esteem	Achievement	Convince oneself of one's achievements Status Show one's importance to others Prestige Social recognition Ego-enhancement Professional/business Status and prestige
Self-actualization	Be true to one's self	Exploration and evaluation of nature Self-discovery Satisfaction of inner desires
To know and understand	Knowledge	Cultural Education Wanderlust Interest in foreign areas
Aesthetics	Appreciation of beauty	Environmental Scenery

that environmental damage which leads to health hazards will result in long-term business failure." They go on to suggest that promoting legal, supervised brothels might limit the health risk to both tourist and provider.

The need for belonging and love relates to the desire for affection, for both giving and receiving love. The organized tour is often mentioned as a method of encouraging and satisfying this need for companionship and social interaction.

This motivation is frequently referred to as the VFR market: visit friends and relatives. Part of this is the ethnic roots market—the desire to visit the homeland or previous residence of oneself or one's ancestors. This segment of the market tends to fall into two groups. First, there are those who were born somewhere else and desire to return to their own homeland. Second, there are

those in later generations who wish to experience the land of their ancestors. For the people in the first segment of the market, the desire is to see people and things and to relive experiences as they are remembered. This desire to recapture previous experiences means that these tourists are willing to adjust to the conditions of the destination visited. They are there, after all, to enjoy again what they remembered from their past. Inconveniences of the homeland can be tolerated. At the same time, however, people in this market segment may have little economic impact on the destination because of the tendency to stay with friends and relatives. Later generations will have the slightly different desire to experience vicariously the land of one's ancestors; however, because the personal experience of one's roots is missing and has been replaced by standards of living learned in

Please Come Again

Vietnam has encountered a variety of political, economic, and social changes that have discouraged vacation travel to the area since the end of the Vietnam War in 1975. The nearly collapsed economy of the country devastated the area and stifled tourism. Connie Mok and Terry Lam wrote an article titled "Hotel and Tourism Development in Vietnam," which discusses the issues surrounding negative experiences guests have had in the past and may still encounter. Vietnam's entry into ASEAN (1995) and its re-established diplomatic relations with the United States is expected to boost tourism. However, the article indicates that even though Vietnam has potential for tourism, ". . . the poor infrastructure, lax legal systems, the lack of accommodation facilities of international standard, and inadequate skilled workers and qualified management people" have caused and will continue to cause a variety of issues for travelers.

In 1993, it was reported that of the 10,500 hotel rooms available in Vietnam, only 4,000 met international standards. The huge boost in tourism has caused hotel development of international hotel rooms to be lax, lacking proper strategic planning. An over-supply of hotels in certain areas is hurting the local economy rather than helping. To add to the trouble, the article mentions, "Domestic air travel is operated mainly by Vietnam Airlines, but the aircraft are old and poorly maintained." Even so, it is projected that by 2010 nine million visitors will travel to Vietnam.

If tourists are dissatisfied with their visit because of the issues surrounding tourism in Vietnam, it could be a huge problem for hotel developers who have quickly responded to the tourism boost based on the projected numbers. Mok and Lam believe that among many solutions necessary to change the attitudes of tourists who visit the area, "Externally, strategic marketing planning and promotion activities are required to improve Vietnam's public image and expand its international market share." Vietnam has great potential in the hospitality industry if it is able to meet the standards necessary to encourage people to come back again, and tell their friends to visit too.

THINK ABOUT THIS:

1. A guest's past experiences have a major effect on their future decisions to travel to the same location twice. If you recently were given a job as a hotel manager in Vietnam, what would be your primary concerns for meeting American standards?

2. How would you encourage guests to come back with friends and family to experience Vietnam in a way that is the most comfortable and enjoyable for them?

Source: Mok, C., and T. Lam. 1998. Hotel and Tourism Development in Vietnam. *Ideas and Trends Hotel Online.* Retrieved March 2008.

---

one's country of birth, it is these accustomed standards of living that are taken on the journey for one's roots. Therefore, living standards are expected to be comparable to those experienced at home. At the same time, however, this segment of the market tends to have a greater impact on the economy if lodging and meals are taken in hotels instead of with family.

Maslow's concept of the need for esteem breaks down into two components: that of *self-esteem* and that of esteem from others. The idea of self-esteem is embodied in such ideas as the need to exhibit strength, achievement, mastery, competence, and independence. This might explain why people take whitewater rafting trips. Esteem from others is explained by such concepts as reputation, prestige, status, and recognition. Travel can certainly boost one's ego, both at the destination and upon one's return. It may be that as people grow older,

their status in society declines. Travel is one way to enhance that status.

Self-actualization can, in fact, be considered the end or goal of leisure. Leisure is the state of being free from the urgent demands of lower-level needs. Vacations offer an opportunity to reevaluate and discover more about the self, to act out one's self-image as a way of modifying or correcting it.

The need to know and understand can be viewed in light of the desire for knowledge. Many people travel to learn of others' cultures. It is also true that contact with people of another culture offers an opportunity to discover one's own culture. This same concept has also been expressed as a motivation for education, wanderlust, and interest in foreign parts. The need for aesthetics is seen in those who travel for environmental reasons—to view the scenery.

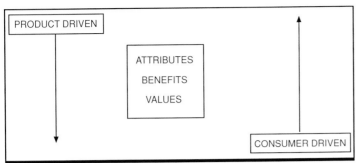

Figure 11.4 Product-Driven vs. Consumer-Driven Approaches.
Source: Cameron, B. 1992. Creative Destinations: Marketing and Packaging:
Who Wants What and Why? An Overview of the Canadian Pleasure Market
Study. 21st Annual Conference Proceedings of the Travel and Tourism
Research Association. 160.

In the words of one researcher, "Any product or service can be broken down into what it is, what it does, and what people get from it" (Cameron, 1992). A product-driven approach is to talk about the attributes, then the benefits, and finally the values. In a consumer-driven approach you start with the values and lead up through the benefits to the attributes (see figure 11.4). Using the Yukon as an example (figure 11.5), the product-driven approach would begin by stressing the attributes of the Yukon: wilderness and history. Messages would then point out the benefits to be gained from these attributes: get away, learn and reconnect with nature. Finally, the values to be gained would be mentioned: discover yourself and explore and grow.

People see vacations as a way of escaping from everyday life rather than as a way of seeking pleasure. © 2009 Rostislav Glinsky. Used under license from Shutterstock, Inc.

The better consumer-driven approach would lead with the values, suggesting the need to discover yourself, explore, and grow. The message would continue by pointing out the benefits to be gained and finally suggest that the wilderness and history of the Yukon is the place to do this.

The traveler, then, is better understood and better appealed to if he or she is recognized as a person consuming products and services. Seeing the traveler in this manner will result in a change of attitude on the part of the observer and enable the marketer to provide a better product or service to the traveler. A second, more tangible benefit to be gained from this approach relates to the idea of prepotency. If one accepts Maslow's idea of *prepotency*—that lower-level needs should be satisfied to some extent before the satisfaction of higher-level needs becomes a concern—we would expect that products and services, including vacations, which are targeted toward the satisfaction of lower-level needs, would be regarded as more of a necessity than a luxury and would, as such, be more resilient to external pressures of time and money.

A number of authors, in fact, have demonstrated that the need to escape (related to the physiological need) is the strongest travel motivation. The importance of "escape" motives continues to be demonstrated by a number of researchers (Hanefores and Mossberg, 1997).

People see vacations as a way of escaping from everyday life rather than as a way of seeking pleasure. It has been suggested that the two motivational factors simultaneously influence the leisure behavior of individuals. Leisure activities are sought because they allow individuals to escape from personal or interpersonal problems. Personal escape items might be such things as (Snepenger, 2006, p. 142):

- To get away from my normal environment
- To have a change in pace from my everyday life
- To overcome a bad mood

Interpersonal escape items can include such things as:

Figure 11.5 Product-Driven vs. Consumer-Driven Approaches: The Yukon Example. Source: Cameron, B. 1992. Creative Destinations: Marketing and Packaging: Who Wants What and Why? An Overview of the Canadian Pleasure Market Study. 21st Annual Conference Proceedings of the Travel and Tourism Research Association. 161.

- To avoid people who annoy me
- To get away from a stressful social environment
- To avoid interactions with others

At the same time people are seeking psychological rewards from participating in leisure activities. These rewards can be personal (to tell others about my experiences, to feel good about myself, to experience new things by myself) or interpersonal (to be with people of similar interests, to bring friends/family closer, to meet new people). The model is illustrated in figure 11.6. The unequal length of the lines indicates the fact that the desire to escape from personal or impersonal environments is greater than the desire to seek personal or impersonal rewards. This has practical implications for tourism businesses. Support for using the Iso-Ahola model as a means of segmenting a market has been demonstrated (Norman and Carlson, 1999; Snepenger et al., 2006).

It would suggest that promoting the need to escape, and getaway vacations, would be particularly effective in triggering the need to travel. It also suggests that the destination is less important than the need to escape. This makes it more difficult to sell the differentiating qualities of a particular destination.

Another model that is worthy of discussion here is Pearce's *Travel Career Ladder* (Kim, Pearce, Morrison, and O'Leary, 1996). This model, which is based on

> *What gives value to travel is fear. It is the fact that, at a certain moment, when we are so far from our own home country . . . we are seized by a vague fear, and the instinctive desire to go back to the protection of the old habits. This is the most obvious benefit of travel. . . . This is why we should not say that we travel for pleasure. There is no pleasure in traveling, and I look upon it as an occasion for spiritual testing. . . . Travel, which is like a greater and graver science, brings us back to ourselves.*
>
> Albert Camus, (1963)

Maslow's Hierarchy of Needs theory, argues that each person has a "travel career" just as they have a "work career." The five levels of the Travel Career Ladder are (figure 11.7):

1. Relaxation
2. Stimulation
3. Relationship
4. Self-esteem and development
5. Fulfillment

There are two sides of the ladder: The left side represents self-directed motivations, and the right is other-directed motivations. People start their travel careers at different levels and may change their levels during their travel careers. Some people "ascend" the ladder predominantly on the left side. Others may go through all the steps on both sides of the ladder. The main point that Pearce's career ladder emphasizes is that people's travel decisions and decision-making processes are not static; they change over a person's lifetime based upon their actual travel experiences. For example, the more experienced travelers become, the more they will act on higher-level needs in the ladder such as fulfillment, self-esteem, and development.

WHY TRAVEL?

We have said that an individual's needs—for safety, for belonging, and so on—can be satisfied by setting different objectives or by taking certain actions. What determines how an individual will seek to satisfy a need? It is proposed that an individual is motivated to satisfy a particular need in a particular way (by taking a vacation, for example) based upon three factors. First, the vacation will be taken if the individual *perceives* that the vacation will satisfy a need important to her. If she feels that taking a cruise will result in her returning relaxed and refreshed, and if it is important to her that

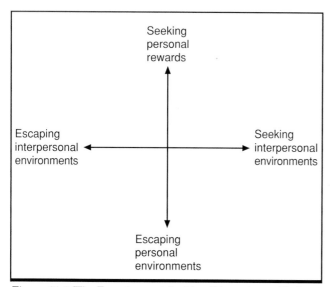

Figure 11.6 The Escaping and Seeking Dimensions of Leisure Motivation. Adapted from: Iso-Ahola, S. E. 1984. Social Psychological Foundations of Leisure and Resultant Implications for Leisure Counseling. In *Leisure Counseling: Concepts and Applications*, E. T. Dowd (ed.). Springfield, IL: Charles C. Thomas. 111.

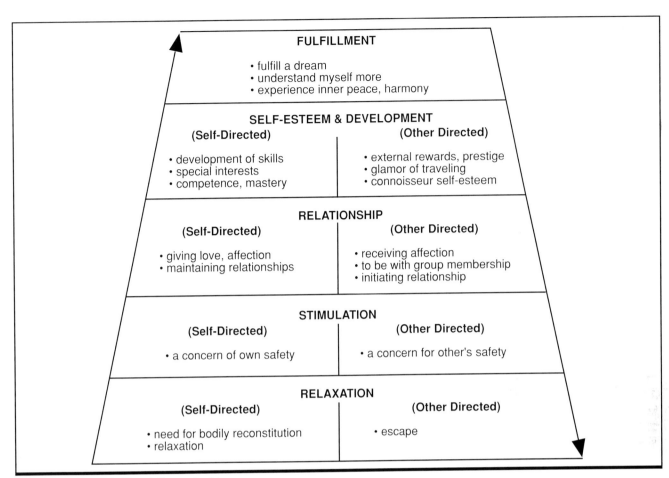

Figure 11.7 Pearce's Travel Career Ladder.

she do something to relax and refresh herself, then she is more likely to take that cruise. (Perception and image is covered in chapter 12.) Second, a particular action will be taken if the individual has *learned* that action will satisfy that need. If she has taken a cruise that has resulted in her returning home refreshed, she will be more inclined to take it again. Third, the decision as to what action to take in order to satisfy a need must be taken within the limitations of the individual's external environment. She may perceive that a cruise will satisfy her need, she may have learned that a cruise will satisfy her need, but if she does not have sufficient time or money or there are strong social or cultural factors that inhibit this option, she may not be able to take the cruise. The effect of the external environment on the individual's decision-making process was considered in chapter 10.

TOURIST'S LEARNING PROCESS

An individual will purchase a specific vacation package or trip if he has learned that the purchase will help satisfy an important need. This process is illustrated in figure 11.8. The tourist weighs various alternatives against a list of criteria important to him to determine which alternatives are most likely to satisfy a particular motive. The inclination that results will have an effect upon the "fit" between motives and alternatives–how well a chosen alternative will meet the motivation. Travelers have a low upper limit on the number of destinations that they perceive they may visit within a specified time period. Most travelers have identified seven or fewer destinations that they list as alternatives. The number of alternatives will vary relative to the characteristics of the travelers. Travelers who have previously visited foreign destinations have a larger number of destinations likely to be visited. Whether or not a destination will be included as an alternative depends in great part upon whether or not a destination has previously satisfied the individual. The level of satisfaction is a function of one's expectations of a situation and one's perception of the actual situation. If the level of expectation is higher than the actual experience, the individual

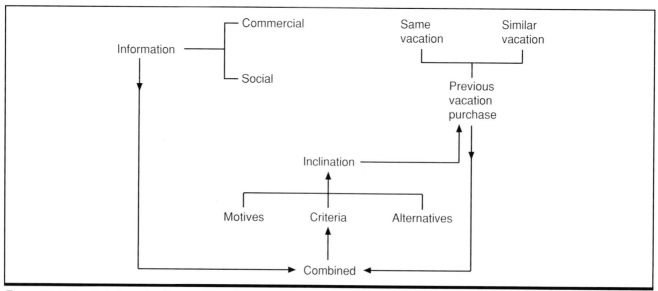

Figure 11.8 Tourist's Learning Process. Adapted from: Howard, J. A., and J. N. Sheth. 1969. *The Theory of Buyer Behavior.* New York: John Wiley & Sons, Inc.

will be dissatisfied. For an individual to be satisfied with a product, service, or situation, the level of actual experience must be equal to or greater than the level of expectation. Tourists can attempt to reduce the psychological risk involved in a purchase by expecting less from the vacation. This, however, is not a popular strategy, especially in travel.

We would expect that as the amount of satisfaction increases, the number of alternatives considered next time decreases. The more an individual is pleased with a vacation choice, the higher that choice will be placed on the list of alternatives, and the fewer will be the other alternatives considered. This places great importance on the level of service given the vacationer to ensure a quality experience and a level of satisfaction that will bring the traveler back. The one exception to this might be the vacation with a high need to know and understand. If this is very important, it may not matter how satisfied he or she is with, for example, a trip to Paris. Having visited that spot, the individual, making the most of limited resources of time and money, may never return to that city.

Serving as a bridge between the motives of an individual and the perceived alternatives are the criteria used for making a decision among those alternatives. A choice is made that the individual believes will produce maximum satisfaction of a need or needs. The criteria used to distinguish between alternatives are learned. These criteria are developed as a result of past experience and from information taken in from either the commercial (business) or social (friends and relatives)

environment. The effect of information on learning will be considered in chapter 12 when we look at the process of perception and image formation.

Learning, based on past experience, can come from having experienced the same thing that is being contemplated or from having experienced something similar. If you stayed in a particular town on vacation and were very satisfied, you learn that visiting that particular town is liable to satisfy you again. Those factors that accounted for your satisfaction—good weather, friendly service—are the criteria by which you determine where to take your next vacation.

On the other hand, by staying at one property of a chain and having a poor experience, you may infer that you would have a similarly poor experience at all properties of that chain and behave accordingly (which, by the way, may not be an accurate representation of what would have happened at another property in the chain). This is known as the psychology of simplification. To make the decision-making process easier, the potential tourist generalizes from what he or she perceives to be similar situations. The more experiences a traveler has, the more firmly established her decision criteria and the easier it is for her to generalize.

The individual moves from what is termed an extensive problem-solving process through a limited problem-solving process to a routine problem-solving process. In the process known as extensive problem-solving, the tourist has little in the way of information or experiences from which to make a decision. The need and, consequently, the search for information is high, and a few decision criteria have been established. We may know what criteria are important to us, but we may be unaware of whether or not they can be satisfied by the various alternatives available. Additionally, as we experience certain destinations or vacations, we may find that the criteria that were important to us previously have become less significant.

Thus, our decision criteria are developed or modified (that is, learned) in great part by our actual experiences. As we become more confident in our decision criteria, decision-making is easier for us. Our experiences, and the resultant generalization from them, are weighed more heavily than any information received. This is due, in part, to the fact that, as our decision criteria are strengthened, our need for information is weakened. Additionally, we have a tendency to filter incoming information so that it will support and reinforce our decisions. This is explored further in chapter 12. This progression leads to a routine problem-solving process whereby little or no information is sought and the decision is made rather quickly in reference to the decision criteria that have been established.

Consistency versus Complexity

The movement described above—from extensive problem solving to routine problem solving—suggests that people seek to maintain consistency in their lives. Indeed, many psychologists adhere to this philosophy. Their idea is that inconsistency leads to psychological tension, which we constantly seek to avoid. Other psychologists argue the opposite. They feel that individuals find change and uncertainty extremely satisfying. This is referred to as the need for complexity.

The aforementioned two concepts are balanced by Mayo and Jarvis in *The Psychology of Leisure Travel* (1981). It is their feeling that individuals vary in the amount of psychological tension they can handle. Too much repetition or consistency can result in boredom for an individual, creating a corresponding amount of psychological tension greater than the optimum for him. He will attempt to introduce some complexity in his life, thereby reducing the tension to an optimum level. Should this level be exceeded by an overly complex situation, the tension level will be greater than the optimum for him. This explains why someone, who for years has driven to a particular vacation spot, will change either the destination or the method of reaching that spot.

Similarly, too much complexity can result in more tension than an individual can handle. She will introduce consistency into the experience to reduce the ten-

Depending upon the extent to which novelty is sought, the attributes of a destination will be evaluated against the need for novelty, in addition to other motives. © 2009 Karl Naundorf. Used under license from Shutterstock, Inc.

sion level. An American tourist in Europe may find the different language and culture (complexity) needs to be balanced by staying in a hotel chain with which she is familiar (consistency). This model may also help explain a person's choice of vacation. The individual who experiences a great deal of consistency in everyday life may compensate by seeking vacations that offer variety. People who have less stimulation in their lives than they desire prefer more novelty and stimulation on their ideal vacation.

This goes back to the studies mentioned earlier that noted novelty as a major push factor influencing travel. What is meant by novelty? It has been proposed that the dimensions of novelty are (Lee and Crompton, 1992):

- Change from routine
- Escape
- Thrill
- Adventure
- Surprise
- Boredom alleviation

It is felt that a tourist has a certain predisposition to either seek or avoid arousal. Depending upon the extent to which novelty is sought, the perceived attributes of a destination will be evaluated against this need for novelty in addition to the strength of other motives and, within the kinds of external constraints noted in chapter 10, a vacation destination will be chosen. Questionnaires have been developed that would allow managers to determine the extent to which novelty is important to a potential tourist. Depending upon the results destinations offering the elements of novelty noted above could be matched with that potential tourist.

SUMMARY

People are motivated to satisfy needs that may be innate or learned. Part of marketing's task is to make people aware of their needs and present them with an objective, the purchase or attainment of which will help satisfy that need. Vacations or trips are ways of satisfying various needs. There are, however, ways other than taking vacations to satisfy those same needs. An individual will purchase a vacation to satisfy a need or needs if he perceives that the vacation will satisfy needs considered important, or if he has learned that a vacation will satisfy those needs under the constraints of external factors such as time, money, and social pressure.

An individual learns of the alternative ways of satisfying her needs from personal experience, from the same or similar experiences, and from information gained from the commercial or social environment. The alternatives considered are linked to the person's motives by a set of decision criteria—guidelines used by the individual to select among alternatives. These guidelines are also learned from the sources described. If an individual has learned that a particular purchase results in satisfaction, strong decision criteria favoring that purchase will have been built up as the number of alternatives considered will have been reduced. There is a great likelihood that a specific motive under the conditions described above will result in a tendency to purchase a particular product, service, or experience.

Trends

Consumer Trends

The Expectation Economy is inhabited by experienced, well-informed consumers with high expectations. Word of mouth travels the world instantly with exceptional performance being noted through a variety of blogs and mags such as TripAdvisor and SeatGuru. As a subtrend, consumers tell each other about the best of the best without feeling the need to actually purchase anything. The armchair traveler is practicing "vicarious consumption" through the eyes of others. Because high expectations often go unmet, well-informed consumers often find themselves in a state of indifference or irritation. This can lead to fake loyalty and postponed purchases. For example, travelers know that Virgin Atlantic, Singapore Airlines, and Emirates offer superior performance but, because these airlines do not fly on all routes, consumers have to settle for subpar airlines. They will switch to these "best in class" companies as soon as they can.

Here are some applications to tourism:

1. Status Symbols—Increasing numbers of consumers will purchase luxury items they can tout as a symbol of their status. Selling to this consumer involves appealing to the emotions of the buyer.
2. Time: The New Currency—Time is increasingly becoming scarce and qualifies as the new status symbol. People want quality time for themselves and their friends and family. Time-intensive experiences that provide emotional internations will appeal to today's consumer.
3. Unfixed Theme—Increased numbers of people are seeking experiences over physical goods. As they collect these experiences, many find it better to use or share rather than own, This has implications for fractional ownership resorts.
4. Eco-Friendly—Consumers will become more aware of their own and travel companies' carbon footprints as they seek out environmentally friendly products, companies, and destinations.

Sources: trendwatching.com/. The Experience Economy. Retrieved 26 March 2008; Heffer, L. 2008. Consumer Trends That Will Impact Luxury Shared Ownership in 2008. *Developments: The Voice of the Vacation Ownership Industry.* 42–43.

ACTIVITIES

1. You are a hotel manager of a resort that has a golf course on site. Create a "green" plan for your golf course. What specific sustainability practices do you feel will be most beneficial to your company in the future?

2. Create a full-page spread for a magazine including images and phrases that encourage people to travel abroad with their families. Attempt to grab someone's attention, and inspire that person to seek further information.

3. Call a few popular hotels in Mexico. Ask them about their security onsite and what they have done to make travelers feel comfortable about visiting there. Ask them about their policies with crime onsite and how they attempt to solve and make up for crime situations that occur.

REFERENCES

Andereck, K. L., and R. C. Knopf. 2004. Exploring the nature of destination drivers. *Measuring the Tourism Experience*. 35th Annual Conference Proceedings of the Travel and Tourism Research Association. CD-ROM, unpaged.

Bansal, H. and H. A. Eiselt. 2004. Exploratory research of tourist motivations and planning. *Tourism Management*, 25: 387–396.

Beach, J., and M. G. Ragheb. (1983). Measuring leisure motivation. *Journal of Leisure Research*, 15 (3): 219–228, reported in J. Swarbrooke, and S. Horner, *Consumer Behavior in Tourism*. Oxford, England: Butterworth Heinemann, 1999, 54.

Bogari, N. B., G. Crowther, and N. Marr. 2004. Motivation for domestic tourism: A case study of the kingdom of Saudi Arabia. *Tourism Analysis*, 8: 137–141.

Cameron, B. 1992. *Creative Destinations: Marketing & Packaging: Who Wants What—and Why? An Overview of the Canadian Pleasure Travel Market*. Proceedings of the 23rd Annual Conference of the Travel and Tourism Research Association, 160.

Cook, S., and S. Hopkins. 2007. *The Ideal American Vacation Trip*. Washington, DC: Travel Industry Association.

Crompton, J. 1979. Motivations for pleasure travel. *Annals of Tourism Research*, 6: 408–424.

Dann, G. 1977. Anomie, ego-enhancement and tourism. *Annals of Tourism Research*, 4: 184–194.

Fakeye, P. C., and J. L. Crompton. 1992. Importance of socialization to repeat visitation. *Annals of Tourism Research*, 19: 364–367.

Goossens, C. 2000. Tourism information and pleasure motivation. *Annals of Tourism Research*, 27 (2): 301–321.

Hanefores, M., and L. L. Mossberg. 1997. Travel Motives and Loyalties. 28th Annual Conference Proceedings of the Travel and Tourism Research Association. 21–30.

Hobson, J. S. P., and U. C. Dietrich. 1994. Tourism, health and quality of life: Challenging the responsibility of using the traditional tenets of sun, sea, sand, and sex in tourism marketing. *Journal of Travel & Tourism Marketing*, 3 (4): 28, 30.

Hyde, K. F., and R. Lawson. 2003. The nature of independent travel. *Journal of Travel Research*, 42: 13–23.

Klenosky, D. 2002. The "pull" of tourism destinations: A means-end investigation. *Journal of Travel Research*, 40: 385–395.

Kotler, P. 1984. *Marketing Management*. Englewood Cliffs, NJ: Prentice-Hall, Inc., 30.

Lee, S. and C. Kim. 1999. Understanding tourist motivations across the globe: perspective on independent and inter-dependent self-paradigms. 30th Annual Conference Proceedings of the Travel and Tourism Research Association. 51–55.

Lee, G., J. T. O'Leary, S. H. Lee, and A. M. Morrison. 2002. Comparison and contrast of push and pull motivational effects on trip behavior: An application of a multinomial logistic regression model. *Tourism Analysis*, 7: 89–104.

Lee, T., and J. Crompton. 1992. Measuring novelty seeking in tourism. *Annals of Tourism Research*, 19: 732–751.

Mayo, E. J., and L. P. Jarvis. 1981. *The Psychology of Leisure Travel*. Boston: C.B.I. Publishing Company, Inc. 172.

McClelland, D. 1953. *The Achievement Motive*. New York: Appleton-Century-Crofts.

Norman, W. C., and M. N. Carlson. 1999. An investigation of the seeking-escaping theory as a segmentation tool in tourism marketing. 30th Annual Conference Proceedings of the Travel and Tourism Research Association. 10–18.

Pearce, P. L., and U.-I. Lee. 2005. Developing the travel career approach to tourist motivation. *Journal of Travel Research*, 43: 226–237.

Snepenger, D., J. King, E. Marshall, and M. Uysal. 2006. Modeling Iso-Ahola's motivation theory in the tourism context. *Journal of Travel Research*, 45: 140–149.

Tran, X., and L. Ralston. 2006. Tourist preferences influence of unconscious needs. *Annals of Tourism Research*, 33 (2): 424–441.

Turnbull, D. R., and M. Uysal. 1995. An exploratory study of German visitors to the Caribbean: Push and pull motivations. *Journal of Travel & Tourism Marketing*, 4 (2): 85–92.

Wright, P. A. 1996. North American ecotourism markets: Motivations, preferences, and destinations. *Journal of Travel Research*, 35 (1): 3–10.

Yiannakis, A., and H. Gibson. 1992. Roles tourists play. *Journal of Travel Research*, 19: 287–303.

Yoon, Y., and M. Uysal. 2005. An examination of the effects of motivation and satisfaction on destination loyalty: A structural model. *Tourism Management*, 25: 45–56.

You, X., J. O'Leary, A. M. Morrison, and G.-S. Hong. 2000. A cross-cultural comparison of travel push and pull factors: United Kingdom vs. Japan. *International, Journal of Hospitality & Tourism Administration*, 1 (2): 1–26.

Yuan, S., and C. McDonald. 1990. Motivational determinates of international pleasure time. *Journal of Travel Research*, 29 (1): 43.

SURFING SOLUTIONS

http://edis.ifas.ufl.edu/AE259 (University of Florida Extension)

http://titaniumenterprises.com.au/_dbase_upl/EPA_ecoBiz_Factsheet.pdf (Club Pelican Golf Course)

http://www.msnbc.msn.com/id/24240009/ (MSNBC)

http://www.visitmexico.com/wb/Visitmexico/Visi_Home (Country of Mexico official tourism site)

ADDITIONAL READING

Choice and Demand in Tourism. 1992. P. Johnson and B. Thomas (eds.). Mansell Publishing Ltd., Villiers House, 41–47 Strand, London WC2N 5JE, U.K.

Economic Psychology of Travel and Tourism. 1995. J. C. Crotts and W. F. van Raaij (eds.). The Haworth Press, 10 Alice Street, Binghamton, NY 13904-1580, 1995.

Leisure Travel: Making it a Growth Market . . . Again. 1991. S. C. Plog, John Wiley & Sons, Inc., New York.

The Seasons of Business: A Marketer's Guide to Consumer Behavior. 1992. J. Waldrop and M. Mogelonsky, American Demographics Books, 127 West State Street, Ithaca, NY 14850.

The Theory of Buyer Behavior. 1969. J. A. Howard and J. N. Sheth, John Wiley & Sons, Inc., New York, NY.

The Whole is More: Living the Travel Experience. 1993. H. Gondek, Vantage Press, Inc., 516 West 34th Street, New York, NY 10001.

chapter *12*

Selecting a Travel Destination

THE IMPORTANCE OF IMAGE

My first rule of travel is never to go to a place that sounds like a medical condition
and Critz is clearly an incurable disease involving flaking skin.

Bill Bryson

PURPOSE

Based upon an understanding of the traveler's search for vacation information, students will be able to
suggest specific strategies to influence where, how, with whom, when, and for how long people vacation.

LEARNING OBJECTIVES

✓ Explain the importance of perception on travel decisions and the interpretation of travel information.
✓ Describe how opinion leaders form a link between the social and commercial environments.
✓ Describe how a person's self-image influences his or her choices of travel destinations and services.
✓ Explain how to use the factors that influence people's sensitivity to information to increase the
  chances of a message being noticed.
✓ Explain the process through which a person forms an image of a travel destination or service.

OVERVIEW

A travel destination is chosen in part based upon our perception of its ability to satisfy our felt needs. This chapter examines the process by which we search for and receive information about potential destinations and how our perception of that information influences the travel decision.

Information is received from both the commercial and social environments. The factors that influence where the information is sought from and how much is taken in are examined. The process by which the information taken is distorted by our perceptual biases is explored. Implications for the marketer seeking to develop a specific image for a destination or to change an unsatisfactory image are pointed out.

THE SEARCH FOR INFORMATION

Once individuals are motivated to travel they embark on an information search to compare alternative destinations. Early attempts to explain decision-making theory were based on the idea that the consumer is a rational decision maker. Recent studies indicate that travel decision making is very complex and involves decisions about several destinations, trip length, activities, accommodations, and so on. It seems that potential travelers constantly move back and forth between searching for information and making subdecisions about the trip (Pan and Fessenmaier, 2006). This has led to a concept known as *case-based planning* (Jun et al., 2007) whereby individuals use their personal memory as the initial knowledge base for planning a new trip. Past experiences are combined with current behaviors to make new travel decisions.

It is probably true that the tourist's memory of a vacation is the most important piece of information used in planning future trips—deciding whether or not to return to a particular destination, for example. Interestingly, tourists who have previously visited a destination do as much external information searching as do first-time visitors. This may be related to the concept of memory distortion. Information or advertising received after the vacation can influence and even distort first-hand memories of the trip. Even a bad experience can be made to seem better and make the tourist want to re-visit the destination (Braun-LaTour et al., 2006).

The information search has three dimensions to it (Fodness and Murray, 1998): spatial, temporal, and operational. The spatial dimension is one of internal (information from personal memory) or external (informa-

tion from the external environment). The potential tourist will first examine his or her own individual experiences. If that destination has not been previously visited or if the trip took place a long time before, then the tourist will turn to an external search for information.

External searches can be on-going or pre-purchase in response to a specific situation. This is the temporal dimension of the search. It may be, for example, that retirees, with both time and money, are continuously scanning newspaper articles or travel brochures for future trips.

Finally, the search has an operational dimension, focusing on specific sources of information. Information will come from two major sources: the *commercial environment* and the *social environment*. The commercial environment refers to information coming from companies, destinations, countries, or tourist businesses. These businesses and organizations have a vested interest in persuading the tourist to buy and profit by such a purchase. The social environment, characterized by friends, relatives, and reference groups, presumably would have nothing materially to gain from the tourist's decision to buy. As such, it is presumed that their information or advice is more objective and worthy of trust. Although friends, relatives, and those in our reference groups may not benefit financially from the decision to buy a particular vacation, they may have their egos stroked if their advice is accepted and a decision is made based on their input.

Tourists seek information in an attempt to reduce risk. Information from professional sources is important before a definite trip decision is made. Once the decision to take a trip is made, the risk for the tourist has increased. As a result, travelers make intensive use of informal information sources that they consider trustworthy (Bieger and Laesser, 2004).

While prospective visitors may not actively search public sources of information—newspapers and news magazines in their search for travel information, they are, nevertheless, influenced by current events. For example, news articles about terrorist attacks in London that occurred in the summer of 2005 would impact an individual's intention to visit.

It is likely that people will spend a longer time on an external search for a tourism purchase. There are several reasons for this. The greater the amount of risk is a purchase, the greater the search. Buying a vacation involves a great deal of risk involving both time and money. For many people the annual vacation is their only chance to get away. If they select a poor vacation, they may have to wait another year for the next opportunity. The vacation is also an expensive proposition—hence the risk. Second, because the purchase of a vacation involves buying an intangible that cannot be seen or touched ahead of time, there is heavy reliance on secondary and tertiary sources of information. It is, thus, likely that the search process will be longer than that for many other consumer products. There is a tendency for many vacationers to select a different vacation destination each time they holiday. This would support the need for a greater information search.

INFORMATION SOURCES

What sources of information are sought when planning a vacation? It is hypothesized that the sources of information used varies depending upon such things as (Fodness and Murray, 1999):

- **Nature of decision making:** The extent to which the trip is a routine, weekend drive, for example, or a first-time cruise.
- **Composition of traveling party:** Whether an individual is traveling alone or with friends and/or family.
- **Purpose of trip:** Whether the trip is business, vacation, or to visit friends and relatives. There are, for example, significant differences in the utilization of information sources between business and leisure travelers of Japan, South Korea, and Australia (Chen 2000). Japanese business travelers, for example, are more likely to use airlines, corporate travel departments, and personal computers while leisure travelers are more likely to seek out information from friends and relatives, newspapers and magazines, travel agencies, and travel guides.
- **Mode of travel:** Whether the mode of travel is personal automobile or public transportation.
- **Stage in the family life cycle:** From households with or without children to retirees.
- **Socioeconomic status**
- **Length of stay**

Much evidence suggests that the social environment—the influence of friends and family—is instrumental in selecting a travel destination. It seems that the commercial environment performs an informing function—it lets people know what is available. The social environment performs an evaluating function; the potential traveler uses it as a means of evaluating the alternatives.

Individuals will use sources if the sources are thought of as credible. It may be that tourists look at a

Knowing how people search for information allows marketers to segment the market based on search behavior and develop strategies that appeal to and reach each segment. © 2009 kristian sekulic. Used under license from Shutterstock, Inc.

small number of credible sources rather than consider all available sources of information. This means that marketers should consider the credibility of a source, as perceived by the tourist, when making the decision as to how to get a message out (Cho and Kerstetter, 2002).

Of increasing importance is the use of social media and social networking sites. Social media allow consumers to be providers rather than just recipients of information. Sites like Trip Advisor and I Go You Go allow consumers to post reviews of their vacation experiences. This increase in information is moving control of the marketing message away from companies and into the hands of the consumer.

Knowing how people search for information can enable marketers to segment the market based on search behavior and develop specific strategies to appeal to and reach each segment. For this to happen there must be a sufficiently large number of people who engage in a certain form of search behavior to make the effort of marketing to them worthwhile. It would also be important to know whether different segments of the market use different types and numbers of information sources. The relative importance of these sources must be known in addition to the length of time taken in the planning process. This latter piece of information is necessary to ensure that information is available at the time when the potential travelers want it. If July vacationers plan their vacations six months in advance, the destinations should target their messages to reach that market in January. Advertising to them beforehand will have little impact because they are not thinking about the vacation. Advertising to them afterward will be too late because they will already have decided where they will vacation.

In general, longer searches using a greater number of sources of information are undertaken by vacationers who want a well-planned trip, seek excitement from their vacation, and are planning longer trips over greater distances.

The role of the retail travel agent in this process has been documented in a series of reports by Louis Harris & Associates since 1971. These reports indicate that, over the past thirty-five plus years, between 30 and 40 percent of those who visit travel agencies have only a general idea of where they want to go and thus rely, to some extent, on the agent's advice in selecting a destination. There is an increased tendency to use travel agents as the distance being traveled increases. While Internet use to plan and book travel has increased in recent years, there are clear indications that many people prefer to deal with a travel agent. According to a 2005 study (http://www.htrends.com/researcharticle17329.html, accessed August 2, 2005) nearly seven out of ten U.S. adults are more comfortable booking travel plans through a traditional travel agent. Travelers like that an agent:

- Asks questions to better understand a traveler's needs
- Is willing to help customize itineraries to best fit those needs
- Is able to book complex itineraries that are hard to book online

When the needs of the traveler are complex, it seems important to people to be able to sit down with a real person.

USE OF THE INTERNET

The year 2007 was the first in which more travel was bought online than offline. It is projected that 60 percent of U.S. travel will be booked online in 2009. In 2005 it was estimated that 56 percent of U.S. adults used the Internet. The Travel Industry Association of America (TIA) estimates that the rapid growth in Internet used in the 1990s has slowed. There are over 101 million "online travelers." Over two-thirds of the 152 million U.S. travelers use the Internet. Frequent travelers–those taking five or more trips a year–have a greater propensity to use the Internet.

To what extent is the Internet used for travel planning? Among the traveling population are adults who took at least one trip of fifty plus miles away from home, one-way (Green and Cooke, 2005, 1):

- Two-thirds are online travelers.
- Fifty-two percent use the Internet and make plans online.
- Forty-three percent use the Internet and make travel reservations/bookings online.
- Twenty percent use the Internet and traveled for business in the past year.
- Sixty-three percent use the Internet and traveled for pleasure in the past year.

By some accounts over 20 percent of all travel revenue comes from Internet bookings (Travel Industry Association of America, 2004; Bai et al., 2003).

Industry tracking has shown that Internet usage is greater than Internet purchases. This suggests either that many Internet users search for more information than they need for purchasing a product or that, after an on-line information search, consumers buy offline.

Individuals with greater levels of experience at the destination are less likely to use and place trust in the Internet. Experienced consumers who were knowledgeable about the destination attributes are more critical of Web site information (Cho and Kerstetter, 2004; Dellaert and Wendel, 2004).

Internet users are more likely to be (Bai et al., 2003; Andereck, Ng, and Knopf, 2003; Beldona, 2005):

- Younger
- Women
- Older Baby Boomers compared to Generation Xers
- Have higher educational levels
- Travelers who stay overnight in commercial lodging establishments
- Air travelers
- To have been on-line for four years or more
- To have made the decision to visit before requesting the state tourism office's official information packet (This suggests that Internet users are making travel destination decisions based on their on-line information search and use other information sources as secondary sources of information.)
- Advance planners (Given the planning horizon of Internet users, information on Web sites needs to be relevant for a six-month time frame.)

Neither sex nor race seems to be a defining characteristic of Internet use.

Concern over security (i.e., providing credit card information on the Web) is the most important reason individuals do not buy on-line. However, this is not a concern to repeat on-line purchasers who are comfortable with providing credit card information (Jun, Vogt, and MacKay, 2004).

The key to increasing purchasing behavior over the Internet is to increase the level of involvement felt by the Internet user. Internet providers need to demonstrate that the product being displayed is personally relevant to the tourist and to reduce the negative effect of Internet use by, for example, making the Web site easy to navigate and sending a confirmation message to assure customers about their booking (Park, Ekinci, and Cobanoglu, 2002). For on-line travelers, the following marketing techniques are successful in eliciting a consumer response (Green and Cooke, 2005, 2):

- Unsponsored search engine results
- E-mail recommendations by friends or colleagues
- Links on Web sites to go to other destinations of interest
- E-mails/newsletters that were requested or "opted in" by the consumer

The fifth annual Corporate Travel Benchmark Survey which tracks business travel patterns at America's leading corporations, indicates that two-thirds of travel reservations at responding corporations are made on-line. This figure is up from the 26 percent on-line adoption rate reported in the first Benchmark Survey in 2001. In many cases companies are requiring on-line booking because of the savings these programs can generate. Savings of up to 14 percent in airfares are reported (http://www.hotelmarketing.com/index.php/content/article/corporations_book_two_thirds_of_reservations_online/, accessed August 16, 2005). In regard to what is purchased on-line, consumers tend, first, to buy airline tickets followed by lodging and car rentals. Package tours—because they are more complicated and more expensive—involve more risk for the travelers and are the least-purchased on-line travel product.

Internet use is also spreading throughout the world. In some countries Internet searches are surpassing personal recommendations as the preferred means of obtaining travel information. In Australia, Canada, China, Denmark, France, Germany, Italy, Japan, South Korea, the Netherlands, Poland, Spain, the United Kingdom, and the United States, more people do Web searches than seek personal recommendations from friends and acquaintances (http://www.emarketer.com/Article.aspx?1003480, accessed July 11, 2005). For the most part, users are satisfied with on-line travel services. Britons, Australians and Americans are the world's most satisfied on-line travelers, while Japanese and Polish consumers are the least. One in five Russians says on-line travel services are "not worth it." There is a greater tendency for younger people to use the Internet. Among British respondents, 60 percent of eighteen- to twenty-nine-year-olds said their use of on-line travel had increased while only 37 percent of older British age groups said the same.

Because the role of a retail travel agent increases in importance as the use of air transportation and the distance traveled increases, it might be better to view the important sources of information for the auto traveler separately from those used by the air traveler.

AUTOMOBILE TRAVEL

A number of studies have been completed on the tourist's use of travel information sources when traveling by automobile. These studies indicate the importance of information from the social environment. Information from family or friends and from personal knowledge is regarded as more significant than that from commercial sources. The non-media preferred commercial sources are billboards and signs. It appears that as motorist travelers become more familiar with the location of establishments in a geographic area, they rely more on previous experience than on physical appearance and on credit-card directories rather than on commercial billboards.

In some countries Internet searches surpass personal recommendations as the preferred means of obtaining travel information. © 2009 Philip Date. Used under license from Shutterstock, Inc.

Invitation for Two

Imagine that you and your boyfriend or girlfriend decide to go out to dinner for a romantic date. You choose a location with a great menu of unique dishes and an extensive wine list, which makes it well worth the money you will spend. You expect to have a private, intimate experience. You arrive and realize that you are the only two guests in the dining room. For a Friday night, you expected to see many couples enjoying each other's company. You didn't want to share chairs with another couple but you did want to feel like you were getting the experience of a night out. A dinner this private could have been created in your own kitchen with a hired chef.

Bruce Wallin, Editorial Director of *Robb Report; Luxury Resorts,* discusses the exclusive nature of luxury resorts in his summer 2008 issue. He writes about his visit to a beach resort at Cabo San Lucas in Baja, California. The extreme exclusivity he found unappealing. A couple was seen sitting together at a candlelight dinner with idle waiters and bussers standing nearby. He comments, "While most people expect privacy from an upscale resort, few want to feel like they are the only ones at the party."

Wallin cites a solution to this issue through the example of the Esperanza resort also located in Cabo San Lucas. He writes that this resort ". . . strikes a successful balance between exclusivity and activity. You will not be trammeled by tequila-crazed teens at Esperanza's ocean-view bar, but you will not be alone there either."

When advertisements grace the glossy pages of magazines, images of romantic vacations typically show a couple walking on the beach alone. This gives the reader a sense of exclusivity that they may be searching for. However, the perception of guests is similar to the couple in the opening scenario. Complete privacy is not anticipated, nor particularly desired.

THINK ABOUT THIS:

1. How would you advertise to members of a market segment who wish to have a private, but not entirely exclusive, vacation?

2. What activities could you offer to satisfy these needs?

Source: Wallin, B. 2008. Not Alone At the Top. *Robb Report Luxury Resorts.* 12.

A link between the social and commercial environment is suggested by a consideration of the role of opinion leaders. *Travel Opinion Leaders (TOL)* are defined as such based on how often they serve as sources of travel information. People are more inclined to be regarded as TOLs the more and the longer trips they take (Oh and Lee, 1995). There is evidence to indicate that the flow of communication is a two-step flow process. The tendency is for influence to flow from the mass media to opinion leaders who are receptive to the idea presented and from these opinion leaders to the general public. Opinion leaders act as channels of information. They tend to be demographically indistinguishable except for higher income or occupational levels, tend to read more media about related consumer issues, are more knowledgeable about new product developments, and participate more often in related consumer activities. Studies of TOLs found that they are active seekers of information but do not seek either personal or media sources of information as being significantly important sources for them. TOLs are more likely to rely on travel brochures and guides, highway welcome/information centers and convention and visitor bureaus than most people. It appears that TOLs may be better able to determine the credibility of various source materials and are not as easily swayed by the advice of friends and relatives as are the general population. Others, after all, look to them for advice—they do not look so much to others.

The idea that a relatively small number of "influentials" can trigger large movements of people to purchase an item is the central thesis of Malcolm Gladwell's book *The Tipping Point.* Critics suggest that the emergence of a trend depends not on the influentials but, rather, on how susceptible people are to what is being talked about or promoted (Thompson, 2008).

SENSITIVITY TO INFORMATION

Thus far we have considered the sources to which potential tourists turn to determine vacation patterns. The personal sources—those from the social environment—have been shown to exert considerable pressure compared with those from the commercial environment. All information from both the commercial and social environments reaches us if we are sensitive to the incoming information. Our sensitivity to receiving incoming information is first a function of how inclined we are to that information. If, for example, we feel strongly inclined toward taking a vacation, we will readily be open to information regarding vacations. If we have a strong preference for a Bahamas vacation, any information about the Bahamas—about travel packages, the weather, the political situation—is liable to receive attention. On the other hand, if we have definitely decided against a European vacation, our preference to go to Europe will be low, as will our sensitivity to information about Europe. Consequently, we will probably ignore any information that would affect those taking a European vacation. Our sensitivity to information is also a function of the ambiguity of the message. If the information received is familiar to us already, it may be too simple and straightforward and thus be ignored. On the other hand, if the information presented—an advertisement, a travelogue, a personal opinion—is too complicated for us to absorb, the high level of ambiguity may lead us to put up a shield to "defend" ourselves, and the information will not get our attention. This process may be thought of as controlling the quantity of information received. In order to gain tourists' attentions, the information presented should be aimed at their capacity to absorb it. Its chances of being taken in will be enhanced if the tourists have a preference for the destination or package being mentioned.

GETTING THE MESSAGE NOTICED

If the decision to travel to a particular destination is linked to our perception of that destination, then an examination of the perception process may help us understand if and how we can change an individual's perception of a destination in order to increase the likelihood of that individual's visiting the destination. Any information from either the social or commercial environment is molded into an image through our perceptual processes. The resultant image is less a function of the promotional message of a destination than of our individual perception of that message. There are many factors that affect consumer sensitivity and perception. Although these elements are working at the same time and although the effect of one often contradicts the effect of another, they are discussed individually.

Technical factors refer to the object, product, or service as it actually exists. The various elements of a particular product or service, such as price, quality, service, availability, and distinctiveness, can be communicated through the product or service itself. These inputs are termed significant stimuli. The elements may also be communicated in a symbolic way through the use of words and/or pictures. There are several factors that are

> *What we're seeking is an experience of being alive, so that our life experiences on the purely physical plane will have resonances within our own innermost being and reality, so that we actually feel the rapture of being alive.*
>
> Joseph Campbell

termed technical. *Size* is an important consideration. To many, size is equated with quality. The larger the company, airplane, or hotel, the better the service is perceived to be. Generally speaking, larger advertisements will receive greater attention. A travel company might use a big advertisement or emphasize the size of its operation to gain more attention and give the impression of quality to the reader. *Color* also attracts more attention than black-and-white. Color advertisements are 50 percent more effective than are black and white ones. The *intensity* of a stimulus also affects the perception of it. The greater the intensity, the more the attention. Intensity can refer to the brightness of colors, the use of certain "strong" words, or the importance of a present or past purchase or experience. Stressing the importance of a decision to buy will increase the attention given a message. It can also refer to repeating the stimulus, thereby intensifying the message. The more a message is seen, the greater the chance that it will attract attention. *Moving objects* attract more attention than stationary objects. This accounts for much of the success of advertising on television. Point-of-purchase displays with moving parts—in a travel agency, for example—can also be used to good effect. The increased popularity of virtual tours over the Internet can have an impact on the tourist. Such virtual tours are shown to result in tourists getting a more vivid image and perceiving the destination as being more attractive (Cho and Fesenmaier, 1999). The *position* of a piece of information can affect whether or not the information will attract attention. In a brochure rack, pamphlets at shoulder height will attract the most attention. When placing advertisements in a newspaper, it is important to consider that the upper part of the page attracts more attention. *Contrast* is another element that affects the attention given a stimulus. By varying the thought, color, size, pattern, or intensity of a stimulus, enough discontinuity may be created between what is expected and what is actually perceived to attract attention. If competing messages are bright, colorful, and somewhat gaudy, a very simple, dignified message may be noticed because of the contrast. The final technical factor is that of *isolation*. Advertisers are fond of putting a border called "*white space*," around their messages to isolate them from other messages on a page. As noted earlier, these elements interact often in contradictory ways. The greatest impact comes when several factors combine to give a more significant effect. This is illustrated in figure 12.1.

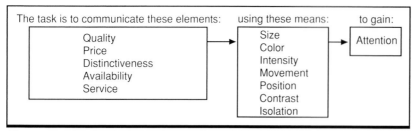

The task is to communicate these elements:	using these means:	to gain:
Quality Price Distinctiveness Availability Service	Size Color Intensity Movement Position Contrast Isolation	Attention

Figure 12.1 Getting Attention.

THE PROCESS OF PERCEPTION

The information-receiving process, described above, controls the quantity of information taken in. The quantity of information received, however, is distorted by how that information is perceived. Two people presented with the same travel advertisement may perceive it differently. One person may view the advertisement positively, the other negatively. Feedback from our motives, the alternatives considered, and the decision criteria used will affect our image of information received. Various studies have shown, in fact, that visiting a destination or staying at a particular lodging chain causes a positive change in the image of that destination or chain. If we are strongly motivated to seek a historical, cultural vacation, one which could readily be satisfied by a trip to the province of Quebec, and if it is important (decision criteria) that we avoid crowds, then an advertisement showing throngs of people at an art festival in Quebec will be perceived negatively. Similarly, an advertisement that stresses the magnificent scenery of the province will not be perceived positively because that image runs counter to that which motivates us.

> Spring is nature's way of saying, "Let's Party!"
> Robin Williams

Although information from both the commercial and social environments is distorted, information received from personal sources is less subject to *perceptual bias*. This is because information from the social environment is regarded more favorably by the individual receiving the information. It should be remembered, however, that before a friend or relative gives us information, he or she has already distorted it to meet his or her value system. A recommendation of a wonderful place to visit, stay, or eat will only be given in those terms if it has met with what our friend determines is a wonderful place to visit, stay, or eat. This, of course, depends upon whether or not our friend perceives that his or her experience satisfied unmet needs. There is also liable to be less distortion when information is actively sought. When the tourist is unsure of which vacation will result in a more satisfying experience—

when preference for any particular vacation is low—there will be less bias in the way information is perceived. In addition, there will be greater reliance upon the social environment for information if the tourist is unsure of the satisfactions from various alternatives and if the purchase is important. To the extent that we are influenced by the social group of which we are a part, our motives will be influenced by the (subjectively weighted) information from our social environment. Similarly, the social environment will affect the alternatives a buyer considers, particularly where experience is lacking. Also, information received will be fed into the buyer's decisions criteria and will influence those criteria in the direction in which the information is perceived. A tourist, for example, may look for the lowest priced hotel. If information is received that suggests that paying a little more will actually be a better value, and if the tourist perceives this to be true, the decisions criterion of "lowest cost" may change.

A link has been established between perception and behavior. We behave—buy, travel, stay at home, and so on—based in part upon our perception of information received. But how do we perceive products, for example, tourist destinations or services?

PERCEPTUAL BIAS

In chapter 11 it was suggested that, in part, a travel purchase is made based on the extent that an individual perceives that the purchase will satisfy his or her needs.

The image that an individual has of a destination plays an important role in determining whether or not a travel purchase will be made.

Erasing What's Written

Opinion leaders are media users who utilize their familiarity of a specific subject to effectively interpret information in order to make the best possible decisions. Opinion leaders are experts in an industry. They are able to form judgments based on their extensive knowledge of their specialized field, and their opinions are often valued.

Travel blogs and forums are channels of communication that are often more respected by the average traveler compared to the advertisements surrounding them every day. When peers share their experiences, it is perceived as "honest"; and when an advertisement is observed, it is considered to be entirely promotional. As Brendan Cooper, Social Media Planner at Porter Novelli, says, "A blogger might be spending more time thinking about you, offering analysis and comment." He continues to discuss "opinion formers" who influence customers through their writings on Internet blogs and forums. He writes, "So you have your list of opinion formers. What happens now? Well, you should start monitoring them, both qualitatively (what they are talking about and quantitatively how many of them are talking about it)."

Advertisements can draw attention to specific destinations and hotels, but they are not the deciding factor between one alternative and another. Major results of final decisions are the opinions of experienced travelers and individuals who have visited the area previously. *Travelpost.com* allows travelers to rank their stay from 1 to 10 and to write a commentary on the reason for the number given. A 1 mark means "stay away" and a 10 ranking means the experience was "perfect."

The Radisson Martinique on Broadway in New York writes on its Web site that it has "historical status and internationally renowned personal service." However, a blogger posted on May 2, 2008, on *Travelpost.com* that she has "NEVER BEEN SO THOROUGHLY DISGUSTED by every aspect of this hotel." She proceeded to remark that she will never stay at another Radisson Hotel again. When prospective guests are searching for reviews on this specific hotel and they come across this information, they may forego the knowledge they gained from advertisements on the official Web site and stay away from the hotel due to this negative review. This is just one opinion from a guest, but it can certainly affect possible sales.

THINK ABOUT THIS:

1. How can hotel managers monitor information written about their hotel on travel blogs and forums and use this information to make improvements?

2. How can a hotel use positive guest feedback through its Web site and advertisements to make the information received by the observer more reliable?

Sources: http://www.utalkmarketing.com/pages/Article.aspx?ArticleID=10178&Title=How_to_indentify_online_opinion_leaders; http://www.travelpost.com/; http://www.radisson.com/newyorkny_broadway.

The key word is "perceive," for we buy based not so much upon what information is actually presented to us, but on how we *perceive* that information. Thus, the image that an individual has of a destination plays an important role in determining whether or not a travel purchase will be made.

It will be recalled that, prior to the search for information, available alternatives are matched with motives considered important to the individual through learned purchase criteria. The result is an initial inclination—positive or negative—toward a particular product or destination (see figure 12.2). The strength of our preference has an effect on how new alternatives are perceived

> I never travel without my diary.
> One should always have something
> sensational to read about.
>
> Oscar Wilde

and even if any new alternatives are considered. For example, if an individual is well-traveled and consequently knows which destinations please and which do not, a strong set of decisions criteria will have been developed: There must be a sunny climate; the culture must be significantly different from my own; and so on. This, in turn, leads to a strong inclination toward certain destinations. The results are:

1. The tourist is less inclined to seek out information about new places.

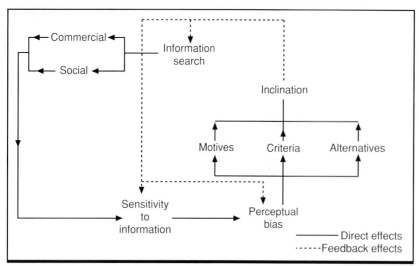

Figure 12.2 Information Sources and Perceptual Biases. Adapted from: Howard, J. A., and J. N. Sheth. 1969. *The Theory of Buyer Behavior.* New York: John Wiley & Sons, Inc.

2. The tourist is less sensitive to any information about vacation spots; the preferred destination is protected by a reluctance to allow in any information about other destinations.

3. Because a strong preference for a particular destination has been developed, any information about that destination is filtered to emphasize the positives while any negatives are rationalized or downplayed. The reverse is also true.

Perception is reality for most people. Irrespective of the reality of the situation people will buy, or not; travel, or not, based upon their perception of the situation. Perception, then, is the same thing as image. An image is "the set of meanings by which an object is known and through which people describe, remember and relate to it" (Chon, 1990). For an individual who has not visited a destination previously, the travel decision must be made on the perceived image of that destination. After a visit occurs, personal experience modifies that image. However, that first visit is made on the basis of whether or not the destination—or, at least, my image of the destination—is likely to meet needs and wants that are important to me. In fact perceptions are the most important factor in several important decisions made by tourists: the choice of a destination, what is purchased while on vacation, and the decision to return.

It is important to consider the factors that influence image formation. According to Gunn (1972) an image evolves at two levels. An *organic image* is formed as a result of general exposure to newspaper reports, magazine articles, television reports, and other specifically non-tourist information. Thus, even the individual who has

never visited a particular country nor even sought out information on that country will have some kind of image, probably incomplete, of that country. At this point, as mentioned earlier, other pieces of the image picture will be added that the individual perceives *should* be there to match the pieces already known in order to make a complete picture. The second level is that of an *induced image*. This refers to an image brought about by tourist-directed information, such as advertisements and travel posters. The organic image tends to develop first and, as such, may be regarded as a stronger influence than the induced one in overall image formation. There is little that can be done to influence the formation of an organic image. Filmmakers may be persuaded to shoot a movie such as *Braveheart* which, although not a travel film, influences people in their image of Scotland. In general, however, little can be done. Marketers do seek, obviously, to induce an image through the production of films, posters, and advertisements. If the organic image is set in an individual's mind, an induced image may be disregarded in favor of the previously held organic image.

The influence of image is suggested in figure 12.3. The organic image is already present to some extent before an individual is motivated to travel. It is based upon the kinds of information suggested above. Being motivated to travel, the individual undertakes an active search for information on the destinations being con-

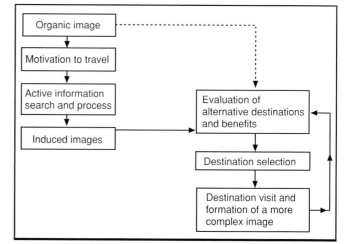

Figure 12.3 A Model of a Tourist's Image Formation Process. Source: Fakeye, P. C., and J. R. Crompton. 1991. Image differences between prospective, first-time and repeat visitors to the Lower Rio Grande Valley. *Journal of Travel Research,* 30 (2): 11.

Bragging Rights

When skimming through *Travel and Leisure* magazine in its European edition published in May 2008, various locations in Europe are advertised. *DiscoverIreland.com* depicts a couple being served tea outside of a castle. A plaque states, "This castle was home to the Bennetts who lived here for three nights last week. Just enough time to learn the true meaning of "Royal Treatment." The bottom corner of the page says, "Your very own Ireland."

A risk is taken when a person invests money into a vacation without truly knowing the product that he or she will receive. Any person who is willing to take the time and spend the money to travel has standards of expectations that coincide with his or her own self-image.

Your father or mother may have told you about a co-worker who strutted around the office on a Monday showing off a golden tan and telling stories of an exotic island or relaxing golf getaway. Prestige is often associated with travel, and guests like to be treated with special considerations. *DiscoverIreland.com* advertises treating guests like royalty and fulfilling any and all desires. This targets individuals who associate travel with a certain level of esteem and a source of self-worth due to monetary success or a variety of other factors signifying achievement.

THINK ABOUT THIS:

1. An individual's self-image is closely tied to his or her travel decisions. What type of imagery and descriptive phrases can be used to promote travel as a function of personal success?

Source: Discoverireland.com. 2008. "Your Very Own Ireland." *Travel and Leisure.* 85.

(or more tangible) and *psychological* (or more abstract) characteristics; that images of destinations also range from those based on common functional and psychological characteristics to those based on more distinctive or unique features (Echtner and Ritchie, 1993). This is illustrated in figure 12.4. On the attribute-holistic continuum, a destination is perceived both in terms of information regarding specific features, such as climate and the friendliness of the people, and an overall sense of the place, such as the general feeling or atmosphere of the destination. One study on Australia identified the following attributes (Ryan and Cave, 2005):

- Friendly
- Sunny
- Scenic
- Good beaches
- Interesting wildlife

The holistic imagery included:

- Adventure
- Laid back
- Rugged

On the functional-psychological component there are characteristics that are directly measurable (low prices) and those that are less tangible (generally safe). Functional and psychological characteristics may be individual attributes or overall impressions. The preceding study had the same functional characteristics as noted under attributes. The psychological characteristics were:

- Friendly
- Relaxed

sidered. This will result in an induced image of the destinations. The organic image, being stronger, will modify as additional information taken in as part of the induced image. Once the destination is selected and the trip taken, the actual personal experiences at the destination have an impact upon the evaluation of future vacation plans.

It is proposed that a destination image has two main components: those that are *attribute-based* and those that are *holistic*. Each of these components contain *functional*

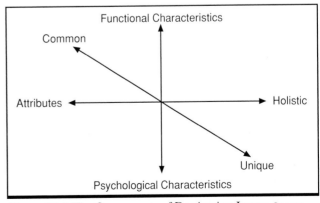

Figure 12.4 The Components of Destination Image. Source: Echtner, C. M., and J. R. B. Ritchie. 1993. The measurement of destination image. *Journal of Travel Research*, 31 (4): 4.

- Adventurous
- Diversity
- No worry

Finally, on the common-unique continuum, both functional and psychological characteristics as well as individual attributes and holistic impressions may be common or consist of unique features. It is argued that, only by considering all of the dimensions noted above can the complete image of a destination be developed. This is important because, as the authors of the study indicate, "if a destination is found difficult to categorize or is not easily differentiated from other similar destinations, then its likelihood of being considered in the travel decision process is reduced" (Echtner and Ritchie, 1993). While most all tourism image studies have focused on the cognitive or belief aspect of image, some argue that image also has an affective component dealing with feelings. Destinations could, for example, be examined on the basis of the following:

- Arousing–Sleepy
- Exciting–Gloomy
- Pleasant–Unpleasant
- Relaxing–Distressing

One such study (Balogu and Brinkberg, 1997) finds that a sample of undergraduates think of Egypt and Morocco as falling between arousing and exciting while Portugal is described as between relaxing and sleepy. The affective image has a greater impact on developing destination image (Yoon and Kimm, 2002).

An image *can* change over time. Research has indicated that, although consumers have stable perceptions about frequently bought products, their image of an infrequently bought product changes over time. Although an image can change over time, can that image *be* changed over time? There is some literature that suggests that an image cannot be changed, but it appears that the task, though difficult, costly, and time-consuming, is not impossible.

IMAGE-SHAPING FORCES

Technical factors are concerned with getting information through to the potential traveler. However, the information and impressions that do get through are distorted by a number of forces into an image. First there is a tendency on our part to *stabilize our perception* even after the original basis for the perception has changed. A traveler may continue to stay at an old favorite hotel where the level of service has declined because the perception re-

Images of destinations range from those based on functional and psychological characteristics to those based on more distinctive or unique features. © 2009 Galyna Andrushko. Used under license from Shutterstock, Inc.

mains in the past. An image, whether positive or negative, may continue long after the factors causing that original image have been changed. This illustrates the difficulty involved in changing an image. Linked with this very closely is that, second, as a creature of habit, a traveler will perceive in a certain *habitual way* until forced to think differently. Stress here is placed on the need for marketers to break through the traveler's "habit barrier" by means of various stimuli mentioned above.

A third shaping force relates to the extent to which individuals have a tendency to be *confident* or *cautious*. The confident individual takes in a complex situation more quickly, can more readily see positive elements in a situation, and can assimilate more detail. Decisions are made faster by confident persons, although those who are cautious make slower decisions and hence their perceptions tend to be more accurate. This factor points to the need to communicate different messages to different segments of an intended market. This, of course, will work only if marketers are able to determine that the more-confident traveler reads different newspapers or magazines or watches different television programs than the more cautious traveler. The amount of information that can be perceived is limited by the fact that we have a *limited span of attention*. This refers to the number of stimuli that can be taken in at the same time. Experiments have shown this number to be approximately eight. This infers that messages should not consist of too many elements for fear that an important element may be missed or that the message may be disregarded because it is too confusing. The tendency to react to a given stimuli in a certain way is referred to as an *individual's mental set.* This suggests a learned response. It may be possible, for example, to suggest in a campaign, "Whenever you think of hotels, think of Hilton." If the campaign has the desired effect, an individual will think of Hilton (the response) whenever she or he thinks of hotels (the stimulus). Parts of this mental set are the *expectations* we bring to a situation.

People tend to perceive what they expect to perceive. There is a tendency to round out a particular image in our minds by adding pieces that we do not have *based upon what we expect to be there.* For example, a highway traveler may see a sign for a motel that advertises an indoor pool. The traveler may expect that if a motel has an indoor pool, it will also have a certain high quality of service in other facilities. This is known as bringing closure to a situation. Another part of our state of readiness is the degree of *familiarity* we have with incoming stimuli. To the extent that we are familiar with the stimulus we will have some idea of how to respond to it. This effect of past experience manifests itself in several ways. First, if we have visited Germany, then information about Germany will be perceived by us, in part, based upon our experience there. If we experienced negatives, we will perceive new information about Germany negatively because it evokes memories of a negative experience. The reverse is also true. In addition, if we perceive new information to be *similar* to an experience with which we are familiar, we will tend to act upon that new information in a way similar to our behavior in our previous experience. For example, assume we perceive Austria and Germany to be similar as vacation destinations, yet we have visited only Germany and were pleased with the experience. Information received about Austria will be perceived positively in light of our German experience. This, of course, can work to encourage or discourage purchase behavior. If we know positive feelings exist for a product or service, we may wish to stress the connection when advertising a new product from the same company. A major selling point in a chain operation is the uniformity of quality standards. The message is that if you stayed at one Holiday Inn and were pleased, you will be pleased when you stay at another Holiday Inn. This can also work in reverse. An unpleasant experience at one chain operation will be generalized into a perception about the entire chain. There are times when an advertiser will have to work hard against this tendency. Some tourists will have a tendency to perceive all "sun 'n fun" destinations as being similar. The task for any one such destination is to show that it is different from the others. A further complicated factor is that stimuli in close proximity to each other tend to be perceived as being similar. Despite the fact that islands in the Caribbean have unique identities because of different historical and cultural influences, the fact that they are relatively close together means they will be perceived as being similar. Again, the marketing task is to differentiate one from another. Another related part of this perceptual process relates to *context.* A stimulus will be perceived relative to the context in which it is viewed. A resort will be judged, in part, by the perceptions of the media in which the resort is advertised. Advertising in a magazine viewed as exclusive will bring a certain perception of exclusivity to the resort.

How consumers perceive a situation is also affected by various *social and cultural factors.* A Mediterranean cruise, for example, will be perceived differently by individuals from different social classes. Males and females will perceive the same advertisement differently. It is also clear that the relative merits of attractions at a particular destination are perceived differently by those from different cultures. The difference in perception necessitates different marketing themes for those different market segments. Even within the same country, a destination will be perceived in different terms by those in different social or cultural groups.

Clear differences have been shown between the perceptions of international and domestic visitors to the same destination (Bonn, Joseph, and Dai, 2005). For example, international visitors to Tampa Bay, Florida, perceived signage, value for the dollar and ground transportation in less favorable terms than did domestic visitors.

PERCEPTION OF DISTANCE

The subject of distance in general and perceptions of it in particular, are very important in relation to the study of tourism. Perception of distance influences three crucial tourism decisions: whether to go or stay, where to go, and which route to take (Walmsley and Jenkins, 1992). Perception of distance (and also price) are barriers to Hawaii vacations.

Much of tourist travel revolves around differences. People may travel to a different climate, from snow to sun; to see different scenery, from plains to mountains; or to experience a different culture, from modern to traditional. By its very nature, then, tourist travel to experience differences implies covering some distance. The distance to be traveled may act as a barrier, depending upon how it is perceived.

The perception of distance is relative to varied socioeconomic factors and the activity being undertaken. © 2009 iofoto. Used under license from Shutterstock, Inc.

The perception of a particular distance is not a constant. For example the homeward-bound journey seems shorter than the outward-bound journey along the same route; short distances tend to be over-estimated to a greater degree than long distances. The perception of a particular distance seems to vary relative to various socioeconomic factors as well as to the activity to be undertaken. It appears that travelers in higher levels of occupation and income are inclined to travel farther. This may, of course, be partially explained by the fact that they can afford to travel farther. However, those who favored active vacations over inactive vacations are inclined to travel long distances. Some researchers feel that occupation is the key, while others link personality variables to the propensity to travel. Others have shown that distance tends to be overestimated relative to reality (Walmsley and Jenkins, 1992).

Although all of the answers are not known, it does seem that distance can be viewed either positively or negatively in terms of its effect on travel. Certainly the greater the distance the greater the financial cost. As such, distance is a limiting factor. It may also be that great distances represent a psychological barrier because of the tediousness involved in traveling in or the fear of being far from home. At the same time, a destination may increase in attractiveness because of the distance that must be traveled to get there. It has been demonstrated that, for some tourists, beyond a certain distance the friction of distance becomes reversed—the farther they go, the farther they want to go. Especially on unplanned trips there may be a tendency to view closer-to-home destinations and attractions as stepping stones to stopping points farther away than as competition for the farther destination.

HOW WE PERCEIVE

It is generally felt that we perceive products and services as consisting of a bundle of benefits or attributes. A vacation package consists of a variety of parts—for example, in a ski vacation, excellent snow conditions, few lift lines, apres-ski entertainment, saunas, continental cuisine, and so on. A significant association between overall preference for a particular brand and preference based on the attributes of that brand has been demonstrated in the choice of an airline, destination, and tourist attraction. Thus, we buy a bundle of benefits. The decision to purchase the overall brand or package will be based upon two factors. First, the skier, for example, must believe that the attributes of the package will help satisfy his or her felt needs. Second, the satisfaction of those felt needs must be important to the skier. The former contributes more to determining an individual's attitude toward a product or service. The implication is that, if we wish to sell a particular vacation, we should sell that vacation as consisting of a number of benefits that will contribute toward the satisfaction of the buyer's needs. As we saw earlier, an individual may be seeking to satisfy several needs at the same time. Our package, therefore, should contain many elements that will aim at satisfying different needs. The provision of American-type meals and English-speaking guides may satisfy primary physiological and safety needs during a trip to Europe, while the inclusion of side trips to certain "name" resorts may help in satisfying the need for status.

Consumers have a tendency to buy things that have attributes consistent with their own perceived image. An individual's total image is made up of several parts. First, the *real self* is the objective person—what the individual is deep down. In reality, few of us know ourselves this well. Yet this true self governs our purchase and travel behavior, even if we are unaware of what it is that moves us in a particular way. Second, there is the *ideal self.* The ideal self is what we would like to be. This aspect of the individual is easier to discover for two reasons that are important to marketers: consumers are more willing to discuss what they aspire to than what they believe *really* motivates them, and by simple observation of purchase behavior much can be learned about what a consumer is striving for. Last, the *self-image*, is how consumers make purchases that will maintain or improve their self-image, as they perceive it. According to Walters (1978), consumers attempt to preserve the self-image in several ways. They:

- Buy products consistent with self-image
- Avoid products inconsistent with the self-image

- Trade up to products that relate favorably to group norms of behavior
- Avoid products that show a radical departure from accepted group norms

Tourists have favorable attitudes to destinations and products that they perceive to be consistent with their own self-image. The reverse is also true. It has, in fact, been demonstrated that pre-visit travel interest and purchase likelihood are positively correlated to self-congruity (where there is a low discrepancy between the self-image of an individual and his or her image of the destination) and ideal congruity (where there is a low discrepancy between the ideal self-image and the image of the product or destination) (Goh and Litvin, 2000).

These three aspects of the self—the real, ideal, and self-image—are totally concerned with the individual. There are two other aspects of the self concerned with external facts. The apparent self—in essence a combination of the real self, ideal self, and self-image—represents how the consumer is seen by outsiders. The impressions that outsiders have of an individual will determine whether or not any commonality of interests or desires is perceived and whether or not any friendships, will develop. This affects purchases because we tend to copy the purchases of those we admire. Thus, the picture of myself that I give to others—made up of my real and ideal selves and my self-image—will tell others if they and I seem to be the same type of person. If we are, buying patterns for a vacation, for example, may influence others to purchase that type of vacation. The *reference-group self* is how we believe others see us. What is believed, however, is more important than what is real, for behavior is predicted on what we *believe* oth-

A ski vacation package consists of snow conditions, lift lines, entertainment, food, lodging, and many other attributes that influence a potential visitor's decision. © 2009 Christophe Testi. Used under license from Shutterstock, Inc.

ers want us to do. The important influence of reference groups will be explored further in chapter 13. This self, then, is a combination of all of these aspects.

Sirgy and Su (Sirgy and Su, 2000) have attempted to link destination image, self-congruity, and travel behavior. To that end, they propose the following:

- Tourists are likely to make inferences about a destination as a direct function of atmospheric (landscape etc.) cues, the quality of services at the destination, the geographic location of the destination, prices of services and facilities at the destination, and the destination's advertising messages and media.

  From a managerial perspective, this means that changes in atmospheric cues, service quality, pricing levels can be made to positively impact the individual's perception of the destination image. Additionally, a communications message can be developed to create or reinforce that image in the minds of potential visitors.

- Travel behavior is affected by the match between the destination visitor image and the tourist's self-concept. This is referred to as the concept of self-congruity. Travel occurs because tourists are motivated to satisfy their need for self-consistency.

  Research can be conducted to determine the extent to which the destination image matches the self-concept of the majority of visitors. If congruence is found, a promotional campaign can be initiated that profiles these types of tourists.

- Travel is also affected by ideal self-congruity—the match between the destination image and the ideal self-image. Traveling to the destination satisfies the tourist's need for self-esteem.

  As above, a campaign could be developed to illustrate a match between the destination and a tourist's ideal self-congruity.

- Travel is also affected by social self-congruity—the degree of match between destination image and tourist social self-image. Travel satisfies the individual's need for social consistency. Similar effects come from the tourist's ideal social self-congruity that satisfies the tourist's need for social approval.

  Tourists might be seen returning from vacation to the envy of their friends.

- Visits to conspicuous destinations are more likely to be influenced by public self-congruity, travels with significant others and for younger tourists while inconspicuous destinations are more likely to be influenced by private self-congruity, travel alone and for older visitors.

■ The more a tourist knows about a destination, the more experience a tourist has, the more involved the tourist is with touring, and the less the time pressure on the visitor, the less the impact of self-congruity.

BENEFIT SEGMENTATION

So far, the link between purchase of a product, attitudes toward that product, and perceptions of that product has been stressed. We have said that individuals perceive products and services in terms of bundles of benefits or attributes. Their likelihood of buying a product is determined by the extent to which they perceive the product to contain sufficient benefits to satisfy their felt needs and also the extent that the satisfaction of those felt needs is important to them. Also, customers buy products that are consistent with their existing self-image or that they feel will allow them to improve their self-image. This is done within the boundaries of what kinds of purchases are sanctioned by their own reference groups. To make an effective marketing application of this process, it would be possible to divide up the tourist potential into segments and develop different vacation alternatives for the different segments based upon the various benefit bundles being sought by each segment. "Market segmentation is a technique used to divide a heterogeneous market into homogeneous sub-groups or market segments" (Davis and Sternquist, 1987). For example, in the skiing market people look for different things from the skiing experience. To some, the quality of the slopes is of prime importance; to others, the apres-ski entertainment is paramount. Each segment looks for different attributes. To the first segment a campaign stressing the quality of the slopes and the short lift lines would work. This campaign would not particularly interest the entertainment skiers. A brochure showing people sipping hot buttered rum around a blazing fire would be more effective.

It has been found that benefit-based market segmentation is a viable means of determining vacation market segments (Loker and Perdue, 1990). For example, visitors to Latin America can be broken down into four segments based on benefits sought:

1. Adventurer
2. Multifarious

> Your world is as big as you make it.
>
> Georgia Douglas Johnson

The benefits people seek are better determinants of behavior than are other approaches. © 2009 Specta. Used under license from Shutterstock, Inc.

3. Fun, relaxation seeker
4. Urbane (Sarigollu and Huang, 2005)

The benefits people seek are better determinants of behavior than are other approaches, and have been shown to predict behavior better than personality and lifestyle, usage, and demographic and geographic measures. These latter describe behavior without explaining it.

It has been demonstrated, for example, that the benefits sought from a specific destination vary by season and for different segments of the market. In the first study (Calantone and Jonar, 1984) visitors to Massachusetts were segmented by benefits sought and, further, by season of the year. Spring visitors were looking for a combination of such things as good road conditions, sporting activities, and historical and cultural attractions. The summer group was also interested in sporting activities and historical and cultural attractions. In addition, however, two new segments appeared—one group looking for a clean and scenic environment at a low cost, and the other a clean environment with a good climate and quality accommodations. The major benefit sought by fall tourists was a clean and inexpensive vacation with a large number of attractions that were cultural and historical. Winter travelers were concerned about climate and relaxation, the extent of commercialization, and the quality of shopping.

The second study (Woodside and Jacobs, 1985) looked at the benefits sought by visitors to Hawaii. It was found that Canadians saw rest and relaxation as the main benefit of a vacation to Hawaii; mainland Americans sought cultural experiences, and Japanese visitors reported family togetherness as the major benefit from the trip.

These findings have implications for product and promotional strategy. Different travel products would be developed for different segments of the market and advertising messages would differ by market segment and by season.

There has been some question as to the individuality of specific destinations in providing unique benefit bundles. Does each destination contain those elements that will satisfy particular felt needs? It has been suggested that socio-psychological motives are unrelated to destination attributes. The emphasis may shift from the destination itself to its function as a medium through which socio-psychological needs can be satisfied. If the "escaping from" motive is more important than the "seeking" motive (as suggested in chapter 11), then destinations are, to a certain extent, interchangeable. Earlier we saw that a large percentage of tourists who use travel agents enter with only a general idea of where they wish to visit. This suggests the difficulty from a marketing viewpoint of establishing a destination as the unique place offering various unique benefits to satisfy particular needs.

MARKETING IMPLICATIONS

Image research does not tell us which of the destination attributes are important to potential visitors. Nor does it indicate which are unique and do a good job of differentiating a destination from its competition in terms of the ability to meet the needs and wants of the guest. The concept of *positioning* takes care of these deficiencies. Positioning is "the process of establishing and maintaining a distinctive place for a destination in the minds of potential visitors within target markets."

QUICK TRIP 12.4

One Summer in Montana

People are more inclined to pay attention to magazine advertisements for vacations that coincide with their idea of what they would like their vacation to be like. If travelers desire to relax on a beach for seven days sipping a Margarita in the sun, a tour into the Alaskan wilderness is probably not for them. They may ignore advertisements that don't depict palm trees and a guest sleeping on a hammock by the shore. It is the challenge of advertisers to change the perceptions of individuals who do not view certain areas as vacation spots worth traveling to.

Montana is advertised as "Big Sky Country." It is the land where the greatest discoveries of dinosaur bones have been found. Attractions such as the Lewis and Clark Trail, Glacier National Park, and Yellowstone National Park are a few of the major appeals for tourists to visit. Montana does not fall under the same category as the Caribbean or Mexico but it certainly has a special experience to offer guests. The Official State Travel Information Site provides information on activities and scenic spots that offer guests reasons for visiting this northwestern state. An advertisement in the May 2008 *Trailer Life* issue depicts a bear peeking around a tree. A quote at the top of the page states, "There's a little live and let live in you. A little bit of wander. Unchanged, unknown. Yet somehow, larger than life. It's the child part. The wild part. The part that keeps us on our toes. Montana. There's a little in us all." The words used are meant to inspire readers to forge into the unknown and discover a part of themselves that is as courageous and adventurous as a child. It encourages people to consider Montana when making their next vacation decision because it is different from the "normal" idea of a vacation filled with images of sun and sand. The advertisement may cause someone to become inspired by the message and decide to take time away in a place he or she never would have deemed worth visiting prior to reading the message. However, if a person prioritized getting a good tan on vacation, he or she may not even look at the message because it is not considered to be a possible option even if the message invokes feelings of being young and adventurous.

THINK ABOUT THIS:

1. How would you inspire prospective vacationers to visit a location that does not fit the "normal" vacation criteria?
2. How would you get them to pay attention and notice advertisements that could persuade them to consider alternative vacation options?

Source: http://visitmt.com/tripplanner/things_to_do.htm. Montana Tourism. 2008. Montana. There's a little in us all. *Trailer Life*. 23.

It is important for a destination to take control of the image it wishes to portray. For example, it has been shown that the image of India that is shown in the Western press is, in many ways, different from that depicted by the Indian government (Bandyopadhyay, and Morais, 2004). While the U.S. media portrayed experiences in India as "bewildering" and "uncertain," the Indian government emphasized the country's "extreme natural and cultural contrasts." In another example, the U.S. media focused on the charm of India's small villages and folkways while the Indian government's promotions ignored such images. Additionally, the American media promoted a royal image of luxury with a focus on "Maharaja palaces" and eco-lodges embedded in historical and natural environments. The Indian government, on the other hand, emphasized India's modern hotels as well as the Western-style amenities that had recently been added to its old hotels.

A similar phenomenon has been found in the depiction of Canada's image (Buzinde, Santos, and Smith, 2004). In this case the image portrayed by the Canadian government is criticized by some who see, in the messages, that ethnic minorities are shown only in supporting roles while the ethnic majority is the only group shown as being able to travel.

The stages involved in developing a positioning strategy for a destination are as follows (Crompton, Fakeye, and Lue, 1992):

1. Identify the competition.
2. What are the strengths and weaknesses of the destination as perceived by the target market?
3. What benefits are being sought by the target market?
4. What are the strengths and weaknesses of the competition as perceived by the target market?
5. How do potential visitors perceive the destination relative to the competition?
6. Select the best position for the destination.

This has very real marketing implications. The concept is known as importance-performance analysis. Effective marketing strategies can be determined only after determining the extent to which potential visitors perceive that our destination contains those attributes that they consider important. This involves a three-step process:

1. What do you, the potential visitor, consider important?
2. Do you *perceive* that we have this?
3. Do we *actually* have this?

Data on the first two items can come from quantitative data or from open-ended comments using impressions of critical incidents recorded by tourists (Pritchard and Havitz, 2006). A model for this process is contained in figure 12.5. This process is illustrated through an examination of a study of Ireland's image by French tourists (O'Leary and Deegan, 2005). A literature search identified a comprehensive list of attributes that could be used to measure destination image. In a survey of potential tourists from France individuals were asked what three words or expressions came to mind when they thought of Ireland (see figure 12.6). Prior to their visit, tourists from France were asked to rate the relative importance of these attributes on a scale of 1 through 5, with 5 being the most important. After their visit, tourists were asked to evaluate the performance of the destination on these same attributes again using a scale of 1 through 5, where 5 indicates "very good."

The first consideration is "what does the market consider important or unimportant?" Potential visitors are particularly interested in scenic beauty, the welcome of the people, potential for discovery and environmental and tranquility factors. Because these items are important to the market, they are important to the destination. Items that are rated low in importance should be ignored by those at the destination. To include them in

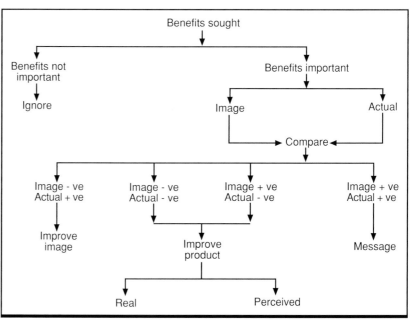

Figure 12.5 Perception–Marketing Implications.

Functional (Physical, Measurable)

   Beautiful scenery
   Pretty towns
   Activities/sports available
   Culture/history
   Litter free
   Environment
   Nightlife/entertainment (pubs, music)
   Services available (restaurants/shopping)
   Access (cost, means)
   Price/quality ratio
   Pleasant climate
   Economic development/urbanization
   Meet family/friends
   Welcome/friendly people
   Calm/tranquility
   Relaxed pace of life
   Discover something new
Psychological (Abstract)

Figure 12.6 List of Attributes Developed for French Tourists. Source: O'Leary and Deegan. 2005.

To make the most of its tourism marketing, Ireland must make sure perceptions and reality match up, and concentrate on those areas deemed most important to visitors. © 2009 Steeve Roche. Used under license from Shutterstock, Inc.

any marketing effort would overload the consumer and may result in the potential visitors "protecting" themselves by ignoring the entire message.

The same strategy is appropriate if the image is positive but the actual situation is negative. In such a situation we may attract visitors because they think they will be made to feel welcome. If we know that our employees do not have enough training to give this expected level of service, dissatisfaction will result unless the product (employee hospitality) is changed.

Tourists compare their initial expectations with their actual experience (or, actually, their *perception* of the actual experience). It has been found that (Chon, 1992):

■ When the expectation of the destination is negative but the perceptions are positive, the tourist is most satisfied;

■ When the expectation is positive and the perception is positive, the satisfaction is moderate;

■ When the expectation is negative and the perceptions are negative, satisfaction is lower than either of the above scenarios;

■ When the expectation is positive but perceptions are negative, the tourist is least satisfied.

This process can be displayed visually in a perceptual map. A perceptual map shows the collective perceptions of a segment of the market for a particular destination on factors considered important to them. A perceptual map of Ireland is shown in figure 12.7. The importance of vacation attributes has been placed on

the horizontal axis and the perception of Ireland for these same attributes has been placed on the vertical axis.

Items in the top left quadrant consist of those attributes that are important to this segment of the market and on which Ireland is perceived as doing a poor job of providing. Ireland is not seen as providing good quality for the money, is not litter-free and is perceived as being costly. These are items where performance must be improved. However, these items must survive a *reality check*. It may be, for example, that lost-cost travel options are

HIGH IMPORTANCE		
Price-quality		B.S.
Litter free		W.
Access (cost, means)		D
		C/T
		C/H
		RPL
		N/E
		E
Low		High
Performance		Performance
S		
PT		
C		
FF		
A/S		
E/D		
LOW IMPORTANCE		

Figure 12.7 A Perceptual Map of Ireland. Source: Adapted from O'Leary and Deegan. 2005.

A Flight, a Hotel Room, and . . .

Uniquely Singapore ran an advertisement in the Spring/Summer 2008 edition of *Girlfriend Getaways* that promotes a six-day/four-night package. This $1,199 vacation includes airfare from Los Angeles, San Francisco, and New York and accommodations at The Ritz-Carlton Millennia. The advertisement includes the Top Ten Reasons to Visit Singapore:

1. Indulge in retail therapy at Orchard Road and Vivocity.
2. Pamper yourself at one of Asia's biggest outdoor spas: Spa Botanica.
3. Savor seafood Singapore-style, including spicy chili crab, black-pepper crayfish, and butter prawns for an unforgettable meal.
4. Take a bumboat ride on the Singapore River.
5. Head to Chinatown, Kampong Glam (Malay Village), and little India for a cultural excursion and a different take on shopping.
6. Check out the Night Safari–world's first night zoo.
7. Party the night away at either Clarke Quay or Boat Quay, Singapore's premiere clubbing zone.
8. Have a Singapore Sling at the Raffles Hotel.
9. Head to Sentosa Island for some R&R and chill out at Café Del Mar.
10. Take a Peranakan Trails tour or a culinary tour.

When travelers book flights and make hotel accommodations, they expect to indulge in a variety of benefits that make the trip worthwhile. Advertising activities and selling a travel package to guests fill expectations that the vacation will potentially satisfy a variety of perceived needs. Vacationers are not likely to travel great distances to lock themselves in their hotel rooms for the duration of the visit. Rather, they expect a bundle of benefits that will grant them a memorable experience. Uniquely Singapore understands this expectation of travelers and encourages guests to immerse themselves in the culture of the city.

THINK ABOUT THIS:

1. What descriptive words are used in the Top Ten Reasons to Visit Singapore in order to target a specific segment of the market?
2. What market is being targeted?
3. What are the benefits of creating vacation packages for guests?

Source: Visitsingapore.com. 2008. Asia's Lifestyle Capital. *Girlfriend Getaway*. 77.

available but tourists are not aware of them. In this case, where the image is negative but, in actuality, low-cost packages are available then the image must be changed. On the other hand, if the country is not litter-free, then the product must be improved.

The product change may, on the other hand, be perceptual. There is a segment of skiers who place high priority on short lift lines. If a ski area is perceived as having long lift lines, it will be necessary to change the product if, in fact, the lines are long. How can a lift line be shortened? A real change would be to open up more hill capacity. This, however, is expensive. A perceived

change would be to make the wait *appear* shorter. Some Michigan ski areas provide entertainers or musicians to provide a diversion for those in line to make the time spent in line seem short.

Ireland is seen as strong on certain attributes deemed important to French tourists: beautiful scenery, welcome, discovery, calm/tranquility, culture/history, relaxed pace of life, nightlife/entertainment and environment. The temptation is to charge full steam ahead with these items as the mainstay of a marketing campaign. Here again, there is the need for a reality check. Are these perceptions truly reflective of Ireland? If the image is positive yet the reality is otherwise, the product needs to be improved. If, on the other hand, these attributes truly are reflective of the destination, they can form the basis for a marketing campaign directed to this segment of the market.

There are certain attributes where Ireland is perceived as doing a poor job: services, pretty towns, climate, family and friends, activities/sports, economic development. However, these are items that score low in importance to tourists from France. As such, they should be given a low priority in terms of improving the product.

Finally, there are items ranked as low in importance and high in performance. It would be foolish to spend time and money to improve things already considered high in performance when they are items not considered important to the tourist.

Through the use of perceptual mapping, destinations can determine how or if they should change their tourism product and advertising.

Branding is one way to improve the image of a destination. Scotland, for example, is seen as "uniquely strong in integrity, inventiveness, tenacity, and spirit."

Destination branding can be defined as: "the set of marketing activities that

1. support the creation of a name, symbol, logo, word mark or other graphic that readily *identifies* and *differentiates* a destination; that
2. consistently convey the *expectations* of a memorable travel *experience* that is uniquely associated with the destination; that
3. serves to *consolidate* and *reinforce* the *emotional connection* between the visitor and the destination; and that
4. reduce consumer *search costs* and *perceived risk*. Collectively, these activities serve to create a *destination image* that positively influences consumer *destination choice*" (Blain, Levy, and Ritchie, 2005).

It appears that most destinations use destination logos, mostly in print and videos. These logos are reflective of the destination's image and are intended to be memorable. If done properly, a logo can bring the many tourism-related businesses at the destination together under a common banner. The actual logo design is typically developed by the marketing department of the tourism destination and does not involve, though perhaps it should, local tourism-related businesses.

SUMMARY

Once people are motivated to go on vacation they begin an information search to compare various alternatives. They seek and receive information from friends and relatives, travel opinion leaders as well as from the commercial environment. The latter has less credibility. Incoming information goes through a two-step process before it has an impact. The first step controls the quantity of information that is received; the second controls the quality of information taken in. It is possible to structure messages such that they have a greater chance of being noticed and giving off the intended message.

Because people perceive a destination as consisting of a bundle of benefits, benefit segmentation is a viable way of segmenting a market. By comparing what is important to the tourist with the perception the tourist has of a particular vacation spot, a perceptual map can be developed to aid in marketing.

Trends

Hotelier's Top Ten Internet Marketing Resolutions

1. I will generate robust Internet marketing ROIs from my hotel's Internet marketing efforts.
2. My Internet marketing budget will take a holistic view of the hotel online environment.
3. I will look at best industry practices by Internet marketing vendors.
4. I will develop a robust Web site re-design and optimization strategy.
5. I will adopt a robust social media strategy.
6. Direct Internet marketing and distribution will be the centerpiece of my Internet strategy.
7. My marketing strategy will provide a Unique Value Proposition to my customers.
8. Electronic Customer Relationship Management will be part of my strategic objectives.
9. I will implement Web site Analytics and Campaign Tracking Functionality on my Web site.
10. I will become a smarter Internet marketer.

Source: Starkov, M., and J. Price. 2008. "Hotelier's 2008 top ten internet marketing resolutions," http://www.tourism exchange.com/exchange/en/newsroom/home/getArticle.jsp? articleID=7259&languageID=1. Retrieved 2 February 2008.

ACTIVITIES

1. Imagine that you are building a resort or hotel in an area you know well. What market is it aimed at? Create a positioning strategy for that destination using the following guidelines:

   a. Identify the competition.
   b. What are the strengths and weaknesses of the destination as perceived by the target market?
   c. What benefits are being sought by the target market?
   d. What are the strengths and weaknesses of the competition as perceived by the target market?
   e. How do potential visitors perceive the destination relative to the competition?
   f. Select the best position for the destination.

2. Create a logo for the above destination. Use this form of branding to reinforce your company image through the use of a symbol.

3. Think of five places you have been and describe them using one word. Come up with a marketing strategy for one of the locations that would change your perception of the location to fit a different image. How might you combat external factors such as climate and how friendly the locals are to visitors?

REFERENCES

1999 U.S. Consumer Survey. *Travel Weekly*, 58 (85): Section 2.

Andereck, K. L., E. Ng, and R. C. Knopf. 2003. Traveler information search: Differences between internet users and non-users. 34th Annual Conference Proceedings of the Travel and Tourism Research Association. CD-ROM, unpaged.

Bai, B., C. Hu, C. C. Countryman, and J. D. Elsworth. 2003. Understanding consumer behavior through online vacation planning. 34th Annual Conference Proceedings of the Travel and Tourism Research Association. CD-ROM, unpaged.

Balogu, S., and D. Brinkberg. 1997. Affective images of tourism destinations. *Journal of Travel Research*, XXXV (4): 11–15.

Bandyopadhyay, R., and D. B. Morais. 2004. Representative dissonance: Differences in the way India is portrayed to the USA tourist market. 35th Annual Conference Proceedings of the Travel and Tourism Research Association. CD-ROM, unpaged.

Beerli, A., G. D. Meneses, and S. M. Gil. 2007. Self-congruity and destination choice. *Annals of Tourism Research*, 34 (3): 571–587.

Beldona, S. 2005. Cohort analysis of online travel information search behavior. *Journal of Travel Research*, 44: 135–142.

Bieger, T., and C. Laesser. 2004. Information sources for travel decisions: Toward a source process model. *Journal of Travel Research*, 42: 357–371.

Blain, C., S. E. Levy, and J. R. B. Ritchie. 2005. Destination branding: Insights and practices from destination management organizations. *Journal of Travel Research*, 43: 337.

Bonn, M. A., S. M. Joseph, and M. Dai. 2005. International versus domestic visitors: An examination of destination image perceptions. *Journal of Travel Research*, 43: 294–301.

Braun-LaTour, K. A., M. J. Grinley, and E. F. Loftus. 2006. Tourist memory distortion. *Journal of Travel Research*, 44: 360–367.

Buzinde, C. N., C. Santos, and S. Smith. 2004. Experiencing the "other" destination imagery in multicultural Canada. 35th Annual Conference Proceedings of the Travel and Tourism Research Association. CD-ROM, unpaged.

Calantone, R. J., and J. S. Johar. 1984. Seasonal segmentation of the tourism market using a benefit segmentation framework. *Journal of Travel Research*, 23 (2): 14–24.

Chen, J. S. 2000. Cross-cultural comparison of the usage of travel information. 31st Annual Conference Proceedings of the Travel and Tourism Research Association. 104–106.

Cho, M. H., and D. Kerstetter. 2004. Moderating effect of source credibility on tourists: prior knowledge and information search behavior. 34th Annual Conference Proceedings of the Travel and Tourism Research Association. CD-ROM, unpaged.

Cho, M. H., and D. Kerstetter. 2002. Sign value and tourists' information search behavior. *Capitalizing on Travel Research for Marketing Success*. 33rd Annual Conference Proceedings of the Travel and Tourism Research Association. CD-ROM, unpaged.

Cho, Y., and D. Fesenmaier. 1999. The effects of virtual tour on the formation of destination image. 30th Annual Conference Proceedings of the Travel and Tourism Research Association. 178–189.

Chon, K. 1990. The role of destination image in tourism: A review and discussion. *The Tourist Review*, (2): 2–9.

Crompton, J. L., P. C. Fakeye, and C. Lue. 1992. Positioning: The example of the Lower Valley in the winter long stay destination market. *Journal of Travel Research*, 31 (2): 20–26.

Davis, B. D., and B. Sternquist. 1987. Appealing to the elusive tourist: An attribute cluster strategy. *Journal of Travel Research*. 25 (4): 26.

Dellaert, B. G. C., and S. Wendel. 2004. Tourists' hedonic and utilitarian use of the internet as a travel information channel. 34th Annual Conference Proceedings of the Travel and Tourism Research Association. CD-ROM, unpaged.

Echtner, C. M., and J. R. B. Ritchie. 1993. The measurement of destination image. *Journal of Travel Research*, 31 (4): 3–13.

Fodness, D., and B. Murray. 1998. A typology of tourist information search strategies. *Journal of Travel Research,* 37 (2): 108–119.

Fodness, D., and B. Murray. 1999. A model of tourist information search behavior. *Journal of Travel Research,* 37 (3): 220–230.

Godwin, N. 2000. Leisure travelers are outpacing business travelers on the Net. *Travel Weekly,* 59 (26): 1, 4.

Goh, H. K., and S. W. Litvin. 2000. Destination Preference and Self-Congruity. 31st Annual Conference Proceedings of the Travel and Tourism Research Association. 197–203.

Green, C. E., and S. D. Cook. *Travelers' Use of the Internet,* Washington, DC: Travel Association of America, 2005 edition.

Gunn, C. A. 1972. *Vacationscape: Designing Tourist Regions.* Austin, TX: University of Texas. 110–113.

Harris, L. & Associates (biennial since 1971). *The Character and Volume of the U.S. Travel Agency Market.*

Jun, S.H., C. Vogt, and K. J. MacKay. 2004. The role of web-based planning and purchasing behaviors in pretrip contexts. 35th Annual Conference Proceedings of the Travel and Tourism Research Association. CD-ROM, unpaged.

Jun, S.H., C. Vogt, and K. J. MacKay. 2007. Relationships between travel information search and travel product purchase in pretrip contexts. *Journal of Travel Research,* 45: 266–274.

Loker, L. E., and R. R. Perdue. 1990. A benefit-based segmentation of a nonresident summer travel market. *Journal of Travel Research,* 31 (1): 30–35.

Miller, J. E. 1995. *Perceptual Mapping.* A travel research seminar presented at the Annual Conference of the Travel and Tourism Research Association.

O'Leary, S., and J. Deegan. 2005. Ireland's image as a tourism destination in france: Attribute importance and performance. *Journal of Travel Research,* 43: 247–256.

Oh, I., and J. Lee. 1995. *Modification of Travel Information Communication Flow.* Poster Presentation at the 26th Annual Conference of the Travel and Tourism Research Association.

Pan, B., and D. R. Fessenmaier. 2006. Online information search vacation planning. *Annals of Tourism Research,* 33 (3): 809–832.

Park, J., Y. Ekinci, and C. Cobanoglu. 2002. An empirical analysis of internet users' intention to purchase vacations online. *Capitalizing on Travel Research for Marketing Success.* 33rd Annual Conference Proceedings of the Travel and Tourism Research Association. CD-ROM, unpaged.

Pritchard, M. P., and M. E. Havitz. 2006. Destination appraisal: An analysis of critical incidents. *Annals of Tourism Research,* 33 (1): 25–46.

Rao, S. R., E. G. Thomas, and R. G. Javalgi. 1992. Activity preferences and trip-planning behavior of the U.S. outbound pleasure travel market. *Journal of Travel Research,* 30 (3): 3–12.

Ryan, C., and J. Cave. 2005. Structuring destination image: A qualitative approach. *Journal of Travel Research,* 44: 143–150.

Sarigollu, E., and R. Huang. 2005. Benefits segmentation of visitors to Latin America. *Journal of Travel Research,* 43: 277–293.

Sirgy, M. J., and C. Su. 2000. Destination image, self-congruity, and travel behavior: toward an integrative model. *Journal of Travel Research,* 38 (4): 340–352.

Stevens, B. F., 1992. Price value perceptions of travelers. *Journal of Travel Research,* 31 (2): 44–48.

Thompson, C. 2008. Is the tipping point toast? *Fast Company.* 75–78, 104–106.

Travel Industry Association of America. 2004. Travelers' Use of the Internet. Washington, DC.

Walmsley, D. J., and J. M. Jenkins. 1992. Cognitive distance: A neglected issue in travel behavior. *Journal of Travel Research,* 31 (1): 24–29.

Walters, C. G. 1978. *Consumer Behavior: Theory and Practice.* Homewood, IL: Richard D. Irwin, Inc. 182–186.

Woodside, A. G., and L. W. Jacobs. 1985. Step two in benefit segmentation: Learning the benefits realized by major travel markets. *Journal of Travel Research,* 24 (1): 7–13.

Yoon, Y., and S. Kimm. 2002. An assessment and construct validity of destination image: A use of second-order factor analysis. *Capitalizing on Travel Research for Marketing Success.* 33rd Annual Conference Proceedings of the Travel and Tourism Research Association. CD-ROM, unpaged.

SURFING SOLUTIONS

http://www.kristofcreative.com/portfolio/advertising/print/ads_travel.shtml (Kristof Creative, Nashville advertising agency)

http://www.phi-marketing.com/tourism-marketing.php (Phi Marketing)

http://www.hospitalitynet.org/news/4035839.search?query=hospitality+advertising (Hospitality net)

ADDITIONAL READINGS

"An Investigation of Consumer Perceptions of, and Preferences for, Selected Tourism Destinations: A Multidimensional Scaling Approach," Jonathan Goodrich, PhD dissertation, State University of New York at Buffalo, 1977.

Psychology of Leisure Travel. 1981. E. J. Mayo and L. P. Jarvis, C.B.I. Publishing Company, Inc., Boston, MA.

"The Relevance of Life Style and Demographic Information to Designing Package Travel Tours," James Abbey, PhD dissertation, Utah State University, 1978.

"A System's Model of the Tourist's Destination Selection Process with particular Reference to the Roles of Image and Perceived Constraint," John Crompton, PhD dissertation, Texas A&M University, 1977.

Tasci, A. D., and W. C. Gartner. 2007. Destination image and its functional relationships. *Journal of Travel Research,* 45: 413–425.

chapter 13

Travel Purchase

THE TRAVELER'S BUYING PROCESS

Today's travelers have a common set of expectations.
Meet those expectations and the client is happy. No complaints.
Fail to meet those expectations, you may lose a client.

The Institute of Certified Travel Agents

PURPOSE

Having learned about how people make travel decisions and destination choices, students will be able to suggest appropriate communications strategies.

LEARNING OBJECTIVES

✓ Describe the buying-process stages that people go through when making travel decisions.
✓ Explain the effectiveness of different communication strategies at each stage of the buying process.
✓ Identify which promotional techniques work best at each stage of the buying process.
✓ Describe some of the models that have been suggested to explain how travelers choose destination areas.
✓ Describe the series of sub-decisions that make up how a vacation decision is actually made.
✓ Explain the influence of family life-cycle stages on vacation sub-decisions.

OVERVIEW

When travelers become aware of a need to travel, they go through a series of stages before committing to a purchase decision. The characteristics of each of these steps is examined. The communications strategy of the marketer depends upon where the target market is in the buying process. Appropriate strategies for each stage in the buying process are outlined.

A number of alternative destination choice process models are described. It is suggested that perceived travel activities and benefits play a key role in the choice of destination areas. It is also pointed out that people's travel decisions and decision-making processes change as they gain more travel experience.

The decision to take a travel trip involves a series of sub-decisions—where to go, when to go, how long to stay, how to travel, and so on. The order in which these sub-decisions are made and the influence of various family members on the sub-decisions is examined.

> We only need travel enough to give our intellects an airing.
>
> Henry David Thoreau

TRAVEL PURCHASE: THE TRAVELER'S BUYING PROCESS

It is easier, less time-consuming, and less costly to sell London as a travel destination than it is to sell Tibet. Part of the reason is that more people know more about and have specific opinions or attitudes about London as a vacation destination than about Tibet. To sell Tibet would require a rather lengthy educational process. Making a travel decision involves "selecting and committing oneself to a course of action

---

QUICK TRIP 13.1

Attention Please!

The first step in the buying process is gaining the attention of the potential customer. Mass media advertising plays a major role in this first stage. Advertisers must make the message memorable to motivate people to seek further information about the destination. This may lead to the actual purchasing of the products/services offered.

Janet Clark published an article on January 15, 2008, titled "Top 10 Memorable Super Bowl Commercials of the Decade." ABC asks for $2.5 million for just half a minute of commercial time during the Super Bowl. Major corporations and companies invest a great deal of money into the advertisements that are squeezed in between timeouts. That is a lot of money to spend just to get people to notice you! Janet Clark considers the following 10 Super Bowl commercials to be the best of the decade:

#10 2005 MasterCard: Mascots
In this commercial you see many food mascots including the Pillsbury dough boy, the chef from Chef Boyardee, the Vlasic Stork, Star-Kist tuna, the Jolly Green Giant, and Mr. Clean. All of these icons are eating dinner together and is one of MasterCard's "priceless" commercials. It definitely was cute, and MasterCard also was able to advertise all the products of different food companies by showing off their mascots.

#9 2002 Quiznos: Toasted or Untoasted
This commercial is advertising Quiznos. A lady is sitting in front of a toasted and untoasted sub; she picks the wrong one and gets shot by a dart.

#8 2003 FedEx: Castaway
A castaway returns a package that he found on his island. He did not open the package, returning it to the person that was supposed to receive it. The recipient opens it in front of him and reveals a cell phone and seeds. This commercial is very funny.

#7 2002 M&M: Complimentary Candy
A guy checks into a hotel and waiting in his room is a big complimentary talking red M&M.

#6 2007 Bud Light: Rock, Paper, Scissors
Two men play Rock, Paper, Scissors to win the last Bud Light. The man who plays rock literally throws a rock at the other man and wins the Bud Light.

(continued)

#5 2006 Ford Hybrid: Kermit the Frog
Kermit the Frog rides his bike through rough terrain, kayaks, and climbs a mountain using transportation that is environmentally friendly saying it's not easy being green. He then reaches the top of the mountain to find the Ford Hybrid and all its features and then says maybe it is easy to be green.

#4 2004 Bud Light: Horny Talking Monkey
A horny talking monkey is shown to a guy's date.

#3 2007 Doritos: Checkout Girl
A Doritos checkout girl gets seductively excited over Doritos flavors while checking out a customer.

#2 2007 GoDaddy.com: Marketing
This commercial is showing a marketing office with a bunch of sexy girls in the room.

#1 2007 Snickers: Kiss
Two men eat the same Snickers and share in a kiss. This commercial got media attention from gay rights activists.

These examples of entertaining commercials draw in the attention of viewers. The publicity generated from this event allows for millions of people to view the message. Yet there are many factors that lie between being made aware of the product and the actual purchase of the product that deal with the stages people go through when making buying decisions.

THINK ABOUT THIS:
1. How do the unique perceptions of individuals influence the amount of information that is taken in?
2. How might an advertiser leave a lasting impression on an observer and inspire the observer to search for further information?
3. How might management identify whether the money spent on advertising was worth the cost incurred?

Sources: http://www.associatedcontent.com/article/533451/top_10_memorable_super_bowl_commercials.html; http://blogcritics.org/archives/2006/02/03/225712.php.

that involves a series of steps or events" (Milman, 1993).

ATTENTION AND AWARENESS

When making a travel purchase, a consumer moves through several stages. The wise marketing manager realizes that different communication strategies are appropriate for different stages of the buying process. Figure 13.1 illustrates the various stages as defined by several authors. When deciding whether or not to visit a previously unknown destination area, an individual may at first be unaware of its potential as a travel destination. The destination area has to be brought to the awareness or attention of the potential traveler. A prime function in communicating to the consumer is to gain attention. Mass media advertising can be very influential at this point. A slogan or a jingle aimed at arousing curiosity can be successful in gaining the viewer's attention. This is the first step in the buying process.

There is no consensus on the relationship, if any, between an individual's prior knowledge of a destina-

tion and the amount of time spent on an information search. Some studies report a negative relationship between the amount of prior knowledge and the amount of external information search, while others report a positive correlation. Perhaps an experienced traveler does not have to collect more information because they already are very familiar with it. On the other hand, it may be that because of their experience, they know where to get specific information and, thus, collect information more efficiently compared to less experienced tourists (Gursoy and McCleary, 2004).

Research has shown that people who are familiar with central Florida were more interested in and likely to revisit it compared to those who were only aware of the destination (Milman and Pizam, 1995). As people move from the awareness stage to the familiarity stage, their interest and likelihood to visit increases. However, the same study found that moving from non-awareness to awareness does not necessarily increase the likelihood of visiting the destination area. This is not surprising. Once aware of a particular destination area, individuals, perhaps based on scanty information, might decide that

Howard/Sheth	Crissy	McDaniel	AIDA	IUOTO	Russ	Cunningham
				Unawareness		
Attention	Awareness	Awareness	Attention	Awareness	Awareness	Awareness
Comprehension		Knowledge		Comprehension		
Attitudes	Interest Evaluation	Liking Preference	Interest Desire		Interest Desire	Interest Evaluation
Intention		Conviction		Conviction		
Purchase	Trial Adoption	Purchase	Action	Action	Action Reaction	Trial Adoption

Figure 13.1 The Traveler's Buying Process. Sources: Howard, J., and J. N. Sheth. 1969; Crissy, W. J. E., R. J. Boewadt, and D. M. Laudadio. 1975; McDaniel, C., Jr. 1979; AIDA, Strong, E. K. 1925; IUOTO (undated); Russ, F. A., and C. A. Kirkpatrick. 1982; Cunningham, W. H., and I. C. M. Cunningham, 1981.

visiting it will not satisfy needs and wants important to them. They "drop out" of the buying process. However, it might call into question the large amounts of money spent on making people aware of destination areas of which they were previously unaware. Targeted advertising oriented toward specific markets and travel opinion leaders (see chapter 12) might be one answer.

At this early point, there is some indication (based on one relatively small sample) that individuals make an initial judgment as to the extent to which the destination area meets their needs. If it does, it is looked at more closely. At this early stage of the process facilitators— "those beliefs about a destination's attributes which help to satisfy a potential traveler's specific motives" (Um and Crompton, 1992)—are influential. Later on in the process inhibitors—"attributes which are not congruent with his or her motives" (Um and Crompton, 1992)— become more influential.

KNOWLEDGE AND COMPREHENSION

The task in the next stage of the buying process is to make the customer *goal directed*. If the potential traveler's attention has been successfully stimulated, she or he seeks out more information on the destination area. The attempt is to become more knowledgeable about what the destination area has to offer, to comprehend what it is all about. The emphasis is on information, and the task of the communicator is to provide sufficient information to direct the potential traveler toward purchase. Experienced travelers are more likely to search for information from external sources than are travelers who are merely "familiar" with the destination. Travelers who are unfamiliar with a destination need information that is relatively simple. Expert tourists prefer detailed information about the destination. Communications to first-time tourists need to focus on being persuasive,

while repeat visitors need to be reminded of the destination as a future alternative (Gursoy and McCleary, 2004; Vogt and Andereck, 2003).

Advertising is again important at this stage. The choice of media is crucial. Media should be chosen that can convey a great deal of information. Brochures or the Web can do this, as can magazine and newspaper advertisements with a great deal of copy. Radio and television cannot provide the large amounts of information needed at this stage. It is important to talk about the destination area in terms of the benefits offered. It will be remembered that destination areas are perceived in terms of their benefits to the individual. To the extent that we understand a message, we are more inclined to pay attention to it.

ATTITUDES, INTEREST, AND LIKING

If the communication so far has been effective, the potential traveler next moves to developing a liking, interest, or attitude about the destination area. The promotional objectives at this stage are to create or reinforce existing positive attitudes or images or to correct negative attitudes or images. A positive attitude is influenced by the individual's tendency or predisposition to visit that particular destination area (see chapter 12). It is also a function of how well we have gained the traveler's attention and provided sufficient information for him to determine whether or not the benefits of the destination area match his needs and wants. Attitudes are difficult to change because new incoming information is often screened to conform to an old attitude. It has been demonstrated that awareness or attention must exist before an attitude can change. The interest in a particular destination area influences how much effort is put into the comprehension of a particular message.

More Money, Less Time

At the conviction stage of the Traveler's Buying-Decision Process, a person is typically constrained by time or money, which deters the person from making the actual purchase. Vacation compression is an issue in American culture today. People may have the means to travel, but they do not have the time available to actually take time off. Americans overwork. They often feel pressured from their jobs if they ask for vacation time or are looked down upon if they take advantage of their allotted vacation allowance. Is there a solution to relaxing without feeling anxious about spending too much time away?

It is the task of hospitality companies to understand the broad topic of vacation compression and create packages that promote weekend travel that makes the most out of each vacationer's time off. Philip S. Gutis of the *New York Times* states, "Travel industry experts say that, in the last several years, Americans have been taking shorter, but more frequent, vacations." Hotels may have found a way to increase occupancy during their slowest days. Hilton Hotels Corporation told Gutis that Saturday, which once had the lowest occupancy rates, now had the highest due to weekend packaging. American Express has created clubs that cater to weekend travelers and allow guests to enjoy a variety of discounts. Cruise Lines International tripled its three- to five-day cruises from 347,000 to 1.2 million between 1980 and 1989.

Furthermore, packaging makes it easy for a potential guest to plan a vacation. Instead of searching various sources of information, a package often includes accommodation, airfare, and activities. Gutis remarks, "The travel industry has introduced a broad range of packages in the last five years intended to make short trips more affordable and accessible." The trend of frequent weekend travel vacations is continuing to rise in popularity. Introducing weekend packages to guests acts as a solution to the negative effects that vacation compression has on the hospitality industry.

THINK ABOUT THIS:

1. As the manager of a hotel, how would you consider approaching the problem of vacation compression?
2. Do you consider weekend packaging to be the best solution?
3. What benefits and activities would you include in a weekend package that would be most valuable to travelers who need a weekend to relax but wish to make the most out of their time away?

Source: http://query.nytimes.com/gst/fullpage.html?res=9C0CE3D6123CF937A25750C0A966958260&sec=&spon=&pagewanted=all.

EVALUATION, PREFERENCE, AND DESIRE

After evaluating various alternatives, the consumer develops a preference or desire for a destination area. The importance of advertising is somewhat less at this stage. The most effective types of messages are *testimonial* and *comparison advertisements*. In a testimonial advertisement, a person, usually a well-known public figure, praises what is being sold. The hope is that if the viewer or reader respects the person in the message, their opinion on the product or service being sold is respected. The same effect can be gained by "testimony" from someone who has already visited the destination area. It is crucial that the spokesperson be believable. It is also important, for maximum impact, that the person chosen to be in the advertisement have some connection with what is being sold. A form of testimonial is the rating found in various guidebooks. To the extent that the rating system is respected, advertising the rating gains the respect of the readers.

In a comparison advertisement, one destination area or facility is mentioned in a promotional message in comparison with another. The destination areas are compared on particular attributes. For this kind of message to work, it is necessary to select, for the basis of comparison, attributes that the customer thinks are important. It is crucial that the destination area being advertised be stronger on those attributes than the competition. The tendency, however, is that visitors shift from the intensive use of travel catalogs and advertisements to sources of advice such as travel agents and automobile associations. The more educated the visitor, the more sources are used.

Another interesting concept at this point is the idea of the *decoy effect*. The hypothesis is that "the introduction of a carefully constructed 'decoy' into a choice set results in a segment of consumers shifting their choice to a higher-priced targeted item" (Josiam and Hobson, 1995). This strategy is outlined in figure 13.2. The "target" is what we want the customer to buy; the "option" is what is initially offered; the "decoy" is offered as an option, but with no intent that people actually buy it. There has been some limited research on the impact of a decoy in making a travel decision that seems to support the hypothesized contention. The implications are obvious. Offering additional choices to customers (decoys) that are within the price range of the destination area being targeted but that offer less perceived value might shift customers to the higher-priced target. In part this is because the value offered relative to the price charged for the decoy is less than that of the target. It is also because customers tend to stay away from extreme options. In the situation displayed in figure 13.2 the low price-low value "option" seems an extreme choice in comparison to the other choices.

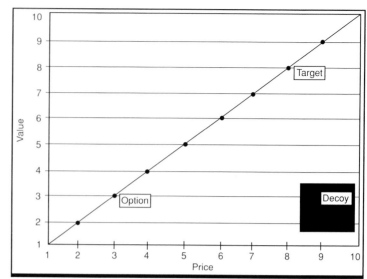

Figure 13.2 The Decoy Effect. Source: Josiam, B. M., and J. S. P. Hobson. 1995. Consumer choice in context: The decoy effect in travel and tourism. *Journal of Travel Research*, 34 (1): 46.

QUICK TRIP 13.3

Make It Better or Lose Me Forever

The main objective during the Attitudes, Interest, and Liking stage of the Traveler's Buying-Decision process is to reinforce existing positive attitudes of a destination and correct any negative attitudes. A customer of Residence Inn Montreal Downtown wrote her complaints about this Marriott location on *my3cents.com* on April 30, 2008. As a longtime Gold member, she expected to be treated with more courtesy than the hotel was willing to give. She booked her reservations and unfortunately did not notice that she purchased her room at a "nonrefundable" rate. When she cancelled her reservation, she was charged for the two nights she originally booked. She asked the hotel to give her a full refund, give her two free nights, or give her extra reward points for two nights. However, the hotel did not fulfill any of these suggested responses to correct the situation. When a customer complains about a bad experience at a hotel, he or she is likely to see the hotel in a better light if courteous and polite employees work to fix the situation in a timely manner. Otherwise, the hotel may lose a customer forever; and when that customer complains to his or her peers, potential customers are lost as well.

Promotional techniques not only solve a situation when concerns arise, but they also encourage guests to stay at the location to begin with. Marriott's Gold Card offers discounts and benefits to members that support traveling to various Marriott locations. The official Web site states, "The Marriott Gold Card program is an exclusive membership program that offers its members generous dining discounts and accommodation benefits throughout all participating Marriott International hotels." This program has a variety of benefits for members that motivate customers to book rooms with Marriott.

THINK ABOUT THIS:

1. Should the hotel have to pay for this woman's mistake?
2. Does the cost of giving this customer a full refund, two free nights, or extra reward points outweigh the potential of losing her as a guest in the future?
3. How does being a loyalty card member influence the attitude of customers and their expectations for special considerations?

Sources: http://www.marriottgoldcard.com/en/program_benefits.php; http://www.my3cents.com/showReview.cgi?id=36523.

INTENTION AND CONVICTION

At this stage in the buying process, the potential travelers are convinced that the benefits of the destination area meet their needs and wants and are almost at the point of purchase. Studies have shown that the intention to purchase precedes the actual purchase.

PURCHASE, TRIAL, AND ACTION

If the potential traveler has reached the conviction stage of the buying process, the barrier to travel is likely to be lack of time or money. It is clear that the motivation is present. The marketing task is to identify the barrier and develop a product to breach it. If the problem is lack of money, a tour package may be successful. Lodging in smaller, cheaper hotels can be suggested. If the problem is one of time, it may be possible to offer a package that capitalizes on the time available. One of the reasons that fly-cruise packages have been developed is to respond to a market that has the money and the motivation, but not the time. Previously, when ships cruised out of New York much time was lost because two days of bad weather often had to be experienced before the ships reached sunny climates. The solution has been to fly travelers to Florida, sail out of a southern port, and give more sun for the time available.

> It's rather nice to think of oneself as a sailor bending over the map of one's mind and deciding where to go and how to go.
>
> Katherine Mansfield

ADOPTION

The final stage of the buying process is the adoption stage. At this point, the traveler has become a repeat purchaser. People return to a destination for several reasons (McKercher and Wong, 2004):

- The risk of a bad experience is less.
- They want to meet the same kind of people.
- They feel an emotional attachment to the place.
- They want to explore the destination more widely.
- They wish to expose the destination to others.

To achieve this end, it is necessary to provide a quality experience to the first-time traveler. It is unlikely that either first-timers or repeat visitors will return to a destination if they are dissatisfied with the experience (Alegre and Cladera, 2006). It is further likely that repeat visits are affected more by how well the destination performs in terms of quality than by overall satisfaction (Um et al., 2006). However, advertising also has a role to play. The necessity for some form of communication

to the purchaser results because of *cognitive dissonance*. Cognitive dissonance occurs after a choice between two or more alternatives has been made. It is a feeling of anxiety, a feeling that perhaps the choice made was not the best one. The amount of dissonance felt is influenced by the type of decision made. The anxiety is stronger if

- The rejected alternative is attractive.
- The decision is important.
- The purchaser becomes aware of negative characteristics in the alternative chosen.
- The number of rejected alternatives increases.
- The alternatives are perceived as being similar.
- The decision made goes against a strongly held belief.
- The decision is a recent one.

Because vacation travel represents an important decision, it has the potential for creating a great deal of anxiety after the purchase has been made. The potential is even greater if the traveler has chosen among a large number of attractive alternate destination areas. The key is to indicate to the traveler as soon as possible after the decision has been made that the decision has been a good one. A note to the purchaser of a package tour or cruise may be sufficient to avoid second thoughts and cancellations. For advertisers, the key is to provide in their advertisements information that purchasers can use to justify to themselves the purchase made, as well as the messages to convince people to buy.

BUYING-COMMUNICATION PROCESSES INTERACTION

Visitors seek information to identify vacation options. The type and amount of information sought varies by the experience level and the motivation of the tourist looking for travel information. People who are more skilled value detailed information for activities and events, while those less skilled are motivated by the availability and offerings. Greater amounts of information intimidate those who are less skilled (Beldona, Morrison, and O'Leary, 2005).

One study of the users of airline Web sites finds two distinct types of users (Chen and Jang, 2004):

1. Bargain Seekers who use the Web as an information channel to find low fares.

110-Year Family Vacation

When there are so many places to see in the world, why travel to the same place twice? When a person decides to revisit a location, it could be for a variety of reasons. The guest is reducing his or her risk by excluding alternatives that might not satisfy his or her wants and needs. Guests may feel that the amount of time they spent at the location was not enough, and they want to explore more of the site. They might want to bring back friends and family to enjoy the experience with them again or they may want to vacation with the same type of people they met on their previous visit. Most important for family resorts, however, is the emotional attachment that is formed to the destination, which brings guests back for yearly visits.

Family resorts like Fern Resort in Orillia, Ontario, Canada, attribute most of their customers to generations of families who have stayed at the resort the same week, year after year. This charming establishment known as "The Land of Rolls and Honey" welcomes guests with a road lined with willow trees leading to the Main Inn. For 110 years, this property has enriched its visitors with a history guests can claim as their own. It is mainly marketed toward families who would like to spend time together in a cost-efficient way. The anxieties of travel can often be attributed to a discomfort with deviation from an individual's normal lifestyle. While time away is necessary, the expectations of relaxation can be compromised due to the difficulty of managing cultural differences. This lakeside property offers an experience that brings customers back because it becomes a "home away from home" rather than a "once in a lifetime" trip. Travelers who yearn for a change in scenery can walk out their back door, replacing a green lawn with a soft-sanded beach slowly washed over by the calm current of Lake Couchiching.

THINK ABOUT THIS:

1. How can a resort manager combat the issue of creating a yearly experience in the exact likeness of the ones before it?
2. When the resort wishes to expand in order to gain a larger market, how might the manager convince guests that the changes will ultimately add value to their experience?

Source: http://www.fernresort.com/.

2. Utilitarians who are more interested in a quality Web site that can help them make a reservation in a user-friendly way.

Beyond that primary need, however, is the fact that there are three nonfunctional elements of the search (Fesenmaier, 1992). Visitors may collect travel information simply to improve their knowledge about a particular place. Second, they may collect it for aesthetic reasons—to get information (primarily pictures) about a special place. Third, the search may allow the armchair traveler to vicariously "experience" vacationing to that spot.

The role of travel information is to minimize risk through information, persuade through image creation, and justify the decision through reminders after the choice is taken. What risks does the visitor take in deciding where to go (Mansfeld, 1992)? First, visitors risk the limited amount of disposable time available to them. For many the vacation is a one-time-only annual event. Make a mistake and you wait a year for the next opportunity. Second, visitors risk the money they have saved over the year for the annual event. Third, there is the risk of choosing a vacation that does not satisfy the needs and wants discussed in chapter 11. Fourth, for those traveling for health reasons, there is the risk of putting one's health at risk. Visitors expose themselves to risk in buying vacations that they hope satisfy various needs and wants important to them. The goal for marketers "is to present the best solution to the problem at the lowest risk" (Lewis, Chambers, and Chacko, 1995).

> Traveling in the company of those we love is home in motion.
>
> Leigh Hunt

Various researchers have differentiated between the early consideration and late consideration stages of the travel decision. Most research suggests that potential tourists in the early consideration or awareness stage focus on the relative merits of the destination. At least one study, however, suggests that specific constraints—lack of travel information and interest—are felt in the early consideration stage (Shin, 1998). There is agreement that, in the late consideration stage, attention is focused primarily on constraints such as access to the destination, financial resources, work obligations, etc. (Shin, 1998).

There is an appropriate and different communications strategy for each stage in the traveler's buying process. This realization is particularly important because it helps in determining why a communications campaign failed. It is fairly easy to determine that a campaign did not work. For example, the promotion to induce travel to a particular destination area can be assumed a failure if there has been no increase in visitors to the destination area after the campaign. A more interesting question is not so much *did* the promotion fail, but *why* did it fail? Were enough people exposed to the message? Was the message memorable? Did it result in a change of attitudes? The only way that campaign managers can determine why the campaign failed is to break the process into its various stages and measure the results of each stage.

The information presented in figure 13.3 refers to this process. At the first stage in the buying process, the objective is to expose the message to a certain number of people. The number of readers or viewers *exposed* to the message serves as a measure of whether or not the campaign reached this objective. At the next level, the objective is to transfer information to those exposed to the message. To determine the effectiveness, it is possible to measure the extent to which people exposed to the message have recalled the essential parts of it.

To measure a change in attitude it is necessary to survey attitudes both before and after a campaign. A similar strategy is necessary to measure whether preferences have been developed. The extent to which a message initiates action can be measured by the percentage of those who send in a response to a particular advertisement or the number who take an advertisement into a travel agent. Last, repeat purchases, signifying the adoption of a product or service,

As international travel increases, the perception of risk associated with travel decreases. © 2009 Lorelyn Medina. Used under license from Shutterstock, Inc.

can be measured by the percentage of visitors who are repeat purchasers.

By being aware of these different stages, communication objectives, and ways to measure their accomplishment, it is possible to determine where things went wrong. For example, it may be that the promotion reached a sufficiently large number of the right kind of people, a large percentage of whom remembered the message. However, it may be that the message was not sufficiently strong to result in a change in attitude about the destination area being promoted. The promotion manager knows that the media used were on target in terms of reaching the right numbers of prospects. The program has to be strengthened to result in an attitude change. A strategy offering cheap package tours would be totally ineffective because the necessary prerequisite steps have not been taken in the minds of the readers.

BUYING PROCESS FEEDBACK

Although each step in the buying process is a prerequisite for the next, there are also *feedback effects* or *loops*. The purchase itself has an effect on attitudes, either a positive or a negative one. Each higher stage thus tends to reinforce the lower stages. For example, study abroad has been shown to result in a change in attitude about foreigners. As international travel increases, the perception of risk associated with travel decreases. The experience is also shown to be a significant and positive predictor of travel attitudes (Sonmez and Graefe, 1995). Holding a positive attitude

Buying Process Stages	Communication Objective	Communication Measurement
Awareness, attention	Exposure	Number of readers/viewers exposed to message
Knowledge, comprehension	Transmission of information	Percentage of readers/viewers who remembered essential parts of the message
Attitudes, interest, liking	Attitude change	Attitude surveys before and after message to determine degree of change
Evaluation, preference, desire	Creation of preferences	Preference surveys before and after message to determine preferences
Intention, conviction	Initiation of action	Number of actions taken in response to a particular message
Purchase, trial, action	Purchase	Number of bookings made
Adoption	Repeat purchase	Percentage of visitors who are repeat purchasers

Figure 13.3 Interaction Between the Buying and Communication Processes.

about a place means that the potential traveler makes more effort to understand the message being presented. Similarly, understanding the vacation attributes of a destination area means that the potential traveler is more inclined to pay attention to advertisements about that destination area.

It is easier to induce a repeat purchase if a good job has been done to satisfy the traveler the first time, than it is to get that first purchase. Satisfying the visitor reinforces each step in the buying process.

The entire buying process can occur in a relatively short period of time. The total trip planning interval (the time between the date that trip planning begins and the date the trip itself begins) can be divided into two parts (Yoon and Holecek, p. 175):

- Information processing interval or time between the date trip planning begins and the date the destination is selected.
- Post decision interval or the time between the date the destination is selected and the date the trip actually begins.

One study finds that almost two-thirds of respondents begin to plan trips only thirty days or less before departure. A destination is selected less than seven days after trip planning begins. The planning interval is longer for summer trips, large parties, outdoor recreation/festival trips, and longer and more expensive vacations. Finally, tourists are more likely to be in a trip planning mode during the first twenty days of any given month than in the latter part of the month (Yoon and Holecek, 2000).

There are obvious implications for destination marketing organizations (DMOs). Much of the budget for many DMOs is in generating and fulfilling inquiries from potential visitors who are in the information processing interval. If, as this study suggests, this interval is non-existent for most travelers, much of this money may be wasted even if prompt responses to inquiries occurs. Similarly, if destination selection occurs shortly after trip planning begins, it would make sense to promote summer visits during the summer season itself rather than in spring, as is often the case.

IMPACT OF THE INTERNET

Given the impact of the Internet on search behavior, it is suggested that the traditional model suggested in the preceding discussion is gradually becoming obsolete.

To summarize that model, travel marketers tended to focus on two points in the purchase process. They created awareness campaigns to promote brand recognition. Second, they engaged in tactical campaigns to capture attention at the time of booking.

Dale A. Brill, Chief Marketing Officer for Visit Florida, suggests a different travel planning model. The steps are (Estis-Green, 2008, 44):

- Pre-market/need trigger
- Search
- Plan
- Pre-validate
- Book
- Post-validate
- Prep
- Experience
- Share

As the tourist takes more responsibility for the search process at each stage of the way social media and social networks (see chapter 12) take on more importance and offer different opportunities for interaction between tourist and destination marketer.

DESTINATION CHOICES

Now that the process by which travelers make purchases is known, it is useful to look at how they choose destination areas, since this choice process triggers the decisions in the next part of the Tourism System Model (Travel). There are models that try to explain how travelers make destination choices.

There are three major theoretical streams regarding information search behavior (Bieger and Laesser, 2004):

1. **Psychological/motivational/individual characteristics approach**—People are *pushed* by their own internal forces and *pulled* by the external characteristics of the destination. There is some indication that the number of previous trips to the destination explains the search for information rather than the socioeconomic characteristics of the travel.
2. **Cost/benefit or economics approach**—Information is sought to reduce risk and will be sought if it is felt that the time and money spent on the search will result in greater benefits to the individual. The more one travels, the more experience is gained and the less important external information becomes.

> A trip is what you take when you can't take any more of what you've been taking.
>
> Adeline Ainsworth

3. **Process approach**—Concentrates on the *process* of the search rather than on the action itself. After the decision is made to take a trip the tourist seeks more information in an attempt to reduce the risk of a bad decision. Getting information from a variety of sources creates some redundancy but verifies information previously received.

Moscardo et al. (1996) have proposed a model that integrates the theories relating to the internal and external constraints that have been discussed in chapters 10 to 13 and other chapters. They propose a simplified *destination choice model* that recognizes the contribution of four distinct bodies of research on tourism (Gilbert, 1991):

1. Travel motivation theories and research (chapters 10 and 11)
2. Destination image and attraction research (chapter 12)
3. Destination choice model research (chapter 12)
4. Market segmentation research (chapters 7, 12, and 14)

The integrative model suggested by Moscardo et al. is shown in figure 13.4. The model suggests that the traveler's desired *activities* and *benefits* provide a link between motivation and destination choice. The components of the model follow:

- **Traveler and socio-psychological variable (A):** This variable includes the needs, wants and motives, and personalities of travelers, and the external influences such as previous travel experience, culture, age, income, education, available time, and family life-cycle stage.
- **Destination marketing variables and external inputs (B):** This includes the marketing by destination areas plus information that travelers get through travel trade intermediaries, word of mouth, and other external sources of information.
- **Images of destination areas (C):** These are the perceptions or images of alternative destination areas. Moscardo et al. suggest that activities and benefits may be the most important attributes of these in influencing destination choice.
- **Destination choice (D):** The choice of a destination area is made on the basis of there being a match between what activities and benefits travelers prefer, and what activities and benefits they perceive that each destination area offers.

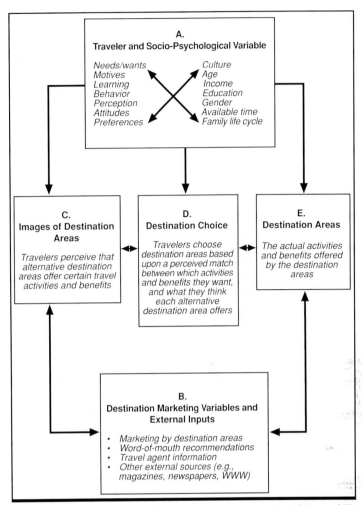

Figure 13.4 A Destination Choice Model Based on Activities and Benefits. Adapted from Moscardo, G., A. M. Morrison, P. L. Pearce, C.-T. Lang, and J. T. O'Leary. 1996. Understanding vacation destination choice through travel motivation and activities. *Journal of Vacation Marketing,* 2 (2): 109–122.

- **Destination areas (E):** The actual activities and benefits offered and promoted by the destination areas.

By studying the model in figure 13.4 in more detail, the suggested process of destination choice can be better understood. The model shows that images of destination areas (C), in terms of which travel activities and benefits they are thought to provide, are formed through the influence of the traveler and socio-psychological variable (A) and marketing variables and external inputs (B). The destination choice (C) is made by a matching process in which travelers consider what they wish to do when they travel (activities) and what benefits they want (from A), and what they perceive each destination area offers in potential activities and benefits (C). Each destination area offers an actual set of travel

One Summer In Oregon

When a potential guest is going through the buying process, it is a series of subdecisions that lead to the actual purchase. It is important for marketers and advertisers to understand these decisions and to communicate appropriately in order to effectively gain customers. This allows for an understanding of why a marketing/advertising campaign failed. Each stage must be broken apart in order to understand why the campaign was not as successful as expected.

The Oregon Tourism Commission began a "We Love Dreamers" advertising campaign in 2006. The official Web site states, "The ad series continues to reinforce what captivates Oregon visitors–from our stunning natural beauty to our unique people, culture, and quality of life." The full-page spread grabs the observers' attention with unique photography and a "quirky" story that adds humor to the culture and history of Oregon. In one advertisement titled "*Mysteries of the Oregon Outback,*" an old woman with a wide smile is seen wearing an outfit that is assumed to be silk pajamas. The advertisement says, "Who is this woman and why is she wielding a cleaver and wearing silk pajamas? For your information, they're not pajamas. They're traditional Chinese garb. And this woman is a highly respected curator of Chinese artifacts who keeps watch over a highly unusual and mysterious museum." The story goes on to tell a tale of a local Chinese medicine man who disappeared a long time ago. His preserved pharmacy was taken over by the women in the image. The spread finishes, "So if you're in the neighborhood, fossil hunting, fishing, rock-climbing, or just enjoying the spectacular scenery, you would be a fool not to stop by the museum called Kam Chung Company. It's the last thing you'd expect to see, but the first thing you might write home about. Start planning your Oregon Wild West Getaway." This interesting and unique advertisement is memorable to the reader.

The campaign is meant to inspire more people to visit the state in order to support the local economy. Destination Marketing Organizations work alongside the Oregon Tourism Commission to "enhance the local economy through purchase of room nights, food and beverage, retail items, transportation, visitor services, etc." The advertising campaign is meant to generate revenue into each of these areas. Understanding how to communicate effectively to potential customers and knowing the decision processes they go through are indicators of how successful the campaign will be.

THINK ABOUT THIS:

1. Why is it important to communicate to potential customers at each level of the buying process, and to be aware of the subdecisions that lead to the actual purchase?

Source: http://industry.traveloregon.com/Resource%20Library/Advertising%20Campaigns.aspx.

---

activities and benefits (E), and may select to emphasize these in its destination area marketing efforts (B).

Feedback in the model occurs in several places. For example, a destination area may complete a marketing research study with travelers (B) and determine that they do not think it is a good place for snorkeling and scuba diving (C). However, the destination area has several significant reef areas, and provides excellent snorkeling and scuba diving opportunities. Therefore, marketing programs are changed to put greater emphasis on these opportunities (B) and a program is initiated to encourage more dive and snorkeling operations (E).

Moscardo et al. admit that their model is a simple one and, in fact, it may be overly simplified. However,

> A journey is like a marriage. The certain way to be wrong is to think you control it.
>
> John Steinbeck

their main argument is that activities and benefits play a key role in destination choice. This is based on a growing amount of research on the role of activities in travel market segmentation (Hsieh, O'Leary, and Morrison, 1992; Morrison, Hsieh, and O'Leary, 1994).

VACATION SUBDECISIONS

Although the vacation buying process has been treated as a series of stages culminating in a buying decision, the vacation purchase is actually comprised of a series of subdecisions. From a marketer's viewpoint, it is important to know the order in which decisions are made and who makes the particular decisions. In this way, a marketing campaign can be developed that is aimed at the decision maker. For example, leisure travelers decide where they want to go and for how long before considering the price of the trip (Travel Industry of America, 2005).

The literature continues to show that as many as two-thirds of all vacation decisions are shared by husband and wife (Nichols and Snepenger, 1999). Joint decision makers plan their vacation earlier and have slightly more information sources compared to husband- or wife-dominated decision makers.

What the order of decisions is, and who the decision maker is varies by which stage in the life cycle the family is in. At the stage in which the couple has been married for less than fourteen years, in which the couple is at most in their mid-thirties and may have young children at home, the decision to vacation tends to be a joint one. Although discretionary income is low, the first subdecision is "where to go," followed by "whether to go." This seems to reflect a more hedonistic attitude, which indicates an expectation to take a vacation despite income restraints. Decisions are next made concerning the amount to spend, the length of time to stay, and the accommodations to be used. In the next stage, in which the couple has been married for fourteen to twenty years, has a mid-forties age median, and has children eighteen years old or more, the husband tends to dominate the decision making slightly. This is due primarily to the vacations being designed around the husband's work schedule. At this stage, the question of whether or not to go is most important, followed by decisions on destination areas, amounts to spend, length of stay, and place to stay. When the spouses are in the mid-fifties and have been married twenty to thirty years, the process is largely wife dominated. This coincides with vacation purchases at a peak and disposable income close to a peak. The wife-dominated decision making continues until the husband is close to retirement; then he exerts a slight dominance, due perhaps to anxiety about financial matters. For couples married for over forty years, when the couple is retired, the wife once again takes over the decision making.

Vacation decision making is increasingly becoming a joint decision rather than being dominated by one spouse. This is, in part, a function of the fact that more women are breadwinners, there are increasing numbers of dual-income families and that people are taking more frequent and shorter vacations. Family vacation decision making can get very complicated because of the dynamics involved between two spouses. The situation gets even more complicated when children are involved.

A destination choice is made through a matching process between what a traveler wishes to do and the benefits s/he perceives a destination offers. © 2009 Christian Noval. Used under license from Shutterstock, Inc.

One study indicates that women, especially those in lower-income brackets, are more likely than men to gather information as a way of persuading their spouses when disagreements arise about where the family should vacation. Interestingly, in another study, almost 60 percent of husbands say they did the research for the family vacation—the same percentage of wives who said *they* did the research. The author suggests looking into two separate campaigns to create independent demand from both husbands and wives so that both come to the family decision-making process with information to influence the vacation decision. Best Western's senior vice president of marketing quotes research indicating that 80 percent of travel decisions are made by the female in the household while Holiday Inn feels that the female is in charge of making accommodations arrangements (Milligan, Litvin, Xu, and Kang, 2004; Kang and Hsu, 2005; Kang and Hsu, 2004).

Vacation dates, for example, are probably determined by job and school dates, and hence decisions on these are husband dominated, with heavy influence by the children. There is some indication that the number of joint decisions is greater in middle-class families than in lower-class ones, but less than in the highest class ones.

A review of figure 13.5 indicates that most vacation subdecisions are joint decisions. These decisions are culturally based. In Mexico, for example, the decision to travel appears to be wife-dominant (Michie and Sullivan, 1990).

The following differences between men and women are postulated (Luntz, 2007, 230):

Subdecision	Standish	Jenkins	Myers	Ritchie	Omura	3M	Kendall, et al.
Whether to go							
Whether to take the children		♀					
How long to stay		♂		♀			
How much to spend	♀	♂		♂			♂
Vacation dates		♂		♂			
Vacation destinations	♀	♀	♀	♀	♀	♂	♀
Mode of transportation	♀	♀					
Route		♂	♂				
Lodging	♀	♀	♀				♂
Activities							♀

Key: ♂ male-dominated decision
♀ joint decision

Figure 13.5 Family Vacation Decision Making. Sources: Standish, T. C. 1978; Jenkins, R. L. 1978; Myers, P. B., and L. W. Moncrief. 1978; Ritchie, J. R. B., and P. Filiatrault. 1980; Omura, G. S., M. L. Roberts, and W. W. Talavzyk. 1979; 3M National Advertising Company. 1972; Kendall, K. W., D. J. Sandhu, and G. Giles. 1983.

- Men decide where to go; women decide where to stay.
- Men want excitement; women want luxury.
- Men are more likely to have the final say over the destination; women have the final say over the hotel.
- He wants to pick where to go; she wants to take care of the details.
- Attention to details is meaningless to men but all-important to women.

INFLUENCE OF CHILDREN

A recent study finds that 68 percent of parents say their children are "very influential" in deciding the family vacation (Milligan, 2005).

Studies by Jenkins (1978) and Ritchie and Filiatrault (1980) indicate that children influence some vacation subdecisions. The children's effect is felt on the decision of whether to go on vacation, what dates and destination areas to choose, what type of lodging is preferred, and which activities to undertake while on vacation. Cultural differences have also been discovered in a study comparing the role of children in Belgium, the United Kingdom, Italy, and France (Seaton and Tagg, 1995). Children from the United Kingdom play a smaller role in family vacation decisions than those from other countries, particularly France and Italy. The children themselves agree that the final decision is a

Children have a great deal of influence on many of decisions made regarding vacations. © 2009 HannaMonika. Used under license from Shutterstock, Inc.

"You're taking the kids?!"

It is difficult to travel long distances with children, but most families vacation in order to spend time together. Family vacation packages such as Hilton's Waikoloa Village three-day offer encourages families to travel because it is worth the hassle of getting there. Offering discounts and including activities with a mix of separate kid and adult entertainment and entire family entertainment add value to the experience. Hilton writes on their Web sites, "Our family friendly resort is designed to make sure everyone, whatever their age, has a fun-packed, stress-free stay. With so many activities to choose from, every day is a new adventure. And when it's time for some grown-up peace and quiet, our Kids Club and entertainment program makes sure the fun can continue." When a family is anxious about traveling with children, special offers like this one make planning a vacation more enticing.

Children have a huge influence over vacation decisions. Most families admit that the location, lodging, and activities of a vacation all revolve around their kids. It is important to involve children in the vacation as much as possible, to make the experience good for everyone. When a child is having fun and busy participating in resort activities, it makes the visit memorable and enjoyable. Understanding the influence that children have on vacation buying decisions is imperative to gaining potential customers. Catering to the needs of family travelers can eliminate the constraints associated with not traveling due to children.

THINK ABOUT THIS:

1. What activities would you include in your family vacation package that would inspire families to travel despite the distance it takes to get there?

Source: http://www.hilton.com/en/hi/hotels/specials_detail_popup.jhtml?ctyhocn=KOAHWHH&promoId=126910023.

joint one between mother and father. Where the decision was not a joint one, the children perceived it as a wife-dominant rather than husband-dominant one. The researchers concluded that involving children in the vacation decision-making process improves the possibility of a child who is happy with the vacation choice, while not involving the children increases the chance that he or she will be one of the small minority who are unhappy while on holiday with the family.

A knowledge of who influences various vacation subdecisions helps marketing managers in selling their products and services. Facilities and messages can be more clearly geared to the decision-maker in an attempt to increase the attention given the message, the comprehension, and ultimately, the final purchase behavior.

SUMMARY

Before making travel bookings, people go through a buying process consisting of a series of stages. Tourism marketers can help "lead" potential visitors through this process by the kinds of messages they design. They must know at which stages people are in the process, and design messages that are appropriate for these stages.

In addition to the buying-process stages, there is also a process that people use to select destination areas for their travel. Scholars have suggested a number of different destination choice process models. The perceived activities and benefits offered by alternative destination areas may play a key role in determining destination choice.

The travel decisions and decision-making processes that people use are not static over time. First, previous experiences and satisfaction with destination areas influence future choices. In addition, people's cumulative travel experiences influence their future travel decisions. Motives for travel and destination choices are affected by people's previous "travel careers."

The decision to travel is actually composed of a series of subdecisions, in which several people's input affects the decision. For family vacations, children have a significant influence on travel decisions.

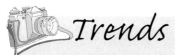 *Trends*

Top Ten Trends in Travel Marketer's Use of Social Media

1. Use of social media is high and growing in all customer segments.
2. It will be necessary to transmit the passion for travel in order to engage a customer base.
3. Trip planning is the ideal point to stimulate traveler interaction.
4. The volume of user-generated contact is high and can be intimidating but is a potent tool if managed properly.
5. Consumer relationships should be interactional, not transactional.
6. The "long tail" of the Internet can be leveraged with niche consumers and suppliers.
7. Social media may one day supplant traditional search engine marketing and search engine optimization.
8. Corporate travel, groups, and meetings all respond to social media.
9. Learning to use this new technology will become increasingly important as the online activity goes mobile.
10. The rivalry between online travel agencies, third-party intermediaries, and travel suppliers will intensify in the social media and social networking arena.

Source: Estis-Green. 2008. The travel marketer's guide to social media and social networks: Sales and marketing in a Web 2.0 world. *Marketing Review*. 45.

ACTIVITIES

1. Most Americans suffer from vacation compression. They are overworked and don't have time to take lengthy vacations. Dual-income families are more likely to take more frequent weekend trips rather than choosing a vacation that requires more time away from their responsibilities. In many cases, money is much less of a constraint than time. Create a vacation package that will give these people the most value for their time. Develop an advertising strategy to promote the package you created. How would you advertise it? Where would you advertise it? To whom would you advertise it?

2. Enter an online travel forum and ask a variety of people who recently traveled the reasons they chose their specific destinations. Ask specific questions that correspond with the Traveler's Buying Process in the text. Did they follow the written guidelines? What were the similarities and differences between the buying-process model and their real-life decision process? Were the decisions mainly based on activities and benefits like the *destination choice model* suggests?

3. Plan a dream vacation. Write a description of the process and the reasons behind your destination decision. Relate your findings to what you learned in this chapter. What factors influenced you the most and what deterred you from choosing various alternatives? How much risk do you associate with this vacation? What effect did this have on your decision-making process as a whole? What does this tell you from a managerial/marketing perspective?

REFERENCES

Alegre, J., and M. Cladera. 2006. Repeat visitation in mature sun and sand holiday destinations. *Journal of Travel Research*, 44: 288–297.

Beldona, S., A. M. Morrison, and J. O'Leary. 2005. Online shopping motivations and travel products: A correspondence analysis. *Tourism Management*, 26: 561–570.

Bieger, T., and C. Laesser. 2004. Information sources for travel decisions: Toward a source process model. *Journal of Travel Research*, 42: 357–371.

Chen, J. S., and S. Jang. 2004. Profiling airline web users: A segmentation approach. *Tourism Analysis*, 8: 223–226.

Crissy, W. J. E., R. J. Boewadt, and D. M. Laudadio. 1975. *Marketing of Hospitality Services: Food, Lodging, Travel*. East Lansing, MI: The Educational Institute of the American Hotel and Motel Association.

Cunningham, W. H., and I. C. M. Cunningham. 1981. *Marketing: A Managerial Approach*. Cincinnati, OH: South-Western Publishing.

Estis-Green. 2008. The travel marketer's guide to social media and social networks: Sales and marketing in a Web 2.0 world. *Marketing Review*. 42–45.

Fesenmaier, D. R. 1992. Researching consumer information: Exploring the role of pre-trip information search in travel decisions. Proceedings of the Annual Conference of the Travel and Tourism Research Association. 32–36.

Gilbert, D. C. 1991. An examination of the consumer behaviour process related to tourism. *Progress in Tourism, Recreation and Hospitality Management*, 3: 78–106.

Gursoy, D., and K. W. McCleary. 2004. Travelers' prior knowledge and its impact on their information search behavior. *Journal of Hospitality and Tourism Research*, 28 (1): 66–94.

Howard, J., and J. N. Sheth. 1969. *Theory of Buyer Behavior.* New York: John Wiley & Sons, Inc.

Hsieh, S., J. T. O'Leary, and A. M. Morrison. 1992. Segmenting the international travel market using activities as a segmentation base. *Tourism Management*, 13: 209–223.

IUOTO (undated). *Study and Analysis of the Long-Term Effectiveness of Promotional Campaigns and Other Tourist Publicity and Advertising Activities.* International Union of Official Tourism Organizations.

Jenkins, R. L. 1978. Family vacation decision-making. *Journal of Travel Research*, 16 (4).

Josiam, B. M, and J. S. P. Hobson. 1995. Consumer choice in context: The decoy effect in travel and tourism. *Journal of Travel Research*, 34 (1): 45–50.

Kang, S. K., and C. H. C. Hsu. 2005. Dyadic consensus on family vacation destination selection. *Tourism Management,* 26: 571–582.

Kang, S. K., and C. H. C. Hsu. 2004. Spousal conflict level and resolution in family vacation destination selection. *Journal of Hospitality and Tourism Research*, 28 (4): 408–424.

Kendall, K. W., D. J. Sandhu, and G. Giles. 1983. Family decision making in the upscale travel market. Proceedings of the Annual Conference of the Travel and Tourism Research Association.

Kendall, K. W., and D. J. Sandhu. 1985. What do you do when you get there?: A family decision making analysis of activity and lodging sub-decisions of vacationers. Proceedings of the Annual Conference of the Travel and Tourism Research Association.

Kim, Y. J., P. L. Pearce, A. M. Morrison, and J. T. O'Leary. 1996. Mature vs. youth travelers: The Korean market. *Asia Pacific Journal of Tourism Research*, 1 (1): 102–112.

Lewis, R. C., R. E. Chambers, and H. E. Chacko. 1995. *Marketing Leadership in Hospitality: Foundations and Practices,* 2nd ed. New York: Van Nostrand Reinhold.

Litvin, S. W., G. Xu, and S. K. Kang. 2004. Spousal vacation-buying decision making revisited across time and place. *Journal of Travel Research*, 43: 193–198.

Luntz, F. 2007. Words that work: The language of travel and tourism. In *2007 Outlook for Travel & Tourism*. 230. Washington, DC: Travel Industry Association.

McDaniel, C., Jr. 1979. *Marketing: An Integrated Approach.* New York: Harper & Row.

McKercher, B., and D. Y. Y. Wong. 2004. Understanding tourism behavior: Examining the combined effects of prior visitation history and destination status. *Journal of Travel Research*, 43: 171–179.

Mansfield, Y. 1992. From motivation to actual travel. *Annals of Tourism Research*, 19: 399–419.

Mathieson, A., and G. Wall. 1992. *Tourism: Economic, Physical and Social Impacts.* London: Longman.

Michie, D. A. 1986. Family travel behavior and its implications for tourism management. *Tourism Management*, 7: 8–20.

Michie, D. A., and G. L. Sullivan. 1990. The role(s) of the international travel agent in the travel decision process of client families. *Journal of Travel Research*, 29 (2): 30–38.

Milligan, M. Family ties: Banking on kids' influence on vacation matters. *Travel Weekly*, online version. Accessed May 17, 2005.

Milman, A. 1993. Maximizing the value of focus group research: Qualitative analysis of consumers destination choice. *Journal of Travel Research*, 32 (2): 61–63.

Milman, A., and A. Pizam. 1995. The role of awareness and familiarity with a destination: The Central Florida case. *Journal of Travel Research*, 33 (3): 21–27.

Morrison, A. M., S. Hsieh, and J. T. O'Leary. 1994. Segmenting the Australian domestic travel market by holiday activity participation. *Journal of Tourism Studies*, 5 (1): 39–56.

Moscardo, G., A. M. Morrison, P. L. Pearce, C.-T. Lang, and J. T. O'Leary. 1996. Understanding destination vacation choice through travel motivation and activities. *Journal of Vacation Marketing*, 2 (2): 109–122.

Moutinho, L. 1987. Consumer behaviour in tourism. *European Journal of Marketing*, 21 (10): 1–44.

Myers, P. B., and L. W. Moncrief. 1978. Differential leisure travel decision-making between spouses. *Annals of Tourism Research*, 5: 157–165.

Nichols, C. M., and D. J. Snepenger. 1988. Family decision making and tourism behavior and attitudes. *Journal of Travel Research*, 26 (4): 2–6.

Nichols, C. M., and D. J. Snepenger. 1999. Family decision making and tourism behaviors and attitudes. In *Consumer Behavior in Travel and Tourism*. New York: The Haworth Hospitality Press. 135–148.

Omura, G. S., M. L. Roberts, and W. W. Talavzyk. 1979. An exploratory study of women's travel attitudes and behavior: Directions for research. *Proceedings of the Association for Consumer Research*, 7.

Pearce, P. L. 1982. *The Social Psychology of Tourist Behaviour.* Oxford, England: Pergamon.

Pearce, P. L. 1988. *The Ulysses Factor: Evaluating Visitors in Tourist Settings.* New York: Springer-Verlag.

Ritchie, J. R. B., and P. Filiatrault. 1980. Family vacation decision-making: A replication and extension. *Journal of Travel Research*, 18 (4): 3–14.

Ross, G. F. 1994. *The Psychology of Tourism.* Melbourne: Hospitality Press.

Russ, F. A., and C. A. Kirkpatrick. 1982. *Marketing.* Boston: Little, Brown and Company.

Schmoll, G. A. 1977. *Tourism Promotion.* London: Tourism International Press.

Seaton, A. V., and S. Tagg. 1995. The family vacation in Europe: Paedonomic aspects of choices and satisfactions. *Journal of Travel & Tourism Marketing*, 4 (1): 1–21.

Shin, H. C. 1998. The specific classification of perceived constraints on the travel decision-making process: Implications for tour developers. 29th Annual Conference Proceedings of the Travel and Tourism Research Association. 300–303.

Sonmez, S. F., and A. R. Graefe. 1995. International vacation decisions and the threat of terrorism. Proceedings of the Annual Conference of the Travel and Tourism Research Association. 236–245.

Standish, T. C. 1978. How the computer views the family vacation travel market. Proceedings of the Annual Conference of the Travel and Tourism Research Association. 9.

Strong, E. K. 1925. *The Psychology of Selling*. New York: McGraw-Hill.

3M National Advertising Company. 1972. *Psychographics and the automobile traveler*. 3M.

Travel Industry of America. 2005. Leisure Travel Planning, Washington, DC.

Um, S., and J. L. Crompton. 1990. Attitude determinants in tourism destination choice. *Annals of Tourism Research*, 17: 432–448.

Um, S., and J. L. Crompton. 1991. Development of pleasure travel dimensions. *Annals of Tourism Research*, 18: 500–504.

Um, S., and J. L. Crompton. 1992. The roles of perceived inhibitors and facilitators in pleasure travel destination decisions. *Journal of Travel Research*, 30 (3): 18–25.

Um, S., K. Chon, and YH. Ro. 2006. Antecedents of revisit intention. *Annals of Tourism Research*, 33 (4): 1141–1158.

Vogt, C. A. and K. L. Andereck. 2003. Destination perceptions across a vacation. *Journal of Travel Research*, 41: 348–354.

Yoon, S., and D. Holecek. Pleasure trip planning behavior– implications for timing tourism promotional messages. *31st Annual Conference Proceedings of the Travel and Tourism Research Association*, 2000, 173–184.

SURFING SOLUTIONS

http://www.travelpod.com/ (Travelpod: The Web's original travel blog)

http://www.blogtoplist.com/travel/ (Blog top list: Travel)

http://www.tourism.gov.on.ca/english/research/travel_activities/index.html (Ontario Ministry of Tourism)

www.ntaonline.com/staticfiles/psychtravel_economic.pdf (Strategic Travel Action Resource)

PART FOUR

Travel

THE CHARACTERISTICS
OF TRAVEL

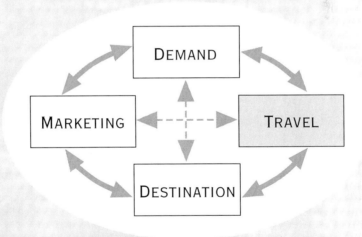

The decisions that travelers make affect their travel purchases and result in certain characteristics of travel. Part Four of *The Tourism System* examines these characteristics in terms of travel purposes and market segments, the geographic dispersion of travel flows, and modes of transportation.

PART THREE

3. Demand:
The Factors Influencing
the Market

LINK THREE

The Travel Purchase

PART FOUR

4. Travel:
The Characteristics of
Travel

chapter 14

Purposes of Travel

THE CHARACTERISTICS OF TRAVELER SEGMENTS

It is not fit that every man should travel; it makes a wise man better, and a fool worse.

William Hazlitt

PURPOSE

Readers will be able to demonstrate their knowledge of tourists by suggesting appropriate vacations, packages, services, and messages to the major segments of the market.

LEARNING OBJECTIVES

✓ Describe the characteristics of the major segments of the travel market.
✓ Suggest appropriate vacations, packages, and services to individual segments of the travel market.
✓ Suggest appropriate messages to engage individual segments of the travel market.

OVERVIEW

The two major classifications of travel purpose are business travel and leisure travel. The patterns and needs of people in both segments are the topic of this chapter. Both segments of the travel market are examined from the viewpoint of traditional segments. Leisure travel is broken down into visit friends and relative, the weekend getaway, and general vacation. Characteristics of the Ideal American Vacation Trip are explored.

Business travel is the "bread-and-butter" market for many tourism-related businesses. Business travel is bro-

ken down into general business; business travel related to meetings, conventions, and congresses; and incentive travel, which is somewhat of a hybrid as the people on the trip are traveling for pleasure although the purchasers of the trip are businesses. The characteristics of those in these market segments are explored in detail.

Business travel is the "bread-and-butter" market for many tourism-related businesses. © 2009 Zsolt Nyulaszi. Used under license from Shutterstock, Inc.

INTRODUCTION

Chapters 10 to 13 have examined how an individual–any individual–makes a travel decision. In order to describe the larger picture of travel flows, it is necessary to describe not individuals but segments of the total travel market. Those travelers relevant to tourism are either tourists, if they are in a destination for more than a day but less than a year, or excursionists, if they arrive and depart the same day. In either case their travel may be for reasons of business or pleasure (see figure 14.1).

THE LEISURE TRAVEL MARKET

In 2006 there were over 2 billion person trips (one person taking one trip) and over one billion household trips

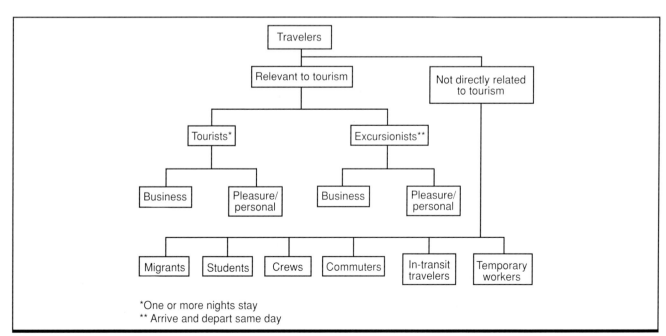

Figure 14.1 Segments of the Travel Market.

(one household taking one trip) in the United States. A trip is defined as travel of more than fifty miles away from home. Leisure trips account for almost three-quarters of all U.S. domestic travel.

The vast majority of trips in the United States are taken by auto. Trips by plane are less than 10 percent of the total number of trips taken. Overnight trips account for half of all person trips. Trips of one or two nights are more common than longer-stay trips. Thirty percent of all trips are taken in summer with about 25 percent in winter and slightly less in spring and fall. Almost 60 percent of all trips are taken within the traveler's own state while an additional almost 20 percent are taken within the traveler's census region.

Over the past decade, leisure travel volume has been increasing while business travel volume has declined.

There are a number of ways to describe the segments that comprise the tourist market. Geodemographics, a proprietary system developed by Claritas, Inc., and dubbed PRIZM, segments the market into neighborhood clusters based on socioeconomic and behavioral data. It is based on the idea that people with similar socioeconomic backgrounds and behavioral profiles select neighborhoods that suit their chosen lifestyles. Certain segments account for a disproportionately large amount of travel activity compared to their share of U.S. households.

PRIZM Social Group	Share of Leisure Trips	Share of Business Trips	Share of U.S. Households
Landed Gentry	12.07%	14.05%	9.07%
Country Comfort	14.3	13.31	10.57
Rustic Living	11.39	12.2	11.26
Middle America	11.28	13.08	10.03

Source: Patkose, M., T. B. Traverse, and S. D. Cook. 2007. *Domestic Travel Market Report 2007 Edition*. Washington, DC: Travel Industry Association. 40, 48.

The Landed Gentry segment consists of wealthy individuals who moved to smaller boomtowns. Many are boomers with college degrees who hold professional jobs. Country Comforts are predominantly white and middle-class homeowners, many of whom live in bedroom communities. They tend to be married, between the ages of twenty-five and fifty-four, with or without children. Rustic Living clusters live in isolated towns and rural villages. This segment has modest incomes, low educational levels, aging homes, and blue-collar occupations. Many are unmarried and tend to spend their leisure time in such traditional small-town activities as fishing and hunting, attending social activities at the local church and veterans club, enjoying country music, and car racing. Middle America consists of middle-class homeowners living in small towns and remote exurbs. They tend to be white, high-school educated, living as couples or larger families, and ranging in age from under twenty-five to over sixty-five. They prefer traditional rural pursuits such as fishing, hunting, making crafts, antique collecting, watching television, and meeting at civic and veterans clubs for recreation and companionship.

SEGMENTS OF THE MARKET

Early attempts to define the U.S. travel market used the stated motivation as the basis for the segmentation. One national probability sample divided the U.S. market into six segments using benefits/motivations. The segments are (Young, Ott, and Felgin, 1978):

- **Friends and Relatives–Nonactive Visitor.** Representing 29 percent of the market, these travelers look for familiar surroundings where they visit friends and relatives. They tend not to participate in any activity.
- **Friends and Relatives–Active City Visitor.** An additional 12 percent of the population also seek out the familiar where they visit friends and relatives. However, this group is more inclined to do such things as sightsee, shop, and engage in cultural activities.
- **Family Sightseers.** Six percent of the market look for new vacation places that would entertain and enrich their children.
- **Outdoor Vacationers.** The 19 percent who fall into this category want clean air, rest and quiet, and beautiful scenery. Recreation facilities are important for the numerous campers who are part of this segment. Facilities for children are also important.
- **Resort Vacationers.** A similar percent–19–fall into this category. They are primarily interested in water sports and good weather. Popular places with a big city atmosphere are preferred.
- **Foreign Vacationers.** Over a quarter–26 percent–consists of people who seek destinations they have never been to before. A foreign atmosphere offering an exciting and enriching atmosphere with beautiful scenery is important. Good accommodations and service are more important than the cost.

More recently it has been suggested that segmentation on the basis of actual behavior is a better reflection of the market. It has been found that what people *say* they want is not necessarily what they actually do.

Trips are taken for various reasons. In terms of percentage of the total, in 2006 the breakdown is:

Leisure (74 Percent of the Total)	Business (26 Percent of the Total)
28 percent: Other Personal/ Leisure	16 percent: General business
26 percent: Visit Friends and Relatives	10 percent: Convention, Seminar, Training Session, Group Meeting
12 percent: Weekend Getaway	
8 percent: General Vacation	

LEISURE TRAVEL

Leisure Travel accounts for almost three-quarters of all trips. This includes trips to visit friends or relatives, a weekend getaway, a general vacation, or a trip for other personal/leisure reasons. Visiting friends or relatives accounts for over one-third of leisure person trips. The vast majority of leisure person trips are taken by car, van, or small truck. Three in ten leisure trips include children. Half of all leisure person trips include an overnight stay. Among these, six in ten last one or two nights while trips of three to six nights are also popular. Most leisure travel occurs in the summer. Dining, shopping, entertainment, and sightseeing are the most common activities on leisure household trips. Almost 60 percent of all leisure trips are to destinations within the traveler's state of residence.

The top five Designated Marketing Areas of origin for leisure travel account for one-sixth of all leisure person trips. They are:

- Los Angeles
- New York
- Chicago
- San Francisco-Oakland-San Jose
- Philadelphia

TRAVEL TO VISIT FRIENDS OR RELATIVES. Trip characteristics are different based on the trip purpose. Households visiting friends or relatives are the most likely to spend less on a trip compared to those traveling for other reasons. Almost three out of every four person trips include staying in someone else's home. Winter is the most popular time to visit friends or relatives, probably due to the end-of-year holidays. Surprisingly, two in five trips in this segment involve only one traveler from the household. This figure is much higher than any other leisure travel segment.

Leisure travel accounts for almost three-quarters of all trips. © 2009 Phil Date. Used under license from Shutterstock, Inc.

One study (Young et al., 1978) finds that there are four types of hosts within this segment of the market—*ambassadors* and *talkers* who act like salespeople, encourage friends and relatives to visit and join their visitors in tourist activities during the visit; magnets, also called reluctant hosts; and *neutrals* who do less selling and tend not to join their guests in activities during the visit. There are other differences among the hosts. Ambassadors and magnets are more likely to have a combination of friends and relatives visit while neutrals and talkers tend to only have friends visit. Those visiting magnets are more likely to be attending a family gathering.

The "Visit Friends and Relatives" (VFR) segment is often reported as a homogeneous market. However, in some cases, VFR is just one of several activities engaged in by tourists. It is suggested that the VFR market is better understood if it is segmented on the basis of the following variables (Moscardo et al., 2000):

- Difference between VFR as a travel activity and as a trip type or motive
- Domestic versus international VFR
- Short-haul versus long-haul VFR trips
- Staying with friends or relatives versus staying in commercial accommodation
- Focus of visit (visiting friends, visiting relatives, visiting both friends and relatives)

Although some discount the economic contribution of the VFR market, thinking they spend little because they stay and eat with friends and relatives, this segment contributes to a destination in several ways (Xinran, Morrison, and O'Leary, 2001):

- They act as a moderator, compensating for seasonal variations.

Family Adventure Travel

In today's busy society, families are finding it more and more difficult to spend time with one another. One niche market in tourism is family adventure trips. TourismReview.com believes that these holiday vacations are largely successful because of the challenges they provide and the camaraderie that results from successfully meeting those challenges. The idea is that families can work and play together to overcome a variety of interactive obstacles. The teamwork required in these activities brings people together.

Several steps can be taken in order to successfully plan an adventure vacation. The first step is to choose the type of vacation that is best for your family. Trips can range from one-day rafting excursions to week-long safaris. When making these crucial decisions, ask yourself how adventurous your family members are, if they would like to spend time outdoors, and if they would like to travel overseas. Other questions include what type of elements your family members enjoy, if they would like more land-based adventures like hiking, or water excursions, and so on.

After you have decided on the type of trip your family would like to take, involve your kids in the trip planning. Getting a child involved in the process will excite and engage them in the trip itself. The next step is to plan a project for the children to focus on throughout their vacation. Ideas include allowing children to use a disposable camera or create a travel journal. While on the trip, make sure your family is properly equipped and remains as comfortable as possible throughout the excursion. Bring lots of bottled water, apply sunscreen on a regular basis, and wear appropriate clothing.

It can be difficult to get children actively involved and engaged in a family vacation, but planning a family adventure can be the perfect solution.

THINK ABOUT THIS:

1. Would these trips be most effectively marketed to the parents or children?
2. In what ways would the message vary depending on which family member you are marketing to?

CHECK THIS OUT:

Check out http://www.wildernesstrips.com and surf the Web to find other adventure trip Web sites.

Source: *TourismReview.com*. 2008. The Trip of a Lifetime—Adventure with Kids?

- International VFRs have longer than average length of stays.
- They are a very effective word-of-mouth channel.

WEEKEND GETAWAY. Half of weekend getaway person trips last only one or two nights with most of the rest being day trips. One in six weekend getaways lasts three nights or more. Those traveling for a weekend getaway are the most likely to dine out, gamble, or engage in nightlife activities. Most involve destinations within the traveler's state of residence.

GENERAL VACATION. General vacations are the most likely to include air transportation or a rental car. The average trip length is four nights although one-fourth last seven or more nights. Nearly half of all general vacation travel is during the summer. Popular activities include sightseeing, beach/waterfront activities, and visiting theme/amusement parks. This segment of the market is the most likely to include children on a household trip.

Various niche markets exist in tourism for general vacations. Some of these are:

- Gen Xers and Millennials
- Travelers with disabilities
- Girlfriend getaways
- Mancations
- Destination weddings
- Procreation vacations
- Babymoons
- Medical/life enhancement travel
- Voluntourism
- Pet travel
- Space tourism
- Culinary travel
- Gay/lesbian market
- Adventure travelers

Here are profiles of four of these segments. A 2004 study published in the *Journal of Travel Research* found that adventure travelers can be classified into six groups:

1. **General Enthusiasts.** These are usually men with some college education and no children under the age of twelve. The general enthusiast is the most likely to take adventure trips, preferring hard adventure like sea kayaking or mountain climbing to soft adventure like camping. He is also likely to want to arrange his own trip, and to travel to non-American destinations like the South Pacific.

2. **Budget Youngsters.** These travelers are generally young (nineteen to thirty-four) and single, with a fairly low income. They prefer to organize their own trips, though they also like to have partially inclusive trips to get professional expertise. The budget youngster prefers to travel with friends to areas around America, perhaps because travel in-country is cheap.

3. **Soft Moderates.** This is a small group composed mostly of middle-aged women who have been highly educated but nevertheless have a low income, because there is only one wage earner in the house. The soft moderate is unlikely to have children under the age of twelve. She prefers soft adventure, like hiking and nature trips, in American destinations. The soft moderate would rather not arrange her own trips, and she desires familiarity, not risk taking.

4. **Upper High Naturalists.** Members of this group are mostly middle-aged, married, and earn high wages. They usually have a dual-income household, but no children under twelve. They prefer both soft and rugged adventures, like hiking or backpacking, and they like to travel with family members and friends. The upper high naturalist seeks novelty trips and exotic destinations like Africa, where she generally stays more than a week and spends more than $1,000.

5. **Family Vacationers.** These travelers, married males, are usually not very excited about their vacations. Family vacationers have generally completed some college and have two incomes in the household to support their children, at least one of which is under age twelve. Favorite travel destinations for the family vacationer include America and South America. These travelers like to have some help in planning their vacations.

6. **Active Soloists.** This group is composed mostly of well-educated middle-income earners without children under twelve. The active soloists distinctly prefer high-risk, high-adventure activities like hang gliding, and they prefer to travel alone or in an organized group. Of all the groups, this group seems to rely on tourist infrastructure the most when making travel arrangements.

Over the last few years, the travel industry has taken note of the fact that gay and lesbian travelers constitute 10 percent of the market—a significant portion. Not only that, but they often travel undaunted after large disasters, and they typically spend more than their

> *Travel is the answer to a dream—a dream of luxury, prestige, in exotic places. It is the ultimate escape from daily routine . . . and travel which is earned through effort salves not only the ego, but the conscience as well.*
>
> Incentive Travel Planner

heterosexual counterparts while on vacation. These realizations have led to a scramble to become gay-friendly, especially among hotels, car rental agencies, and popular tourist destinations.

Philadelphia is one city that's taken the gay-traveler initiative. In November of 2003, the city unveiled a $900,000, three-year campaign created to attract gay and lesbian vacationers. Clever ads featuring Ben Franklin and Betsy Ross holding rainbow props combine with a witty slogan—"get your history straight and your night life gay"—to emphasize Philadelphia's gay-friendly attractions. With the new campaign, the city hopes to tap into the profits that gay-friendly cruises and resorts have long enjoyed.

The majority of industry experts agree that travel for gays and lesbians nowadays is more enjoyable and simpler than it was only ten years ago. Nevertheless, "there are still a lot of hurdles to overcome within organizations and corporations," said Tom Roth, president of Community Marketing, a San Francisco-based research organization that specializes in gay travel. "Often it boils down to personal feelings."

Men's vacations are fast becoming more than just a fishing trip. A "male" vacation nowadays allows guys the time and opportunity to stretch, explore, and express themselves in new ways. Some incarnations of the new traveling man:

- **Metro Man.** He seeks fine dining, spa visits, etiquette and wine lessons, and consultations with a personal shopper. This is a self-improvement vacation that blends relaxation with interesting new experiences.
- **Adventure Man.** A fellow with a hefty bank account, Adventure Man looks for trips like helicopter skiing, yachting, and chartered safaris in Africa. He doesn't mind bringing the kids along—in fact he finds it a more rewarding vacation with them there.
- **Corporate Man.** He could also be called Junket Man. Mixing business with pleasure, Corporate Man makes the most of each destination. Marketers try to draw him in with ads like the Floridian ad showcasing a business-suit-clad man holding swim fins and a sign saying "Bring your other suit."

- **Speed Man**. He is affluent, and he loves to race. Vacations at places like the Skip Barber Racing School satisfy his need for speed, as do piloting lessons. For him, racing school may simply be a $1,000-per-week vacation, or it could be the beginning of a $30,000-per-year "hobby."

It used to be extremely difficult to be a wheelchair-bound traveler. Now, disabled travelers of all types are having an easier time of it, due to the Americans with Disabilities Act of 1990 and the Air Carrier Access Act of 1986. Nevertheless, there are still hurdles in the way of the millions of blind, deaf, and wheelchair-dependent travelers that roam the world each year.

Luckily, with the right resources, these hurdles don't present a major problem. Tony Schrader, a fifty-four-year-old lawyer from Austin, Texas, has been a paraplegic for most of his life. He's an avid traveler who has been with his wife to St. Petersburg, Cozumel, and London, among a host of other places. How did he surmount the marble staircases inside the State Hermitage Museum while he was in Russia? Simple—two volunteers carried him up, at the request of his private guide. What about the sandy beaches in Cozumel, Mexico? A local van with a power lift was waiting at the shore to meet the small boat that carried Schrader from the cruise ship. In London, the narrow streets were not a problem; black cabs equipped with ramps ferried him around the city.

This market is likely to grow larger, studies suggest, especially as the Baby Boomer generation ages, and technological advances make the lives of disabled people more mobile and convenient. The Society for Accessible Travel and Hospitality in New York estimates that nearly 75 percent of the 54 million disabled Americans have the financial and physical ability to make a trip. However, only about 11 million travel at least once a year.

TRAVEL FOR PERSONAL OR OTHER LEISURE REASONS. Trips for general personal or other leisure reasons tend to be just for the day and to destinations in the household's state of residence.

IDEAL AMERICAN VACATION TRIP. A recent study, mentioned in chapter 10, identified the characteristics of the Ideal Vacation Trip. The ideal trip involves rest and relaxation, spending time with one's spouse, partner, or family, exploration and discovery, luxury, adventure,

Important elements of the ideal trip include: rest and relaxation, and spending time with one's significant other. © 2009 Monkey Business Images. Used under license from Shutterstock, Inc.

and socialization. The most important elements are rest and relaxation and spending time with significant others. Travelers indicated they want to spend less time with extended family and more time with their partner.

At the destinations, which favor beaches and international spots, they want an easy travel experience, a sense of fun and adventure and a local flavor. They want more sightseeing, beaches/waterfront activities, entertainment, culinary or wine-related activities, and nature and arts/cultural activities. Interestingly, they would like to double the length of their most recent trip. Less than half of those surveyed said their last trip was close to their ideal and over one-quarter said their last trip was not close to their ideal. This suggests that there is significant room for improvement.

Eight specific motivational groups were identified.

> The whole object of travel is not to set foot on foreign land; it is at last to set foot on one's own country as a foreign land.
>
> G. K. Chesterton

- **Experiential.** Enthusiastic travelers interested in long, ideally international, trips that give them the freedom to have new, different experiences
- **Family focused.** Want to travel with family members to family-friendly destinations that offer numerous activities
- **Casual travelers.** Young, mostly males, who seek rest and relaxation
- **Trail blazers.** Older, outdoor enthusiasts who want adventure, to connect with nature and less interested in creature comforts
- **Reconnectors.** Mainly females who want rest and relaxation and time with their spouse/significant other in romantic, low-key settings such as beaches, cruise ships and dining out

Medical Tourism

An interesting new segment of the travel market is medical tourism. State-of-the-art hospitals are luring American travelers to their overseas locations with low prices and packages that include side trips to local attractions. This new trend is being fueled by medical-savvy consumers who have discovered that the costs of transportation, accommodations and a few days of vacation total less than the same procedure would cost them in the United States.

Some experts believe medical tourism began long ago when wealthy Romans traveled to other countries to seek healing waters at spas. The trend experienced its first real boom when European couples traveled to Italy and Belgium to receive in vitro fertilization and other reproductive therapies that were difficult or impossible to obtain in their own countries. Many developing nations have recognized the potential profit that lies in advancing their health care systems.

An article in *TourismReview.com* predicts that by 2012 Asia's medical tourism market will generate more than $4.4 billion. Similar operations in India are growing by roughly 30 percent annually; and South Africa, Israel, Columbia, and Spain are developing impressive reputations for administering IVF procedures. Critics of the new medical tourism trend argue that once these American consumers travel back to the United States, they have little legal defense against their doctors and have few alternatives to take if anything goes wrong; but these possible consequences have yet to deter many from making their trips abroad. There are roughly two types of medical tourists: the leisure tourist who gets a small treatment on the side, and the more serious medical patient who comes for an important surgery but is also looking for a taste of vacation. Medical tourism will be an interesting segment to keep an eye on in the future. Who knows what will come next?

THINK ABOUT THIS:

1. How can international doctors and medical companies advertise to interested individuals appropriately?
2. What dangers do you foresee with this type of tourism?

CHECK THIS OUT:

Try to find any type of overseas medical tourism advertised online.
Try http://www.spa-resorts.cz/.
Also check *TourismReview.com*. 2008. Ethical Pitfalls of Transplant Tourism, by Arthur R. Derse, MD, JD.

Source: *TourismReview.com*. 2008. Vacations or Surgery? Both! by Louisa Kamps.

- **Affluentials.** Younger segment looking for relaxation, adventure, and luxury with their significant other in international luxury or upscale resort destinations
- **Back to basics.** Frugal travelers looking for rest and relaxation from inexpensive vacations through package deals
- **Quintessential travelers.** Highly motivated, passionate travelers interested in all types of destinations (especially international spots) and activities and who like to get involved in the research and planning part of the trip

THE MARKET TO 2010

The potential of the U.S. market for leisure travel can be viewed in light of the following (Canadian Tourism Commission, 1998):

- Real Gross Domestic Product Growth Forecast in terms of annual compound rate from 2000 to 2010 is projected at 2.0 percent for the United States compared to 3.1 percent for the world as a whole.
- In 1997 the average age of the 268 million people in the United States was 36. By 2007 the population will increase to 290 million with an average age of 37.4. At the time, with a median age of 36.9, almost half of the population will be 37 or older.
- The Baby Boomers represent two segments: an older group of 34 million people born between 1946 and 1954 and a younger group of 42 million born between 1955 and 1964. The former segment has an economic advantage over the younger group as most workers reach their peak earning power between the ages of 45 and 54.
- Boomers are saving for retirement.

- States with a population growth of more than one million between 1995 and 2015 are:
  - ☐ California
  - ☐ Texas
  - ☐ Florida
  - ☐ Georgia
  - ☐ N. Carolina
  - ☐ Washington
  - ☐ Arizona
  - ☐ Virginia
  - ☐ Tennessee
  - ☐ Colorado

THE FAMILY MARKET

Over 90 percent of all adults agree that the interests of their kids are important when planning vacations. The impact of children on the household travel plans is noted in chapter 10. There is also agreement that children are influential in the selection of destinations (64 percent), accommodations (40 percent), and vacation packages (38 percent). Interestingly, about eight out of every ten children across key age categories (6–17) say they really like taking family vacations. What do the kids say is important to them? The following (70–85 percent agreement) has high appeal:

Attribute	High Appeal
Experimentation	Theme parks
Fantasy/Ambiance	Beach
	Water parks
	Place never visited
Physical Activities	Snorkeling
	Swimming
Other	Doing things with family

The family is an extremely crucial market to tourism interests. © 2009 Monkey Business Images. Used under license from Shutterstock, Inc.

Over 60 percent of families feel that their freedom and flexibility is reduced when traveling with children. This might be an opportunity for destinations to program family activities as well as opportunities for parents to be away from the kids.

QUICK TRIP 14.3

Merging Business with Leisure

The line between business and leisure travel continues to blur as more business travelers are seeking rest and relaxation on their trips. Fifty-two percent of travelers surveyed by Deloitte said they extended an average of 3.2 business trips for vacation/leisure over the past year. In addition, almost half had a family member or friend join them for at least one of these trips. Even intended leisure trips are morphing into business trips. One-third of respondents stated that they answer work phone calls, listen to voice mails, and check e-mails when they are on vacation.

One way business travelers are making a business trip feel a bit more like a vacation is by bringing the kids along. Hotels have recognized this growing trend and begun to adapt accordingly. At 90 percent of Westins properties, children can have a day of supervised recreation. Over twenty of Hilton's resorts have programs in which kids can play games and engage in activities with local flair like hula dancing and salsa making. At seventeen Hyatt hotels, kids can learn about local geography and crafts. Twenty-one Ritz hotels provide a full day of diversions like etiquette lessons, nature walks, and scavenger hunts. Business and leisure travel seem to be merging so much that maybe one day the two categories will not exist and the idea of "travel" will include both work and play. It is up to individuals to determine what separation they would like between their two worlds. But overall, you should make it your business to have a little fun.

THINK ABOUT THIS:

1. Is it necessary for there to be a clear line between business and leisure time?
2. What are the disadvantages of blurring this boundary?

Sources:

Travel Industry Prospects Bright Despite Economic Uncertainty: Many Expect To Travel at Least as Much For Holidays and in Coming Year. 2007.

http://deloitte.com/dtt/press_release/0,1014,sid%253D2283%2526cid%253D236153,00.html.

The family is an extremely crucial market to tourism interests. Because these parents are of the Baby Boomer generation, they make up a high percentage of the population. They feel the need to get away from job stress and spend time alone with the family. They tend to take shorter and more frequent vacations, closer to home, to maximize the use of their time. To attract this market, destinations are adding such features as baby-sitting, children's menus, and even children's dining rooms.

Within this group there are several subsegments:

- Husbands and wives without children. This represents 29 percent of the nation's households.

- Husbands and wives with children. Twenty-five percent of all households fall into this category.

- Grandparents with grandchildren. In the United States about 3 million children under the age of 18 live full-time with their grandparents. In households where both parents work it is becoming increasingly common for grandparents to take their grandchildren on vacation.

- Single parents with children.

GROUP TOURS

Package travel has become a significant factor in the expansion of mass tourism markets to both domestic and

QUICK TRIP 14.4

Luxury Business Travel?

The life of a business traveler can be full of frustrations and complications. In an effort to deliver a more personalized experience, hosts of airports, airlines, hotels and travel services have created a unique experience in an attempt to simplify the life of a business traveler. A South America–based company, Blue Parallel, will expedite you through the airport, provide cell phones when you reach the limo at your international location, set you up with a personal assistant, arrange your stays at five-star hotels, and coordinate off-site corporate meetings. Many companies are catching on to this new trend and taking it upon themselves to plan every detail of your business trip.

New high-class amenities are also entering the business traveler's life. "Flatbeds" provided on long-haul flights provide the opportunity to stretch out and relax. Multicourse meals are prepared in partnership with celebrity chefs in premium-class cabins. Entertainment systems can now include high-resolution LCD screens, noise canceling headphones, and USB ports for charging personal MP3 players. International cities are also paying attention to this new trend by providing services to assist guests with their stay and tips on how to easily navigate the city.

Although companies are doing their best to satisfy the business traveler's every need, airlines are having trouble retaining their high-paying clientele. Many business travelers are platinum members on a variety of airlines but lately have been less loyal to any particular company. One avid business traveler said he is tired of the inconveniences of airline travel today and will sway his loyalty depending on who provides more convenient flights or more comfortable seating. Airlines are struggling to attract the lucrative long-haul business traveler. The problem is that so many of the carriers have out-of-date technology and amenities. Even when updated, these airlines fall far behind some of their international rivals, and the costs of upgrading can be too high. Standard business class fare today must include lie-flat seats, gourmet food and wine service, and extensive entertainment options. Those who cannot provide will not be able to woo the business travelers to their airline.

THINK ABOUT THIS:

1. Obviously, business travel is becoming much more pleasure focused. Is it appropriate for business professionals to be receiving this kind of treatment when on a business trip? Why or why not?

CHECK THIS OUT:

The article recommends checking out SeatGuru (http://www.seatguru.com), which offers interactive seating charts of nearly every plane in the air today.

Sources:

The Wall Street Journal. 2008. Global Business Travel. Raising the Bar on Business Travel.

Battle for the Business Class Traveler, by Marnie Hunter. Retrieved 28 April 2008, http://www.cnn.com/2008/TRAVEL/business.travel/03/21/business.class/index.html.

international destinations in the past sixty years. Some argue that package travel has been declining because of changing tourist preferences towards more individualized and independent travel experiences while others counter that package travel has a considerable economic impact in the United States through job creation and income generation. United States and Canadian tour companies operate over half a million tour departures with 23 million passengers every year. Well over half are one-day trips. However, taking into account the number of people on a given tour and the tour length, 80 percent of passenger-days (one passenger taking a trip for one day) and 90 percent of the revenues are accounted for by multi-day trips. (For example, one passenger taking a six-day trip accounts for six passenger-days) (Davidson-Peterson Associates, *1995 Economic Impact Study*, 1996).

THE GAMING MARKET

In 1931 gaming was legalized in Nevada (Rohs, 1995). For forty-five years this was the only legal location for gaming in the United States. Nevada was joined by Atlantic City in the mid-1970s. By 2003 the gaming market of $72.9 billion was distributed in this way (Miller & Associates, Inc., 2005):

- $28.6 billion   Commercial casinos
- $19.9   Lotteries
- $16.8   Indian casinos
- $3.78   Parimutuel wagering
- $2.7   Charitable games and bingo
- $851 million   Card rooms
- $128 million   Legal bookmaking

In the 1996 election voters in Ohio, influenced by strong opposition from the governor of the state and the mayor of Cincinnati, rejected a constitutional amendment to allow riverboat casinos in Cleveland, Cincinnati, Youngstown, and Lorain. However, a number of other initiatives were supported by voters. Michigan approved a plan that would allow casinos to be constructed in Detroit; Arizona approved more Indian casinos in the state; Arkansas residents authorized casinos in Hot Springs, subject to local voter approval; six Louisiana parishes voted to keep legalized gambling while twenty-three others voted to approve floating casinos.

Since the late 1980s, gambling has grown significantly in the United States. Much of this gambling

> ... [T]wo U.S. tourists in Germany ... were traveling on a public bus when one of them sneezed. A German turned around and said, sympathetically, "Gesundheit." The U.S. tourist commented, "How nice that he speaks English."
>
> Sharon Ruhley, "Intercultural Communication"

activity occurs while Americans are traveling away from home. One-half of all gambling travelers gambled in the Western census region (51 percent), which includes Nevada (40 percent). The South captured 19 percent of all gambling travelers, followed by the Northeast (17 percent) and the Midwest (13 percent). Most gambling on trips occurs within the same region where the traveler lives. The West (32 percent) and the Midwest (31 percent) garner the highest shares of *non-resident* gambling visitors. Overall, gambling travelers are older, are less likely to be married or to have children in their households and are less educated than their non-gambling counterparts. Nonetheless, household incomes are similar for the two groups, even though a higher share of gamblers are retired.

Gamblers actually fall into two groups: where gambling is the only activity on the trip (39 percent) and where gambling is one of multiple activities on the trip (61 percent).

It has become apparent that casino gambling is accepted as a form of entertainment. Secondly, entertainment means more than gaming. It is more than slot machines. It is fake volcanoes, jousting machines, and dancing water fountains in Las Vegas, for example.

There are two types of casino locations:

1. Transient. Serving the day-tripper market; people travel to the site by car or bus and use little lodging or off-premises food facilities. Most Indian casinos and many riverboats fall into this category.
2. Destination casinos. The premiere example continues to be Las Vegas. Over 40 percent arrive by air while slightly less than that number drive to the destination. People stay an average of four days, 90 percent staying in hotels.

Over 70 percent of Canadians gamble in a given year. While playing the lottery is the most popular gambling activity, in-province casino gambling ranks fourth, out-of-province casino gambling is listed ninth while out-of-country casino gambling is tenth. It appears that there are two distinct segments—those who prefer to stay inside the province and others who prefer to visit casinos outside the province.

A study of Alberta residents finds differences between casino travelers and non-travelers and of travelers for whom a casino visit was a major trip activity versus those for whom it was a minor activity. Travelers to casinos are more likely to be female, to have a university

Nude Travelers

Many travelers are disgruntled over the fees being charged for checking a second piece of luggage, but there is a select group of people unaffected by the increased cost of traveling by air. Travelers seeking a nudist destination won't be needing the extra space in their suitcases. "Clothing-optional" vacations are becoming more popular as tourists seek to add a new dimension to their out-of-town experience. The average person may picture a nudist colony being in the middle of the woods occupied with hippies, volleyball courts, and RV parks. Although these developments still exist, the new trend is toward high-end travel with upscale hotels, resorts, and even some luxury cruise lines. Companies are beginning to see the profit potential in this new market as many travelers want to shed their clothing but not their luxury lifestyles.

In 2003 an all-inclusive, nude only, luxury resort opened along the Mayan Riviera in Mexico. When staying at this $300-a-night hotel, guests are greeted with champagne, have rose petals spread across their beds, and are offered reading materials and towels while relaxing by the pool. A similar resort can be found in the Desert Hot Springs, California, with room rates ranging from $269 to $900 a night. Guests can expect to have Egyptian bed linens, flat-screen TVs, and natural mineral water pumped into their showers. Other upscale resorts will set aside blocks of rooms for nude guests while some have started the process by allowing topless pools. The housing market has also caught sight of this trend, and a new clothing-optional condo resort in Arizona has recently sold over one hundred condos.

The nude recreational industry has jumped from being a $200 million market in 1992 to a $440 million market in 2007, and it is still growing strong. Nude vacation options range from yoga retreats and mountain biking adventures to bed and breakfasts and cruise lines. A new German travel operator is arranging nude flights to take travelers to clothing-optional retreats. Nude vacationers say that what they enjoy most is liberation from the typical pretenses of society.

THINK ABOUT THIS:

1. From the hotel's perspective, what issues could you see arising from this type of tourism?

CHECK THIS OUT:

SpaFinder.com, an online spa search engine, recently created a separate category for "nudist spa vacations" after noticing an increase in searches for the term. Since November, searches on SpaFinder.com for such trips have averaged about 720 a month.

Source: No Shoes, No Shirt, No Worries, by Michelle Higgins. Retrieved April 27, 2008, http://travel.nytimes.com/2008/04/27/travel/27nude.html.

education, and to have management or professional occupations. There are differences depending upon whether the trip is a major or a minor activity. Risk taking is a major motivation for those travelers for whom casino gaming is a major trip activity. They also demonstrate a desire to escape their regular lives (Hinch and Walker, 2004).

THE SENIOR TRAVEL MARKET

By the year 2025 there will be twice as many people in the United States sixty-five and older as there are teens. This segment has been called a number of things:

- Mature market
- Muppie market (mature, upscale, post-professional)
- Senior market
- Maturing market

One significant study (Shoemaker, 2000) profiles changes in Pennsylvania residents fifty-five and over in the last ten years. The study finds that, for the most part, the motivation and attitudes to travel as well as behavior while on vacation have remained remarkably stable over time. This suggests that, as people age, individuals attempt to maintain past patterns of behavior. Thus, marketing programs aimed at the older traveler may need to be updated, but probably do not require major surgery.

The study also finds that the senior market can be segmented on the basis of motivation. Three sub-segments are suggested:

1. **The Escape and Learn Group,** comprising 46 percent of the sample, who want to visit new places, experience new things, and escape everyday routine.
2. **The Retirees,** 19 percent of the sample, who take trips where they stay in one place for a period of time.
3. **Active Storytellers,** 35 percent, who want to experience new things, visit museums and historic sights, and meet people and socialize.

The influence of seniors as a market segment in tourism will grow over the next several decades. By the year 2000 people age fifty or more made up 38 percent of the population and accounted for 75 percent of the country's wealth (van Harssel & Theobald, 1994). By the year 2030 there will be 65 million older adults in the United States. Many older people have the time, money and desire to travel. They hold a large share of the country's discretionary income because their children are grown and they no longer have house payments. Because they are time-flexible they can fill the times of low occupancy felt by many businesses and tourist destinations.

Seniors will be increasingly important for two reasons. First, there will be more of them. Second, their lifestyles are different from those of previous generations. They are increasingly independent about how they choose to live, and enjoy, their lives. Two demographic items are of particular importance. There will be a high proportion of singles in this population and a higher proportion of women than men.

This is because they live longer than men, marry men older than themselves, and more widowers remarry than do widows.

The *Escape and Learn Group* is one sub-segment of the senior travel market. © 2009 Mayskyphoto. Used under license from Shutterstock, Inc.

A national study of older pleasure travelers sponsored by the American Association of Retired Persons (AARP) and American Express (van Harssel & Theobald, 1994) provides a picture of this market segment. The primary motivators include:

- Needing to change routines
- Seeing new things
- Visiting friends and relatives
- Meeting new people and experiencing new cultures
- Expanding knowledge
- Creating memories

At the same time they expressed concern about such things as:

- **The single supplement penalty.** The cost of a single room is often more than half the cost of a double room. While some tour operators offer assistance in finding a roommate the process is not easy and the result not always compatible.
- **Health/mobility constraints.** While 60 percent of those age sixty-five or older report no activity limitations, they do consider health a problem with travel as it prevents them from enjoying the trip or engaging in some activities.
- **The fear of falling ill.** The prospect of having a doctor or nurse close by helps alleviate concern.
- **Uncertainty about political conditions.** Many choose not to travel internationally when there is a question regarding the country's economic or political situation.
- **Quality and quantity of information.** There was a problem in getting information about upcoming events or trips. More aggressive promotion is needed to reach this group.
- **The pace of itineraries.** People indicated they needed more time to get ready when they were part of a tour. Scheduling was also a problem—packing too many things into a short period of time.
- **Language.** Language is seen as a major barrier to traveling internationally. Tour guides are seen as important in helping overcome this concern.
- **Packing and unpacking.** A more leisurely trip is preferred over tours that go to a new city every day.
- **Meals.** Lack of variety is a problem. Most evening meals consist of chicken dinners while a greater choice at breakfast is desired.
- **Concerns related to transportation.** More help is desired when getting on and off buses. Communication is really important. One participant said, "I re-

The Solo Traveler

Travelers typically come in pairs, if not groups. In the past, people traveling on their own have had few options except for the package tour in which an individual can expect to be lost in a crowd of couples. Today things are changing and new avenues are opening up for those who care to explore alone. According to the Travel Industry Association, roughly one in ten leisure travelers chooses to make his or her trek alone, and the travel industry is beginning to take note of this new market opportunity.

Intrepid Travel has introduced singles-only trips focusing on off-the-beaten-path excursions to places like Peru and Nepal. To make the journey a little less painful for one's pocketbook, travelers can share rooms so they are not forced to incur otherwise large hotel bills. Another agency, Absolute Travel, is pairing compatible travelers up who would rather not journey alone. Spas and resorts are also creating packages for the individual traveler. Some hotels are lowering their prices for single individuals and encouraging guests to explore the area by themselves.

The popularity of these new travel deals boosts the independence of solo travelers while helping them feel less like loners. An even more unique niche market is travel agencies that cater to single women, like Adventure Women and Country Walkers. The women on these trips say they enjoy having the company of people who are not "couples." Many of the women travel alone when their husbands are traveling for business, while others are just there to enjoy the journey. Agencies say these new opportunities are a great advancement from what once existed for single travelers. In the past, trips for singles were typically composed of a group tour to some beach resort, but now the opportunities are endless and individuals can travel just about anywhere and find special deals along the way.

THINK ABOUT THIS:

1. What are some other ways the tourism industries could make single travelers feel more comfortable and welcome?

2. How can hotels and resorts adapt to this new market trend?

Source: One Is No Longer the Loneliest Number, by Michelle Higgins. Retrieved 2 December 2007, http://travel.nytimes.com/2007/12/02/travel/02prac.html.

member hearing an announcement on the bus. I did not understand what was said. That can really throw you into a panic."

MINORITY TRAVEL PATTERNS

Most Americans, regardless of ethnicity, share similar travel habits. Most vacation, and use cars; a typical trip includes two people, an overnight stay, and the primary activity is shopping.

The three largest minority groups in the United States—African-Americans, Hispanics, and Asian-Americans—will make up 35 percent of the population in the United States by 2020. African-Americans are slightly more likely than the other groups to travel on business, especially to seminars and conventions. They are also more likely to add on vacation travel to business trips. They are more prone to taking group tours and less likely to use recreational vehicles (RVs). The most popular destinations for African-Americans are Texas, Georgia, and other southern states. Washington, DC, and Maryland are also popular in addition to trips to the Caribbean.

Hispanics are more likely to travel with children than are other groups. They also take longer trips and are more likely to take a plane trip and stay at a hotel or motel. Hispanics, already a majority in New Mexico, Hawaii and California, will constitute the majority in Texas by 2010 and will represent the largest minority group in the United States by 2013. When considering vacations, they are likely to want to explore their adopted country before venturing internationally. The only exception to this would be the desire to visit the country they were born in. California, Nevada, Florida, Arizona, Texas, and New Mexico are popular destinations in the United States while the Caribbean, Mexico, and South America are favored international destinations.

Asian-Americans use rental cars more than the average, are more likely to travel alone and are the biggest spenders of the three ethnic groups. California, Nevada, Hawaii and the Far East are popular.

THE CRUISE MARKET

Only 8 percent of the U.S. population has ever taken a cruise. The growth potential appears to be excellent as cruise lines have begun to look at less traditional demographic groups. For example, the Cruise Lines International Association (CLIA) reports that only 36 percent of people who cruise are 60 years of age or older. Those

The top three benefits of cruising are the ease of visiting several destinations, the many activities, and the reasonable price in relation to value. © 2009 Bryan Busovicki. Used under license from Shutterstock, Inc.

under 40 make up one in five cruisers while over a third are between 40 and 59 years old. In fact, among first-time cruisers, slightly less than half are under 40 years of age.

The CLIA identifies six market segments:

1. **Enthusiastic Baby Boomers.** Excited about cruising, they live intense, stressful lives and want to escape and relax when on vacation. This segment accounts for 20 percent of cruisers, 15 percent of all cruising days. Forty-six percent of them are first-time cruisers.

2. **Restless Baby Boomers.** The newest cruisers, they like to try new vacation experiences and, while they enjoy the cruise experience, cost may be an inhibiting factor. Making up one-third of all cruisers and 17 percent of all cruising days, almost 60 percent are first-timers.

3. **Luxury Seekers.** They want to be pampered, want deluxe accommodations, and are willing and able to pay for it. Thirty percent of these cruisers are first-timers. They comprise 14 percent of the market and account for 18 percent of all cruising days.

4. **Consummate Shoppers.** Committed to cruising they seek the best value (though not necessarily the cheapest price). Accounting for 16 percent of the market and accounting for one-fifth of all cruising days, 20 percent of them are first-time cruisers.

5. **Explorers.** Well-educated, well-traveled, they are interested in different and exotic destinations. Twenty percent are first-timers. They are 11 percent of the market and account for 18 percent of all cruising days.

6. **Ship Buffs.** The most senior segment, they cruise extensively and will continue because of the pleasure and comfort it brings them. Only 6 percent of the market, this segment accounts for 11 percent of cruising days. Thirteen percent are first-timers.

Several attitudes are common to all six segments:

- Sixty percent like to experiment with new and different things
- In choosing a cruise over 70 percent say the destination is the most important factor, followed by cost and time of year (each 60 percent), and cruise line or ship (57 percent)

The top three benefits of cruising are the ease of visiting several destinations (91 percent), the many activities (83 percent), and the reasonable price in relation to value (83 percent).

CANADIAN PLEASURE MARKET

The Canadian pleasure market is made up of the following segments of the population (Cameron 1992):

- Family value makes up 17 percent of the population yet comprises only 10 percent of all travel. They are more traditional than experimental, feel uncomfortable when stared at in a crowd, do not enjoy even a small amount of danger, the unpredictable, or doing things on the spur of the moment.
- No surprises account for 15 percent of the population and 19 percent of those who travel. They share a similar approach to life to the family value segment, though are not as extreme in their actions or lack of actions.
- Active players, at 15 percent of the population, are 14 percent of all travelers. They, as distinct from the previous two segments, enjoy a small element of danger. They like to be in style and enjoy the unpredictable. Being part of a group is very important to them.
- Packaged sun and services represent 14 percent of the population in general and 12 percent of the travel population in particular. They also like to be in style but do not score high on any of the other factors mentioned.
- History and hospitality, 14 percent of the population, account for 17 percent of all travelers. They are more traditional, are the least likely segment to enjoy a small amount of danger, do not like the unpredictable and do not care to be in style.

- Culture and nature seekers make up 13 percent of both the general and travel populations. They are the most likely to be in style and experimental, do not feel that being part of a group is important and are less likely to feel that everything is changing too fast and to pay whatever it costs to get the best quality. They are not concerned with security and enjoy the unpredictable and a small amount of danger.
- Knowledge and experience, at 12 percent of the population, comprise 15 percent of all travelers. They are experimental, do not believe things are changing too fast and are not concerned with security. They like the unpredictable and a small amount of danger.

Four travel philosophies were identified.

1. Organized variety travelers (29 percent) like to travel throughout the country to a different place each trip.
2. Independent variety travelers (29 percent) feel that money spent on travel is well spent, enjoy making plans, and make them as they go. Inexpensive travel is important.
3. Familiar independent travelers (24 percent) stay places they have been before and stay put at a destination. They prefer short trips over one long trip, find making arrangements bothersome and don't feel the need to travel on vacation.
4. Organized and familiar travelers (18 percent) feel it is worth paying for extras. They like the travel arranged before the trip begins and prefer it be done by others.

About 30 percent of travelers are described as "knowledge seekers," interested in new and different lifestyles, new foods, and foreign destinations. They also feel that history is important. One in four are breakaway travelers, looking to escape the ordinary and somewhat daring and adventuresome while slightly fewer are players. They are likely to gamble, participate in and watch sports, and like to feel at home when away. Finally, one in five are described as social, visiting family, friends and relatives.

A recent study of seniors in Ontario (Joppe, Athanassakos, and Forgacs, 2003) projects travel patterns to the year 2026. By 2026 more than half of Canadian seniors will be located in Ontario.

In 2000, there were approximately 23.3 million Canadians aged 18 years or older. Statistics Canada projects that the number of Canadians aged 18 years or older will grow from 23.3 million in 2000 to 29.6 million by the year 2026. Age becomes a determining factor for travel patterns as people become older. The incidence of travel drops significantly over 60, with the drop becoming more prominent after the age of 70. Despite this, the number of traveling seniors in Ontario alone is expected to grow from 1.1 million in 2000 to 2.4 million by 2026.

Destination choices also change with age. Seniors are less likely to vacation in Canada compared to the rest of the population, but are equally likely to travel to the U.S. or to other overseas destinations. This changes after the age of 70 when travel within Canada is preferred. In terms of international destinations, the over-70 group tends to visit Florida, Hawaii and the United Kingdom.

Seniors are more likely than the general population to take both getaway trips and vacations in the spring and especially in the fall seasons. They also take a large number of warm weather trips in winter.

The top travel driver for seniors is overwhelmingly to visit friends and relatives (VFR) followed by rest/relax/recuperating, spending time with family away from home, spending time with friends, visiting historical sites, seeing natural wonders/natural sites, and escaping winter weather. It is expected that VFR will be the major motivator for the next 25 years. The importance of rest/relax/recuperate drops for those over 70 years of age due to the fact that many of the younger seniors are still in the workforce and experiencing workplace stress.

There will be a movement away from outdoor activities (especially strenuous ones) towards cultural activities over the next 25 years. In addition to outdoors activities like sunbathing and swimming, seniors like to view wildflower, flora and wildlife, golf, watch birds and freshwater fish. Seniors also like to visit small towns and villages, take day trips in their own vehicles along scenic coastlines and join guided bus day tours in a city. Cruises also remain important to this segment. The demand for all of these activities will grow from this segment of the population.

"BEAM ME UP, SCOTTY"

This phrase from *Star Trek* may be said sooner than we think. Dennis Tito became the first person to pay for a ticket into space on April 28, 2001, after he paid $20 million to accompany a Russian rocket to the International Space Station. There are three potential opportunities for space tourism (Couch, 2001):

1. Terrestrial Space Tourism such as tours to observe a shuttle launch at the Kennedy Space Center, or the Russian Space Tour consisting of a nine-day visit to the Yuri Gagarin Cosmonaut Training Center in Moscow.
2. High-Altitude and Suborbital Space Tourism taking people off the ground to experience weightlessness.
3. Orbital Space Tourism—actually taking tourists into space.

One estimate of demand for space tourism indicates that, at ticket prices of $10,000, $100,000 and $1 million, there is a high probability of passenger demand of 6,000, 60 and 20 per year respectively.

THE BUSINESS TRAVEL MARKET

In most developed countries, business travel is the "bread-and-butter" market for tourism for much of the year. This is certainly the case in the United States, Canada, and the United Kingdom. For example, within the European Union, business travel accounts for 48 percent of all air passenger trips. Just as it is inadequate to use the "jumbo jet" approach to analyzing pleasure/personal travel markets, it is equally wrong to view the business travel market as an amorphous mass that cannot be further segmented. In fact, this first major travel market has many component segments, and the number of segments appears to grow from year to year. The business-related travel market segments can be broadly categorized as follows:

- Regular business travel
- Business travel related to meetings, conventions, and congresses
- Incentive travel

The third category of incentive is really a "hybrid" segment because it is a type of pleasure travel that has been financed for business reasons. Thus, the persons on incentive trips are pleasure travelers and the purchasers are businesses.

Over one in five adults travel for business each year, taking 127 million trips of more than fifty miles away from home. This includes travel for general business purposes or to attend a convention or seminar (14 percent) and travel combining business and pleasure (8 percent). Business travel is a $153 billion segment of the U.S. domestic travel market. Business travel accounts for almost one-third of all domestic travel spending in the United States. Business travelers are more

likely to be male with nearly half being Baby Boomers. Technologically savvy, almost all members of this group own personal computers while most have a high-speed Internet connection. They like frequent-traveler programs, in-room Internet access, and hotel fitness centers. Frequent business travelers (more than ten business trips a year) make up less than 20 percent of all business travelers yet take more than half of all business trips.

An increasingly popular trend is for the traveler to add a pleasure piece to the business trip with many taking a spouse, child, or other family member or friends along. It is estimated that 15 percent of all business trips includes a child (Patkose, Stokes, and Cook, 2004).

The top ten cities for general business travel are (Milligan, 2005):

1. Chicago
2. Los Angeles-Long Beach
3. Washington
4. New York
5. Atlanta
6. Houston
7. Boston (metro area)
8. Minneapolis-St. Paul
9. Dallas
10. Denver

Business travelers are more important to travel suppliers than their total numbers would indicate. They use airlines, rental cars, hotels, and travel agents to a greater extent than pleasure travelers. Business travelers, for example, account for over 40 percent of all airline trips and hotel stays, and account for almost two-thirds of rental car revenues. In selecting an airline, business travelers are primarily concerned with the convenience of the airline schedule. To a lesser extent, low or discount fares and the on-time departure record of the airline influence their choice. Reasonable rates, on the other hand, are the most important factor when choosing a car rental company. This is followed in importance by the convenience of the location and the condition of the cars. Location is the number one factor in selecting a hotel, followed by clean, comfortable rooms and room rates.

Compared to the pleasure traveler, the business traveler is more time sensitive; service quality is more important than price; and she or he is more experienced and demanding. Approximately one-third of all business travelers belong to frequent-flyer programs, an average of two programs each. However, this figure increases to half when looking at air business travelers. To a majority of travelers, this is a major factor in their choice of an airline. Belonging to a frequent-flyer program means that credit is collected for mileage flown on that particular airline. After a specified number of miles have been flown, the traveler can qualify for upgrades to first class and free trips. In recent years, airlines have reduced the attractiveness of their awards, making it necessary to fly greater distances in order to obtain a particular reward. There are two factors that, if enacted, will have a tremendous negative impact on travelers and the industry. First, passengers of many airlines have accumulated significant amounts of travel that, if and when these amounts show up on the company's balance sheet as a liability, will have a significant impact on the airline. Second, it is only a matter of time before the Internal Revenue Service looks at these rewards and begins to tax them. As part of the effort to reduce corporate travel costs, some companies are seeking to have the award given to the company rather than to the individual.

They are increasingly looking for value when flying. Forty percent use full-fare tickets, a significant reduction from previous years. Two-thirds say they are willing to use no-frills carrier for short flights. The more frequent flyers are less willing to make this switch. When selecting a carrier for long-haul flights, business travelers seek convenient schedules, seat comfort, and service. Schedules are more important for short-haul flights over fares, service, and punctuality.

A survey of business travelers finds that 25 percent indicate that leg room would be the hardest airline amenity to give up, closely followed by frequency of available flights. Comfortable bedding is the hotel amenity that matters most. In terms of car rental, expedited pickup and drop-off are the favored amenities (Holly, 2003).

Two-thirds of North American and half of European business travelers use the Internet for flight information. However, only 9 percent use the Internet to make flight reservations. Most prefer to use a travel agent. Security does not seem to be a problem with this group.

Business travel is a nondiscretionary expenditure. The business traveler must travel to specific places to do business. For the pleasure tourist, taking a vacation is a discretionary purchase—one that he or she does not need to make. As a result, business travel is more stable and less price resistant than vacation travel. Business trips are taken consistently throughout the year, while pleasure trips tend to be concentrated in the summer months.

People traveling on business tend to get frustrated with the many demands of travel that are beyond their control. Principal among these are the time required to travel, the long waits, and the delays of arrivals and departures. They also have more personal frustrations—being away from home and families, being alone, and living out of suitcases. More and more people are taking kids with them on their business trips.

More and more companies are concerned about the high cost of travel and are putting more time and effort into controlling their corporate travel costs (Jones, 1996). The most common restrictions on business travelers are travel per diems, restrictions on the type of airfare class, and requirements that travel be approved by upper management (Patkose, Stokes, and Cook, 2004).

The use of technology to replace business travel in the United States seems to have leveled off with just under one-third of travelers reporting the use of teleconferencing, Webcasting, or videoconferencing to replace at least one business trip. However, nearly half of U.S. workers are traveling less frequently for business than they did five years ago. Additionally, a recent study of U.K. business travelers finds that half indicate they are traveling less because of technology, specifically remote access and virtual private networking (VPN). Videoconferencing helps a third of them travel less. One-quarter claim their health is suffering because of time spent away from home. As technology becomes more efficient in time and money spent, its use as a travel alternative becomes increasingly apparent. However, less than a third of business travelers feel that such technology is more effective than face-to-face meetings (Quest, 2005; Patkose, Stokes, and Cook, 2004).

Travel remains the third-largest controllable expense at U.S. corporations. Sixty percent of companies have a formal written travel policy and 30 percent have informal guidelines. Almost 80 percent of companies require employees to take the "lowest logical" airfare. There is movement away from upscale accommodations and toward more moderate or economy class accommodations. More than 60 percent require employees to stay at hotels in which the company or travel agency has corporate or negotiated rates. Rental car use is also regulated. Over three-quarters of companies impose a size limit on cars rented by employees. American Express estimates that U.S. companies lose $15 billion a year to deviations from corporate policy. To combat the problem, a number of companies are experimenting with systems that allow corporate travelers to make their travel plans on their personal computers, but only within the parameters of corporate policy.

> Commuter—one who spends his life
> In riding to and from his wife;
> A man who shaves and takes a train,
> And then rides back to shave again.
>
> E. B. White

However, according to the consulting firm Runzheimer International, companies—even those serious about managing travel costs—often overlook meal expenses because many corporate cultures consider business meals a perk for travelers who have to spend many days on the road.

The business executive travel market is proving to be more "segmentable" today, with many airlines and hotels making specific efforts to cater to these higher echelon persons. Airlines have been offering first-class seat service and first-class passenger lounges in airport terminals to these travelers for many years. More recent innovations include special check-in arrangements, bigger seats, and sleeper seats. Many hotel chains have begun to allocate whole floors or wings of their buildings for those business travelers seeking greater luxury in their accommodations. The rooms or suites are more spacious and contain more personal giveaways; the hotels provide their guests with complimentary drinks and express check-in, check-out service. Normally the airlines and hotel companies add a surcharge to their regular prices for the extra comforts and convenience provided to executive travelers. They have achieved considerable marketing success in doing so.

While we have been talking about the business traveler, there are actually several segments to this market, each with distinct characteristics. Business travelers can be divided into segments as follows:

- Frequent business traveler
- Women business travelers
- Luxury business traveler
- International business traveler
- Occupational designation

On average, business travelers take an average of 5.4 trips per year. However, an average frequent traveler takes twenty-three business trips annually. Frequent travelers (ten+ trips a year on average) continue to be an influential segment. Although frequent travelers make up only 14 percent of all business travelers, they account for 54 percent of all trips. The number of frequent travelers has grown marginally with the growth in total business travelers from 6 million individuals two years ago to 6.2 million in this survey period.

In 1970, women accounted for 1 percent of all business travelers. This figure increased to 50 percent by the year 2000. Typically, the female business traveler:

> They may be 60, they seem (to act) 50 and they'd like to be marketed to as if they were 40.
>
> Jeff Hamblin, executive vice president for the Americas, British Tourist Authority

- Is married, over the age of forty, with no children in the household
- Is not a member of a hotel frequent guest program
- Does not book online
- Eats at a restaurant away from the hotel when traveling with colleagues and in a hotel restaurant when traveling alone
- Sees as the top benefits from travel being with new people, experiencing new destinations, and having time for self
- Tries to incorporate some leisure time into a business trip
- Values responsive service, a hotel located near business, and affordable rates
- Is looking for convenience, such as express check-in and check-out and late check-out

Female business travelers can actually be grouped into three segments based on the amount of travel done. The occasional business traveler, two to four business trips a year, makes up 48 percent of the segment; the periodic business traveler, five to ten business trips a year, comprises 28 percent of all female business travelers; the constant business traveler, eleven plus business trips a year, makes up 24 percent of the market. The constant female business traveler, compared to the occasional female business traveler, is more likely to:

- Add a weekend to a trip (61 percent to 54 percent)
- Add a vacation day to a trip (44 percent to 37 percent)
- Value late check-out (70 percent to 49 percent)
- View business travel as a way to meet new people and network (92 percent to 87 percent)
- Experience a new destination (83 percent to 77 percent)
- Consider that business travel makes their job more interesting (92 percent to 80 percent)
- Value responsive service (76 percent to 60 percent)

As hotels sought to attract this segment of the market, several mistakes were made. Early attempts to provide "women's floors" and pink wallpaper were viewed by many women as patronizing. They were concerned about such things as security, however. This has resulted in such things as a "club floor"—open to both sexes—and accessed by a special key. More hotels are building suites so that women can hold meetings in their rooms without having a bed in view.

Room service hours have been expanded as many women dislike eating alone in public. Lighting in hallways and parking lots is getting brighter.

According to the *Official Airline Guide* (Dorsey, 1996), the "typical" international business traveler is a married man over the age of forty-five holding a director-level position at a company with fewer than one-hundred employees. This "typical" traveler takes close to twenty trips a year and states that home and family are priorities over work. This person will travel with a laptop computer but prefers watching videos and making phone calls in the air. The ideal in-flight companion is an empty seat. This person is tempted to give up a seat on an overbooked flight although an upgrade on the next flight is also of interest. Executive airline lounges are favored for the opportunity to sit in peace and quiet, use the telephone, and get a free drink.

The traveler prefers to make air arrangements by going to a travel agent, looking at a printed flight guide, and having a secretary take care of things. Airlines are chosen on the basis of convenient schedules, on-time performance, and modern planes. Frequent-flyer membership also plays a role. United States travelers are likely to belong to five or more such programs. They belong so they can jump ahead of others on an airline's waiting list. Flight upgrades are also important. The traveler prefers to use mileage awards for personal and leisure travel rather than to save the company money on business travel.

When making hotel arrangements, the preference is to contact the hotel directly, use a travel agent, or consult an independent hotel guide.

Over half of all travelers fall into the highest occupational groupings of professional/managerial with almost equal percentages found in the other classifications of lower manager/technical, sales/clerical, blue collar, and retired/unemployed. Business travel is most prominent in the health, legal, and educational fields, with manufacturing following this group.

QUICK TRIP 14.7

Voluntourism

Volunteering while on vacation was once a job for nonprofits, small adventure companies, and a few motivated backpackers. Today the trend is encouraging a variety of travelers to give back to the communities they visit. A survey conducted by *Condé Nast Traveler* and MSNBC discovered that while only 14 percent of Americans have taken a volunteer holiday, 55 percent say they would like to. Of those who have participated in such a trip, 95 percent say they are likely to do it again. Brian Mullis, president of Sustainable Travel International says that "travelers are looking for a sense of purpose in their leisure activities; they are looking at new ways of distributing wealth. The age of checkbook philanthropy is morphing into the age of participatory philanthropy." Travelers are now asking what they can do that will actually have an impact and be meaningful to the community they are working in. Volunteer programs exist but many tourists find ways to volunteer independently. Proponents of voluntourism say one of the benefits is that Americans' interactions with foreign communities breaks down stereotypes and cultural barriers. The American traveler may develop a new perspective while the foreigners may gain a new image of Westerners.

Voluntourism is even entering the luxury market as high-end travel agencies arrange volunteer experiences for their customers. Ritz-Carlton Hotels has launched Give Back Getaways, connecting guests staying at its properties around the world with volunteer opportunities. Sue Stephenson, who runs the company's philanthropy programs, says, "Our guests want pampered experiences, but they also want the chance to do something in the community."

Regardless of how you may choose to volunteer your time or money, it is important to confirm that your efforts are going toward the right causes. Put some time into researching the program you would like to work with, and ensure that what you will be doing is meeting the needs of the community.

THINK ABOUT THIS:

1. Do you think many travelers would participate in voluntourism mainly to feel good about themselves, or to actually help a community and make an impact?

2. How could tourist destinations, hotels, and resorts advertise this kind of opportunity?

Source: *Condé Nast Traveler*. Voluntourism. Retrieved May 2008, http://www.concierge.com/cntraveler/articles/12200?pageNumber=2.

It is expected that the number of business travelers will not grow much, if any, but that those who do travel will, on average, take more trips. It is anticipated that there will be an increased need to have access to more information regarding available choices. This is driven by the fact that companies are increasingly looking for the best value options in travel as they seek to contain their travel costs. There is a particular interest in technology as more companies are moving into the area of online or data-on-disk products. The latter is more popular at the moment as companies are concerned about the cost if all employees have online accessibility.

Four factors influence the future of business travel:

1. Economy
2. Regulation
3. Globalization
4. Automation

As a general rule, the rate of growth of the economy determines the level of business travel and the extent to which that level changes. Business travel activity tends to match the growth of the economy when overall economic performance is weak, but business travel moves ahead of the rate of growth of the economy during times of economic stability and expansion. The U.S. market follows this pattern more strongly than does the European market. The strong signs for business travel are strong trade, investment, and output growth, while the weak signs are high interest rates and unemployment levels.

The second factor affecting the future of business travel is regulation. Its impact is felt in two areas: (1) deregulation of travel and (2) government policy regarding the treatment of business travel expenses for tax purposes. In 1978, deregulation came to the U.S. air industry. Airlines were free to set rates based on market demand without their being subject to government approval beforehand. As a result, many new airlines came into being and many went out of business. Increased competition kept fares between many major cities low. Airline deregulation is evolving much more slowly in Europe. It remains to be seen whether air fares there will be reduced significantly.

Business travel is treated as a business expense. Limiting the tax deductibility of business meals to 50

Over half of all travelers fall into the highest occupational groupings of professional/manager. © 2009 Yuri Arcurs. Used under license from Shutterstock, Inc.

percent of the cost of the meal has not seemed to limit travel but has changed the way clients are entertained. For example, by bringing a speaker into a meeting, the entire cost of the meal can be deducted. Various attempts have been made to limit the tax deductibility of meetings abroad. Any attempt to do this would have an impact on the amount and type of travel undertaken.

The economies of countries are increasingly interdependent. With this globalization comes a greater need for international business travel.

An increasing number of people combine business and pleasure by adding a few days of pleasure to the beginning or end of a regular business trip or attendance at a business-related convention or meeting. In fact, in 1994, 8 percent of all U.S. travelers combined their vacation trip with some business or convention attendance. Over half of these vacation person trips were taken over a weekend or long weekend. Travel promoters at travel destinations should realize that business travelers provide a three-part opportunity. First, the business traveler visits to carry out his or her work-related activities. Second, the traveler and his or her spouse may be convinced to spend pleasure travel before or after the meeting, convention, or other business-related activity. Third, she or he may be attracted to return to the destination in the future on a pleasure or business trip.

CONVENTIONS AND CONGRESSES

Over 50 million people a year attend North American conventions and trade shows, generating over $80 billion annually. On average, each convention delegate spends almost $950 per event, over $260 a day. Associations represent 70 percent of that total. Meetings represent 25 percent of air travel revenue and over one-third of hotel revenue, even more at business hotels. The largest associations are represented by the American Society of Association Executives (ASAE). Their members are 204 million strong and hold 12,500 membership-wide conventions each year, involving 22 million delegates. They have another 230,000 educational seminars with almost 67 million delegates.

Associations also increasingly hold trade shows. The average members-only show is booked an average of three years ahead of time and consists of an average of 133 exhibitors, over 4,000 attendees, and requires 64,000 square feet of space.

The number one factor considered by associations when they look at potential venues is the quality of service at the hotel. The services considered important are, in order of importance:

1. No-smoking rooms
2. Concierge
3. Twenty-four-hour room service
4. Gift shop

The second most important factor is the presence of adequate meeting facilities. When considering meeting space, association executives are concerned with light and temperature controls; variety in table size and chair types; overhead projectors, projector screens, and flip charts; and the availability of a variety of microphones.

The top ten cities for conferences and conventions are:

1. Chicago
2. Las Vegas
3. Washington
4. Orlando
5. Atlanta
6. Dallas
7. San Francisco
8. Nashville
9. San Diego
10. New Orleans

The major cities for trade shows are (Miller & Associates, Inc., 2005):

City	Percentage of total trade show business
Las Vegas	18
Chicago	18
New York	10.5
Atlanta	7
Dallas	6.5
Anaheim	6
Orlando	5
New Orleans	4
San Francisco	4

The following trends are predicted by the International Association of Convention & Visitor Bureaus (IAVCB) (Miller & Associates, Inc., 2005):

- Second- and third-tier cities will increasingly compete with first-tier cities for convention business due to increased supply of facilities in recent years.
- Meeting planning cycles will continue to shorten as meeting planners believe (often mistakenly) that prices will be less if they book at the last minute. In the United States planners are booking 15 to 60 days in advance instead of the usual 90 to 150 days. Even larger meetings are being booked one to three years in advance instead of the former three to six years.
- Planners are blocking fewer hotel rooms, fearful that attendees find their own, less expensive accommodations on the Internet. They are working with hotel companies to offer incentives to attendees to stay at the conference hotel.

Over half of all conventions are held at downtown hotels, followed by resorts and conference centers. What will these planners want in the near future? They are looking for more sophisticated use of technology. They want to register online; they want to lay out their meeting room setup electronically on the hotel's blueprints; they want modem hookups and cellular phone service. In this increasingly fragmented market, there is a desire for educational programs more tightly focused on particular interests. This means more small breakout sessions devoted to specialized topics. Baby boomers want fewer weekend meetings, an opportunity to include their families, and a greater emphasis on learning. While more than half of ASAE associations offer spouse programs, only 13 percent have something directed at children. Over one-third offer pre- or post-trips in conjunction with the meeting. This is an excellent way for someone to combine business and pleasure. There is also a demand for a greater variety of price and quality alternatives when it comes to accommodations.

Convention locations usually change from year to year as attendees do not want to return to the same spot each year. Many associations have a policy of rotating the meeting destination on a geographic basis—East one year, West the next, Midwest the third.

Attendance at corporate meetings is required. As a result, the choice of destination has no effect on the number of people attending. Many corporate meetings are held at the same place year after year if the host hotel can show it can deliver quality service. The site chosen is usually close to the corporate facility. The dollar and time cost of traveling to the meeting is thereby minimized. Because the accent at a corporate meeting is on work, privacy and a lack of distractions are appreciated more than recreational facilities and sightseeing opportunities.

The Society of Incentive and Travel Executives defines incentive travel as "a global management tool that uses an exceptional travel experience to motivate and/ or recognize participants for increased levels of performance in support of organizational goals" (Jones, 1996). It is one of the fastest-growing segments of the industry. The United States is responsible for just over half of world demand, Europe is responsible for an additional 40 percent, and Japan and Australia account for the rest.

As standards of living have increased, traditional incentives such as cash and merchandise have proven less effective in motivating employees to work harder or to sell more. Travel is touted as doing a better job of satisfying people's needs for achievement, recognition, and rewards than cash or merchandise. Indeed, the four most important attributes of company incentive travel programs are a sense of achievement, a sense of pride, reward for effort, and recognition among colleagues (Sheldon, 1995). It has been shown that, for salespeople, the most effective motivational rewards are (in order):

1. Travel incentives
2. Cash
3. Merchandise

While incentives have traditionally been targeted toward salespeople, an increasing number of programs are being developed for nonsalespeople. Programs are either organized within the company sponsoring the trip or by an outside incentive travel house, of which there are over one hundred in the United States. It is argued by many that programs are more successful when organized in-house because the organizers have a better understanding of the characteristics of the workforce and can do a better job of targeting rewards to motivate them.

Over 40 percent of companies use group travel awards, with just under half finding that group travel is either extremely or very effective as an incentive. Annually, they spend just short of $10 billion on travel awards (Miller & Associates, Inc., 2005).

- Incentive users have more dealerships and fewer distributorships, although the use of incentive travel is not dependent upon the type of industry in which the company operates.
- A corporate travel department is more likely to be present in a company that uses incentive travel.

However, it is not known whether the presence of a travel department leads a company to develop incentive travel programs or whether the presence of incentive travel programs leads the company to establish a travel department.

- Cash and merchandise are more likely than travel to be used to motivate managers and nonsalespeople.
- For incentive travel programs, the most common criterion was for employees to reach a specified dollar amount of sales, while for cash or merchandise it was more common for employees to have to increase sales by a certain percentage.
- The most likely companies to use incentive travel are those that are in the service sector with a strong national or international presence, have a large in-house corporate travel program, and have a strong sense of corporate culture.

The people who "buy" destinations for incentive trips are influenced by:

1. **Budget.** However, incentive trip planners look for high quality rather than low prices.
2. **Time of year.** Employee participation on incentive trips tends to take place in that particular industry's slow season. The most popular months for incentive travel are February and April. Planners would look at destinations that are attractive during these months.
3. **Participant background.** The level of sophistication and previous travel experiences of the likely participants are considered.
4. **Incentive history of the users and the competition**. Previously used destinations are less likely to produce spirited competition than are new destinations.
5. **Accessibility.**
6. **Facilities.** These can include hotel rooms, meeting rooms, restaurants, and local transport.
7. **Activities.** Recreation and sports facilities are considered.

SUMMARY

While it is unwise to generalize, a review of the major segments of the tourism markets is key to getting the big picture of why people travel. Understanding the profiles of these segments gives an indication of how to appeal to the various markets.

 *Trends*

Top Trends in a Post 9/11 World

1. Slower growth in travel volume reflects a mature industry, numerous challenges, and a slowdown in the economy.
2. As airlines become profitable, old problems resurface.
3. U.S. lodging market remains strong.
4. Leisure travel increases while business travel is stagnant.
5. Increased interest in gambling, performance arts activities, dining, entertainment, shopping.
6. Declining interest in outdoor recreation, historic sites, and nightlife.
7. People seek more control by driving more than flying, and by staying close to home.
8. Travelers seek connections—families become more important.
9. People cut costs—reduced budgets.
10. People stay close to home.

Sources:

2008 Outlook for U.S. Travel and Tourism, 2007 Travel Outlook Forum, Charlotte, North Carolina, October 2007.
2007 Outlook for U.S. Travel and Tourism, 2007 Travel Outlook Forum, Charlotte, North Carolina, October 2006.

ACTIVITIES

1. Develop a package suitable for students seeking a spring break experience and families looking for a holiday getaway. Why are the elements of the packages suitable for the two market segments?
2. Devise a suitable way to present these packages to the two market segments. Justify your answer.
3. Online, find a travel destination advertisement. Notice the market segment this ad is targeting. How is it attracting a certain type of tourist? Why, in your opinion, is the ad effective? How might it be improved?

REFERENCES

Ahmad, I. 1993. Selling black history in Alabama. *American Demographics*, 15 (1): 49–50.

ASTA agents reveal most popular family vacations. 1999. *Travel Weekly*. 57. Based on ASTA/Fodor's Hot Spots Survey.

Cameron, B. 1992. *Creative Destinations: Marketing and Packaging: Who Wants What—and Why? An Overview of the Canadian Pleasure Market Study*. 21st Annual Conference Proceedings of the Travel and Tourism Research Association. 154–167.

Canadian Tourism Commission, American Travel to Canada—The Market to 2010, Ottawa, Canada, 1998.

Cook, S. 1995. 1996 outlook for travel and tourism: Basics for building strategies. *1996 Outlook for Travel and Tourism*. Proceedings of the 21st Annual Outlook Forum at the Travel Industry National Conference, Washington, DC: Travel Industry Association of America. 5.

Couch, J. I. 2001. The market for space tourism: Early indications. *Journal of Travel Research*, 40: 213–219.

Davidson-Peterson Associates. 1996. *1995 Economic Impact Study of Leisure Travelers & Group Tour Takers*, National Tour Association/International Association of Convention and Visitor Bureaus.

Dorsey, J. 1996. OAG creates typical traveler profile. *Travel Weekly*. 69.

Executive Summary, The Changing Nature of Female Business Travelers, New York University/Wyndam Hotels & Resorts, 1999.

Godsman, J. E. 1995. 1996 outlook for the cruise industry. *1996 Outlook for Travel and Tourism*. Proceedings of the 21st Annual Outlook Forum at the Travel Industry National Conference. Washington, DC: Travel Industry Association of America. 32, 36.

Hinch, T., and G. J. Walker. 2004. Casinos and travel: A comparative study of market profiles and motivations. 35th Annual Conference Proceedings of the Travel and Tourism Research Association. CD-ROM, unpaged.

Holly, T. A. 2003. Tracking the trends. *TravelAgent*. 86.

IATA survey finds business travelers are value-savvy. 1998. *Travel Weekly*. 5.

Jones, D. 1996. SITE redefines incentive travel. *Travel Weekly*. 49.

Jones, D. October 21, 1996. Survey: Firms tightening up on expenses. *Travel Weekly*. 55–56.

Joppe, M., A. Athanassakos, and K. Forgacs. 2003. The Senior's Market in 2026: A Projection of Their Profile and Behaviour. 34th Annual Conference Proceedings of the Travel and Tourism Research Association. CD-ROM, unpaged.

Mason, P. 1993. The changing family vacation market. *Travel Printout*, 23 (11).

Mason, P. 1995. 1996 outlook for leisure travel. *1996 Outlook for Travel and Tourism*. Proceedings of the 21st Annual Outlook Forum at the Travel Industry National Conference. Washington, DC: Travel Industry Association of America. 80–98.

August 11, 1996. Minority travelers are a diverse force on the road. *The Seattle Times*.

Marzella, D. 2000. New perspectives on family travel. *Travel Marketing Decisions*, 5 (1): 8.

Milligan, M. 2005. Study shows business travel picking up steam. *Travel Weekly*, 64 (7): 2 (1).

Moscardo, G., P. Pearce, A. Morrison, D. Green, and J. T. O'Leary. 2000. Developing a typology for understanding visiting friends and relatives. *Journal of Travel Research*, 38 (3): 251–259.

Oppermann, M. 1996. *Meeting Planners' Decision Attributes and Perceptions of Convention Cities*. 25th Annual Conference Proceedings of the Travel and Tourism Research Association. 233–237.

Patkose, M., A. M. Stokes, and S. D. Cook. Business and Convention Travelers: 2004 Edition. Washington, DC, Travel Industry Association of America.

Quest, R. Tech trims down business travel. CNN.com, Internet posting February 18, 2005.

Reese, W. S. 2004. Are senior leisure travelers different? *Journal of Travel Research*, 43: 11–18.

Richard K. Miller and Associates, Inc. 2005. *The 2005 Travel & Leisure Market Research Handbook*. Loganville, GA. 209–215.

Rohs, J. J. 1995. 1996 outlook for gaming. *1996 Outlook for Travel and Tourism*. Proceedings of the 21st Annual Outlook Forum at the Travel Industry National Conference. Washington, DC: Travel Industry Association of America. 114–119.

1996. Runzheimer survey: Meals are often-overlooked expense. *Travel Weekly*. 53.

Sheldon, P. J. 1995. The demand for incentive travel: An empirical study. *Journal of Travel Research*, 33 (4): 23.

Shoemaker, S. 1994. Segmenting the U.S. travel market according to benefits realized. *Journal of Travel Research*, 32 (3): 8–21.

Survey of Business Travelers, 1999 Edition. Washington, DC: Travel Industry Association of America.

Tasci, A. D. A., A. Aziz, and D. F. Holecek. 2003. Characteristics and potential of midwestern package travelers. 34th Annual Conference Proceedings of the Travel and Tourism Research Association. CD Rom version, unpaged.

TravelScope Special Report on Gambling. Washington, DC: Travel Industry Association of America, 1995.

Van Harssel, J., and W. Theobold. 1994. The senior travel market: Distinct, diverse, demanding. *Global Tourism: The Next Decade*. Oxford, England: Butterworth-Heinemann, Ltd. 363–377.

Whitehead, L. 1995. 1996 outlook for business travel. *1996 Outlook for Travel and Tourism*. Proceedings of the 21st Annual Outlook Forum at the Travel Industry National Conference. Washington, DC: Travel Industry Association of America. 99–109.

Xinran, L., A. M. Morrison, and J. T. O'Leary. 2001. Does the visiting friends and relatives' typology make a difference? *Journal of Travel Research*, 40: 201–212.

Young, S., L. Ott, and B. Feigin. 1978. Some practical considerations in market segmentation. *Journal of Marketing Research*, 15: 405–42.

SURFING SOLUTIONS

www.btonline.com/ (*Business Travel*)
www.rainbowadventures.com/ (Adventures for Women)
www.studyabroad.com/ (Study Abroad)
www.family.disney.comCategories/Travel/ (Family travel)
www.eldertrek.com/ (Senior travel)

ADDITIONAL READING

The 55+ Traveler, U.S. Travel Data Center, 1100 New York Avenue, N.W., Washington, DC 20005-3934, April 1995.

The Congress Bibliography, The Main Association of Convention Professionals, G. C. Fighiera, Via Natale Sandre 15, 10078 Venaria Reale, Torino, Italy, 1995.

Global Tourist Behavior, M. Uysal (ed.). International Business Press, 10 Alice Street, Binghampton, NY 13904-1580, 1994.

Group Travel Report, The National Tour Foundation, 546 Main Street, P.O. Box 3071, Lexington, KY 40596-3071.

Harrah's Survey of Casino Entertainment, Harrah's Marketing Communications, 1023 Cherry Road, Memphis, TN 38117, 1996.

International Travel-Tourism Profiles, Statistics Canada, Pacific Region, 340F-757 West Hastings Street, Vancouver, BC, Canada V6C 3C9, March 1993.

Legalized Casino Gambling in Canada: An Overview, Industry, Science and Technology Canada, Ottawa, Ontario, Canada K1A 0H5, September 1990.

The Meeting Spectrum: An Advanced Guide for Meeting Professionals, R. R. Wright, Rockwood Enterprises, P.O. Box 370126, San Diego, CA 92137, 1988.

Special Interest Tourism, B. Weiler and C. M. Hall (eds.). John Wiley & Sons, Inc., 605 Third Avenue, New York, NY 10158, 1992.

Tourism to the Year 2000: Qualitative Aspects Affecting Global Growth, World Tourism Organization, Capitan Haya, 42, E-28020 Madrid, Spain, 1991.

chapter *15*

The Geography of Travel

CHARACTERISTICS OF TRAVELER FLOWS

If you wish to travel far and fast, travel light.
Take off all your envies, jealousies, unforgiveness, selfishness and fears.

Cesare Pavese

PURPOSE

Applying specific models used to explain existing travel patterns, students will be able to predict future travel patterns and new travel market opportunities.

LEARNING OBJECTIVES

✓ Explain the impact of demand/origin and demand/resource factors on travel flows.
✓ Indicate the magnitude of worldwide travel flows and identify the major reasons for these flows.
✓ Project future major travel flows.

OVERVIEW

Tourist flows, both domestic and international, are not random. The movement of travelers when measured and explained, can be used as a basis for forecasting future tourist movements. The characteristics of traveler flows is the subject of this chapter.

International tourists are described and recent trends noted. The origins of these visitors and reasons behind these trends are explored. The size and characteristics of travel flow between the countries in North America are covered in detail.

Domestic travel within North American countries is the next topic of this chapter. The major characteristics of domestic travel are examined.

A profile is given of the major European and Asian tourism countries.

INTRODUCTION

The study of tourist movements is important for several reasons. For those at a destination it is vital to know the origins of the visitors. By knowing where the market comes from, marketing plans can be drawn up to reach potential travelers. Also, by studying the geographic characteristics of existing tourists, it may be possible to identify additional untapped market areas. For example, we may note that visitors to a particular "sun and fun" destination tend to come from cold-weather cities within a 600-mile radius of the destination. Further analysis might show several large cold-weather centers of population within 600 miles where there is no marketing effort at present. These would be potential areas for expansion of the marketing effort.

From a theoretical viewpoint the study of tourist flows is also important. By analyzing existing tourist flows, general principles can be developed to explain the movements of tourists. By applying these principles to other destinations, we can forecast potential future tourist movements. This kind of information is important not only to those who market destinations, but also vital to people who plan airline routes and develop attractions for the tourist areas of the future.

THEORETICAL MODELS OF TRAVEL FLOWS

The study of traveler flows has been called by many the geography of travel/tourism or simply *tourist geography*.

As Matley (1976) notes, there is obviously an "uneven spatial distribution of international tourist activities." He attributed this to the following factors:

- The uneven distribution of tourism resources between destinations
- The wide variety of activities in which travelers participate
- Changes in season
- Weather
- International and domestic political situations
- Economic changes in countries of origin and destination
- Fluctuations in monetary exchange rates
- Increases or decreases in the prices of tourist services
- The staging of special, short-duration attractions and events

> The fool wanders, a wise man travels.
>
> Thomas Fuller

A number of authors and researchers have attempted to explain past travel-flow patterns and the unevenness by developing and using theoretical models.

The hypothesis put forward by Williams and Zelinsky (1970) is that travel flows are not random but have distinctive patterns that can be explained by several identifiable factors. They suggest that these factors include:

1. **Spatial distance.** The travel time and costs involved when going between origin and destination points.

2. **Presence or absence of past or present international connectivity.** The existence of economic, military, cultural, and other ties or linkages between countries. The flow of travelers between Canada and the United States and between Canada and the United Kingdom are good examples of strong international connectivity.

3. **Reciprocity of travel flows.** The belief that a flow in one direction creates a counterflow in the opposite direction. Williams and Zelinsky have found that this is a poor predictor of travel flows between two countries.

4. **Attractiveness of one country for another.** The attractive features of one country can induce travel; these include such items as a favorable climate; cultural, historical, and sporting attractions; and so on. The attractiveness of Florida, Hawaii, and the Caribbean to North Americans is a good example of this, as is the climatic attractiveness of Spain

and other Mediterranean countries to northern Europeans.

The attractiveness of one country for another is very much a matter of contrast. What makes Colorado attractive to Texans in winter is that Colorado has mountains and climate suitable for skiing while Texas does not. Americans are attracted to Europe in great part because of the belief that Europe is "old" while the United States is thought of as "new." There is some evidence that the greater the cultural distance between host and visitor, "the more time will be spent in planning the trip, the more use will be made of travel packages and tour operators, and people will travel in larger numbers to fewer destinations and in shorter trips" (Crotts, 2004).

5. **Known or presumed cost of a visit within the destination country.**

6. **Influence of intervening opportunities.** The influence of attractions and facilities between the origin and destination points that cause travelers to make intermediate stops and even to forego the journey to their original destination.

7. **Impact of specific, nonrecurring events.** The influence of major international events such as the Olympic Games, the World's Fair, and the World Cup of Soccer can cause temporary increases in travel between a destination and various points of origin.

8. **The national character of the citizens of originating countries.**

9. **The mental image of the destination country in the minds of the citizens of originating countries.**

Williams and Zelinsky developed and tested their hypothesis by examining the flows of travelers between fourteen destinations, including the United States, Japan, the United Kingdom, France, the Netherlands, Benelux, West Germany, Scandinavia, Austria, Switzerland, Italy, Iberia, Greece, and South Africa. These authors illustrated the relationships of the flows between individual pairs of origins and destinations. They developed a model with which they calculated the actual and expected travel flows between individual pairs of origins and destinations. They then computed a relative acceptance index (an RA) by dividing the difference between the actual and expected flows by the expected flows. Williams and Zelinsky found strong interactions between several origin and destination pairs, including the United States and Japan, the United Kingdom and South Africa, and France and Iberia. It is probable, however, that the authors have created an artificial situation by limiting their analysis to only fourteen countries.

The simplest model of a travel flow consists of an *origin point*, a *destination*, and a *transportation link*. This basic system has been adapted by introducing the two factors of the resistance of the link (a function of distance and cost) and the propensity to participate at the origin. The basic equation (Chubb, 1969) is that the flow for a link is equal to P (propensity to participate) × resistance of the link.

This gravity model is an adaptation of Newton's Law of Universal Gravity, which states that two bodies attract each other in proportion to the product of their masses and inversely by the square of their distance apart. The propensity to travel may, for example, be a measure of the population at the origin—the more people who live in the country of origin, the greater number of potential tourists to travel from that country of origin to a particular destination. The number of travelers is tempered by the time and money it takes to travel from origin to destination. This model assumes that tourist flows decrease as distance from the origin increases. This tends to be true; however, for many people, after a certain point, distance becomes an attraction rather than a deterrent. The farther a destination is, the more status might be given by traveling there. It is speculated that this might be the case where the travel is for a generic reason. For example, take the case of people traveling from Britain to Spain for beaches and sun. The fact that "everybody goes to Spain" may induce people seeking the sun to travel farther. There is more status in traveling to Greece or the Caribbean for a suntan than to Spain. (Cost factors also come into play in understanding the reasons behind such movements.)

The model also assumes a two-way flow. We have seen, however, that tourism flows tend to be one way from generating areas to destination areas. A last proviso is that the model predicts relative flows rather than absolutes. The model might, for example, predict that the flow of tourists between countries A and B would be twice that between countries A and C. It would not predict the actual number of tourists who would travel between these countries.

> Perhaps travel cannot prevent bigotry, but by demonstrating that all peoples cry, laugh, eat, worry, and die, it can introduce the idea that if we try and understand each other, we may even become friends.
>
> Maya Angelou

Traveling Out of Your Comfort Zone

The Middle East is a region practically ignored by Western travelers. Although the area is brimming with culture, beautiful scenery, and history, few Americans venture into this foreign land. Many Westerners tend to label all of the Middle East as a scary and unknown area while millions of people are traveling to the region annually, harm-free. A group of foreign correspondents decided to illustrate the beauty of traveling to a few of these exotic locations to prove that the rewards can greatly outweigh the risks.

In Iran, American travelers are generally treated very well due to the fact that seeing a Westerner is a rare occurrence, and the Iranian people are very gracious. Local authorities are determined to improve tourism in the area so they are handing out cash bonuses to travel agents who are able to attract Americans and Europeans to the country. Currently, American tourists are required to travel with a guide and a visa ($229), which can take a few months to acquire.

Sacred religious sites have continued to attract tourists to Israel despite the risks. Security guards are present at the entrances to all public buildings, and before loading a public bus all passengers must first pass through a metal detector. Most highways have English signs but hiring a guide to navigate the area is recommended.

Yemen has experienced a few terrorist attacks recently but thousands of European tourists travel to the region unharmed annually. Unlike its surrounding neighbors, Yemen has yet to become rich through the discovery of oil so its old-world appeal attracts visitors to this historic and preserved country. Once again, hiring a guide is suggested.

The Middle East may appear to be a world away from America and not at all the ideal place for a leisure vacation, but millions of tourists are visiting the region annually. These travelers are experiencing sights, sounds and tastes that Americans are missing out on. Although venturing to the Middle East may be out of your comfort zone, the rewards may outweigh the risks and make the trip worth taking.

Annually, millions of tourists experience the sights and sounds of the Middle East. © 2009 javarman. Used under license from Shutterstock, Inc.

THINK ABOUT THIS:

1. Terrorist attacks occur around the globe, but tourism is rarely affected in these places. What makes individuals shy away from the Middle East?

Source: The Middle East: Traveling Outside the Comfort Zone. Retrieved May 2008. http://www.concierge.com/cntraveler/articles/12201?pageNumber=1.

This concept of "distance decay"—the idea that the demand for travel between two points declines as distance and cost in terms of both time and money increases—becomes more complicated when we take into account how easy it is for tourists to visit the destination. Destinations that are easy for people to visit tend to attract families, while those with weak market access attract couples and seniors who may need to travel farther to get the feeling that they have "escaped" from their home environment (McKercher and Kew, 2003). In terms of international travel a variety of factors, including the political situation, the amount of marketing done, and the number and type of attractions all complicate the situation. An interesting aspect of the distance decay effect is that, especially for pleasure trips, the farther people travel to get to a destination the more places they tend to visit at that destination.

A model of tourist flows is shown in figure 15.1. To understand tourist flows, it is necessary to examine factors at the origin, the destination, and in-transit routes that influence these flows.

DEMAND AND ORIGIN FACTORS

The demand for tourism occurs at the origin. Demand is either effective or actual—the number of people who actually travel. *Suppressed demand* comes from the number of people at the origin who, for one reason or

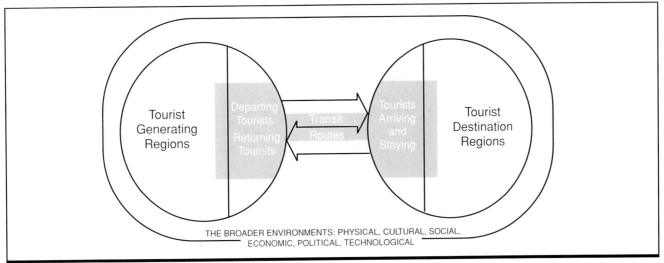

Figure 15.1 The Tourism System. Source: Leiper, N. 1979. The framework of tourism. *Annals of Tourism Research,* 6 (1): 400.

another, do not travel. If, however, the factors that prevented them from traveling (lack of income or time, for example) were removed, they would be inclined to travel. This is referred to as *potential demand. Deferred demand,* on the other hand, refers to demand that is put off because of a scarcity of supply. There may, for example, be a lack of package tours to where the tourist wants to travel. Both potential and deferred demand can be converted into *effective demand* by, for example, an increase in income or the development of package tours to specific destinations. Last, these people who have, and will continue to have, no desire to travel exhibit a category of no demand.

Travel propensity is used as a measure of actual demand. The travel propensity of a population is the percentage of the population that actually take a trip or are tourists. The net travel propensity refers to "the percentage of the population who take at least one tourism trip in a given period of time, while gross travel propensity gives the total number of trips taken as a percentage of the population" (Boniface & Cooper, 1987). As more people take second and even third vacation trips each year, the gross travel propensity becomes more important. Dividing the gross travel propensity by the net gives the *travel frequency*—the average number of trips taken by the population.

Because of suppressed demand and no demand, the maximum net travel propensity is likely to be 70 to 80 percent. In the United States, for example, about two-thirds of the population travel away from home each year, while four out of five Swedish residents take a holiday of four nights or more every year. On the other hand, one in three Italians take a holiday each year.

Gross travel propensity, however, can exceed 100 percent if many in the population take more than one trip a year.

The travel propensity for a given population is determined by a number of factors (Boniface and Cooper, 1987). The demand for tourism is, first, a function of the country of origin's level of economic development. As a country moves toward a developed economy, more people move from employment in the primary sector (fishing, agriculture, etc.) to employment in the secondary or manufacturing sector, and, eventually, in the tertiary or service sector. The percentage of the population that is economically active increases from 30 percent or less in developing countries to 50 percent or more for such things as recreation and tourism. Paid vacations, a healthier population, and greater educational opportunities all combine to produce a greater demand for travel and tourism.

Second, the demand for tourism is affected by the growth, development, distribution, and density of the population. Population growth is important in terms of the number of people and the relationship between births and deaths. As a society progresses, it tends to move from a stage characterized by high birth and death rates to continued high birth rates while death rates decline due to improved health care. The country still cannot afford to care for its growing population, and tourism is a luxury. As countries continue to develop, birth rates decline, and both birth and death rates stabilize at a low level. The population increasingly can afford to travel.

The distribution of the population between urban and rural areas has a significant impact upon the demand for travel and the travel patterns. Densely populated rural areas tend to indicate a population dependent upon agriculture with neither the time nor the money to travel. In contrast, densely populated urban areas suggest an industrialized society with the time, money, and motivation (the "escape from the urban jungle" mentality) to travel. The distribution of a population also affects travel patterns. In the United States, two-thirds of the population is concentrated in the eastern one-third of the country. A major travel flow in the United States is from the populated East to the open spaces of the West.

The politics of the country of origin also affects travel patterns. Countries can, and do, act to control such things as the amount of currency that can be taken out of the country as a deterrent to people's traveling abroad. In 1966, for example, the British government imposed a 50 pound travel allowance in an attempt to curtail travel abroad. (Interestingly enough, this policy encouraged package tour operators to put together creative packages to maximize value within the travel allowance. In 1967, 18 percent more British tourists traveled to the United States than in the previous year). The Japanese were not allowed by their government to travel abroad for pleasure until 1964 following the Tokyo Olympics.

Chinese citizens can only travel to countries given Approved Destination Status (ADS) by their government. Seven guidelines must be met. The countries should (Kim et al., 212):

1. Generate outbound tourists to China
2. Have a favorable political relationship with China
3. Have attractive resources and facilities for Chinese travelers
4. Offer guaranteed safety and freedom of discrimination for Chinese travelers
5. Be easily accessible by transportation
6. Should have a balance of tourist expenditures with China
7. Should exhibit reciprocal market share between tourists visiting China compared to Chinese tourists visiting there

In 2008, the China National Tourism Administration (CNTA) and the U.S. Department of Commerce signed a memo of understanding (MOU) that formally sanctions group travel to the United States and also permits America's destinations to market themselves in China. The Department of Commerce expects Chinese

> When you travel, remember that a foreign country is not designed to make you comfortable. It is designed to make its own people comfortable.
>
> Clifton Fadiman

visitation to the United States to reach 579,000 by 2011.

Patterns of international travel are affected by patterns of domestic tourism. On a worldwide basis, domestic tourism far exceeds international tourism, although the relative percentages of domestic to international tourism vary by country.

Tourism demand is a function of the demographics and lifestyles of the population. This was explored in great detail in chapter 10. It is, in part, a measure of the amount of *discretionary income* enjoyed by the population. Discretionary income is the amount of money left over when taxes have been paid and the basics of life have been provided for. The number of employed and the types of jobs they have are important demographic considerations, also. These factors are closely related to income. Education is also important. Education broadens the mind and leaves the individual more aware of travel opportunities, while stimulating the desire to travel. The number of paid holidays affects travel demand. Greater numbers of paid holidays or entitlements encourage travel. However, the high cost of travel may mean that more of this entitlement is spent at home. We are seeing, in industrialized nations, more demands for blocks of time that could be used for short vacations. The stage in the family life cycle will influence the type of vacation chosen. The young adult has the need for independence and a fair amount of free time tempered by a lack of money. There is great demand for budget vacations using surface transportation and self-catering accommodations. Patterns change with the arrival of marriage and, even more dramatically, with the appearance of children. Marriage may bring high income, especially with more and more dual-income families. Travel abroad may increase. As children arrive on the scene, families are constrained by more responsibility and less discretionary time and money. Vacations are role-related, with an emphasis on domestic holidays, self-catering, and visiting friends and relatives. With the advent of the empty nest and retirement, people again have the time and, importantly, the money to travel. The currency exchange rate between pairs of destinations and the countries of origin are also important.

Finally, travel demand is a function of the *values and lifestyles* of the population. How important is travel to them? What do they like to do on vacation? An examination of the culture of the country (see chapter 10) can reveal different values regarding travel, both domestically and internationally.

DESTINATION AND RESOURCE FACTORS

While factors at the origin "push" people to travel, destination characteristics "pull" them to vacation. Basically, visitors seek what they cannot get at home. A number of factors help pull visitors.

Climate is a key factor. Everything from sunbathing to skiing is dependent on climatic factors. Climate is the major determinant of the length of the season for many destinations. When the snow is gone, so is the ski season.

The climates of the world are displayed in figure 15.2. The significance for tourism for each of the ten regions is shown in table 15.1. Three major factors determine the kind of weather, water temperature and physical conditions tourists encounter at a destination: water currents, wind, and mountains.

Because land surfaces heat and cool faster than large bodies of water, the oceans act as a source of heat. Both coastal areas and islands enjoy temperate conditions compared to the extremes experienced by large land masses. The Gulf Stream, which brings warmth from the ocean, brings relatively mild winters to much of western Europe.

Generally speaking, in the Northern Hemisphere oceans revolve clockwise; in the Southern Hemisphere they generally revolve counterclockwise. There are five major ocean currents (see figure 15.2). The Gulf Stream, mentioned above, consists of warm North Atlantic current originating in the Caribbean. It helps moderate

QUICK TRIP 15.2

Global Warming and Tourism

Climate is an essential component for the success of the tourism market. Whether going to the beach or a ski resort, weather matters to tourists. Global warming has been gradually affecting the tourism industry through changing weather and climate conditions. In 2004, the U.N. World Tourism Organization held the first conference on climate change and tourism, placing more awareness on global warming and acknowledging the impact this phenomenon could have on one of the world's fastest-growing industries. The conference recognized that the tourism industry is not only affected by the changing climate but is also contributing to the emission of greenhouse gases. It was thus determined that the tourism industry must take immediate steps in discovering ways to reduce emissions and plan for future environmental changes.

Environmental campaign groups have recognized that the airline industry is responsible for a large amount of global greenhouse gas emissions; the world's 16,000 commercial jet planes generate more than 600 million tons of carbon dioxide per year. Cruise ships are also feeling the pressure to reduce emissions. Ships that carry up to 5,000 tourists create massive amounts of waste and are also the largest contributors to greenhouse gases in the industry.

Consumers are becoming more aware of these issues and voicing their concerns. Many are demanding fuel taxes and stricter regulation on the transportation industry. Environmentally friendly Westerners are flying less while some Europeans are suggesting it is immoral to fly during holiday vacations. New resorts and hotels are attempting to convince travelers they are environmentally sensitive. When built, large resorts, golf courses, and other tourist attractions' emissions are extremely high. Operating these tourist developments creates high consumption of energy and water, thus emitting even more and contributing to global warming. Regardless of the damaging effects these projects may have on the environment, with convincing PR efforts many of these large polluters can camouflage themselves as ecotourism resorts. The tourism industry is extremely sensitive to changing climate conditions and yet it is a large contributor to global warming; something must be done.

THINK ABOUT THIS:

1. Since it appears that the most popular forms of travel are large contributors to global warming, how can tourists be eco-friendly and still travel?
2. How can travelers be sure they are staying at an eco-friendly hotel or traveling in an eco-friendly manner if companies are working to deceive consumers into believing that they are environmentally aware when they really are not?

Source: *TourismReview.com.* 2008. Tourism Feels the Heat of Global Warming, by Anita Pleumarom. http://www.twnside.org.sg/.

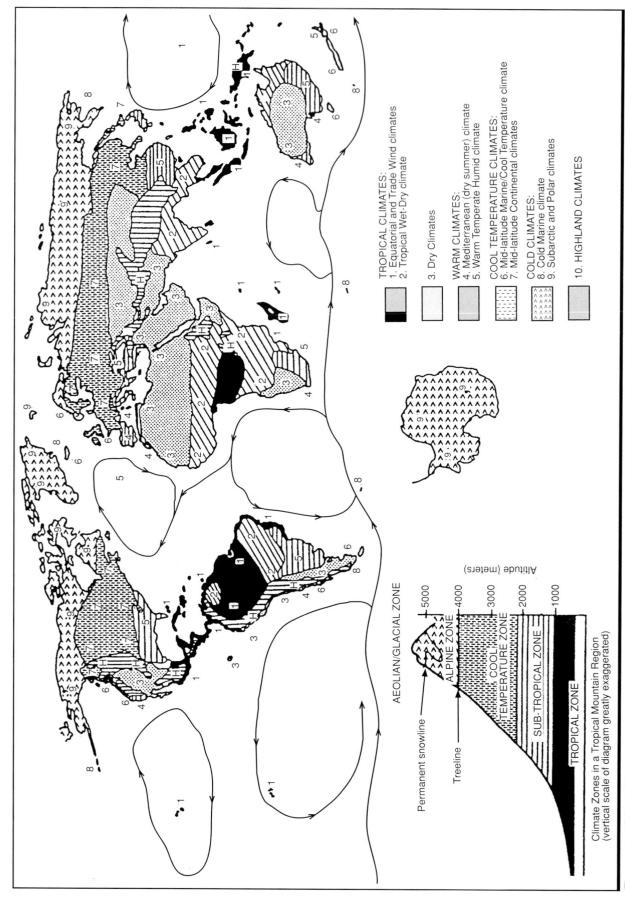

Figure 15.2 World Climates. Source: Adapted from Boniface, B. G., and C. P. Cooper. 1987. *The Geography of Travel and Tourism*. London, England: Heinemann Professional Publishing, 23.

Table 15.1
World Climatic Regions and Their Implications for Tourism

Climatic Region	Significance for Tourism
1. Tropical trade wind and equatorial climates	High temperatures discourage high activity. Warm year-round water temperatures encourage beach tourism.
2. Tropical wet-dry climates	Dry season suitable for sightseeing, safaris, and beach tourism. High rainy season temperatures and storms discourage tourists.
3. Dry climates	Plentiful sunshine encourages outdoor recreation most of the year. Problems with water supply, dust storms, and high summer heat.
4. Mediterranean climate	Beach tourism most of the year.
5. Warm temperature humid climate	High summer temperatures may deter active recreation. Water sports most of the year.
6. Cool temperature climate	Beach activities only in the summer. Favors strenuous outdoor recreation. All-weather indoor facilities desirable.
7. Mid-latitude continental climates	Outdoor recreation in the summer. Skiing and snow-based activities in the winter.
8. Cold marine climate	Unfavorable for recreation. Rich bird and marine animal life.
9. Subarctic and polar climates	Adventure holidays requiring much advance preparation. Canoeing and fishing in some areas in the summer.
10. Highland climates	Recreation including trekking, climbing, and naturalists. The thin air may restrict strenuous activities. Mountains in tropical countries offer relief from summer heat, while in middle latitude countries snow cover encourages winter sports.

Source: Adapted from Boniface, B. G., and C. P. Cooper. 1987. *The Geography of Travel and Tourism.* London, England: Heinemann Professional Publishing. 24–25.

temperatures as far north as Great Britain and Norway. The Japan current is also a warm current. It comes from the Equator past Japan and helps moderate Alaska's coastal temperatures. The Peru-Chile current consists of cold water along the Peruvian and Chilean coastline. The California current is a cold current flowing southward along the Pacific Coast of North America that causes land temperatures to be fairly constant. The Benguela is a cold Antarctic current along the southwest African Coast. Knowing this, and looking at the Pacific Ocean, we can understand why it is much colder in Los Angeles than at the southern tip of Japan even though both are at approximately the same latitude. Warm water flows from the Equator along the western shore of the Pacific up past the Philippines and Japan until it reaches the ice around the northern shores of Alaska. As a result it is cold as it continues south along the west coasts of Canada and the United States. On the other hand the eastern shores of the United States, benefiting from the Gulf Stream, are warmer than the Atlantic European coastal resorts. For similar reasons the waters along the east coasts of South America, Africa, and Australia are warmer than on the west coasts of these continents.

> To my mind, the greatest reward and luxury of travel is to be able to experience everyday things as if for the first time, to be in a position in which almost nothing is so familiar it is taken for granted.
>
> Bill Bryson

Winds generally move west to east above the Tropics in the Northern Hemisphere and below the Tropics in the Southern Hemisphere. The zone between the Tropic of Cancer (23.5 degrees north of the Equator) and the Tropic of Capricorn (23.5 degrees south of the Equator) experiences a warm climate all year long. The farther from the Equator, the shorter is the summer and the greater the difference in day length between summer and winter.

The upper-air currents (the jet stream) are particularly strong. Between the Tropics the steady humid winds (trade winds) usually move east to west. The impacts are felt on flying time and on local climate. Flying against the wind (San Francisco to Tokyo) takes longer than flying with the wind (Tokyo to San Francisco).

The local climate is affected as air in the wind current picks up and drops moisture as it goes. Looking at the West Coast of North America we can see that the air is moist from the Pacific Ocean. As it blows east it brings moisture to the western coast until it reaches the third influencing element: mountains. For every 1,000 feet (305 meters) in elevation the air temperature drops 3.5 degrees F (1.5 degrees C). As the air cools, the moisture it carries drops as rain or snow. The western or windward side of the mountains are lush and green while the sheltered or leeward side of the range is dry as little moisture makes it over the mountain. Denver faces this situation in its position relative to the Rocky Mountains. In addition to the Rockies, which include the Sierra Nevada range between California and Nevada, the major mountain ranges are the north/south-running Sierra Madres, a continuation of the Rockies chain in Mexico; the Andes, a north/south continuation of the Rockies/Sierra Madres in South America; the Alps, an east/west European chain; and the Himalayas, an east/west Asian chain.

In Europe, as a result of prevailing winds and the Alps, a moist westerly wind comes from the Atlantic Ocean across Great Britain and the west coast of Europe until it hits the mountains. Because of the height of the Alps and conflicting air currents from northern Europe, the air slows and backs up onto itself. As a result there is a great deal of fog and dampness from Ireland to the Alps. In contrast, on the southern side of the Alps little moisture makes it over the mountains. The relatively small amount of water produced by the Mediterranean has little negative impact. As a result Greece and the southern parts of Italy and the Balkans are very dry.

The combination of climate and land surface produces conditions that affect the type of tourism appropriate to the location. The land surface of the earth is either mountains, plateaus, hill lands, or plains. Approximately three-quarters of the earth is mountain or hill land. These are suitable for recreation all year long. In winter, skiing and other snow-based recreation is possible, while the clear, crisp air at other seasons allows opportunities for such things as walking, sightseeing, and photography. As noted above, mountains can provide relief from the summer heat for those in the lowlands. The lack of population adds to the attractiveness of these areas. Most of the world's population lives on the plateaus and plains. Coastal plains are ideal for tourism development providing, as they do, access to beach and sea. Inland waters are also attractive to tourists, allowing a variety of recreational pursuits in addition to their attractiveness as a scenic resource.

The impact of climate change on tourist destinations is the focus of a number of studies. Many governments and scientists see it as a significant social and environmental issue. There are some who say that, in order to manage the effects of climate change, developed countries—by 2050—will have to reduce CO_2 emissions by a factor of four. Were this to happen, would it

> To travel is to discover that everyone is wrong about other countries.
>
> Aldous Huxley

mean the end of tourism's growth? One scenario (Ceron and DuBois, 2007) suggests that the decrease could be accommodated by having more people take longer holidays than are taken now but for longer stays and less often. Traveling to exotic destinations will be seen as an exceptional, once-in-a-lifetime experience. In short, the authors suggest that people will still travel but that travel habits will have to be modified.

We can distinguish between climate-dependent and weather-sensitive tourism. In the former case, the weather itself attracts visitors to the destination. Changes in the climate will impact the number and pattern of tourist arrivals. In the case of weather-sensitive tourism, weather conditions play a role in what types of tourist activities can be undertaken at the destination. If and when global warming becomes an issue for tourism, we can expect that (Amelung et al., 2007):

- The countries of northern Europe (whose residents tend to visit countries in the Mediterranean in the summer) will have improved summer weather.
- Traditional sun and sand southern destinations may become too hot for comfort in the summer peak season. Will this result in reduced flows from North to South (or even a reversal) in summer months?
- Southern destinations, on the other hand, may experience more pleasant spring and fall seasons.

Traditionally, summer is the season for school vacations. If schools are flexible relative to the times when students are in school, travel flows may be reduced in

In addition to climate and natural resources, culture, history, ethnicity and accessibility are major factors that draw visitors to a destination.
© 2009 digitalsport-photoagency. Used under license from Shutterstock, Inc.

the summer but increase in the shoulder seasons of spring and fall. Overall, demand may even out across several months while aggregate demand remains the same. If, however, countries maintain the traditional summer school vacation time in the summer, tourist flow will redistribute spatially. Destinations that are too hot in the summer will suffer cuts in visitor numbers with little increase in the colder months. Countries experiencing better summer conditions will see an increase in tourist visits while being unable to shift demand to the (improved) seasons of spring and fall.

Small island developing states such as Barbados have expressed concern that damage to coastal tourism is very likely with changes to the beach, sea level rise, and damage to marine ecosystems.

While climate and natural resources are major factors in drawing visitors to a destination, visitors are also attracted by culture, history, ethnicity, and accessibility of a destination.

Being safe getting to, and while staying at, the destination has taken on new meaning in light of recent terrorist attacks. Air passenger flows from the United Kingdom to various destinations were negatively impacted by the 1988 Lockerbie air disaster (in which all passengers and crew and eleven people on the ground were killed as a result of a terrorist bomb) and the 1990–1991 Persian Gulf crisis. However, U.K. air passenger flows quickly returned to normal. A similar picture is seen when the numbers of Americans flying to Europe in 1986 are examined. However, the significant downturn in travel after the 9/11 bombings of 2001 in the United States took longer to come back to pre-9/11 levels. Some indications are that it took 18 months while others note that the United States has not fully recovered. Other factors may be involved including the perception that it is difficult to get a visa to visit the United States; the country is not hospitable to tourists; other countries have lowered visa requirements for international visitors; and there are new, emerging tourist destinations. As outbound international travel from the United States decreased, domestic travel to many regional destinations, including Hawaii, increased. Beginning in 2009, travelers from the twenty-seven countries participating in the VisaWaiver program (countries where visas are not required for visitors to the United States) will have to provide the United States with basic identification information at least three days prior to their arrival. This registration will be good for two years unless the traveler's passport expires sooner. It remains

> *Like all great travelers, I have seen more than I remember and remember more than I have seen.*
> Benjamin Disraeli

to be seen whether the implementation of this policy will negatively impact visitor flows to the United States.

After more recent bombings in Madrid and London, travel bounced back relatively quickly. In the case of Madrid, hotel occupancies returned to pre-attack levels within six months (Coshall, 2003). More than three-quarters of terrorist events caused a significant decline in tourist demand, the median length of the decline being one to three months. The negative impact is greater if both tourists and residents are harmed and the event results in bodily harm rather than "just" property loss. Tourist destinations can recover if such acts are not repeated.

TRANSIT ROUTES

While tourists may have the means and the motivation to travel, and while destinations may have features likely to attract visitors, tourists must be able to reach the places where they want to go. That is the function of the *transit route* that links origin to destination.

The vast majority of travel between origin and destination is by road. For tourists, the advantage of traveling by car is that they have the flexibility of stopping where they wish, when they wish, for as long as they wish. It also allows for the transport of sizable (depending upon the size of the car) amounts of luggage. Travel by coach is more restrictive; however, the number of destinations served by coach is significantly greater than are served by other means of transportation.

In the mid-nineteenth century rail travel opened up areas that were previously inaccessible. Some lines added special carriages, raised to allow viewing of the scenery. Trains offer a relaxing way to travel with the opportunity to get up and walk around.

Air travel ushered in the era of mass tourism. The speed and the range of the jet aircraft opened up large areas of the world to millions of people. The individual with two weeks' annual holiday can get to the destination within a few hours instead of the several days that it might have taken by road or rail.

Traveling by sea is now essentially limited to cruising and ferry crossings. The major selling point for the cruise is relaxation, luxury, and comfort.

The travel route and mode of transportation are decided upon by the visitor after evaluating the options in terms of availability, frequency, price, speed, and comfort. The various modes of transportation are covered more fully in chapter 16.

Traveling to the 2008 Beijing Olympics

Approximately two million visitors flowed into China for the 2008 Beijing Olympics. Questions regarding China's lacking aviation systems were answered through the building of a new terminal at Beijing airport. To handle the demands of international travelers attending the Olympic Games, Beijing opened the world's largest air passenger terminal. The country's aviation traffic has grown 17 percent annually for the last five years, so the expansion of this airport is well overdue.

When preparing for the upcoming Olympic Games, Chinese authorities were concerned about increased violent attacks against tourists. Authorities were unsure whether these attacks were due to an eroding economy, desperate citizens, or an increased confidence in Chinese attackers. Crimes against foreigners carry a heavier punishment; Chinese citizens cannot carry guns; and police watch groups are vigilant. Authorities still claim the region is safe for travelers, but U.S. officials remind tourists to be cautious.

When traveling to China, it is important to remember the cultural differences in etiquette. When attending a banquet, it is not necessary to eat everything, but it is important to try a variety of foods and put something on your plate. Bargaining in China is appropriate except in large department stores. Try to develop a friendly rapport with the store merchant and do not be afraid to ask for a better price. When eating at a Chinese restaurant, be sure not to point, stab, or lick your chopsticks and make sure not to stick them upright into your rice bowl, as this is how the Chinese honor the dead. The Chinese maintain a great deal of respect for their elders by helping them upstairs, giving up their seats, or opening doors. It is respectful to keep public displays of affection to a minimum, as many elderly people are unaccustomed to such behavior. A final etiquette tip is to tip. Although guidebooks recommend not tipping at restaurants, the Chinese are well aware that Westerners tip regularly and it is unlikely they will refuse the gesture.

THINK ABOUT THIS:

1. Do you think the recent increase in violence, travel frustrations, or China's distinctive culture deterred many foreigners from attending the Olympics?

Sources:

China, Air Travel and the 2008 Beijing Olympics, by David Armstrong. Retrieved 30 January 2008. http://www.msnbc.msn.com/id/22803912/.

10 Chinese Etiquette Tips, by May-lee Chai and Winberg Chai. Retrieved 19 March 2008. http://www.msnbc.msn.com/id/23615910/.

Crimes against Tourists on the Rise in China, Associated Press. Retrieved 18 March 2008. http://www.msnbc.msn.com/id/23678400/.

TRAVEL FLOWS

TRENDS

In examining the trends in mass-market holidays over the past several decades, three items are worthy of note:

1. People have ventured farther from home.
2. There has been a constant north-south movement.
3. Despite a recent loss of market share, Europe has maintained its prominent role as a destination and region of origination.

In 1970 the main direction of inclusive air charter flights was north-south, with traffic being centered in Spain and, to a lesser degree, Italy. Spain was linked to the eight major European markets, the most important being the United Kingdom. In fact the U.K.-Spain route was the most important in terms of volume, accounting for over one-quarter of total traffic within Europe between countries that had at least 1 percent of the market.

Movements became more complex in the 1970s as new destinations opened up. The U.K.-Spain route, while still important, saw its market share drop to 20 percent. Links between the United Kingdom and France and the United Kingdom and the Netherlands fell below 1 percent, as did those between Scandinavia and Italy. Greece not only emerged as a new destination, but as the second most important after Spain. Of its four markets—United Kingdom, France, the then West Germany, and Sweden—the United Kingdom was the most important. During this time major flows also developed between the United Kingdom and two new destinations: Malta and Portugal.

The north-south movement intensified as new southern destinations were developed and Norway emerged as a growing originating country. The reasons for these changing flows can be explained by developments in the countries of origin, in the destinations, and in the linkages themselves. Population growth in the countries of origin is one reason for the growth. More people with more discretionary income produced a larger potential market. Complementarity is another reason. The north-south traffic is strong because of the movement from colder, northern countries to warmer, southern areas around the Mediterranean coast. The distances involved and the fact that certain markets, in particular the United Kingdom, are insular explain the rise in importance of *inclusive tour charters*. The long coastline of Spain and the short distances involved between airport and hotel, together with the close proximity of other tourism features, lead to an ease of packaging. The availability of surplus military aircraft also helped spur the development of package tours. The Berlin Airlift of 1947 and 1948 showed the advantage of having a pool of operators able to move large quantities of items on short notice. The movement of large numbers of people was seen as an appropriate use of their skills in peacetime.

Yet why did the United Kingdom develop a strong inclusive tour charter package (ITC) movement when France, for example, did not? To answer this question, it is necessary to examine the characteristics of the countries more closely. First, France has an attractive coastline of its own. Second, it is relatively close to and has overland links with other Mediterranean countries. Third, the French are very individualistic. Fourth, there have been a number of industry practices that induced the potential for ITCs. These included such things as high commissions by travel agents and restrictive practices by government authorities and parent airlines. The net result was that, in 1980, the proportion of French tourists taking an organized tour was 5 percent, while 50 percent of all British holidays abroad involved inclusive tours.

This kind of analysis shows many of the factors that must be considered in explaining and understanding the reasons for tourist flows. Only with such an understanding can future flows be predicted.

GLOBAL TRAVEL FLOWS

Tourism is the world's largest industry and generator of jobs. To put that in perspective, if tourism were a coun-

> The World is a book, and those who do not travel read only a page.
>
> St. Augustine

try, it would have the third largest economy in the world, behind the United States and Japan. Since World War II, international tourism has grown tremendously, showing annual average growth rates in tourist arrivals of just

QUICK TRIP 15.4

International Tourism Expected to Surpass Pre-9/11 Levels

The terrorist attacks of September 11, 2001, left a devastating impact upon the U.S. travel market as international and local travelers developed a fear of flying. In 2002, overseas tourism fell to a level that was 19 percent below pre-9/11 numbers. This decline, coupled with a slowing economy, created a plethora of challenges for the travel market. Gas prices peaked, spending slowed, and consumers lost confidence in the market. Finally, for the first time since the 2001 attacks, the number of international tourists traveling to America should surpass pre-9/11 levels in 2008. On another positive note, $107.4 billion worth of travel receipts were collected in 2006, representing a 5 percent increase from the previous year and a new record high since the terrorist attacks.

Although this increase in international travelers is not affecting every region of the United States, the Commerce Department estimates there will be a 21 percent increase nationally in foreign visitors over the next five years. In the future, travelers from China, India, and Brazil are expected to help raise these numbers. According to the department, Mexico, South Korea, Australia, Spain, Ireland, India, China, Denmark, and the Dominican Republic sent more tourists to the United States in 2006 than they ever had before, with the majority of the tourists coming from Canada and Mexico. It has taken years and a struggling economy, but the travel industry is beginning to rise again. In 2006, roughly 51.1 billion international travelers visited the United States, just under the number of tourists visiting in 2000.

THINK ABOUT THIS:

1. Are you surprised it took this long to surpass pre-9/11 travel levels? Why or why not?

Source: International Tourism to Pass Pre-9/11 Levels, Associated Press. Retrieved 2 March 2007. http://www.msnbc.msn.com/id/17421641/.

over 7 percent from 1950 to 1990. In the 1990s, however, growth slowed to less than 6 percent a year, a reflection of a maturing market. International tourism receipts are increasing at a faster rate than arrivals. In part, this reflects the influence of Asian and Pacific countries, whose tourists spend proportionately more when on vacation than do visitors from other regions (Vellas and Becherel, 1995).

Tourism experienced a number of challenges as we entered a new century. Fears that airplanes might fall out of the sky as computers malfunctioned when the computer clocks switched to 2000 were unfounded. Terrorist attacks in the United States in September 2001 had a chilling effect on international travel, which was already suffering due to a weak economy. Shortly thereafter, an outbreak of Severe Acute Respiratory Syndrome (SARS) in East Asia caused additional concern.

According to the World Tourism Association (UNWTO) this caused a pent-up demand for travel that began to be released in 2005, resulting in 2007 international arrivals close to 900 million. Spending increased from $846 in 2006 to $898 million in 2007. This number is expected to grow to over $1.156 billion by 2020. Three-quarters of that total will be intraregional while the remaining 25 percent will be long-haul travel. Growth is linked to the world economy in general and the state of the economies in the major industrialized countries in particular, the major generating markets for international tourism. In fact, nearly 30 percent of international departures come from the world's top seven markets.

In 2006, Europe accounted for over half the world's market share of international arrivals. The relatively strong showing by Europe is due to the propensity of Europeans to travel and the fact that countries in Europe are smaller than in other regions of the world. A trip of one hundred miles in the United States, for example, might get an individual into another state. This would be recorded as a domestic arrival. In Europe, if that one hundred-mile trip meant traveling to another country, it would be classified as an international arrival. The Americas remain a distant second in both international arrivals and receipts, while also experiencing a loss of market share.

Among those regions that have been increasing their share of world arrivals since 1975, the East Asia and Pacific region has made the most significant gains. It is projected that this region will pass the Americas by 2010 to follow Europe in terms of market share. The

region has also seen significant increases in its share of tourist receipts. Africa has also increased its share while less dramatic increases were posted by South Asia and the Middle East. It is projected by the UNWTO that, by 2020, the market share of the 1.6 billion international arrivals will be:

- 45.9 percent   Europe
- 25.4 percent   East Asia and the Pacific
- 18.1 percent   Americas
- 5.0 percent   Africa
- 2.2 percent   Middle East
- 0.7 percent   South Asia

The Middle East will experience the greatest regional annual growth rate followed closely by East Asia and the Pacific. Europe will experience the slowest average annual growth rate. This is because the base is much larger for Europe and considerably smaller for the Middle East.

In Europe, the fastest-growing subregion is Eastern Mediterranean Europe. Western Europe is experiencing the poorest growth due to saturation levels and overvalued currencies in certain destinations. The latter can be corrected while the former cannot. However, Western and Southern Europe together account for about two-thirds of European arrivals and over 70 percent of international tourism European receipts. Eastern and Central Europe benefit from Western tourist flows and long-distance travel.

The United States, Canada, and Mexico together represent about two-thirds of total arrivals in the Americas. This share of the total has gone down in recent years. Growth in the region, however, is most evident in South America. Significant increases are also projected for Latin America.

In East Asia and the Pacific, the fastest-growing subregion is Australasia and other Pacific Islands. Northeastern Asia, however, is the most visited subregion, accounting for more than half of all arrivals in the region.

In the African region, South Africa is showing most growth as a result of strong demand in both leisure and business travel. The market share in Northern Africa has been declining due to negative results from both

Algeria and Morocco while East Africa is experiencing a sustained growth in arrivals from Europe.

Middle East growth has been fueled by Egypt, which accounts for almost half of the increase in arrivals and 80 percent of the increase in receipts for the region. Although the proportion of intra-regional traffic in the region has been declining (as long-haul travel has been increasing), it is still important. In fact, Egyptians and Saudi Arabians together account for more than 20 percent of all tourists in the Middle East. Egypt is both the largest generator and recipient of tourists. Tourism to Saudi Arabia is strictly for business or religious purposes.

The growth in South Asia is a product of strong increases to India, a sustained growth of long-haul leisure travel from Europe, the Middle East, and East Asia.

The top tourism destinations, money earners, and spenders in 2006 are shown in table 15.2. The top three countries are France, Spain, and the United States. France attracts the most international arrivals while the United States receives the most in receipts. This is a reflection of the fact that the United States attracts more higher-spending, long-haul traffic than does either France or Spain.

An attempt has been made to forecast outbound short- and long-haul travel in the year 2010 (Frechtling, 2000). There is a difference between short-haul and long-haul volume. For the purpose of this study, "short-haul" travel is defined as travel to countries in the same World Tourism Organization (UNWTO) subregion as the generating country while "long-haul" travel is defined as travel to countries outside the generating country's UNWTO subregion. For example, travel from France to Germany would be short-haul while travel from France to Canada would be long-haul.

The forecasted top international generating countries are outlined in table 15.3.

Most countries' outbound long-haul travel will grow faster than short-haul travel. Israel, Sweden, and Venezuela are exceptions. Most countries' long-haul traffic will grow at a slower pace in the next decade compared to the last one. Australia, Canada, Mexico, and the United Kingdom are the exceptions on this point. Similarly, except for France, Germany, Sweden, and the United Kingdom, most countries' short-haul traffic will be less in the next decade than in the previous one.

Table 15.3
Top International Generating Countries

Origin Country	Forecast 2010 (million) Long-haul	Forecast 2010 (million) Short-haul	1998–2010 Change (million) Long-haul	1998–2010 Change (million) Short-haul
United States	55.8	41	23.5	7.8
United Kingdom	29.4	95.3	18.6	55.4
Japan	20.1	16.3	7.8	5.3
Germany	16.9	140.4	9.2	65.2
France	15.5	28.4	8.7	10.7
Canada	8.3	13.2	3.5	−0.8
Australia	5.4	4.6	0.6	1.4

Source: Frechtling, D. 2000. International travel generating markets to 2010. 31st Annual Conference Proceedings of the Travel and Tourism Research Association. 327, 328.

Table 15.2
Top Tourism Destinations, Money Earners, and Spenders, 2006

Country	International Arrivals (millions)	Rank	International Receipts (U.S. billions)	Rank	International Expenditures (U.S. billions)	Rank
France	79.1	1	42.9	3	32.2	4
Spain	58.5	2	51.1	2	*	
United States	51.1	3	85.7	1	72	2
China	49.6	4	33.9	5	24.3	6
Italy	41.1	5	38.1	4	23.1	7
United Kingdom	30.7	6	33.7	6	63.1	3
Germany	23.6	7	32.8	7	74.8	1
Mexico	21.4	8	*		*	
Austria	20.3	9	16.7	10	*	
Russian Federation	20.2	10	*		18.8	9
Australia	*		17.8	8	*	
Turkey	*		16.9	9	*	
Japan	*		*		26.9	5
Canada	*		*		20.5	8

*Did not make the top ten in this category.

Source: World Tourism Organization, *Tourism Highlights, 2007 Edition*.

Thus, though growth is expected in outbound volume, both long-haul and short-haul traffic will slow for most countries. The rates of growth of long-haul traffic are related to growth in gross domestic product (GDP). GDP is also an explanatory factor in about half of the short-haul models although age cohorts are much more important in explaining short-haul growth than in explaining long-haul. The sixty-five and older age group is an especially important factor.

The author concludes that the United States will continue to be the largest source of long-haul traffic with Japan, the United Kingdom, and France in the second tier; developing countries, despite large growth *rates*, will be small generators of long-haul travel; the sixty-five and older age group is a large and growing segment regarding the generation of long-haul travel.

In terms of short-haul travel, the United Kingdom and Germany will be the major sources while Israel and Venezuela will show the largest *rates* of growth; developing countries will be small generators of traffic; the retired age cohort is a major determining factor; and short-haul demand is sensitive to factors other than income and population, such as inflation and exchange rates.

According to the World Tourism Organization (UNWTO, 1997) the world's top destinations in the year 2020 will have many of the same players but in a different order (see table 15.4). Based on destinations growing at a rate above the world average between 1994 and 2004, the UNWTO identifies the following countries (see table 15.5) as the world's top emerging markets (Source: UNWTO for TMT 2005 edition):

> A journey is like marriage. The certain way to be wrong is to think you control it.
>
> John Steinbeck

Table 15.4
Top Destinations in the Year 2020

Country	Tourist Arrivals (millions)	% Growth Rate per annum. (1995–2010)
China	137.1	8.0
United States	102.4	3.5
France	93.3	1.8
Spain	71.0	2.4
Hong Kong SAR	59.3	7.3
Italy	52.9	2.2
United Kingdom	52.8	3.0
Mexico	48.9	3.6
Russian Federation	47.1	6.7
Czech. Republic	44.0	4.0

Source: World Tourism Organization. 1997. Travel to surge in the 21st century. *WTO News*. 1.

Table 15.5
World's Emerging Tourism Destinations

Country	Absolute Increase in International Tourism Arrivals, 1994–2004 (thousands)
China	21,727
Spain	17,510
Angola	13,125
Ukraine	11,913
Turkey	9,743
Croatia	6,427
Saudi Arabia	5,255
Hong Kong (China)	4,842
Thailand	4,785
United Arab Emirates	3,556

UNITED STATES

The United States attracted two million fewer overseas visitors in 2007 compared to 2000 despite favorable exchange rates. This is attributed to increased security, visa restrictions, and the image of America as a hospitable place to visit. Overseas travelers account for almost 45 percent of arrivals and over 80 percent of spending. Canadians make up approximately 30 percent of all international arrivals and over 10 percent of all spending, while Mexico accounts for about one-quarter of international arrivals and less than 10 percent of all spending.

Europe generates approximately 20 percent of all international arrivals in and one-third of total receipts to the United States. Almost three-quarters of all European travelers to the United States come from just five countries—the United Kingdom, Germany, France, Italy and the Netherlands. Most are repeat visitors. In 2005, the top overseas generators of tourists were:

- The United Kingdom
- Japan
- Germany
- France
- Australia
- Italy

Japan is the strongest market to the United States from Asia. Travel from Latin America to the United States has grown by a third in the past decade. The United States is the most popular long-haul destination from this region (Miller & Associates, Inc., 2005). The top states for spending by international travelers are:

- Florida
- California
- New York
- Hawaii
- Texas
- Nevada
- Massachusetts
- Illinois
- Washington, DC
- Arizona

CANADA

In 2007, there were over 30 million trips by nonresidents to Canada and more than 50 million trips by residents of Canada. Almost 85 percent of trips by nonresidents are taken by U.S. residents. Three-quarters of all U.S. resident trips are by automobile, over 40 percent being same-day trips. Approximately 15 percent of U.S. resident trips involve plane travel. Of the non-Canadian, non-U.S. resident trips, two-thirds are direct into Canada while the remainder come into Canada by way of the United States.

Of the 50 plus million trips by Canadian residents, 85 percent are accounted for by trips returning from the United States. Of this total, almost 70 percent involve automobiles. Seventy percent of the automobile trips are same-day trips. Of the 15 percent of all trips that involve Canadians returning from other countries, over 85 percent involve direct flights into Canada. The remainder come in through the United States.

United States travelers are the major international market for Canada. Of the more than 4.5 million non-U.S. visitors to Canada in 2007, just over half came from Europe. Tourists from the United Kingdom make up almost 40 percent of this total with an additional 15 percent coming from France and 13 percent traveling from Germany. Over one-quarter of non-U.S. tourists in 2007 came from Asia with Japan and Korea making up 40 percent of the Asian total. Almost as many travelers—about 5 percent of the non-U.S. total—visited from Mexico as came from all of Oceania.

The challenge for Canada is to persuade American domestic vacationers to go North to experience the adventure of international travel without the risks, costs, and time commitment of going overseas. The need is to differentiate on the basis of such things as the unspoiled outdoors, safe and clean cities, coastal villages, and heritage and cultural centers.

Many people see Canada as an exciting tourist destination. Significant increases from Asian countries such as South Korea, Taiwan, China, and Thailand are expected by the Conference Board of Canada. South Korea is already a larger market for Canada than either Italy or the Netherlands. As the economies continue to expand in these countries and a growing middle class emerges, Canada should continue to receive healthy increases from these markets in the first decade of this century.

Of the main inbound markets, Japan is expected to provide the largest increase in pleasure travelers to Canada. Smaller markets in Asia and South America are also showing strong growth. While Europe will continue to be the number one overseas destination for Canadians into the new century, its overall market share will also decline.

The challenge for Canada is to persuade American domestic vacationers to go North to experience the adventure of international travel without the risks, costs and time commitment of going overseas. © 2009 Kenneth V. Pilon. Used under license from Shutterstock, Inc.

While operators believe that summer travel will continue to be the most important season in the next century, winter and off-season travel are expected to show some growth if the right products are in place. With a renewed emphasis by city tourism organizations on the colder season market (festivals, sports), this situation is likely to change.

In January 2005, the Chinese government granted Canada "approved destination status." This, in effect, eases restrictions on Chinese residents traveling to Canada. In 2004, Canada had 77,000 visitors from China. The World Tourism Organization estimates 100 million Chinese tourists a year by 2020 (*Aviation Daily*, 2005).

Canada outbound travel is about 20 percent of total national person trips, while it is only 5 percent in the United States (Smith and

Xie, 2003). Florida continues to be the prime outbound sun destination in the new century. Many Canadians have assets in this state, and this will keep them going back. Florida and other southern states are the only sun destinations that can be reached by car. While uncertainty exists with respect to Cuba as a destination, U.S. tour operators believe it is only a matter of time before Americans will be able to travel to that country. If this does occur, the impact on the Canadian market could be significant. With Europeans and South Americans making Cuba an increasingly popular destination for their vacations, the demand for hotel space has already exceeded the supply during peak season. If sufficient political stability is achieved in some of the Central American countries such as El Salvador, Guatemala, and Nicaragua, most tour operators believe that tourism can make a rebound in these countries. When this does occur, there will also be an impact on tourism demand from Canada and the United States on destinations such as Cuba, Mexico, and the Dominican Republic.

Europe remains a major destination for Canadians in the summer. Canada's main European travel markets are Germany, the United Kingdom, and France. Secondary markets such as Italy, Spain, and the Netherlands will not be growing their populations in sufficient numbers to become main target markets for Canada.

TOURIST FLOWS TO AND FROM MAJOR TOURISM COUNTRIES

Five *European countries* are highlighted because of their importance as originators of and/or destinations for in-

> *The traveler sees what he sees. The tourist sees what he has come to see.*
>
> G.K. Chesterton

ternational tourists: France, Germany, Italy, Spain, and the United Kingdom.

FRANCE. France has been losing tourists due to competition from other Mediterranean countries as a result of lower exchange rates. Taking one measure aimed at improving the situation, the French Minister of Tourism in 1996 decided to create a five-star category for the country's luxury properties. Other countries, most notably Spain and Italy, have been accused of drawing potential tourists away, in part because they have a five-star designation. In the minds of many tourists, a four-star property in France is thought of as having less quality than a five-star hotel in Spain.

While an increasing number of French people are taking vacations abroad, nine out of ten French people vacation in France for their summer holidays. Internationally, they travel to Spain, Italy, Germany, and the United Kingdom. The major international tourists visiting France come from other European countries, specifically Germany, the United Kingdom, Belgium, and the Netherlands. This has resulted in a balance of payment surplus double that of the automobile industry, the next most important export industry. The most popular destinations in France remain the seaside resorts.

About 60 percent of the French population take an annual holiday of four or more nights. More of them are taking second holidays with half staying with friends or relatives or using a second home, whether taking the vacation in France or abroad. There is a movement toward French travelers organizing their own vacations, preferring to book a flight only rather than a complete package. These travelers also will deal directly with tour operators. The market responds to discount holidays through last-minute bookings as operators offer special "last-minute" prices on tour packages.

GERMANY. Germans are the world's most prolific international travelers. Approximately three-quarters of the population each year make at least one vacation trip lasting five days or more. The reasons are twofold: Germans have both the time and the money. In addition to having approximately six weeks paid vacation a year, the German economy has been very strong for the past decade. In addition to a primary vacation, there has

Many U.S. tour operators believe it is only a matter of time before Americans will be able to travel to Cuba. © 2009 Jose Miguel Hernandez Leon. Used under license from Shutterstock, Inc.

> *The worst thing about being a tourist is having other tourists recognize you as a tourist.*
>
> Russell Baker

been a trend toward second and third trips of eight to ten days duration as well as city breaks of four to five days in length. Since the early 1970s, the proportion of trips abroad compared to domestic vacations has increased from 50 percent to approximately two-thirds. Almost 10 percent of the German population have vacationed in the United States or Canada at least once.

The largest group of travelers are those between twenty and twenty-nine years of age. Age groups with the highest propensity to travel will continue to do so as they age. In addition, there will be a further increase of travel propensity from those currently in the sixty-and-older age category (Travel Industry Association of America, undated). As in most other cases, the more education a person has, the more likely he or she will travel. As might be expected, travel propensity is also positively linked to income. Travel propensity is highest in Berlin and Hamburg although, in absolute numbers, the most travelers are from North Rhine-Westphalia.

Over 60 percent of all holidays are taken in July/August/September while an additional 20-plus percent occur in April/May/June. Twice as many holiday makers from the former West Germany prefer staying in hotels as in bed and breakfasts or inns. Almost equally popular as staying at an inn is renting an apartment or house.

While the automobile's travel market share has remained unchanged since the 1970s at about 60 percent, air transportation's market share has almost doubled. The amount of air travel has tripled in relation to travel by train. There is a trend to travel by rail for second and third holidays. There also has been an increased interest in package tourism, which now accounts for almost half of all main holiday trips. For domestic trips, over three-quarters of all Germans travel independently. However, travel agencies book more than 85 percent of all business trips as well as those to visit friends and relatives.

According to the U.S. Commerce Department's Office of Tourism Industries, German travelers will probably stay in midpriced or budget properties, rather than with friends and family, and travel for more than three weeks. The survey of German travelers who took long-haul trips in the past three years and who are planning to take a long-haul trip in the next two years found that Germans are extremely active on vacation. The most popular activities include shopping, dining, beach activities, and visiting national parks. They spend less time

visiting cities and travel to more scenic areas of the United States. The German traveler of the future is more likely to have children living at home and less disposable income. The biggest potential markets for the United States are small towns, ethnic cultures, religious tours, and nature-oriented activities. Crime continues to be the major single barrier to German travel to the United States.

ITALY. The major markets for Italy are Switzerland, Germany, France, and Austria. The vast majority of international visitors to Italy select it because of its art cities. The most negative features, according to tourists, are the means of transport and infrastructure (almost half noted this), strikes, petty crime and various inefficiencies, and the lack of information on artistic and cultural opportunities. Geographically, there is a north-south split in visited destinations. Southern regions receive only 10 percent of all visits while the north and central regions serve as the main areas for tourists.

One-third of all Italians take an annual holiday of four days or more. Increasing numbers are taking more than one trip a year. They are expressing an interest in ecotourism or green tourism, a growth that is linked to the expansion of protected areas in Italy. There is a trend toward shorter average stays but in better hotels.

SPAIN. Over 80 percent of the visitors to Spain come from other European countries, mainly France, Portugal, Germany, and the United Kingdom. The automobile remains the favorite way to enter the country, accounting for half of all annual visitors, 60 percent in the peak summer months. Just over one-third of all international travelers come by plane. Recent promotional campaigns by the government have focused on cultural tourism, ecotourism, and leisure.

In the Balearics, the focus is on the traditional "sun, sea, and sand." The growth experienced in the islands has led to deterioration of the environment. Tour operators, who control almost 90 percent of tourism flows, greatly influence the development of new destinations. There does seem to be an understanding that, in order to compete, the islands must place a renewed emphasis on quality that seeks to attract market segments with higher buying power, that spreads the seasonal effect, and that opens up new channels of distribution.

UNITED KINGDOM. Tourism is one of the key drivers of the British economy. It is also one of the fastest-

> Travel is more than the seeing of sights; it is a change that goes on, deep and permanent, in the ideas of living.
>
> Miriam Beard

growing industries with one in five of all new jobs created in the tourist industries.

Travel by U.K. residents far outstrips that by overseas visitors. Eighty percent of all outbound travel is for leisure. Over three-quarters of outbound travel is to short-haul destinations in Europe. The United States is the most popular long-haul destination for British tourists, capturing over one-quarter of all long-haul British travelers. Britain remains the top overseas market for the United States. They enjoy shopping, city sightseeing, visiting historic sites and amusement parks, and going to the beach. It should be noted that North American visitors spend proportionately more than other tourists. The top countries of origin are:

1. The United States
2. France
3. Germany
4. Irish Republic
5. The Netherlands

Canada ranks number ten in terms of country of origin.

Tourism faces a number of challenges in the future:

- Greater propensity to travel overseas
- Limited growth from traditional European markets
- More available international destinations, creating more competition for the North American, Far Eastern, and Australian markets
- Price competitiveness problems compared to other European countries, particularly in the hotel sector
- Congested air and land transportation
- Excessive peak-season demand
- Coastal area and river water pollution
- Reduced state financial support for development and marketing

EMERGING MARKETS

The significance of two emerging economies—China and India—justifies the inclusion of these two potential tourism powerhouses.

CHINA. In 2007, 132 million visitors traveled to China and spent $42 billion. The World Tourism Organization (UNWTO) estimates that, by 2015, China will be the world's number one tourist destination country.

The leisure travel market in China opened up in the early 1990s when Chinese residents were allowed to take leisure tours to Malaysia, Singapore, and Thailand for the first time. Prior to this, outbound travel was permitted only for government business and visiting relatives overseas. Between 1994 and 2004, outbound travel grew at a rate of 24 percent annually. In recent years, the Chinese outbound travel market has expanded at an average rate of 34 percent. In 2005, 40 million Chinese traveled overseas. It is expected that by 2020 there will be 115 million departures from China each year. The long-haul pleasure market is dominated by large groups traveling on package tours. However, special-interest travel, luxury travel, and travel to explore the culture

The World Tourism Organization estimates that by 2015, China will be the world's number one tourist destination country. © 2009 Jarno Gonzalez Zarraonandia. Used under license from Shutterstock, Inc.

and lifestyles of a destination are beginning to appear. The market is at the same time very demanding and extremely price-sensitive.

The major factor in growing the outbound Chinese market has been the liberalization of regulations by the Chinese government. As noted earlier, once a destination country is given approved destination status (ADS), Chinese travel agents are allowed to market group leisure trips to these countries and exit procedures for travelers wishing to visit are simplified. Over eighty countries, including Canada, have ADS agreements with China. The granting of ADS can have a major impact on travel flows. For example, within three years of being granted ADS, travel from China to Australia and New Zealand doubled and tripled, respectively, while Japan saw a 75 percent increase four years after being granted ADS.

Only 4 percent of China's urban population have traveled overseas, suggesting that the growth potential is very large. This potential is being aided by an increase in international air access with new routes being proposed to the United Kingdom, the United States, and Europe.

Travel to Hong Kong and Macau accounts for 70 percent of all departures with an additional 19 percent going to other Asian countries. Europe has a 7 percent market share; the Americas receives 3 percent with Oceania getting about 1 percent of the market. As a measure of the growth of international travel, we can consider the growth of China in international spending. In 1995 China was ranked fortieth in terms of international spending; by 2004 it was ranked number seven. The World Travel and Tourism Council (WTTC) estimates that China will be in second spot by 2015, behind the United States, but ahead of Japan.

The Chinese travel to Hong Kong primarily for shopping and to Macau for gambling and entertainment. Travelers to Southeast Asia go for the scenery, history, shopping, beach resorts, and as a warm winter getaway destination. Russia appeals to older Chinese seeking culture and history.

Trip duration, while trending up, tends to be shorter compared with other international markets. There is a growing demand for off-season travel because of the cheaper prices compared to peak season. The Chinese—being very industrious—tend to book both domestic and overseas trips at the last minute as they will not schedule trips long in advance when something may come up at work. As previously noted, they are very cost-conscious. In addition, they are very safety-conscious and will only consider destinations they see as safe and clean. Because Chinese cities are crowded and polluted and many people live in small apartments, they are attracted to places that have lovely scenery, fresh air, and wide open spaces. They are also fascinated by history, literature, and celebrities in the worlds of entertainment and sports. The United Kingdom has taken advantage of this by developing theme tours targeting this market based on such diverse figures as William Shakespeare and Harry Potter.

Growing markets are evident in the following areas:

- Golf—Scotland is targeting the Chinese golf market, with complete golf packages, including Mandarin-speaking tour guides.
- Backpacking and trekking among young urbans.
- Skiing—With two million downhill skiers, the number is expected to expand by 20 to 30 percent annually such that, by 2011, it is expected that China will have the world's largest ski industry.
- Health and wellness—Spas are becoming big business in China.

QUICK TRIP 15.5

Shark Attacks Deterring Tourists

A popular strip of Mexico's coastline serves as a relaxing refuge for surfing enthusiasts and Hollywood stars. No one could recall ever hearing about a shark attack in Zihuatanejo, Mexico, until three attacks took place in less than one month, two of which were fatal. On average, only four fatal shark attacks occur each year across the globe. This year the only other reported attack took place in Solana Beach, California, only a few months earlier. Researchers are trying to discover why the sharks suddenly became so aggressive, and in the process tourists have been frightened away from the area. In an attempt to ease concerns, Mexican officials strung lines of baited hooks far off the shoreline and slaughtered dozens of sharks, which attracted a great deal of international criticism.

Although officials are concerned about attracting more tourists to the area, biologists are reminding the public to keep the events in perspective. Regardless of the recent attacks, a traveler is more likely to be affected by food poisoning when visiting Mexico than by being attacked by a shark. One has a better chance of getting hurt by driving to the beach than by getting in the water. Biologists also say killing the sharks will not help much and officials should focus on keeping people out of the water until more information is discovered.

The International Shark File says attacks have been increasing over the last century due to more water sport activities such as surfing. Logically, when there are more people in the water the chances of an attack increase. Mexican experts are planning a catch-and-release study to determine which species of sharks are attack prone in order to learn more about these recent disasters. For now, the tourism industry in this region of Mexico will continue to suffer until travelers' worries are alleviated.

THINK ABOUT THIS:

1. How can a popular tourist destination recover from a dramatic situation such as this one?
2. What can the area do to encourage travelers back to the region?

Source: Fatal Shark Attacks Spook Mexican Resort Area, by Alexandra Olson. http://www.usatoday.com/travel/news/2008-05-28-mexico-shark-attacks_N.htm?csp=34.

Although the United States does not have approved destination status (ADS), the China National Tourism Administration (CNTA) and the U.S. Department of Commerce recently signed a memorandum of understanding (MOU) under which Chinese leisure travelers may travel to the United States in group tours.

The Chinese are attracted to modern cities, advanced technology, a well-developed economy, and Western lifestyle. Travelers want to see famous cities like New York, Washington, DC, Los Angeles, and San Francisco. Las Vegas is popular as it gives Chinese tourists a chance to experience American "decadence" firsthand. Despite the desire to visit the United States, the lack of ADS and the difficulty in obtaining visas for travel currently dissuade most potential visitors.

INDIA. The outbound travel market in India has been growing at just under 20 percent annually in recent years. Three million travelers ventured outside India in 2006. This growth is fueled by growing personal incomes among a privileged social class for whom international travel has become a natural part of their lifestyle. The outbound market tends to be young people who are looking for experiences, adventure, and status. Many want to experience life outside of India. Indians love to shop and want the access to better products as well as better prices. As in China, many live in crowded cities. This sparks the desire for a more relaxing and peaceful vacation. Because so many Indians have emigrated to other countries, the VFR motivation is strong.

Asia draws 50 percent of the Indian market followed by Europe, the Middle East, and Australia. Canada and the United States attract 4 to 6 percent of the market each.

Five market segments have been identified of approximately equal size:

- Family Vacation Seekers
- Business Opportunity Seekers
- Status Seekers
- Adventure Seekers
- Social/Fun Seekers

SUMMARY

Travel movements occur because of the interaction between the characteristics of the origin, the destination, and the transit routes that join them. By examining existing flows of tourists both within and between countries it is possible to develop principles and models to explain traveler movements. These principles can then be used to explore the potential for movements between tourists and new destinations.

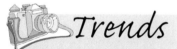

Trends

Top Ten Emerging Destinations

According to the Cool Hunters, the little-known travel executives who help discover new tourist destinations, here are the top ten places that will become emerging destinations in coming years:

1. Honduras: A cutting-edge Costa Rica.
2. Providence, Rhode Island, United States: A cultural center with $500 million in revitalization projects.
3. Newfoundland, Canada: A Canadian island attracting second-home owners.
4. Montenegro: A newly independent nation where Sophia Loren used to vacation.
5. Rwanda: A picture of Africa few have discovered.
6. Seychelles: An Indian Ocean alternative to the Maldives.
7. Saadiyat Island, Abu Dhabi: The flash of Dubai with more culture.
8. Almaty, Kazakhstan: Luxury destination swimming in new oil money.
9. Sanya, Hainan Island, China: The Hawaii of China.
10. Boracay, Philippines: A regional vacation spot reengineered for luxury seekers.

Source: The Contenders. 2007. *Wall Street Journal.* P6–P7.

ACTIVITIES

1. Discuss with a partner places you have traveled and what encouraged you to visit particular regions.

2. What drew you to the area or pushed you away from your home?

INTERNET ACTIVITIES

3. Research group trips or tours to exotic countries. Is an emphasis placed on safety in these advertisements?

4. How often do these Web sites discuss the risks of traveling abroad?

REFERENCES

1995. Canada outbound. *Travel & Tourism Analyst*, (5): 24–36.

Amelung, B., S. Nicholls, and D. Viner. 2007. Implications of global climate change for tourism flows and seasonability. *Journal of Travel Research*, 45: 285–296.

Aviation Daily. 2005. China approves Canada as tourism destination. *Aviation Daily*, 358 (14): 3.

Belle, N., and B. Bramwell. 2005. Climate change and small island tourism: Policy maker and industry perspectives in Barbados. *Journal of Travel Research*, 44: 32–41.

Bonham, C., C. Edwards, and J. Mak. 2006. The impact of 9/11 and other terrible global events on tourism in the United States and Hawaii. *Journal of Travel Research*, 45: 99–110.

Boniface, B. G., and C. P. Cooper. 1987. *The Geography of Travel and Tourism*. London, England: Heinemann Professional Publishing. 9.

Ceron, J. P., and G. DuBois. 2007. Limits to tourism? A back-casting scenario for sustainable tourism mobility in 2050. *Tourism and Hospitality Planning & Development*, 4 (3): 191–209.

Chubb, M. 1969. RECYS-SYMAP–Michigan's computerized approach to demand distribution prediction. *Predicting Recreation Demand*, Technical Report No. 7, Michigan State University. 23–33.

Coshall, J. T. 2003. The threat of terrorism as an intervention on international travel flows. *Journal of Travel Research*, 42: 4–12.

Coulomb, F. 1995. Recent trends in French tourism. *An Encyclopedia of International Tourism–I–Tourism Trends in Western Europe*. Paris, SERDI, 72.

Crotts, J. C. 2004. The effect of cultural distance on overseas travel behaviors. *Journal of Travel Research*, 43: 84.

Erdmann, R. 1996. *Measuring Tourism Impacts: Impact of Japanese Long-Haul Tourism*. 25th Annual Conference Proceedings of the Travel and Tourism Research Association. 50.

Europe in the 21st Century. Ottawa, Canada, The Conference Board of Canada, 1998.

Frechtling, D. 2000. International travel generating markets to 2010. 31st Annual Conference Proceedings of the Travel and Tourism Research Association. 322–331.

Gut, P., and S. Jarrell. 2007. Silver lining on a dark cloud: The impact of 9/11 on a regional tourist destination. *Journal of Travel Research*, 46: 147–153.

India Consumer & Travel Trade Research. Ottawa, Canada, Canadian Tourism Commission, 2007.

Kim, S. S., Y. Guo, and J. Agrusa. 2005. Preference and positioning analyses of overseas destinations by mainland Chinese outbound pleasure tourists. *Journal of Travel Research*, 44: 212–220.

Klemm, K. 1995. Trends in tourism: Germany. *An Encyclopedia of International Tourism–I–Tourism Trends in Western Europe*, Paris, SERDI, 102.

Lim, C., and M. McAleer. 2005. Analyzing the behavioral trends in tourist arrivals from Japan to Australia. *Journal of Travel Research*, 43: 414–421.

Matley, I. M. 1976. *The Geography of International Tourism*. Washington, DC: Association of American Geographers, Resource Paper no. 76–1, 11.

McKercher, B., and A. A. Kew. 2003. Distance decay and the impact of effective tourism exclusion zones on international travel flows. *Journal of Travel Research*, 42: 159–165.

OTTI–Office of Travel & Tourism Industries, www.tinet.ita. doc.gov/, accessed August 18, 2005.

Pyszka, R. H. 1990. *Americans as International Travelers: The Search for Understanding*. 21st Annual Conference Proceedings of the Travel and Tourism Research Association. 255–256.

Richard K. Miller & Associates, Inc. 2005. *The 2005 Travel & Leisure Market Research Handbook*, Loganville, GA.

Sakia, M., J. Brown, and J. Mak. 2000. Population aging and Japanese international travel in the 21st century. *Journal of Travel Research*, 38 (3): 212–220.

Statistics Canada. 2007. *International Travel: Advance Information*. Ottawa, Canada: Statistics Canada.

The American Market Evolution to 2010. Ottawa, Canada, Canadian Tourism Commission, 1998.

Travel Industry Association of America. Emerging international tourism markets: trends and insights, 2004.

Travel Industry Association. 2006. *The Economic Review of Travel in America*. Washington, DC: Travel Industry Association.

Travel Trade Research in China. Ottawa, Canada, Decima Research for the Canadian Tourism Commission, 2006.

Travel Weekly, TIA Study: U.S. is losing its share on inbound tourists. January 31, 2005, 64 (5): 12(1).

Undated. *Selling to Germany: Marketing the U.S. Travel Product*. Washington, DC: Travel Industry Association of America. 9, 12.

Undated. *Selling to Japan: Marketing the U.S. Travel Product.* Washington, DC: Travel Industry Association of America. 2, 12.

Uysal, M., D. R. Fesenmaier, and J. T. O'Leary. 1994. Geographic and seasonal variation in the concentration of travel in the United States. *Journal of Travel Research*, 32 (3): 61–64.

Williams, A. V., and W. Zelinsky. 1970. On some patterns in international tourist flows. *Economic Geography*, 46 (4): 549–67.

World Tourism Organization. 2005. *Tourism Market Trends 2005 Edition*. Madrid, Spain: UNWTO.

World Tourism Organization. 2007. *Tourism Highlights 2007 Edition*. Madrid, Spain: UNWTO.

World Tourism Organization. 2008. Tourism 20/20 vision, http://www.unwto.org/facts/eng/vision.htm. Accessed March 4, 2008.

Yelton, L., A. M. Stokes, and S. D. Cook. Japan Travel Demand: Trends and Insights, 2004 Edition, Washington, DC: Travel Industry Association of America.

Yelton, L., A. M. Stokes, and S. D. Cook. U.K. Travel Demand: Trends and Insights, 2004 Edition, Washington, DC: Travel Industry Association of America.

Zang, J., and C. Jensen. 2007. Comparative advantage explaining tourism flows. *Annals of Tourism Research*, 34 (1): 223–243.

SURFING SOLUTIONS

http://www.the-times.co.uk/ (*Sunday Times*)
http://tinct.ita.doc.gov/ (U.S. Department of Commerce/Tourism)
http://www.conferenceboard.ca/ (Conference Board of Canada)
http://www.mexico-travel.com/ (Mexico Ministry of Tourism)
http://www.oecd.org/ (OECD)

ADDITIONAL READING

An Encyclopedia of International Tourism—I—Tourism Trends in Western Europe, F. Vellas (ed.) (Paris, SERDI, 1995). Future editions are planned on other areas of the world.

Annual European Travel Commission Report, European Travel Commission, 2 Rue Linois, 75015 Paris, France.

Explorations: Travel Geography and Destination Study, J. L. Landry, and A. H. Fesmire, Prentice Hall Career and Technology, Englewood Cliffs, NJ 07632, 1994.

International Tourism Reports, The Economist Intelligence Unit Ltd., 40 Duke Street, London W1A 1DW, U.K.

Tourism in China: Geographic, Political and Economic Perspectives, A. A. Lew and L. Yu (eds.). Westview Press Inc., 500 Central Avenue, Boulder, CO 80301.

Tourism in Europe: Structure and Developments. W. Pompi and P. Lavery (eds.). University of Arizona Press, 1230 North Park Avenue, Tucson, AZ 95719, 1993.

Tourism Today: A Geographical Analysis, 2nd edition, D. Pearce, Longman Scientific and Technical, Fourth Avenue, Harlow, Essex CM19 5AA, U.K., 1995.

Travel Industry World Yearbook, The Big Picture, S. R. Waters, Child & Waters, Inc., P.O. Box 610, Rye, NY 10580, annual.

Travel-log Statistics Canada, Ottawa, Canada K1A 0T6.

US Travel Data Center, 2 Layfayette Centre, 1133 21st Street, N.W., Washington, DC 20036 has the following reports:

- Summary and Analysis of International Travel to the United States.
- Outlook for International Travel to and from the United States.
- Historical Arrivals Data Base.
- Reviews of the Market (for 25 countries).
- USTTA Office of Research Mailing List.
- In-flight Survey of International Air Travelers.

World Travel and Tourism Review: Indicators, Trends and Issues, Volume 3, 1993. J. R. B. Ritchie and D. E. Hawkins, editors in chief, University of Arizona, 1230 North Park Avenue, Tucson, AZ 95719, June 1993.

ANNUAL TOURISM STATISTICS ARE AVAILABLE FROM:

The World Tourism Organization (WTO) publishes a *Yearbook of Tourism Statistics*, a comprehensive analysis of data for 150 countries. Its *Compendium of Tourism Statistics* is a pocketbook statistical guide to 180 countries.

The Organization for Economic Co-operation and Development (OECD) publishes *Tourism Policy and International Tourism in OECD Countries*. It covers the main generators and receivers of international tourism and includes statistics in addition to detailed sections on government policy and planning.

WTO's *Travel and Tourism Barometer* monitors arrivals, overnight stays and receipts for major destinations.

The Web site for WTO is http://www.world-tourism.org/.

chapter *16*

Modes of Travel
TRAVEL ALTERNATIVES

Airplane travel is nature's way of making you look like your passport photo.

Al Gore

PURPOSE

Through an understanding of a model of travel mode selection, students will be able to explain how tourists travel.

LEARNING OBJECTIVES

✓ Show how a knowledge of the criteria people use to select their preferred modes of transportation can be used to influence that choice.
✓ Identify the reasons for the changes in passenger use of the various transportation modes.
✓ Show how the characteristics of demand and supply affect the marketing of passenger transportation.

OVERVIEW

The means travelers use to reach their destinations is the subject of this chapter. A model is presented to explain the reasons people select one transportation mode over another. Marketing implications for the various modes are suggested. An in-depth treatment of each travel mode is provided. The rise and fall of travel by rail is chronicled and its competitive edge today defined. The major change through which ocean liners have gone is the shift from scheduled ocean liner service to cruise ships. The reasons and ramifications are explained. Automobile travel is the single most predominant mode in North America. The extent and advantages of automobile travel to the visitor are covered in a section that includes material on recreational vehicles and rental cars. The airplane has had a revolutionary impact on tourism. The history, scope, and significance of travel by air is an important part of this chapter. The importance of bus travel is indicated by the fact that the industry annually carries more passengers and provides service to more destinations than any other common carrier mode.

The interaction between demand and supply and its impact for transportation marketing completes this topic.

MAJOR TRANSPORTATION MODES

There can be no doubt that the development of new transportation modes, routes, and alternatives has opened up the world to tourism. People travel either in their own private mode of transportation or alternatively use a group travel mode offered by a common carrier. Figure 16.1 defines today's major travel alternatives.

TRANSPORTATION MODE SELECTION DECISIONS

MODEL

There are a variety of ways people can travel between two destinations.

Why do people select one transportation mode over another for business and pleasure/personal trips? Many theories have been put forward on mode selection decision processes. It is suggested that mode selection is influ-

enced by four variables—characteristics of the mode, destination features, characteristics of those taking the trip, and characteristics of the trip itself (Kelly et al., 2007). In terms of the mode, people are influenced by such things as travel time, cost, frequency, convenience, flexibility, comfort, and safety of the various options available.

Factors at the destination also influence choice. These include whether development at the destination is dispersed or compact. The latter would lead to people taking a car while the latter would incline people toward taking public transportation. The presence or lack of transportation infrastructure is also a factor. The presence of no-vehicle cones, constraints on parking, and the availability of walking and biking trails all have an impact. Parking fees and the availability of public transportation also are part of the decision.

Socioeconomic variables—how much money people can afford to spend, how able they are to walk—as well as situational factors, motivation for travel, and personal values and attitudes factor into the equation. Some people are strongly committed to the idea of public transportation while others are not. A business traveler is unlikely to have the same value perceptions as a pleasure traveler. Speed/time and departure/arrival times may be all important to the business traveler, while cost/price may be the pleasure traveler's first criterion.

Finally, the characteristics of the trip come into play. These include the size and composition of the travel

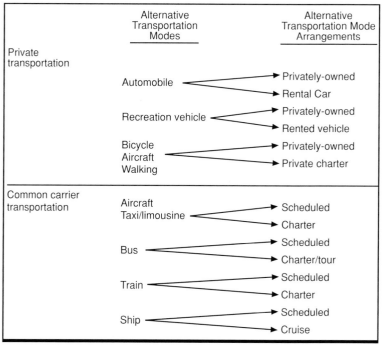

Figure 16.1 Travel Alternatives.

Ecotourism

In February of 2008, journalists and investors gathered at a London airport to witness a 747 plane lift off in the world's first biofuel demonstration flight. Regardless of the fact that only one of the plane's engines was running on the new fuel and it was mixed with standard jet fuel, the event was still extremely significant. Air travel is the fastest-growing source of greenhouse gases, and companies are scurrying to find the best alternatives to lessen their carbon footprint. The biofuel used in this particular takeoff was a mixture of coconut and babassu oil and although developers do not believe this particular mixture could satisfy the airlines' demand, it is a start in the right direction. Creators of the fuel believe that algae will be the fuel of the future.

Some environmental groups protest the continuing research for such new fuels stating that land being used to create produce for these fuels takes away from land capable of producing food. Because there is a finite amount of land for food, using the land for expanded production of fuel drives deforestation, which accounts for about one-fourth of the world's global emissions. In light of the growing food shortage and rising food prices, some analysts are suggesting that the search for an alternative fuel be placed on hold. Proponents of the biofuel industry claim they are receiving too much negative press for their efforts and too much of the blame for the food crisis.

Airlines believe they are not seeing a major decline in flyers so they are feeling less of a pressure to examine alternative fuel options. Others say that as the public becomes more environmentally aware, the airline industry could suffer. A British survey conducted in 2007 stated that 54 percent of the British population felt guilty about flying, which was an increase from the previous year's statistics. Environmentalists are hoping that as consumers become more aware of the carbon footprint they are leaving behind when flying they may switch to other modes of transportation or to short-haul destination trips.

THINK ABOUT THIS:

1. Would you adjust travel plans to reduce your carbon footprint?

Source: Trying to Lighten that Carbon Footprint, by Jennifer Conlin. Retrieved 4 May 2008, http://travel.nytimes.com/2008/05/04/travel/04green.html?scp=9&sq=business+travel&st=nyt.

party, how long the stay is, how accessible the accommodations are, what activities will be undertaken during the vacation, and whether or not several destinations will be visited. People who intend to take part in activities that require a great deal of equipment are more likely to use private transportation. Traveling to a destination using public transportation may, in fact, constrain people in their choice of activity.

One useful classification of selection variables and values has been put forth by Sheth (1975). He suggests that travelers choose a travel mode based upon the actual performance compared to the desired performance on five dimensions, namely the functional, aesthetic/emotional, social/organizational, situational, and curiosity utilities of the alternative modes. The *functional utility* of a mode is simply its likely performance for a specific purpose. Departure and arrival times, safety records, the directness of routes, and the absence of stops or transfers are examples of functional considerations. The functional utility is the *net* outcome of the positive and negative evaluations the user makes of a particular mode.

Aesthetic or *emotional* reasons relate to such things as fear and social concerns that affect fundamental values of the individual. Often users associate strong emotional feelings derived from early experiences with a mode of travel. Associations are also developed by early childhood socialization processes. These values often manifest themselves in terms of such things as style, interior/exterior decoration, comfort, luxury, and safety.

Social or *organizational utilities* refer to the stereotypes that various transportation modes have. For example, motor coach tours and cruises have been stereotyped as being a mode of transportation and vacation type for persons of retirement age. This may dissuade younger people from taking motor coach tours and cruises.

Situational utilities refer to the locational convenience of the mode and its terminal facilities to the traveler—the *total* set of activities associated with a trip. This might relate to the time in getting to and from the airport as a disincentive to fly. It is similar to the functional utilities except that the stress is on the activities that are antecedent and subsequent to the actual travel itself.

Curiosity utility concerns the traveler's tendency to try something because it is new and different. This feeling is usually short-lived.

The model presumes that the individual has desired expectations on these five utilities and that the discrepancy between the image or perception of the utility and the actual experience determines the extent to which that mode of travel is acceptable or not.

Certain supply-oriented and trip-purpose/traveler-profile factors influence the traveler's utility assessments. The availability of the mode–the number and convenience of flights, for example–influences the perception of functional and situational utilities. Mode design, including the variety of products or services offered to customers, affects the image of functional, curiosity, and aesthetic/emotional utilities. The way the mode is operated–on-time departures, quality of services, careful handling of the traveler's luggage–influence perceptions of functional and situational utilities. For example, advertisements for cruises that show young people on-board having a great time may dispel perceptions that cruises are just for older people. These supply-oriented factors combine to generate differential psychological utilities for different travel modes. These factors often create mass acceptance or rejection of a mode in the marketplace.

> The only way of catching a train I have ever discovered is to miss the train before.
> G. K. Chesterton

In a similar fashion, various demand-oriented factors produce differential psychological utilities for the same mode among a cross-section of users, leading to acceptance by some and rejection by others. Differences can be expected on the basis of personal demographics, lifestyle, familiarity and satisfaction of the traveler with a particular mode, and the purpose of the trip. For example, income level will influence the mode of transportation chosen. A person who values status will select a way of traveling that reflects that self-image. A person traveling from New York to London on business may choose to fly but, when traveling the same route on vacation, may choose to sail on the Queen Mary.

Last, there is the impact of unexpected events. A death in the family requiring attendance at a funeral will influence a person to fly to the destination, even if the cost is perceived as too high or if the individual is afraid of flying.

Sheth's explanation of the transportation mode selection decision-making process is illustrated in figure 16.2.

TRAVEL BY TRAIN

It seems fitting to begin our review of individual transportation modes by talking about trains. They opened up the North American continent from its Atlantic to Pacific coasts, and they were the major stimulant in the nineteenth and early twentieth centuries to vacations within the United States, Canada, and Europe. The first transcontinental route in the United States was completed in 1869. Britain had its first organized tour on the train in 1841 when Thomas Cook put together an excursion between Leicester and Loughborough. In 1851, 3 million English took the train to the Great Exhibition that was being staged in London. The train was also instrumental in Britain for spurring the development of many of its seaside resorts.

In the United States in 1929, the first year for which comprehensive train statistics are available, approximately 780.5 million paying passengers took the train. The heyday of the train in most of the major developed countries lasted approximately one hundred years, from the 1830s to the 1930s. In the 1920s and 1930s the automobile began to gain more popularity as a passenger transportation mode, mainly drawing away traffic from the train. Rail passenger traffic in the United States began to decline in the 1920s during what some persons have called the "age of abundant energy." In the late 1950s the number of route miles served by trains in the United States was surpassed by the number served by airlines. By 1963 the number of passengers carried intercity by airlines passed the number carried by trains. It was not until the mid-1970s to the early 1980s, which could be referred to

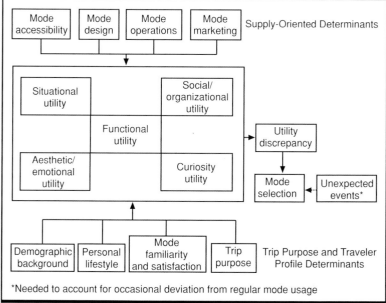

Figure 16.2 Travel Mode Selection Model. Source: Sheth, J. N. 1975. A Psychological Model of Travel Mode Selection. In *Advances in Consumer Research, vol. 3*. Proceedings of the Association for Consumer Research, Sixth Annual Conference. 426.

as the "age of uncertain energy," that the slide in the popularity of the train as a passenger transportation mode seemed to be halted.

The demise of the railway as a passenger travel mode was so alarming that in 1958 the U.S. Interstate Commerce Commission (ICC) ordered a detailed study of the situation. The results of this study became known as the Hosmer Report, and it predicted the eventual disappearance of the train as a passenger travel mode in the United States. The recommendations of the Hosmer Report were never officially accepted, and it was not until 1970 that the federal government took some concrete action to improve the failing rail-passenger travel business. In October 1970, the Rail Passenger Service Act became law. The act created the National Railroad Passenger Corporation, now commonly known as Amtrak. Amtrak began its operations in May 1971, and it was intended to be a profit-making corporation. In 2006, Amtrak had 21,000 route miles across forty-six states and, in that year, carried over 24 million passengers to five hundred destinations. Approximately 70 percent of the miles traveled by Amtrak trains are on rails owned by other railroads for which freight takes precedence over passengers. Due to wear and tear on those tracks, train speeds are low and on-time performance is poor. In 2006, Amtrak had revenues of $2,042.6 million and total expenses of $3,110.6 million for a year-end loss of just over one million dollars (National Railroad Passenger Corporation, 2007).

Canada's equivalent of Amtrak, Via Rail Canada is an independent crown corporation created in 1978. In 2007 it carried almost 4.2 million passengers, earning revenues of $285.6 million and expenses of $486.2 million for a deficit of over $200 million (Canadian). The Canadian network is made up of four main product groups:

1. Quebec City-Windsor Corridor, which accounts for about 85 percent of the corporation's ridership and 70 percent of its income
2. Western services between Toronto and Vancouver, a line especially popular with tourists, both domestic and international
3. Eastern services, linking the Atlantic regions with central Canada by way of the Montreal-Halifax and Montreal-Gaspe routes
4. Northern services in Quebec, Ontario, Saskatchewan and British Columbia, often traveling through sparsely populated regions

Key financial information, contained in annual reports follows:

	1990	1999	2004	2007
(in millions of Canadian dollars)				
Key Financial Indicators				
Total operating revenue	142.8	220.6	259.5	285.6
Cash operating expenses	493.3	389.1	444.6	486.2
Total passengers carried (000's)	3,536	3,757	3,887	4,181
On-time performance (%)	88	84	70	77

Source: Annual Reports, http://www.viarail.ca/pdf/an2007/VIARail_review_en.pdf.

Both Amtrak and Via Rail have the sole national responsibility for marketing and providing intercity passenger rail transportation. Since their inception both organizations have been successful in increasing passenger volumes that had been falling continuously beforehand. They have done so primarily by improving the equipment and services they offer, and by more effectively promoting the benefits of traveling by train.

Several attempts have been made to determine why travelers select the train as a transportation mode. Four factors seem to emerge consistently:

1. Cost/price
2. Comfort
3. Safety
4. The ability to see the area through which the train is passing

Via Rail's onboard surveys of business travelers have identified user cost, convenience, travel time, and comfort as being of prime importance. A survey of Amtrak users has indicated that travelers favored the train for the following reasons:

- Safety
- Ability to look out of trains and see interesting things en route
- Ability to get up and walk around
- Arriving at the destination rested and relaxed
- Personal comfort

One study of Amtrak passengers identified two market segments: "Enthusiasts" and "Functionalists" (Hallab and Uysal, 2004).

Enthusiasts make up over 70 percent of the passengers surveyed. They value the experience of traveling by train, and travel for relaxation. Both segments identify interpersonal as the main reason for travel. Although there are no differences demographically, enthusiasts place more emphasis on "Educational," "Nature," "Culture," and "Recreational" attributes than did func-

Touring Europe at Two Hundred Miles an Hour

Getting *to* Europe still requires a plane, but there appear to be more options when it comes to getting *around* Europe. High-speed rail operators have been ambitiously adding routes and cutting travel times in an attempt to attract short-haul airline travelers away from the hassles and frustrations of the air travel industry. New perks such as DVD movie rentals, free newspapers, more leg room, and plush accommodations are luring many customers away from flying and onto the train.

Eurostar reported a 15 percent increase in ticket sales after its recent reduction in travel time while the airline industry's passenger growth rate has fallen by 2 percent over the past two years. The two-hundred-mile-per-hour trains are not expected to attract long-distance travelers but should appeal to tourists looking to make multiple stops across the country.

Train travelers can also avoid airport security hassles and delays. Train stations are often more convenient, typically located in city centers. Another deterrent from air travel is the new "no frills" systems becoming more prevalent; European airlines are charging passengers for checking bags, checking in at the airport, and even for using credit cards. A recent increase in fees and surcharges has been raising airline fares and may push more customers onto the train. Rail travel, conversely, has been offering more perks. Trains also allow customers to stay better connected while they travel and carry up to two pieces of luggage for no extra charge. Travelers can use their cell phones where a signal is available. Drawbacks for the railway industry are the prices and route structures. Short-distance trips can be more cost-efficient if taken by air and many cities are not directly connected by train. Regardless of the advantages and disadvantages to rail travel, the future of the industry looks hopeful.

THINK ABOUT THIS:

1. Do you think the trend to take a train as opposed to flying will catch on?
2. What do you think are the biggest obstacles facing the rail industry?

Source: *The Wall Street Journal.* Personal Journal, March 12, 2008. Touring Europe at 200 Miles an Hour, by Darren Everson.

tionalists. They also place more emphasis, compared to functionalists, on comfort and staff friendliness. For both, price is the most important factor in selecting the train as a mode of transportation.

Negative factors often associated or perceived with rail travel are slowness in reaching the destination, relatively inflexible departure times, and a lack of quality in food service. Trains are certainly perceived as being a very safe mode of transportation and are thought to attract a significant "fear of flying" market. Recent promotions by Via Rail and Amtrak have emphasized the rest and relaxation benefits of taking the train. They have also begun to point out that the downtown-to-downtown routing of trains actually saves passengers time.

In Germany, France, and Japan, high-speed trains have been developed and are in operation. These trains travel faster than the automobile, and they actually cut down on the time that passengers would take to drive between the major cities. In France the TGV and in Japan the Shinkansen (Bullet Train) have an average speed of 186 mph, while German and Italian trains travel at speeds of 155 mph. In 2009 a marketing alliance of seven high-speed train operators was formed with an online reservations system for booking international train fares. Known as Railteam, the alliance consists of Eurostar; France's SNCF; Germany's Deutsche Bahn; and operators from Austria, Belgium, Switzerland, and the Netherlands. Travelers are able to travel to more than one hundred destinations on one ticket. This development is significant as it will make it easier for trains to compete with air travel. It is estimated that, at point-to-point journeys of under four-and-a-half hours, trains achieve a 50 percent market share when competing with air.

Amtrak introduced the American Flyer between Washington, DC, and Boston in January 2000. The time from Boston to New York was reduced from four to three hours as average speed increased from 100 to 135 mph. From New York to Washington travel time was cut from three to two-and-a-half hours as average speed increased from 125 to 150 mph.

Beginning in the 1970s British Rail became more marketing-oriented in an attempt to increase its share of the tourist market. Their policies were helped by shortages of gas and the subsequent increase in prices that had a dampening effect on travel by private automobile. Package holidays were developed with hotel companies, while other programs were aimed at the rail enthusiasts who were mainly interested in the trip itself. Originally organized as charters, these excursions were later provided on scheduled services. Longer packages, which offered travelers a short break away from home, were introduced. The high-speed train—capable of speeds of 125 mph—now offers a service competitive in time from city center to city center with that of the airlines.

Changes in the travel patterns of U.S. travelers to Europe have forced rail companies to create new products. Americans tend to take shorter trips to Europe and to go more often. They are also more adventurous. As a result Rail Europe created three new programs: the Europass, rail and drive, and the regional rail pass. The Europass covers travel to France, Germany, Italy, Spain, and Switzerland from five to fifteen days within a two-month period. The rail and drive program combines elements of rail travel and car rental while regional passes focus on one area within Europe.

Before leaving the subject of rail travel, the role of railways as tourist attractions should be highlighted. Short-duration train excursions through scenic surroundings have been proven to be major attractions to pleasure travelers in recent years. For example, two major excursions of this type in Canada are the Algoma Central Railway in Ontario and the Royal Hudson Steam Train in British Columbia. The Strasburg Railroad in Pennsylvania is a U.S. example of a popular train excursion of this type. The experience of riding aboard the Orient Express, made famous by mystery writer Agatha Christie, was reintroduced in 1983 after a complete restoration of the train.

TRAVEL BY SHIP

Travel by ship did in fact precede travel by train, but it was not until the mid-nineteenth century that travel by ocean liner began to show its greatest prominence. Although ocean liners used to provide an important link for passengers between continents, water transport today plays two main roles in travel and tourism—ferrying and cruising.

The steamship era had its beginnings in the 1840s. Sir Samuel Cunard pioneered the first transatlantic scheduled liner trips at that time. Cruising began as one way to use surplus tonnage. The industry received a major boost with Prohibition in the United States in the 1920s. Non-U.S.-flagged ships could board passengers for prohibition-beating cruises. As a result, the number of cruisers increased. A similar effect was felt when, in the 1960s, the U.K. government placed strict currency restrictions and exchange regulations on those citizens leaving the country. However, U.K.-flagged ships were exempt from these restrictions, and an increase in passengers resulted, in part because of this loophole. Just as the automobile led to the demise of the train, the introduction of intercontinental commercial airline service precipitated the rapid decline in the use of ships as a scheduled passenger transportation mode. In 1957, transatlantic ship traffic reached a new post-World War II high as some 1,036,000 passengers were transported on ocean liners. Although travel by ship remained strong for several years thereafter, the aircraft had by 1958 eclipsed it in terms of volumes of transatlantic passengers.

Transatlantic scheduled passenger ship traffic declined rapidly. Passenger departures from New York fell from approximately 500,000 in 1960 to 50,000 in 1975. So great has been the decline in scheduled liner passenger transport volumes that it has almost completely disappeared in this modern-day era.

The cruise industry consists of five segments (Bjornsen, 2003). The budget segment accounts for about 5 percent of the industry and consists of older, smaller ships charging $80 to $125 per day, per passenger. The contemporary segment, about 60 percent of the industry, consists of new, large and mega ships sailing three to seven days and charging between $100 and $150 per passenger, per day. The premium segment,

The majority of train travelers value the experience and travel for relaxation. © 2009 olly. Used under license from Shutterstock, Inc.

about 30 percent, sails for seven to fourteen days on new, medium and large ships charging $150 to $300 per passenger, per day. The niche segment accounts for less than 5 percent of the total, consisting of small ships sailing for seven days and up and charging anywhere from $200 to $900 per passenger, per day. Finally, the luxury segment, accounting for approximately 2 percent of the total industry, consists of small and medium ships sailing for seven days and up and charging anywhere from $300 to $2,000 per passenger, per day.

Just over 70 percent of the demand for cruises is from North America, 20 percent from Europe, and the remainder from the rest of the world. Over the past two decades, the North American share of demand has been losing ground to a corresponding increase from Europe (Duval, 2007). There has been a substantial increase in annual demand from people in the United Kingdom, Germany, and especially Japan. The latter two show the most potential for growth (Cartwright and Baird, 1999). The major cruise routes of the world are illustrated in figure 16.3. The major oceans and seas in the world are:

> My experience of ships is that on them one makes an interesting discovery about the world. One finds one can do without it completely.
>
> Malcolm Bradbury

Pacific Ocean	63,986,000 square miles
Atlantic Ocean	31,744,000
Indian Ocean	23,350,000
Arctic Ocean	5,541,000
Caribbean Sea/Gulf of Mexico	1,450,000
Mediterranean Sea	1,145,000

Since 1980, the cruise industry has had an average annual growth rate of 7.9 percent per annum. Since 1970, an estimated 76 million passengers have taken a deep-water cruise (2+ days). Of this number, 60 percent of the total passengers have been generated in the past ten years. Thirty-three percent of total passengers have been generated in the past five years alone.

Cruise Lines International Association (CLIA) estimates that 51 million Americans have cruised at least once, 17 percent of all Americans, and that annually about 13 million Americans take a cruise (CLIA, 2006). CLIA Member Lines represent 95 percent of North American-marketed berths. From a capacity standpoint, utilization is consistently around 90 percent. The Caribbean represents the number one destination with almost 50 percent of all passengers and 46 percent of capacity placement. The

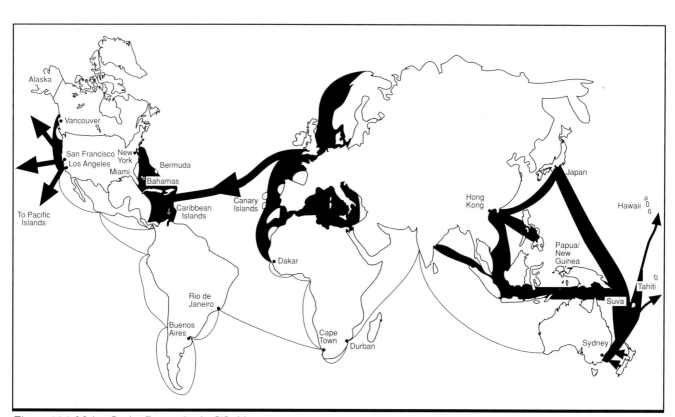

Figure 16.3 Major Cruise Routes in the World. Source: Christopher, J. *The Business of Tourism*, 2nd ed. London: Pitman Publishers.

Caribbean, which primarily attracts the North American market, is followed in popularity by the Mediterranean, with about 20 percent of all passengers, and Alaska with 10 percent of the total. British cruisers sail the Mediterranean, followed by the Caribbean and the Atlantic Islands.

The Caribbean was the first area to develop. It is fairly close to its North American market. The islands of the Caribbean were developed by different Western nations, thus providing contrasts in style. Additional attractions include the fact that English is the predominant language, and the U.S. dollar is accepted nearly everywhere. The Caribbean is not a year-round cruising area due to the hurricane season from June to November. The Panama Canal is important for positioning cruises between the Caribbean and Alaska during the switch from the winter to the summer season.

The Mediterranean/Black Sea/Red Sea area is linked to the Greek Islands. There is an extension to the Holy Land and Egyptian coast. Political events in the former Soviet Union opened up the Black Sea as a cruise destination. The United States is well represented in terms of passengers to this area due to large numbers of U.S. citizens with ancestors in this region. The region is easily reached from Northern European ports, and summer is the preferred season, though there is no particular season for Mediterranean cruising.

Alaska offers scenery, wildlife, and a mild summer climate. Recent concern for the environment means the number of large cruise ships is limited. The short season runs from only May to September and puts increased pressure on port facilities. Growth of this market is constrained by the ability of the infrastructure to cope.

The Eastern Atlantic is one of the earliest cruise areas. Destinations are either mature holiday destinations in their own right, or major cities where cruises are a welcome but marginal addition The year-round cruising accounts for about one percent of world market, but 21 percent of the U.K. market. Growth is anticipated and the area has the infrastructure to cope. Cruise companies know the area well, it gets good repeat business and the region has the facilities to handle cruise ships.

Asia represents the fastest growing destination as more Western cruisers visit the area and the local Asian market is growing rapidly. See table 16.1 for results of a survey of cruisers that identified the main categories of attractions and area attractiveness (Cartwright and Baird, 1999). Based on responses by cruisers, researchers were able to allocate scores to various areas with ten being the highest and zero the lowest. Norway, for ex-

ample, is rated very high in terms of scenery and wildlife and very low for the other categories. Cruise executives can use this type of information to identify strengths and weaknesses in the cruises they offer to different destinations.

QUICK TRIP 16.3

Space Tourism

Ever been tempted to travel at twice the speed of sound to about thirty-seven miles above the earth? Well, your dreams can soon come true for the small price of $100,000. Companies in the space tourism race are already experiencing price wars years before their privately financed rocket planes are ready for takeoff. XCOR Aerospace is developing a vehicle predicted to cost less than $10 million to build and to be more compact than propeller planes. The planes will carry only the pilot and a single passenger and the entire expedition, of traveling to thirty-seven miles above Earth, should take under half an hour. An XCOR test pilot says the best part of the experience is getting to ride up front, like a copilot, instead of in the back like cargo.

British billionaire Sir Richard Branson is also developing a Galactic spaceship capable of holding six passengers and designed to travel at about four times the speed of sound and reach true space, about sixty miles above Earth. Estimated cost of this new spacecraft? Roughly $50 million and a traveling fee of $200,000. The profits from this new type of tourism are expected to be substantial, with estimates reaching the hundreds of millions of dollars in the next decade.

Congress and federal regulators have designed a simple system for protecting travelers' safety by making passengers sign releases acknowledging that they understand the inherent risks in strapping themselves inside a modified rocket. Companies hope to avoid lawsuits by offering training to travelers and supplying basic information about the vehicle's safety record.

Another designing team says the only way we are going to have a really robust space industry is to develop an actual mass market for space tourism.

THINK ABOUT THIS:

1. What are the characteristics of space tourism that would attract someone to that kind of travel?

Source: *The Wall Street Journal.* Marketplace, March 26, 2008. Economy Fare ($100,000) Lifts Space-Tourism Race, by Andy Pasztor.

Table 16.1
Main Categories of Attractions and Area Attractiveness

Area	Scenery and wildlife	Lifestyle	Shopping	Culture and history	Activities
Caribbean	2	3	2	2	1
Mediterranean	1	3	1	5	0
Alaska	8	2	0	0	0
Asia	1	5	2	2	1
Eastern U.S. Seaboard/Bermuda	2	3	1	3	1
Panama Canal	4	1	1	3	2
U.S. West Coast	0	4	0	4	0
Eastern Atlantic	2	5	0	3	0
Baltic	0	4	0	6	0
Norway	9	1	0	0	1
Hawaii	3	3	0	2	0
South America	4	4	0	2	0
Black Sea	0	5	0	5	0
British Isles	2	4	9	4	0
Africa	6	3	0	2	0

According to one study of cruise passengers, the most important factors determining whether or not people will take a cruise are marital status (singles have higher probability of taking a cruise), income (above $50,000), previous cruise experience, cost, duration of the cruise, visiting new destinations and the availability of a pre-cruise or post-cruise package (De La Vina and Ford, 2001).

CRUISER SEGMENTS. Six segments are identified within the recent cruiser market.

1. **Restless Baby Boomers** are newest to cruising. They represent 33 percent of total cruisers and 17 percent of total cruising days. Fifty-nine percent of this segment are first timers. They have enjoyed their cruise experience and would like to cruise again but cost may be an impediment. They are also at a point in time when they may be trying different vacation experiences. Marketing messages to this segment need to reinforce the affordability of cruising and its superiority over other vacation experiences.

2. **Enthusiastic Baby Boomers** are already convinced and excited about cruising and its many activities. This segment represents 20 percent of the market and account for 15 percent of total cruising days. Forty-six percent are first timers. They live intense, stressful lives and look to vacations generally, and cruises in particular, for the escape and relaxation they offer. Marketing messages to this segment need to underscore the fun and excitement of cruises, cruising as a way to "get away from it all" and cruising as a family experience.

3. **Luxury Seekers**, 14 percent of cruisers and 18 percent of total cruising days, can afford and are willing to spend money for deluxe accommodations and pampering. Thirty percent are first timers. Marketing messages to this segment need to address their desire for luxury and extravagance, recognizing that they are sophisticated in their experience and expectations.

4. **Consummate Shoppers** are looking for the best value (not necessarily the cheapest) in a vacation and in a cruise. Members of this segment are very committed cruisers. Cruising has met their needs versus other types of vacations. Marketing messages need to continue to reinforce the value theme and highlight promotions with special rates. This segment represents 16 percent in terms of number, 20 percent of total cruising days and 20 percent are first-timers.

5. **Explorers** are well-educated, well-traveled individuals with an intellectual interest and curiosity about different destinations. Marketing messages stressing new destinations with opportunities to explore and learn about the area should appeal to this segment. This segment represents 11 percent of the total cruisers, 18 percent of total cruising days and 20 percent are first-timers.

6. **Ship Buffs**, 6 percent of all cruisers and 11 percent of total cruising days, are the most senior segment; they have cruised extensively and expect to continue because they find the on-board experience of cruising so pleasurable and comfortable. Messages to this segment need to do little more than reinforce the ship experience as one they know and enjoy. Thirteen percent of this segment are first-timers.

Although this group is only 6 percent of all cruisers, the fact that they tend to take more and longer cruises accounts for the 11 percent of total cruising days they contribute.

The size of the market is limited by a number of negative perceptions about cruising. First, there is the association with ships of isolation, storms, and seasickness. While the number of outbreaks of illness has declined in recent years, ships are vulnerable because of the close quarters and the fact that there are many elderly passengers. The Center for Disease Control (CDC) runs a Vessel Sanitation Program that performs unannounced inspections of ships docked in U.S. ports and publishes sanitation ratings in a document sent to travel agents. However, the agency's mission is more advisory than regulatory. It relies on voluntary compliance as many ships are of foreign registry and sail in international waters. The CDC also helps in designing ships' galleys and sanitation systems and trains kitchen crews in food handling and hygiene.

It does not appear that the age or passenger-carrying capacity of the ship affects its vessel sanitation score. There is a weak indication that larger cruise ships and a moderate indication that higher per diem prices produce better sanitation scores (Marti, 1995). The key seems to be that modern equipment can and has been installed on older ships to help ensure sanitary conditions. Further, higher prices might mean that more money is available for training and the production of a higher quality cuisine. The key is management.

The dominance of Americans in the cruise market has meant that strict standards have been imposed on all foreign flag carriers that operate out of U.S. ports. There are strict standards expected in the areas of hygiene, safety, and financial protection for passengers in case of the collapse of the carrier. Additional barriers that have to be overcome to induce people to cruise are that cruising is seen as:

- Expensive with no general awareness of the less expensive options
- Exclusively for the rich
- Suitable for couples, not children
- Claustrophobic with many people believing there is no quiet space (Cartwright and Baird, 1999)

Three-quarters of all embarkations are from ports in the United States. The most important areas for cruises from the United States are the Caribbean, the Mexican Riviera, and Alaska. Seventy percent of all passengers leaving the United States cruise in these areas. The popularity of the Caribbean has been built on warm winter weather, good sailing conditions, the ability to visit a number of varied ports in a relatively short time, and the capacity of Miami International Airport to bring in passengers. Fifty-six percent of U.S. cruise passengers sail from Florida—Miami, Port Everglades, Port Canaveral and Tampa. Just over 10 percent sail from California—Los Angeles, Long Beach, San Diego and San Francisco—and these are largely to the Mexican Riviera. In recent years California has been gaining market share at the expense of Florida.

Cruises to Alaska originate in San Francisco, Seattle, and Vancouver, Canada. Because of the Passenger Service Act of 1886, foreign vessels may sail from Seattle, but those passengers may not disembark in Alaska, another U.S. port. Passengers must return to Seattle via a foreign port. Since most vessels operating out of the United States are foreign, this poses a problem for Seattle. A popular package to Alaska is the seven-day fly and cruise package that involves a one-way trip by ship and a fly or land return. This type of tourism must originate in neighboring Vancouver, Canada. Restrictions on the number of cruise ships into Glacier Bay have placed limits on the growth of this market.

One of the reasons for the growth of the U.S. market to the Caribbean was the deregulation of the airlines in 1978 that allowed cruise operators to offer cheap fly-cruise packages. Flights from northern cities were heavily subsidized. By flying to Florida, the time spent in warm weather was maximized. In theory, deregulation in Europe could offer the same boost to Mediterranean cruising. However, deregulation in Europe must take into account the diversity of national markets and cannot benefit from the economies of scale enjoyed in the United States. The Mediterranean cruise industry took off in the late 1960s and early 1970s as lines expanded their fleets. The extra capacity generated additional interest from tour operators in Germany and the United Kingdom. This interest coincided with significant growth in the overseas inclusive vacation market.

While Germany and the United Kingdom make up the largest market segments for Mediterranean cruises, the development of the market differs greatly in both countries. In the United Kingdom tour operators set up their own cruise divisions, negotiating charter deals with cruise lines. The initial effect was to increase the size of

Cruise operators are looking to larger ships to spread overheads and to capitalize on economies of scale. © 2009 Ramunas Bruzas. Used under license from Shutterstock, Inc.

the market. However, lack of expertise and experience in operating a cruise ship meant that the narrow profit margins that were a result of concentrating on volume and market share put companies at risk. Tour operators now have no operating responsibility for the cruise and tend to feature cruises in their vacation brochures on an open-sale basis with no charter commitments. A major problem for cruise operators in the United Kingdom is the difficulty of selling a rather sophisticated travel product through retail travel agents. By some estimates less than one in ten travel agents are productive in terms of cruise sales, lacking the expertise or experience to sell cruises.

In Germany tour operators dominate the cruise booking market. In part this is because a flight must be packaged in to get the vacationer from Germany to the Mediterranean. About 75 percent of the Mediterranean cruise market travels on tour-operated chartered ships.

Incentive travel accounts for 15 percent of all cruise berths, perhaps more in the United States. Yet, because cruise lines tend to be registered in foreign countries, they have been unable to penetrate the business or convention markets to a larger extent. Legal restrictions prevent the tax deductibility of convention-oriented expenses if they are incurred with a cruise on a non-U.S. flag vessel.

Most cruise-line marketing has been oriented to capturing market share from other lines rather than to increasing the size of the total market. In the United States, travel agents sell about 95 percent of all sea vacations. Some lines have successfully found themselves a market niche. Premier Cruise Lines has developed a unique package by combining three days in Walt Disney World with four days of cruising. In addition to appealing to families who want a balanced vacation, the competition will find the product truly difficult to duplicate. Another niche has been developed by Windstar Sail Cruises. Aimed at the affluent active vacationers who would normally not cruise, Windstar markets cruises on a sail-cruising ship, which offers a wide variety of water sports activities and visits to remote, small islands that traditionally ships do not visit.

Excess capacity in the industry has meant that operators are looking to larger ships to spread overheads and capitalize on economies of scale. The cruise ships being built now tend to be in the 40,000-ton range. The commercial life of a cruise ship is about twenty years, but there is increased pressure on them to make a profit by the third year of operation. This has resulted in a selling orientation on the part of the operators to fill their berths through heavy price discounting. The cor-

Riverboat cruises combine nostalgia with viewing scenic surroundings. © 2009 Anne Kitzman. Used under license from Shutterstock, Inc.

responding battle for market share has done little to expand the size of the market for cruises.

Larger ships mean lower cost per berth and maximum revenue per berth. Many larger ships are too big to go through the Panama Canal. A consequence of their size is that they are able to visit fewer ports of call. Some destinations have upgraded their harbor areas to accommodate the larger vessels.

Ships are also becoming smaller with the development of a number of ships with a capacity of 150 passengers or less to cruise the more remote waters of the world.

Cruises share a kinship with other unique transportation offerings, such as traveling on the Orient Express train, in that they are more of a vacation experience than a transportation mode. The romance of cruising has been heavily promoted, and this has been helped along by a popular television program, "The Love Boat." Today cruise ships are like portable resort hotels that ply the waters of the Caribbean, Mediterranean, and other regions.

Special interest or hobby-type cruises have grown, packaging such things as the theater, gourmet dining, bridge, flower arranging, aquasports, jazz, country and western music, and many other themes and activities. This ties in closely with the trend toward more vacation travel for the purpose of learning or improving upon a leisure-time or recreation activity.

The ship remains an important passenger transportation mode in its role as a ferry service. The "floating bridge" is an essential complement to the automobile, recreational vehicle, and bus in many parts of the world, including the English Channel, the Irish Sea, the Hebridean Islands of Scotland, the North Sea, the Maritime provinces and British Columbian coast in Canada, and on the Great Lakes.

As with its "partner" in history, the train, the ship also has considerable importance in tourism as an attraction. Examples of short-duration sightseeing cruise-ship attractions are abundant in North America and elsewhere. Characteristically, these cruises are for a day or less. Viewing scenic surroundings is the major focus of many of these operations, including those featuring the Thousand Islands (New York–Ontario), the Mississippi River, Muskoka Lakes (Ontario), Niagara Falls (New York–Ontario), and many others. Other cruises combine nostalgia with scenic viewing. Steamer and riverboat cruises are examples of these. One study of a restored steamer sightseeing cruise operation indicated that its appeals were in learning about the history of steamships and the history of the surrounding area, seeing the scenic beauty of the area, watching the visible operations of steam engines, and using its dining/bar service.

Many destinations seek to develop cruising as a way of bringing economic benefits to the destination. The economic benefits of cruising to destinations can be determined only after a full consideration of the costs and benefits (Dwyer and Forsyth, 1996). Cruise ship expenditures can be divided into passenger expenses and operator expenses. The former includes such things as international air fares to the point of embarkation, internal travel, add-on expenditures such as accommodation in the port prior to departure as well as direct expenditures on excursions and shopping.

Cruise operators also make a number of expenditures. These include charges for the port and terminal, towage payments and stevedoring charges. Goods and services must be purchased to provision the ship. If any crew members are local, their wages represent an economic impact. Usually, however, a foreign crew means that crew expenditures in port are the only economic benefit to the destination. In addition to such things as ship maintenance and the cost of maintaining a local office, various taxes will be levied.

The basic differences between land-based and cruise holidays are that land-based vacations bring tourists to a fixed infrastructure where tourists are a captive market. With a cruise, the accommodation moves and tourists spend relatively short periods of time in any one place. Cruises operate on fixed routes. As such, the cruise ships and their passengers have a great deal of impact on the place, but there is little time for the place to impact the cruiser. Land-based holidays provide employment to local staff in hotels, while cruise ships pick their staff from around the world, lessening the economic benefits to the port of call. The situation is similar in en-

clave resorts in developing countries where staff may be shipped in and out (Cartwright and Baird, 1999).

TRAVEL BY AUTOMOBILE

The introduction of the automobile precipitated the demise of the train in most developed countries. As mentioned earlier, the automobile as a passenger travel mode gained its momentum as far back as the 1920s. Lundgren (1973) refers to the period after this as the automobile-based travel-system era characterized by "individual travel diffusion." He explained this point as follows:

> The private motor car siphoned off a larger portion of the potential travel market from the established mechanisms and routes toward a new tour destination concept with quite different distance dimensions. Thus, the (international) tourist dollar became diffused over wider territories (Lundgren, 1973).

The advent of the automobile, therefore, spread the benefits of tourism more widely and provided more and more people with the means to travel individually or in private, smaller groups. Nonprivate group travel had been a characteristic of the railway and steamship era that preceded the automobile. Due to the nature of the railroad's infrastructure and the limited routing possibilities by water, travel patterns were very predictable. People could only get to the destinations to which the trains and steamships would take them. Many famous resort areas, resort hotels, and city center hotels flourished at important destination and staging points for the trains and steamships. With the increased popularity of the automobile, the attractiveness of these areas and facilities began to decline, and many of them suffered significantly.

The automobile brought about a more random pattern of travel movements, opened up new destinations,

> A route differs from a road not only because it is solely intended for vehicles, but also because it is merely a line that connects one point with another. A route has no meaning in itself; its meaning derives entirely from the two points that it connects. A road is a tribute to space. Every stretch of road has meaning in itself and invites us to stop. A route is the triumphant devaluation of space, which thanks to it has been reduced to a mere obstacle to human movement and a waste of time.
>
> Milan Kundera

and spurred the development of elaborate networks of new automobile-oriented facilities and services along highways and roads. The tourist court, motel, and the motor hotel were three of the new facility types that developed in the United States and Canada after World War II. In fact, the whole development pattern in North America was fashioned directly and indirectly to accommodate the private automobile.

Traveling by automobile is now the single most predominant travel mode in North America. Most travel surveys have shown that automobile trips account for over 85 percent of the pleasure and personal and business trips taken by Canadians and 75 percent of intercity passenger miles in the United States. The nuclear family unit traveling by private automobile has been the major source of pleasure and personal travel demand and the marketing target for a majority of tourist-oriented businesses in the United States and Canada. It is not difficult to see why, considering the statistics that have been discussed earlier.

Just as they have done with the trains, many experts have tried to explain why the automobile is selected over other modes of transportation. One such report found the major attractive attributes of the automobile to be as follows:

- Control of the route and the stops en route
- Control of departure times
- Ability to carry baggage and equipment easily
- Low out-of-pocket expense of traveling with three or more persons
- Freedom to use the automobile once the destination is reached

Other surveys have shown that many persons perceive the automobile to be a relatively safe mode of transportation, and others indicate that people like driving as a recreational experience.

Two other important aspects of automobile travel that remain to be discussed are recreation vehicles and car rentals, or as they are called in Britain "car hires." These two areas have developed so extensively in North America and elsewhere that they are now both significant elements of tourism.

The major U.S. car rental companies and some of their operating characteristics are noted in table 16.2. Most transactions occur at airports, the exception being Enterprise, which specializes in local business. Note that several companies aim at the business traveler while others target leisure customers.

The car rental industry relies upon the auto manufacturers for their cars. As such, the strength of the auto-

Table 16.2
U.S. Car Rental Companies: A Comparison (2006)

	Systemwide revenue (000)	Total fleet	Total locations	% Business travel revenue
Hertz	$5,950,000	400,000	7,400	50
Avis	$4,711,950	505,200	2,035	60
National	$1,851,300	140,000	2,050	30
Budget	$1,600,000	144,800	1,798	50
Alamo	$1,089,000	80,000	1,157	20

Source: *Business Travel News.* 2006. 2006 Business Travel Survey. 24.

owning business impacts car rental companies. When manufacturers experience a strong retail demand for cars they do not need to offer incentives to car rental companies to buy large supplies of cars to keep the factories open. The result is that car rental companies keep their fleets in service longer, resulting in fleets with higher mileage caps. In addition, rental companies can experience difficulties in getting some of the more popular models. Recent changes in the rental car business have included significant shifts in car fleets toward smaller and more fuel-efficient models. Fly-drive packages offering rental cars together with flights have made significant gains in popularity as more travelers have begun to substitute air travel for travel by the private automobile.

The recreational vehicle, or RV, is an extension of Northern Americans' love affair with the automobile. The President's Commission on Americans Outdoors found that 43 percent of American adults consider driving for pleasure a main recreational pastime. RVs offer the opportunity to combine driving and camping. RVs have grown tremendously in popularity in recent years. There has been an increased interest in touring the country in rented recreational vehicles.

RVs offer the opportunity to combine driving and camping. Their popularity has grown in recent years. © 2009 Condor 36. Used under license from Shutterstock, Inc.

Since World War II, camping has grown rapidly in popularity in North America and elsewhere. The United States has more than 14,000 public and private parks and commercial campgrounds containing about a million campsites. Canada has been said to have 250,000 campsites and Mexico 10,000 campsites. The increasing popularity of the RV led directly to a number of new camping phenomena during the 1990s, including the franchised, condominium, and time-sharing condominium campgrounds. In a condominium campground the RV owner buys the site and pays a monthly fee for the maintenance of the common areas. In a time-share operation, the use of the site for one or more weeks each year is purchased.

Yet another phenomenon to which the RV has led is that of many European visitors to Canada and the United States renting these vehicles for cross-continent trips. Many companies have been formed to provide this service to overseas pleasure travelers.

TRAVEL BY AIR

Continuing our chronology of transportation modes, the airplane had a revolutionary impact on tourism from World War II onward. This point was already highlighted in chapter 15 where the plane's refashioning of the global travel market was mentioned.

The history of air transportation can be divided into at least three parts: pre-World War II, World War II, and post-World War II. The first period, from 1918 to 1938, was a period of infancy for the scheduled airlines of North America, while the modern era can be termed the mass air-travel era. The present era has been marked by steadily improving aircraft technology and the advent of air charters and the packaged vacation, or as it has sometimes been called, the "inclusive" or "all-inclusive" vacation.

A few dates in history allow us to put the facts to be discussed later in perspective:

1918   The first scheduled domestic air service in the United States is on the New York–Philadelphia–Washington route.

1939   Pan American operates the first Transatlantic passenger flight using a "clipper" flying boat.

1946   BOAC (now British Airways) offers its first Transatlantic passenger service.

1946   BEA (now also a part of British Airways) offers its first passenger service to Europe.

1970   The first of the widebodied jets is introduced into service.

As was just pointed out, the modern era of air travel really began at the end of World War II. Between 1945 and 1960 we have seen that travelers increasingly switched from trains and ships to automobiles and airplanes. By the late 1950s the number of route miles served by airlines surpassed those served by train for the first time. By the early 1960s the number of passengers carried intercity by airlines was greater than that carried by trains. (Both numbers pale, however, compared to those route miles served and passengers carried by bus.) In the 1960s this trend continued, and airfare reductions further stimulated air travel. The 1970s was the decade of the wide-bodied jets, and it was then that the "mass tourism" phrase was coined. Various operating statistics for the top international and U.S. airlines for 2004 are shown in tables 16.3 and 16.4 respectively.

In 2005 the major U.S. scheduled airlines lost $10 billion due, in large part, to increases in fuel costs. Airlines spent an average of more than $70 per barrel on jet fuel in 2005. Analysts estimate that airlines can break even when fuel prices are $60 per barrel. The U.S. airline industry has not been profitable since 2000. Foreign airlines were more successful in offsetting

Table 16.3
Operating Statistics–International Airlines

	Passenger revenue ($000)	Traffic in RPM (000)	Net earnings ($000)	Load factor (%)
Air France/KLM	20,064,580	117,601	1,081,000	80.6
Deutsche Lufthansa AG	14,269,100	67,266	536,556	75
British Airways	12,192,000	69,251	834,860	75.6
Japan Airlines System	11,484,100	62,354	401,488	67.5
Qantas Airways	7,003,970	47,970	581,863	77

Source: *Business Travel News.* 2006. 2006 Business Travel Survey. 20.
RPM = Revenue Passenger Miles

Table 16.4
Operating Statistics–U.S. Airlines

	Passenger revenue ($000)	Traffic in RPM (000)	Net earnings ($000)
American	18,860,000	147,320	861,000
Delta	14,600,000	103,742	3,800,000
United	12,914,000	114,046	21,000,000
Northwest	10,237,000	75,820	2,600,000
Continental	10,235,000	71,261	68,000

Source: *Business Travel News.* 2006. 2006 Business Travel Survey. 14.
RPM = Revenue Passenger Miles

higher fuel costs with passenger fuel surcharges. European carriers made about $1.3 billion while Asian carriers made $1.5 billion. Business travel is more price sensitive than previously assumed in the 1990s. Airlines are slowing domestic growth and are more willing to lose passengers on routes that are marginal in profitability. They are moving to increase traffic at their hubs and are increasingly looking to improve yield by expanding international traffic. While most of the major carriers succeeded in reducing labor costs, distribution costs increased from 2 percent to over 10 percent. Fuel costs increased in 2003 by anywhere from 20 percent to over 50 percent.

> I feel about airplanes the way I feel about diets. It seems to me that they are wonderful things for other people to go on.
>
> Jean Kerr

Much of the strength of the industry in terms of profitability, is in long-haul traffic as low-cost carriers dominate the shorter routes. Europe is seeing less restrictive ticketing regulations, stricter passenger rights, continuation of the move to eliminate base commissions paid to travel agencies and, most important of all, industry consolidation.

The International Civil Aviation Organization estimates that, in 2005, North America and Asia/Pacific each accounted for 34 percent of world passenger traffic. Europe has 23 percent of all traffic while Latin America/Caribbean, Middle East, and Africa account for five, three, and two percent respectively (Hanlon,

QUICK TRIP 16.4

Baggage Becomes a Big Ticket Item

What is the newest controversy in the airline industry? Pack light or pay up. Big name airlines are demanding that passengers pay a fee of $50 roundtrip for checking a second piece of luggage. Some are even charging for the first piece! Smaller airlines are implementing a charge for the third piece of baggage checked.

These courageous moves are an attempt to help the bottom line without raising ticket prices. Airlines are constantly threatened by high fuel prices and the chance of recession curbing travel, so carriers have been desperate for a way to keep themselves out of bankruptcy. The carriers have attempted to "up sell" fliers by selling first-class upgrades, alcoholic drinks, and day passes to airport clubs. Other attempts to cut costs have left customers with a bare-bones flying experience. Many previously free services are being eliminated and customers can now expect to be charged for anything more than basic transportation. Several costs affecting the consumer include the use of skycaps, telephone reservations, and on-board meals. Even the request for an assigned seat, exit row, or bulkhead legroom are coming with an extra charge. Fliers have adapted so far and the concept of giving travelers the chance to improve their experience has been popular.

Baggage policies and pricing vary on these new policies. At Delta Air Lines Inc. a third checked bag that weighs seventy-one pounds and is oversize costs $660 roundtrip. Cheaper discounters like Skybus Airlines Inc. charges customers $10 to check even one bag and $50 for an oversize bag. Southwest and JetBlue Airways Corp. demand $100 for an oversize bag while United, American, Delta, and Continental charge $200 per oversize bag.

Some complain this new pricing strategy targets leisure travelers more than it does business travelers. Leisure travelers are more likely than business travelers to be carrying more than one bag. United says that one out of every four customers checks multiple bags, and that customer is typically leisure traveler.

The airline claims that the second-bag fee will generate over $100 million in annual revenue. Golfers, skiers, and musicians will also be hit hard with these new policies. The fees are providing more than an afternoon annoyance for travelers; they are calling into question exactly what should be included in basic air travel. So be aware the next time you are packing for that relaxing Mexico vacation, you may want to throw that fifth pair of shoes out of your suitcase.

THINK ABOUT THIS:

1. What should come with the cost of an airline ticket? What amenities/perks should or should not be included?

2. What constitutes "basic air travel"? Is it fair that airlines are beginning to charge for some of these basic necessities?

Source: *The Wall Street Journal*. Personal Journal, March 22, 2008. Baggage Becomes a Big Ticket Item, by Scott McCartney.

1999). Transpacific routes are the fastest growing international routes in the world. In fact in 1995, for the first time, more passengers were carried across the Pacific than across the Atlantic. It is difficult to operate nonstop transpacific routes between Asian countries and the United States. The longest nonstop commercial service in operation is New York to Singapore—18 and a half hours. This next decade will see the introduction of advanced-technology, long-range aircraft capable of flying nonstop on these routes. This will undoubtedly make transpacific travel more enticing to the pleasure traveler. For the airlines, nonstop service offers greater economic performance as more fuel is used on takeoffs and landings than when the plane achieves cruising altitude. For this reason, the cost per unit goes down as the length of the flight increases. The unit operating costs in Europe are 40 to 50 percent higher than comparable airlines in the United States.

In 1978 the U.S. airline industry was deregulated. The National Transportation Act of 1988 accomplished the same thing in Canada. The impact of *deregulation* was explored in more detail in chapter 4.

Air transportation can be broken down into scheduled and nonscheduled or charter operations. Scheduled services fly on defined routes and times on the basis of published timetables irrespective of passenger-load factors. Scheduled airlines may be publicly or privately owned. The amount of private vs. public ownership will vary with the political philosophy of the host country. In most countries, the public airline will be the national flag carrier and is usually the only airline designated for international flights. In the United States, the airlines are privately owned.

The number of national flag carriers remaining totally in state ownership is shrinking year by year. State ownership is the exception in north, south, and central America. In Europe, British Air and Lufthansa are the only major flag carriers without government involvement. Governments in the Middle East and Africa are keen to privatize but the fact that the airlines are operating at a loss tends to deter most purchasers. Privatization continues to increase in the Far East. Of the top 100 airlines, 62 are in 100 percent private ownership, 18 are in partial privatization, and 20 in full state ownership. Privately owned take nine out of the top ten slots (Hanlon, 1999).

United States carriers are designated as either major carriers, national carriers, or regional carriers. Carriers are classified as major carriers if they have annual gross revenues of over $1 billion. They include United, American, and Continental Airlines. National carriers have annual gross revenues of $75 million to $1 billion. Companies that run commuter airlines are now classified as regional air carriers. A large regional airline is one whose annual gross revenue falls between $10 and $75 million, while a small regional is one with annual gross revenues of less than $10 million. The market share of the major U.S. airlines in 2007 was (*Wall Street Journal*, 2008):

- 17.1 percent   American
- 14.5   United
- 12.8   Delta
- 10.4   Continental
- 9.0   Northwest
- 8.9   Southwest
- 7.6   U.S. Airways

(Note: At the time of writing, Northwest and Delta were poised to merge.)

In Canada, airlines are designated as Level I, II, III, or IV carriers, depending upon their size. There are two Level I carriers in Canada: Air Canada and Canadian Airlines.

Charter airlines fly only on routes where they can generate high passenger-load factors—typically 85 to 90 percent. Because they are not obligated to fly regardless of load factor, their revenues per flight are much higher than those of scheduled airlines. Additionally, they keep costs low by saving on marketing, offering less in the way of service both in the air and on the ground, and having lower overhead costs. In this way they can offer, in many cases, substantial fare savings over scheduled airlines. As a result, charters tend to operate to high-volume destinations. A recent trend has been the tendency for tour operators to form or take over their own charter airlines in order to ensure seat availability for their passengers. Prior to the 1960s, charters could operate only through closed groups made up of members of a club or organization whose main purpose was something other than low-cost travel. Many bogus clubs were formed, and policing became increasingly difficult. The 1970s saw a liberalization of charter restrictions. The scheduled airlines had a difficult dilemma. They did not wish to discount prices for passengers who were willing to pay the higher fares, but they wished to capture a share of the market. One answer was the *advanced purchase excursion fare (APEX)*, which required passengers to book and pay for their trip in advance.

Increased capacity brought about by deregulation has meant that scheduled airlines were forced to reduce prices to attract the traveler. The result was that charter flights lost their price competitive edge in many cases.

Charters remain popular in Europe, where deregulation is moving more slowly than in the United States. The success of charter airlines in Europe will depend upon their ability to move with the changing demands of the market. This might mean selling seats only (instead of an air-land package), offering scheduled flights, and new, less crowded destinations. There will also be a demand for more activity holidays, winter vacations, and more flexible packages, such as multi-center and fly-drive options. Increased demands for higher-quality service will also challenge charter operators.

A major problem for airlines—particularly in North America—is the safety of air travel. While flying is still much safer than traveling by car, the high profile of one air crash puts concern into the minds of many travelers. The safety record for major airlines is slightly less than for so-called upstart airlines. The Federal Aviation Administration defines an aircraft accident as "an incident in which any person suffers death or serious injury as a result of being in or in direct contact with an aircraft."

New aircraft are being developed that are safer and more fuel efficient. The newest 747 (400) jet airliner can fly from New York to Tokyo entirely by computer and, if necessary, even land automatically. It offers more range, better fuel economy, and lower operating costs. Its 8,400-mile range almost doubles that of the original 747, while it consumes one-third less fuel. One factor that makes it particularly safe is the triple and quadruple redundancy of its systems. Complete failure of any one system is a million-to-one possibility. Bigger planes are in the works. Airbus has in production a new full-length, double-decker super jumbo, with one level of 300 people stacked atop another in a three-class layout, or 400 on each level on all economy flights. Boeing's version of a super jumbo, designed to seat 500 or more, involves stretching both decks of the 747. The super jumbos are too big to taxi around most airports and to park at their gates so airports would have to build structures to handle them. The airlines have their own set of demands for the super jumbos. The turnaround time of these planes—the time it takes to refuel, clean, and restock the jet and put it in the sky—must be no longer than it takes now for a 747 (about 100 minutes). The operating cost is very important to the airlines as it varies significantly by type of plane. For example, in 1995 dollars, the hourly operating cost for a 747 is $6,686 compared to $1,409 for a DC-9.

In the United States and in Europe the major carriers are facing increased competition from low-fare competitors. In the United States, of the top 1,000 city pairs, major carriers faced competition from low-fare competi-

tors on 50 percent of the routings in 2000. That percentage increased to 80 percent by 2005.

Until recently the major carriers controlled most of the landing slots at the half-dozen most crowded airports in the United States. This allowed them to protect

QUICK TRIP 16.5

The High Price of Airline Travel

Many travelers rely on the convenience and reliability of the airline industry as a mode of constant transportation. The question now is for how long each airline will be able to survive. Financially speaking, the airlines are running out of breathable air. Since 2001, 123,000 U.S. airline workers have lost their jobs in the airlines' attempt to cut costs and stay afloat. Those employees left standing have experienced both wage and benefit decreases; and although productivity is up and capital spending and operating expenses have been reduced, the bottom line is still feeling the pressure. *TourismReview.com* says the problem is not a failure to manage controllable costs but, instead, an assortment of costs that are beyond the airlines' control and nearly impossible to transfer.

Federally imposed taxes and fees are accounting for 26 percent of a domestic roundtrip ticket. Security costs are also high; although Congress has agreed that airport security should be handled financially by the federal government, airlines are still being forced to pay this hefty price tag. Fuel is the third factor affecting airline costs. Even as companies become more fuel efficient, it is unlikely that they will ever be able to beat the increasing barrel prices.

Regardless of these increasing costs, airline ticket prices have been falling for years. A ticket today costs half of what it did in 1978. In the savagely competitive business environment, a great deal of pressure is placed on airlines to provide lower and lower prices. The problem is that these slashed prices are not adequate to cover the industry's basic costs. So eventually, the costs will have to rise and what will consumers do then?

THINK ABOUT THIS:

1. Many people wonder at what point consumers will alter their spending on fuel. Similarly, at what point would individuals alter their travel plans because of increased ticket prices?

Source: *TourismReview.com*. 2008. Airlines to Airports: We have a Problem, by James C. May.

themselves from low-cost competition. In addition they maintained "fortress" hubs from which they controlled as much as 80 percent of the traffic. Finally, they dominated long-haul, coast-to-coast routes as well as traffic from midsized cities to their hubs. This is no longer the case for these three items. Low-fare carriers are able to do a better job of keeping their costs down. This can be seen from the following illustration showing airline average costs in the first quarter of 2004 (per available seat mile):

JetBlue	6.1 cents
Southwest	7.7
American	9.5
Continental	9.8
United	10.2
Northwest	10.2
Delta	10.7
US Airways	11.7

Miller & Associates, Inc. 2005.

Concern has also been expressed over security at airports. The General Accounting Office reported the existence of security deficiencies at U.S. high-security airports. Chief among these were ineffective passenger screening and inadequate controls over personnel identification systems and over access to those parts of the airport where aircraft operate. Concern for safety has been felt in the response of travelers to terrorist threats. Direct and indirect security costs total more than $3.8 billion for the entire airline industry. That figure equates to 48,000 airline jobs or 349,000 commercial flights.

Because airlines are limited in their ability to adjust to these new levels by increasing seat densities, much of the capacity growth will come from more flights on existing and new routes. The fear is that congestion in the skies over the region will follow the lead of Europe and will become a problem. It is estimated, for example, that congestion problems in Europe are costing the airlines $5 billion each year.

Various communities continue to explore the possibility of rail services linking airports and replacing some short-haul feeder services. A major difficulty for airlines is the time it takes getting from the airport to the business district, usually in the city center. In Europe the development of high-speed trains has extended rail's competitiveness for distances up to three hundred miles. The major disadvantage comes when passengers are making onward connections.

Capacity constraints at European airports is a major problem. In order to gain access to a congested airport,

Flights between tourist destinations are limited by the number of take-off and landing slots available at the airports. © 2009 Xavier Marchant. Used under license from Shutterstock, Inc.

many regional airlines are going into partnership with a major airline. Flights between tourist destinations are limited by the number of airline take-off and landing slots available at the airports. European slot policy has been self-administered through the International Air Transport Association (IATA), the airlines trade association, under the principle of grandfather rights and "effective use." The former concept means that an airline that held the slot last year is entitled to do so next year. The idea of "effective use" is that preference is given to an airline that wishes to use the slot more intensively (daily rather than weekly or throughout the season rather than only in the peak). Thus, daily scheduled carriers are favored over charters, and incumbents are favored over new entrants into the field. Recent European Union regulations essentially follow the IATA guidelines.

In 2008, an "Open Skies" agreement was signed between the United States and eleven European Union (EU) countries where the United States had restrictive agreements or none at all that allow airlines to fly between any of the affected countries. Before this agreement, for example, British Air could fly between Britain and the United States. Now it can fly between France and the United States. This is regarded as the first step in negotiations intended to open up the U.S. domestic market.

In the United States, the IATA system is not employed because of anti-trust laws, and slots tend to be allocated on a first-come, first-served basis. Since 1986 the Federal Aviation Administration (FAA) has allowed slots to be sold for money rather than traded in the "one for one" IATA system. A peak-time slot can cost several millions of dollars.

Destinations that rely on air traffic coming from congested airports are especially vulnerable to the scarcity of take-off and landing slots (Debbage, 2002).

The air transportation industry is facing a number of challenges:

- Reconciling the benefits of globalization and growth with the need to retain local identity and individuality
- Protecting against sudden and damaging worldwide financial shocks
- Protecting the natural environment
- Dealing with the potential use and misuse of "interconnectability"
- Re-defining the role of the state in the modern economy
- Infrastructure

Protests at meetings of the World Trade Organization have focused on the fact that the global market is not just about an economic system and that it will foster the development of a set of cultural "global" cultural values. The challenge for the airline industry is to encourage flexible bilateral agreements beneficial to all negotiating parties. After the Asian financial crisis in the late 1990s there was serious re-trenching on the part of some airlines and the transfer of capacity to mature markets such as the North Atlantic. Airlines are increasingly dependent on the available discretionary income because leisure travel seized the majority share of the world air travel market some time ago. Any future financial shock will significantly affect the size origin and profitability of that market.

The challenge of connectivity among airlines is how to use it profitably. There will be many additional alliances and mergers among the world's airlines. IATA is also very much involved in e-commerce to set standards and has proposed the development of an international e-ticket interlining facility.

As noted earlier, around the world governments are returning entire sectors of the economy to private hands and the discipline of market forces. In aviation governments are shedding themselves of airlines. IATA is concerned about two issues in this regard. First is to ensure that liberalization proceeds in a manner which produces the best balance of benefits to consumers, airlines, and the public interest. Second, that the critical elements of global industry systems which allow airline products and services to be so universally available and efficient are preserved.

> I dislike feeling at home when I am abroad.
>
> George Bernard Shaw quoted in "The Quotable Traveler"

The concern for infrastructure comes from the forecast that over the foreseeable period demand for aviation products and services will continue to double every ten to fourteen years. Aviation growth will be limited if governments simply ignore the necessary improvements to aviation infrastructure or privatize it without adequate safeguard.

In summary, the airplane has in the post-World War II era taken over as the major international and intercontinental transportation mode. It also predominates among the common carriers in domestic transportation in the United States and Canada. It is a particularly important mode for the business travelers who have the time factor as a major consideration. Additionally, charter flights, since their introduction, have become increasingly important as vacation travel modes, particularly in Europe.

TRAVEL BY BUS AND MOTORCOACH

The third principal common-carrier mode is the bus. The term bus is used to describe intercity travel while *coach* or *motorcoach* describe charter or tour travel.

Only 15 percent of person-trips on Greyhound were for pleasure travel, excluding visits to friends and relatives. This compares to 43 percent of total person-trips in the United States for this purpose. As can be seen, most travel by bus is of the intercity type.

In 1983 the bus industry in the United States was deregulated. Prior to that time an Interstate Commerce Commission-licensed bus company or tour broker had to prove need before receiving authority to operate. At that time few motorcoach operators employed marketing representatives. Many had a small individual tour program, and most had a larger group tour program. The majority were still charter operators, while many operated regular group service as well. Tour brokers were generally smaller operations, many tied to a retail travel agency.

The impact of deregulation can be seen in the growth of motorcoach companies. In 1983 there were 1,500 motorcoach companies licensed by the ICC. Today there are almost 3,600 private motorcoach companies operating 38,000 motorcoaches in the United States and Canada. Only 1 percent of the industry consists of large carriers, defined as those operating more than one hundred motorcoaches. However, they account for 25 percent of the motorcoaches and employees in the industry. One-third of all miles are logged on charters, while less than 10 percent are accounted for by tours and sightseeing trips. The largest companies in North America are Greyhound Lines, Inc., Coach USA, Inc., and Boston Coach, while the major tour operators are Grey Line Worldwide and Trafalgar Tours. Tour brokers were deregulated out of existence. Many became tour operators or tour organizers.

Britain's state-owned bus industry was sold to private investors and deregulated in the mid-1980s. Instead of the initial plan of hundreds of small operators each owning a few vehicles, a few large companies have most of the business and many small operations have been driven out of business or were taken over by larger concerns. There are almost 600 million passenger trips by motorcoach in the U.S. and Canada each year.

About half of the motorcoaches used in the United States are for scheduled intercity service. An additional one-third are used for charters. The rest are used for tours, shuttle and commuter service.

For the purposes of tourism, the potential lies with the use of coaches for touring vacations. People go on tours for reasons that are practical and emotional. The practical benefits are convenience, expertise, safety, and price.

Tours are convenient in that the vacation can be spent concentrating on the experience rather than on making the arrangements. Having someone else doing the driving is important in terms of dealing with city traffic, driving in unfamiliar areas, and spending time reading maps rather than enjoying the scenery. Tours offer the convenience of being picked up and delivered to hotels, sights, and entertainment. Accommodation and event tickets are guaranteed, which is particularly important for high-season events or times. Last, the idea of the baggage being taken care of is appreciated. This is particularly true for single women and older people.

People who take tours feel that they can see and do more than if they were traveling alone. There is the feeling that the operator has the expertise to select the best places to see. Because of this, participants can actually see more because they do not have to spend time evaluating all of the options. Also, there is safety in numbers. This is particularly true for older or female travelers and for urban or unfamiliar destinations.

The fixed price of a tour is an important feature. The most important part, however, is not the absolute price but the fact that the costs are known beforehand. There is little or no danger of being halfway through one's vacation and running out of money because of poor budgeting. The tour is prepaid. The only other costs are some meals, sightseeing, and shopping.

People also take tours for emotional reasons: companionship, an opportunity to learn, shared activities, and security. Tours offer the opportunity to meet new people and make new friends. Many see it as an opportunity to get an overview of a destination—to discover and learn. Adventure touring is important to younger travelers, while historical touring is mentioned by older tourists.

Group travel is seen as a way of participating in activities with others who have the same interests. This can include physical activity tours such as skiing or water sports, as well as theater, garden, or historic homes tours. In all of this, there is the opportunity to be further educated in a particular area.

The senior motorcoach market has been broken down into three segments:

1. **Dependents** are older and have a lower educational level than either of the other two segments. They account for over half of the entire market. They tend to be price conscious as well as rather demanding.
2. **Sociables** account for less than 20 percent of the market. They enjoy evening entertainment and group activities. Because they are younger seniors, they may well be interested in more physically active social programs compared to the others. This segment has higher incomes than the other two segments.
3. **Independents**, 30 percent of the total, are concerned about health and safety issues. They are younger, have a higher education and a moderate income. They are the least demanding of the three segments (Hsu and Lee, 2002).

The security angle comes from the feeling of being an insider even in an unfamiliar place. This is an emotional appeal compared to the physical feeling of safety, explored previously. In light of the terrorist attacks of 9/11, changes have been made so travelers feel secure traveling by motorcoach.

Table 16.5
Reasons Why Clients Choose a Motorcoach Tour

Reason	Under 50	50+
Make new friends	91%	72%
More convenient	91	67
Safe	83	61
Learn more	86	51
Less expensive	74	54

Increased concern about security is one reason that educational groups, senior citizens and travel clubs have cut back on travel.

The negative images that people have about tours fall into four categories: perceptions of the bus, the tour experience, the group concept, and the types of people who take tours. For a number of people, tours are associated rather negatively with buses. The term *motorcoach* is used by the industry to designate touring buses. Particularly in Europe most coaches are extremely comfortable with videos, attendants who serve drinks, and reclining seats. However, despite the fact that such equipment is available in the United States (albeit on a lesser scale), the image brought to mind is too often the school or commuter bus. The bus is seen as too slow, too confining, and too uncomfortable. It is viewed as a cheap and old-fashioned way to travel. Travelers also have a negative image of bus terminals and view this as an undesirable place to start a vacation. Additionally, some people—particularly men—dislike the idea of giving up control to the coach driver. They complain about not being able to control the lights, the fans, or where and when to stop.

For people who do not take tours, the experience itself is perceived negatively. Touring, to many, is equated with regimentation, inflexibility, and passivity. The tour is seen as a shallow, boring, and impersonal experience. There are also those who think that, rather than receiving the advantages of group power, being part of a group involves getting second-class treatment from hotels and restaurants. Yet another barrier to be overcome in selling tours is the group aspect of the tour. There is a fear of not relating well to other members of the group. To many people, a vacation involves having personal space and freedom. Being part of a group limits both. Last, many have a negative perception of the kinds of people who take tours. People who travel as part of a group are seen by many, stereotypically, as infirm, older, inexperienced travelers. This translates into a personality profile of tour-goers as passive and lacking in self-confidence.

To rid itself of these negatives, those who package tours need to be more innovative in upgrading the image and the content of tours. Perhaps even the word *tour* needs to be changed into "adventure holiday," "expedition," "discovery trip" or "excursion." Different modes of transportation can be used in conjunction with each other: air to get the traveler there and coach to see the destination.

Hub-and-spoke concepts can be used to bring people to a destination where they can relax on their own. Shorter mini-trips can be packaged with more free time, and tours themed around recreational activities can be developed to appeal to the younger, more active crowd.

Contiki Holidays has identified four categories of eighteen- to thirty-five-year-old travelers who might be good candidates for motorcoach tours (*Travel Weekly*, 1994). They are overseas students attending school in the United States, international visitors who want to see the country, younger American travelers who want to mix with an international group, and young people who might otherwise have planned a cross-country driving trip. It notes the advantage of being able to see as much of the country as possible and traveling great distances without the problems associated with road travel, such as breakdowns, finding affordable accommodations, and getting lost.

MARKETING OF PASSENGER TRANSPORTATION

Transportation marketing seeks to satisfy the needs and wants of the traveler by providing the right mix of services. To appreciate the difficulties involved, it is necessary to consider the characteristics of supply and demand for passenger transportation.

CHARACTERISTICS OF DEMAND

The demand for passenger transportation has a number of characteristics, all of which affect the way a company markets. First, demand is instantaneous. For carriers there is great uncertainty as to what the demand will be on a particular day at a particular time between points.

> Travel as tourism has become like the activity of a prisoner pacing a cell much crossed and grooved by other equally mobile and "free" captives. What was once the agent of our liberty has become a means for the revelation of our containment.
>
> Eric J. Leed

While past trends are useful, they cannot be totally reliable. When demand is greater than supply, travelers are unhappy. By the time adjustments are made to supply more capacity, customers may have changed carriers or found an alternate means of transportation. The tendency, then, would be to provide more capacity than needed. Overcapacity shows up in the load factor. In a perfect match of supply and demand, the load factor would be 100 percent. Anything less indicates the measure of overcapacity. The challenge in marketing is to create programs to fill each plane, train, ship, or bus on each trip.

Overcapacity is the result, not only of instantaneous demand, but also of the variability of demand. Demand for transportation is not the same each hour of each day of each month. It shows what is known as peaks and valleys. At certain times of the day or week or month, there is great demand; at other times the demand is light. Yet sufficient planes, boats, trains, buses, and terminal facilities have to be provided to cover peak demand. The result is that excess capital has to be invested. As a result, the costs of operation are increased. How should demand be priced? Should the peak traveler pay more than the off-peak traveler? Peak-load pricing states that those traveling at peak times should pay more for the extra capacity provided to meet peak demand. Some off-peak pricing is found in the airline industry and with passenger trains. Reduced midweek and night fares are an attempt at peak pricing.

Another characteristic of demand is that there is, in fact, more than one type or segment of demand for transportation. In its simplest terms, demand is either business demand or pleasure demand. The motivations, frequencies, and responses to price are different. The motivation for the business traveler is *derived*–that is, the demand for travel exists because of the desire to do business in a particular territory. Demand for the pleasure travel is *primary*–the motivation is to travel to a vacation spot. The distinction is important because derived demand tends to be affected more by factors external to the transportation industry. No matter how good the services between New York and Detroit, if business is bad in Detroit, travel demand may go down. A reduction in fares, for example, may affect primary demand but may not affect derived demand.

The business traveler travels more frequently than does the pleasure traveler. This makes the business traveler very valuable to the airline. Frequent-flier programs, which offer rewards based on miles traveled, have been targeted toward the business traveler in an attempt to capture customer loyalty. As mentioned above, derived demand may not be affected by changes in price. The company may absorb a fare increase as a cost of doing business. The business traveler may choose a more convenient, but more expensive, flight since the company and not the individual is paying for it.

In some situations people can substitute one mode of transportation for another: train for plane, bus for train,

Business travel is essential to the airline industry. © 2009 Galina Barskaya. Used under license from Shutterstock, Inc.

and so on. This affects the way transportation is marketed. *Elasticity* is the economic term for the sensitivity of travelers to changes in price and service. An elastic demand is sensitive to substitution; an inelastic demand is not. The extent of elasticity is dependent upon the price of the other mode of transportation and the type of demand. Pleasure travel is more price elastic than is business travel; primary demand is more price elastic than is derived demand. When people choose how to travel, the decision is made on the basis of price, prestige, comfort, speed, and convenience. Amtrak could successfully compete with the plane on certain distances on the basis of these factors.

Competition also exists within one mode between carriers. Generally prices and the speed of the journey are the same or similar among competing carriers. Carriers must then market on the basis of the factors mentioned above: prestige, comfort, and convenience. Often a small change in departure time can capture a significant number of passengers. This explains much of the congestion at airports at certain times–everyone wants to offer flights at what are felt to be the most convenient times for the traveler.

Another aspect of demand is that some transportation modes offer more than one type of service. Airline passengers can fly economy, business class, or first class; trains also offer various classes of service. The different types of service are in competition with each other. Airlines, for example, have to decide the proportions of first class, business class, and economy or tourist class seats to offer on a plane. They then decide what additional services are necessary to justify the price differential–more legroom, better meals, free drinks, and the like.

Demand for transportation is also affected by the relationship between the price charged and the income level of the traveler. Pleasure travel is income elastic; that is, the demand for travel is affected by changes in the traveler's income. Economists say that demand is elastic when a reduction in price results in more demand that will result in more revenue. (Revenue equals price times number demanded.) The company gains revenue because the increased demand brought about by a drop in price makes up for the reduced price. Similarly, an inelastic demand is one where a reduction in price results in less revenue generated. More passengers may be attracted but not in sufficient numbers to offset the loss of revenue brought about by the reduction in price. Pleasure travel is discretionary—the traveler has a choice of whether or not to travel. An increase in price may mean the traveler will postpone the vacation.

Business travel is also influenced by the income of the company. Much business travel is essential; some is discretionary. Businesses may turn to *teleconferencing* as a way of reducing the travel bill if costs increase too much. Last, the demand for travel makes itself felt in a demand for nonprice items. The frequency of departures, the condition of the equipment, the service of the employees, on-time performance—the whole package— is often more important than the price. Companies have to find out what is important to the different segments of the market they are going after (the list will be different for each) and seek to provide it.

CHARACTERISTICS OF SUPPLY

Just as the marketing of transportation is affected by the characteristics of demand, so is it influenced by the supply characteristics. The supply of transportation is unique in eight distinct ways. First, the transportation industry is a *capital-intensive* industry. Terminals and equipment cost a great deal of money. The costs are also *indivisible*—airlines cannot put "half a plane" in the air if the plane is only half full. Because the industry is capital-intensive and much of the capital is borrowed, many of the costs of running a transportation company are fixed; interest on the debt must be paid in full, irrespective of the number of passengers and revenue. This puts a great deal of pressure on management to fill seats that would otherwise be empty. This may affect both the promotional and pricing decisions.

Related to this previous point is the fact that transportation costs are "*sunk*" with few alternatives. The cost of a plane is sunk in that the company has incurred the cost of it. It is up to the company to generate revenue to pay for the plane. It is not like a light that can be turned off, thereby saving money. Planes also have few alternative uses. It can fly; it might be possible to sell it as a unique type of restaurant, but essentially all the company can do with it is fly it. This puts additional pressure on the company to use the resource rather than have it lie idle. The large amounts of sunk costs also mean that there is a tendency to use old equipment rather than invest in more modern (and more expensive) equipment.

Another characteristic of supply is that, although demand is instantaneous, supply is not. There is a long time between planning for a piece of equipment and placing the order for it, between placing the order and getting it, and between putting it into service and scrapping it. Thus, while demand can shift very quickly, it takes a great deal of time to adjust supply. A company must live with its mistakes for a very long time.

Because of the high level of fixed costs, the *incremental costs* of operation are small. The incremental cost is the cost of adding one more unit. The running costs of adding another passenger car to a train, another bus to a route, or even a plane between two points is small compared to the costs of an actual piece of equipment. If a plane is scheduled to fly anyway, the cost of an additional passenger is incredibly small—an extra snack and some services. This means that, above a certain point, it makes economic sense to reduce the price charged in order to get some revenue coming in. This is the rationale behind discount fares. Airlines can predict, based on past records, how many seats on a particular flight will sell within a week before a flight. The people who book within a week before a flight are usually business people. Assume, for example, that on a particular flight 80 percent of the seats will be bought at the regular fare in the last week before the flight. This means that the airline can sell up to 20 percent of the seats at a discount for people who will book and pay for tickets more than seven days before a flight.

Another characteristic is that *supply cannot be stored* for future use. A grocery store can sell a can of dog food today, tomorrow, or the next day. Every seat on a plane or train or bus must be sold only for that trip. The sale that is lost today is lost forever. This puts additional pressure on management to sell, sell, sell.

Transportation services must be *available on a continuous basis*. The traveler expects the same level of service whether it is day or night, summer or winter, if the plane is full or almost empty. Because transportation is expected to be reliable on a continuous basis, there is little opportunity to cut costs for inferior service at odd hours. This adds to the cost of providing the service.

Last, there is the problem of *labor*. In transporting people, the company take on a great responsibility. Often the service—whether in operations or in maintenance—is offered twenty-four hours a day. Employees must be equally alert, no matter what the time. There are strict rules about the amount of time that pilots, drivers, or operators can be on duty at any one stretch. The Federal Aviation Administration (FAA) limits pilots to thirty hours of flying in any seven-day period. Although the operating costs are small compared to the sunk costs, they can still be considerable. Airline pilots are paid well for their skills. A further complication is that there is little opportunity for the substitution of capital for labor. This is, after all, a service business.

Marketing has the task of ensuring that there is sufficient demand to utilize the supply of equipment and facilities fully. It must also ensure that there is enough of the right kind of supply to meet the demands of the passengers. Just as demand influences supply, so supply influences demand. The demand for vacations in Jamaica will influence a decision to operate flights to Jamaica; however, the existence of flights to Jamaica at the time and prices appropriate to the market will stimulate demand. Marketing brings supply and demand together.

MARKETING STRATEGIES

In marketing, the offerings of a firm are known as the four "p's": product, promotion, place, and price. In tourism it is appropriate to change the "product" to include service and to replace "place" with distribution.

Service refers to getting the ideal mix of services to satisfy existing or potential customers. This means offering transportation at the right times, in the right kinds of equipment, while giving a level of service before, during, and after the journey that will meet the needs of the customer—all while making profit.

Most carriers use a linear route structure—the equipment travels from one point to another, turns around, and travels back. In the airline industry most fuel is used at takeoff and landing. Also, the speed of travel by plane is only appreciated on longer flights. Thus, for reasons of cost and customer benefit, jet aircraft operate in the most efficient manner when they fly on long-hauls. A piece of equipment may, however, make an intermediate stop. While this increases the time and fuel costs, it can add significant additional revenue.

The emphasis has moved away from line networks as costs are high because station costs are spread over a few flights using each airport. Thus, marketing is difficult and the average cost is also high. In addition, cockpit crews either have long stopovers or need to be ferried to their next flight. In either case, labor costs are high. Flights, especially those at the tail ends of routes, tend to operate with low load factors. Yields tend to be poor because of the low frequency of flights and the fact that line networks do not appeal to business travelers.

The airlines also operate what is known as a hub-and-spoke concept. Airlines have identified several major cities that serve as hubs (as in hub of a wheel) for them. Smaller towns serve as the spokes of a wheel connected to these hubs. Airlines attempt to have passengers fly into their hub city on a smaller or commuter plane for connection to a larger plane for travel to their ultimate destination. Colorado Springs is a spoke city for the Denver hub, which is itself a spoke city for

Chicago, which is a spoke city (on United) for London. Increasing hub development will result in more convenient service for passengers. There will be more nonstops as smaller cities become hubs and displace larger cities as connecting points. In hub and spoke, flights radiate from a central hub to various outlying spokes thereby multiplying the number of city pairs an airline can serve (Hanlon, 1999).

If there are n spokes, an airline can provide service for $\frac{n(n-1)}{2}$ city pairs. When added to the n city pairs to and from the hub itself, the possible city pair markets are $\frac{n(n+1)}{2}$ (see below).

Table 16.6
Possible City Pair Markets

Number of spokes	max. # connecting markets	# of local markets	max # city pair markets
n	$\frac{n(n-1)}{2}$	n	$\frac{n(n+1)}{2}$
5	10	5	15
10	45	10	55
20	190	20	210
40	780	40	820
80	3160	80	3240

Hub and spoke is the predominant pattern in international operations. Since each country claims sovereignty for service above its country, international flights can only be flown with the consent of the governments involved, and only airlines registered in the states involved are licensed to travel that route. Thus, national airlines operate most of the flights to and from their home country.

An airline needs a hub located along one of the main flows of traffic that carry the maximum amount of connecting traffic. The ideal is to have a hub that can carry both north-south and east-west traffic. This explains why many important hubs in the United States are to be found toward the center of the country, and why some airports along the eastern or western seaboards have not, for the most part, emerged as major hubs, as their suitability for domestic linkages is limited to those on the north-south axis.

There are three tactics that airlines are using to extend their network (Hanlon, 1999):

1. **Franchising**—where one airline allows another to use its name, uniforms and image. The practice is widespread in North America but is in its infancy elsewhere.

2. **Block spacing**—where one airline sets aside a number of seats on some of its flights for use by another airline. The other airline then markets the seats to its own customers. This option is used when the airline to whom the seats are allocated is unable to serve the airport itself.

3. **Code-sharing**—one airline allows another to offer a flight under its own flight code, even though it does not operate the service. This practice is becoming widespread worldwide. In the U.S. regional industry, about 96 percent of passengers fly on code-sharing airlines.

Major air carriers have made increasing use of *code-sharing agreements* with regional airlines. Code-sharing involves the joint use by a regional carrier of a major airline's two-letter designation on its air routes and usually involves a commuter traffic fleet at the major's hub. In this way, the regionals serve as feeder lines to the majors. In 1994 there were 280 alliance agreements; by 2007 this number increased to over 500. The major global airline alliances are:

ONEWORLD
Aer Lingus
American
British Airways
Cathay Pacific
Draonair
Finnair
Iberia
Japan Airlines
LAN Airlines
Malev
Qantas
Royal Jordanian

SKYTEAM
Aeroflot
Aeromexico
Air France
Alitalia
China Southern
Continental
CSA Czech Airlines
Delta
Korean
KLM
Korean Air
Northwest

STAR ALLIANCE
Air Canada
Air China
Air New Zealand
All Nippon Airways
Asiana Airlines
Austrian Airlines
bmi
LOT Polish Airlines
Lufthansa
Scandinavian Airlines
Shanghai Airlines
Singapore Airlines
Spanair
South African Airlines
Swiss
TAP Portugal
Thai Airways
THY Turkish Airlines
United Airlines
US Airways
Varig

Airline Alliance Survey, 2007. Retrieved 25 April 2008, http://www.flightglobal.com/alliances.

Five major alliances—Star, Oneworld, Qualiflyer, Sky Team and Wings—account for 60 percent of all air travel. It is hoped that alliances will result in seamless travel across the group network, better customer service at ticketing and check-in, and a wider route network for collecting mileage points and loyalty rewards. The potential benefits of airline alliances to travelers are many, and include (Weber, 2005):

- Ease of transfers between flights
- Smoother baggage handling
- One-stop check-in
- Better assistance in case of problems
- Respectful treatment
- Consistently high service quality
- Ability to earn frequent flyer miles or points
- Improved connections
- Expanded route network
- Access to partner lounge

In contrast to findings from previous research that indicate that the ability to earn frequent flyer miles or points and an expanded route network are the benefits travelers are most aware of, one study finds that travelers' convenience is seen as a more important benefit of airline alliances. Differences also appear depending upon the travelers' country of origin. Importance ratings are lower for those in Western countries compared to Asian residents in all but two factors: respectful treatment and the ability to earn frequent flyer miles.

The concept has been taken internationally. United States airlines have pursued code-sharing agreements protected from anti-trust violations with international airlines in an attempt to secure gate rights at international airports. The Department of Transportation (DOT) finds that code-sharing produces substantial benefits for U.S. passengers although participating U.S. airlines do not benefit as much as their foreign partners. For example, the DOT reported that a code-sharing arrangement between British Airways and USAir resulted in an estimated annual gain to British Airways of $27.2 million and an annual benefit to USAir of only $5.6 million. The partnership has since been dissolved. DOT also indicates that Asia is the next hot spot for code-sharing alliances.

The first *frequent flyer program* was introduced by American Airlines in 1981. The idea was successful in building brand loyalty to a single airline. In an attempt to minimize the cost of passengers flying with accumulated miles, airlines have placed restrictions on the use of this free travel.

Service must be provided on the right kind of equipment. Equipment has two facets that must be matched: identifying the operating costs of one piece of equipment over another while offering equipment that will attract the traveler. One example is the Concorde. While this supersonic aircraft could draw passengers because of its speed and unique shape, the operating costs are so high that the potential market is relatively small. Both British Airways and Air France have discontinued Concorde.

Scheduling is a major marketing weapon for carriers. Traveling from point A to point B leaves little opportunity for differentiating one firm from another. Offering departure times most convenient for the passenger is one way to do this. Unfortunately, everyone wants to do this. The result, certainly in the airline industry, is severe congestion at the most popular times. Generally speaking, the demand for business travel peaks on Monday mornings and Friday evenings, Sunday afternoons, and early evenings.

Service can also be altered by such things as upgrading the quality of the interior of the vehicle. Research has shown that for short-haul flights, business travelers prefer punctuality (65 percent), schedules (52 percent), competitive fares (37 percent), comfort of seat/legroom (33 percent), and staff service (32 percent). However, for long-haul flights the passengers' priorities change. Comfort of seat/legroom is rated as most important (63 percent) followed by punctuality (43 percent), schedules (38 percent), staff service (34 percent), and competitive fares (32 percent). SAS used results like this to change the interior of their intercontinental planes. They had found, additionally, that on 767s people are less comfortable in the middle seats. Given the importance of the airplane in making a trip of five hours or more, they removed the middle seats from their business class cabin. Service could also be altered by providing tie-ins with other modes, such as fly/cruise or rail/drive.

Promotion can be seen as the communications link between carrier and passenger. It is the responsibility of the carrier to communicate its message effectively. If the passenger has not understood, it is the fault of the carrier. To this end, it is important that clear promotional objectives be defined. These objectives should identify which target markets are to be reached, what tasks have to be done to reach the markets, who is to perform the task, and when they have to be completed. It is vital that the promotional theme be in synch with the marketing plan, which, in turn, must be consistent with the overall objectives of the carrier. A carrier may, for example, feel that, in order to meet its financial targets, it must emphasize quality and service. The way then, to reach the target is to stress quality and service. These concepts become the essence of the marketing campaign. As part of that plan, communicating the ideas of service and quality to the public becomes the promotional objective.

Distribution involves the mechanisms by which passengers can obtain the information they need to make a trip choice and, having made that choice, make the necessary reservations. *Direct distribution* occurs when passengers get in touch with the carriers directly. *Indirect distribution* is when the sale is made through an intermediary.

This latter has taken four forms. First is the emergence of independent companies to handle all aspects of travel. It might involve a wholesaler who arranges the specific tour, for example; it might be a retail travel agent who serves as an independent distributor for a wholesaler or carrier; it may be one of the wholesaler-retailers who package their own tours or who buy packages from other wholesalers for distribution.

A second movement has been the marketing of tourism, either regionally or nationally. Countries, provinces, and states promote travel to their particular destinations. This effort supplements the marketing plans of the carriers. In some cases the marketing effort of the carrier can dovetail with that of the destination.

A third trend has been the coordination of marketing plans by various private-sector companies. Tie-ins between airlines and hotels or bus lines and various attractions are becoming more prevalent.

Last, there is the movement toward *vertical integration.* Airlines have moved in to take control of hotels and car-rental agencies. This has been an attempt to develop a "one-stop travel shop" experience for the traveler. The strategy backfired a number of years ago for United Airlines, which formed Allegis—an amalgamation of airline, hotel, and car-rental companies. Under stockholder pressure they were forced to divest themselves of the non-airline parts of the company.

When the majority of airline passengers consisted of people traveling on business and rather wealthy tourists, the airlines felt that the demand for travel was inelastic. That is, if prices were reduced, any increase in number of passengers would not produce more revenue. Because of this and a fear that open pricing would lead to price wars that might result in bankruptcy for smaller airlines, airline pricing was closely controlled. Pricing was a reflection of operating costs. The average costs of carriers serving particular markets were calculated, and a reasonable return on investment was added to come up with the price that could be charged. With deregulation a new era has come to pricing in transportation in general and in the airline industry in particular.

Three economic concepts are important when looking at pricing alternatives. They are the ideas of differential pricing, the contribution theory, and the incremental concept. Underlying *differential pricing* is the idea that there is not one demand curve, but many. A separate demand exists for coach than exists for first class; separate demand exists for travel from Denver to New York than from New York to Denver. As such, carriers can calculate how price-sensitive demand is in one particular class or on one particular route and price accordingly. The demand for business travel, for example, is probably less sensitive to price changes than the demand for pleasure travel on that same route at that same time. A higher price can be charged where demand is inelastic.

The idea of *contribution theory* is that prices should be set at the level that contributes most to paying off costs while still allowing traffic to move. The fare charged might be low on a route where the demand is elastic and higher where demand is inelastic. In effect, segments of the market that are price inelastic are subsidizing others that are price elastic. How low should the price be? Low enough to ensure the passenger travels while contributing as much as possible to paying off fixed costs.

Tied to the ideas above is the *incremental concept*. Incremental costs are those incurred by running an additional service. The operating costs of a particular plane or train are its incremental costs. Each fare should cover its incremental costs while contributing as much as possible to fixed costs and ensuring that the traffic moves. It is up to management to analyze each route and each segment of the market to price accordingly.

SUMMARY

Developments in transportation impact where tourism is developed and the type of development that occurs.

Destinations have to ensure that access to the destination is made as easy as possible for their visitors. It is necessary to know the barriers that inhibit the use of a particular transportation mode to develop programs to overcome them.

Trends

Top Ten Trends Affecting the Travel Industry

Jim Dullum

1. Mergers and industry consolidation continue.
2. Small airline carriers are experiencing big growth.
3. Cruises are offering better routes, upgraded onboard IT, and flexible services.
4. Bankruptcies continue in the airline sector.
5. Airlines will continue trying to grab the high-mileage flier with special deals.
6. Travel distribution companies are offering deeper discounts, no service charges, and GDS bypass.
7. More travel companies are looking to reduce costs by outsourcing functions such as call centers, internal processes, and IT shops.
8. Open Skies and Airline Ownership Rights initiatives require ownership of U.S. carriers to open up to 50 percent plus from outside investors.
9. Security for positive identification, including biometrics, is moving forward, but no standard is in place. Nations are looking to airports like Schipol and Ben Gurion for the answers.
10. Companies want to reduce long-term legacy maintenance costs to allow greater investment in business initiatives. This goal is especially true for airlines, where maintenance costs are quickly approaching 85 percent.

Source: Retrieved 25 April 2008, http://www.eds.com/industries/transportation/trends.aspx.

ACTIVITIES

1. In small groups or as a class, discuss different ways students have traveled. Have individuals' modes of travel changed since increasing fuel costs? Discuss how students believe their travel choices will be affected over the next few years.
2. Think of a place in the United States you would like visit. Then online, compare flight, train, and bus travel to the area in terms of time, cost, convenience, and comfort. Which would you choose and why?

REFERENCES

Bjornses, P. 2003. "The growth of the market and global competition in the cruise industry," paper presented at the Cruise and Ferry Conference, Earls Court, London.

2006 Business Travel Survey, May 29, 2006. *Business Travel News*.

Blum, E. December 2, 1996. Dickinson book: Lines could see 'lost profits.' *Travel Weekly*. 46.

Cartwright, R., and C. Baird. 1999. *The Development and Growth of the Cruise Industry*. Oxford, England: Butterworth-Heinemann. 144–150.

CLIA 2006 Cruise Market Profile. 2006. Fort Lauderdale, FL.

Debbage, K. G. 2002. Airport runway slots. *Annals of Tourism Research*, 29 (4): 933–951.

(December, 1992). *Transportation Issues*. United States General Accounting Office.

De La Vina, L., and J. Ford. 2001. Logistic regression analysis of cruise vacation market potential: Demographic and trip attribute perception factors. *Journal of Travel Research*, 39: 406–410.

Duval, D. T. 2007. *Tourism and Transport: Modes, Networks and Flows*. Clevendon, England: Channel View Publications.

Dwyer, L., and P. Forsyth. 1996. *A Framework for Assessing the Economic Significance of Cruise Tourism*. 27th Annual Conference Proceedings of the Travel and Tourism Association. 161–169.

Hallab, Z., and M. Uysal. 2004. Market profile: The case of rail passengers on Amtrak the crescent. 35th Annual Conference Proceedings of the Travel and Tourism Research Association. CD-ROM, unpaged.

Hanlon, P. 1999. *Global Airlines*, 2nd ed. Oxford, England: Butterworth Heinemann. 14, 23.

Hsu, C. H. C., and E.-J. Lee. 2002. Segmentation of senior motorcoach travelers. *Journal of Travel Research*, 40: 364–373.

Kelly, J., W. Haider, and P. W. Williams. 2007. A behavioral assessment of tourism transportation options for reducing energy consumption and greenhouse gases. *Journal of Travel Research*, 45: 297–309.

Lundgren, J. O. J. 1973. The development of the tourist travel systems. *The Tourist Review*, 1: 10.

March 4, 1996. International traveler's priorities. *Travel Weekly*. 33.

Marti, B. E. 1995. The cruise ship sanitation program. *Journal of Travel Research*, 33 (4): 29–38.

Mergers benefit airlines; fliers lose. 2008. *Wall Street Journal*. D1, D4.

Miller, R. K. & Associates, Inc. *The 2005 Travel & Leisure Market Research Handbook*, Loganville, GA. R. K. Miller & Associates, Inc. 2005, 110.

Motorcoach Census report: Travelers prefer to take the bus. 2000. *Travel Weekly*. 6.

Nathan & Associates, Inc. 2006. *Motorcoach Census 2005: Benchmarking Study of the Motorcoach Industry in the United States and Canada*. Washington, DC: American Bus Association.

National Railroad Passenger Corporation. Amtrak's annual report, 2006, Washington, DC, 2007.

Nomani, A. Q. January 3, 1997. Airline pacts antitrust question sparks controversy. *Wall Street Journal*. A10.

October 7. CLIA survey aims to help agents identify 'likely' cruisers. *Travel Weekly*. 1.

Robinson, R. 1995. *Creating Beneficial Partnerships with Other Leading Marketers, Presentation*. 1995 Annual Conference of the Association of Travel Marketing Executives.

September 25, 1995. Holland America Line president pulls no punches. *Tour & Travel News*. 25, 29.

Sheth, J. N. 1975. A psychological model of travel mode selection. *Advances in Consumer Research*, 3. Proceedings of the Association for Consumer Research, Sixth Annual Conference. 426.

The Future of the Airline Industry. P. J. Jeanniot, O.C., Director General and CEO, International Air Transport Association, to the Economist Global Airlines Conference, Langham Hilton, London, May 16, 2000.

Undated. *Achieving Comfortable Flight, Pathways Systems*. Natural History Museum of Los Angeles County, Massachusetts Institute of Technology, University of California at Berkeley.

Weber, K. 2005. Travelers' perceptions of airline alliance benefits and performance. *Journal of Travel Research*, 43: 261.

SURFING SOLUTIONS

http://www.iecc.com/airline/ (Airlines)
http://www.greyhound.com/ (Bus)
http://www.amtrak.com/ (Train)
http://www.viarail.ca/ (Train)
http://www.cruise-news.com/ (Ship)

ADDITIONAL READING

Air Travel Survey, Air Transport Association, 1301 Pennsylvania Avenue, N.W., Suite 1100, Washington, DC 20004-1707, annual.

Airline Deregulation in Canada. J. Christopher, National Technical Information Service, Springfield, VA 22161, March 1989.

"Airports for the Twenty-first Century," Sir John Egan, *Viewpoint*, 1 (1): 50–55, World Travel and Tourism Council, P.O. Box 6237, New York, NY 10128.

U.S. International Air Travel Statistics, Volpe National Transportation Systems Center, Center for Transportation Information, DTS-44, Kendall Square, Cambridge, MA 02142.

World Air Transport Statistics, annual statistical digest on the world's airlines—traffic, capacity, financial results and operating fleet. Available from the Publications Department, International Air Transport Association, 2000 Peel Street, Montreal, Quebec, Canada H3A 2R4: Tel. (514) 844-3210; FAX (514) 844-5286.

Additional Sources

Data Sources on the Web

The following are some key data sources and gateways to more information about tourism on the Internet.

CAB Abstracts, CAB International: http://www.cabi.org/datapage.asp?iDocID=165

C.I.R.E.T. (International Center for Research and Study on Tourism): http://www.ciret-tourism.com/

Facts & Figures, World Tourism Organization (UNWTO): http://unwto.org/facts/menu.html

Hospitality NET™, Hospitality Net: http://www.hospitalitynet.org/index.html

Insight & Market Intelligence, VisitBritain: http://www.tourismtrade.org.uk/MarketIntelligenceResearch/

Market Intelligence, European Travel Commission: http://www.etc-corporate.org/modules.php?name=Content&pa=showpage&pid=18&ac=8

PATA Intelligence, Pacific Asia Travel Association: http://www.pata.org/patasite/index.php?id=39

Research and Publications, U.S. Travel Association: http://www.tia.org/researchpubs/index.html

Sampling of Key Tourism Publications, US AID: http://www.nric.net/tourism/tourism_pubs.htm

TINET, Travel and Tourism Research Programs: U.S. Office of Travel & Tourism Industries (OTTI): http://tinet.ita.doc.gov/research/index.html

Tourism, European Commission: http://ec.europa.eu/enterprise/tourism/index_en.htm

Tourism Research Australia: http://www.tra.australia.com/

Tourism Research Links by René Waksberg: http://www.waksberg.com/

Travel & Tourism Research Association: http://www.ttra.com/

Tourism Research, World Travel & Tourism Council: http://www.wttc.org/eng/Tourism_Research/

Tourism Books

There are now well over 1,000 books on tourism and it is impossible to list them all here. The authors have included a short and select list of books below that provide good additional reading relevant to the main topic areas within *The Tourism System*. There are many other excellent tourism books that are not listed.

Tourism Management, Policy, Planning and Development

Burns, P., and M. Novelli. 2008. *Tourism Development: Growths, Myths, and Inequalities*. CABI.

Edgell, D. L., A. M. Delmastro, G. Smith, and J. R. Swanson. 2007. *Tourism Policy and Planning*. Butterworth-Heinemann/Elsevier.

Hall, C. M. 2008. *Tourism Planning: Policies, Processes & Relationships*. Pearson Prentice Hall.

Holden, A. 2007. *Environment and Tourism*. Routledge.

Honey, M. 2008. *Ecotourism and Sustainable Development: Who Own Paradise?* 2nd ed. Island Press.

Jenkins, J. M. 2007. *Tourism Planning and Policy*. John Wiley & Sons.

Mason, P. 2008. *Tourism Impacts, Planning and Management*, 2nd ed. Butterworth-Heinemann/Elsevier.

Mill, C. R. 2007. *Resorts: Management and Operation*. Wiley.

Page, S. 2007. *Tourism Management: Managing for Change*. Butterworth-Heinemann/Elsevier.

Weaver, D. 2005. *Sustainable Tourism*. Butterworth-Heinemann/Elsevier.

Tourism Marketing, Promotion and Distribution

Baker, B. 2007. *Destination Branding for Small Cities*. Creative Leap Books.

Davidson, R., and T. Rogers. 2006. *Marketing Destinations for Conferences, Conventions and Business*. Butterworth-Heinemann/Elsevier.

Deuschl, D. E. 2005. *Travel and Tourism Public Relations: An Introductory Guide for Hospitality Managers*. Butterworth-Heinemann/Elsevier.

Fyall, A., and B. Garrod. 2005. *Tourism Marketing: A Collaborative Approach*. Multilingual Matters Limited.

Gorham, G., and S. Rice. 2007. *Travel Perspectives: A Guide to Becoming a Travel Professional*, 4th ed. Delmar Cengage Learning.

Kolb, B. 2006. *Tourism Marketing for Cities and Towns: Using Branding and Events to Attract Tourists*. Butterworth-Heinemann/Elsevier.

McCabe, S. 2008. *Marketing Communications in Tourism and Hospitality: Concepts, Strategies and Cases*. Butterworth-Heinemann/Elsevier.

Morgan, N., A. Pritchard, and R. Pride. 2004. *Destination Branding*, 2nd ed. Elsevier.

Morrison, A. M. 2009. *Hospitality and Travel Marketing*, 4th ed. Delmar Cengage Learning.

Pike, S. 2008. *Destination Marketing: An Integrated Marketing Communications Approach*. Butterworth-Heinemann/Elsevier.

TOURISM MARKETS AND CONSUMER BEHAVIOR

Buckley, R. 2006. *Adventure Tourism*. CABI.

Carlsen, J., and S. Charters. 2007. *Global Wine Tourism*. CABI.

Durham, S. 2008. *Ecotourism and Conservation in the Americas*. CABI.

March, R. S., and A. Woodside. 2006. *Tourism Behaviour: Travellers' Decisions and Actions*. CABI.

Novelli, M. 2005. *Niche Tourism: Contemporary Issues, Trends and Cases*. Butterworth-Heinemann/Elsevier.

Pearce, P. L. 2005. *Tourist Behaviour: Themes and Conceptual Structures*. Channel View Publications.

Reisinger Y., and L. W. Turner. 2003. *Cross-Cultural Behaviour in Tourism*. Butterworth-Heinemann/Elsevier.

Smith, M., and L. Puczkó. 2008. *Health and Wellness Tourism*. Butterworth-Heinemann/Elsevier.

Swarbrooke, J., and S. Horner. 2006. *Consumer Behaviour in Tourism*, 2nd ed. Butterworth-Heinemann/Elsevier.

Weaver, D. 2007. *Ecotourism*. Wiley Australia.

PERIODIC PUBLICATIONS ON TOURISM

The following is just a very short selection of publications on tourism statistics and trends that appear periodically. There are many other such publications; with almost every country producing an annual digest of inbound and domestic tourism volumes and characteristics.

Outlook for Travel and Tourism, U.S. Travel Association, http://www.tia.org/researchpubs/index.html

Tourism in OECD Countries 2008: Trends and Policies: OECD, http://www.oecd.org/document/38/0,3343,en_2649_37461_40116454_1_1_1_37461,00.html

Travelers Use of the Internet, U.S. Travel Association, http://www.tia.org/researchpubs/index.html

UNWTO Tourism Barometer, World Tourism Organization, http://unwto.org/facts/menu.html

UNWTO Tourism Highlights, World Tourism Organization, http://unwto.org/facts/menu.html

ACADEMIC JOURNALS IN TOURISM

The following is a list of nearly 50 academic research journals, mainly focused on tourism. There are additional journals with more of a concentration on hospitality management and in languages other than English. These journal links change frequently, but they were current at the time of publication.

ACTA Turistica (Croatia): http://www.utilus.hr/

ANATOLIA: An International Journal of Tourism and Hospitality: http://www.anatoliajournal.com/

Annals of Tourism Research: http://www.elsevier.nl:80/inca/publications/store/6/8/9/

ASEAN Journal of Hospitality & Tourism: http://www.aseanjournal.com/

Asia Pacific Journal of Tourism Research: http://www.tandf.co.uk/journals/titles/10941665.asp

Cornell Hospitality Quarterly: http://www.sagepub.com/journalsProdDesc.nav?prodId=Journal201681&

Current Issues in Tourism: http://www.multilingual-matters.net/cit/default.htm

Festival Management & Event Tourism: http://www.cognizantcommunication.com

Hospitality and Tourism Educator: http://www.chrie.org/i4a/pages/index.cfm?pageid=3392

International Journal of Hospitality & Tourism Administration: http://www.haworthpress.com/store/product.asp?sku=J149

International Journal of Tourism Research: http://www3.interscience.wiley.com/journal/10009388/home?CRETRY=1&SRETRY=0

Journal of China Tourism Research: http://www.haworthpress.com/store/product.asp?sku=J536

Journal of Convention & Event Tourism: http://www.haworthpress.com/store/product.asp?sku=J452

Journal of Ecotourism: http://www.multilingual-matters.net/jet/default.htm

Journal of Heritage Tourism: http://www.tandf.co.uk/journals/journal.asp?issn=1743-873X&subcategory=SS500000

Journal of Hospitality & Leisure Marketing: http://www.haworthpress.com/store/product.asp?sku=J150

Journal of Hospitality & Tourism Management: http://www.australianacademicpress.com.au/Publications/Journals/JHTM/hospitality.htm

Journal of Hospitality & Tourism Research: http://www.sagepub.com/journalsProdDesc.nav?prodId=Journal200848&

Journal of Information Technology & Tourism: http://ojs.modul.ac.at/index.php/jitt/index

Journal of International Volunteer Tourism and Social Development: http://www.tandf.co.uk/journals/journal.asp?issn=1754-6362&subcategory=SS500000

Journal of Leisure Research: http://www.nrpa.org/content/default.aspx?documentId=508

Journal of Park and Recreation Administration: http://www.sagamorepub.com/ebooks/

Journal of Policy Research in Tourism, Leisure and Events: http://www.tandf.co.uk/journals/titles/19407963.asp

Journal of Sport & Tourism: http://www.tandf.co.uk/journals/journal.asp?issn=1477-5085&subcategory=SS500000

Journal of Sustainable Tourism: http://www.multilingual-matters.net/jost/default.htm

Journal of Teaching in Travel & Tourism: http://www.haworthpress.com/store/product.asp?sku=J172

Journal of Travel & Tourism Research: http://stad.adu.edu.tr/

Journal of Tourism and Cultural Change: http://www.multilingual-matters.net/jtc/default.htm

Journal of Tourism History: http://www.tandf.co.uk/journals/titles/1755182X.asp

Journal of Travel Research: http://jtr.sagepub.com/

Journal of Travel & Tourism Marketing: http://www.haworthpress.com/store/product.asp?sku=J073

Journal of Vacation Marketing: http://jvm.sagepub.com/

Leisure Sciences: http://www.tandf.co.uk/journals/TF/01490400.html

Leisure Studies: http://www.tandf.co.uk/journals/journal.asp?issn=0261-4367&subcategory=SS500000

Managing Leisure: http://www.tandf.co.uk/journals/routledge/13606719.html

Scandinavian Journal of Hospitality and Tourism: http://www.tandf.co.uk/journals/journal.asp?issn=1502-2250&subcategory=SS500000

Tourism Review: http://info.emeraldinsight.com/products/journals/journals.htm?PHPSESSID=hq5d9q5lktl5mk5obigdh509u0&id=tr

Tourism Analysis: http://www.cognizantcommunication.com

Tourism, Culture & Communication: http://www.cognizantcommunication.com

Tourism Economics: http://www.ippublishing.com/te.htm

Tourism Geographies: http://www.tandf.co.uk/journals/journal.asp?issn=1461-6688&subcategory=SS500000

Tourism and Hospitality: Planning & Development: http://www.tandf.co.uk/journals/journal.asp?issn=1479-053X&subcategory=SS500000

Tourism in Marine Environments: http://www.cognizantcommunication.com

Tourism Management: http://www.elsevier.com/wps/find/journaldescription.cws_home/30472/description#description

Tourism Recreation Review: http://www.trrworld.org/

Tourism Review International: http://www.cognizantcommunication.com

Tourist Studies: http://www.sagepub.com/journalsProdDesc.nav?prodId=Journal201263&

Travel Medicine and Infectious Disease: http://www.elsevier.com/wps/find/journaldescription.cws_home/643125/description#description

Visitor Studies: http://www.tandf.co.uk/journals/journal.asp?issn=1064-5578&subcategory=SS500000

Glossary

- **Accreditation (Chapter 4):** Accreditation is a process by which an association or agency evaluates and recognizes a program of study or an institution as meeting certain predetermined standards or qualifications (American Society of Association Executives). For example, Destination Marketing Association International (DMAI) accredits DMOs in North America and Europe.
- **All-inclusive package (Chapter 9):** This is a vacation or holiday package that includes a complete range of tourism services in the price. Items normally included are air fares, ground transfers and baggage handling, accommodation, meals, local sightseeing, recreational activities and entertainment.
- **Alternative tourism (Chapter 6):** This term refers to various forms of low-impact or "soft" tourism. These forms of tourism provide an alternative to mass and resort tourism which may have a high and negative impact on the environment and local peoples.
- **Balance of payments (Chapter 2):** A type of economic accounting system, this is the difference between what a country exports (sells) to other countries and what it imports (buys) from other countries. When a country exports more than it imports, it has a positive balance of payments or trade. A negative balance of payments is where a country imports more than it exports.
- **Benchmarking (Chapter 1):** Continuously measuring the elements, services and practices at a specific tourist destination with those destinations recognized as being the leaders in tourism.
- **Benefit segmentation (Chapter 12):** A process used to divide travelers into groups of people who are seeking similar benefits from their trips.
- **Bilateral agreement (Chapter 4):** An agreement between two countries, often in trade or transportation. Bilateral air agreements are an example; these agreements mainly address the questions of which airlines can fly between the two countries and to which airports they are allowed to fly.
- **Brands, regional destination (Chapter 7):** A marketing concept in which tourism destination areas join together in multi-destination partnerships and promote a region under a single brand name. Examples include El Mundo Maya in Central America and the Alps of Europe in Western Europe.
- **Business travel market (Chapter 14):** Travel where the primary motivation is to conduct business. This includes regular business or corporate travel, incentive travel, and travel related to meetings, conventions, congresses, trade shows and exhibitions.
- **Carriers (Chapter 9):** These are companies that provide transportation for visitors and include airlines, railroad companies, bus operators, ferry services, canal systems, and other transportation providers.
- **Carrying capacity (Chapter 2):** A measurement that indicates the ability of an environment or natural resource to accommodate a certain type of use. There is also the concept of social carrying capacity, which refers to a society's capacity to cope with a certain type of activity.
- **Certification (Chapter 4):** Certification is a process by which an individual is tested and evaluated to determine his or her mastery of a specific body of knowledge, or some portion of a body of knowledge (American Society of Association Executives). For example, The Travel Institute certifies retail travel agents with the Certified Travel Counselor (CTC) designation.
- **Code sharing (Chapter 4):** One common feature of a strategic alliance between two airline companies. This arrangement allows one airline to use its own two-character code (e.g., NW for Northwest) to advertise a flight as its own, when the flight is actually being operated by its partner airline (e.g., DL for Delta).
- **Cognitive dissonance (Chapter 13):** A feeling of anxiety or doubt that people experience after they have made purchases. This anxiety revolves around whether they have selected the best tourism destination area or other travel service.
- **Collateral, printed (Chapter 8):** Printed materials produced by tourism organizations including visitor guides, calendars of festivals and events, and maps.

- **Commission (Chapter 9):** An amount of money, normally expressed as a percentage of the fare, rate or price, paid to a retail travel agency by suppliers, carriers, and other intermediaries such as tour operators.
- **Computer reservation systems (CRS) (Chapter 9):** A computer system operated by an airline, hotel chain, rental car, or other travel company which allows retail travel agencies to check the availability and prices, and make reservations for their clients. Some systems also provide access for individual travelers.
- **Consolidator, travel (Chapter 9):** A special form of travel agent. These are private firms that buy unsold airline seats, cruise berths, and other types of travel options in bulk and sell these at a discount to retail travel agencies and individual travelers. The "consolidator" term comes from the combination of these firms' bookings to qualify for group or discounted prices.
- **Convention-meeting planners (Chapter 9):** Employees of corporations, associations, government agencies, and other non-profit groups who plan and coordinate meetings, conventions, conferences, exhibitions or trade shows.
- **Conversion study (Chapter 8):** A research technique used to determine the percentage of people who request travel information materials that actually visit the destination or use the service after being sent the materials.
- **Corporate travel department (Chapter 9):** Special departments created by corporations, government agencies, and non-profit organizations to coordinate and control all of the travel by employees and associates of the organization. These departments establish organization-wide travel policies and negotiate the best prices on travel. Their jobs are sometimes referred to as travel management.
- **Cost-benefit analysis (Chapter 2):** An economic analysis technique used to determine which economic sector produces the most benefit in terms of foreign exchange, employment, taxes, or income generated relative to the costs of development.
- **Culture (Chapter 10):** A set of beliefs, values, attitudes, habits, and forms of behavior shared by a society and passed from generation to generation (Bennett and Kassasjian).
- **Culture commodification (Chapter 1):** When local culture is turned into an attraction for tourists it becomes a commodity.
- **Database marketing (Chapter 8):** A process increasingly being used in tourism to encourage repeat usage. Computer technology allows the manipulation of relational databases on past and potential visitors or guests, and is facilitating this process.
- **Decoy effect (Chapter 13):** The introduction of an offer into a set of alternative choices that results in a segment of consumers shifting their choice to a higher priced targeted item (Josiam and Hobson).
- **Demonstration effect (Chapter 2):** An economic phenomenon that occurs when local residents, exposed to goods imported for visitor use, begin to demand those goods for themselves. This automatically increases the demand for imports.
- **Destination area (Chapter 1):** A geographic area, ranging in size from an individual community to a group of several countries, where there is a concerted effort to develop and market tourism.
- **Destination competitiveness (Chapter 1):** A destination's ability to increase tourist expenditure, to increasingly attract visitors while providing them with satisfying memorable experiences, and to do so in a profitable way, while enhancing the well-being of local residents and preserving the natural capital of the destination for future generations (Ritchie and Crouch, 2003).
- **Destination management company (DMC) (Chapter 9):** Also known as inbound tour operators, receptive tour operators or receptive services operator. These are companies who provide sightseeing, guiding, and transportation services within specific destination areas. Other types of DMCs specialize in catering to meeting and incentive travel groups.
- **Destination marketing organization (DMO) (Chapter 8):** Government and non-governmental organizations with the responsibility of marketing specific tourism destinations to the travel trade and individual travelers. These organizations operate at all geographic levels from multi-country regions (e.g., European Travel Commission) to individual communities (e.g., convention and visitors bureaus or CVBs).
- **Destination mix (Chapter 1):** The combination of attractions, events, and services that a destination provides for visitors. The destination mix includes attractions and events, facilities, infrastructure, transportation, and hospitality resources.
- **Distribution mix (Chapter 9):** The combination of direct and indirect (through travel trade intermediaries) distribution that a tourism organization

selects to use to market its services or destination area. This includes distribution through the Internet.

- **Domestic tourism (Introduction):** The combination of internal tourism (visits by residents of a country within their own country) and inbound international tourism (visits to a country by non-residents of that country) (World Tourism Organization/UNWTO).

- **Dynamic packaging (Chapter 9):** A feature on a Web site that allows a customer or a travel agent to assemble a tailor-made package by selecting from a menu of different travel options and arrangements.

- **Economic feasibility study (Chapter 6):** A study to determine the economic feasibility of a tourism development project opportunity. A project is economically feasible if it provides a rate of return acceptable to the investors in the project.

- **Ecotourism (Chapter 6):** Nature-based tourism that involves education and interpretation of the natural and cultural environment, and that is managed to be ecologically and culturally sustainable (adapted from Australian National Ecotourism Strategy).

- **Environmental impact analysis (Chapter 6):** An analysis which identifies in advance factors that may affect the ability to build a proposed tourism development and the environmental attributes that will be affected by the development (Manning and Dougherty).

- **Environmental scanning (Chapter 7):** A technique used to identify and analyze the impact of external environmental forces on a tourism organization's marketing. These external forces include legislation and regulation, political situations, social and cultural characteristics, economic conditions, technology, transportation, and competition.

- **Escorted tour (Chapter 9):** A type of organized tour that includes the services of a tour director or manager who accompanies an individual or group throughout the tour.

- **Facilities (Chapter 1):** Part of the destination mix, facilities include the physical facilities and services provided in lodging, food and beverage, and support businesses (e.g., souvenir and duty-free shops).

- **Familiarization tour or trip (Chapter 8):** Also known as a "fam," these trips are organized for selected tour operators or wholesalers, retail travel agents, or travel writers. Having experienced the destination or travel service first hand, the intermediaries are in a much better position to sell it. Familiarization tours may involve the inspection of facilities, visits to tourism attractions, and contacts with the local travel trade (e.g., inbound tour operators). Fams may be conducted in small groups or on an individual basis. Cruise ship "fams" for travel agents are often conducted at cruise ports.

- **Family life cycle (Chapter 10):** Distinctive stages through which families progress over time. These stages are given certain titles or labels, and range from the "bachelor" to "solitary survivor" stages.

- **Focus group (Chapter 8):** A marketing research technique involving a small group of people, typically 8–12 persons. A moderator is used to lead the group to reach a consensus on one or more questions or issues.

- **Foreign independent tour (FIT) (Chapter 9):** A service provided by retail travel agencies and some tour operators in which all the air travel and land arrangements are made for an individual customer in the traveler's destination of choice.

- **Frequent flyer program (FFP) (Chapter 7):** Recognition programs that were first introduced in the early 1980s to reward frequent travelers and to build loyalty among these travelers with the airline. Frequent flyer miles are the "currency" of these programs.

- **Frequent guest program (FGP) (Chapter 7):** Guest recognition programs that were first introduced in the early 1980s to reward frequent travelers and to build loyalty among these travelers with the hotel chain. These programs reward guests with room upgrades, free stays, merchandise, or frequent flyer miles.

- **Fulfillment (Chapter 8):** The process used by tourism organizations to send printed collateral materials to people who request them.

- **Group inclusive tour (GIT) (Chapter 9):** An all-inclusive package with a specified minimum size (number of travelers) involving one or more groups traveling on scheduled or chartered air service (Morrison).

- **Global distribution systems (GDS) (Chapter 9):** Computerized reservation systems that are global in their coverage. Three of the major systems are Amadeus, Sabre, and Travelport (Galileo and Worldspan).

- **Ground or land tour arrangements (Chapter 9):** Travel arrangements made for group or individual travelers at a destination. These include items such as airport transfers, lodging, meals, entertainment, sightseeing, ground transportation by coach or other means.

- **Hierarchy of needs, Maslow's (Chapter 11):** A theory of motivation suggested by Maslow in which needs are arranged in a hierarchy ranging from physiological to psychological needs.
- **Horizontal integration (Chapter 9):** The acquisition and ownership of similar businesses by one organization in the tourism distribution channel, e.g., an airline buying another airline.
- **Hospitality resources (Chapter 1):** Refers to the general feeling of welcome that people receive while visiting a destination area. It is the way that tourism services are delivered by the service providers, as well as the general feeling of warmth from the local resident population.
- **Import substitution (Chapter 2):** An economic strategy aimed at minimizing the leakage from a destination area's economy caused by imported goods and services.
- **Inbound tour operator (Chapter 9):** Tour operators who provide the ground or land tour arrangements within specific destinations for group and individual travelers. They are also called receptive tour, receptive services operators, or destination management companies (DMCs).
- **Incentive travel planning company (Chapter 9):** A specialized tour wholesaler who primarily serves corporate clients and arranges trips that are given to certain of their client's employees or dealers as a reward for outstanding sales or work performance.
- **Input-output analysis (Chapter 2):** An economic analysis technique which examines the interactions among different economic sectors. It is used to determine the impacts of tourism on the other economic sectors of a destination area.
- **Interlining (Chapter 4):** Travel by an air passenger on two or more airlines on a trip. More broadly, interlining refers to cooperative agreements between two or more airlines.
- **Internal tourism (Introduction):** Visits by residents of a country within their own country (World Tourism Organization/UNWTO).
- **International tourism (Introduction):** The combination of inbound and outbound tourism for a particular country.
- **Internet (Chapter 8):** A worldwide network of connected computer networks. Also known as "cyberspace" or the "information superhighway," one of the most popular Internet functions is the World Wide Web.
- **Invisible export (Chapter 2):** Because of the intangible nature of tourism services, it is said to be an invisible export when foreigners visit another country and spend money there. Tourism is not a physical good that must be shipped out to other countries.
- **Leakage (Chapter 2):** An economic term that refers to the monetary value of goods and services that must be imported to service the needs of tourism.
- **Leisure travel market (Chapter 14):** Travel where the primary motivation is to take a vacation or holiday, or to travel for some other personal (non-business) reason.
- **Marketing mix (Chapter 7):** The combination of factors that tourism marketing managers use to attract visitors. These factors include product, price, place, promotion, packaging, programming, partnership, and people (McCarthy; Morrison).
- **Marketing plan (Chapter 7):** A written document that describes the actions that a tourism organization will undertake to achieve its marketing goals and objectives, usually for a period of one year.
- **Market segmentation (Chapter 7):** The division of the tourism market into groups which share common characteristics.
- **MICE markets (Chapter 9):** An acronym for the meetings, incentives, conventions/conferences, and exhibition or exposition markets.
- **Motivation (Chapter 11):** A physiological or psychological drive in a person to take action to satisfy a need.
- **Motives (Chapter 11):** People's personal desires or drives to satisfy their wants (Morrison).
- **Multiplier effect (Chapter 2):** An economic term that describes the indirect and induced effects of income and employment generated by tourism. Income multipliers measure the amount of local income generated per unit of visitor expenditure (Wanhill, 1994).
- **Multilateral agreement (Chapter 4):** An agreement between several countries, often in trade or transportation. The General Agreement on Tariffs and Trade (GATT) is one example.
- **National tourism (Introduction):** The combination of internal tourism (visits by residents of the country within their own country) and outbound international tourism (visits by the residents of the country to other countries) (World Tourism Organization/UNWTO).
- **Needs (Chapter 11):** Gaps between what people have and what they would like to have (Morrison).

Online travel agencies (Chapter 9): Online databases and reservations services that allow travelers to make travel reservations in their own homes or offices via computer modems and the Web. Examples include Expedia.com, Travelocity.com, and LastMinute.com.

Open Skies agreement (Chapter 4): "Open Skies" agreements are bilateral or multilateral agreements between countries that liberalize air travel between or among the signing countries.

Packaging (Chapter 7): The assembly of travel packages that combine the services and products of several tourism organizations into a single-price offering.

Perception (Chapter 12): The mental process in which people employ their five senses (sight, hearing, taste, touch, and smell) to develop images of tourism destinations and services.

Plurilateral agreements (Chapter 4): Plurilateral air services agreements are situations where groups of countries get together to negotiate and sign such agreements.

Positioning (Chapter 7): A marketing process used by tourism organizations to create a unique perception or image in the targeted visitor's mind.

Primary research (Chapter 8): Also known as original research, this is information collected for the first time by an organization or individual.

Principals, travel (Chapter 8): A term in travel used to refer to suppliers and carriers who use retail travel companies as their agents.

Receptive tour operator (Chapter 9): Tour operators who provide the ground or land tour arrangements within specific destinations for group and individual travelers. They are also called inbound tour operators (ITOs) or destination management companies (DMCs).

Relationship marketing (Chapter 8): Marketing activities in which a tourism organization engages to build and enhance long-term relationships with individual visitors and other organizations.

Representative firms (Chapter 8): Companies that represent a tourism destination area or tourism organization in a foreign country, and which provide public relations and other promotional services.

Retail travel agency (Chapter 9): In essence, they are the department stores of tourism. They provide thousands of "travel shops" for suppliers, carriers, destination marketing organizations (DMOs), and the other travel trade intermediaries, and receive commissions or fees for their services. A customer can buy all types of travel services at an agency including tickets for planes and railways, hotels and resorts, cruises, packages and tours, car rentals, and travel insurance.

Satellite tourism accounting (Chapter 2): An economic accounting system for complex service sectors such as tourism. For tourism, this means adding up the impacts of tourism that have traditionally been allocated to other economic sectors.

Situation or SWOT analysis (Chapter 7): A marketing analysis technique used to analyze the strengths, weaknesses, opportunities, and threats of a tourism destination area or tourism organization.

SMERF markets (Chapter 9): An acronym commonly used in tourism for meetings and other events held by social, military, educational, religious, or fraternal groups.

Social media/social networking sites (Chapter 12): Social media allow consumers to be providers rather than just recipients of information. Sites like Trip Advisor and I Go You Go allow consumers to post reviews of their vacation experiences. This increase in information is moving control of the marketing message away from companies and into the hands of the consumer.

Strategic alliances (Chapter 7): These are long-term agreements between companies or countries to invest in joint marketing programs. Strategic alliances have been especially popular among airline companies, e.g., the Star Alliance.

Strategic planning (Chapter 5): A long-range planning process used in overall tourism planning where the time frame is three or more years into the future.

Superstructure (Chapter 6): Generally considered to imply building construction for tourism development.

Suppliers (Chapter 9): Tourism organizations that provide facilities and services within and between tourism destinations. These include hotels, restaurants, attractions, car rental firms, casinos and other gaming operations, and cruise lines.

Sustainable tourism development (Chapter 6): Using the natural and cultural resources of a destination area to support tourism without compromising their carrying capacities, this is their ability to continue to contribute towards tourism activity.

- **System (Introduction):** A set of interrelated elements and components that work together toward common goals or objectives. Von Bertalanffy defines a system as "a set of elements standing in interrelation among themselves and with the environments."
- **Testimonial (Chapter 13):** A format used in advertising in which a celebrity, satisfied customer, or other person "endorses" or recommends a specific product, service, or destination area.
- **Timesharing (Chapter 4):** Also known as interval ownership, this is a procedure where the ownership of a hotel or resort is split among multiple owners according to time intervals such as weeks.
- **Tourism (Introduction):** Tourism comprises the activities of persons traveling to and staying in places outside their usual environment for not more than one consecutive year for leisure, business and other purposes not related to the exercise of an activity remunerated from within the place visited (World Tourism Organization).
- **Tourism product (Chapters 1 and 6):** A term that is roughly synonymous with the destination mix, meaning all the facilities and services offered for the visitors to a destination area.
- **Tourism system (Introduction):** A systematic approach to the study of tourism consisting of four main elements (demand, travel, destination, and marketing) and four major links (the travel purchase, the shape of travel, the tourism product, and the promotion of travel). The tourism system approach emphasizes the interdependency in tourism; that it consists of several interrelated elements working together to achieve common purposes.
- **Tour operator (Chapter 9):** Tour operators assemble the numerous components of travel into packaged vacations/holidays or tours and offer these for sale through retail travel agencies. Tour operators are tour wholesalers, but also operate all or part of their tours by providing tour escorts or managers, and ground/land tour arrangements.
- **Tour wholesaler (Chapter 9):** Tour wholesalers assemble the numerous components of travel into packaged vacations/holidays or tours and offer these for sale through retail travel agents. They do not provide tour operating services.
- **Travel career ladder (Chapter 13):** A concept developed by Philip Pearce which suggests that people's needs, travel decisions and decision-making processes are not static; they change over a person's lifetime based upon their actual travel experiences.
- **Travel trade intermediaries (Chapter 9):** A term used to collectively refer to all the travel distribution channels including retail travel agencies, tour wholesalers and operators, corporate travel departments, incentive travel planning companies, convention/meeting planners, and online travel companies.
- **Vertical integration (Chapter 9):** The acquisition and ownership by one organization of all or part of a tourism distribution channel, e.g., a tour operator buying a hotel company or airline.
- **Visioning (Chapter 5):** A process used in long-term or strategic planning in which the desired future situation for the destination area or tourism organization is determined.
- **VFR (Chapter 14):** An acronym used for people who are visiting their friends or relatives in a destination area.
- **Wants (Chapter 11):** People's desires for specific satisfiers of their needs, e.g., specific tourism facilities, services, or destination areas (Kotler).
- **Web (Chapter 8):** An Internet function which provides a worldwide collection of sites containing text, graphics, sound, and video that are created in hypertext and can be accessed through the use of Universal Resource Locators (URLs) or domain names.
- **Word of mouth (Chapter 8):** Recommendations given about tourism destinations or services by people to their friends, relatives, or business colleagues.
- **World Heritage List (Chapter 4):** A list of natural and cultural sites (maintained by UNESCO) whose outstanding values should be preserved for all humanity and to ensure their protection through a closer cooperation among nations (UNESCO World Heritage Centre).

Index